IMMIGRATION LAW

IMMIGRATION LAW

Kevin Browne, LLB, Solicitor

Published by

College of Law Publishing,
Braboeuf Manor, Portsmouth Road, St Catherines, Guildford GU3 1HA

British Library Cataloguing-in-Publication Data

A catalogue record for this book is available from the British Library.

ISBN 978 1 910019 05 4

Typeset by Style Photosetting Ltd, Mayfield, East Sussex

Printed in Great Britain by Polestar Wheatons, Exeter

Preface

This book is intended to provide an introduction to immigration law and practice. I hope that it will be of use to students studying in this area, as well as practitioners who are new to the various topics covered or who wish to update their knowledge.

After a short, practical introduction in **Chapter 1** (which includes a list of useful websites at **1.2.8**), the book deals with British nationality and the right of abode in the United Kingdom in **Chapter 2**. This is followed by a detailed analysis of immigration controls in **Chapter 3**. The unique immigration status of EEA nationals and their family members is considered in **Chapter 4**, along with how a family member of a British citizen who has engaged Treaty rights might use EU rather than domestic law to enter the UK. The next four chapters then address the key immigration categories of entry to the UK. Asylum seekers and refugees are considered in **Chapter 9**. Enforcement of immigration law, the appeals system and judicial review are dealt with in the last three chapters. In each chapter I have tried to present the information in a logical, structured order with practical examples. I would welcome comments from readers which can be sent via CLP (clponline.co.uk).

Immigration law and practice constantly change. At least one major piece of legislation is introduced each year and, as at October 2013, there had already been eight statements of changes to the Immigration Rules in 2013. In this edition, I have included the new criminality requirement for naturalisation, revisions to the grounds for refusal, developments in EU law, the introduction of the genuineness requirement to additional categories, changes to employment categories and various human rights issues.

New cases in this edition include: B2 *v Secretary of State for the Home Department* (2013) and *GI v Secretary of State for the Home Department* (2012) (naturalisation); *SS (Nepal) v Entry Clearance Officer* (2013) and *JK (India) v Secretary of State for the Home Department* (2013) (refusal grounds); *Aladeselu v Secretary of State for the Home Department* (2013), *Soares v Secretary of State for the Home Department* (2013) and *RM (Zimbabwe) v Secretary of State for the Home Department* (2013) (EEA family members); *MM (Lebanon) v Secretary of State for the Home Department* (2013), *Ahmed (benefits: proof of receipt; evidence) Bangladesh* (2013), *R (on the application of Bibi) v Secretary of State for the Home Department* (2013) and *Mundeba (s.55 and para 297(i)(f))* (2013) (family reunion); *KS (Burma) v Secretary of State for the Home Department* (2013), *SK (Zimbabwe) v Secretary of State for the Home Department* (2012), *AA-R (Iran) v Secretary of State for the Home Department* (2013), *AH (Article 1F (b) – 'serious') Algeria* (2013) and *Al-Sirri v Secretary of State for the Home Department* (2013) (asylum); *RS (immigration/family court liaison: outcome) India* (2013) and *R (on the application of Nagre) v Secretary of State for the Home Department* (2013) (deportation); and *R (on the application of Khan) v Secretary of State for the Home Department* (2013) (appeals).

I would like to thank David Stott, Sue Hall and the team at CLP for all their hard work on this title.

I would also like to thank my wife, children, colleagues and past students for their help and inspiration.

This edition is dedicated to Alistair, Mary, Chris, Tom, Phil, Harry and Rene. All much missed.

Kevin Browne
The University of Law,
London

Contents

Table of Cases

Table of Statutes

Page numbers in bold refer to text of legislation in the Appendices

Table of Secondary Legislation

Page numbers in bold refer to text of legislation in the Appendices

Table of Abbreviations

AI(TC)A 2004	Asylum and Immigration (Treatment of Claimants, etc) Act 2004
BNA 1981	British Nationality Act 1981
BOCs	British overseas citizens
BOTCs	British overseas territories citizens
CPR 1998	Civil Procedure Rules 1998
CUKC	citizen of the UK and colonies
DfWP	Department for Work and Pensions
ECHR	European Convention on Human Rights
ECtHR	European Court of Human Rights
ECJ	European Court of Justice
ECO	Entry clearance officer
EEA	European Economic Area
EU	European Union
FCA	Financial Conduct Authority
HA 1985	Housing Act 1985
HMRC	HM Revenue and Customs
HND	Higher National Diploma
HRA 1998	Human Rights Act 1998
IA 1971	Immigration Act 1971
IA 1988	Immigration Act 1988
IAA 1999	Immigration and Asylum Act 1999
IAC	Immigration and Asylum Chamber
IANA 2006	Immigration, Asylum and Nationality Act 2006
I(EEA) Regs 2006	Immigration (European Economic Area) Regulations 2006
NHS	National Health Service
NIAA 2002	Nationality, Immigration and Asylum Act 2002
NVQ	National Vocational Qualification
SIAC	Special Immigration Appeals Commission
UNHCR	United Nations High Commissioner for Refugees

CHAPTER 1

INTRODUCTION

1.1 PUBLIC LAW AND PRACTICAL PROBLEMS

This book aims to provide an introduction to immigration and nationality law and practice.

This is a public law subject, dealing with relations between the State and the individual, concerned fundamentally with the exercise of discretion by officials. It is easy to understand the practical problems which arise in this area of the law, as it concerns the individual's ability to live, work and enjoy family life in the country of his or her choice. In practice, it involves a great deal of client contact, argument with officials, advocacy in tribunals and familiarity with a wide range of legal sources. It therefore calls upon the full range of legal skills.

1.2 SOURCES OF IMMIGRATION LAW AND GENERAL PRINCIPLES

1.2.1 Legislation

The main piece of legislation dealing with immigration law is the Immigration Act 1971 (IA 1971). This replaced existing immigration controls and introduced the concept of the right of abode in the United Kingdom (UK). The starting point for any immigration practitioner is the following general principles set out in s 1:

(1) All those who are in this Act expressed to have the right of abode in the United Kingdom shall be free to live in, and to come and go into and from, the United Kingdom without let or hindrance except such as may be required under and in accordance with this Act to enable their right to be established or as may be otherwise lawfully imposed on any person.

(2) Those not having that right may live, work and settle in the United Kingdom by permission and subject to such regulation and control of their entry into, stay in and departure from the United Kingdom as is imposed by this Act ...

As to s 1(1) and the right of abode in the UK, see **1.4.1**.

Section 1(2) establishes what are known as immigration controls: see **1.4.2**.

The IA 1971 has been amended by numerous subsequent Acts, almost on an annual basis.

British nationality law is dealt with mainly in the British Nationality Act 1981 (as amended). This Act came into force on 1 January 1983 and Pt 1 sets out the provisions which determine whether or not a person is a British citizen. The date is significant, as different tests apply to determine British citizenship depending on whether or not the individual was born before 1983 (ie up to and including 31 December 1982) or after 1982 (ie from and including 1 January 1983). Note that British citizenship is also affected by whether or not the person was born in the UK. Full details are to be found in **Chapter 2**.

A British citizen has the right of abode in the UK. Therefore a British citizen is not subject to immigration controls. So a preliminary question for an immigration practitioner to answer when seeing a new client is whether or not the client is a British citizen.

1.2.2   The Immigration Rules

Whilst the IA 1971 (as amended) is the framework of immigration law, it does not contain any detail. This is because ss 1(4) and 3(2) permit rules to be laid down and amended by the Secretary of State as to the practice to be followed in the administration of the Act for regulating the entry into and stay in the UK of persons not having the right of abode. These are the Immigration Rules. A copy can be found in **Appendix 1**. Quickly skim through the contents to get some idea of their wide coverage.

The Immigration Rules structure the discretion given by the IA 1971 to grant leave to enter, to vary leave, or to make a deportation order. They bind immigration officers, but not the Home Secretary who, in the exercise of his discretion, may, in appropriate circumstances, depart from the Rules he has laid down, for instance granting leave to remain in the UK when the Rules would require refusal. They are, therefore, not rules of law in the strict sense (R v Secretary of State for the Home Department, ex p Hosenball [1977] 3 All ER 452; Odelolar v Secretary of State for the Home Department [2008] EWCA Civ 308). But as the Rules are laid before and approved by Parliament, published Government policy guidance cannot add requirements that are not in the Rules themselves: see Secretary of State for the Home Department v Pankina [2010] EWCA Civ 719 and R (on the application of Alvi) v Secretary of State for the Home Department [2012] UKSC 33.

Nevertheless, a lawyer can base his advice on the Rules because they are normally followed by the immigration authorities, and because failure to apply them may give grounds for appeal or judicial review (see **Chapters 11** and **12**).

The current Rules are cited as the Statement of Changes in Immigration Rules 1994 (HC 395). As the Rules are not delegated legislation, they are cited as a House of Commons Paper and not as a statutory instrument. Later amendments to the Rules are cited similarly.

1.2.3   Home Office practices

Since the Home Office has considerable discretion not governed by the Rules, it is inevitable that informal practices evolve in order to ensure that comparable cases are treated in like ways. An example is the concession for visitors who wish to enter or remain to care for a sick relative (see **5.12**). These practices are not generally binding, although under the administrative law doctrine of legitimate expectation, a decision which disregards them may be quashed as unreasonable (R v Secretary of State for the Home Department, ex p Asif Mahmood Khan [1984] 1 WLR 1337).

The Home Office has made public some of the internal instructions to staff on the handling of immigration cases. These are available via the Internet (see **1.2.8**).

1.2.4   Case law

Immigration cases have in recent years formed the largest single category of applications to the High Court for judicial review. In addition, cases may reach the higher courts by way of appeal. These cases may be reported in the standard series of law reports, but may also be found in the specialist Immigration and Nationality Law Reports (INLR), published six times a year by Jordans, and the Immigration Appeal Reports (Imm LR), published quarterly by The Stationery Office.

1.2.5   EU law

Nationals of EU and EEA Member States (see the list in **Appendix 2**) have special rights under EU law (eg under Article 45 TFEU (freedom of movement of workers)). These rights are set out in detail in EU Regulations and Directives. The rights often have direct effect and so override conflicting provisions of UK immigration law. The UK Government will try to ensure that legislation and the Immigration Rules give effect to EU law, but be aware that UK provisions may be open to challenge.

In addition, there is a considerable body of case law of the European Court of Justice (ECJ) on the meaning and effect of Treaty provisions and legislation. This is binding on UK courts. Directives, Regulations, EU judgments, etc can be found on the European Union on-line website at www.europa.eu.

Probably the most significant Directive is Directive 2004/38/EC of the European Parliament and Council. A copy appears at **Appendix 3**. This sets out the terms and limits of the right of free movement. It has been implemented into domestic law by the Immigration (European Economic Area) Regulations 2006 (I(EEA) Regs 2006) (see **Chapter 4** and **Appendix 4**).

It is important to note that a family member of a British citizen may sometimes be able to use EU law rather than domestic UK immigration law to enter the UK. The most common example is where a British citizen goes to work in another EEA country, thereby exercising and engaging EU Treaty rights. The British citizen marries or enters into a civil partnership with a non-EEA national. The couple then want to travel to the UK to live together. The British citizen has a right of abode in the UK and so is not subject to immigration controls (see **1.2.1** and **Chapter 2**). His or her spouse or civil partner may be able to seek entry to the UK under EU law rather than domestic law (see **4.4.12** and **8.2** respectively).

1.2.6 The European Convention on Human Rights and the Human Rights Act 1998

The Human Rights Act 1998 (HRA 1998) interprets, rather than incorporates, the European Convention on Human Rights (ECHR). Although the legislation requires UK courts to apply Acts of Parliament even if they are incompatible with the Convention, it contains a number of measures which will enable practitioners to rely on the Convention in immigration cases. In outline these are as follows.

Section 3 requires UK courts to try to interpret an Act of Parliament in a way which is compatible with listed Convention rights, whether or not the Act is ambiguous.

Section 4 enables the courts to make a declaration that an Act is incompatible with Convention rights. The court must still apply the Act in the case before it, but s 10 enables the Government to introduce fast-track delegated legislation to alter the law.

Section 6 is probably the most far-reaching provision. It states that it is unlawful for public authorities (such as the Home Office) to act in a way which infringes Convention rights, unless required to do so by Act of Parliament. So, when exercising a discretion, the Home Secretary must take Convention rights into account and, if statute permits it, must avoid decisions which infringe them. As the Immigration Rules themselves are made in the exercise of a discretion, both the Rules and decisions made under them are open to challenge if they infringe Convention rights. So, in applying the Rules and exercising powers, the Secretary of State must respect Convention rights, whether or not the Rules explicitly refer to them: see *R (Syed) v Secretary of State for the Home Department* [2011] EWCA Civ 1059.

So immigration lawyers need a good working knowledge of human rights. The main Convention rights that might be relevant are set out in **Appendix 5**. Detailed references to human rights cases and principles can be found in the **Chapters 9, 10** and **11**.

1.2.7 Practitioner texts

The practitioner in immigration law relies heavily on a limited number of secondary sources. These include:

(a) *Macdonald's Immigration Law and Practice* (Butterworths): the leading practitioner text;

(b) *Butterworths Immigration Law Service*: in the form of a loose-leaf encyclopaedia, particularly useful as a source for Home Office practices;

(c)   *Tolley's Immigration and Nationality Law and Practice*: a quarterly journal;

(d)   *Immigration, Nationality and Refugee Law Handbook* (Joint Council for the Welfare of Immigrants): an invaluable practical guide (*JCWI Handbook*);

(e)   Fransman, *British Nationality Law* (Butterworths);

(f)   Webb and Grant, *Immigration and Asylum Emergency Procedures* (Legal Action Group).

1.2.8   Websites

There are many useful websites, most of which have links to other, related sites. You might start with the following:

Home Office: www.ukba.homeoffice.gov.uk

International Group: www.ukvisas.gov.uk

European Union on-line: www.europa.eu

Immigration and Asylum (Chamber) Tribunal: www.justice.gov.uk

European Court of Human Rights: www.echr.coe.int

Ministry of Justice: www.justice.gov.uk

The Supreme Court: www.supremecourt.gov.uk

Joint Council for the Welfare of Immigrants: www.jcwi.org.uk

Refugee Council: www.refugeecouncil.org.uk

UNHCR UN Refugee Agency: www.unhcr.org

Electronic Immigration Network: www.ein.org.uk

1.3   INSTITUTIONS

1.3.1   The Home Office

Under the IA 1971, the Home Secretary has overall responsibility for the administration of immigration control. The Act designates the Home Secretary as the person who makes the Immigration Rules, appoints immigration officers, and takes specific decisions such as the decision to deport. The law generally recognises that, in practice, the Home Secretary acts through civil servants (*Carltona Ltd v Commissioner of Works* [1943] 2 All ER 560). However, there is a division of functions under s 4 of the IA 1971. The immigration service is specifically made responsible for granting leave to enter the UK, whilst the Home Office in general deals with the subsequent variation of leave.

1.3.2   The immigration service

The immigration service consists of immigration officers, chief immigration officers and inspectors appointed by the Home Secretary. As explained in **1.3.1**, they are responsible for control on entry to the UK. They operate from the various ports of entry (including airports). Division of functions between the immigration service and the Home Office in general is not always clear-cut, as the Home Secretary may validly delegate some functions (eg the decision to deport overstayers) to the immigration service (*Oladehinde v Secretary of State for the Home Department; Alexander v Secretary of State for the Home Department* [1990] 3 WLR 797).

1.3.3   The UK Border Agency

Until 2013 the UK Border Agency (UKBA) was a shadow agency of the Home Office. It was responsible for managing border controls, as well as enforcing immigration and customs regulations. It considered applications for permission to enter or stay in the UK, citizenship and asylum.

1.3.4   The Identity and Passport Service

This is an executive agency of the Home Office. It issues UK passports.

1.3.5   International Group

The International Group is part of the Home Office. It operates visa offices, manned by entry clearance officers, in 250 locations throughout the world. The largest handles 300,000 applications a year; the smallest fewer than 10.

1.3.6   The First-tier Tribunal (Immigration and Asylum Chamber)

Many, but not all, of the decisions made by an official in an immigration context are appealable to the First-tier Tribunal (Immigration and Asylum Chamber). Any further appeal on a point of law is to the Upper Tribunal and the Court of Appeal. See further **Chapter 11**.

1.4   IMMIGRATION CONTROLS

1.4.1   Right of abode in the UK

As we have seen, a British citizen has a right of abode in the UK. So, if a British citizen leaves the UK, he is free to return at any point in time and enter the UK via an airport or a port. Subject to producing evidence of that right of abode, usually by way of a British passport, he is not subject to immigration controls. This applies equally to a British citizen born abroad who travels to the UK for the first time.

Note that certain Commonwealth citizens also have a right of abode in the UK (see **2.3**). Also, EEA nationals are not subject to domestic UK immigration laws when entering the UK under EU law (see **Chapter 4**).

1.4.2   Entry clearance, leave to enter and leave to remain in the UK

Immigration controls are dealt with in detail in **Chapter 3**. However, it is important to grasp the following points at this stage. As a general rule, immigration controls may exist at three particular points in time, namely:

(a)   before a person travels to the UK. This is known as entry clearance and most persons, apart from some people who wish to enter for less than six months, must obtain it;

(b)   on arrival in the UK at the port of entry. This is known as leave to enter the UK. All people who are subject to immigration controls must obtain permission to enter the UK when first arriving;

(c)   after arrival, if an extension of the initial limited time granted for the stay is required.

1.4.3   Visa nationals

A 'visa national' is a person who always needs entry clearance in advance of travelling to the UK for whatever purpose. The entry clearance document he needs to obtain from the British High Commission or embassy in his own country before travelling is a visa, and this will state the purpose of the entry to the UK, for example as a visitor or student, etc. Most visas appear as a stamp in the person's passport. A list of countries whose nationals must obtain visas appears in Appendix 1 to the Immigration Rules (see **Appendix 1** to this book).

Upon arriving at a UK port of entry, a visa national usually requires leave to enter the UK, that is, he must convince the immigration officer that entry is pursuant to the terms of his visa. If leave is given, a stamp to that effect is put in his passport.

> **EXAMPLE**
>
> Kim is Chinese. He is a visa national. He wishes to come to the UK for a holiday. If he is to be given leave to enter the UK, he must, as a general rule:
>
> (a)   obtain a visa in China before travelling; and
>
> (b)   on arrival in the UK, convince the immigration officer that he is entering as a genuine visitor.

1.4.4 Non-visa nationals

A non-visa national is a person who is not on the visa list. He does not require entry clearance in advance of travelling to the UK for short-term purposes, ie a stay of up to six months in the UK, such as a visitor (see **Chapter 5**). However, he will require it for long-term purposes (ie a stay of more than six months), for example as an employee or a businessman, or if he wishes to stay permanently in the UK. The entry clearance document he needs to obtain from the British High Commission or embassy in his own country before travelling is an entry certificate. This will state the purpose of the entry to the UK, for example 'settlement as spouse', and usually appears as a stamp in the person's passport.

Upon arriving at a UK port of entry, a non-visa national will require leave to enter the UK, ie he must convince the immigration officer that entry is pursuant to the Immigration Rules.

EXAMPLE

Bob is an American. He is a non-visa national. He wishes to come to the UK for a holiday (ie for up to six months). He does not have to obtain an entry certificate in America before travelling but, on arrival, he must convince the immigration officer that he is entering as a genuine visitor, if he is to be given leave to enter. But if Bob wanted to enter and stay for more than six months, he would need to obtain an entry certificate before travelling to the UK.

1.4.5 Settled status

A person with 'settled status' (also known as unconditional leave, permanent stay, permanent residence, indefinite leave and settlement) does not have the right of abode in the UK and so, in theory, can be deported (see **Chapter 10**). This is a person who is legally in the UK without any conditions or restrictions being placed on his residence. Hence, it is not limited in time. If a person with settled status leaves the UK, he will be subject to immigration control on return, ie he will need leave to enter the UK on the basis that he is returning to reside again (see **3.8.3**).

1.4.6 Summary: who does what?

- Entry clearance officer (ECO) – visas and entry certificates;
- Immigration officer – leave to enter the UK;
- Home Office – extension of stay in UK, including switching of category.

BRITISH NATIONALITY AND RIGHT OF ABODE

2.1 INTRODUCTION

The law relating to nationality or citizenship forms the background to immigration law because a person's right to live in the country of his choice often depends on his nationality. This is true in UK law, in that a British citizen has a right to live in the UK.

There are two categories of people who have a statutory 'right of abode in the UK': all British citizens (see **2.2**) and certain Commonwealth citizens (see **2.3**). A person with the right of abode can freely enter the UK (ie he is not subject to immigration controls (see **1.4** and **Chapter 3**)). Moreover, he cannot be excluded from the UK (ie he cannot be removed or deported (see **Chapter 10**)). Nationals of the EEA do not have the right of abode, although they have a right of entry to and residence in the UK under EU law (see **Chapter 4**).

2.2 BRITISH CITIZENSHIP

British nationality law has changed considerably over the last century. For an historical analysis, see **2.4**. The British Nationality Act 1981 (BNA 1981) was implemented on 1 January 1983, thereby creating the nationality of British citizenship. The starting points for determining whether a person is a British citizen or not is to ask two questions:

(a)   was he born before 1983 or after 1982; and

(b)   was he born in the UK or elsewhere?

There is a summary of the key requirements at **Appendix 6**.

2.2.1 People born in the UK before 1983

A person is a British citizen if, before 1983 (ie, up to and including 31 December 1982), he was born in the UK.

2.2.2 People born outside the UK before 1983

A person is a British citizen if, before 1983, he was born outside the UK and:

(a)   his father was born in the UK; *or*

(b)   his father was registered or naturalised (see **2.2.6.1** and **2.2.7**) as a British citizen in the UK before the child's birth (if a father becomes British after the child's birth, this does not retrospectively make the child British); *and*

(c)   his parents were married, or subsequently marry in a country where that marriage operates to legitimise the child.

So, before 1983, a father could pass on his British citizenship acquired in the UK only to his legitimate child. An illegitimate child could not 'inherit' British citizenship through his father.

> **EXAMPLES**
>
> 1. Joshua was born in 1962 in the UK. He is therefore a British citizen (see **2.2.1**). In 1980 he married Grace (who is not a British citizen). In 1981 their daughter, Sophie, was born outside the UK. Sophie is a British citizen as her father was born in the UK and married to her mother at the time of Sophie's birth.
>
> 2. Harry was born in 1961 in the UK. He is therefore a British citizen (see **2.2.1**). In 1979 he started a relationship with Lynda (who is not a British citizen). In 1981 their son, Michael, was born outside the UK. In 1982 Harry and Lynda married in a country where their marriage operated to legitimise Michael who thereby became a British citizen.
>
> 3. James was born in 1960 in the UK. He is therefore a British citizen (see **2.2.1**). In 1978 he started a relationship with Lilly (who is not a British citizen). In 1981 their daughter, Katie, was born outside the UK. James and Lilly never marry. Katie is not a British citizen on these facts.

Before 1983, a mother could not pass on her British citizenship acquired by her birth, registration or naturalisation in the UK to any child born outside the UK. However, in those circumstances, the Home Office allowed for the child to be registered as British, and this is now possible pursuant to BNA 1981, s 4C (see **2.2.6**).

> **EXAMPLE**
>
> Ruby was born in 1959 in the UK. She is therefore a British citizen (see **2.2.1**). In 1980 she married Gary (who is not a British citizen). In 1982 their son, Simon, was born outside the UK. Although Ruby is a British citizen at the time of her son's birth, she cannot pass that citizenship on to him. However, she could have applied to register him as a British citizen whilst he was a child, or he may do so as an adult: see **2.2.6**.

2.2.3   People born in the UK after 1982

A person is a British citizen if, after 1982 (ie, from and including 1 January 1983), he was born in the UK and at the time of his birth either of his parents was:

(a)   a British citizen; *or*

(b)   settled in the UK. (As to settled status, see **1.4.5** and **3.8**. Note that for these purposes a Commonwealth citizen with the right of abode (see **2.3**) is treated as 'settled'.)

Note that until the Nationality, Immigration and Asylum Act 2002 (NIAA 2002) came into force on 1 July 2006, a 'parent' in this context did not include a father of a child who was not married to the child's mother. However, the BNA 1981, as amended by the NIAA 2002, provides at s 50(9A) that from 1 July 2006 a child's father is:

(a)   the husband, at the time of the child's birth, of the woman who gives birth to the child (and remember that if the parents subsequently marry that may operate to legitimise the child); or

(b)   where a person is treated as the father of the child under s 28 of the Human Fertilisation and Embryology Act 1990, that person; or

(c)   where neither paragraph (a) nor (b) applies, any person who is proven to be the father by the production of either a birth certificate identifying him as such that is issued by the competent registration authority within 12 months of the birth of the child to which it relates, or such other evidence (eg a DNA test report or court order) as may satisfy the Secretary of State on this point.

This means that subject to satisfying (c) above, an illegitimate person born in the UK on or after 1 July 2006 is a British citizen if his father was either a British citizen or settled at that time. What if an illegitimate person can meet these requirements but he was born in the UK before July 2006? In these circumstances the person may apply to register as a British citizen which the Home Office may grant at its discretion. Note that in addition to the usual requirements, if the applicant is a child the consent of all parties with parental responsibility must be given.

EXAMPLES

1. Evie was born in 1965 in the UK. She is therefore a British citizen (see **2.2.1**). In 1990 she gave birth to her daughter, Charlotte, in the UK. Charlotte is a British citizen as her mother was a British citizen at the time of Charlotte's birth.

2. Chloe was born outside the UK in 1967 as a visa national. In 1970 she entered the UK with her family for the purposes of settlement. She had indefinite leave to remain in the UK when she gave birth to her son, Lewis, in 1987 in the UK. Lewis is a British citizen as his mother was settled in the UK at the time of his birth.

3. John was born in 1970 in the UK. He is therefore a British citizen (see **2.2.1**). In 1995 he married Helen (who is not a British citizen). In 1997 their daughter, Sally, was born in the UK. Sally is a British citizen as her father was a British citizen and married to her mother at the time of Sally's birth.

4. Oliver was born outside the UK in 1980 as a visa national. In 1992 he entered the UK with his family for the purposes of settlement. He had indefinite leave to remain in the UK when his girlfriend, Jessica, gave birth to his son, Alfie, in 2008 in the UK. Jessica had limited leave to remain in the UK at that point in time. Alfie is a British citizen if Oliver and Jessica subsequently marry in a country where their marriage operates to legitimise him; or if Oliver is named as his father on his birth certificate that was issued within one year his birth; or if the Secretary of State accepts other evidence that Oliver is his father.

5. What if, in Example 4, Alfie had been born before 1 July 2006? In those circumstances Alfie could be registered as a British citizen at the discretion of the Secretary of State. See further **2.2.6**.

Note that if, at any time after his birth but before he reaches 18, either of his parents becomes a British citizen or settled in the UK, he may be able to register as a British citizen (see **2.2.6.1**).

2.2.4 People born outside the UK after 1982

A person is a British citizen if, after 1982, he is born outside the UK, and:

(a) his father or mother was a British citizen otherwise than by descent by birth in the UK (see **2.2.5**); *or*

(b) his father or mother was a British citizen otherwise than by descent (see **2.2.5**), having been registered or naturalised (see **2.2.6.1** and **2.2.7**) as a British citizen in the UK before the child's birth (if either parent becomes British after the child's birth, this does not retrospectively make the child British).

As noted at **2.2.3**, until the NIAA 2002 came into force on 1 July 2006, a 'parent' in this context did not include a father of a child who was not married to the child's mother.

This means that subject to satisfying condition (c) of s 50(9A) of the BNA 1981 (**2.2.3**), an illegitimate person born outside the UK on or after 1 July 2006 is a British citizen if his father was a British citizen otherwise than by descent (see **2.2.5**), or registered or naturalised as a British citizen before the child's birth.

> **EXAMPLES**
>
> 1. Amelia was born in 1970 in the UK. She is therefore a British citizen otherwise than by descent (see **2.2.5.1**). In 1990 she gave birth to her son, Charles, outside the UK. Charles is a British citizen (by descent: see **2.2.5.2**) as his mother was a British citizen otherwise than by descent at the time of Charles's birth.
>
> 2. Benjamin was born in 1972 in the UK. He is therefore a British citizen otherwise than by descent (see **2.2.5.1**). In 1997 he married Adela, a visa national. In 1999 their daughter, Ramona, was born outside the UK. Ramona is a British citizen (by descent: **2.2.5.2**) as her father was a British citizen otherwise than by descent and married to her mother at the time of Ramona's birth.
>
> 3. Ethan was born in the UK in 1980. He is therefore a British citizen otherwise than by descent (see **2.2.5.1**). In 2007 his girlfriend, Alice, gave birth to his son, Zach, outside the UK. Alice is a visa national. Zach is a British citizen by descent (see **2.2.5.2**) if Ethan and Alice subsequently marry in a country where their marriage operates to legitimise him; or if Ethan is named as his father on his birth certificate that was issued within one year his birth; or if the Secretary of State accepts other evidence that Ethan is his father.

2.2.5   British citizenship: what about subsequent generations?

2.2.5.1   British citizen otherwise than by descent

A person who acquires British citizenship by birth in the UK (see **2.2.1** and **2.2.3**), or as a child by registration in the UK (see **2.2.6.1**) or as an adult by naturalisation in the UK (see **2.2.7**), is classified as a *British citizen otherwise than by descent*. This means he can automatically pass on British citizenship to a child born outside the UK in the circumstances described at **2.2.2** and **2.2.4** above.

2.2.5.2   British citizen by descent

Where a person is born outside the UK (see **2.2.2** and **2.2.4**) and acquires British citizenship only because one or both of his parents is a British citizen, he is classified as a *British citizen by descent*. This means that he cannot automatically pass on British citizenship to any child who is also born abroad. However, some second-generation children can be registered abroad at the British consulate as British citizens (by descent) if:

(a)   one of the parents is a British citizen by descent; and

(b)   the British parent has a parent who is or was British otherwise than by descent; and

(c)   the British parent had at some time before the child's birth lived in the UK for a continuous period of three years, not being absent for more than 270 days in that period.

In addition an applicant aged 10 or over will have to satisfy the Secretary of State that he is of good character (see **2.2.7.1(f)**). In these circumstances a child is registered as a British citizen by descent – the registration takes place outside the UK and is based not on any residence in the UK by the child but by his British parent in the past before the child's birth.

What if (a) and (b) are met but not (c)? It will be possible to register the child in the UK as a British citizen if during his childhood his father and mother come and live in the UK with him for a continuous period of three years and are not absent during that time for more than 270 days. Note that the requirement is that both parents live in the UK unless one of them is dead or the couple have divorced. In addition an applicant aged 10 or over will have to satisfy the Secretary of State that he is of good character (see **2.2.7.1(f)**). In these circumstances a child is registered as a British citizen otherwise than by descent because the registration takes place in the UK and is based on the family's residence in the UK.

> **EXAMPLE**
>
> James was born in Germany in 1975. His father, Larry, was born in London, England in 1945. Larry had married James's mother in 1965. In 1990, James married Steffi, a German national. In 2005, their son, Thomas, was born in Germany.
>
> Larry was born before 1983 in the UK and is therefore a British citizen otherwise than by descent. His son, James, was born outside the UK before 1983 and is therefore British by descent. Thomas can be registered as a British citizen by descent if James has lived in the UK at some time for a continuous period of three years before Thomas's birth.
>
> What if James has not lived in the UK for the requisite period before Thomas's birth or, alternatively, the family are just about to move to the UK to live there permanently? If James, Steffi and Thomas all come to live in the UK whilst Thomas is still a child and do so for a continuous period of three years, Thomas may be registered as a British citizen otherwise than by descent.

Can a British citizen by descent apply for naturalisation as a British citizen (see **2.2.7**) in order that his children born abroad automatically become British citizens? No, held the Court of Appeal in the case of R v *Secretary of State for the Home Department, ex p Azad Ullah* [2001] INLR 74.

2.2.6 Registration as a British citizen

2.2.6.1 Child born in the UK after 1982

A child can apply to register as a British citizen, pursuant to s 1(3) and (4) of the BNA 1981, if he was born in the UK after 1982 and, after his birth:

(a) one of his parents becomes a British citizen or settled in the UK (see **3.8**) before he is 18; or

(b) he remains in the UK for the first 10 years of his life and is not absent for more than 90 days each year during that period. By s 1(7), a longer period of absence may be acceptable.

In addition, an applicant aged 10 or over will have to satisfy the Secretary of State that he is of good character (see **2.2.7.1(f)**).

Such a person is a British citizen otherwise than by descent (see **2.2.5**).

2.2.6.2 Child born outside the UK before 1983

As we saw at **2.2.2**, a British mother could not before 1983 transmit her British citizenship acquired in the UK to her child born outside the UK. However, by concession, the Home Office did allow such a child to be registered as British (by descent), provided the application was made before the child reached 18. What if no such registration occurred, given that the concession, by its very nature, expired at the end of 2000? Section 4C of the BNA 1981 now gives a right to such a person born before 1 January 1983 to apply to register as a British citizen. An applicant under s 4C has to satisfy the Secretary of State that he is of good character (see **2.2.7.1(f)**) before being registered.

Such a person is a British citizen by descent (see **2.2.5**).

2.2.7 Naturalisation

If a foreign national adult living in the UK has settled status (see **1.4.5** and **3.8**), he may wish to apply to become a British citizen (otherwise than by descent) by a process known as naturalisation. Under s 6 of the BNA 1981, the Home Secretary has a discretion to grant a certificate of naturalisation to any person aged 18 or over who is not a British citizen. The grant of British citizenship under s 6 is not a fundamental human right: R v *Secretary of State for the Home Department, ex p Al Fayed* [2001] Imm AR 134 and R (AHK) v *Secretary of State for the Home Department* [2009] EWCA Civ 287. As Blake J stated at first instance in AHK (in a judgment entitled *MH v Secretary of State for the Home Department* [2008] EWHC 2525, at [41]): 'In general terms ... no claimant [under s 6] has a right to British citizenship, but only a right to have an application fairly considered under the statutory scheme.'

The requirements are slightly different, depending on whether or not the applicant is married to or in a civil partnership with a British citizen at the time the application is made. Broadly, those requirements are as follows.

2.2.7.1   If the applicant is married to, or in a civil partnership with, a British citizen

The applicant:

(a)   must be settled (see **3.8**) at the time of the application;

(b)   must have been living in the UK legally for at least three years continuously before making the application;

(c)   must have been physically present in the UK on the date three years before the application is made. The start of the qualifying period of three years is the day after the corresponding application date. So, for example, if the application is received by the Home Office on 5 January 2014, the three-year qualifying period starts on 6 January 2011;

(d)   must not have been absent for more than 270 days in total during the three-year qualifying period, and not more than 90 days in the year immediately before the application. The Home Office has indicated that it will normally disregard 30 days and 10 days respectively over these limits, provided all the other requirements are met. If the absences are greater than that, see the Home Office guidance, 'Naturalisation Booklet – The Requirements' on the Home Office website (see **1.2.8**). What is the purpose of this residence requirement? Home Office guidance is that it allows an applicant to demonstrate close links with, and commitment to, the UK, and enables the Home Secretary to assess the strength of that commitment as well as the applicant's suitability on the other grounds;

(e)   must have sufficient knowledge of the English language and sufficient knowledge about life in the UK. How can an applicant demonstrate this? The answer is to be found in the British Nationality (General) Regulations 2003 (SI 2003/548, as amended), reg 5A. Broadly, the requirements are that the applicant either:

(i)   passes a formal test known as the 'Life in the UK Test'; or

(ii)   has already satisfied the Secretary of State that he has sufficient knowledge of language and life in the UK when granted indefinite leave to remain (see **3.8.7**); or

(iii)   attends a course at an accredited college where the course materials include 'Citizenship Materials for English for Speakers of Other Languages (ESOL) Learners', can demonstrate relevant progress on that course, and is awarded an ESOL qualification in speaking and listening. In order to demonstrate relevant progress on the course, the applicant's ability is assessed before the course starts and he must achieve at least one grade higher by the end of the course, eg if the applicant is assessed as being below Entry 1, he must attain his qualification at Entry 1, 2 or 3.

What is the 'Life in the UK Test'? The test has to be taken on a computer and consists of 24 questions, such as: where is the Prime Minister's official home in London, and is it true or false that UK citizens can vote in an election at the age of 18? It is based on the Government handbook, 'Life in the United Kingdom: A Guide for New Residents'. It can be taken only at an official testing centre. Note that in Wales and Scotland the test can be taken in Welsh or Scottish Gaelic, as appropriate. Full details are on the website, www.lifeintheuktest.ukba.homeoffice.gov.uk.

If an applicant already has sufficient knowledge of English (Welsh or Scottish Gaelic) then, as we have seen, passing the Life in the UK Test will satisfy both requirements. If an applicant is unsure of his language ability, he can obtain an initial assessment from any further education college or learndirect centre (www.learndirect.com).

In what circumstances will the Home Office waive these requirements? If the applicant is aged over 65; suffers from a long-term illness or disability which severely restricts his ability to attend ESOL classes or to prepare for the test; is deaf, mute or suffers from any speech impediment which limits his ability to converse in the relevant language; or suffers from a mental impairment and is thereby unable to speak or learn the relevant language. Home Office guidance is that if an applicant claims to have a physical disability or a mental impairment, he must provide original and current medical evidence from a medical practitioner. This must state the condition and explain why it is unreasonable to expect the applicant to take the Life in the UK test or attend an ESOL course; and

(f) must show good character. This requirement is not defined in the BNA 1981. In *R (Thamby) v Secretary of State for the Home Department* [2011] EWHC 1763 Parker J stated, at [41]:

> It is a term capable of carrying a range of meanings, and requires an exercise in evaluation to apply it. It is established that this means that the proper approach of the courts to considering the standard of good character adopted by the Secretary of State and the application of the concept in a particular case is to ask whether the standard and its application were such as could reasonably be adopted in the circumstances: *ex p Al Fayed* [2001] Imm AR 134, [41] (Nourse LJ), [93] (Kennedy LJ) and [97] (Rix LJ). It is open to the Secretary of State, so long as she acts rationally, to adopt a high standard of good character, and one higher than other reasonable decision-makers might have adopted: *ex p Al Fayed* at [41] (Nourse LJ).

The applicant must disclose on the application form details of all criminal convictions both within and outside the UK. These include road traffic offences. Fixed penalty notices are not normally taken into account unless the applicant has had more than one in the previous 12 months.

So what convictions affect an application? **Table 2.1** gives examples of sentences, along with the relevant sentence-based threshold. In calculating the threshold, it is the prison sentence that counts, not the time served. Note that a suspended sentence counts as if it were a prison sentence.

Table 2.1 Criminality requirement

Sentence	Impact on nationality application
4 years' or more imprisonment	Application should be refused, regardless of when the conviction occurred
Between 12 months' and 4 years' imprisonment	Application should be refused unless 15 years have passed since the end of the sentence
Up to 12 months' imprisonment in the last 7 years	Application should be refused unless 7 years have passed since the end of the sentence.
A non-custodial offence	Application should be refused if the conviction occurred in the last 3 years.

2.2.7.2 If the applicant is neither married to, nor in a civil partnership with, a British citizen

The applicant:

(a) must have been settled (see **3.8**) for at least one year before the application;

(b) must have been living in the UK legally for five years continuously before making the application;

(c) must have been physically present in the UK on the date five years before the application is received by the Home Office;

(d) must not have been absent for more than 450 days in total during the five-year qualifying period, and not more than 90 days in the year immediately before the application is made (see **2.2.7.1(d)** for Home Office policy where this is exceeded);

(e)   must have sufficient knowledge of the English language and sufficient knowledge about life in the UK (see **2.2.7.1(e)**);

(f)   must show good character (see **2.2.7.1(f)**); and

(g)   must show an intention to live in the UK. Home Office guidance is that this requirement is usually met if the applicant's stated intention is to have his home or, if more than one, his principal home in the UK. Factors affecting this will include whether a home here (owned or rented) has already been established and the reason for any past or intended future absences.

2.2.7.3   EEA nationals

Certain EEA nationals are treated as settled for the purposes of naturalisation: **3.8.9**.

2.2.8   Formalities for registration and naturalisation

These are governed by the BNA 1981 and the British Nationality (General) Regulations 2003 (SI 2003/548). In particular, applicants of full age are required to make an oath of allegiance and pledge. The latter states that the person will respect the rights and freedoms of the UK and will uphold its democratic values, observe its laws, and fulfil the duties and obligations of citizenship.

2.2.9   Deprivation of citizenship obtained by registration or naturalisation

This is governed by s 40 of the BNA 1981 and the British Nationality (General) Regulations 2003 (SI 2003/548). The Secretary of State may by order deprive a person of his British citizenship status if satisfied that it would be conducive to the public good. Home Office guidance is that this can be done in cases involving national security, terrorism, serious organised crime, war crimes and unacceptable behaviour such as preaching *jihad*.

The Secretary of State may also by order deprive a person of his British citizenship status where it was obtained by registration or naturalisation, if satisfied that such was obtained by means of fraud, false representation or concealment of a material fact.

The Secretary of State may not make either of the above orders if it would make a person stateless: see *Al-Jedda v Secretary of State for the Home Department* [2010] EWCA Civ 212. The Court held that the burden is on the appellant to show on the balance of probabilities that he will become stateless. See also *B2 v Secretary of State for the Home Department* [2013] EWCA Civ 616 for a discussion of the meaning of statelessness under the BNA 1981.

Before making a deprivation order the Secretary of State must give the person concerned written notice specifying that a decision has been made to make the order and the reasons for it. The notice must also advise the person of his right to appeal (see **Chapter 11**). Does the fact that the person has to conduct his appeal from outside the UK render the exclusion decision procedurally unfair? No, held the Court of Appeal in *GI v Secretary of State for the Home Department* [2012] EWCA Civ 867. On appeal, the Tribunal has to ask itself 'does the evidence in the case establish that citizenship was obtained by fraud?' If it does then it has to answer the question 'do the other circumstances of the case point to discretionary deprival?' See *Arusha and Demushi (deprivation of citizenship – delay)* [2012] UKUT 80 (IAC).

2.3   COMMONWEALTH CITIZENS WITH RIGHT OF ABODE

There are two categories of Commonwealth citizens who have the right of abode in the UK, ie the right to enter the UK without being subject to immigration controls (see **1.4** and **Chapter 3**). There is a list of Commonwealth countries in **Appendix 9**.

2.3.1   Parental link

The first category concerns those Commonwealth citizens with a 'parental link' to the UK. The requirements are that:

(a)   the person was a Commonwealth citizen on 31 December 1982, and continues to be such; and

(b)   either parent was born in the UK. 'Parent' in this context includes the mother, but not the father, of an illegitimate child.

EXAMPLE

Bill was born in New Zealand in 1979. His mother, Ada, was born in London, England. His father was a citizen of New Zealand. Assuming that Bill is a citizen of New Zealand under that country's nationality laws and so remained, Bill was a Commonwealth citizen on 31 December 1982. Bill cannot be a British citizen by descent as his father was not British and, before 1983, mothers could not pass on their citizenship (see **2.2.2**). However, as a Commonwealth citizen, he has the right of abode in the UK by virtue of his mother's birth in the UK. Query if Ada registered him as British in these circumstances before he reached 18 or, if she failed to do so, whether he can now apply (see **2.2.6.2**).

2.3.2   Acquired by marriage

The second category concerns those Commonwealth citizen women who acquired the right of abode by marriage. The requirements are that:

(a)   the woman was a Commonwealth citizen on 31 December 1982 and continues to be such; and

(b)   on or before 31 December 1982, she married a man who at the time of the marriage was either:

   (i)   born, registered or naturalised in the UK, or

   (ii)   was a Commonwealth citizen with a right of abode through a parental link (see **2.3.1**).

Note that any subsequent divorce or the death of the husband does not affect her status.

EXAMPLES

1.   Anna was a citizen of Barbados on 31 December 1982 and continues to be such. In 1980 she married Frank. He had been born in the UK in 1960. Anna acquired the right of abode in the UK by marrying Frank.

2.   Barbara was a citizen of Fiji on 31 December 1982 and continues to be such. In 1975 she married Luke. He had been born in Fiji in 1955 and was a Fijian national. His mother had been born in the UK. Provided Barbara can produce evidence that Luke was a Commonwealth citizen with the right of abode by his parental link (see **2.3.1**), she acquired the right of abode by marrying him. There is no requirement that Luke must have obtained his own certificate evidencing his right of abode.

2.3.3   Certificate of entitlement

A Commonwealth citizen with the right of abode will travel under his or her own country's passport. Before travelling to the UK for the first time, he or she should apply to the British High Commission for a certificate showing that right of abode.

To get the certificate in the first category, the applicant will need to produce:

(a)   evidence of being a Commonwealth citizen on 31 December 1982 and that he remains a Commonwealth citizen;

(b)   his own full birth certificate naming the appropriate parent;

(c)   the appropriate parent's full UK birth certificate; and

(d)   if claiming through the father, the parent's marriage certificate or evidence of relationship.

A check should always be made to see if the applicant can claim British citizenship (see **2.2.2**).

To get the certificate in the second category, the applicant will need to produce:

(a)   evidence of being a Commonwealth citizen on 31 December 1982 and that she remains a Commonwealth citizen;

(b)   her marriage certificate; and

(c)   evidence that her husband was either British by birth, registration or naturalisation in the UK (eg his UK birth, registration or naturalisation certificate), or a Commonwealth citizen with his own right of abode (as above).

2.3.4   Excluded Commonwealth nationals

It is important to note that as Cameroon, Mozambique, Namibia, Pakistan and South Africa were not members of the Commonwealth on 31 December 1982, nationals of those countries cannot take advantage of the above provisions.

2.3.5   Deprivation of right of abode

Section 2A of the IA 1971 gives the Secretary of State power to remove this right of abode if it is conducive to the public good to remove or exclude the Commonwealth citizen from the UK. There is a similar power for deprivation of British citizenship (see **2.2.9**).

There is a right of appeal to the IAC or, if issues of national security arise, to the Special Immigration Appeals Commission (see **Chapter 11**).

2.3.6   Flow diagram: summary

We have seen that before 1983 some Commonwealth citizens acquired the right of abode in the UK. The requirements are summarised in the flow diagram at **Appendix 10**.

2.4   HISTORICAL BACKGROUND

One of the difficulties in understanding the law in this area is that a person's citizenship may change over time. Someone born in the UK in 1940 would have had the status of 'British subject' at common law. Under the British Nationality Act 1948, he would have become a citizen of the UK and colonies (CUKC). Under the BNA 1981, he would become a British citizen. The problem is that his current citizenship status is defined in the legislation in terms of his earlier status. Thus, it is necessary to know a little of the history of citizenship law – in particular, three major developments, illustrated in the diagram below.

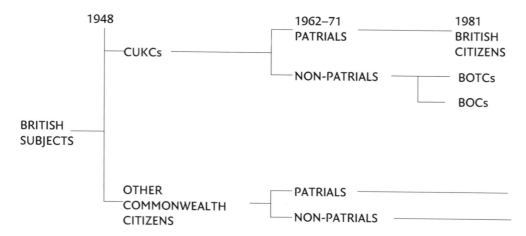

The terms used in the diagram have the broad meanings set out in **2.4.1** to **2.4.7** below.

2.4.1 British subjects

Before 1948, anyone who owed allegiance to the Crown, regardless of the Crown territory in which he was born.

2.4.2 CUKCs

After 1948, anyone connected with the UK or a Crown colony (such as Hong Kong).

2.4.3 Commonwealth citizens

After 1948, anyone having citizenship of an independent Commonwealth country, according to the law of that country. Independent Commonwealth countries included the former Dominions (eg Canada, Australia, New Zealand) and also former colonies (eg Jamaica) when they gained independence. On independence, existing citizens who were CUKCs might lose that status by becoming citizens of the newly independent Commonwealth country. The current list of countries whose citizens are Commonwealth citizens is given in **Appendix 9**. In addition, anyone who has British citizenship, British overseas territories citizenship or British overseas citizenship (see **2.4.5** to **2.4.7** below) is also a Commonwealth citizen.

2.4.4 Patrials

Anyone who under the IA 1971 had the right of abode in the UK. Until 1962, Commonwealth citizens and CUKCs could enter the UK freely. From that year, controls were introduced which were finally enacted in the 1971 Act. The controls extended to both CUKCs and Commonwealth citizens, but CUKCs and Commonwealth citizens who had a close connection with the UK were recognised as 'patrials', having the right of abode.

2.4.5 British citizens

Anyone who at 1 January 1983 was a CUKC with right of abode in the UK, and anyone who acquired British citizenship after that date (eg by birth in the UK, see **2.2.1**). British citizenship and the following categories of citizenship were created by BNA 1981.

2.4.6 British overseas territories citizens (BOTCs)

Anyone who at 1 January 1983 was a non-patrial CUKC, with a close connection with a colony, together with those later becoming BOTCs (eg by birth in the colony). The list of British overseas territories is given in **Appendix 11** to this book. By the Overseas Territories Act 2002, all BOTCs were granted British citizenship.

2.4.7 British overseas citizens (BOCs)

Anyone who at 1 January 1983 was a non-patrial CUKC, but without a close connection with a colony. This category included CUKCs living in a colony which gained independence, who did not acquire citizenship of the newly independent country (eg those of Asian origin in former colonies in East Africa).

This list is not exhaustive. There are other minor categories such as British protected persons, British nationals (overseas) and British subjects under the 1981 Act.

The following other major categories of citizens were unaffected by these changes in UK law.

2.4.8 Irish citizens

Citizens of the Republic of Ireland. They were not Commonwealth citizens under the British Nationality Act 1948. They are not subject to immigration controls (see **3.9**, Common Travel Area), but may be liable to deportation (see **Chapter 10**).

2.4.9 Aliens

Broadly, anyone who does not fall into the above categories. Immigration controls were introduced for aliens in 1905. They do not have the right of abode. However, UK law does permit dual nationality, so that someone who lacks the right of abode as an alien, may nevertheless have it if he can also claim British citizenship.

2.5 SUMMARY OF BRITISH CITIZENSHIP

A summary of British citizenship is set out in **Table 2.2** below.

Table 2.2 Summary of British Citizenship

	British citizen otherwise than by descent	British citizen by descent
Born in the UK before 1983	X	
Born in the UK after 1982 and either parent a British citizen or settled in the UK.	X	
Born in the UK after 1982 and subsequently either parent becomes a British citizen or settled in the UK before applicant is 18.	X	
Born in the UK after 1982 and remains in the UK for the first 10 years of life, and is not absent for more than 90 days each year during that period.	X	
Born outside UK before 1983 and father born, registered or naturalised in the UK and married to mother (or parents subsequently marry in a country where that marriage operates to legitimise the child).		X
Born outside UK before 1983 and mother born, registered or naturalised in the UK and registered child before reached 18 (or registers subsequently).		X
Born outside UK after 1982 and either parent a British citizen otherwise than by descent		X
Born outside UK after 1982 and one parent a British citizen by descent; and the British parent has a parent who is or was British otherwise than by descent; and the British parent had at some time before the child's birth lived in the UK for a continuous period of three years, not being absent for more than 270 days in that period.		X
Born outside UK after 1982 and one parent a British citizen by descent; and the British parent has a parent who is or was British otherwise than by descent; and the family lives in the UK during applicant's childhood for a continuous period of three years and is not absent during that time for more than 270 days.	X	
Naturalised in UK	X	

CHAPTER 3

IMMIGRATION STATUS

3.1 IMMIGRATION CONTROLS

As we saw at **1.4**, a person with the right of abode in the UK (British citizens – see **2.2** – and certain Commonwealth citizens – see **2.3**) can enter without being subject to any immigration controls. All that person has to do is produce documentary evidence of that right of abode, usually a British passport or a Commonwealth country passport with a certificate of the right of abode.

Nationals of the EEA may enter the UK under EU law (see **Chapter 4**) rather than domestic UK law.

Everyone else is subject to immigration controls. Full details are given at **3.4**.

3.2 IMMIGRATION RULES

3.2.1 An overview

You will find it useful to take a brief look at the contents of the Immigration Rules. You will see that they start with a brief introduction, and importantly there are some useful definitions of key terms in para 6. The Rules are then divided into 13 Parts, each Part dealing with a discrete topic. So, for example, Part 1 sets out the general provisions regarding leave to enter or remain in the UK.

3.2.2 Structure

Parts 2 to 8 of the Rules set out the various different categories of entry to the UK. Why is the structure of the Rules for some categories different from others? This is because some categories require entry clearance, whilst a few do not for non-visa nationals. Also, some categories can lead to settlement, whilst others cannot.

Look at Part 2 and the category of 'general visitor' at para 41. You should already appreciate that only a non-visa national can enter as a general visitor without obtaining entry clearance (see **1.4.2**). So why does the paragraph state that it deals with 'The requirements to be met by a person seeking leave to enter the United Kingdom as a general visitor'? For the answer we need to go back to para 26, which provides that 'An application for entry clearance will be considered in accordance with the provisions in these Rules governing the grant or refusal of leave to enter.' So, a visa national general visitor must satisfy the entry clearance officer that he meets the requirements of para 41 in order to get his visa before travelling to the UK. Then, on arrival at a UK airport or port, he may have to satisfy the immigration officer that he meets the requirements of para 41 in order to get leave to enter the UK. Any such leave will be granted pursuant to para 42, and so will be for a period not exceeding six months and subject to a condition prohibiting employment (see **3.3.1**). As a general visitor cannot subsequently apply for settlement, that is the basic structure of the provisions dealing with a visitor.

In 2008 the Government introduced a points system for entry to work in the UK (see Part 6A, dealt with in **Chapter 7**). It took that opportunity to restructure the paragraphs dealing with those categories, which now clearly state which requirements are for entry clearance etc. Likewise, when in 2012 the Government made significant changes to most family reunion routes into the UK (see **Chapter 8**), it modernised the structure and content of the new requirements.

3.2.3 Legal status of the requirements

After entering the UK an entrant does not commit a criminal offence by no longer meeting any particular requirement. For example, a student may no longer be following any course of study at all (see *OO v Secretary of State for the Home Department* [2008] EWCA Civ 747). However, if that comes to the attention of the Home Office, it may end the leave by what is known as curtailment (see **3.7**). If an application is made to extend or vary the leave (see **3.6**) it is likely to be refused.

3.3 CONDITIONS OF LIMITED LEAVE

By s 3(1) of the IA 1971, a person granted limited leave to enter or remain in the UK may be subject to all or any of the following conditions:

(a)   a condition restricting his employment or occupation in the UK;

(b)   a condition requiring him to maintain and accommodate himself, and any dependants of his, without recourse to public funds;

(c)   a condition requiring him to register with the police;

(d)   a condition requiring him to report to an immigration officer or the Secretary of State; and

(e)   a condition about residence.

3.3.1 Restricting employment or occupation

The category of entry will determine the nature of this condition, and the answer can be found by looking at the relevant paragraph under which leave is granted. So, as we saw at **3.2.2**, a general visitor's limited leave is subject to a condition prohibiting employment. That is because a general visitor should not work at all. A student may work only within prescribed guidelines (see para 95 and **6.6.4**). An entrepreneur is not permitted to take employment, other than working for the business or businesses which he has established, joined or taken over (see para 245M and **7.4**).

Note that para 6 defines 'employment' as including paid and unpaid employment, paid and unpaid work placements undertaken as part of a course or period of study, self-employment and engaging in business or any professional activity.

3.3.2 Not to have recourse to public funds

3.3.2.1 What are public funds?

All entrants with limited leave are subject to a condition not to have recourse to public funds. This is because all entrants are supposed to be self-sufficient and able to maintain and accommodate themselves and any dependants. So what count as public funds? All that follow:

(a)   housing of homeless persons under Pts VI or VII of the Housing Act 1996 and under Pt II of the Housing Act 1985;

(b) the non-means tested welfare benefits of attendance allowance, carer's allowance, child benefit, personal independence payment, and disability living allowance;

(c) the means-tested benefits of universal credit, income support, income-related employment and support allowance, income-based jobseeker's allowance, council tax benefit and a council tax reduction under a council tax reduction scheme, housing benefit, State pension credit, child tax credit and working tax credit; and

(d) a Social Fund payment.

The following do not count as public funds:

(a) the National Insurance-based welfare benefits of contribution-based jobseeker's allowance, contributory employment and support allowance, State pension and bereavement benefits;

(b) National Health Service treatment and education for a child at a local authority maintained school.

3.3.2.2 Additional public funds

Very often entry to the UK is for the purposes of family reunion (see **Chapter 8**), for example a child joining a parent who is already settled in the UK. The person settled in the UK is often known as the 'sponsor'. If a sponsor already receives public funds, will entry clearance be refused? Paragraph 6A makes an important qualification to this condition. It states that

> For the purpose of these Rules, a person (P) is not to be regarded as having (or potentially having) recourse to public funds merely because P is (or will be) reliant in whole or in part on public funds provided to P's sponsor unless, as a result of P's presence in the United Kingdom, the sponsor is (or would be) entitled to increased or additional public funds (save where such entitlement to increased or additional public funds is by virtue of P and the sponsor's joint entitlement to benefits under the regulations referred to in paragraph 6B).

So, for example, if P seeks entry clearance to live permanently with his sponsor (S) in the UK, the application will not necessarily fail if S already receives one or more of the public funds. It will fail, however, if S becomes entitled either to an increase in the amount of his existing public funds, or to another public fund because of P's joining S in the UK.

Paragraph 6B provides as follows:

> Subject to paragraph 6C, a person (P) shall not be regarded as having recourse to public funds if P is entitled to benefits specified under section 115 of the Immigration and Asylum Act 1999 by virtue of regulations made under subsections (3) and (4) of that section or section 42 of the Tax Credits Act 2002.

Normally a person with limited leave to enter or remain in the UK is excluded from claiming mainstream welfare benefits (including those on the public funds list) by s 115 of the IAA 1999. However, a claim might be made by such a person if he meets the exceptions in subsections (3) and (4). Also, if the person has a partner who is entitled to apply for child and/or working tax credits, uniquely the application can be made jointly, and both count when the tax credits are calculated under the 2002 Act.

Paragraph 6C provides as follows:

> A person (P) making an application from outside the United Kingdom will be regarded as having recourse to public funds where P relies upon the future entitlement to any public funds that would be payable to P or to P's sponsor as a result of P's presence in the United Kingdom (including those benefits to which P or the sponsor would be entitled as a result of P's presence in the United Kingdom under the regulations referred to in to paragraph 6B).

What is the effect of paragraph 6C? First, note that it only concerns an application by P for entry clearance. That application will be refused if P shows that he will be adequately maintained in the UK only by relying upon his or his sponsor's future entitlement to any public funds, including tax credits or those payable to him under the IAA 1999, s 115(3) and (4).

This form of sponsorship should not be confused with the more formal and detailed sponsorship of students and workers, etc under Part 6A of the Immigration Rules (see **Chapters 6** and 7). Also see **3.4.4**.

For further details on this topic, see Chapter 10 of *Welfare Benefits*.

3.3.3 Registration with the police

Adult nationals of certain countries are listed in Appendix 2 to the Immigration Rules (see **Appendix 1** to this book) as they are required to register with the police within seven days of arriving in the UK (see Part 10 of the Rules). To register they need to produce their passports and pay a registration fee. If they are staying in the Metropolitan Police area in London, they should register at the Overseas Visitors Records Office, Brandon House, 180 Borough High Street, London, SE1 1LH. Otherwise they should contact their local police station for the address and opening hours of the nearest police registration office.

3.3.4 Reporting to an immigration officer or Secretary of State

This condition and the next (**3.3.5**) were introduced by s 16 of the UK Borders Act 2007. The Government's view was that without these powers it was difficult for the Home Office to maintain contact with foreign nationals during the currency of their limited leave, and to enforce their removal should that leave be curtailed (see **3.7**). The Government stated that it would apply these conditions to foreign national criminals, who cannot currently be removed due to the ECHR, and to certain children about whom there are particular concerns or who have been placed on discretionary leave (see **9.10**) with a view to their removal when they reach 18.

3.3.5 Residence

See **3.3.4** above.

3.3.6 Consequences of breach of a condition

Although it is an offence under s 24(1)(b) of the IA 1971 for a person with limited leave knowingly to breach a condition of leave, it is unusual for the Home Office to prosecute. Government policy is that if the breach is sufficiently serious, the person should be removed from the UK (see **10.2**).

3.4 ENTRY CLEARANCE

3.4.1 The general rule

The entry clearance procedure is, in effect, a form of pre-entry control, in which a UK official known as a visa or entry clearance officer (ECO) acts as an immigration officer, applying the Immigration Rules, but usually in the country in which the entrant is living before travel to the UK.

The form of clearance depends on the nationality of the entrant. The Immigration Rules specify countries whose nationals (known as 'visa nationals') require entry clearance in the form of a visa (usually stamped on the passport). A list of these countries is given in Appendix 1 to the Immigration Rules (**Appendix 1** to this book). In the case of some 'non-visa nationals', entry clearance is required for a stay of more than six months (see **2.1**). In this case, the entry clearance is shown by a different stamp, known as an entry certificate (see para 25 of the Immigration Rules).

An applicant for entry clearance as a visitor must apply to a particular designated post. However, any other type of application must be made to the appropriate designated post in the country or territory where the applicant is living. Applicants from certain countries can apply on-line at www.visa4uk.fco.gov.uk, although it should be noted that the website currently only supports applications made in English. Once they have submitted their on-line applications they are given an appointment to produce their original passports and supporting documents, and pay the appropriate fees if they have not already done so on-line. At that appointment the applicant's biographic and biometric data are collected (see **3.4.3**). These are then transmitted to the UK for checks.

Nationals listed in Appendix T of the Immigration Rules must undergo compulsory screening for active pulmonary tuberculosis if applying to enter the UK for more than six months.

Forms and guidance notes for making an application in writing can be found at www.ukvisas.gov.uk/en/howtoapply/vafs.

3.4.2   Leave under the Immigration and Asylum Act 1999

The IAA 1999 provides for greater flexibility in the way permission to enter the UK and to remain may be granted. Instead of leave to enter always having to be given in writing at a port of entry, the IAA 1999 allows for additional ways of giving leave to enter to be specified, eg that a visa or other entry clearance is to be treated as leave to enter. This means that holders of visas, for example, will be able to pass through the port control with only a quick check on identity and on the rightful ownership of the travel document and entry clearance, unless there is a need to examine for, among other matters, change of circumstances.

Most entry clearance now takes effect as leave to enter as well. This means that there are two significant dates to look out for on a visa or entry certificate, namely, the *effective date* and the *expiry date*. In most cases, the effective date will be the date on which the entry clearance is issued. However, some people may not intend or be able to travel to the UK immediately following their application, and in these circumstances an ECO will usually exercise his discretion to defer the effective date for up to three months after entry clearance has been authorised. So, in order to avoid the cost of making an unnecessary application for an extension of stay, an applicant should always confirm his date of travel.

For applicants in categories that require a qualifying period to be met before applying for settlement, or who have a limit imposed on their total length of stay in that category, their leave to enter will normally begin on the date they arrive in the UK within the three-month limit. This ensures that the maximum leave to which they are entitled is given.

The expiry date on a visa or entry certificate reflects the date on which the entry clearance and leave to enter are no longer effective. After this date the entry clearance will not be valid for travel to the UK, neither will it confer leave to enter.

3.4.3   Biometric information

All applicants are now routinely required to provide 10-digit fingerscans and a digital photograph when applying for UK entry clearance. The applicant attends a pre-arranged appointment. Fingerprints are taken on a glass screen scan. A digital photograph is taken. The biometric data are stored on a central government database in the UK and checked against UK government records.

3.4.4   Financial undertakings

Often entry clearance is sought for the purposes of immediate or ultimate settlement (eg child joining parent in UK, or grandparent joining grandchild in UK or spouse joining partner in UK, etc). The person based in the UK is usually known as 'the sponsor'. See the definition in Immigration Rules, para 6. This does not necessarily mean that that person has signed a written agreement with the DfWP to be financially responsible for the entrant. As para 35 of the Immigration Rules states: 'A sponsor of a person ... may be asked to give an undertaking in writing to be responsible for that person's maintenance [and] accommodation ...'. However, it will always be required when the adult dependent relative of a British citizen or a person settled in the UK seeks entry clearance to settle in the UK (see **8.11.6**). As to what constitutes a written undertaking, see *Ahmed v Secretary of State for Work and Pensions* [2005] EWCA Civ 535.

The Home Office uses Sponsorship Undertaking Form SU07. It can be found on the Home Office website (see **1.2.8**).

3.4.5 Refusal of entry clearance

3.4.5.1 Mandatory grounds

The general grounds for refusal of entry clearance (and leave to enter) are set out in para 320 of the Immigration Rules. Some of these are described as mandatory grounds, although in such cases an ECO should always consider any human rights grounds (in particular the right to family life under Article 8 ECHR) which would justify issuing the entry clearance.

Mandatory grounds for refusal are given in para 320(1)–(7D). These include that entry clearance must be refused in the following circumstances:

(a)   Where entry clearance is being sought for a purpose not covered by the Rules.

(b)   Where the applicant is currently the subject of a deportation order (see **10.1**) or has a relevant criminal conviction (see **Appendix 8**).

(c)   Where the applicant has failed to produce a valid national passport or other document satisfactorily establishing his identity.

(d)   Where the Secretary of State has personally directed that the exclusion of a person from the UK is conducive to the public good.

(e)   Where the Medical Inspector has confirmed that, for medical reasons, it is undesirable to admit a person seeking entry clearance to the UK and an ECO is satisfied that there are no strong, compassionate reasons justifying admission.

(f)   Where false representations have been made or false documents have been submitted (whether or not material to the application, and whether or not to the applicant's knowledge), or material facts have not been disclosed, in relation to the application. This includes false representations made in order to obtain supporting documents for an application, for example using false representations to obtain a genuine qualification.

Home Office guidance is that a false representation is made when an applicant or third party lies or makes a false statement in an application, either orally or in writing. To refuse the application, an ECO must be satisfied to a high standard that a false representation has been made. It is irrelevant that the applicant might later in interview correct the false statement. As the Court of Appeal observed in *SS (Nepal) v Entry Clearance Officer* [2013] All ER (D) 314 (Jul), an applicant has to be honest throughout the process; otherwise, an applicant would be permitted to lie on the application form and when found out could later make a true statement. That is contrary to common sense.

The Home Office gives the following two examples of false representations:

(i)   A visa applicant states that he is a project manager for a company, earning a significant salary. It is discovered that he is in fact the cleaner for the company on a low salary.

(ii)   An applicant applies for entry clearance on the basis of his marriage to a British citizen, and states in his application form that he has never been married before. But a marriage certificate is received from another wife, which is verified, showing that he is already married.

Does a false statement mean one made dishonestly? Yes: see *AA (Nigeria) v Secretary of State for the Home Department* [2010] EWCA Civ 773. This is because 'a false representation stated in all innocence may be simply a matter of mistake, or an error short of dishonesty' (per Rix LJ at [68]).

What is a false document? Home Office guidance is that this includes a genuine document which has been altered or tampered with; a counterfeit document (one that is completely false); a genuine document that is being used by an impostor; a genuine document which has been fraudulently obtained or issued; and a genuine document which contains a falsified or counterfeit visa or endorsement.

Must the applicant have created the false document or even be aware that it is false? No, as Rix LJ observed in *Adedoyin v Secretary of State for the Home Department* [2010] EWCA Civ 773:

> 67. First, 'false representation' is aligned in the rule with 'false document'. It is plain that a false document is one that tells a lie about itself. Of course it is possible for a person to make use of a false document (for instance a counterfeit currency note, but that example, used for its clarity, is rather distant from the context of this discussion) in total ignorance of its falsity and in perfect honesty. But the document itself is dishonest. It is highly likely therefore that where an applicant uses in all innocence a false document for the purpose of obtaining entry clearance, or leave to enter or to remain, it is because some other party, it might be a parent, or sponsor, or agent, has dishonestly promoted the use of that document. The response of a requirement of mandatory refusal is entirely understandable in such a situation. The mere fact that a dishonest document has been used for such an important application is understandably a sufficient reason for a mandatory refusal. That is why the rule expressly emphasises that it applies 'whether or not to the applicant's knowledge'.

See also *JK (India) v Secretary of State for the Home Department* [2013] EWCA Civ 1080.

What about material facts that have not been disclosed? Here the ECO will need to show that the withheld information would have been relevant to his decision. Note that an ECO cannot refuse an applicant on this ground if he has not indicated to the applicant the kind of information that is relevant to the application. The Home Office gives the following example. The wife of a man in the UK who has limited leave to remain as a highly-skilled worker (see **7.3**), applies to join her husband as his dependant, but does not mention that the marriage has broken down. The husband has sent a letter stating that the marriage no longer subsists.

(g)   Where the applicant has previously breached the UK's immigration laws and was over 18 at the time of the most recent relevant breach. That breach must be the result of overstaying by more than 90 days; breaching a condition attached to leave; being an illegal entrant; or using deception in an application for entry clearance, leave to enter or remain (whether successful or not). All of these are dealt with in **Chapter 10**.

Are there any exceptions to this? Yes, but these result in time limits being imposed on the applicant applying again.

Table 3.1 below summarises the position.

Table 3.1 Time limits applicable where there are exceptions to mandatory refusal on ground (g)

Exceptions	Length of ban
Left the UK voluntarily and not at the expense (directly or indirectly) of the Secretary of State	12 months from date left the UK
Left the UK voluntarily; at the expense (directly or indirectly) of the Secretary of State; and the date the person left the UK was no more than 6 months after the date on which the person was given notice of the removal decision, or no more than 6 months after the date on which the person no longer had a pending appeal, whichever is the later	2 years from date left the UK
Left the UK voluntarily and at the expense (directly or indirectly) of the Secretary of State	5 years from date left the UK
Removed or deported from the UK	10 years from date left the UK
Used deception in an application for entry clearance	10 years from date deception used

EXAMPLES

1. Alan overstays his leave by 50 days before departing the UK voluntarily. He pays his own travel costs (so not at the expense (directly or indirectly) of the Secretary of State). As Alan overstayed for less than 90 days, he will not in these circumstances be subject to any ban.

2. Brenda overstays her leave by 100 days before departing the UK voluntarily. She pays her own travel costs (so not at the expense (directly or indirectly) of the Secretary of State). As Brenda overstayed for more than 90 days, any application she makes for entry clearance within 12 months of leaving the UK will, in these circumstances, be subject to mandatory refusal.

If an applicant has previously been refused entry clearance because a false document was used or a false representation was made, the applicant may claim that he was unaware that the document or representation was false. Unless the applicant can prove this, he must be automatically refused entry clearance under this ground for 10 years from the date the deception was used.

Note that where more than one breach of the UK's immigration laws has occurred, only the breach which leads to the longest period of absence from the UK is relevant. The Home Office gives the following example. An applicant left the UK voluntarily at her own expense in January 2008 and applied for entry clearance using false documents in February 2008. Any subsequent entry clearance application must be automatically refused for 10 years, until February 2018. This is the longer refusal period where deception has been used in an entry clearance application. The shorter refusal period of one year for leaving the UK voluntarily is not applicable.

(h)   Where the applicant has failed, without providing a reasonable explanation, to comply with a request made on behalf of the ECO to attend an interview.

Note that only ground (c) above applies to an application for entry clearance and leave to enter as a family member under Appendix FM of the Immigration Rules (see **Chapter 8**).

3.4.5.2   Discretionary grounds

The general grounds on which entry clearance (and leave to enter) should normally be refused are set out in para 320(8)–(20) of the Immigration Rules, and these include the following:

(a)   Failure to supply any information, documents, copy documents or medical report that has or have been formally requested.

(b)   Where the applicant has previously contrived in a significant way to frustrate the intentions of the Immigration Rules by:

   (i)   overstaying; or
   (ii)   breaching a condition attached to his leave; or
   (iii) being an illegal entrant; or
   (iv)   using deception in an application for entry clearance, leave to enter or remain, or in order to obtain documents from the Secretary of State or a third party required in support of the application (whether successful or not);

and there are other aggravating circumstances, such as absconding, not meeting temporary admission or reporting restrictions or bail conditions, using an assumed identity or multiple identities, switching nationality, making frivolous applications or not complying with the re-documentation process.

All cases must be considered on their merits, taking into account family life in the UK and the level of responsibility for the breach in the case of children.

There is, of course, an overlap here with the mandatory ground for refusal highlighted at (g) in **3.4.5.1**. Home Office guidance is that where an applicant falls to be refused under the mandatory ground, an ECO must also consider whether it is also appropriate to refuse the applicant on this discretionary ground. If an applicant is exempt from the mandatory ground refusal, an ECO must consider whether a refusal under this discretionary ground is appropriate.

(c)   Refusal by a sponsor to give, if requested to do so, an undertaking in writing (see **3.4.2**) to be responsible for that person's maintenance and accommodation for the period of any leave granted.

(d)   Refusal to undergo a medical examination when required to do so.

(e)   Relevant criminal convictions as detailed in **Appendix 8**.

(f)   Where, from information available, it seems right to refuse the application on the ground that exclusion from the UK is conducive to the public good; if, for example, in the light of the character, conduct or associations of the person seeking leave to enter, it is undesirable to grant the application. The Home Office gives the following examples: where a person's admission could adversely affect the conduct of foreign policy; where there is reliable evidence that a person has been involved in criminal activities, even though he has not been convicted; where the person's admission would be contrary to internationally agreed travel restrictions; where the person's admission might lead to infringement of UK law; where the person's admission might lead to an offence being committed by someone else; and where a person's activities are such that his presence in the UK is likely to cause a public order concern. What is involved is an evaluation of risk to the public. The question the ECO must answer is whether or not there a substantial risk of disorder: see *CB (United States of America) v Entry Clearance Officer (Los Angeles)* [2008] EWCA Civ 1539.

(g)   Where one or more relevant NHS body has notified the Secretary of State that the person seeking entry or leave to enter has failed to pay a charge or charges with a total value of at least £1,000 in accordance with the relevant NHS regulations on charges to overseas visitors.

Note that only ground (b) above applies to an application for entry clearance and leave to enter as a family member under Appendix FM of the Immigration Rules (see **Chapter 8**).

3.5 LEAVE TO ENTER

3.5.1 The general rule

Leave to enter is dealt with in paras 7–11 of the Immigration Rules. Everyone must, on arrival in the UK, produce a passport or other document establishing his nationality and identity. On examination by an immigration officer, the entrant must furnish such information as may be required to enable the officer to decide whether he requires leave to enter, whether leave should be given, and the terms of leave. It is para 2(1) of Sch 2 to the IA 1971 which gives an immigration officer the power to examine any person who arrives in the UK and sets out the purpose for which such an examination is conducted, namely to determine whether:

(a)   he is or is not a British citizen; and, if not,

(b)   if he may or may not enter the UK without leave; and, if not,

(c)   if he has been given leave which is still in force, or should be given leave and for what period or on what conditions (if any), or should be refused leave.

If it is concluded that a person is a British citizen, the immigration officer takes no further action. If he is not a British citizen, however, he will be examined to determine whether or not he requires permission to enter the UK. This permission is called leave to enter. If a person qualifies for leave to enter then the immigration officer will go on to decide the length of the leave and any conditions, such as permission to work, which will apply. Finally, if a person does not qualify for leave to enter then the immigration officer may refuse leave to enter.

These controls do not, however, apply to persons arriving from another part of the Common Travel Area (see **3.9**).

3.5.2 Documentary evidence

Documentary evidence to be produced to an immigration officer may include:

(a)   a UK passport: required to be produced by a British citizen as evidence of his right of abode;

(b)   a certificate of entitlement issued by the UK Government: evidence of right of abode which may be produced as an alternative to (a) above (by a Commonwealth citizen who has the right of abode, see **2.3**);

(c)   entry clearance in the form of a visa or entry certificate;

(d)   a non-UK passport or identity card: identity cards may be used as a substitute for a passport by EEA nationals.

3.5.3 Grant of limited leave

The immigration officer grants leave by written notice, usually in the form of a stamp on the entrant's passport. The stamp gives the date and port of entry, the time limit of the leave, and any conditions imposed, but does not indicate the Rule under which leave has been granted.

However, if a person's entry clearance also takes effect as leave to enter the UK (see **3.4.2**), an immigration officer may still question that person to establish that he is the rightful holder of the document, that the document does take effect as limited leave, that the passport is genuine and that there are no circumstances under which the entry clearance should be cancelled (see **3.5.4**).

3.5.4 Refusal of limited leave

An immigration officer may refuse leave to enter the UK on exactly the same grounds that an ECO may refuse entry clearance (see **3.4.5**).

Paragraph 321 of the Immigration Rules provides three instances where a person seeking leave to enter the UK who holds an entry clearance which was duly issued to him and is still current may be refused leave to enter. These are where an immigration officer is satisfied of any of the following:

(a)   False representations were made or false documents were submitted (whether or not material to the application, and whether or not to the holder's knowledge), or material facts were not disclosed, in relation to the application for entry clearance.

(b)   A change of circumstances since it was issued has removed the basis of the holder's claim to admission, except where the change of circumstances amounts solely to the person becoming over age for entry in one of the categories contained in paras 296 to 316 of the Rules since the issue of the entry clearance.

(c)   Refusal is justified on grounds of restricted return ability; on medical grounds; on grounds of criminal record; because the person seeking leave to enter is the subject of a deportation order; or because exclusion would be conducive to the public good.

Paragraph 321A sets out the grounds on which a person's leave to enter which is in force on his arrival in, or whilst he is outside, the UK may be cancelled by an immigration officer. These include that:

(a)   There has been such a change in the circumstances of that person's case since the leave was given, that it should be cancelled.

(b)   False representations were made or false documents were submitted (whether or not material to the application, and whether or not to the holder's knowledge), or material facts were not disclosed, in relation to the application for leave.

(c)   For medical reasons it is undesirable to admit the person.

(d)   The Secretary of State has personally directed that exclusion is conducive to the public good.

After admission, any extension of the time limit, or variation of conditions, is dealt with by an application to the Home Office (see **3.6**).

3.5.5   Temporary admission

If a decision on whether to grant leave cannot be reached quickly, the immigration officer will usually issue a notice of temporary admission (in Form IS96). This tells the entrant that he is liable to detention, but may physically enter the UK without having leave to enter. He may be directed to reside at a particular place, and is asked to report back to an immigration officer at a specified time. He may not take employment.

As an alternative to temporary admission, the entrant can be detained, but may apply to an Immigration Judge for bail if he remains detained seven days after his arrival in the UK.

3.5.6   Entry without a passport

By s 2(1) of the Asylum and Immigration (Treatment of Claimants, etc) Act 2004 (AI (TC)A 2004), a person commits an offence if, when seeking leave either to enter or remain in the UK or asylum, he does not have with him a passport (or similar immigration document) which is in force and satisfactorily establishes his identity and nationality or citizenship. By s 2(4) various defences may be raised, such as proving a reasonable excuse for not being in possession of the required document. The defendant has the legal burden of proving the defence on the balance of probabilities: see R v Navabi and Embaye [2005] EWCA Crim 2865.

However, note that by s 2(7) the fact that a document was deliberately destroyed or disposed of is not such a reasonable excuse unless it is shown that the destruction or disposal was for a reasonable cause, or that it was beyond the control of the person charged with the offence. So what is a 'reasonable cause'? By s 2(7)(b) this does not include the purpose of (i) delaying the handling or resolution of a claim or application or the taking of a decision, (ii) increasing the chances of success of a claim or application, or (iii) complying with instructions or advice given by a person who offers advice about, or facilitates, immigration into the UK, unless in the circumstances of the case it is unreasonable to expect non-compliance with the instructions or advice.

3.6   LEAVE TO REMAIN IN THE UK: EXTENSION OR VARIATION OF EXISTING LEAVE

3.6.1   Application made to Home Office

The general framework is laid down by s 3(3) of the IA 1971, which provides that limited leave may be varied, whether by restricting, enlarging, or removing the time limit, or by adding, varying, or removing conditions. If the time limit is removed, the leave becomes indefinite and any conditions cease to have effect. Indefinite leave cannot be varied.

Application for variation is made to the Home Office. Immigration officers have no powers to deal with variations. Application should be made before expiry of the time limit on leave, because overstaying is a criminal offence, and may result in refusal of the application to extend leave.

If the application is granted, an appropriate entry is made in the applicant's passport and that is returned with a covering letter. Any refusal (see **3.6.5**) is notified to the applicant by letter, stating the reasons for the refusal and setting out any rights of appeal (see **Chapter 11**).

3.6.2 Effect of application on existing leave

By s 3C of the IA 1971, when a person applies for variation of his leave before that leave expires, but it then expires before a decision is taken, the leave is automatically extended to the point at which the appropriate period for appealing a refusal expires (see **Chapter 11**). This will protect the immigration status of that person and prevent him from becoming an overstayer. All conditions attached to the leave will still apply. So if a person who entered the UK as a fiancé(e) subsequently applies to stay as a spouse following the marriage, until the variation is granted by the Home Office, the applicant cannot lawfully work (see **8.4.10**). A person will not be able to submit further applications during the leave as extended under this section, although he would be able to vary his original application: this is to ensure that all issues raised are covered by one decision and consequently one appeal (see further **Chapter 11**).

3.6.3 Switching categories

In many cases, an entrant will apply to vary his leave by switching from one category of entry to another. For example, someone who has entered as a student may wish to remain as the spouse of someone living in the UK. In every case, it will be necessary to check the detailed provisions of the Rules relating to the new category.

Is there any danger in applying to switch categories? The danger is that the Home Office may refuse the application and curtail the existing leave (see **3.7**).

3.6.4 Procedure for variation

3.6.4.1 Specified forms

Paragraphs 34 and 34A to 34J of the Immigration Rules lay down the procedure that must be followed for most applications to the Home Office (apart from EEA matters: see **3.6.4.3**). First, certain applications must be made on the form specified by the Home Office. The main forms are:

FLR(M): application for an extension of stay in UK as the partner of a person present and settled here, the partner of a person with limited leave as a refugee or with humanitarian protection, or on the basis of a right to family and/or private life.

FLR(O): application for extension of stay in UK for any purpose not covered by other application forms.

SET(DV): application for indefinite leave to remain in UK as a victim of domestic violence.

SET(M): application for indefinite leave to remain in UK as the spouse, civil partner or unmarried partner of a person who is present and settled here.

SET(O): application for indefinite leave to remain in UK on completion of five years of continuous leave to remain in UK in categories such as Tier 1 entrepreneur or investor migrant and person with UK ancestry. The form is also used to apply for indefinite leave to remain in one of the following categories: long residence in UK, bereaved partner, and any other purpose or reason not covered by other application forms.

SET(F): application for indefinite leave to remain in UK as a family member (other than husband or wife or unmarried partner) of a person present and settled in UK.

BUS: application for an extension of stay (FLR) or for indefinite leave to remain in UK (SET) as a sole representative.

Tier 1 (entrepreneur): application to switch or extend stay as an entrepreneur.

Tier 1 (graduate entrepreneur): application for leave to remain as a graduate entrepreneur.

Tier 1 (investor): application to switch or extend stay as an investor.

Tier 2 Migrant: application to switch or extend stay as a Tier 2 Migrant.

PBS (dependant): application for extension of stay as dependant of person granted leave to remain under points-based system.

Tier 4 (general): application to switch or extend stay as a student.

Tier 5 (temporary worker): application for leave to remain as Tier 5 worker.

3.6.4.2 Following the specified forms procedure

It is absolutely vital that an applicant follows the specified form procedure or his application will be invalid. An invalid application is returned to the applicant and treated as if it was never made. Of course, if a valid application is not made in time, the applicant becomes an overstayer liable to removal from the UK (see **3.6.5** and **Chapter 11**).

What will make an application invalid? Any of the following:

(a)   failing to use the specified form;

(b)   failing to pay the specified fee, or paying it in a manner not specified in the form and/or guidance notes;

(c)   failing to complete in full those parts of the specified form marked as mandatory. Every question in these parts of the form must be answered and all the information required given;

(d)   failing to provide biographical or biometric information as required;

(e)   failing to provide any photographs or documents specified as mandatory (see, for example, *R (Fu) v Secretary of State for the Home Department* [2010] EWHC 2922);

(f)   failing to sign the form as required;

(g)   failing to deliver the form in the manner stated on it.

As the requirements for an application to be valid are part of the Immigration Rules there is an element of discretion, but Home Office guidance is that this is limited to exceptional circumstances, such as where an applicant is unable to sign the form or to provide photographs because of a serious illness or accident.

It is vital that the Home Office receives the specified form before the applicant's current leave expires. If possible, therefore, it should be delivered by hand to the public enquiry office and a receipt obtained. If it is posted, the application is treated as made on the day it was posted by reference to the postmark.

If an application is rejected but then re-submitted, and fully complies with the requirements of para 34A, the date of application is the date that it is re-submitted.

Note that if parts of a specified form which are not designated as mandatory are incomplete, a Home Office caseworker may attempt to obtain the missing information from the applicant, or consider the application on the basis of the information provided, but the application will be valid.

3.6.4.3 EEA forms

Note that the following four forms all relate to EEA nationals (see **Chapter 4**) and are not forms specified under para 34.

EEA1: application for a registration certificate by an EEA national.

EEA2: application for a residence card by a non-EEA family member of an EEA national.

EEA3: application for permanent residence by an EEA national.

EEA4: application for permanent residence by a non-EEA family member of an EEA national.

3.6.5 Refusal by Home Office

In addition to the grounds for refusal of extension of stay for the various immigration categories set out in Parts 2 to 8 of and Appendix FM to the Immigration Rules, para 322 provides a list of grounds similar to those used by entry clearance officers and immigration officers to refuse entry clearance (see **3.4.4** and **3.5.4**).

The provisions concerning the refusal of an application made by an overstayer were amended in July 2012. Now an application for further leave to remain after the applicant's previous period of leave has expired by more than 28 days will be refused. Note, however, the following concessions:

(a) Where an applicant submits an application before his previous period of leave to enter or remain expires, but the application is rejected as invalid after his leave expires, the 28-day window in which the application may be submitted as an overstayer will start from the date on which the application was rejected, rather than when leave expired.

(b) The Home Office caseworkers have discretion to consider exceptional cases. Applicants who have overstayed by more than 28 days may provide evidence of exceptional circumstances which prevented them from submitting their application in time. Home Office guidance is that the threshold here is high, but it could include delays resulting from:

   (i) serious illness which meant that the applicant or his representative was unable to submit the application in time (where supported by appropriate medical documentation);

   (ii) travel or postal delays, which meant that the applicant or his representative was unable to submit the application in time; or

   (iii) inability to provide necessary documents. This would apply only to exceptional or unavoidable circumstances beyond the applicant's control, such as the Home Office being at fault in the loss of, or delay in returning, travel documents; or delay in the applicant being able to replace documents following loss as a result of theft, fire or flood (where supported by evidence of the date of loss and the date replacement documents were sought).

(c) A breach of immigration laws by remaining in the UK beyond a period of leave to enter or remain will not be a determinative factor when considering applications in the following circumstances:

   (i) the applicant has a dependent child under the age of 18 years who is a British citizen or who has lived in the UK for at least the preceding seven years, and it would be unreasonable to expect the child to leave the UK (see EX.1 at **8.5.1**); or

   (ii) the applicant has lived in the UK for more than 20 years; or

   (iii) the applicant is seeking leave to remain as a bereaved partner (see **8.7**) or as a victim of domestic violence by her partner (see **8.8**).

3.6.6 Overstaying: a summary

Note that by para 6 of the Immigration Rules, 'overstayed' and 'overstaying' mean that an applicant for leave to remain has stayed in the UK beyond the latest of:

(a) the time limit attached to the last period of leave granted; or

(b) the period that his leave was extended under ss 3C or 3D of the IA 1971 (see **3.6.2**); or

(c) the date that an applicant receives the notice of invalidity declaring that an application for leave to remain is not a valid application, provided the application was submitted before the time limit attached to the last period of leave expired (see **3.6.4.2**).

3.7 CURTAILMENT OF EXISTING LEAVE TO ENTER OR REMAIN

If a person enters the UK in one category and before his limited leave expires he applies to switch to another category, there is a danger not only that the application might be refused but also that the existing leave might be curtailed (or the applicant removed from the UK).

> **EXAMPLE**
>
> Bob enters the UK as a student with 12 months' limited leave. After three months he applies to remain in the UK as the spouse of a British citizen. The suspicion may well be that he never intended to leave the UK because he always intended to marry. Not only might his leave be curtailed, but alternatively he may be removed from the UK as an illegal entrant (see **Chapter 10**).

The power to curtail a person's leave is contained in s 3(3)(a) of the IA 1971. It may be used when a person has failed to comply with certain requirements of the Immigration Rules or has lost the justification for his presence here, eg an employee's job ends. It is only available when a person has limited leave. Guidance from the Home Office is that curtailment should not normally be used unless the person has at least six months' leave outstanding.

Paragraph 323 of the Immigration Rules allows curtailment, for example, if:

(a) false representations have been made or material facts not disclosed in order to obtain leave to enter or a previous variation of leave;

(b) the person has failed to comply with any conditions attached to his leave;

(c) the person has failed to maintain and accommodate himself and any dependants without recourse to public funds;

(d) the person ceases to meet the requirements of the Rules under which that leave was granted;

(e) the person has, within the first six months of being granted leave to enter, committed an offence for which he is subsequently sentenced to a period of imprisonment.

As curtailment is a matter of Home Office discretion it is not automatic. The burden of proof rests with the Secretary of State. Very often a person will be removed rather than his leave curtailed, eg where a person has failed to disclose relevant facts or has made false representations in order to obtain leave, consideration may be given to curtailing any subsisting leave, but it is more usual to proceed directly to administrative removal (see **Chapter 10**) or, in the case of leave to enter, removal for illegal entry (also **Chapter 10**). Equally, although leave may be curtailed where a person fails to observe the conditions of his leave to enter or remain, normally the Home Office proceeds direct to administrative removal for breach of conditions (see **Chapter 10**). Curtailment therefore is normally considered only where the person's actions are not so serious as to merit enforcement action, but where it would be inappropriate to let him remain for the duration of his leave.

Note that by s 3D of the IA 1971, a person's leave is deemed to continue if he makes an appeal whilst in the UK against curtailment (see **Chapter 11**).

3.8 SETTLEMENT

3.8.1 What is it?

A person is settled according to the definition in s 33(2A) of the IA 1971 if he is ordinarily resident in the UK without being subject under the immigration laws to any restriction on the period for which he may remain. The status will be acquired by a person given unlimited leave who satisfies the 'ordinary residence' test (see **3.8.2**). A person who has been given indefinite leave to remain in the UK would not be 'settled' in the UK under the IA 1971, if he has emigrated to another country and is no longer ordinarily resident in the UK.

A person who is settled in the UK has, subject to the Immigration Rules, the right to continue to live in the UK. Unlike a person with right of abode, he may be deported (see **Chapter 10**).

3.8.2 Ordinarily resident

This is a condition of settled status. It has a quite distinct meaning. Case law from various fields suggests that a person can be 'ordinarily resident' without having the right, or the intention, to reside here permanently. All that is necessary is that a person resides in a place with a 'settled purpose' (eg to undertake a course of education). It is possible to have ordinary residence in more than one place at the same time. A person may be ordinarily resident in the UK even though temporarily absent (eg on holiday). Generally, however, for purposes other than exemption from deportation, a person cannot be so resident at a time when he is in breach of immigration laws (eg overstaying) (see the IA 1971, s 33(2)).

EXAMPLES

(1) Erasmus has been in the UK for the last eight years, periodically renewing his leave to remain.

   He is 'ordinarily resident' in the UK, but not 'settled' as he is subject to limited leave.

(2) Farooq was given indefinite leave to remain in the UK 10 years ago, but emigrated six years ago. He is now here for a holiday, having been admitted as a visitor.

   He is not 'ordinarily resident'. Neither is he 'settled', as his indefinite leave to remain was not renewed on his return to the UK.

(3) As (2), but Farooq has been admitted as a student, with 12 months' leave.

   He is 'ordinarily resident' but not 'settled'.

3.8.3 Returning resident rule

If a person with settled status leaves the UK and returns within two years, his leave will continue, leave to enter has to be given again and his settled status in effect confirmed. This is usually automatic under para 18 of the Rules, dealing with 'returning residents', provided that the entrant satisfies the immigration officer that he had indefinite leave to enter or remain in the UK when he last left, that he has not been away for longer than two years, and that he now seeks admission for the purpose of settlement. If a person is returning periodically only for a limited period simply to show residence in the UK within two years of each departure, then eventually he or she is likely to be denied the benefit of para 18 of the Immigration Rules.

What if a person with settled status does not return to the UK within two years of last leaving it? See para 19 of the Immigration Rules.

3.8.4 Who is treated as settled under the Immigration Rules?

Note that the Immigration Rules use the term 'settled' to cover British citizens (see **2.2**) and Commonwealth citizens who have the right of abode (see **2.3**), as well as those people who have indefinite leave.

3.8.5 Entry clearance

Only certain family members of a person already settled in the UK may apply for entry clearance for the purposes of settlement in the UK with that relative. These are dealt with in **Chapter 8**.

3.8.6 Switching where permitted

Some categories of entrants with limited leave are by their very nature temporary and so cannot lead to settlement, eg visitors (see **Chapter 5**) and students (see **Chapter 6**). However, most other categories may lead to settlement, and the answer is always found by studying the appropriate Immigration Rules. For example, a Tier 1 (Entrepreneur) Migrant can apply for settlement under para 245DF. See further **Chapters 7** and **8**.

3.8.7 Knowledge of language and life in the UK

Any individual between the ages of 16 and 65, who has entered the UK with limited leave and subsequently applies for settlement, must satisfy the English language and life in the UK requirements detailed in Appendix KoLL of the Immigration Rules.

3.8.8 The long-residence rules

Even where the requirements of the Immigration Rules for a switch to settled status are not met, it may be possible to obtain indefinite leave by virtue of long residence in the UK. Pursuant to the Immigration Rules, paras 276B and 276ADE, it is Home Office practice to consider this in cases where the applicant has been continuously resident in the UK either for 10 years lawfully (see **3.8.8.2**), or for 20 years lawfully or unlawfully based on his private life (see **3.8.8.3** and **8.13**).

3.8.8.1 Key requirements

Both provisions share the key requirement of 'continuous residence'. By para 276A(a), this means residence in the UK for an unbroken period. Does that mean that the applicant must not have been absent from the UK at all? No, for these purposes a period is not considered broken where an applicant is absent from the UK for six months or less at any one time, provided that the applicant has existing limited leave to enter or remain on his departure and return. So in what circumstances is a period broken? This occurs if the applicant:

(a) has been administratively removed or deported (see **Chapter 10**), or has left the UK having been refused leave to enter or remain here; or

(b) has left the UK and, on doing so, evidenced a clear intention not to return; or

(c) left the UK in circumstances in which he could have had no reasonable expectation at the time of leaving that he would lawfully be able to return; or

(d) has been convicted of an offence and was sentenced to a period of imprisonment or was directed to be detained in an institution other than a prison (including, in particular, a hospital or an institution for young offenders), provided that the sentence in question was not a suspended sentence; or

(e) has spent a total of more than 18 months absent from the UK during the period in question.

For the long residence provision based on 10 years' continuous residence (see **3.8.8.2**) there is an additional key requirement of 'lawful residence'. By para 276A(b), this means residence which is continuous residence pursuant to:

(a) existing leave to enter or remain; or

(b) temporary admission within s 11 of the 1971 Act (see **3.5.5**) where leave to enter or remain is subsequently granted; or

(c) an exemption from immigration control, including where an exemption ceases to apply if it is immediately followed by a grant of leave to enter or remain. People exempt from immigration control include diplomats and members of the armed forces. These are beyond the scope of this book.

Is an applicant no longer lawfully resident if at any point he became an overstayer? Yes, held the Court of Appeal in *MD (Jamaica) v Secretary of State for the Home Department* [2010] EWCA Civ 213, as para 276A(b) has an exhaustive definition of lawful residence. However, Home Office guidance is that if an applicant has a single short gap in lawful residence through making one single previous application out of time by a few days (not usually more than 10 days late, unless there are extenuating reasons for this such as a postal strike, hospitalisation or an administrative error by the Home Office), caseworkers may exercise discretion to grant indefinite leave to remain, provided the application meets all the other requirements. An application by a claimant with more than one gap in his lawful residence is normally refused, as he would not have shown the necessary commitment to ensuring he has maintained lawful leave throughout his time in the UK.

3.8.8.2 Ten years' residence provision

By para 276B, the requirements to be met by an applicant for indefinite leave to remain on the ground of long residence in the UK are that:

(a)   he has had at least 10 years' continuous lawful residence in the UK (see **3.8.8.1**);

(b)   having regard to the public interest, there are no reasons why it would be undesirable for him to be given indefinite leave to remain on the ground of long residence, taking into account his:

    (i)   age, and

    (ii)   strength of connections in the UK, and

    (iii) personal history, including character, conduct, associations and employment record, and

    (iv)   domestic circumstances, and

    (v)   compassionate circumstances, and

    (vi)   any representations received on the person's behalf; and

(c)   the applicant does not fall for refusal under the general grounds for refusal (see **3.6.5**);

(d)   the applicant has sufficient knowledge of the English language and sufficient knowledge about life in the UK by passing the test known as the 'Life in the UK Test' (see **3.8.7**), unless he is under the age of 18 or aged 65 or over at the time he makes his application.

What is the Home Office guidance on the public interest factors in para 276B(ii) ((b) above)?

(a)   Age may be a relevant factor if the applicant is an unaccompanied child under the age of 18, or if the applicant or his dependants have spent their formative years in the UK and adapted to life here.

(b)   The family life a person has in the UK must be taken into account in assessing the strength of that person's connections to the UK. This may be particularly strong if he is married to or has established a similar relationship with a settled person. The person may have other close relatives settled in the UK. The strength and closeness of the relationship will determine how strong a factor this may be. Similarly, if a person's close relatives are not in the UK, this may call into question the strength of the person's connection to the UK.

Owning property or a business may support the view that an applicant has shown long-term commitment and a connection to the UK. However, on its own, this would not be a significant factor. Factors such as the length of time the individual has owned the business or property, or whether the business is legally operating, must be considered. If someone mentions his business interests as proof of commitment to the UK, he must provide supporting documentary evidence. The applicant will be required to show further proof of strong connections to the UK.

If the applicant has contributed positively to society, for example through significant investment or charitable work, this may be another factor in his favour, although this is unlikely to be decisive on its own.

(c)   Character, conduct and associations go beyond criminal convictions and enable the caseworker to consider whether the applicant's activities in the UK or abroad make it undesirable to grant indefinite leave. This could include concerns about the applicant on the basis of national security, war crimes, crimes against humanity and serious criminality, whether convicted or not. As to applicants with a conviction, see para 276B(iii).

A history of anti-social behaviour or low-level criminality might be a ground to refuse indefinite leave, especially if it has led to the issuing of an anti-social behaviour order (ASBO).

The applicant's employment record will often be a significant consideration. The caseworker must consider what the person has been doing while he has been in the UK, and what economic contribution, if any, he has made. Whilst not having a sound employment record is not in itself a reason to refuse leave, a sound employment record, along with strong ties with the UK, would count in a person's favour, if he has not been a burden on public finances but has, in fact, contributed through income tax and national insurance contributions.

(d)   If the applicant has dependent children who have adapted to life in the UK, this could be a factor against refusal. The presence of another settled person who is routinely dependent on the applicant, for example a disabled relative, might also be a factor against refusal.

(e)   It is not possible to define all potential compassionate circumstances, but it might, depending on the situation, include significant or serious illness, frailty and particularly difficult family circumstances.

(f)   All representations raised on behalf of the applicant must be carefully assessed, even if these have been dismissed in previous applications. The caseworker must weigh those factors against the compassionate circumstances, if any, and all the other circumstances of the case, and then decide whether a grant of indefinite leave would be against the public interest.

Note that if the applicant cannot meet the requirements of paras 276B(iii) and/or (iv), he may under para 276A2 be granted an extension of his stay on the ground of long residence in the UK for a period not exceeding two years.

The application will be refused if the applicant does not meet the requirements for indefinite leave to remain or further leave to remain on the ground of long residence in the UK.

3.8.8.3   Private life under Article 8 ECHR

In July 2012 the Immigration Rules were amended by the introduction of this category. It replaced a provision based on 14 years' (lawful or unlawful) continuous residence. Broadly, it provides that at least 20 years' continuous residence (lawful or unlawful) in the UK will, subject to certain requirements, normally be necessary to establish a claim to limited leave to remain in the UK on the basis of the Article 8 ECHR right to respect for private life. Alternative provisions allow an applicant to be granted limited leave to remain in the UK on the basis of private life after seven years' continuous residence if he is under the age of 18; or if he has spent at least half of his life in the UK if he is aged between 18 and 24; or if the applicant has less than 20 years' continuous residence in the UK but has no ties (including social, cultural or family) with his country of origin. See further **8.13**.

3.8.9   EEA nationals

Nationals of the EEA do not need leave to enter or remain while exercising rights in EU law (see **Chapter 4**). Does this mean that while in the UK they have no restriction on the period for which they can remain and are therefore 'settled' under UK immigration law? The answer is, 'No'. However, by reg 15(1) of the I(EEA) Regs 2006 (see **4.4.9** and **Appendix 4**), EEA nationals acquire the right to reside in the UK permanently where, as a general rule, they have resided in the UK in accordance with the Regulations for a continuous period of five years. In limited circumstances, the right to reside in the UK permanently may be acquired more quickly, eg under reg 15(1) by a worker or self-employed person who has ceased activity as defined in reg

5. People falling within reg 15(1) are treated as settled for the purposes of applying for naturalisation (see **2.2.7**).

3.8.10 Criminality requirement for settlement

In April 2011 the Government introduced a requirement that any person applying for settlement under the Immigration Rules must show that he does not have any relevant convictions as detailed in Part 9. Are criminal convictions imposed outside the UK relevant? Yes, as para 6 of the Immigration Rules provides that 'conviction' means conviction for a criminal offence in the UK or any other country. Home Office guidance is that offences do not need to have an identically named provision or carry similar penalties as in the UK, provided that there is a comparable offence, for example homicide and murder. However, offences which do not constitute a criminal offence in the UK are ignored, such as homosexuality and proselytising (attempting to convert someone to another religion). The details are in **Appendix 8**.

3.9 THE COMMON TRAVEL AREA

The Common Travel Area consists of the UK, Ireland, the Channel Islands and the Isle of Man. The basic principle, set out in s 1(3) of the IA 1971, is that persons arriving on local journeys to the UK from elsewhere in the Common Travel Area are not subject to immigration control, and no leave to enter is required. Control operates only on initial entry to the Area from outside. This is subject to some exceptions, for example under the Immigration (Control on Entry through the Republic of Ireland) Order 1972 (SI 1972/1610). This subjects some persons to immigration control (such as visa nationals without a visa for entry to the UK). If such persons enter the UK, for example, from Ireland, they are illegal entrants, even though they have never been examined by the immigration service. The 1972 Order also imposes conditions in other cases (eg where a person who is not Irish, and does not have the right of abode in the UK, travels to the UK from outside the Area, via the Republic). Usually such persons will have deemed leave to enter for three months, with a prohibition on employment and business for non-EEA nationals. As the person will not have passed through immigration control, there will be no indication of these conditions on his passport.

CHAPTER 4

EEA Nationals

4.1 WHO ARE EEA NATIONALS?

'EEA nationals' are nationals of the Member States of the European Union together with Iceland, Liechtenstein and Norway (which are parties to the European Economic Area Agreement). See **Appendix 2** to this book for the full list of relevant countries.

Note that by an Agreement on the Free Movement of Persons made between the EC (now EU) and the Swiss Confederation (Cm 4904), Swiss nationals and their family members were from 1 June 2002 given broadly similar rights of entry to and residence in the UK as are enjoyed by EEA nationals. See the Immigration (Swiss Free Movement of Persons) (No 3) Regulations 2002 (SI 2002/1241).

4.2 WHAT IS THEIR IMMIGRATION STATUS?

Nationals of the EEA have a hybrid status. They do not have the right of abode possessed by British citizens but, unlike other aliens, they do not require leave to enter or remain while exercising rights in EU law (s 7(1) of the IA 1988). Paragraph **4.3** outlines their rights in EU law. These have been implemented in UK law by the I(EEA) Regs 2006, considered in detail in the rest of this chapter.

4.3 RIGHTS UNDER EU LAW

Article 20 TFEU states that:

1. Citizenship of the Union is hereby established. Every person holding the nationality of a Member State shall be a citizen of the Union. Citizenship of the Union shall be additional to and not replace national citizenship.

2. Citizens of the Union shall enjoy the rights and be subject to the duties provided for in the Treaties.

Article 21(1) TFEU provides that:

Every citizen of the Union shall have the right to move and reside freely within the territory of the Member States, subject to the limitations and conditions laid down in the Treaties and by the measures adopted to give them effect.

It can be seen that Article 21 TFEU provides for a right of residence and movement of EEA nationals throughout the EU. Directive 2004/38/EC of the European Parliament and Council of 29 April 2004 sets out the terms and limits of this right of movement. It is a consolidation and modernisation of existing EU secondary legislation in this area. It has been implemented into domestic law by the I(EEA) Regs 2006 (see **4.4**). This book will look at the detail of the 2006 Regs. There is a chart at **4.5** which sets out where the 2006 Regs implement the 2004 Directive. A copy of the Directive is set out in **Appendix 3**.

More detailed treatment of this topic is to be found in Part III of **Legal Foundations**. The following is a summary of the main principles.

4.3.1 Free movement of workers

Article 45 TFEU requires free movement for workers within the Union. Article 45(3) TFEU provides that this entails the right to:

(a)   accept offers of employment;

(b)   move freely within the EU for this purpose;

(c)   stay in a Member State for employment;

(d)   remain after employment, subject to conditions.

4.3.2 Self-employed activities and establishment of businesses

Article 49 TFEU requires abolition of restrictions on the freedom of establishment of EU nationals. This freedom includes the right to pursue activities as self-employed persons, and to set up and manage undertakings such as companies or firms.

4.3.3 Provision of services

Article 56 TFEU requires abolition of the restrictions on freedom to provide services within the Community in respect of nationals of Member States who are established in a State of the Community other than that of the person for whom the services are intended.

Article 57 TFEU states that the provider of a service (including industrial, commercial, craft, and professional activities) may temporarily pursue his activity in a State where the service is provided. Permanent provision of the service would involve 'establishment'.

Freedom of movement extends not only to the providers, but also to the recipients of services. In Joined Cases 286/82 and 26/83 *Luisi (Graziana) and Carbone (Giuseppe) v Ministero del Tesoro* [1984] ECR 377, the ECJ held that this covered tourists, and those who travel for medical treatment, education or business.

Does the EEA national have to travel to another EEA country and provide services there? 'No', held the ECJ in *Alpine Investments BV v Minister van Financiën* (Case C-384/93) [1995] ECR I-1141 – an offer to provide services over the telephone to potential recipients established in other Member States is sufficient. On a proper construction, Article 56 applies to services which a provider supplies, without moving from the Member State in which he is established, to recipients established in other Member States.

4.3.4 When the 2004 Directive applies

The 2004 Directive applies only to EEA nationals exercising Treaty rights. So a non-EEA national cannot directly benefit from it. This is because the Directive determines how, and under what conditions, EEA citizens can exercise their right to freedom of movement within the territory of the Member States. Accordingly, the Directive concerns the travel and residence of an EEA citizen in a Member State other than that of which he is a national: see *McCarthy (European citizenship)* [2011] 3 CMLR 10. A non-EEA national may only indirectly benefit from the Directive if he is the family member of an EEA national (see **4.4.6**).

An EEA national will exercise his Treaty rights by, for example, moving to another EEA country and living there. This is the combined effect of Articles 20 and 21 TFEU (see **4.3**). The EEA national might take employment pursuant to Article 45 TFEU (see **4.3.1**), or run a business under Article 49 (see **4.3.2**). His right of entry to and residence in the host EEA country will be governed by the 2004 Directive as implemented into the domestic law of the host EEA country; as we saw at **4.3**, in the UK that means the 2006 Regs.

EXAMPLES

(1) Abdus is a citizen of Pakistan. He is a single man. He travelled from Pakistan and entered Spain, an EEA country, pursuant to domestic Spanish immigration laws. Abdus is not an EEA national. He cannot exercise Treaty rights.

(2) Marie is a French national living in Paris. She is single and an EEA national. She has a right of entry to and residence in the other EEA countries. She travels to Madrid, Spain (an EEA country) and starts working there. She is thereby exercising her Treaty rights.

(3) Boris is a German national living in Berlin. He travels to Jamaica and works there for several years. He marries Alisha, a Jamaican national. The couple decide that they want to live together in Germany. As Jamaica is not an EEA country, Boris has not exercised his Treaty rights. Alisha will have to comply with domestic German law to enter and live with Boris there.

(4) Marie, from example (2) above, meets Abdus from example (1) in Spain. They fall in love and marry. The couple subsequently decide to live together in France. As Marie is an EEA national who has exercised her Treaty rights, Abdus, as her spouse, can benefit indirectly. Rather than applying under domestic French immigration law to enter France with Marie, he can choose to rely on EU law and enter as the spouse of an EEA national. See further **4.4.6** and **4.4.7**.

4.4 THE IMMIGRATION (EUROPEAN ECONOMIC AREA) REGULATIONS 2006

The I(EEA) Regs 2006 enact EU law rights of free movement in UK law. A copy may be found at **Appendix 4** to this book. The immigration adviser can refer directly to the I(EEA) Regs 2006 but should be aware that, in the event that they fail to give effect to EU law, EU law will prevail. In addition, EU case law may affect the interpretation of the Regulations.

All references in the rest of this chapter are to the I(EEA) Regs 2006 unless otherwise stated.

4.4.1 Right of admission for EEA nationals (reg 11(1))

An EEA national must be admitted to the UK if he produces on arrival a valid national identity card or passport issued by an EEA State.

4.4.2 Right of admission for family members of EEA nationals (reg 11(2))

A person who is not an EEA national must be admitted to the UK if he is a family member of an EEA national and he produces on arrival a valid passport or an EEA family permit (see **4.4.7**), a residence card (see **4.4.8**) or a permanent residence card (see **4.4.10**).

The family member may be travelling with the EEA national to the UK, or joining the EEA national who is already in the UK. If the family member is travelling independently of the EEA national and not joining him in the UK then the Immigration Rules apply.

4.4.3 Initial right of residence for three months (reg 13)

An EEA national and his family member(s) are entitled to reside in the UK for a period not exceeding three months. The only condition is that the EEA national and any family member must not become an unreasonable burden on the social assistance system of the UK (see further **4.4.5.4**).

4.4.4 Residence beyond three months (reg 14)

An EEA national is entitled to reside in the UK for a period exceeding three months if he is a qualified person. Indeed, he has the right to reside in the UK for as long as he remains a qualified person. His family member(s) have the same right.

It is important to appreciate that the family member's right to reside is dependent upon the EEA national having a right to reside. The problem that arises if the EEA national dies or leaves the UK, etc is considered at **4.4.11**.

4.4.5   Who is a qualified person? (reg 6)

A qualified person is an EEA national who is in the UK in any of the following categories:

(a)   a jobseeker;

(b)   a worker;

(c)   a self-employed person;

(d)   a self-sufficient person; or

(e)   a student.

4.4.5.1   Jobseeker

A 'jobseeker', as defined in reg 6(4), is an EEA national who enters the UK in order to look for employment. He must be able to provide evidence that he is seeking employment and that he has a genuine chance of securing employment.

There is no set limit on the amount of time an EEA national can spend looking for employment, although six months is often used as a rule of thumb. This is because in the case of *R v IAT, ex p Antonissen* [1991] 2 CMLR 373, the ECJ stated that:

> it is not contrary to the provisions of Community law governing the free movement of workers for the legislation of a Member State to provide that a national of another Member State who entered the first State in order to seek employment may be required to leave the territory of that State (subject to appeal) if he has not found employment there after six months, unless the person concerned provides evidence that he is continuing to seek employment and that he has genuine chances of being engaged.

4.4.5.2   Worker

Regulation 4(1)(a) defines a worker by a simple cross-reference to Article 45 TFEU (see **4.3.1**), namely an employee.

So what constitutes employment? Does it include part-time employment? Yes, held the ECJ in *Levin v Secretary of State for Justice* [1982] ECR 1035, although it will not include activities on such a small scale as to be regarded as purely marginal and ancillary. Work means to pursue an economic activity.

Note that by reg 6(2), an EEA national who has worked in the UK but is currently not working may in certain limited circumstances still be classified as a worker, eg if he is temporarily unable to work due to illness or accident. So a woman who ceases work because she is pregnant does not retain the status of a worker since pregnancy is not an illness: see *JS v Secretary of State for Work and Pensions* [2011] EWCA Civ 806. An employed woman will, of course, still remain a worker whilst on maternity leave.

Also note the definition of a worker who has ceased activity in reg 5(2)–(5). This includes, for example, an EEA national who has resided in the UK for more than three years and worked for at least 12 months before ceasing work when reaching retirement age, and also an EEA national who has resided in the UK for at least two years prior to termination of his work or self-employment due to a permanent disability. The definition is important, as such a person may acquire permanent residence in the UK (see **4.4.9**).

What is the difference between a worker who is 'temporarily' unable to work due to illness or accident (reg 6(2)(a)) and a worker with a 'permanent' incapacity to work (reg 5(3))? According to Blake J in *FMB (Uganda) v Secretary of State for the Home Department* [2010] UKUT 447 at para 23 'if a person's inability or incapacity is not permanent, then it should be regarded as temporary'. This was approved by the Court of Appeal in *De Brito v Secretary of State for the Home Department* [2012] EWCA Civ 709.

4.4.5.3   Self-employed person

Regulation 4(1)(b) defines a self-employed person by a simple cross-reference to Article 49 TFEU (see **4.3.2**).

Note that by reg 6(3), an EEA national who is temporarily unable to work due to illness or accident retains the stautus of a self-employed person.

Also note the definition of a self-employed person who has ceased activity in reg 5(2)–(5). This includes, for example, an EEA national who has had to stop work due to a permanent incapacity, and either he resided in the UK for more than two years before that incapacity or the incapacity results in him becoming entitled to a pension payable in whole or part by a UK institution. The definition is important, as such a person may acquire permanent residence in the UK (see **4.4.9**).

4.4.5.4   Self-sufficient person

A 'self-sufficient person', as defined in reg 4(1)(c), is an EEA national who has (i) sufficient resources not to become a burden on the social assistance system of the UK during his period of residence; and (ii) comprehensive sickness insurance cover in the UK. Guidance from the Home Office is that, for example, a retired person would be self-sufficient if he could demonstrate that he was in receipt of a pension and/or had sufficient funds or income from investments not to become a burden on the UK's social assistance system. Can resources supplied by another person be taken into account? Yes: see *Commission v Belgium* [2006] ECR I-2647.

Is a set amount of money required to demonstrate self-sufficiency? Directive 2004/58 EC, Article 8(4) prohibits this. However, reg 4(4) provides that a person's resources are regarded as sufficient if they exceed the maximum level of resources which a UK national and his family members may possess if he is to become eligible for social assistance under the UK benefit system.

If an EEA national claims a UK 'minimum subsistence benefit' like income support or income-based jobseeker's allowance, at what point might he become an unreasonable burden on the UK's welfare benefits system? The UK Government should carry out a proportionality test, and recital 16 of the 2004 Directive suggests that the following questions need to be posed and answered:

(1)   Duration
   •   For how long is the benefit being granted?
   •   Outlook: is it likely that the EEA citizen will get out of the safety net soon?
   •   How long has the residence lasted in the UK?

(2)   Personal situation
   •   What is the level of connection of the EEA citizen and his family members with the society of the UK?
   •   Are there any considerations pertaining to age, state of health, family and economic situation that need to be taken into account?

(3)   Amount
   •   Total amount of aid granted?
   •   Does the EEA citizen have a history of relying heavily on social assistance?
   •   Does the EEA citizen have a history of contributing to the financing of social assistance in the UK?

Only receipt of social assistance benefits can be considered relevant to determining whether the person concerned is a burden on the UK's social assistance system. As long as the beneficiaries of the right of residence do not become an unreasonable burden on the social assistance system of the UK, they cannot be expelled for this reason.

Is the requirement that the EEA national has comprehensive sickness insurance cover in the UK strictly enforced? Yes. It is not a mere formality but an integral part of the concept of self-sufficiency under the Regulations: see *Kamau (Kenya) v Secretary of State for the Home Department* [2010] EWCA Civ 1302.

4.4.5.5   Student

A 'student', according to reg 4(1)(d), is an EEA national who:

(a)   is enrolled, for the principal purpose of following a course of study (including vocational training), at a public or private establishment which is financed from public funds; or otherwise recognised by the Secretary of State as an establishment which has been accredited for the purpose of providing such courses or training within the law or administrative practice of the part of the UK in which the establishment is located;

(b)   has comprehensive sickness insurance cover in the UK; and

(c)   assures the Secretary of State, by means of a declaration, or by such equivalent means as the person may choose, that he has sufficient resources not to become a burden on the social assistance system of the UK during his period of residence.

4.4.6   Who is a family member of an EEA national?

Under reg 7, as a general rule, the following are family members of an EEA national:

(a)   his spouse or his civil partner;

(b)   direct descendants (children, grandchildren, etc) of him, his spouse or his civil partner who are–

(i)   under 21, or

(ii)   dependants of him, his spouse or his civil partner;

(c)   dependent direct relatives in his ascending line (parents, grandparents, etc) or that of his spouse or his civil partner.

As to (a), what if an EEA national has more than one lawful spouse or civil partner? Only one counts. Why? Because reg 2 provides that a spouse or civil partner does not include the spouse or civil partner of an EEA national where a spouse or civil partner is already present in the UK.

4.4.6.1   Spouse or civil partner

A spouse or civil partner ((a) in **4.4.6** above) will not cease to be a family member in the event of marital breakdown or separation as long as the EEA national continues to exercise Treaty rights in the same Member State: see *Diatta v Land Berlin* [1985] ECR 567 and *Amos v Secretary of State for the Home Department* [2011] EWCA Civ 552. The right of residence will continue until any divorce is finalised by decree absolute, or until a civil partnership is dissolved. See further **4.4.11**.

4.4.6.2   Marriage or civil partnership of convenience

Note that by reg 2, a 'spouse' does not include a party to a marriage of convenience; and a 'civil partner' does not include a party to a civil partnership of convenience.

The 'convenience' referred to involves the non-EEA national seeking to obtain a right of residence in the UK under EU law by marriage to, or entering into a civil partnership with, an EEA national. That might occur whilst the parties are outside the UK, and so the non-EEA national seeks to enter under an EEA family permit (see **4.4.7**), or whilst they are in the UK. The objective is to avoid UK domestic immigration law. Typically, but not always, it takes place after the non-EEA national has been refused entry clearance or leave to remain in the UK.

Article 35 of the 2004 Directive (see **Appendix 3**) allows the UK Government to refuse, terminate or withdraw any rights conferred on the non-EEA national in these circumstances, provided that is a proportionate response, taking into account Article 8 of the ECHR (see

Appendix 5), and subject to the safeguards in Articles 30 and 31 of the Directive. Further details may be found in Pt 4 of the I(EEA) Regs 2006 (see **Appendix 4**).

What factors might suggest a marriage or civil partnership of convenience? In *TC (Kenya) v Secretary of State for the Home Department* [2008] EWCA Civ 543, the Court of Appeal indicated that these may include the fact that the marriage occurs after the non-EEA national has been refused leave to remain under domestic law; that the application for a residence certificate or card (see **4.4.8**) is made quickly after the marriage or civil partnership ceremony; a lack of financial support between the parties; a considerable difference in age or background between the parties; no common language; the limited time that the parties to the relationship spend together; lack of cohabitation; the length of time which any party spends abroad without any compensating cohabitation whilst in the UK; the fact that the couple never go away together on holiday; one party being vague about the other's movements; the lack of credibility or reliability of a party as a witness; and limited (or no) supporting evidence from family and friends about the relationship between the parties.

The Home Office has published its policy in this area. Factors taken into account by an ECO when considering an application for a family permit include:

(a) *Evidence of previous relationship.* In all cases, in order to refuse on the basis of a marriage of convenience, an ECO must be satisfied that there is little or no evidence of a relationship between the applicant and the EEA national. An applicant might provide email exchanges, letters, joint bank accounts, photographs, etc to show evidence of their relationship.

There are a number of other factors which may cause an ECO to suspect that the applicant is party to a marriage of convenience. The following may raise doubts as to the credibility of a relationship:

(b) *The applicant has an adverse immigration history.* The applicant may have had previous entry clearance applications refused or had otherwise attempted to gain entry or leave to remain in the UK, eg a failed asylum application.

(c) *Intention to live together in the UK.* The applicant and the EEA national should generally intend to live together in the UK. This should be evidenced by a clear commitment from both parties that they will do so following the outcome of the application.

(d) *Claims of previous marriage.* The applicant may have previously claimed to be married to someone else. In such cases they should produce documentary evidence of that marriage being dissolved.

(e) *Reason to question the plausibility of the marriage.* For example, factors may include considerable differences in age and background or where the applicant and EEA national have no common language.

(f) *A sum of money has been handed over in order for the marriage to be contracted.* This would not include money given in the form of a dowry in the cases of nationals of countries where the provision of a dowry is common practice.

Guidance on the point may be found at COM (2009) 313 Final. This confirms that the 2004 Directive does not prevent Member States from investigating individual cases where there is a well-founded suspicion of abuse; for instance, where the couple are inconsistent about their respective personal details, about the circumstances of their first meeting or about other important personal information concerning them. The guidance also includes the following example:

> S, a third country national, was ordered to leave in one month as she had overstayed her tourist visa. After two weeks, she married O, an EU national who had just arrived to the host Member State. The authorities suspect that the marriage might have been concluded only to avoid expulsion. They contact the authorities in O's Member State and find out that after the wedding his family shop was finally able to pay a debt of 5000 EUR, which it had been unable to repay for two years.

They invite the newly-weds for an interview, during which they find out that O has meanwhile already left the host Member State to return home to his job, that the couple is not able to communicate in a common language and that they met for the first time one week before the marriage. There are strong indications that the couple may have married with the sole purpose of contravening national immigration laws.

In *Papajorgji (EEA Spouse – Marriage of Convenience) Greece* [2012] UKUT 38, the Tribunal held that when an applicant applies for a family permit, there is an evidential burden on the ECO to justify having a reasonable suspicion that the marriage or civil partnership was entered into for the predominant purpose of securing residence rights. Only then is the burden of proof on the applicant because reasonable suspicions have arisen, and the matter will be resolved against him unless those suspicions are determined in his favour.

4.4.6.3 Direct descendants

The direct descendants ((b) in **4.4.6** above) of the EEA national, his spouse or civil partner also count. So this will include children, grandchildren, great-grandchildren, etc who are either under 21 years of age or dependent on the EEA national, his spouse or civil partner. As to dependency, see **4.4.6.7**.

'Children' include step-children, and adopted children provided that the adoption is recognised by the UK.

4.4.6.4 Dependent direct relatives in ascending line

The parents, grandparents, etc of the EEA national and his spouse or civil partner count. As to dependency, see **4.4.6.7**.

4.4.6.5 Family members of a student after three months

Whilst the list of those who constitute family members in **4.4.6** above is the general rule, there is a major exception. Once a student has been residing in the UK for a period of three months, his family members are limited to (i) his spouse or his civil partner, and (ii) his dependent children or those of his civil partner.

4.4.6.6 Other (extended) family members

What about direct descendants (children, etc) aged 21 or over, or direct relatives in the ascending line (parents, etc) who cannot show dependency? What about other relatives, such as brothers and sisters, uncles and aunts, cousins, etc? These may fall within reg 8, which deals with 'extended family members'. These are any of the following:

(a) a person who is a relative of an EEA national, his spouse or his civil partner and –
   (i) who is residing in a country other than the UK and who is either dependent upon the EEA national or a member of his household,
   (ii) who satisfied the condition in para (i) and is accompanying the EEA national to the UK or wishes to join him here, or
   (iii) who satisfied the condition in para (i), has joined the EEA national in the UK and continues to be either dependent upon him or a member of his household;
(b) a person who is a relative of an EEA national, or his spouse or his civil partner and, on serious health grounds, who strictly requires the personal care of the EEA national, his spouse or his civil partner;
(c) a person who is a relative of an EEA national and who would meet the requirements in the Immigration Rules (other than those relating to entry clearance) for indefinite leave to enter or remain in the UK as a dependent relative of the EEA national were the EEA national a person present and settled in the UK (see **8.11**);
(d) a person who is the partner of an EEA national (other than a civil partner) and who can prove to the decision maker that he is in a durable relationship akin to marriage or a civil

partnership with the EEA national. The Home Office advises that the test it imposes is similar to that in the Immigration Rules, Appendix FM (see **8.3.1**). Note that the fiancé(e) or proposed civil partner of an EEA national is not his or her family member under EU law. Such a person would have to apply under the Immigration Rules, Appendix FM (see **8.3.5.1**).

In category (a), when is someone a member of the EEA national's household? Home Office guidance is that the family member should normally have lived with the EEA national under the same roof for at least six months.

In category (a), evidence is required of recent dependency or recent household membership. Historic but lapsed dependency or membership is irrelevant to the Directive policy of removing obstacles to the Union citizen's freedom of movement and residence rights: see *Bigia v Entry Clearance Officer* [2009] EWCA Civ 79 and *SM (India) v Entry Clearance Officer* [2009] EWCA Civ 1426.

Are there two or four different ways of meeting (a)? The Upper Tribunal held that there are four ways, in *Storey v Secretary of State for the Home Department* [2012] UKUT 79, each of which requires proving a relevant connection both prior to arrival in the UK and in the UK, namely: prior dependency and present dependency; or prior membership of a household and present membership of a household; or prior dependency and present membership of a household; or prior membership of a household and present dependency.

It does not matter whether it is the EEA national or his extended family member who arrives in the UK first: see *Aladeselu v Secretary of State for the Home Department* [2013] EWCA Civ 144.

Note that in *Secretary of State for the Home Department v Islam & Another* [2012] EUECJ C-83/11 the Court of Justice stated that the dependence must exist in the country from which the family member in question comes, at least at the time when such a family member makes an application for entry.

EXAMPLES

(1) Marta is a citizen of Latvia. Her cousin, Mikhaila, a non-EEA national, has lived with her in the capital, Riga, for the last two years. Marta may seek to enter the UK as an EEA national. Mikhaila could travel with her to, or soon afterwards seek to join her in, the UK as her extended family member, as someone who was and will remain a member of Marta's household.

(2) Patrik is a citizen of Slovakia. His aunt, Kata, a non-EEA national, has lived in another part of Slovakia for the last 12 months. She has been financially dependent on Patrik during that time and remains so. Patrik may seek to enter the UK as an EEA national. Kata could travel with him to, or soon afterwards seek to join him in, the UK as his extended family member, as someone who is financially dependent on Patrik.

(3) Mahbur, a Bangladeshi national, marries Molly, an Irish national who is working in the UK. Following that marriage, Mahbur's brother, Muhammad, in Bangladesh becomes financially dependent on the couple. He may apply for an EEA family permit in order to enter and reside in the UK as Molly and Mahbur's dependant.

Does it count if the applicant is dependent on the spouse or civil partner of the EEA national or a member of his household? This might arise where the EEA national and his spouse or civil partner live separately, perhaps for work reasons, before moving to the UK. The Court of Appeal answered the question in the negative in *Soares v Secretary of State for the Home Department* [2013] EWCA Civ 575. Dependence or household membership can only count when it relates to the EEA national.

What are the requirements in order to meet category (b) above? The Tribunal in *TR (reg 8(3) EEA Regs 2006) Sri Lanka* [2008] UKAIT 00004 held that the 'serious health grounds' need to be significantly beyond ordinary ill-health and require detailed medical evidence in support. Personal care must be provided on a day-to-day basis and relate either or both to the physical and mental tasks and needs required for a person to function. 'Strictly' is a restrictive or limiting requirement and imports a need for complete compliance or exact performance, and reinforces the need for personal care to be provided on a day-to-day basis. Home Office guidance is that this would include an applicant who is totally dependent on his EEA national family member, or his spouse or civil partner, for basic everyday care, like helping with personal hygiene or preparing meals.

For further Home Office guidance on extended family members, see **4.4.6.8** below.

4.4.6.7   Meaning of dependency

Some of the above categories have a test of dependency on the EEA national. Guidance from the Home Office is that the dependency may be one of choice rather than necessity, but the definition of 'dependency' includes only financial dependency and not emotional dependency. Financial dependency might be shown by the family member being unemployed.

According to the case of *Lebon* [1987] ECR 2811, the status of 'dependent' family member is the result of a situation characterised by the fact that material support for that family member is provided by the EEA national, or by his spouse or partner. In order to determine whether a family member is dependent, it must be assessed in the individual case whether, having regard to his financial and social conditions, he needs material support to meet his essential needs in his country of origin or the country from which he came at the time when he applied to join the EEA national (ie not in the host Member State where the EEA national resides).

In the case of *Jia* [2007] ECR I-0001, when addressing the concept of dependency, the Court did not refer to any level of standard of living for determining the need for financial support by the EEA national. The 2004 Directive does not lay down any requirement as to the minimum duration of the dependency, or the amount of material support provided, as long as the dependency is genuine and structural in character.

In *Bigia v Entry Clearance Officer* [2009] EWCA Civ 79, the Court stated that the dependency test was met where the EEA national provided his adult daughter with rent-free accommodation and sent her money on a regular basis for 'bills, daily expenses and clothes'. She had no other source of income. The Court concluded that without that support she would be unable to meet her essential needs.

4.4.6.8   Home Office guidance on extended family members

Guidance from the Home Office is that Directive 2004/38 refers in Article 3 only to facilitating the entry and residence of extended family members. When deciding whether to issue a residence card, the Home Office must assess whether refusal would deter the EEA national from exercising his EU Treaty rights, or would create an effective obstacle to the exercise of those rights. An example is given that it might be appropriate to issue a residence card where the family member was very elderly or incapacitated. In assessing such a case, the Home Office states that it would be important to consider whether there were relatives to care for the person in the home country.

In considering cases under reg 8, the Home Office normally refuses those who have, for example, their own family unit (unless there are sufficient compassionate circumstances), or who lived as part of the EEA national's household many years ago.

4.4.7   Does a family member need a travel document? (reg 12)

To be admitted to the UK, a family member should apply to an ECO for a travel document known as an EEA family permit before travelling to the UK. It is required only where the family member is not an EEA national. In order to obtain the permit the family member will have to produce documentation demonstrating the relationship with the EEA national (eg marriage certificate, etc).

4.4.8 How can an EEA national or family member confirm his right of residence?

Under regs 16 and 17, an EEA national or a non-EEA family member entitled to residence may apply to the Secretary of State for a residence certificate or residence card respectively. A residence certificate or card is normally valid for five years.

A family member may find it useful to obtain a residence card, particularly when applying for employment, as it confirms his entitlement to take employment in the UK. Also, if he leaves the UK, it will prove his right of re-entry (otherwise he will need to obtain an EEA family permit: see **4.4.7**).

4.4.9 Permanent right of residence in UK (reg 15)

The following persons may acquire the right to reside in the UK permanently:

(a)   an EEA national who has resided in the UK in accordance with the 2006 Regulations for a continuous period of five years;

(b)   a family member of an EEA national (who is not himself an EEA national) who has resided in the UK with the EEA national in accordance with the 2006 Regs for a continuous period of five years;

(c)   a worker or self-employed person who has ceased activity;

(d)   the family member of a worker or self-employed person who has ceased activity;

(e)   a person who was the family member of a worker or self-employed person where –

   (i)   the worker or self-employed person has died,

   (ii)   the family member resided with him immediately before his death, and

   (iii) the worker or self-employed person had resided continuously in the UK for at least the two years immediately before his death, or the death was the result of an accident at work or an occupational disease;

(f)   a person who –

   (i)   has resided in the UK in accordance with the 2006 Regulations for a continuous period of five years; and

   (ii)   was, at the end of that period, a family member who has retained the right of residence.

So as to (a), this would include an EEA national who works in the UK for two years and then is unable to work for the next three years due to illness – this person would initially be a worker as defined in reg 6(1)(b) and would remain a worker when subsequently temporarily unable to work due to illness under reg 6(2)(a). The Home Office may well require medical evidence that there was a genuine inability to work during those three years. These are the facts of *FMB (Uganda) v Secretary of State for the Home Department* [2010] UKUT 447.

Note that as to (b) above (and subject to reg 10: see **4.4.11**), the family member must have held that status for five years. So an extended family member who was in a durable relationship with an EEA national but whose relationship breaks down before he fulfils the five-year requirement is excluded: see *CS (Brazil) v Secretary of State for the Home Department* [2009] EWCA Civ 480.

In (b) above, does the 'residing with' requirement relate just to presence in the UK or does it require living in a common family home? In *PM v Secretary of State for the Home Department* [2011] UKUT 246, the Tribunal held the former. So, in respect of a spouse, (b) is met where the couple entered a genuine marriage; both parties have resided in the UK for five years since the marriage; the EEA national's spouse has resided as the family member of a qualified person or otherwise in accordance with the Regulations and the marriage has not been dissolved.

Obviously, if the parties have separated there may be an issue as to whether the marriage is one of convenience (see **4.4.6.2**). But that did not apply in the case as there was genuine matrimonial cohabitation for some time, a child had been born to the couple and there were continuing social relations by the parties to the marriage in the context of contact with the child.

Note that as to (c) above (a worker or self-employed person who has ceased activity), this category of person is defined by reg 5. So, for example, it includes a worker or self-employed person who has to stop work as a result of a permanent incapacity (see **4.4.5.2**) and who had resided in the UK continuously for more than two years prior to his work ending.

So if an EEA national with the right of permanent residence in the UK under (c) marries or enters into a civil partnership with a non-EEA national, that spouse or civil partner acquires the permanent right of residence in the UK under (d): see *RM (Zimbabwe) v Secretary of State for the Home Department* [2013] EWCA Civ 775.

Some of the above categories are based on a period of continuous residence in the UK. What about any periods of absence? Regulation 3 provides that continuity of residence is not affected by:

(a)   periods of absence from the UK which do not exceed six months in total in any year;

(b)   periods of absence from the UK on military service; or

(c)   any one absence from the UK not exceeding 12 months for an important reason, such as pregnancy and childbirth, serious illness, study or vocational training, or an overseas posting.

Is any period of continuous residence in the UK broken if the person is imprisoned? Yes, see *C v Secretary of State for the Home Department* [2010] EWCA Civ 1406, as 'the worker is not legally resident in the host state as an EEA worker during the period of imprisonment and that any period, which includes that period of imprisonment, cannot be part of the necessary "continuous" period for the purpose of calculating the five years continuous legal residence necessary to acquire the right permanently to reside here' (per Longmore LJ at [47]).

Can the right of permanent residence be lost once acquired? Yes, but only through absence from the UK for a period exceeding two consecutive years.

4.4.10   How can an EEA national or family member confirm his permanent residence?

Under reg 18, an EEA national or non-EEA family member entitled to permanent residence can apply to the Secretary of State for a document certifying permanent residence or a permanent residence card respectively.

A document certifying permanent residence does not have an expiry date. A permanent residence card is valid for 10 years and is renewable.

4.4.11   What is the status of a family member who has not acquired permanent residence on the death or departure from the UK of the qualified person, or the termination of marriage or civil partnership?

Until a family member acquires his own right of permanent residence he is in a vulnerable position: what if the qualified person dies or leaves the UK? If his right of residence is dependent on marriage to, or on a civil partnership with, a qualified person, what is his immigration status when that relationship formally ends?

The answer is to be found in reg 10, which allows certain family members to retain the right of residence. This includes, for example, under reg 10(2), a person who:

(a)   is a family member of a qualified person when the qualified person dies;

(b)   resided in the UK in accordance with the 2006 Regs for at least the year immediately before the death of the qualified person; and

(c)   if he had been an EEA national himself, would qualify as a worker, a self-employed person or a self-sufficient person as defined by reg 6, or who is the family member of such a person.

A non-EEA ex-spouse or ex-civil partner may retain the right of residence under reg 10(5) if:

(a)   he ceased to be a family member of the qualified person on the termination of their marriage or civil partnership;

(b)   he was residing in the UK in accordance with the 2006 Regs at the date of the termination;

(c)   had he been an EEA national himself, he would qualify as a worker, a self-employed person or a self-sufficient person as defined by reg 6 (or as the family member of such a person); and

(d)   either –

(i)   the marriage or civil partnership had lasted for at least three years prior to the initiation of the proceedings for its termination, and the parties had resided in the UK for at least one year during its duration;

(ii)   he has custody of a child of the qualified person;

(iii)   he has the right of access to a child of the qualified person, where the child is under the age of 18 and where a court has ordered that such access must take place in the UK; or

(iv)   his continued right of residence in the UK is warranted by particularly difficult circumstances, such as he or another family member having been a victim of domestic violence while the marriage or civil partnership was subsisting.

For (b) above, the applicant will need to demonstrate that at the date of termination his ex-spouse or ex-civil partner was a qualified person. So, if the EEA national was then working, his payslips, bank statements, accounts, letters from employers or customers may help if the applicant can obtain such. On any appeal to the Tribunal (see **Chapter 11**) the applicant may be able to apply for a witness summons requiring his ex-spouse or ex-civil partner to attend and give evidence. Additionally, or alternatively, a direction may be sought requiring the Secretary of State to provide any information necessary for the determination of the appeal: see *Amos v Secretary of State for the Home Department* [2011] EWCA Civ 552.

Home Office guidance is that it will normally revoke, or refuse to issue or renew, a residence card where a family member's marriage to, or civil partnership with, a qualified person terminates, or there is evidence that the EEA national has left the UK, unless the family member has retained the right of residence under reg 10.

The burden is on the applicant to show that the conditions under which the right of residence is said to be retained are met: *Okafor v Secretary of State for the Home Department* [2011] EWCA Civ 499.

Can a family member who retains the right of residence ever acquire permanent residence? Yes, after five years' continuous residence in the UK, provided that has been in accordance with the 2006 Regs (see **4.4.9**).

4.4.12   British citizens who exercise Treaty rights and then return to the UK (reg 9)

If a British citizen travels to another EEA country to work or otherwise exercise Treaty rights, he is entitled to be accompanied by, or later joined by, his family members. Equally, if a British citizen travels to the UK from an EEA country after exercising Treaty rights there as a worker or self-employed person, his family may accompany him. So, for example, the Indian spouse of a British citizen who has worked in another EEA country may take advantage of Article 44

TFEU, acquiring rights of residence in the UK itself beyond those given by UK immigration law – see *R v Immigration Appeal Tribunal and Surinder Singh, ex p Secretary of State for the Home Department* [1992] 3 CMLR 358. The facts of the case were as follows.

Mr Singh, an Indian national, married a British citizen in the UK in 1982. At no time did the authorities allege that the marriage was a sham. It appears that Mr Singh was lawfully in the UK, but his immigration status is not clear from the case report. In 1983 Mr and Mrs Singh went to Germany, where they were both employed for two years. At the end of 1985 the couple returned to the UK to open a business. The ECJ held that the provisions of the Council Regulations and Directives on freedom of movement within the EU for employed and self-employed persons provide that Member States must grant the spouse and children of such a person rights of residence equivalent to those granted to the person himself. A national of a Member State might be deterred from leaving his country of origin in order to pursue an activity as an employed or self-employed person as envisaged by the Treaty in the territory of another Member State if, on returning to the Member State of which he is a national in order to pursue an activity there as an employed or self-employed person, the conditions of his entry and residence were not at least equivalent to those which he would enjoy under the Treaty or secondary law in the territory of another Member State. He would in particular be deterred from so doing if his spouse and children were not also permitted to enter and reside in the territory of his Member State of origin under conditions at least equivalent to those granted them by EU law in the territory of another Member State.

Regulation 9 is said to give effect to the *Surinder Singh* judgment.

4.4.12.1   Regulation 9(2)(a)

Where a UK national is residing in an EEA State as a worker or self-employed person, or was so residing before returning to the UK, he is entitled to be accompanied by his family members (spouse, civil partner, partner in a durable relationship, child under 21, etc: see **4.4.6**).

The Home Office advises that the UK national must either have been employed in an EEA State other than on a transient or casual basis, or have established himself there as a self-employed person. As a rule of thumb it is said that the UK national should have carried out such an activity for at least six months. It might be less if he was required to return to the UK earlier for a good reason, eg health grounds.

Does reg 9(2)(a) require that the UK national must be residing in an EEA State as a worker or self-employed person immediately before returning to the UK? No, held the Upper Tribunal in *OB (Morocco) v Secretary of State for the Home Department* [2010] UKUT 420. In the case the UK national married a national of Morocco in August 2006 whilst both were in the Republic of Ireland. The couple stayed there until July 2008. During that time the UK national worked from November 2006 to April 2007. In July 2008 the UK national returned to Northern Ireland, UK (where she had previously lived) to live and work there permanently. Her husband joined her and in September 2008 he applied for a residence card as the spouse of a UK national who had exercised Treaty rights. This application was granted. The Tribunal stated that the link between the UK national's right under EU law to reside and work in the Republic of Ireland and her right to return to the UK accompanied by her family members had not been broken. Further, in general, a period of interruption of employment for maternity and child rearing purposes, temporary illness or involuntary unemployment would also not break such a link.

Does it make any difference if the British citizen deliberately went to another EEA country and worked there in order that he might use EU rather than domestic law to bring a family member back to the UK? No, held the ECJ in *Secretary of State for the Home Department v Akrich* [2003] 3 CMLR 26, provided the British citizen was properly a worker and, in the case of a spouse or civil partner, the relationship is genuine and not one of convenience. As to the latter, see **4.4.6.2**.

4.4.12.2 Regulation 9(2)(b)

If the family member of the UK national is his or her spouse or civil partner, there are additional requirements. Either:

(a)   the couple are living together in the EEA State before the UK national returns to the UK; or

(b)   the couple entered into the marriage or civil partnership and were living together in the EEA State before the UK national returned to the UK.

4.4.12.3 Rights of family members

Home Office guidance is that because EEA nationals have an initial three-month right of residence in the UK (see **4.4.3**), there is no requirement for the British citizen to be the equivalent of a qualified person on arrival back in the UK. However, the first two questions on the application form for an EEA family permit are: what is the main purpose of your visit to the UK, and how long do you intend to stay in the UK? Detailed disclosure is then required of the couple's financial situation, as well as details of where they intend to live in the UK, etc. If an ECO takes the view that after three months in the UK the British citizen will not then be the equivalent of a qualified person (see **4.4.4**), it is possible that the application may be refused. However, note that Home Office guidance is that where the ECO has strong grounds to doubt that the EEA (or thereby British) national is, or will be, a qualified person, he should first interview the couple.

Additionally, a family permit might be refused on public policy, public health or public security grounds (see **4.4.14**) or, where the non-EEA national is the spouse or civil partner of the British national, on the ground that the relationship is one of convenience (see **4.4.6.2**).

On entering the UK the family member will be entitled to a residence card (see **4.4.8**) and, in due course, permanent residence (see **4.4.9**) under the same conditions as any family member of an EEA national.

If the family member of the UK national is his spouse or civil partner, he has the choice of entry under EU law or domestic law (see **8.3**). If he chooses EU law and is successful, he will be issued with a family permit and a residence card. He may qualify for permanent residence after five years.

4.4.13 Derivative rights (reg 15A)

In 2012 the 2006 Regs were amended (see the Immigration (European Economic Area) (Amendment) Regulations 2012 (SI 2012/1547)) to give effect to the judgments of the ECJ in Case C-200/02 *Chen*, Case C-310/08 *Ibrahim* and Case C-480/08 *Teixeira*. Broadly, these cases established the right of entry and residence for primary carers of self-sufficient EEA national children, children of EEA national workers or former workers where the child is in education in the UK, primary carers of children of EEA national workers or former workers where that child is in education in the UK, and dependent children under the age of 18 of those primary carers.

In 2012 the 2006 Regs were further amended (see the Immigration (European Economic Area) (Amendment) (No 2) Regulations 2012 (SI 2012/2560)) to give effect to the judgment of the ECJ in the case of *Zambrano v Office national de l'emploi (ONEm)* (Case C-34/09) [2011] 2 CMLR 46. This provides that if a child in the UK is a British citizen, his primary carer (usually a parent) is a non-EEA national and there is no other parent, guardian or carer on whom the child is dependent or who could care for the child if the primary carer left the UK, the carer will have a right of residence.

Regulation 15A sets out the conditions which a person must satisfy in order to qualify for a derivative right of residence. Why derivative? Because the right does not stem directly from the 2004 Directive. As a result the person's wider family members have no right of entry to the UK and the person cannot acquire permanent residence here.

4.4.14   Summary of key terms

'Qualified person'	An EEA national who is exercising Treaty rights as a jobseeker; worker; self-employed person; a self-sufficient person or student.
'EEA family permit'	A form of entry clearance issued to a non-EEA national who is the family member of an EEA national.
'Registration certificate'	This is issued to an EEA national who is exercising Treaty rights (reg 16).
'Residence card'	This is issued to a non-EEA national who is the family member of a qualified person (reg 17).
'A document certifying permanent residence'	This is issued to an EEA national who has been residing in the UK for at least five years exercising Treaty rights (reg 18).
'A permanent residence card'	This is issued to a non-EEA national who is the family member of a qualified person, when he has resided for at least five years with a qualified person, who, during those five years has exercised Treaty rights (reg 18).

4.4.15   Excluding and removing an EEA national from the UK

Regulation 19 of the I(EEA) Regs 2006 provides for the exclusion and removal of an EEA national or his family member who has ceased to qualify, or whose removal is justified on the grounds of public policy pursuant to reg 21. Note that protection from removal is enhanced if the person has a permanent right of residence after five years ('serious grounds of public policy or public security' are required under reg 21(3))) and further enhanced after continuous residence of 10 years ('imperative grounds of public security' are required under reg 21(4))). As to the meaning of these terms, see *VP (Italy) v Secretary of State for the Home Department* [2010] EWCA Civ 806 and *FV (Italy) v Secretary of State for the Home Department* [2012] EWCA Civ 1199. Further, note that in *HR (Portugal) v Secretary of State for the Home Department* [2009] EWCA Civ 371 it was held that both these qualifying periods must consist of lawful residence and so do not include time spent in prison. Can time spent in the UK before a period of imprisonment be included in a qualifying period? The matter has been referred to the ECJ: see *Onuekwere (Nigeria)* [2012] UKUT 269 and *MG (Portugal)* [2012] UKUT 268.

For a person to be excluded or removed on public policy grounds under reg 21, he must present a serious threat to the fundamental interests of society by his personal conduct. Guidance from the Home Office provides that previous criminal convictions are not in themselves sufficient grounds, unless the offence(s) are particularly serious (eg rape, murder, drug smuggling) and it is likely that the person will reoffend. A person charged with minor customs offences is not refused admission on that basis alone, whereas a person who is the leader of an extreme political party might present such a threat. Facilitation of illegal entry may, in itself, be sufficient grounds to refuse admission to EEA nationals. National security may also fall under this heading.

Public security under reg 21 does not necessarily equate with national security. Public security may also be a matter of personal security within society. Certain medical conditions (eg drug addiction or profound mental disturbance) may pose a threat to public policy or public security. These conditions might provide reasons for exclusion on public policy or public security grounds, but not on public health grounds.

As to public health, only a disease that has epidemic potential as defined by the World Health Organisation, or a disease to which s 38 of the Public Health (Control of Disease) Act 1984 applies (detention in hospital of a person with a notifiable disease), will constitute a ground for a decision to exclude or remove. However, if the person concerned is in the UK, any disease occurring after the initial three-month period does not count.

Home Office guidance is that once it is established that the threat posed by a person is sufficient in principle to justify his deportation on grounds of public policy or security under EU law, there will be a presumption that the public interest requires deportation. Regulation 21(5)(a) of the I(EEA) Regs 2006 requires such a decision to deport to comply with the principle of proportionality. Regulation 21(6) lists the type of considerations that must be taken into account, such as age; state of health; family and economic situation; length of residence in the UK; social and cultural integration into the UK and the person's links with his country of origin. The proportionality test under EU law requires that any interference with a person's free movement rights must be both appropriate in the circumstances of the case and go no further than is necessary to achieve the public policy or public security need; and the consideration of proportionality encompasses human rights considerations.

4.5 CHART CROSS-REFERENCING KEY ASPECTS OF 2006 REGULATIONS AND 2004 DIRECTIVE

Coverage	2006 Regulations	2004 Directive
Definitions	reg 2 'EEA national'	Art 2 'Union citizen'
	reg 7 'family member' reg 8 'extended family member'	Art 2 Art 3(2)
Right of entry	reg 11	Art 5
Initial right of residence up to 3 months	reg 13	Art 6
Right of residence for more than 3 months	reg 14	Art 7
Issue of residence cards	reg 17	Art 10
Retention of right of residence by family members on death or departure of qualified person	reg 10	Art 12
Retention of right of residence by family members on formal ending of marriage or registered civil partnership with qualified person	reg 10	Art 13
Right of permanent residence	reg 15	Arts 16, 17 and 18
A document certifying permanent residence	reg 18	Art 19
A permanent residence card	reg 18	Art 20
Continuity of residence	reg 3	Art 21
Protection against expulsion	reg 21	Art 28
Public health	reg 21	Art 29

CHAPTER 5

VISITORS

5.1 INTRODUCTION – WHO IS A VISITOR?

A person may want to enter the UK temporarily as a visitor for many different reasons – for a holiday, to visit family or friends, to conduct some sort of business, to have private medical treatment, get married or enter into a civil partnership, etc. Part 2 of the Immigration Rules deals with these different routes into the UK for a visitor, and we shall look at the key categories in this chapter.

5.1.1 Entry clearance

Except in the case of visa nationals (see **1.4.3**), no entry clearance is required for a visit to the UK of up to six months. So it is possible for non-visa nationals (see **1.4.4**) to arrive in the UK and seek leave to enter. It may, however, reduce any potential problems for those who are not simply tourists, if entry clearance is obtained in advance.

5.1.2 Leave to enter and conditions

Most kinds of visitors under Part 2 will be given leave to enter the UK for a period not exceeding six months, subject to a condition prohibiting employment (see **3.3.1**). Like all limited leave entrants, all visitors will also be subject to the condition not to have recourse to public funds (also see **3.3.2**).

5.1.3 Frequency of visits

Is there any restriction on the number of visits a person may make to the UK? Is there any requirement that a specified period of time must elapse between successive visits? The answer to both these questions is 'No'. Home Office guidance is that a person who has made a series of visits to the UK with only brief intervals between them would not, in the absence of any other relevant factors, be refused entry as a visitor. However, an immigration officer will consider the stated purpose of a visit in light of the length of time that has elapsed since previous visits. As a rule of thumb, a visitor should not normally spend more than six out of any 12 months in the UK. See further *Sawmynaden (Family visitors – considerations)* [2012] UKUT 00161 (IAC).

Note that the Home Office accepts that, occasionally, a business visitor (see **5.6**) may be required to stay for a period of weeks or even months in the UK, for example where machinery is being installed or faults are being diagnosed and corrected. An immigration officer should be satisfied, however, that a person's presence in the UK on business for more than six out of any 12 months does not mean that he is basing himself here and holding down a specific post which constitutes employment, and which would therefore require the individual to seek entry under the points-based system (see **Chapter 7**).

5.2 GENERAL VISITOR

For the purposes of paras 41 to 46 of the Immigration Rules, a general visitor includes a person living and working outside the UK who wishes to enter or remain in the UK as a tourist.

5.2.1 Requirements

The requirements to be met by a person seeking leave to enter the UK as a general visitor are set out in para 41, namely, that he:

(a)   is genuinely seeking entry as a general visitor for a limited period as stated by him not exceeding six months, or not exceeding 12 months in the case of a person seeking entry to accompany an academic visitor (see **5.6.2**), provided in the latter case that the visitor accompanying the academic visitor has entry clearance (para 41(i)); and

(b)   intends to leave the United Kingdom at the end of the period of the visit as stated by him (para 41(ii)); and

(c)   does not intend to take employment in the United Kingdom (para 41(iii)); and

(d)   does not intend to produce goods or provide services within the United Kingdom, including the selling of goods or services direct to members of the public (para 41(iv)); and

(e)   does not intend to undertake a course of study unless that is 'permitted study' (see **5.2.6**) (para 41(v)); and

(f)   will maintain and accommodate himself and any dependants adequately out of resources available to him without recourse to public funds or taking employment; or will, with any dependants, be maintained and accommodated adequately by relatives or friends (para 41(vi)); and

(g)   can meet the cost of the return or onward journey (para 41(vii)); and

(h)   is not a child under the age of 18 (see **5.3**) (para 41(viii)); and

(i)   does not intend to do any of the activities provided for in paras 46G(iii), 46M(iii) or 46S(iii) (see **5.6**) (para 41(ix)); and

(j)   does not, during his visit, intend to marry or form a civil partnership, or to give notice of marriage or civil partnership (see **5.7**) (para 41(x)); and

(k)   does not intend to receive private medical treatment during his visit (see **5.8**) (para 41(xi)); and

(l)   is not in transit to a country outside the Common Travel Area (see **5.11**) (para 41(xii)); and

(m)   where he is seeking leave to enter as a general visitor to take part in archaeological excavations, provides a letter from the director or organiser of the excavation stating the length of the visit and, where appropriate, what arrangements have been made for the person's accommodation and maintenance.

5.2.1.1   Home Office policy

What should have struck you when reading the requirements in para 41 for a general visitor, is that most concern the applicant's intention. So he must *genuinely* be seeking entry as a general visitor and *intend* to leave the UK at the end of his visit, and he must *not intend* to take employment, etc whilst in the UK. It is therefore not surprising that the Home Office's policy focuses as follows on the credibility of a passenger seeking entry to the UK:

> The fact that a passenger claiming to be a visitor may be able to produce a return ticket (and other supporting evidence) does not guarantee that he intends to abide by his conditions of stay or that his intention to leave at the end of his visit is genuine. All documents produced by a passenger should be assessed in conjunction with any other evidence, however circumstantial, which may be relevant to the case.

> If there are any doubts as to a passenger's intentions, it is essential to obtain and record not only his statements as to his intentions but also full details of his background.

> A visitor's proposed purpose in coming to the United Kingdom must bear some reasonable relationship to his financial means and his family, social and economic background. Previous immigration history and evidence of a pattern of family migration, both here and abroad, are also matters to be taken into account.

> If a passenger or his sponsor is shown to have attempted to deceive the immigration officer or some other person in some material respect or where there are material discrepancies between what the passenger and his sponsor say, when the sponsor can reasonably have been expected to know the facts, these are again grounds for doubting the passenger's credibility and not therefore being satisfied as to his intentions.

EXAMPLE

Ada, aged 22, is a non-visa national. She arrives in the UK without an entry certificate. She informs the immigration officer that she is visiting her sister in the UK for six months. When questioned, she discloses that:

(a) she recently lost her job;

(b) she will be looking after her sister's children whilst she is in the UK because her sister and brother-in-law have just got jobs;

(c) her sister will not pay her but will provide her with food and accommodation;

(d) she has only a few pounds in cash on her;

(e) her sister bought her a one-way ticket to the UK.

The immigration officer may decide that she does not meet the requirements of para 41, as follows:

(a) Ada is not genuinely seeking entry as a general visitor for six months; rather, her purpose is to enter the UK to be a childminder for her sister and brother-in-law indefinitely.

(b) Ada does not intend to leave the UK after six months, especially as she has no return ticket and no apparent means of saving enough money to buy one whilst in the UK.

(c) Ada intends to take unpaid employment.

(d) Ada has no evidence to support her claim that she will be maintained and accommodated adequately by her sister.

(e) Ada has no evidence that she can meet the cost of her return journey after six months.

Note that, in addition, the immigration officer will have consulted the Home Office guidance on a general visitor acting as a temporary childminder for a relative. This will give an additional reason for refusing the application, as the childminding arrangement appears to have come about simply to enable Ada's sister and brother-in-law to take gainful employment.

5.2.2 Leave to enter

By para 42, a person seeking leave to enter to the UK as a general visitor may be admitted for a period not exceeding six months (or not exceeding 12 months in the case of a person accompanying an academic visitor – see **5.6.2**), subject to a condition prohibiting employment (see **3.3.1**). Like all limited leave entrants, he will also be subject to the condition not to have recourse to public funds (also see **3.3.2**).

5.2.3 Multi-entry visa

Visit visas are normally valid for six months, 12 months, two years, five years and 10 years. A visa is valid for unlimited journeys within its period of validity. However, a person with a visit visa may remain in the UK for a maximum of only six months on any one visit, or until the visa expires if less than six months.

5.2.4 Written statements and undertakings

As we have seen at **5.2.1**, a general visitor must demonstrate that he intends to enter the UK for the purpose of a visit, say with family or friends, or simply as a tourist, and that he will leave the UK. Home Office guidance is that in exceptional circumstances, where the application would normally be refused but the person is given the benefit of the doubt, it may ask the applicant to sign a written statement of his declared intentions. If a person then acted in contradiction to such a written statement by applying in the UK for leave to remain, the Home Office would normally refuse that leave under para 322(7) of the Immigration Rules (see further **3.6.5**).

Applications for leave to enter as a general visitor are often supported by a family member or a friend in the UK. Such a person may offer to sponsor the proposed visitor formally, ie enter into a written undertaking to be responsible for the visitor's maintenance and accommodation during the visitor's stay (see **3.3.2**).

5.2.5 Leave to enter as visitor under Approved Destination Status Agreement with China

This Agreement allows groups of Chinese tourists to enter the UK. A very limited number of designated tour operators have been accredited and trained by the British Embassy in China, and these may submit visa applications to the British Embassy for each member of the proposed tour group. The details are to be found in para 56G.

5.2.6 Permitted study

A visitor may undertake up to 30 days of recreational, English language or academic study whilst in the UK provided that is not the main purpose of his visit. Home Office guidance is that recreational study means leisure and holiday-type courses such as pottery or horse riding. Any other study (including any English language) may only take place at an institution that holds a licence under Tier 4 (see **Chapter 6**) or which is accredited by a Home Office-approved body (see further para 43A of the Immigration Rules).

5.3 CHILD VISITOR

A child is a person under the age of 18. A child might be travelling to the UK alone or with an adult. Usually the purpose of the visit is to see family, but it may be for some short-term educational reasons.

5.3.1 Requirements

By para 46A, the requirements to be met by a person seeking leave to enter the UK as a child visitor are that he:

(a)   is genuinely seeking entry as a child visitor for a limited period as stated by him not exceeding six months (or not exceeding 12 months to accompany an academic visitor – see **5.6.2**, provided the child visitor has entry clearance) (para 46A(i)); and

(b)   meets the requirements of para 41(ii)–(iv), (vi)–(vii) and (x)–(xii) (see **5.2.1**) (para 46A(ii)); and

(c)   is under the age of 18 (para 46A(iii)); and

(d)   can demonstrate that suitable arrangements have been made for his travel to, and reception and care in, the UK (see **5.3.1.1**) (para 46A(iv)); and

(e)   has a parent or guardian in his home country or country of habitual residence who is responsible for his care (see **5.3.1.2**) (para 46A(v)); and

(f)   if a visa national (see **5.3.1.3**) –

    (i)   holds a valid UK entry clearance for entry as an accompanied child visitor, and is travelling in the company of the adult identified on his entry clearance who is on the same occasion being admitted to the UK, or

    (ii)   holds a valid UK entry clearance for entry as an unaccompanied child visitor (para 46A(vi)); and

(g)   if he has been accepted for a course of study (see **5.3.1.4**), this is to be provided by an institution which is –

    (i)   the holder of a Sponsor Licence for Tier 4 of the Points Based System, or

    (ii)   Accreditation UK, the Accreditation Body for Language Services (ABLS), the British Accreditation Council (BAC) or the Accreditation Service for International Colleges (ASIC), or

    (iii)   the holder of a valid and satisfactory full institutional inspection, review or audit by one of the following bodies: the Bridge Schools Inspectorate; the Education and Training Inspectorate; Estyn; Education Scotland; the Independent Schools Inspectorate; Office for Standards in Education; the Schools Inspection Service or the Education and Training Inspectorate Northern Ireland (para 46A(vii)); and

(h)   if he is undertaking an exchange or educational visit only, this is to be provided by a school specified in para 46A(viii).

Some of these requirements are explored further below.

5.3.1.1   Suitable travel, reception and care arrangements in UK

Home Office guidance is that where there are no other factors which give cause for concern, this requirement may simply involve the inclusion of the child in the travel and accommodation arrangements of the parent(s), relative(s) or friend(s) accompanying him, or a letter from a relative or friend at the UK address, inviting the child to visit.

What evidence will an ECO require for entry clearance purposes? He will need the name, address and landline telephone number of the parent or carer in the child's home country, the host in the UK and the person accompanying the child. Where these details are missing or unclear, or other factors raise concerns about the child's welfare, further enquiries will be undertaken to confirm the identity and residence of the host and that the child is expected in the UK. The application will be refused if the ECO remains concerned about the child's welfare in the UK.

Where an immigration officer considering leave to enter has concerns about the child's welfare, the Home Office's policy is that both the social service departments in the host's area and those local to the port of entry should be contacted so that enquiries can be made to ascertain the host's suitability.

5.3.1.2   Parent or guardian responsible for child's care in home country or country of habitual residence

In the majority of cases where an application is being made for entry clearance abroad, the parent or guardian will be the person making the application on behalf of the child, and this requirement should be met. Otherwise, provided there are no other factors which give cause for concern, a letter from the parent or guardian confirming his relationship to the child and consenting to the child's application is normally sufficient.

What if the child's parents are divorced? Written consent must be given by the parent who has residence or legal custody, or sole responsibility of the child.

5.3.1.3   A child who is a visa national

Where a child is travelling in the company of an adult, he must hold a visa which identifies the adult with whom he seeks to enter the UK. The identification is by way of the adult's passport number, initial and surname, which is included on the child's visa document.

Where a child is travelling unaccompanied, his visa will state this.

5.3.1.4   Accepted for a course of study

A child visitor may be given entry clearance to study in the UK for up to six months, provided the institution he intends to attend meets the requirements of para 46A(vii) (see **5.3.1** above, at (g)) (for further details, see **Chapter 6**).

5.3.2   Leave to enter

By para 46B, a person seeking leave to enter the UK as a child visitor may be admitted for a period not exceeding six months, or not exceeding 12 months in the case of a child visitor accompanying an academic visitor (see **5.6.2**) subject to a condition prohibiting employment (see **3.3.1**). Like all limited leave entrants, a child visitor will also be subject to the condition not to have recourse to public funds (also see **3.3.2**).

5.4   PARENT OF A CHILD AT SCHOOL IN UK

This category allows entry to the UK of the parent of a child under 12 who is at school in the UK. Paragraph 56A sets out the following requirements:

(a)   the parent meets the requirements set out in para 41(ii)–(xii) (see **5.2.1**) (para 56A(i)); and

(b)   the child is a Tier 4 (Child) Student attending an independent fee-paying day school (see **Chapter 6**) (para 56A(ii)); and

(c)   the child is under 12 years of age (para 56A(iii)); and

(d)   the parent can provide satisfactory evidence of adequate and reliable funds for maintaining a second home in the UK (para 56A(iv)); and

(e)   the parent is not seeking to make the UK his main home (para 56A (v)); and

(f)   the parent was not last admitted to the UK under the Approved Destination Status Agreement with China (see **5.2.4**) (para 56A(vi)).

5.4.1   Home Office policy

Home Office policy is that this category allows for a parent to stay with a young child at school in the UK, provided that the child is under 12, attending a private day school, the parent of the child is not working, there is evidence of adequate and reliable funds for maintaining a second home in the UK, and there is no reason to believe that the family is seeking to make its principal home in the UK.

As to the maintenance requirements for child students accompanied by parents with whom they are living, see **Chapter 6**.

5.4.2 Entry clearance and leave to enter

By para 56B, a person seeking leave to enter or remain in the UK as the parent of a child at school, may be admitted or allowed to remain for a period not exceeding 12 months, subject to a condition prohibiting employment and study (see **3.3.1**). Like all limited leave entrants, the parent will also be subject to the condition not to have recourse to public funds (also see **3.3.2**).

Entry clearance is mandatory for visa nationals and for all those seeking entry for up to the maximum of 12 months.

Leave to enter may be granted for six months, or for the maximum of 12 months if the parent has entry clearance in this category.

5.5 STUDENT VISITOR

This category allows a person to enter the UK either:

(a)   as a visitor, but also to undertake a short period of study which must be completed within that person's six months' limited leave; or

(b)   as a student to study on a course of six months' duration or less, provided he does not intend to take part-time employment, or undertake a paid or unpaid work placement as part of that course. Only a Tier 4 (Adult) Student (see **Chapter 6**) may work part-time or take up a work placement.

5.5.1 Requirements

Paragraph 56K sets out the following requirements, namely, that the student visitor:

(a)   is genuinely seeking entry as a student visitor for a limited period as stated by him, not exceeding six months (para 56K(i)); and

(b)   has been accepted on a course of study which is to be provided by an institution which is:

    (i)   the holder of a sponsor licence for Tier 4 of the points-based system (see **Chapter 6**), or

    (ii)   Accreditation UK, the Accreditation Body for Language Services (ABLS), the British Accreditation Council (BAC) or the Accreditation Service for International Colleges (ASIC), or

    (iii)   the holder of a valid and satisfactory full institutional inspection, review or audit by one of the following bodies: Bridge Schools Inspectorate; the Education and Training Inspectorate; Estyn; Education Scotland; the Independent Schools Inspectorate; Office for Standards in Education; the Quality Assurance Agency for Higher Education; the Schools Inspection Service or the Education and Training Inspectorate Northern Ireland, or

    (iv)   an overseas Higher Education Institution offering only part of its programmes in the UK, holding its own national accreditation and offering programmes that are of a level equivalent to a UK degree (para 56K(ii)); and

(c)   intends to leave the UK at the end of his visit as stated by him (para 56K(iii)); and

(d)   does not intend to take employment in the UK (para 56K(iv)); and

(e)   does not intend to engage in business, to produce goods or provide services within the UK, including the selling of goods or services direct to members of the public (para 56K(v)); and

(f)   does not intend to study at a maintained school (para 56K(vi)); and

(g)   will maintain and accommodate himself and any dependants adequately out of resources available to him without recourse to public funds or taking employment; or will, with any dependants, be maintained and accommodated adequately by relatives or friends (para 56K(vii)); and

(h)   can meet the cost of the return or onward journey (para 56K(viii)); and

(i)   is not a child under the age of 18 (see **5.3**) (para 56K(ix)); and

(j)   meets the requirements set out in para 41(ix)–(xii) (see **5.2.1**) (para 56K(x)).

5.5.2 Entry clearance and leave to enter

By para 56L, a person seeking leave to enter to the UK as a student visitor may be admitted for a period not exceeding six months, subject to a condition prohibiting employment (see **3.3.1**). Like all limited leave entrants, the student visitor will also be subject to the condition not to have recourse to public funds (also see **3.3.2**).

Only a visa national must obtain entry clearance before travelling to the UK in this category.

5.5.3 English language course concession

From January 2011 the Government announced a concession for an applicant seeking entry as a student visitor to undertake a course in English language only. This can be longer than six months but no more than 11 months. The applicant must still meet all the other requirements of the student visitor category.

For the purposes of this concession the student must be learning English as a foreign language. Mixed courses with only a portion of time spent learning English do not qualify.

Non-visa nationals must obtain prior entry clearance if they wish to undertake an English language course that is for longer than six months.

5.6 BUSINESS VISITOR

Who is a business visitor? Surprisingly, Part 2 of the Immigration Rules creates a wide category, as we shall see below. However, any business visitor must satisfy three key tests, namely, that:

(a)   he is based abroad and has no intention of transferring his base to the UK, even temporarily;

(b)   he will not receive his salary from a UK source; and

(c)   he will not be involved in selling goods or services direct to members of the public.

5.6.1 Requirements

Paragraph 46G sets out the requirements for business visitor, namely, that he:

(a)   is genuinely seeking entry as a business visitor for a limited period as stated by him –

    (i)   not exceeding six months, or

    (ii)   not exceeding 12 months if seeking entry as an academic visitor (see **5.6.2**) (para 46G(i));

(b)   meets the requirements of para 41(ii)–(viii) and (x)–(xii) (see **5.2.1**) (para 46G(ii));

(c)   intends to do one or more of the following during his visit –

    (i)   to carry out a 'permissible activity' as defined in para 46G(iii)(a) (see **5.6.3**),

    (ii)   to take part in a location shoot as a member of a film crew (see **5.6.4**),

    (iii)   to represent overseas news media, including as a journalist, correspondent, producer or cameraman, provided he is employed or paid by an overseas company and is gathering information for an overseas publication,

    (iv)   to act as an academic visitor, but only if he has been working as an academic in an institution of higher education overseas, or in the field of his academic expertise immediately prior to seeking entry,

    (vi)   to be a secondee to a UK company which is directly contracted with the visitor's overseas company, with which it has no corporate relationship, to provide goods or services, provided the secondee remains employed and paid by the overseas company throughout the secondee's visit (see **5.6.6**),

(vii) to undertake some preaching or pastoral work as a religious worker (see **5.6.7**), provided his base is abroad and he is not taking up an office, post or appointment,

(viii) to act as an adviser, consultant, trainer, internal auditor or troubleshooter (see **5.6.8**) to the UK branch of the same group of companies as the visitor's overseas company, provided the visitor remains employed and paid by the overseas company and does not undertake work, paid or unpaid with the UK company's clients,

(xi) to receive specific, one-off training on techniques and work practices used in the UK (see **5.6.9**), where:

(1) the training is to be delivered by the UK branch of the same group of companies to which the individual's employer belongs; or

(2) the training is to be provided by a UK company contracted to provide goods or services to the overseas company; or

(3) a UK company is contracted to provide training facilities only, to an overseas company; or

(4) the training is corporate training provided for the purposes of the person's employment overseas and delivered by a UK company that is neither part of the person's employer's corporate group nor whose main activity is the provision of training.

5.6.2 Academic visitor

An 'academic visitor' is defined in para 6 as a person who is from an overseas academic institution, or who is highly qualified within his own field of expertise, seeking leave to enter the UK to carry out research and associated activities for his own purposes.

An academic visitor must either be a person on sabbatical leave from an overseas academic institution who wishes to make use of his leave to carry out research in the UK (research for a book, for example), or an academic (including a doctor) taking part in a formal exchange arrangement with a UK counterpart, or an eminent senior doctor or dentist coming to the UK to take part in research, teaching or clinical practice, or coming to share knowledge or experience, or to hold informal discussions with their UK counterparts, or taking part in a single conference or seminar that is not a commercial or non-profit venture.

Note that academic visitors must not receive funding for their work from any UK source, although the Home Office states that payments of expenses or honoraria to cover their needs whilst in the UK may be disregarded, as may payments on an exchange basis. The applicant must not intend to take up employment or engage in any work other than the academic activity for which he is being admitted, and he must not be filling a normal post or a genuine vacancy.

An academic visitor is not permitted to switch into employment under the points-based system (see **Chapter 7**).

Note that a doctor applying to enter the UK to take the Professional and Linguistic Assessment Board (PLAB) Test, or wishing to undertake a clinical attachment, and a dentist wanting to undertake dental observer post, must meet the requirements of paras 75A and 75G respectively.

5.6.3 'Permissible activity'

What activities may a business person carry out during his six months' limited leave? By para 46G(iii)(a) these are:

(a)   to attend meetings, conferences and interviews, provided they were arranged before arrival in the UK and, if the applicant is a board-level director attending board meetings in the UK, provided he is not employed by a UK company (although he may be paid a fee for attending the meeting);

(b)   to attend trade fairs for promotional work only, provided he is not directly selling;

(c)   to arrange deals, or negotiating or signing trade agreements or contracts;

(d)   to carry out fact-finding missions;

(e)   to conduct site visits;

(f)   to work as a driver on a genuine international route delivering goods or passengers from abroad;

(g)   to work as a tour group courier, provided the applicant is contracted to a firm with headquarters outside the UK, is seeking entry to accompany a tour group, and will depart with that tour or another tour organised by the same company;

(h)   to speak at a one-off conference which is not organised as a commercial concern, and is not making a profit for the organiser;

(i)   to represent a foreign manufacturer by:

(i)   carrying out installing, debugging or enhancing work for computer software companies,

(ii)   servicing or repairing the manufacturer's products within the initial guarantee period, or

(iii) being briefed on the requirements of a UK customer, provided this is limited to briefing and does not include work involving use of the applicant's expertise to make a detailed assessment of a potential customer's requirements;

(j)   to represent a foreign machine manufacturer, as part of the contract of purchase and supply, in erecting and installing machinery too heavy to be delivered in one piece;

(k)   to act as an interpreter or a translator for visiting business people, provided they are all employed by, and doing the business of, the same overseas company;

(l)   to erect, dismantle, install, service, repair or advise on the development of foreign-made machinery, provided he will do so in the UK for up to only six months.

Note that the Home Office accepts that it is reasonable to expect those coming to the UK as business visitors in order to attend meetings, etc, to want to make use of their laptops/ Blackberrys whilst here. Provided this is solely to enable such visitors to keep up to date with their own workload abroad, or to liaise with contacts in the UK, the Home Office does not consider this to be 'work' for the purposes of the Immigration Rules.

5.6.4   Taking part in a location shoot as a member of a film crew

A film crew includes actors, producers, directors and technicians for these purposes. The purpose of entry must be to take part in location shoots only here in the UK, and the film crew must be employed or paid by an overseas company.

5.6.5   Visiting professor

Paragraph 6 defines a 'visiting professor' as a person who is seeking leave to enter the UK as an academic professor to accompany students who are studying here on Study Abroad Programmes.

5.6.6   Secondee

This provision relates specifically and only to the situation where a UK company is to provide goods or services to an overseas company on a direct contractual basis (not vice versa), and where there is no corporate relationship between the two companies, ie they are not part of the same group of companies. The individual must be seconded in a supernumerary capacity for the purpose of assisting the UK company to deliver the contract, for example to clarify his company's specifications. The secondee must remain employed and paid by the overseas company throughout his visit.

Where a person is employed by an overseas company and is being seconded to a UK company which is related to the overseas employer, he must apply under Tier 2 of the points-based system as an intra-company transfer migrant (see **7.9**).

5.6.7 Religious worker

A religious worker, visiting the UK for a particular event, such as a conference, may also undertake some preaching or pastoral work during the course of his visit, provided he is based abroad and does not intend to take up an office, post or appointment in the UK.

A person coming to the UK to fill a vacancy or work temporarily as a religious worker should apply under Tiers 2 and 5 respectively of the points-based system (see **Chapter 7**).

5.6.8 Adviser, consultant, trainer or troubleshooter

The provision relates only to a person who is employed by an overseas company and who is coming to provide advice, consultancy, training or troubleshooting services to its UK branch. The applicant cannot conduct work, paid or unpaid, for or on behalf of the UK branch, including, but not limited to, providing services for the UK branch to other companies, working in a supernumerary capacity (eg internship, project-managing, or by way of short-term temporary cover for the UK branch) or having direct involvement in producing goods for the UK company's clients. The applicant must remain employed and paid by the overseas company throughout the visit, and typically his visit would be of a one-off short-term nature.

Where a person is employed by an overseas company and is being transferred to fill a skilled post in a UK entity that is related to the overseas company, he must apply under Tier 2 of the points-based system as an intra-company transfer migrant (see **7.9**).

5.6.9 One-off training on techniques and work practices

This provision allows a person to enter the UK for specific, one-off training in techniques and work practices used in the UK. The training might typically be classroom-based and/or involve familiarisation or observation. Home Office guidance is that the provision applies in the following circumstances:

(a)   Where the visitor is an employee from the same group of companies overseas as the UK company and the training is to be provided in-house. For example, where an overseas branch sends an employee to find out about the UK branch's marketing systems.

(b)   Where the training relates to a product or service that has been sold by a UK company under contract to the overseas company and the latter is to receive training on its use. In this instance the two companies do not need to be related corporately. For example, training on how to use a piece of computer software that has been purchased.

(c)   Where a company has contracted to provide training facilities only, and no tuition, to an overseas company, the trainees and the trainers from the overseas company will be business visitors. For example, provision of a classroom or piece of equipment.

(d)   Where the visitor is an employee from the same group of companies overseas as the UK company, and is participating in a corporate training exercise provided to the UK company by an outside provider.

A person seeking to enter the UK for training other than in the above circumstances – most commonly for English language training – must qualify to do so either as a Tier 4 Student (see **Chapter 6**), or as a student visitor (see **5.5**).

5.6.10 Leave to enter

By para 46H, a person seeking leave to enter to the UK as a business visitor may be admitted for a period not exceeding six months, subject to a condition prohibiting employment (see **3.3.1**). Like all limited leave entrants, the business visitor will be subject to the condition not to have recourse to public funds (also see **3.3.2**).

An academic visitor (see **5.6.2**) without entry clearance may be admitted for a period not exceeding six months, but with entry clearance may be admitted for up to 12 months.

5.6.11 Multi-entry visa

Business visit visas are normally valid for six months, 12 months, two years, five years and 10 years. The visa will be valid for unlimited journeys during its period of validity.

5.7 MARRIAGE AND CIVIL PARTNERSHIP VISIT

If a person wishes to enter the UK to marry or to enter into a civil partnership, this route may be used, provided, of course, that the couple do not intend to stay in the UK after the marriage or civil partnership ceremony.

If the couple wish to remain in the UK permanently, the applicant should apply as a fiancé(e) or proposed civil partner (see **8.7**).

5.7.1 Requirements

Paragraph 56D sets out the requirements, namely, that the person seeking leave to enter the UK as a visitor for marriage or civil partnership must:

(a) meet the requirements set out in para 41(i)–(ix) and (xi)–(xii) (see **5.2.1**) (para 56D(i));

(b) show that he intends to give notice of the marriage or civil partnership, or marry or form a civil partnership, in the United Kingdom within the period for which entry is sought (para 56D(ii));

(c) produce satisfactory evidence, if required to do so, of the arrangements for giving notice of marriage or civil partnership, or for his wedding or civil partnership to take place, in the United Kingdom during the period for which entry is sought (para 56D(iii)); and

(d) hold a valid United Kingdom entry clearance for entry in this capacity (para 56D(iv)).

5.7.2 Entry clearance and leave to enter

Entry clearance is mandatory for all applicants.

By para 56E, a person seeking leave to enter the UK as a visitor for marriage or civil partnership may be admitted for a period not exceeding six months, subject to a condition prohibiting employment and study (see **3.3.1**). Like all limited leave entrants, the visitor in this category will be subject to the condition not to have recourse to public funds (also see **3.3.2**).

5.8 PRIVATE MEDICAL TREATMENT VISIT

This provision allows a person who is genuinely seeking entry for the purpose of receiving private medical treatment in the UK to do so. The ECO and immigration officer must be satisfied that he does not intend to seek free treatment under the National Health Service (NHS); that he des not represent a danger to public health; that the treatment is of finite duration; and that he has sufficient funds available to pay for the cost of treatment and all other expenses until the treatment ends.

Although any initial leave is for a maximum of six months, Home Office guidance is that where a bona fide passenger returns to the UK to continue private medical treatment after a previous stay here for the same purpose, no account will be taken of the normal six-month time limit for visitors.

5.8.1   Requirements

Paragraph 51 sets out the requirements to be met by a person seeking leave to enter the UK as a visitor for private medical treatment, namely, that he:

(a)   meets the requirements set out in para 41(iii)–(vii), (ix)–(x) and (xii) for entry as a general visitor (see **5.2.1**) (para 51(i));

(b)   in the case of a person suffering from a communicable disease, has satisfied the medical inspector that there is no danger to public health (see **5.8.1.1**) (para 51(ii)); and

(c)   can show, if required to do so, that any proposed course of treatment is of finite duration (see **5.8.1.2**) (para 51(iii));

(d)   intends to leave the UK at the end of his treatment (para 51(iv));

(e)   can produce satisfactory evidence (see **5.8.1.3**), if required to do so, of –

(i)   the medical condition requiring consultation or treatment, and

(ii)   satisfactory arrangements for the necessary consultation or treatment at his own expense,

(iii)   the estimated costs of such consultation or treatment,

(iv)   the likely duration of his visit, and

(v)   sufficient funds available to him in the UK to meet the estimated costs and his undertaking to do so (para 51(v)).

5.8.1.1   No danger to public health

A person suffering from a communicable disease may be given leave to enter if he satisfies the port medical inspector that there is no danger to public health. However, an applicant who otherwise meets all the requirements of para 51 may still be refused entry under para 320(7) if the port medical inspector confirms that his admission is undesirable for medical reasons (see **3.4.5.1**).

5.8.1.2   Proposed course of treatment is of finite duration

Home Office guidance is that a commonsense view should be taken of the meaning of 'finite'. A long period of treatment, although not precisely defined, may be acceptable, provided that there is a clear need for the patient to be in the UK to receive that treatment and he has sufficient funds. It is reasonable to scrutinise carefully the likely duration and success of, for example, fertility treatment which could have been going on for some years without success. It would be acceptable (with the applicant's consent) to approach the consultant direct to ask about the likelihood of eventual success of the treatment.

5.8.1.3   Evidence

What evidence is required? The Home Office guidance is as follows:

> A letter from a registered medical practitioner who holds an NHS consultant post or who appears in the Specialist Register of the General Medical Council, providing full details of the nature of the illness; the proposed treatment; the frequency of the consultations (whether weekly, monthly etc); the likely duration of the treatment; details of the cost of the treatment and confirmation that all expenses are being met and, where treatment amounts to private visits to a consultant for what appears to be a relatively minor ailment, details of the progress being made. An original letter on headed notepaper giving a private practice or hospital address and describing the signatory as a consultant is normally taken as sufficient evidence of that status.

> Evidence of the applicant's ability to pay for the treatment and to support and accommodate himself and any dependants without working or recourse to public funds needs to be provided. Where the applicant is, or appears to be, sponsored, fresh confirmation of the sponsor's willingness and financial ability to meet the likely costs is obtained. The applicant will if he is dependent upon funds from abroad, be asked to prove that the funds are transferable as certain countries operate strict exchange controls.

5.8.2   Leave to enter

By para 52, a person seeking leave to enter the UK as a visitor for private medical treatment may be admitted for a period not exceeding six months, subject to a condition prohibiting employment and study (see **3.3.1**). Like all limited leave entrants, the visitor in this category will be subject to the condition not to have recourse to public funds (also see **3.3.2**).

5.8.3   Extension of limited leave

Given that a person's treatment may take longer than six months, a visitor in this category may apply to the Home Office to extend his limited leave. The requirements for an extension of stay as a visitor to undergo or continue private medical treatment are set out in para 54, and are that the applicant:

(a)   meets the requirements set out in para 41(iii)–(vii), (ix)–(x) and (xii) (see **5.2.1**), and para 51(ii)–(v) (see **5.8.1**) (para 54(i));

(b)   has produced evidence from a registered medical practitioner who holds an NHS consultant post, or who appears in the Specialist Register of the General Medical Council, of satisfactory arrangements for private medical consultation or treatment and its likely duration; and, where treatment has already begun, evidence as to its progress (para 54(ii)); and

(c)   can show that he has met, out of the resources available to him, any costs and expenses incurred in relation to his treatment in the UK (para 54(iii)); and

(d)   has sufficient funds available to him in the UK to meet the likely costs of his treatment and intends to meet those costs (para 54(iv)); and

(e)   was not last admitted to the UK under the Approved Destination Status Agreement with China (see **5.2.5**) (para 54(v)).

5.9   SPORTS VISITOR

This provision is intended for sportspersons coming to the UK usually for a one-off event, or a series of linked events. Sportspersons coming to base themselves in the UK permanently or temporarily to work should apply under Tier 2 or Tier 5 respectively of the points-based system (see **Chapter 7**).

5.9.1   Who is a sportsperson?

Home Office guidance is that the following people may qualify for entry as a sportsperson:

(a)   amateurs and professionals coming to the UK to take part either as individuals or as a team in a specific event or tournament, such as Wimbledon, or a series of events;

(b)   members of the technical or support staff of amateurs or professionals, who are attending for the same event. Examples of such staff include team managers, personal coaches, doctors, physiotherapists, dieticians, bodyguards and press officers. Also polo grooms, provided they are not intending to base themselves at the stables for the season;

(c)   officials, including those officials coming on a voluntary basis, attending the same event as the sportsperson. Examples include linespersons and umpires;

(d)   amateurs and professionals coming for a specific one-off charity sporting event or exhibition match, either as individuals or as members of an overseas team, provided the organisers are not making a profit and the sportsperson is not receiving a fee. An example would be the London Marathon;

(e)   those seeking entry for personal appearances and promotions such as book signings, television interviews, negotiating contracts or to discuss sponsorship deals;

(f)   sportspeople seeking entry for 'trials', provided that the trial is not in front of an audience, either paying or non-paying;

(g)   those coming for training for short periods (whether as an individual or as part of team), provided that they are not basing themselves in the UK, are not being paid by a UK sporting body or joining a UK team, and that any matches they are involved in are of the friendly or exhibition type.

What is the difference between an amateur and professional sportsperson? Paragraph 6 defines an amateur as a person who engages in a sport or creative activity solely for personal enjoyment and who is not seeking to derive a living from the activity. So, by contrast, a professional is a person paid a salary for participation in sport, such as someone contracted to play for a sport or club.

5.9.2   Requirements

By para 46M, the requirements to be met by a person seeking leave to enter the UK as a sports visitor are that he:

(a)   is genuinely seeking entry as a sports visitor for a limited period as stated by him, not exceeding six months (para 46M(i)); and

(b)   meets the requirements of para 41(ii)–(viii) and (x)–(xii) (see **5.2.1**) (para 46M(ii)); and

(c)   intends to do one or more of the following during his visit (see **5.9.3**)–

    (i)   to take part in a sports tournament, a particular sporting event or series of sporting events in which the applicant is taking part either as an individual or as part of a team; making personal appearances and promotions, such as book signings, television interviews, guest commentaries, negotiating contracts or to discuss sponsorship deals; taking part in 'trials', provided it is not in front of an audience, either paying or non-paying; undertaking short periods of training, either as an individual or as part of a team, provided the applicant is not intending to settle in the UK, being paid by a UK sporting body, or joining a UK team where they are involved in friendly or exhibition matches,

    (ii)   to take part in a specific one-off charity sporting event provided no payment is received other than for travelling and other expenses,

    (iii)   to join, as an amateur, a wholly or predominantly amateur team, provided no payment is received other than for board and lodging and reasonable expenses,

    (iv)   to serve as a member of the technical or personal staff, or as an official, attending the same event as a visiting sportsperson coming for one or more of the purposes listed in (i), (ii) or (iii) (para 46M(iii)).

5.9.3   What are permissible activities for a sports visitor?

The question is largely answered in **5.9.1** above. But what about participation in competitions that do not fall within the definition of 'sports', such as a chess tournament? Home Office guidance is that this may qualify, provided the applicant does not receive any fee or sponsorship for his participation, although he may receive cash prizes, board, lodging and living expenses.

What counts as a series of events? This is defined by para 6 as two or more linked events, such as a tour or rounds of a competition, which do not add up to a league or a season, eg football teams coming to the UK to participate in pre-season friendly matches against English clubs in competitions. This also includes those coming for a series of events that, although not part of the same competition, are being held in the UK at the same time. For example, the AEGON Tennis Championship is held immediately before Wimbledon, and the Home Office would not expect players to return home and seek fresh entry clearance.

5.9.4   Leave to enter

By para 46N, a person seeking leave to enter the UK as a sports visitor may be admitted for a period not exceeding six months, subject to a condition prohibiting employment and study (see **3.3.1**). Like all limited leave entrants, the sports visitor will be subject to the condition not to have recourse to public funds (also see **3.3.2**).

5.10 ENTERTAINER VISITOR

This provision is intended for entertainers and their entourages, who wish to come to the UK (usually) for a one-off event or a series of events. Entertainers who wish to base themselves in the UK permanently or temporarily to work should apply under Tier 2 or Tier 5 respectively of the points-based system (see **Chapter 7**).

5.10.1 Requirements

By para 46S, the requirements to be met by a person seeking leave to enter the UK as an entertainer visitor are that he:

(a)   is genuinely seeking entry as an entertainer visitor for a limited period as stated by him, not exceeding six months (para 46S(i)); and

(b)   meets the requirements of para 41(ii)–(viii) and (x)–(xii) (see **5.2.1**) (para 46S(ii));

(c)   intends to do one or more of the following during his visit (see **5.10.2**) –

    (i)   to take part as a professional entertainer in one or more music competitions, and/or

    (ii)   to fulfil one or more specific engagements as either an individual amateur entertainer or as an amateur group, and/or

    (iii)   to take part, as an amateur or professional entertainer, in a cultural event (or one or more of such events) that appears in the list of permit free festivals in Appendix R to the Immigration Rules, and/or

    (iv)   serve as a member of the technical or personal staff, or of the production team, of an entertainer coming for one or more of the purposes listed in (i), (ii), or (iii) (para 46S(iii)).

5.10.2 Who is an entertainer visitor and what activities can he carry out?

Home Office guidance is that an entertainer visitor includes the following:

(a)   professional entertainers coming to take part in music competitions;

(b)   internationally famous people coming to the UK to take part in broadcasts or public appearances, provided they are not performing or not being paid;

(c)   those undertaking an audition, provided this is not performed in front of an audience (either paying or non-paying);

(d)   amateur entertainers seeking entry as an individual performer for a specific engagement;

(e)   amateur entertainers seeking entry as part of a group, such as a choir or youth orchestra coming for a specific engagement. This can include conductors, choreographers, stage managers and other non-performing staff supporting the group;

(f)   professional entertainers taking part in a charity concert or show where the organisers are not making a profit and no fee is to be paid to the entertainer;

(g)   members of the technical or support staff of amateurs or professionals who are attending the same event, such as make-up artists, personal bodyguards and press officers;

(h)   officials attending the same event as the entertainer, such as choreographers and stage managers.

The definitions of 'amateur' and 'professional' are the same as for a sports visitor – see **5.9.1**.

5.10.3 Leave to enter

By para 46T, a person seeking leave to enter the UK as an entertainer visitor may be admitted for a period not exceeding six months, subject to a condition prohibiting employment and study (see **3.3.1**). Like all limited leave entrants, the entertainer visitor will be subject to the condition not to have recourse to public funds (also see **3.3.2**).

5.11 VISITOR IN TRANSIT TO COUNTRY OUTSIDE THE COMMON TRAVEL AREA

Who is a visitor in transit? This refers to any passenger whose sole purpose is to pass through the UK within 48 hours and who either:

(a)   arrives at one port or airport and needs to transfer to another port or airport to continue his journey; or

(b)   wishes to spend the time between his arrival and embarkation outside the transit area (ie pass through immigration controls at the port or airport).

As to the Common Travel Area, see **3.9**.

5.11.1 Requirements

Paragraph 47 sets out the requirements to be met by a person (not being a member of the crew of a ship, aircraft, hovercraft, hydrofoil or train) seeking leave to enter the UK as a visitor in transit to another country. He must:

(a)   be in transit to a country outside the Common Travel Area (para 47(i)); and

(b)   have both the means and the intention of proceeding at once to another country (para 47(ii)); and

(c)   be assured of entry there (para 47(iii)); and

(d)   intend and be able to leave the United Kingdom within 48 hours (para 47(iv)).

5.11.2 Leave to enter

A person seeking leave to enter the UK as a visitor in transit may be admitted for a period not exceeding 48 hours with a prohibition on employment.

5.12 PROSPECTIVE ENTREPRENEUR

The prospective entrepreneur category allows an individual entrepreneur to come to the UK to secure funding to set up a business here.

5.12.1 Who is a prospective entrepreneur?

At the time of applying for entry clearance, the applicant must be in discussions with a Home Office-designated funding body to secure funding in order to join, set up or take over, and be actively involved in the running of, a business in the UK.

Which funding bodies are designated? These are:

(a)   registered venture capitalist firms regulated by the Financial Conduct Authority (FCA);

(b)   UK entrepreneurial seed funding competitions which are listed as endorsed on the UK Trade & Investment website; and

(c)   one or more UK government departments.

What is a venture capitalist firm? It is a company that draws on private equity funds to invest in new businesses with high growth potential and in exchange takes a stake in the business (which it subsequently hopes to sell at a profit). A registered firm is one regulated by the FCA.

What UK entrepreneurial seed funding competitions are listed as endorsed on the UK Trade & Investment website? See **7.4.2.2**.

5.12.2 Requirements

By para 56O, the requirements to be met by a person seeking leave to enter the UK in this category are as follows:

(a)   The applicant must provide an original, signed letter on headed paper supporting the application from one or more of the Home Office-designated funding bodies (see **5.12.1**).

(b)   That letter must be dated no earlier than three months before the date of the application. It must be signed by an authorised official and contain the information set out in para 56O(b). This includes, by sub-para (iv), a commitment by the individual(s) and/or organisation(s) supporting the applicant to decide within six months of the applicant entering the UK whether or not to provide a minimum of £50,000 funding for the proposed business. Note that if more than one individual and/or organisation is supporting the applicant, each amount proposed may be less than £50,000 provided that the total amount is at least £50,000.

(c)   The applicant's primary intention in applying must be to secure funding in order to join, set up or take over, and be actively involved in the running of, a business in the UK.

(d)   The applicant must intend to carry out one (or more) of the permitted activities listed. Currently these activities are: attending meetings (which may be arranged when in the UK, including interviews arranged before coming to the UK, or conferences); attending trade fairs (provided this is restricted to promotional work and does not involve selling directly to members of the public); arranging deals, or negotiating or signing trade agreements or contracts; conducting site visits; speaking at a one-off conference (which is not organised as a commercial concern and is a 'one-off'); undertaking fact-finding missions; purchasing, checking details of, or examining goods; and recruiting staff for the proposed business activity which is the object of the application.

(e)   The applicant must intend to leave the UK at the end of the period of the visit as stated by him, unless he makes a successful application for leave to remain as a Tier 1 (Entrepreneur) Migrant (see **7.4**) before the end of the period of the visit.

(f)   The applicant must maintain and accommodate himself and any dependants adequately out of resources available to him without recourse to public funds or taking employment; or will, with any dependants, be maintained and accommodated adequately by relatives or friends.

(g)   The applicant must not intend during his visit to:
    (i)   take employment in the UK;
    (ii)   produce goods or provide services within the UK, including the selling of goods or services direct to members of the public;
    (iii)   undertake a course of study;
    (iv)   marry or form a civil partnership, or to give notice of marriage or civil partnership; or
    (v)   receive private medical treatment.

(h)   The applicant must not be under the age of 18.

(i)   The applicant must not be in transit to a country outside the Common Travel Area.

(j)   The applicant must hold a valid UK entry clearance for entry in this capacity.

Note that, as to requirement (g), a prospective entrepreneur is also not allowed to undertake activities permitted under the business (see **5.6**), sports (see **5.9**) or entertainer (see **5.10**) categories, apart from those set out in requirements (c) and (d).

5.12.3 Leave to enter

By para 56P, a person seeking leave to enter to the UK in this category may be admitted for a period not exceeding six months, subject to a condition prohibiting employment and study (see **3.3.1**). Like all limited leave entrants, he will also be subject to the condition not to have recourse to public funds (see **3.3.2**).

5.12.4 Switching to Tier 1 (Entrepreneur) Migrant

If, after entering the UK, the applicant secures funding then he may be able to apply to switch to the Tier 1 (Entrepreneur) Migrant category (see **7.4**). Otherwise he must leave the UK at the end of his limited leave.

5.12.5 Alternative entry as a business visitor

If an applicant is unable to satisfy the requirements for this category, he might consider entering the UK as a business visitor instead (see **5.6**). Note, however, that a business visitor is not allowed to switch into the Tier 1 Entrepreneur category whilst in the UK.

5.13 VISITOR UNDERTAKING PERMITTED PAID ENGAGEMENT

What if a UK Higher Education Institution wants to pay a visiting academic to examine its students, chair a selection panel, or give one or more lectures? Or what if a person wants to pay an advocate to act for him at a court or tribunal hearing, arbitration or other form of alternative dispute resolution process in the UK? Or say that a UK-based arts or sports organisation or broadcaster wants to pay a professional artist, entertainer or sportsperson to carry out activities relating to his main profession.

Note that Home Office guidance is that this category would include, for example, artists, sculptors and photographers who are exhibiting and selling their works; authors doing book-signings and/or participating in literary prize panels; entertainers giving one-off or a short series of performances; and sportspersons carrying out broadcasting or other activities relating to their field of sport.

The above engagements will be possible, provided the activity will last no longer than one month in the UK and the requirements of para 56X of the Immigration Rules are met. Leave will be subject to a condition prohibiting study and recourse to public funds.

This is an alternative route to requiring sponsorship under the points-based system for these activities (see **Chapter 7**).

5.14 VISITORS AS CARERS

There is no provision in the Immigration Rules for leave to enter or remain to be granted solely to allow a person to care for a friend or relative in the UK. Applications for leave to enter as a carer may thus be refused on the ground that there is no provision for this in the Rules. However, where an applicant wishes to care for a friend or relative for a short period, the application may be considered under the requirements of the rules relating to visitors. Applications from persons already in the UK in a temporary capacity seeking leave to remain to care for a sick relative or friend who is suffering from a terminal illness, such as cancer or AIDS, or who is mentally or physically disabled, are dealt with outside the Immigration Rules under the Secretary of State's discretion. If leave to remain is granted, it is made clear to the applicant that it is only in a temporary capacity and that, once alternative arrangements have been made or if the patient should die, the 'carer' is expected to return home. An extension of stay on this basis will not lead to settlement.

Where the application is to care for a sick or disabled relative, leave for three months is usually granted. Where it is decided to grant leave for three months exceptionally, outside the Rules, the applicant is informed that leave has been granted on the strict understanding that, during this period, arrangements must be made for the future care of the patient by a person who does not require leave to remain outside the Immigration Rules. However, applications for leave to remain in order to care for a sick or disabled friend are normally refused save in an emergency (eg the patient has suddenly fallen ill and there is insufficient time to arrange permanent care, or there is nobody else in the UK to whom the patient can turn). In those circumstances, leave to remain may be granted for a period of three months. An extension of further leave will not be given unless there are wholly exceptional circumstances.

When the Home Office is considering whether a period of leave should be granted, it takes into account the following:

(a)   the type of illness/condition (this should be supported by a doctor's letter); and

(b)   the type of care required; and

(c)   the care which is available (eg from the social services or other relatives/friends); and

(d)   the long-term prognosis.

In cases where there are sufficient exceptional compassionate circumstances to continue the exercise of discretion, leave to remain may be granted for up to 12 months.

CHAPTER 6

STUDENTS

6.1 WHO IS A STUDENT?

6.1.1 Tier 4 of the points-based system

Part 6A of the Immigration Rules deals with the points-based system of entry to the UK. Students come within Tier 4. The other tiers deal with working and conducting business in the UK (see **Chapter 7**).

There are two main types of student categories in Tier 4. First, an adult student, known in the Immigration Rules as a Tier 4 (General) Student. Here an adult is any person coming to the UK for post-16 education. We shall focus on this category in this chapter, as it attracts a large number of applicants. Secondly, a child student or a Tier 4 (Child) Student. This category covers children aged between 4 and 17 who wish to enter the UK for their education. Note that a child aged between 4 and 15 may be educated only at an independent fee-paying school. The details of this second category, which has a limited number of applicants, are beyond the scope of this book.

The following special considerations apply to a student aged 16 or 17:

(a) If he wants to study a course at National Qualification Framework (NQF) level 3 or above, he can apply as an adult or a child student, but if the course is longer than two years, the Home Office recommends that the application is made as an adult student. If he is proposing to study a course below NQF level 3, he must apply as a child student. Note that the NQF sets out the levels against which a qualification may be recognised in England, Wales and Northern Ireland. Broadly, the levels are as follows: 1 (GCSE at grades D–G), 2 (GCSE at grades A*–C), 3 (A Level), 4 (Certificate of Higher Education), 5 (HND, HNC), 6 (Bachelor's degree), 7 (Master's degree) and 8 (Doctorate). Full details can be found at www.qcda.gov.uk.

(b) If he wants to study for an English language qualification at the Common European Framework of Reference for Languages (CEFRL) level A2 or above, he must apply as an adult student. Note that the CEFRL provides a basis for the mutual recognition of language qualifications in the EEA.

For further details of the courses that may be studied, see **6.3.2.4**.

All students can enter to study at a Home Office-approved education provider only (see **6.2**). This is otherwise known as sponsorship.

6.1.2   Entry clearance

All Tier 4 students must apply for entry clearance. As part of the visa or entry certificate application they must produce certain documentation (see **6.3.2**) from the Home Office-approved educational institution at which they will be studying in the UK.

6.2   SPONSORSHIP: APPROVED EDUCATION PROVIDER

6.2.1   Obtaining a licence from the Home Office

All education providers that want to provide courses for international students need a licence from the Home Office (known as 'highly trusted sponsor' status). One key step is for the provider to obtain a satisfactory review or inspection by one of the publicly recognised inspection bodies approved for Tier 4 purposes (namely Ofsted and its equivalents in the devolved administrations, the Quality Assurance Agency and the Department for Education-approved inspectorates for independent schools). In addition, a provider must be able to show that it has allocated a number of key roles to its staff using the Home Office online sponsorship management system; it can comply with its sponsorship duties; and it has the appropriate human resource systems in place to be able to monitor its students' attendance.

For ease of reference, throughout the rest of this chapter we shall refer to an approved education provider as the 'sponsor'.

6.2.2   Sponsorship duties

The key duties of a sponsor are to keep copies of all students' passports, to keep up-to-date contact details for students, and to tell the Home Office if a student has any unauthorised absences, fails to enrol on his course or stops his studies.

6.2.3   Tier 4 register

Once a sponsor has a licence, it is added to the Tier 4 register with details of its name and location. The register can be found on the Home Office website (see **1.2.8**).

6.3   TIER 4 (GENERAL) STUDENT

6.3.1   Requirements

Paragraph 245ZV provides that to qualify for entry clearance as a Tier 4 (General) Student, an applicant must meet the following key requirements:

(a)   The application must not fall for refusal under the general grounds for refusal (see **3.5.4**).

(b)   The applicant must have a minimum of 30 points under paras 113 to 119 of Appendix A ('Sponsorship' – see **6.3.2**).

(c)   The applicant must have a minimum of 10 points under paras 10 to 13 of Appendix C ('Maintenance' – see **6.3.3**).

(d)   The applicant must, if required to do so on examination or interview, be able to demonstrate, without the assistance of an interpreter, English language proficiency of a standard to be expected from an individual who has reached the standard specified in his CAS (see **6.3.2.1**). Home Office guidance is that the applicant will not be subject to a test at the standard set for his CAS.

(e)   The ECO must be satisfied that the applicant is a genuine student (but note that this requirement does not apply to 'low risk' students: see **6.3.2.2**). Home Office guidance is that refusal on this ground will normally occur only after the applicant has been interviewed. In 2012 the Government announced that following a successful pilot, a targeted interview system for students was being introduced, concentrating on so-called high-risk applicants. An applicant may be interviewed (in person or on the telephone) and asked a number of questions about his immigration and education history, study and post-study plans, as well as his financial circumstances. One thing the ECO will look for is the standard of English used by the applicant at the interview (see (d) above). Up to 14,000 students are expected to be interviewed each year. See further **6.3.4**.

An applicant therefore needs to score 40 points to qualify. Although the wording of para 245ZV(b) and (c) suggests that a range of points may be available to collect to meet the minimum required, the tests in Appendix A and Appendix C in fact only have 30 and 10 points available each, so either the applicant scores the necessary number of points by meeting the tests or he does not.

6.3.2 Sponsorship points

A Tier 4 (General) Student is awarded 30 points only if he has obtained from a sponsor a confirmation of acceptance for studies.

6.3.2.1 The Confirmation of Acceptance for Studies

Once a sponsor has been granted a licence, the sponsor can access the Home Office's IT sponsorship management system. This may be used to create and assign a Confirmation of Acceptance for Studies (CAS). This is therefore not an actual certificate or paper document. It is a virtual document similar to a database record. Each CAS has a unique reference number and contains information about the course of study for which it has been issued and the student's personal details.

An application for entry clearance or leave to remain must be made no more than three months before the start date of the course of study as stated on the CAS. A CAS expires if it is not used to apply for entry clearance or leave within six months of being issued. In addition, a CAS can be used only once.

Before allocating a CAS, the sponsor must ensure that the student is competent in English language at a set minimum level. This is met if the student is a national of a Home Office-recognised majority English-speaking country (see the list at **7.4.3.2**) or has successfully completed an academic qualification, at least equivalent to a UK Bachelor's degree, which was taught in a Home Office-recognised majority English-speaking country (see the list at **7.4.3.3**). Otherwise, the student must have passed an approved English language test that is still within its validity date. Normally a student must demonstrate knowledge of English equivalent to level B2 of the Council of Europe's Common European Framework for Language Learning, or above. Details are on the Council's website at www.coe.int/T/DG4/Linguistic/CADRE_EN.asp. A list of Home Office-approved test providers and their contact details are on the Home Office website.

6.3.2.2 Supporting documents

In order to be awarded points, the applicant must also supply documentary evidence, such as qualification certificates and references, that he used to obtain the offer of the place on the course from the sponsor. The specified documents are listed in para 120-SD of Appendix A to the Immigration Rules.

Note that students who are nationals of the countries listed in Appendix H to the Immigration Rules – currently Argentina, Australia, Barbados, Botswana, Brunei, Canada, Chile, Hong Kong, Japan, Malaysia, New Zealand, Singapore, South Korea, Taiwan, Trinidad and Tobago, and the United States of America – who apply for entry clearance in their country of nationality or for leave to remain in the UK, are treated by the Home Office as 'low risk' and so generally do not have to produce any supporting documents (see also **6.3.3.2**) unless required by the Home Office to do so. Evidence of the student's nationality will be his passport. A 'low risk' student has to confirm that he meets the points requirements on his visa or entry clearance application form and that he has the required documentary evidence. Entry clearance officers do spot checks and sometimes require such a student to send the documents.

6.3.2.3 Re-sitting examinations or repeating course module

If an applicant is re-sitting examinations or repeating a module of a course, he must not previously have re-sat the same examination or repeated the same module more than once. If this requirement is not met, no points will be awarded.

If a student's leave will expire before he is able to re-sit an exam, he will not get an extension as a Tier 4 student unless he scores the required points. It is therefore not possible for a student to remain in the UK just to re-sit an exam. Such a student is expected to leave the UK and revise for the re-sit in his own country (or at least outside the UK). The student should then seek entry to take the re-sit exam as a student visitor (see RS (Pakistan) v Secretary of State for the Home Department [2011] EWCA Civ 434 and **5.5**).

6.3.2.4 Academic requirements and approved qualifications

Points are awarded only if the course in respect of which the confirmation is issued satisfies each of the following requirements:

(a)   The course must meet the Home Office's minimum academic requirements and must lead to an approved qualification. The minimum academic requirement is that the course must be a full-time course of study, as either:

  (i)   a full-time course of study that leads to a UK-recognised bachelor degree, postgraduate degree, postgraduate diploma or postgraduate certificate;

  (ii)   an overseas course of degree level study that is recognised as being equivalent to a UK Higher Education course and is being provided by an overseas Higher Education Institution; or

  (iii) a full-time course of study involving a minimum of 15 hours per week organised daytime study and, except in the case of a pre-sessional course, lead to a qualification below bachelor degree level.

  The following are approved qualifications:

  (i)   level 3 or the same as or above on the NQF (see **6.1.1**);

  (ii)   short-term study abroad programmes in the UK as part of a qualification at an overseas higher education institution, as long as the qualification is confirmed as the same as a UK degree level by the National Academic Recognition Information Centre for the United Kingdom (UK NARIC) (see **7.3.2.1**).

  (iii) an English language course at level B2 or above of the CEFRL (see **6.1.1**).

(b)   Other than when the applicant is actually on a work placement (see **6.6.2**), all study that forms part of the course must take place on the premises of the sponsor.

6.3.3 Maintenance points

6.3.3.1 How much maintenance?

To score the required 10 points, the level of maintenance funds that the applicant will have to show that he has available depends on two factors: how long the course is, and where the course is being studied.

If the applicant has already paid to his sponsor some of his course fees (this may include expenditure on study materials, such as books, purchased from the sponsor), that amount may be deducted from the total required provided that it is confirmed in the CAS or the student is able to produce an original paper receipt issued by his sponsor.

What if the Tier 4 (General) Student will be staying in accommodation provided by his sponsor (eg halls of residence) and he has already paid towards it? In these circumstances, up to a maximum of £1,000 may be deducted from the total required (but no more than that, even if the student has paid in excess of £1,000). Again, either the amount paid must be included in the student's CAS, or the student must produce the sponsor's original written receipt.

If the applicant is receiving all or any of his funding from an official financial sponsorship or government sponsor, see **6.3.3.3**.

Table 6.1 below sets out the details regarding maintenance funds.

Table 6.1   Amount of maintenance funds dependent on length of course and location

Length of course	Location	Amount of maintenance funds needed
Nine months or less	Inner London	Course fees and £1,000 to cover living costs for each calendar month (or any part of a month) of the course
Nine months or less	Outer London or anywhere else in the UK	Course fees and £800 to cover living costs for each calendar month (or any part of a month) of the course
More than nine months	Inner London	First year's course fees and £9,000 to cover living costs for the first nine months in the UK
More than nine months	Outer London or anywhere else in the UK	First year's course fees and £7,200 to cover living costs for the first nine months in the UK

When is a Tier 4 (General) Student considered to be studying in Inner London? The answer is if more than 50% of his study time is spent in any of the following London boroughs: Camden, City of London, Hackney, Hammersmith and Fulham, Haringey, Islington, Kensington and Chelsea, Lambeth, Lewisham, Newham, Southwark, Tower Hamlets, Wandsworth and Westminster.

6.3.3.2   Supporting documents

The money to be used for the applicant's maintenance must be in the form of cash. Shares, bonds, pension funds and similar savings accounts are not acceptable.

The applicant will need to produce documentary evidence to show that the minimum level of maintenance funds has been available to him for a consecutive period of at least 28 days ending no more than 31 days before the date of the application. Provided it covers that period, any of the following documents are acceptable (provided it meets all of the detailed requirements of para 1B of Appendix C to the Immigration Rules):

(a)   personal bank or building society statements;

(b)   a building society pass book;

(c)   a letter from the applicant's bank confirming that the funds are available;

(d)   a letter from a financial institution regulated either by the Financial Conduct Authority or, in the case of overseas accounts, the home regulator (official regulatory body for the country the institution is in and where the money is held) confirming that the funds are available;

(e)   a letter from a financial institution regulated either by the Financial Conduct Authority or, in the case of overseas accounts, the home regulator (official regulatory body for the country the institution is in and where the money is held) confirming that the funds are available as a loan.

The applicant's specified financial documents must be from institutions acceptable to the Home Office. A check should always be made in Appendix P to the Immigration Rules, where there are lists of financial institutions approved or not approved for certain countries (currently Sri Lanka, Bangladesh, Cameroon, India, Ghana, Pakistan, Iran and The Philippines).

What if a student is relying on money held by a parent or legal guardian? In addition to providing the above evidence of available funds, the applicant will have to produce:

(a)   evidence of the relationship, eg the student's birth certificate showing the names of his parent(s), or the student's certificate of adoption showing the names of his parent(s) or legal guardian, or a court document naming his legal guardian. The original document or a notarised copy must be produced;

(b)   a letter from his parent(s) or legal guardian confirming the relationship and consenting to the student using their funds to study in the UK.

Remember that if the student is 'low risk' (see **6.3.2.2**) he will have to produce documentation only if required.

6.3.3.3   Official financial sponsorship

An applicant might receive financial help from the UK Government, his home government, the British Council or any international organisation, company or university.

Details must either be set out in the CAS, or a letter is required from any official financial sponsor confirming the length of the sponsorship, that it will cover all of the applicant's fees and living costs, or the amount available. The applicant must produce evidence to meet any shortfall.

6.3.3.4   Family members

If an applicant is bringing any family members (spouse, civil partner, unmarried or same-sex partner and children under 18) with him, he will have to demonstrate that additional maintenance funds are available (see **6.8**).

6.3.4   Genuine student

Home Office guidance is that when assessing whether the applicant is a genuine student, the ECO must consider the application in the round and might take into account factors such as:

(a)   the immigration history of the applicant in the UK and other countries; and

(b)   the applicant's education history, study and post-study plans. So an ECO might ask: How long has elapsed since the applicant last studied? Does the applicant have sound reasons for returning to, or commencing, formal study in this area, particularly after any significant gap? What is the applicant's knowledge of, and level of research undertaken into, the proposed course of study and sponsoring institution, and living arrangements in the UK? What are the applicant's personal circumstances, and would these make it difficult to complete a full-time course of study? What is the relevance of the course to the applicant's post-study plans?

Home Office guidance is that whether the applicant has the academic ability to study the proposed course is not a relevant consideration for the ECO and should not form part of any conclusion reached. The academic ability of the applicant is a judgement for the sponsor to make with the benefit of its educational expertise. Similarly, the fact that the course does not represent academic progression is not a decisive factor.

The relevance of the course to post-study plans, or vagueness about the nature of post-study plans, should not be used as a sole reason to refuse an applicant; rather, it is one of a range of factors to be considered. In this context, whether the course will add to the applicant's employability, or whether the course could be undertaken more cheaply in the applicant's home country, should not be taken into account.

For those considered to be genuine students, intention to leave the UK at the end of the course is not relevant as there are many bases on which an individual might lawfully remain in the UK.

6.4 LEAVE TO ENTER THE UK

If granted entry clearance, how long will a Tier 4 (General) Student get as limited leave in the UK? The answer depends on the nature and length of the course, as set out in **Table 6.2** below.

Table 6.2   Amount of limited leave

Length of course	Amount of limited leave granted
Less than six months	The full length of the course plus one month after the end of the course
At least six months but less than 12 months	The full length of the course plus two months after the end of the course
12 months or more	The full length of the course plus four months after the end of the course
Postgraduate doctor or dentist	The full length of the course (up to a maximum of three years) plus one month after the end of the course

Note that if a Tier 4 (General) Student has an official financial sponsor (see **6.3.3.3**) who pays all his fees and living expenses but limits the time the student may study in the UK, the permission to stay is limited to the same length of time plus the usual post-course period specified in **Table 6.2**.

6.5 EXTENDING LIMITED LEAVE

After finishing one course, a Tier 4 (General) Student may wish to take another course. In these circumstances the student will need to meet the same requirements as he did to secure entry clearance (see **6.3.1** above). The only difference will be as to the level of maintenance required if the student has within the last four months completed a course of at least six months' duration. In such a case, the figures in **Table 6.3** below will apply.

Table 6.3   Amount of maintenance funds required for extending limited leave

Length of course	Location	Amount of maintenance funds needed
Two months or less	Inner London	Course fees and £1,000 to cover living costs for each calendar month of the course up to a maximum of two months
Two months or less	Outer London or anywhere else in the UK	Course fees and £800 to cover living costs for each calendar month of the course up to a maximum of two months
More than two months	Inner London	First year's course fees and £2,000 to cover the first two months of living costs in the UK

Length of course	Location	Amount of maintenance funds needed
More than two months	Outer London or anywhere else in the UK	First year's course fees and £1,600 to cover the first two months of living costs in the UK

Note that there are limits as to how long a Tier 4 (General) Student may study in the UK. Generally, it is for a maximum of three years studying at below degree level and five years at degree level or above. In certain circumstances this may be extended to six years when doing a master's degree and eight years for a PhD (see para 245ZX(h)(ha) of the Immigration Rules). Note that the five years or more limits operate in addition to the maximum time permitted for studying at below degree level.

6.6 WHAT CAN A TIER 4 (GENERAL) STUDENT DO IN ADDITION TO STUDYING?

6.6.1 Students' union sabbatical officer

A students' union sabbatical post is a full-time, salaried, elected executive union position. A Tier 4 (General) Student may take up this post for a maximum of two years, either during his course of study or in the academic year immediately after he graduates. The post must be at the institution which is the student's sponsor.

6.6.2 Work placement

A course of study for a Tier 4 (General) Student may include a work placement, but it must not exceed one-third of the length of a non-degree course or half of the length of a degree course in the UK, unless the student is doing a course where there is a statutory requirement for it to contain a specific period of work placement.

For example, if a degree course is two years long, the first year of the course might involve full-time study and the last year might involve a work placement.

In addition, the work placement must form an assessed part of the course.

A sponsor remains responsible for the student throughout the term of his work placement, and must continue to comply with all the sponsor duties throughout this time.

6.6.3 Extra studies

Tier 4 (General) Students are allowed to undertake supplementary courses, for example evening classes. These do not need to relate to the course of study for which the student was granted entry clearance or leave. No permission is needed and the student does not have to inform his sponsor.

6.6.4 Employment

A Tier 4 (General) Student following a course with a sponsor which is a UK higher education institution, or on a short-term study abroad degree programme at an overseas higher education institution, or at a publicly-funded further education college, may work whilst in the UK. This is in addition to any work placement (see **6.6.2**) he is doing as part of his course. However, the student must not fill a full-time, permanent vacancy (other than on a recognised Foundation Programme).

Students may work full time during vacations, but only part time for a prescribed maximum number of hours during term time. What are the limits?

(a)   Students following a course at NQF 6 (Bachelor's degree level) or above with a sponsor which is a UK higher education institution, or undertaking a short-term study abroad degree programme at an overseas higher education institution, can work for no more than 20 hours per week in term time.

(b) Students following a course at NQF 3, 4 or 5 (below degree level) with a sponsor which is a UK higher education institution can work for no more than 10 hours per week in term time.

(c) Students following a course at any level with a sponsor which is a publicly-funded further education college can work for no more than 10 hours per week in term time.

The following categories of employment are not permitted at any time:

(a) self-employment;

(b) employment as a doctor in training (other than on a recognised Foundation Programme);

(c) employment as a professional sportsperson (including a sports coach); and

(d) employment as an entertainer.

6.7 CONDITIONS ATTACHED TO LEAVE

A Tier 4 (General) Student's limited leave is subject to the following conditions:

(a) no recourse to public funds (see **3.3.2**);

(b) registration with the police, if this is required (see **3.3.3**);

(c) no employment except:

    (i) (as detailed at **6.6.4**),

    (ii) employment as part of a course-related work placement (see **6.6.2**),

    (iii) employment as a Student Union Sabbatical Officer, for up to two years, provided the post is elective and is at the institution which is the applicant's sponsor (see **6.6.1**);

(d) no study except:

    (i) study at the institution that the Home Office records as the migrant's sponsor;

    (ii) supplementary study (see **6.6.3**).

Note the effect of condition (d)(i) is to tie the student's leave to his sponsor. So a student cannot lawfully change courses and study with a different sponsor without obtaining a CAS from the new sponsor and further leave to remain from the Home Office.

6.8 FAMILY MEMBERS OF A TIER 4 (GENERAL) STUDENT

6.8.1 Entry clearance and leave to remain and permission to work

Can all Tier 4 (General) Students bring their family members to the UK? No. So who can? Only either:

(a) students sponsored by a higher education institution on a course at NQF level 7 or above that lasts 12 months or more; or

(b) Government-sponsored students following a course that is longer than six months.

Who are family members? If subject to immigration controls, the spouse, civil partner, unmarried or same-sex partner ('the Partner') and children under 18 will require entry clearance in order to enter the UK as the family member. If relevant, they should subsequently apply for an extension at the same time as the Tier 4 (General) Student.

Note that such a family member is able to work in the UK.

6.8.2 Partner

6.8.2.1 Requirements

The requirements are set out in para 319C, as follows:

(a) The applicant must not fall for refusal under the general grounds for refusal (see **3.5.4**) and, if applying for leave to remain, must not be an illegal entrant (see **10.2.2**).

(b) The applicant must be the spouse or civil partner, unmarried or same-sex partner of a person who:

   (i) has valid leave to enter or remain as a Tier 4 (General) Student; or

   (ii) is, at the same time, being granted entry clearance or leave to remain as a Tier 4 (General) Student.

(c) An applicant who is the unmarried or same-sex partner of a Tier 4 (General) Student must also meet the following requirements:

   (i) any previous marriage or civil partnership or similar relationship by the applicant or the Tier 4 (General) Student with another person must have permanently broken down;

   (ii) the applicant and the Tier 4 (General) Student must not be so closely related that they would be prohibited from marrying each other in the UK; and

   (iii) the applicant and the Tier 4 (General) Student must have been living together in a relationship similar to marriage or civil partnership for a period of at least two years (see further **Chapter 8**).

(d) The marriage or civil partnership, or relationship similar to marriage or civil partnership, must be subsisting at the time the application is made.

(e) The applicant and the Tier 4 (General) Student must intend to live with the other as their spouse or civil partner, unmarried or same-sex partner throughout the applicant's stay in the UK.

(f) The applicant must not intend to stay in the UK beyond any period of leave granted to the Tier 4 (General) Student.

(g) There must be a sufficient level of funds available to the applicant, as set out in Appendix E.

6.8.2.2 Maintenance funds

As to (g) in **6.8.2.1** above, the same requirements for available maintenance funds apply to a Partner as to an applicant (see **6.3.3**). Appendix E to the Immigration Rules (see **Appendix 1**) sets out the following requirements:

(a) If the Tier 4 Migrant is studying in Inner London, there must be £600 in funds for each month for which the applicant would, if successful, be granted leave, up to a maximum of £5,400.

(b) If the Tier 4 Migrant is not studying in Inner London, there must be £450 in funds for each month for which the applicant would, if successful, be granted leave, up to a maximum of £4,050.

> **EXAMPLE**
> Anne applies for entry clearance as a Tier 4 (General) Student. She has a CAS issued by an Inner London-based sponsor. She has a place on a 24-month master's degree course. She does not have an official financial sponsor. She has not yet paid anything towards her course fees or the accommodation arranged by her sponsor. Her civil partner, Brenda, will be travelling with her. In addition to meeting the requirements of para 319C(a)–(f) above, what maintenance funds under (g) do they need to have available? Anne needs the amount of her first year's course fees and £9,000 to cover living costs for the first nine months in the UK (see **6.3.3.1**). As she will get 28 months' leave (see **6.4**), there must be the maximum additional amount available for Brenda of £5,400.

6.8.2.3 Leave and conditions

If the application is successful, the Partner is granted entry clearance and leave to remain for a period which expires on the same day as the leave granted to the Tier 4 (General) Student.

That leave will be subject to conditions not to have recourse to public funds and registration with the police, if this is required (see **3.3.2** and **3.3.3** respectively).

6.8.3 Child

6.8.3.1 Requirements

The requirements are set out in para 319H, as follows:

(a) The applicant must not fall for refusal under the general grounds for refusal (see **3.5.4**) and, if applying for leave to remain, must not be an illegal entrant (see **10.2.2**).

(b) The applicant must be the child of a parent who:

    (i) has valid leave to enter or remain as a Tier 4 (General) Student; or

    (ii) is, at the same time, being granted entry clearance or leave to remain as a Tier 4 (General) Student.

(c) The applicant must be under the age of 18 on the date the application is made, or if over 18 and applying for leave to remain, must have, or have last been granted, leave as the child of a Tier 4 (General) Student.

(d) The applicant must not be married or in a civil partnership, must not have formed an independent family unit, and must not be leading an independent life. See further **Chapter 8**.

(e) The applicant must not intend to stay in the UK beyond any period of leave granted to the Tier 4 (General) Student parent.

(f) Both of the applicant's parents must either be lawfully present in the UK, or being granted entry clearance or leave to remain at the same time as the applicant, unless:

    (i) the Tier 4 (General) Student is the applicant's sole surviving parent; or

    (ii) the Tier 4 (General) Student parent has and has had sole responsibility for the applicant's upbringing (see **Chapter 8**); or

    (iii) there are serious or compelling family or other considerations which would make it desirable not to refuse the application and suitable arrangements have been made in the UK for the applicant's care (see **Chapter 8**).

(g) There must be a sufficient level of funds available to the applicant, as set out in Appendix E.

It is important to note the effect of (c) above in respect of a child now aged 18 or over. That child will still qualify for an extension of leave in this category, provided he had previously obtained such leave when under 18.

6.8.3.2 Maintenance funds

As to (g) in **6.8.3.1** above, the additional available maintenance funds are exactly the same as for any Partner (**6.8.2.2**).

EXAMPLE

Lewis applies for entry clearance as a Tier 4 (General) Student. He has a CAS issued by an Outer London-based sponsor. He has a place on a 12-month master's degree course. He does not have an official financial sponsor. He has not yet paid his course fees. He is not using accommodation arranged by his sponsor. His wife, Alice, and 6-year-old son, John, will be travelling with him. In addition to meeting the requirements of paras 319C and 319F(a)–(f) respectively, what maintenance funds under (g) do they need to have available? Lewis needs the amount of his course fees and £7,200 to cover living costs for the first nine months in the UK (see **6.3.3.1**). As he will get 16 months' leave (see **6.4**), there must be the maximum additional amount available for his wife, Alice, of £4,050 and also the maximum additional amount available for his son, John, of £4,050.

6.8.3.3   Leave and conditions

If the application is successful, the child is granted entry clearance and leave to remain for a period which expires on the same day as the leave granted to his Tier 4 (General) Student parent. This will be subject to conditions of no recourse to public funds and registration with the police, if this is required (see **3.3.2** and **3.3.3** respectively).

6.9   WHO CAN SWITCH TO BECOME A TIER 4 (GENERAL) STUDENT?

The following migrants already in the UK may switch from their current category and apply for leave to remain as a Tier 4 (General) Student, namely a:

(a)   Tier 2 General Migrant (see **7.9**);

(b)   Tier 2 Intra-Company Transfer Migrant (see **7.9**);

(c)   Tier 2 Minister of Religion (see **7.10**);

(d)   Tier 4 Child Student (see **6.1.1**).

6.10   TIER 4 (GENERAL) STUDENT SWITCHING TO ANOTHER CATEGORY

A Tier 4 (General) Student may be able to switch categories whilst in the UK. The most usual routes would be into the category of a Tier 1 (Entrepreneur) Migrant (see **7.4**), Tier 1 (Investor) Migrant (see **7.5**), Tier 2 Migrant (see **7.7**), the spouse, or civil partner or the same-sex partner of a person settled in the UK (see **Chapter 8**).

Note that if a Tier 4 (General) Student switches to a category that may lead to settlement, the time spent in the student category cannot count towards the time needed to qualify for settlement.

6.11   SUMMARY OF POINTS AND EVIDENCE REQUIRED FOR A TIER 4 (GENERAL) STUDENT

Points	How obtained	Evidence required
30	Sponsorship – studying a course that meets the Home Office's minimum academic requirements and leads to an approved qualification with a licensed education provider (see **6.3.2**).	Confirmation of acceptance for studies from the sponsor with supporting documents (see **6.3.2**).
10	Maintenance – having enough cash available to pay course fees and monthly living costs (see **6.3.3**).	Bank statement or letter confirming level of cash funds (see **6.3.3.2**). It must be shown that the applicant has held the money for at least 28 days ending no more than 31 days before the date of the application.

6.12 SUMMARY OF DIFFERENT TYPES OF STUDENT CATEGORIES

Category	Key details
Child visitor (see **5.3**)	Aged 17 or less and coming to UK to do a course of study for up to six months.
Tier 4 (Child) Student	Aged between 4 and 17. If aged between 4 and 15 must be entering UK to be educated at an independent fee-paying school.
Student visitor (see **5.5**)	Aged 18 or over, coming to UK to do a course for up to six months and not working whilst in UK.
Tier 4 (General) Student	Adult student coming to UK for post-16 education.

CHAPTER 7

EMPLOYMENT, BUSINESS AND INVESTMENT

7.1 INTRODUCTION

7.1.1 Who can work, conduct business or invest in the UK?

In this chapter we shall consider entry to the UK for the specific purpose of working, conducting business or investing.

Nationals of the EEA can work, conduct business and invest in the UK exercising their EU Treaty rights (see **Chapter 4**). If a UK business wants to employ an EEA national, it will not have to use any of the domestic law routes of entry dealt with in this chapter.

A general visitor (see **5.1.2**) is prohibited from working. A student (see **6.6.4**) is restricted as to what work he may do. But the following people may freely carry out any of these activities:

(a) anyone admitted for settlement (see **Chapter 8**);

(b) anyone given limited leave with a view to settlement, eg spouses, civil partners and those in a non-marital relationship (see **Chapter 8**);

(c) refugees and those granted humanitarian protection (see **Chapter 9**);

(d) anyone admitted, without prohibition on employment, as the dependant of someone with limited leave in the UK, eg the spouse or civil partner of a Tier 1 or Tier 2 Migrant (see **7.6** and **7.8.9**).

7.1.2 Overview of the categories covered in this chapter

A person seeking to enter the UK may fall into one of the following categories:

(a) A person with officially recognised 'exceptional talent' in the field of science, humanities, engineering or the arts; an entrepreneur (business person); a graduate with officially recognised entrepreneurial skills; and an investor. These are known as *Tier 1 Migrants*. They form part of a points-based system detailed in paras 245AA to 245DF.

In the Immigration Rules, these Tier 1 Migrants (apart from the graduate entrepreneur) are normally given limited leave initially for three years. This may be extended for two years, followed by an application for settlement. Note that in certain circumstances an entrepreneur or investor may be able to apply for settlement earlier. The graduate entrepreneur may be allowed two periods of limited leave to remain of 12 months, but is expected either then to depart the UK or to switch into another category, such as an entrepreneur.

See further **7.2**.

(b)   A skilled (general) worker, minister of religion or sports person. These applicants are known as *Tier 2 Migrants* and form part of the points system detailed in the Immigration Rules, paras 245G to 245HF. Each person must have a UK-based sponsor who is licensed by the Home Office. Limited leave is initially for three years. This may be extended for two years, followed by an application for settlement. See further **7.8**.

(c)   Temporary work in the creative and sporting sector, charity and religious workers, government authorised exchange workers, workers under an international agreement and workers under a youth mobility scheme. These are known as *Tier 5 Migrants* and form part of the points system detailed in the Immigration Rules, paras 245ZI to 245ZS. Each category has its own sponsorship arrangements. As this tier provides for temporary work only, leave is usually limited to one or two years and cannot lead to settlement. See further **7.12**.

(d)   A sole representative of an overseas firm who will establish a wholly-owned subsidiary or branch in the UK. This is a long-standing category and it is not part of the points system. The requirements are set out in para 144 of the Immigration Rules. A person who meets the requirements is given three years' limited leave. That may be extended for two years, followed by an application for settlement. See further **7.13**.

(e)   A Commonwealth citizen with a UK-born grandparent. This is a long-standing category reflecting the UK's historical links with the Commonwealth. It is not part of the points system. The requirements are set out in para 186 of the Immigration Rules. A person who meets the requirements may enter the UK to look for, or take up, work. Five years' limited leave is given, after which an application for settlement can be made. See further **7.14**.

Note that at the time of writing the Government has indicated that it does not intend to implement Tier 3 for low-skilled workers for the foreseeable future.

7.2   OVERVIEW OF TIER 1

7.2.1   A profile of each category

7.2.1.1   Exceptional talent

This category allows a person who is internationally recognised as a world leader or potential world-leading talent in the field of science, humanities, engineering or the arts to work in the UK, provided he has the official endorsement of a Home Office-specified Designated Competent Body (DCB).

7.2.1.2   Entrepreneur

This category might otherwise be called the 'business person' route into the UK. The individual (or team of two entrepreneurs) must be investing in the UK. How? By either setting up a new business, or joining or taking over an existing business. Note that the minimum investment in a business is either £200,000 from any source, or £50,000 from a Home Office-approved source such as a registered and regulated venture capital firm.

7.2.1.3 Investor

This category is for an individual who is able to make substantial financial investment of at least £1,000,000 in the UK.

7.2.1.4 Graduate entrepreneur

This category allows a graduate from a Home Office-approved UK Higher Education Institution, who has been identified as having developed world-class innovative ideas or entrepreneurial skills, to stay in the UK after graduation to establish one or more businesses in the UK. Leave is normally only for 12 months (with the possibility of one 12-month extension) and then the person is expected to depart the UK or switch into another category, such as an entrepreneur.

7.2.2 Common features: entry clearance

7.2.2.1 Points system

An entrepreneur and a graduate entrepreneur are required to score 95 points from three different areas, namely, attributes (a minimum of 75 points), English language (10 points) and maintenance (10 points).

A person with exceptional talent and an investor are required to score 75 points for attributes. These categories are not subject to the English language and maintenance requirements in order to obtain entry clearance. However, a person with exceptional talent will need to meet the English language requirement when applying for an extension of leave (see **7.3.3**).

7.2.2.2 Attributes

Briefly, the specific attributes for each category are as follows:

(a)   Person with exceptional talent – the applicant must have the official endorsement of a Home Office-specified DCB.

(b)   Entrepreneur – the applicant must have access to at least £200,000 that is in a regulated financial institution, being disposable in the UK to invest in business; or £50,000 in a Home Office-approved source such as a registered and regulated venture capital firm.

(c)   Investor – the applicant must have access to either £1 million that is in a regulated financial institution and disposable in the UK; or personal assets exceeding £2 million and at least a £1 million loan from a regulated financial institution.

(d)   Graduate entrepreneur – the applicant must have the official endorsement of a Home Office-approved UK Higher Education Institution.

Full details are set out below, where each category is considered further.

7.2.2.3 English language test for entrepreneur and graduate entrepreneur

An entrepreneur and a graduate entrepreneur must have a minimum level of English language. This requires scoring 10 points by an entrepreneur either passing a Home Office-prescribed English language test, or being a national of a Home Office-designated majority English-speaking country or having a Home Office-recognised degree that was taught in English. Only the last applies to a graduate entrepreneur. Further details are given at **7.4.3** and **7.7.3**.

7.2.2.4 Available maintenance funds test for entrepreneur and graduate entrepreneur

An entrepreneur and graduate entrepreneur must be able to demonstrate that he can support himself in the UK. This requires scoring 10 points for available maintenance funds of at least £3,100 and £900 respectively. Further details are set out at **7.4.4** and **7.7.4**.

7.2.2.5 Self-assessment

A Tier 1 applicant may assess the likely number of points he will score by using the Home Office online points-based calculator. This is at www.ukba.homeoffice.gov.uk/pointscalculator.

7.2.2.6 Forms and guidance notes

Applicants can find application forms and guidance notes on the Home Office website.

7.2.2.7 Not liable to refusal on general grounds

An applicant will fail if his application is liable to be refused under the general grounds in Part 9 of the Immigration Rules (see **3.4.5**).

7.2.3 Common features: extension of leave

Just before the initial limited leave of a Tier 1 person with exceptional talent, entrepreneur and investor expires, an application should be made to extend it. Basically the applicant will have to demonstrate that the original requirements have been met, eg an exceptional talent migrant must show that he is economically active in his expert field and still endorsed by his DCB; an entrepreneur must show that the full amount of cash has been invested in business in the UK; and an investor must show that he has invested at least £750,000 within three months.

Before the leave of a graduate entrepreneur expires, an application should be made to switch categories (assuming the person wishes to remain in the UK). Note that a graduate entrepreneur may be granted only one extension of 12 months' limited leave to remain in this category.

An applicant will fail if his application for an extension is liable to be refused under the general grounds in Part 9 of the Immigration Rules (see **3.4.5**) or he is an illegal entrant (see **10.2.2**), or if he is in the UK in breach of immigration laws, except that any period of overstaying for 28 days or less is ignored.

See further **7.3.3, 7.4.5, 7.5.3** and **7.7.2**.

7.2.4 Common features: limited leave conditions

In each category it will be a condition of a person's limited leave that he does not have recourse to public funds (see **3.3.2**).

A person must also register with the police if this is necessary under the Immigration Rules, para 326 (see **3.3.3**).

Additionally, it is a condition of an entrepreneur's limited leave that he does not take employment other than working for the business or businesses that he has established, joined or taken over, nor as a professional sportsperson (including as a sports coach).

Also, it is a condition of the limited leave of a person with exceptional talent that he does not take employment as a doctor or dentist in training, or as a professional sportsperson (including as a sports coach).

Additionally, it is a condition of a graduate entrepreneur's limited leave that he works for the business or businesses that he has established, and that any other employment must not exceed 20 hours per week. Also, he must not take employment as a doctor or dentist in training, nor as a professional sportsperson (including as a sports coach).

7.2.5 Common features: settlement

As a general rule, once a person with exceptional talent, entrepreneur and investor has spent a continuous period of five years in the UK in that category, an application may be made for settlement.

Note that an entrepreneur can apply to settle more quickly if he creates 10 jobs or turns over £5 million in a three-year period. See further **7.4.6**.

Note also that an investor is able to settle here faster if he invests larger sums of money. Those who invest at least £5 million can apply to settle after three years, whilst those investing £10 million or more can apply to settle after two years. See further **7.5.4**.

Obviously, a graduate entrepreneur cannot apply for settlement. He may, of course, be able to switch into another category, such as an entrepreneur, which may ultimately lead to settlement.

7.2.6 Common features: family members

Who are the family members of a Tier 1 applicant? The answer is his spouse, civil partner, unmarried or same-sex partner, and children under 18.

Does a family member have to obtain entry clearance? Yes. The requirements are in the Immigration Rules, paras 319A–319K. See further **7.6**.

7.2.7 Common features: verification of documentation

Each application form and the relevant Immigration Rules (Appendix A for attributes, Appendix B for English language and Appendix C for maintenance) lists the various specified documents (see **3.6.4.1**) that are needed. Where a Home Office officer has a reasonable doubt that a specified document is genuine, it is normal practice to verify the document with an independent person or government agency.

There are three possible outcomes of a document verification check:

(a)   If the document is confirmed as genuine, the application will proceed unaffected.

(b)   If the document is confirmed as false, the application will be refused, whether or not the document is essential to the application.

(c)   If the verification check is inconclusive then that document will be ignored as evidence for scoring points.

7.3   TIER 1: (EXCEPTIONAL TALENT) MIGRANT

7.3.1   Overview

An applicant must be internationally recognised in his field as a world-leading talent and be endorsed by a Home Office-specified DCB.

7.3.2   The attributes

An applicant must score 75 points for the specific attribute of having been issued with the endorsement of a Home Office-specified DCB. Each DCB's criteria for the endorsement of an applicant are set out in Appendix L to the Immigration Rules.

What DCBs have been specified by the Home Office? Currently, just four, namely: the Arts Council for arts and culture applications; The British Academy for humanities and social science applications; The Royal Society for natural sciences and medical science research applications; and The Royal Academy of Engineering for engineering applications.

So what steps must an applicant take? An application must be submitted to the Home Office and not to the DCB. The Home Office sends the relevant documentation to the applicant's chosen DCB, which will advise the Home Office whether the applicant meets its endorsement criteria. If so, the Home Office will then consider the application, taking into account whether the DCB has endorsed the applicant, make its decision and notify the applicant of the result.

7.3.3   Post-entry: extension

Just before the initial three years' limited leave of a person with exceptional talent expires, an application should be made to extend it under the Immigration Rules, para 245BD.

An applicant will fail if his application is liable to be refused under the general grounds in Part 9 of the Immigration Rules (see **3.4.5**) or he is an illegal entrant (see **10.2.2**), or if he is in the UK in breach of immigration laws, except that any period of overstaying for 28 days or less is ignored.

The applicant must have earned money in the UK as a result of employment or self-employment in his expert field as endorsed by his DCB; and the DCB must not have withdrawn its endorsement. See para 6 of Appendix A to the Immigration Rules as to the specified documents the applicant must produce to prove his earning.

The applicant must now satisfy the English language test (the details are at **7.4.3**).

Note that only Tier 2 (General) Migrants and Tier 5 (Temporary Worker) Migrants who are sponsored researchers may switch into this category whilst in the UK.

7.3.4 Post-entry: settlement

Once a person with exceptional talent has spent a continuous period of five years in the UK in that category, an application may be made for settlement under the Immigration Rules, para 245BF. The applicant will have to show that he:

(a)   does not fall for refusal under the general grounds for refusal (see **3.4.5**) and is not an illegal entrant (see **10.2.2**);

(b)   has spent a continuous period of five years lawfully in the UK as a Tier 1 (Exceptional Talent) Migrant;

(c)   has earned money in the UK as a result of employment or self-employment in his expert field as endorsed by his DCB (see para 6 of Appendix A to the Immigration Rules as to the specified documents the applicant must produce to prove this), and the DCB has not withdrawn its endorsement; and

(d)   has sufficient knowledge of the English language (see **7.4.3**) and sufficient knowledge about life in the UK (see **3.8.7**).

If an applicant has any family members (spouse, civil partner, unmarried or same-sex partner and children under 18) living with him, they may be able to apply for settlement at the same time (see **7.6**).

7.3.5 Tier 1 (Exceptional Talent) Migrant annual limit

At the time of writing, the Government has stated that for each of the periods ending 6 April 2012 to 5 April 2013 and 6 April 2013 to 5 April 2014, the maximum number of endorsements in this category will be 1,000 divided as follows:

(a)   The Arts Council has 300 places;

(b)   The British Academy has 200 places;

(c)   The Royal Society has 300 places; and

(d)   The Royal Academy of Engineering has 200 places.

7.4 TIER 1: ENTREPRENEUR

7.4.1 Overview

This category might otherwise be called the 'business person' route into the UK.

The applicant (or a team of two entrepreneurs) must either be setting up a new business, joining or taking over an existing business by investing in it.

How much is required? A minimum of £200,000 from any source or £50,000 from a Home Office-approved source such as a registered and regulated venture capital firm.

In addition, the applicant must be able to speak English and have enough money to support himself and any dependants.

See the flow diagram summary at **Appendix 12**.

The investment must be in one or more UK businesses. A business is considered to be in the UK only if:

(a)   it is trading within the UK economy;

(b)   it has a registered office in the UK, except where the applicant is registered with HM Revenue and Customs (HMRC) as self-employed and does not have a business office;

(c)   it has a UK bank account; and

(d)   it is subject to UK taxation.

Multinational companies that are registered as UK companies with either a registered office or head office in the UK are acceptable.

Where two entrepreneurs apply as a team, each must separately pass the English language and maintenance tests.

7.4.2   The entrepreneur attributes

An applicant must score 75 points for specific attributes regarding the level of his investment, where the money is held and the fact that it is disposable in the UK.

The details are set out in Table 4 of Appendix A to the Immigration Rules (see **Appendix 1** to this book).

7.4.2.1   Points

The points required for specific attributes are shown in **Table 7.1** below.

Table 7.1   Entrepreneur – specific attributes points

Investment	Points
The applicant has access to not less than £200,000; or	25
The applicant has access to not less than £50,000 from:	
(a) one or more registered venture capitalist firms regulated by the Financial Services Authority; and/or	
(b) one or more UK entrepreneurial seed funding competitions listed as endorsed on the UK Trade & Investment website; and/or	
(c) one or more UK government departments, and made available by the department(s) for the specific purpose of establishing or expanding a UK business.	
The money is held in one or more regulated financial institutions	25
The money is disposable in the UK	25

It can be seen that to score the required 75 points the applicant must meet all three requirements. We shall now look at each in more detail.

7.4.2.2   The applicant has access to the prescribed investment

First, let us consider the £200,000 route.

An applicant must demonstrate that he has at least £200,000 of his own money available to make a fresh investment into business in the UK. Home Office guidance is that the applicant may include money made available by one or more other people ('a third party or parties'). This includes another investor or corporate body, as well as an applicant's spouse, civil partner, unmarried or same-sex partner. In those circumstances the applicant must also provide a declaration from each third party that the money is available to the applicant, together with confirmation from a legal representative that the declaration document is valid (see **7.4.2.5**).

Secondly, what about the £50,000 alternative route?

An applicant must demonstrate that he has access to at least £50,000 to invest in business. Those funds can be made up of any combination of the three prescribed sources. But an applicant cannot use any of his own funds to meet this requirement.

What is a venture capitalist firm? It is a company that draws on private equity funds to invest in new businesses with high growth potential, and in exchange it takes a stake in the business (which it subsequently hopes to sell at a profit). A registered firm is one regulated by the Financial Conduct Authority (FCA).

What UK entrepreneurial seed funding competitions are listed as endorsed on the UK Trade & Investment website? At the time of writing these are TechStars London, Oxygen Accelerator, Wayra and Seedcamp (at www.ukti.gov.uk/uktihome/item/128990.html).

Where a UK government department is providing all or some of the funds specifically for the purpose of setting up or expanding a business in the UK, the funding package may be considered for the award of points here.

Note that a prospective entrepreneur visitor (see **5.12**) may seek to switch into this category on the basis of having secured funding of at least £50,000 from one or more of the three prescribed sources.

Also note that a Tier 1 (Graduate Entrepreneur) Migrant (see **7.7**) may seek to switch into this category on the basis of having at least £50,000 of his own money to invest and/or already invested in UK business. This may include money made available by third parties.

7.4.2.3 The money is held in one or more regulated financial institutions

The financial institution or institutions that provide confirmation that the money is available to the applicant must be regulated by the home regulator, ie an official financial regulatory body in the country where the financial institution operates and the funds are located. This body must be appropriate to the type of financial transaction. For example, where a financial institution does business in the UK, the appropriate regulator is the FCA.

7.4.2.4 The money is disposable in the UK

If the money is held in the UK then it must be with an institution that is regulated by the FSA. Where the money is held outside the UK, all of the amount required to qualify must be freely transferable to the UK and able to be converted to pounds sterling.

If the money is held overseas but in an institution that has a presence in the UK and is regulated by the FCA, the Home Office requires no further evidence that the money can be transferred into the UK. In all other cases that evidence is needed by way of a document from the bank or financial institution.

Funds in a foreign currency are converted into pounds sterling using an official exchange rate currency converter recognised by the Home Office at www.oanda.com. This is done on the date on which the application is made.

7.4.2.5 Specified documents

To satisfy each of the three requirements and thereby score 25 points for each, the applicant must produce the documents specified in para 41-SD of Appendix A to the Immigration Rules. These include, for example, an original letter, on official headed paper, from each financial institution holding the applicant's funds, confirming that the stated amount of money is available and disposable in the UK.

Each letter must have been produced within the three months immediately before the date of the application. Each letter must also confirm that the institution is regulated by the appropriate body. Details of the amount of money being provided by any third party must also be given.

If the applicant is relying on third-party funding, he must supply a declaration from every third party that they have made the money available for the applicant to invest in a business in the UK, and a letter from a legal representative confirming the validity of signatures on each third-party declaration provided.

7.4.2.6 Team of two entrepreneurs

The required investment funds can be shared by an entrepreneurial team of two people. Each member of the team may apply to come to the UK in this category using the same investment funds.

Where two applicants apply using funds from a third party, each provider of funds must confirm that both applicants have equal access to, and are able to dispose of, the money in the UK.

7.4.2.7 Genuine application

The entry clearance officer (ECO) must be satisfied that:

(a)   the applicant genuinely intends and is able to establish, take over or become a director of one or more businesses in the UK within the following six months;

(b)   the applicant genuinely intends to invest the funds; and

(c)   that those funds are genuinely available to the applicant, and will remain available to him until such time as it is spent by his business or businesses.

'Available to him' in this context means that the funds are in his own possession, or in the financial accounts of a UK-incorporated business of which he is the director, or available from any declared third party or parties.

The ECO must also be satisfied that the applicant does not intend to take any other employment in the UK.

In making this assessment, the ECO will assess the balance of probabilities and may take into account the following factors:

(a)   the evidence the applicant has submitted;

(b)   the viability and credibility of the source of the funds;

(c)   the viability and credibility of the applicant's business plans and market research into his chosen business sector;

(d)   the applicant's previous educational and business experience (or lack thereof);

(e)   the applicant's immigration history and previous activity in the UK.

If the ECO is not satisfied with the genuineness of the application, no points will be scored for specific attributes.

7.4.3 English language

An applicant must score 10 points for English language. There are three different ways in which an applicant might achieve this, as set out in Appendix B to the Immigration Rules (see **Appendix 1** to this book). In summary these are that the applicant:

(a)   has passed a Home Office-approved English language test;

(b)   is a national of a Home Office-designated majority English-speaking country; or

(c)   holds a degree accepted by the Home Office as taught in English that is equivalent to a UK Bachelor's degree or above.

7.4.3.1 English language Home Office-approved test

An applicant must demonstrate knowledge of English equivalent to level B1 (intermediate) of the Council of Europe's Common European Framework for Language Learning, or above. Details are on the Council's website at www.coe.int/T/DG4/Linguistic/CADRE_EN.asp. A list of Home Office-approved tests may be found in Appendix O to the Immigration Rules.

Ten points are be awarded for passing an English language test only if the applicant has the relevant level of English language required and provides with his application the original English language test document which is within its validity date and clearly shows:

(a)   the applicant's name;

(b)   the qualification obtained, which must meet or exceed the relevant level in all four components (reading, writing, speaking and listening), unless the applicant was exempted from sitting a component on the basis of a disability; and

(c)   the date of the award.

7.4.3.2 National of a Home Office-designated majority English-speaking country

Nationals of Home Office-designated majority English-speaking countries automatically meet the English language requirement. To prove their nationality they must produce a current valid original passport or travel document.

Nationals of the following countries are designated for these purposes by the Home Office:

Antigua and Barbuda
Australia
The Bahamas
Barbados
Belize
Canada
Dominica
Grenada
Guyana
Jamaica
New Zealand
St Kitts and Nevis
St Lucia
St Vincent and the Grenadines
Trinidad and Tobago
United States of America

7.4.3.3 Degree accepted by the Home Office as taught in English

An applicant meets the English language requirement if he can produce an academic qualification (not a professional or vocational qualification) from an educational establishment in a Home Office-prescribed country listed below. These are deemed by the National Academic Recognition Information Centre for the United Kingdom (UK NARIC) to meet or exceed the recognised standard of at least a Bachelor's degree in the UK.

Academic qualifications from the following countries count:

Antigua and Barbuda
Australia
The Bahamas
Barbados
Belize
Dominica
Grenada

Guyana
Ireland
Jamaica
New Zealand
St Kitts and Nevis
St Lucia
St Vincent and the Grenadines
Trinidad and Tobago
United Kingdom
United States of America

The applicant should produce with his application the original certificate of the award. If he cannot do so, see para 7(ii)(2) of Appendix B to the Immigration Rules. What if an applicant's relevant qualification was taught in English but not in one of the above countries? Points will be awarded if the qualification is equivalent to at least a UK bachelor's degree and the degree was taught to a competent standard of English equivalent to level B1 on the Council of Europe's Common European Framework of Reference for Languages. In these circumstances an applicant should use the Home Office's points-based calculator on its website (see **7.2.2.5**).

7.4.4 Available maintenance funds

Applicants must be able to support themselves for the entire duration of their stay in the UK without needing public funds (see **3.3.2**). An applicant must score 10 points for having available sufficient maintenance funds. As to what constitute 'sufficient' funds, the requirement is set out in Appendix C to the Immigration Rules (see **Appendix 1** to this book).

An applicant must have at least £3,100 of personal savings. The applicant must demonstrate that he has held at least that amount for a consecutive 90-day period of time, ending no earlier than 31 days before the date of his application. So access to a bank overdraft facility in excess of that amount will not satisfy this requirement: see R *(Adeyemi-Doro) v Secretary of State for the Home Department* [2011] EWCA Civ 849.

Points will be awarded only if the Home Office receives the specified documentary evidence of the applicant's personal savings as set out in para 1B of Appendix C to the Immigration Rules. So, for example, where an applicant produces personal bank or building society statements, or building society passbooks, these must clearly show the applicant's name; the account number; the date; the financial institution's name and logo; transactions covering the 90-day period; and a balance that does not fall below £3,100.

If an applicant is bringing any family members (spouse, civil partner, unmarried or same-sex partner and children under 18) with him, he will have to demonstrate that additional maintenance funds are available. See **7.6**.

The applicant's specified documents must be from institutions acceptable to the Home Office. A check should always be made in Appendix P to the Immigration Rules, where there are lists of financial institutions approved or not approved for certain countries (currently Sri Lanka, Bangladesh, Cameroon, India, Ghana, Pakistan, Iran and The Philippines).

An applicant may not use any moneys included in his investment as evidence of maintenance funds.

7.4.5 Post-entry: extension

Just before the initial three years' limited leave of an entrepreneur expires, an application should be made to extend it under para 245DD of the Immigration Rules.

An applicant will fail if his application is liable to be refused under the general grounds in Part 9 of the Immigration Rules (see **3.5.4**) or he is an illegal entrant (see **10.2.2**), or if he is in the

UK in breach of immigration laws, except that any period of overstaying for 28 days or less is ignored.

Basically, the applicant has to demonstrate that the original requirements have been met, ie the entrepreneur must show that the full amount of £200,000 or £50,000 (as appropriate) in cash has been invested in business in the UK and the applicant must again score at least 75 points. See **7.4.5.1**.

As the applicant will have satisfied the English language test when applying for entry clearance, that requirement does not apply again.

The applicant will have to demonstrate that he has maintained and will continue to maintain himself (and any dependants): see **7.4.5.6**.

7.4.5.1   Attributes for an extension

An applicant must score 75 points for specific attributes in relation to the investment steps he has taken since entering the UK.

The details are set out in Table 5 of Appendix A to the Immigration Rules (see **Appendix 1 to** this book), as shown in **Table 7.2** below.

Table 7.2   Entrepreneur – attributes points for an extension

Investment and business activity	Points
The applicant has invested, or had invested on his behalf, not less than £200,000 or £50,000 (as appropriate) in cash directly into one or more businesses in the UK.	20
The applicant has: (a) registered with HMRC as self-employed; (b) registered a new business in which he is a director; or (c) registered as a director of an existing business. Where the applicant's last grant of entry clearance, leave to enter or leave to remain was as a Tier 1 (Entrepreneur) Migrant, this condition must have been met within six months of his entry to the UK (if he was granted entry clearance in this category and there is evidence to establish his date of arrival to the UK), or, in any other case, the date of the grant of leave to remain.	20
On a date no earlier than three months prior to the date of application, the applicant was: (a) registered with HMRC as self-employed; (b) registered a new business in which he is a director; or (c) registered as a director of an existing business.	15
The applicant has: (a) established a new business or businesses that has or have created the equivalent of at least two new full-time jobs for persons settled in the UK; or (b) taken over or joined an existing business or businesses, and his services or investment have resulted in a net increase in the employment provided by the business or businesses for persons settled in the UK by creating the equivalent of at least two new full-time jobs. Where the applicant's last grant of entry clearance or leave to enter or remain was as a Tier 1 (Entrepreneur) Migrant, the jobs must have existed for at least 12 months of the period for which the previous leave was granted.	20

It can be seen that to score the required 75 points the applicant must meet all four requirements. We shall now look at each in more detail.

7.4.5.2 Invested at least £200,000 or £50,000 (as appropriate) cash in UK business

The applicant must show that the full amount of £200,000 or £50,000 (as appropriate) in cash has already been invested in business in the UK. If the entrepreneur is no longer involved in a business, evidence of the investment must still be produced.

What property, if any, purchased by the applicant counts as an investment? Home Office guidance is that only commercial premises count, and it does not include the value of any residential accommodation, nor property development or property management. If the applicant has bought property which includes residential accommodation for himself and his family, the value of that part is excluded.

If the applicant has made the investment in the form of a director's loan, does that count? Yes, but only if it is unsecured and ranks after any third-party creditors of the company. The original legal agreement between the applicant and the company must be provided.

What other documentary evidence is required? If the business is a registered company that is required to produce audited accounts, these must be provided. Businesses that are not required to produce audited accounts must provide their unaudited management accounts, together with a certificate of confirmation from an UK regulated accountant. Audited accounts, or management accounts accompanied by an accountant's certificate, must show how much the applicant has invested in the business.

For each business that an applicant relies on to claim points, the documents specified by para 46-SD of Appendix A to the Immigration Rules must be provided.

7.4.5.3 Registration requirement

Self-employed applicants must provide either their original welcome letter from HMRC, or any Small Earnings Exemption Certificate from HMRC.

A director of a new or existing company must provide his Current Appointment Report from Companies House.

Each document must be dated no more than six months after the date the applicant entered the UK (or, where there is no evidence of that, the date his entry clearance was granted).

7.4.5.4 Engaged in a business activity

Although an applicant does not have to be engaged in the same business in which he was working when he first entered the UK, he must still be either a self-employed business person or a director of a company at the time the extension application is made. A self-employed person might prove this by producing evidence of payment of Class 2 National Insurance Contributions. A director should produce his Current Appointment Report from Companies House. The report must show that the applicant is a director of the business, and that it is actively trading and not struck off, dissolved or in liquidation. As proof that the applicant is still engaged in business the specified evidence must be dated no earlier than three months prior to the date of application.

7.4.5.5 Created at least the equivalent of two new full-time jobs

What is the purpose of this requirement? The Home Office states that the creation of employment for settled workers shows the applicant's contribution to the UK economy. However, the jobs do not have to exist at the time of the application. The requirement is that during the entrepreneur's three years' limited leave he must have created jobs that existed for at least 12 months of that period.

A self-employed applicant must employ the settled workers directly. If the applicant is a director of a business, he must show that his business has created the new posts for settled workers.

What is a full-time job? The Home Office considers a 30-hour working week to be full-time. But can part-time work form part of the total number of hours of employment created? Yes. Does the employment created need to be in a single period? No, it can be made up of shorter periods. Does it need to be for any particular number of workers? No, a single person may be employed for this time, or several people. But in all cases the employment must comply with UK regulations.

The Home Office gives the following useful examples:

(a)   The working hours of two part-time workers may be combined to add up to 30 hours a week or more and form the equivalent of one full-time post.

(b)   A worker who is employed for part of a year and then leaves the job may be replaced by another worker so that the employment as a whole adds up to at least 12 months. However, if there is a gap between one worker leaving a post and another worker starting employment, the period when the post is not filled will not be counted in the 12-month period. Only periods during which a worker is employed in a post will qualify for the award of points.

(c)   If a single worker is employed for 24 months, this employment will qualify for the award of points. The employment can also be made up of a six-month period for one worker and an 18-month period for another.

(d)   If four workers are employed for 26 weeks (six months) each, their hours of employment may be added together for the award of points.

What documents need to be produced? These include copies of the documents kept by the employer as evidence that the employee is a settled worker; documents registering the employee with HMRC; Form P11 (a report to HMRC recording the earnings of each separate employee); and payslips.

How does an applicant who has taken over or joined an existing UK business show that he has created new posts that result in a net increase? The applicant must produce a duplicate Form P35 (this is an annual return made to HMRC listing the names of employees of the business) and an original accountant's letter verifying that the new posts have been created.

7.4.5.6   Available maintenance funds

The level of funds required on an extension application is £900. The same documentation (see **7.4.4**) is required, evidencing that the applicant has held at least that amount for a consecutive 90-day period of time, ending no earlier than 31 days before the date of his application.

If an applicant has any family members (spouse, civil partner, unmarried or same-sex partner and children under 18) living with him, he will have to demonstrate that additional maintenance funds are available. See **7.6**.

7.4.6   Post-entry: settlement

Once an entrepreneur has spent a continuous period of five years in the UK in that category (or three years in the circumstances set out in **Table 7.3** below), an application may be made for settlement under the Immigration Rules, para 245DF. The applicant will have to show that he:

(a)   does not fall for refusal under the general grounds for refusal (see **3.5.4**) and is not an illegal entrant (see **10.2.2**);

(b)   scores 75 points for specific attributes (see **7.4.6.1**); and

(c) has sufficient knowledge of the English language and sufficient knowledge about life in the UK (see **3.8.7**).

If an applicant has any family members (spouse, civil partner, unmarried or same-sex partner and children under 18) living with him, they may be able to apply for settlement at the same time, provided they have lived together in the UK for at least five years (see **7.6**).

An entrepreneur's child may apply for settlement at the same time as the entrepreneur, as long as the child meets the requirements of the Immigration Rules.

7.4.6.1 Specific attributes for settlement

An applicant must score 75 points for specific attributes in relation to the investment steps he has taken since entering the UK. The details are set out in Table 6 of Appendix A to the Immigration Rules (see **Appendix 1** to this book), as shown in **Table 7.3** below.

Table 7.3   Entrepreneur – attributes points for indefinite leave to remain

Investment and business activity	Points
On a date no earlier than three months prior to the date of application, the applicant was: (a) registered with HMRC as self-employed; (b) registered a new business in which he is a director; or (c) registered as a director of an existing business.	20
The applicant has: (a) established a new business or businesses that has or have created the equivalent of at least two new full-time jobs for persons settled in the UK; or (b) taken over or joined an existing business or businesses, and his services or investment have resulted in a net increase in the employment provided by the business or businesses for persons settled in the UK by creating the equivalent of at least two new full-time jobs. Where the applicant's last grant of entry clearance or leave to enter or remain was as a Tier 1 (Entrepreneur) Migrant, the jobs must have existed for at least 12 months of the period for which the previous leave was granted.	20

The applicant has spent the specified continuous period lawfully in the UK in this category, with absences from the UK of no more than 180 days in any 12 calendar months during that period.
The specified continuous period is:
(a) three years if the number of new full-time jobs referred to above is at least 10;
(b) three years if the applicant has:
   (i) established a new UK business that has had an income from business activity of at least £5 million during a three-year period in which the applicant has had leave as a Tier 1 (Entrepreneur) Migrant;
   (ii) taken over or invested in an existing UK business and his services or investment have resulted in a net increase in income from business activity to that business of £5 million during a three-year period in which the applicant has had leave as a Tier 1 (Entrepreneur) Migrant, when compared to the immediately preceding three-year period; or
(c) five years in all other cases.
	35

It can be seen that to score the required 75 points the applicant must meet all three requirements. The first 40 points are the same as for an extension (see **7.4.5.3** and **7.4.5.4**). Securing the remaining 35 points will determine when the application can be made. The specified documents in para 46-SD of Appendix A to the Immigration Rules must be provided.

7.5   TIER 1: INVESTOR

7.5.1   Overview

This category is for an individual who is able to make a substantial financial investment of at least £1 million in the UK.

An applicant does not have to meet any English language requirement because he is investing in the UK and may choose whether or not he wants to work. In addition, given the level of investment, he does not have to demonstrate that he has enough money to maintain himself (and any dependants).

7.5.2   The investor attributes

An applicant must score 75 points for either having access to £1 million that is in a regulated financial institution and disposable in the UK, or having personal assets exceeding £2 million and at least a £1 million loan from a regulated financial institution. These attributes are set out in Table 7 of Appendix A to the Immigration Rules (see **Appendix 1** to this book) as follows:

The applicant:

(a)   has money of his own held in a regulated financial institution and disposable in the UK amounting to not less than £1 million; or

(b)   (i)   owns personal assets which, taking into account any liabilities to which they are subject, have a value of at least £2 million; and

(ii)   has money under his control held in a regulated financial institution and disposable in the UK amounting to not less than £1 million which has been loaned to him by a UK regulated financial institution.

7.5.2.1   The £1 million route

The applicant must show that he can make an investment of at least £1 million in the UK. The money may already be in the UK or held overseas at the time of application. If it is not in pounds sterling, the applicant must convert its value into that using the Oanda website (see **7.4.2.4**) on the date on which the application is made.

Can an applicant rely on money that he owns jointly with his spouse, civil partner, unmarried or same-sex partner? Yes – see paras 61 and 61-SD of Appendix A to the Immigration Rules.

An applicant must produce the documents specified in para 64A-SD of Appendix A to the Immigration Rules to earn 75 points by this route. In summary, these include:

(a)   A portfolio report or breakdown of investments in a letter produced by a UK regulated financial institution covering the three consecutive months in the period immediately before the application.

If the money has already been invested in the UK in the last 12 months or is held abroad, but in either case the applicant has such a report, he may use it as evidence that the money is available. Alternatively, the applicant may supply a breakdown of his investments in a letter from an authorised financial institution.

Only investments made in the UK within the 12 months immediately before the date of the application are eligible for the award of points. What investments count? Those in government bonds, share capital or loan capital in active and trading companies registered in the UK.

(b) Where the applicant manages his own investments or has a portfolio manager who does not operate in the UK, he must produce documentary evidence of his holdings. This may include certified copies of bonds, share certificates and audited accounts. All documents must cover the three consecutive months in the period immediately before the application.

(c) If the funds are in a bank account, the applicant must provide personal bank statements from a bank that is regulated by the official regulatory body for the country in which the institution operates and the funds are located. These must show the amount of money available in the name of the applicant and/or his spouse, civil partner, unmarried or same-sex partner. Consecutive bank statements covering the three months immediately before the date of application are required. Alternatively a letter from that bank may be acceptable.

What if the money has not been held in a portfolio or bank account for at least three months prior to the application? Then the applicant will have to provide evidence of the source of the money as outlined in **Table 7.4** below.

Table 7.4   Investor – sources of funds

Source of funds	Supporting evidence key points
Gift	The original irrevocable memorandum of gift and a letter from a legal adviser confirming that it is valid and binding according to the laws of the country in which it was made.
Deeds of sale	The original deeds of sale of assets (such as property or business) and a letter from a legal adviser confirming that the sale was genuine and that the money is available to the applicant.
Evidence from a business	Business accounts and a letter from a legal adviser confirming that the applicant can lawfully extract the money from the business.
Will	A notarised copy of the will and a letter from a legal adviser confirming the validity of the will.
Divorce settlement	A notarised copy of the terms of the divorce settlement and a letter from a legal adviser confirming that the document is valid.
Award of winnings	A letter from the organisation issuing the financial award or winnings and a letter from a legal adviser confirming the money has been transferred.

In all other cases the applicant will need to produce original documentation as evidence of the source of the money, together with independent supporting evidence. For example, if the money was received as a result of court action, the Home Office requires original documents in the form of a letter of confirmation of the court proceedings and a suitable letter from the applicant's solicitor.

(d) Applicants who have funds that are not held in the UK, or who have a portfolio of investments that are not in the UK, must provide a letter from their bank or financial institution confirming that the money can be transferred into the UK.

7.5.2.2   The £2 million route

If an applicant intends to borrow money from a UK regulated financial institution to make an investment in the UK, his level of personal net worth must be at least £2 million. Applicants may borrow all of their £1 million investment funds. Can assets held by the applicant's spouse, civil partner, unmarried or same-sex partner, either jointly or in the partner's own name, be taken into account when assessing the applicant's net worth? Yes. But applicants cannot mix personal funds and borrowed funds in order to meet the total £1 million investment required for the award of 75 points.

The applicant will need to produce a letter from a UK regulated financial institution which confirms the following:

(a)   that not less than £1 million is available for the applicant to borrow;

(b)   the money is available on the date that the letter is issued;

(c)   the institution is a UK regulated financial institution;

(d)   the applicant's personal net worth is at least £2 million; and

(e)   that the institution will confirm the content of the letter to the Home Office if required to do so.

How should the authorised financial institution calculate the applicant's personal net worth? It should add up the applicant's assets and deduct from that his liabilities. Assets may include personal cash, investments and property belonging to the applicant and/or his spouse, civil partner, unmarried or same-sex partner. Liabilities may include mortgages and loans.

7.5.3   Post-entry: extension

Just before the initial three years' limited leave of an investor expires, an application should be made to extend it under para 245ED of the Immigration Rules.

An applicant will fail if his application is liable to be refused under the general grounds in Part 9 of the Immigration Rules (see **3.5.4**) or he is an illegal entrant (see **10.2.2**), or if he is in the UK in breach of immigration laws, except that any period of overstaying for 28 days or less is ignored.

Basically, the applicant has to demonstrate that the original requirements have been met, ie the investor has made the required investment, and the applicant must again score at least 75 points. The attributes are set out in Table 8 of Appendix A to the Immigration Rules (see **Appendix 1** to this book), as shown in **Table 7.5** below.

Table 7.5   Investor – attributes for extension

Assets and investment	Points
The applicant: (a) has money of his own under his control in the UK amounting to not less than £1 million; or (b) (i) owns personal assets which, taking into account any liabilities to which they are subject, have a value of not less than £2 million; and (ii) has money under his control held in a regulated financial institution and disposable in the UK amounting to not less than £1 million which has been loaned to him by a UK regulated financial institution.	30
The applicant has invested not less than £750,000 of his capital in the UK by way of UK government bonds, share capital or loan capital in active and trading UK registered companies other than those principally engaged in property investment.	30
The investment referred to above was made within three months of obtaining entry clearance, leave to enter or leave to remain as a Tier 1 (Investor) Migrant, and the investment has been maintained for the whole of the remaining period of that leave.	15

It can be seen that to score the required 75 points the applicant must meet all three requirements. We shall now look at each in more detail.

7.5.3.1   £1 million in the UK

The first requirement has two alternatives that reflect the same original attributes (see **7.5.2.1** and **7.5.2.2**). An applicant will be awarded 30 points if he can show that he has £1 million or more in the UK. This should consist of money invested here and any further money necessary to bring the total funds to at least £1 million. This is a requirement for all applicants who used their own money, or joint money, or who borrowed their investment money for the initial application. See further **7.5.3.3**.

7.5.3.2 Invested at least £750,000 in a specified manner

The Home Office's stated policy is that the money must have been invested in ways that help to stimulate growth in the UK as directly as possible. To be awarded 30 points the applicant must have invested not less than £750,000 of his capital in the UK by way of UK government bonds, share capital or loan capital in active and trading companies that are registered in the UK.

7.5.3.3 Investment made within three months and maintained

An applicant must show that he invested at least the required £750,000 within three months of entry clearance.

The Home Office will accept investments made in the required form in the previous 12 months. Moreover, the applicant must show that his investment was kept at no less than £750,000 during his limited leave.

Can an applicant change investments within those permitted? Yes.

What if the value of any investment in stocks or shareholdings is reduced by fluctuations in share prices? If this occurs the applicant must correct it by the next reporting period, so that the overall value of the investments is maintained at no less than £750,000.

To be awarded 15 points an applicant will have to produce a portfolio of investments totalling at least £750,000, duly certified as correct by a UK regulated financial institution.

In addition, if the investments amount to between £750,000 and £1 million, the applicant must provide evidence of the balance of the funds (such as documents confirming the purchase of assets, like property, in the UK; or a letter from a financial institution that holds the money on deposit).

7.5.4 Post-entry: settlement

Once an investor has spent a continuous period of five years in the UK in that category (or a shorter period of two or three years in the circumstances set out in **Table 7.6** below), an application can be made for settlement under para 245EF of the Immigration Rules.

The applicant will have to show that he:

(a) does not fall for refusal under the general grounds for refusal (see **3.5.4**) and is not an illegal entrant (see **10.2.2**);

(b) scores 75 points for specific attributes; and

(c) has sufficient knowledge of the English language and sufficient knowledge about life in the UK (see **3.8.7**).

If an applicant has any family members (spouse, civil partner, unmarried or same-sex partner and children under 18) living with him, they may be able to apply for settlement at the same time (see **7.6**).

Home Office guidance is that the partner of an investor may apply for settlement at the same time as the investor, provided they have lived together in the UK for at least five years before applying for settlement.

An investor's child may apply for settlement at the same time as the investor, as long as the child meets the requirements of the Immigration Rules.

7.5.4.1 Specific attributes for settlement

An applicant must score 75 points for specific attributes in relation to the investment steps he has taken since entering the UK. The details are set out in Table 9 of Appendix A to the Immigration Rules (see **Appendix 1** to this book), as shown in **Table 7.6** below.

Table 7.6   Investor – attributes points for indefinite leave to remain

Assets and investment	Points

The applicant:
 	
(a) (i) has money of his own under his control in the UK amounting to not less than £10 million; or
 	
      (ii) (1) owns personal assets which, taking into account any liabilities to which they are subject, have a value of not less than £20 million; and
 	
            (2) has money under his control and disposable in the UK amounting to not less than £10 million which has been loaned to him by a UK regulated financial institution;
 	
      or
 	
(b) (i) has money of his own under his control in the UK amounting to not less than £5 million; or
 	
      (ii) (1) owns personal assets which, taking into account any liabilities to which they are subject, have a value of not less than £10 million; and
 	
            (2) has money under his control and disposable in the UK amounting to not less than £5 million which has been loaned to him by a UK regulated financial institution;
 	
      or
 	
(c) (i) has money of his own under his control in the UK amounting to not less than £1 million; or
 	
      (ii) (1) owns personal assets which, taking into account any liabilities to which they are subject, have a value of not less than £2 million; and
 	
            (2) has money under his control and disposable in the UK amounting to not less than £1 million which has been loaned to him by a UK regulated financial institution.
	20

The applicant has invested not less than 75% of the specified invested amount of his capital in the UK by way of UK government bonds, share capital or loan capital in active and trading UK registered companies, and has invested the remaining balance of the specified invested amount in the UK by the purchase of assets or by maintaining the money on deposit in a UK regulated financial institution. The specified invested amount is: (a) £10 million if the applicant scores points from (a)(i) or (ii) in the box above; (b) £5 million if the applicant scores points from (b)(i) or (ii) in the box above; or (c) £1 million if the applicant scores points from (c)(i) or (ii) in the box above.	20

Assets and investment	Points
The applicant has spent the specified continuous period lawfully in the UK, with absences from the UK of no more than 180 days in any 12 calendar months during that period. The specified continuous period must have been spent with leave as a Tier 1 (Investor) Migrant and/or as an Investor, of which the most recent period must have been spent with leave as a Tier 1 (Investor) Migrant. The specified continuous period is: (a) two years if the applicant scores points from (a)(i) or (ii) in the first box above; (b) three years if the applicant scores points from (b)(i) or (ii) in the first box above; or (c) five years if the applicant scores points from (c)(i) or (ii) in the first box above.	20
The applicant has maintained the full specified invested amount referred to in the relevant part of the second box above throughout the relevant specified continuous period referred to in the third box above, other than in the first three months of that period and, in relation to time spent with leave as a Tier 1 (Investor) Migrant, has provided specified documents to show that this requirement has been met. When calculating the specified continuous period, the first day of that period will be taken to be the day three months before the full specified amount is invested.	15

7.6 FAMILY MEMBERS OF A TIER 1 MIGRANT

7.6.1 Entry clearance and leave to remain

If subject to immigration controls, the spouse, civil partner, unmarried or same-sex partner ('the Partner') and children under 18 of a Tier 1 Migrant will require entry clearance in order to enter the UK, and should usually subsequently apply for an extension at the same time as the Tier 1 Migrant. The requirements are set out in the Immigration Rules, paras 319A–319K.

7.6.1.1 Partner

The requirements are set out in para 319C as follows:

(a) The applicant must not fall for refusal under the general grounds for refusal (see **3.5.4**), and if applying for leave to remain must not be an illegal entrant (see **10.2.2**) nor in the UK in breach of immigration laws, except that any period of overstaying for 28 days or less is ignored.

(b) The applicant must be the spouse or civil partner, unmarried or same-sex partner of a person who:

    (i) has valid leave to enter or remain as a Tier 1 Migrant; or

    (ii) is, at the same time, being granted entry clearance or leave to remain as a Tier 1 Migrant.

(c) An applicant who is the unmarried or same-sex partner of a Tier 1 Migrant must also meet the following requirements:

    (i) any previous marriage or civil partnership, or similar relationship by the applicant or the Tier 1 Migrant with another person must have permanently broken down;

    (ii) the applicant and the Tier 1 Migrant must not be so closely related that they would be prohibited from marrying each other in the UK (see **8.3.5.3**); and

    (iii) the applicant and the Tier 1 Migrant must have been living together in a relationship similar to marriage or civil partnership for a period of at least two years (see further **8.3**).

(d)   The marriage or civil partnership, or relationship similar to marriage or civil partnership, must be subsisting at the time the application is made (see **8.3.5.5**).

(e)   The applicant and the Tier 1 Migrant must intend to live with the other as his spouse or civil partner, unmarried or same-sex partner throughout the applicant's stay in the UK (see **8.3.5.9**).

(f)   The applicant must not intend to stay in the UK beyond any period of leave granted to the Tier 1 Migrant.

(g)   If the applicant's partner is a Tier 1 Entrepreneur Migrant, there must be a sufficient level of funds available to the applicant, as set out in Appendix E.

As to (g) above, the same requirements for available maintenance funds for an applicant (see **7.4.4**) apply to a partner. Appendix E to the Immigration Rules (see **Appendix 1** to this book) sets out the following requirements:

(a)   Where the Tier 1 Entrepreneur Migrant to whom the application is connected is outside the UK, or has been in the UK for a period of less than 12 months, there must be £1,800 in funds.

(b)   Where the Tier 1 Entrepreneur Migrant to whom the application is connected has been in the UK for a period of 12 months or more, there must be £600 in funds.

(c)   Where the applicant is applying as the partner of a Tier 1 Entrepreneur Migrant, the relevant amount of funds must be available to either the applicant or the Tier 1 Entrepreneur Migrant.

(d)   Where the Tier 1 Entrepreneur Migrant is applying for entry clearance or leave to remain at the same time as the applicant, the amount of funds available to the applicant must be in addition to the level of funds required separately of the Tier 1 Entrepreneur Migrant.

> **EXAMPLES**
>
> Adam applies for entry clearance as a Tier 1 Entrepreneur Migrant. His civil partner, Brian, will be travelling with him. In addition to meeting the requirements of para 319C(a)–(f) above, what maintenance funds do they need to have available? Adam needs £3,100 for himself (see **7.4.4**). As he is applying from outside the UK there must be an additional £1,800 available for Brian.
>
> Janet has been in the UK for the last two years as a Tier 1 Entrepreneur. She recently married David, a foreign national. He is outside the UK and is applying for entry clearance to join Janet in the UK. In addition to meeting the requirements of para 319C(a)–(f) above, there must be £600 in maintenance funds available for David.

If the application is successful, the Partner is granted entry clearance and leave to remain for a period which expires on the same day as the leave granted to the Tier 1 Migrant (but if the Tier 1 Migrant already has indefinite leave to remain, the Partner will be granted limited leave for a period of three years). That leave will be subject to conditions not to have recourse to public funds and registration with the police, if this is required (see **3.3.2** and **3.3.3** respectively). The Partner will be free to work in the UK, but not normally as a doctor or dentist in training (see para 319D(iii) of the Immigration Rules).

7.6.1.2   Child

The requirements are set out in para 319H as follows:

(a)   The applicant must not fall for refusal under the general grounds for refusal (see **3.5.4**), and if applying for leave to remain must not be an illegal entrant (see **10.2.2**) nor in the UK in breach of immigration laws, except that any period of overstaying for 28 days or less is ignored.

(b)   The applicant must be the child of either:

(i)   one parent who has valid leave to enter or remain as a Tier 1 Migrant, or is, at the same time, being granted entry clearance or leave to remain as a Tier 1 Migrant where –

(1)   that parent is the applicant's sole surviving parent, or

(2)   that parent has and has had sole responsibility for the applicant's upbringing (see **8.9.4.3**), or

(3)   there are serious and compelling family or other considerations which would make it desirable not to refuse the application and suitable arrangements have been made for the applicant's care (see **8.9.4.4**); or

(ii)   parents –

(1)   one of whom has valid leave to enter or remain as a Tier 1 Migrant and one of whom has leave as the partner of a Tier 1 Migrant, or

(2)   who are at the same being granted entry clearance or leave to remain as a Tier 1 Migrant and as the partner of a Tier 1 Migrant, or

(3)   where one parent has valid leave to enter or remain as the partner of a person who has either limited leave to enter or remain as a Tier 1 Migrant, indefinite leave to remain as a Tier 1 Migrant, or who has subsequently become a British Citizen.

(c)   The applicant must be under the age of 18 on the date the application is made, or if over 18 and applying for leave to remain, must have, or have last been granted, leave as the child of a Tier 1 Migrant.

(d)   The applicant must not be married or in a civil partnership, must not have formed an independent family unit, and must not be leading an independent life. See further **8.9.4.6**.

(e)   The applicant must not intend to stay in the UK beyond any period of leave granted to the Tier 1 Migrant parent.

(f)   If the applicant's parent is a Tier 1 Entrepreneur Migrant, there must be a sufficient level of funds available to the applicant, as set out in Appendix E.

(g)   An applicant who is applying for leave to remain must have, or have last been granted leave as the child of a parent who had leave under any category of the Immigration Rules.

(h)   All arrangements for the child's care and accommodation in the UK must comply with relevant UK legislation and regulations.

It is important to note the effect of (c) above in respect of a child now aged 18 or over. That child will still qualify for an extension of leave in this category, provided he had previously obtained such leave when under 18.

As to (f) above, the same requirements for available maintenance funds for an applicant (see **7.4.4**) apply to a child. For details of (f) and Appendix E, see **7.6.1.1**. In addition, note that the required funds must be available either to the child, or to the parent who is the Tier 1 Entrepreneur Migrant or to the child's other parent. In the case of the other parent, he or she must either be lawfully present in the UK, or being granted entry clearance or leave to enter or remain, at the same time.

EXAMPLES

Mona applies for entry clearance as a Tier 1 Entrepreneur Migrant. Her daughter, Janice, will be travelling with her. Janice's father is dead. In addition to meeting the requirements of para 319H(a)–(e) above, what maintenance funds need to be available? Mona needs £3,100 for herself (see **7.4.4**). As she is applying from outside the UK there must be an additional £1,800 available for Janice.

> Clive has been in the UK for the last three years. He applies to switch to a Tier 1 Entrepreneur worker. Clive's wife and 6-month-old baby live with him. What maintenance funds do they need to have available? Clive needs £900 for himself (see **7.4.5.6**). As Clive has been in the UK for longer than 12 months, he needs £600 for his wife and £600 for his child.

If the application is successful, the child is granted entry clearance and leave to remain for a period which expires on the same day as the leave granted to his Tier 1 Migrant parent or partner, as appropriate. This will be subject to conditions of no recourse to public funds and registration with the police, if this is required (see **3.3.2** and **3.3.3** respectively).

7.6.2   Settlement by a partner

Once a Tier 1 Migrant is in a position to apply for settlement, the applicant's partner may apply for settlement at the same time, provided the couple have lived together for at least five years (or later when that requirement is met).

All the requirements are set out in the Immigration Rules, para 319E, as follows:

(a)   The applicant must not fall for refusal under the general grounds for refusal (see **3.5.4**) and must not be an illegal entrant (see **10.2.2**).

(b)   The applicant must be the spouse or civil partner, unmarried or same-sex partner of a person who is being, or has been, granted indefinite leave to remain as a Tier 1 Migrant (or who has subsequently become a British citizen).

(c)   The applicant must have, or have last been granted, leave as the partner of the Tier 1 Migrant who is being or has been granted indefinite leave to remain (or who has subsequently become a British citizen).

(d)   The applicant and the Tier 1 Migrant must have been living together in the UK in marriage or civil partnership, or in a relationship similar to marriage or civil partnership, for a period of at least five years. During that time the applicant must have had continuous leave as the partner of the Tier 1 Migrant and met all of the requirements of para 319C(a)–(e) (see **7.6.1.1**).

(e)   The marriage or civil partnership, or relationship similar to marriage or civil partnership, must be subsisting at the time the application is made (see **8.3.5.5**).

(f)   The applicant and the Tier 1 Migrant must intend to live permanently with the other as spouse or civil partner, unmarried or same-sex partner. See further **8.3.5.9**.

(g)   The applicant must have sufficient knowledge of the English language and sufficient knowledge about life in the UK (see **3.8.7**) (unless the applicant is aged 65 or over at the time the application is made).

7.6.3   Settlement by a child

Once a Tier 1 Migrant is in a position to apply for settlement, the applicant's children may apply for settlement at the same time, provided the following requirements in the Immigration Rules, para 319J are met:

(a)   The applicant must not fall for refusal under the general grounds for refusal (see **3.5.4**) and must not be an illegal entrant (see **10.2.2**).

(b)   The applicant must be the child of:

(i)   a parent who has been granted or is at the same time being granted indefinite leave to remain as a Tier 1 Migrant where –

(1)   that parent is the applicant's sole surviving parent, or

(2)   that parent has and has had sole responsibility for the applicant's upbringing (see **8.9.4.3**), or

(3)   there are serious and compelling family or other considerations which would make it desirable not to refuse the application and suitable arrangements have been made for the applicant's care (see **8.9.4.4**); or

(ii)   a parent who is at the same time being granted indefinite leave to remain as the partner of a person who has indefinite leave to remain as a Tier 1 Migrant, or who has subsequently become a British citizen.

(c)   The applicant must have, or have last been granted, leave as the child of the Tier 1 Migrant who is being granted indefinite leave to remain.

(d)   The applicant must not be married or in a civil partnership, must not have formed an independent family unit, and must not be leading an independent life (see **8.9.4.6**).

(e)   Both of an applicant's parents must either be lawfully present in the UK, or being granted entry clearance, limited leave to remain, or indefinite leave to remain at the same time as the applicant, unless:

(i)   the Tier 1 Migrant is the applicant's sole surviving parent;

(ii)   the Tier 1 Migrant parent has and has had sole responsibility (see **8.9.4.3**) for the applicant's upbringing; or

(iii)   there are serious and compelling family or other considerations which would make it desirable not to refuse the application, and suitable arrangements have been made for the applicant's care (see **8.9.4.4**).

(f)   The applicant must have sufficient knowledge of the English language and sufficient knowledge about life in the UK (see **3.8.7**), unless the applicant is under the age of 18 at the time the application is made.

(h)   All arrangements for the child's care and accommodation in the UK must comply with relevant UK legislation and regulations.

7.7   TIER 1: (GRADUATE ENTREPRENEUR) MIGRANT

7.7.1   Overview

This category allows a graduate from a Home Office-approved UK Higher Education Institution who has been identified as having developed world-class innovative ideas or entrepreneurial skills to stay in the UK after graduation to establish one or more businesses in the UK.

Leave is normally only for 12 months (with the possibility of one 12-month extension) and then the person is expected to depart the UK or switch into another category, such as an entrepreneur.

7.7.2   The attributes

An applicant must score 75 points for specific attributes regarding his endorsement. The details are set out in Table 10 of Appendix A to the Immigration Rules. Note that these cover the requirements for initial leave and an extension in this category.

7.7.2.1   Points

The points required for specific attributes are shown in **Table 7.7** below.

Table 7.7   Graduate entrepreneur – specific attributes points

Criterion	Points
The applicant has been endorsed by a UK Higher Education Institution which: (a) has Highly Trusted Sponsor status under Tier 4 of the Points-Based System, (b) is an A-rated Sponsor under Tier 2 of the Points-Based System if a Tier 2 licence is held, (c) is an A-rated Sponsor under Tier 5 of the Points-Based System if a Tier 5 licence is held, and (d) has established processes and competence for identifying, nurturing and developing entrepreneurs among its undergraduate and postgraduate population.	25
(a) If the applicant's previous grant of leave was not as a Tier 1 (Graduate Entrepreneur) Migrant, the endorsement confirms that, within the 12 months immediately before the date of the endorsement, the institution has awarded the applicant a UK recognised Bachelor degree, Masters degree or PhD (not a qualification of equivalent level which is not a degree), or (b) If the applicant's previous grant of leave was as a Tier 1 (Graduate Entrepreneur) Migrant, the endorsement is from the same institution which provided the endorsement for that previous grant of leave.	25
The endorsement must confirm that the institution has assessed the applicant and considers that: (a) the applicant has a genuine, credible and innovative business idea, and (b) the applicant will spend the majority of his working time on developing business ventures, and (c) if the applicant's previous grant of leave was as a Tier 1 (Graduate Entrepreneur), he has made satisfactory progress in developing his business since that leave was granted and will, on the balance of probabilities, qualify for leave to remain as a Tier 1 (Entrepreneur) Migrant within the next 12 months.	25

It can be seen that to score the required 75 points the applicant must meet all three requirements. We shall now look at each in more detail.

7.7.2.2   Endorsement

Table 7.7 shows which UK Higher Education Institutions may be eligible to provide endorsements. In order to be approved, the institution must confirm to the Home Office that it wishes to take part in the scheme and that it has established processes and competence for identifying, nurturing and developing entrepreneurs among its undergraduate and postgraduate population.

It should be noted that the Government has capped the number of possible endorsements at 2,000 annually.

7.7.2.3   Qualification

To be awarded the points for this requirement the endorsement from the UK Higher Education Institution must confirm that within 12 months immediately before the date of the endorsement it has awarded the applicant a UK recognised Bachelor degree, Master's degree or PhD. Note that the date of award is taken as the date on which the applicant was first notified in writing by the awarding institution that the qualification had been awarded.

7.7.2.4 Business idea

To be awarded the points for this requirement, the endorsement from the UK Higher Education Institution must confirm that the institution has assessed the applicant and considers that he has a genuine, credible and innovative business idea, and that he will spend the majority of his working time on developing business ventures.

Note that on an application for an extension of leave in this category, the endorsement must confirm that the applicant has made satisfactory progress in developing his business and will, on the balance of probabilities, qualify for leave to remain as a Tier 1 (Entrepreneur) Migrant within the next 12 months.

7.7.2.5 Content of endorsement

The above points will be awarded only if:

(a) the endorsement is issued to the applicant no more than three months before the date of application;

(b) the endorsement has not been withdrawn by the relevant Higher Education Institution at the time the application is considered by the Home Office; and

(c) the applicant provides the original endorsement which sets out the information prescribed by para 70(c) of Appendix A to the Immigration Rules.

7.7.3 English language

If an applicant successfully achieves 75 points for attributes, he will automatically satisfy the English language requirement. This is because he will have shown that he was awarded a degree level qualification taught in English (see **7.7.2.3**).

7.7.4 Available maintenance funds

As the applicant is already in the UK, normally as a Tier 4 (Student), his application is for leave to remain in this category and so he must have at least £900 of personal savings. The applicant must show that he has held at least that amount for a consecutive 90-day period of time, ending no earlier than 31 days before the date of his application. He must produce documents demonstrating this as specified in para 1B of Appendix C to the Immigration Rules.

If the applicant has, or wishes to be joined by, any family members, additional maintenance funds will be required (see **7.6.1**).

7.8 OVERVIEW OF TIER 2

7.8.1 A profile of each category

7.8.1.1 Tier 2 (General) Migrant and Tier 2 (Intra-company Transfer) Migrant

A Tier 2 (General) Migrant must have a job offer from a UK-based employer which holds an appropriate licence from the Home Office. However, note that migration here is only for the purpose of filling gaps in the UK labour force that cannot be filled by the resident workforce. So there are tests that have to be met to demonstrate that. In particular, the Tier 2 (General) Migrant must be skilled. How skilled? The job skill level must be at graduate level or above (apart from some shortage occupations: see **7.9.3.1**).

The Tier 2 Intra-company Transfer category is for existing employees of multi-national companies who are being transferred from outside the EEA by their overseas employer to a training position or skilled job in a related UK entity. The transfer must be for training purposes, or to fill a specific vacancy at graduate level or above that cannot be filled by a British or EEA worker.

The applicant must be paid at or above the appropriate rate for the job in accordance with codes of practice in Appendix J to the Immigration Rules (see **7.9.1**).

7.8.1.2 Minister of religion

This category is for a religious worker within a recognised religion and anyone who ministers, whether regularly or occasionally, and/or performs pastoral duties.

Note that Tier 5 (see **7.12**) will cover ministers of religion entering the UK on a temporary basis as religious workers in a non-pastoral role, whose duties include performing religious rites.

7.8.1.3 Sports person

This category is for an elite sports person or a coach who wishes to be based in the UK. The person must be internationally established at the highest level, and his employment should make a significant contribution to the development of the particular sport at the highest level in the UK.

7.8.2 Common features: entry clearance

7.8.2.1 Sponsorship

A Tier 2 Migrant cannot apply for entry clearance without a certificate of sponsorship issued by a UK-based sponsor which has been licensed by the Home Office (see **7.8.3**). Note that a certificate of sponsorship does not guarantee that entry clearance will be given.

7.8.2.2 The points system

Each Tier 2 Migrant is required to score 70 points from three different areas, namely, attributes (50 points), English language (10 points) and maintenance (10 points).

Note, however, that an intra-company transfer migrant who does not wish to remain in the UK beyond three years only has to score 60 points from two different areas, namely, attributes (50 points) and maintenance (10 points).

7.8.2.3 Attributes

For each category an applicant must score 50 points for specific attributes. Briefly, these are as follows:

(a)   General migrant – attributes are based on sponsorship and annual salary.

(b)   Minister of religion and sports person – the only attribute concerns sponsorship.

Full details are set out below, where each category is considered in detail.

7.8.2.4 English language

A Tier 2 Migrant (apart from an intra-company transfer migrant) must have a minimum level of competence in the English language. This requires scoring 10 points for either:

(a)   passing a prescribed English language test at the required minimum level (as set out in **Table 7.8** below); or

Table 7.8   English language test requirements

Entry Clearance Applicant	Council of Europe's Common European Framework for Language Learning Level
Tier 2 (General)	B1
Tier 2 (Minister)	B2
Tier 2 (Intra-company Transfer)	A1
Tier 2 (Sports Person)	A1

(b)   being a national of a Home Office-designated majority English-speaking country (see the list at **7.4.3.2**); or

(c)   having obtained a Home Office-recognised academic qualification (not a professional or vocational qualification) which is deemed by UK NARIC to meet or exceed the recognised standard of a Bachelor's degree in the UK (see **7.4.3.3**).

Note that an intra-company transfer migrant needs to demonstrate the required English language skills only if he wishes to stay in the UK beyond three years.

7.8.2.5   Available maintenance funds

A Tier 2 Migrant must be able to demonstrate that he can support himself in the UK. This requires scoring 10 points for available maintenance funds of at least £900 of personal savings. These must have been held for a consecutive 90-day period of time, ending no earlier than 31 days before the date of the application. Alternatively, if the Tier 2 Migrant has an A-rated sponsor (see **7.8.3**), that sponsor may provide a written undertaking that, should it become necessary, it will maintain and accommodate the migrant until the end of the first month of the migrant's leave. The undertaking may be limited, provided the limit is at least £900.

If any family members (see **7.8.9**) of the Tier 2 Migrant are travelling with him, each must have available savings of at least £600, which must have been held for a consecutive 90-day period of time, ending no earlier than 31 days before the date of the application. Alternatively, if the Tier 2 Migrant has an A-rated sponsor (see **7.8.3**), that sponsor may provide a written undertaking that, should it become necessary, it will maintain and accommodate the dependant until the end of the first month of the migrant's leave. The undertaking may be limited, provided the limit is at least £600 per dependant.

The details are otherwise the same as for Tier 1 (see **7.4.4**).

7.8.2.6   Forms and guidance notes

Applicants can find detailed guidance and application forms on the Home Office website (see **1.2.8**).

7.8.2.7   Not liable to refusal on general grounds

An applicant will fail if his application is liable to be refused under the general grounds in Part 9 of the Immigration Rules (see **3.5.4**).

7.8.2.8   Length of initial limited leave

All Tier 2 Migrants, apart from an intra-company transfer migrant in the Short Term Staff, Graduate Trainee or Skills Transfer sub-categories, are granted leave up to three years with the possibility of extending for a further two years and then applying for settlement.

A Tier 2 Intra-company Transfer Migrant in the Short Term Staff, Graduate Trainee or Skills Transfer sub-categories will be granted leave no longer than 12 months. Then he must leave the UK and he will not be able to reapply for further leave under an Intra-Company Transfer category (other than in the Long Term Staff sub-category) until 12 months after his last leave as an intra-company transfer migrant expired.

7.8.3   Common features: sponsorship

7.8.3.1   An appropriate sponsor

Each Tier 2 Migrant must be sponsored as shown in **Table 7.9** below.

Note that if the sponsor is a limited company, the applicant must not own more than 10% of the sponsor's shares (unless he is applying as an intra-company transfer migrant or as a general migrant with an annual salary of at least £152,100).

Table 7.9   Tier 2 Migrant – appropriate sponsors

Tier 2 category	UK-based sponsor
General migrant	A genuine organisation or sole trader operating legally in the UK.
Intra-company transfer migrant	An UK entity with a direct link by common ownership or control with the overseas entity where the migrant is currently working. For definitions of common ownership or control see **Appendix 13**.
Minister of religion	A genuine religious institution, which is a registered, excepted or exempt UK charity according to the relevant charity legislation in force in its part of the UK, or is an ecclesiastical corporation (either corporation sole or body corporate) established for charitable purposes.
Sports person	A genuine club, or equivalent, which has a recognised governing body. A list of approved bodies is expected to be published by the Home Office in due course.

7.8.3.2   How to become a sponsor

Sponsorship applies to Tiers 2, 4 (see **Chapter 6**) and 5 (see **7.12**). Full details are beyond the scope of this book and the Home Office-published guidance on its website (see **1.2.8**) should be consulted.

In outline, a prospective sponsor must apply for a licence for each Tier that it requires and indicate the number of certificates of sponsorship it intends to issue. The application must be made online, and the applicant must pay a prescribed fee and submit certain specified documents. Once licensed, a sponsor can issue certificates of sponsorship up to a set number. A licence lasts for four years, unless it is withdrawn or surrendered before then.

A licensed sponsor is rated A or B according to the Home Office's assessment of any risk posed. A sponsor that is B-rated must comply with a time-limited action plan, which will set out the steps it needs to take in order to gain or regain an A-rating. If the sponsor does not comply with this action plan, it is likely to lose its licence altogether.

7.8.3.3   Duties of a sponsor

A licensed sponsor must comply with certain duties, including reporting the following situations to the Home Office:

(a)   the migrant does not turn up for his first day at work;

(b)   the migrant is absent from work for more than 10 working days without permission;

(c)   the migrant's contract of employment ends, including if he resigns or is dismissed;

(d)   the name and address of any known new employer;

(e)   any significant changes in the migrant's circumstances, for example change of job or salary;

(f)   any suspicions that the migrant is breaching the conditions of his leave;

(g)   any significant changes in the sponsor's circumstances, for example if it stops trading or becomes insolvent, or substantially changes the nature of its business, or is involved in a merger or is taken over.

A sponsor must also keep proper records of the migrants it sponsors, including contact details and the migrant's identity card details.

7.8.3.4 Certificates of sponsorship

A licensed sponsor will provide its proposed Tier 2 Migrant with a certificate of sponsorship. But this is not an actual certificate or a paper document. It is a unique reference number that the sponsor issues to the migrant, along with details of the sponsorship. This information needs to be produced to the ECO with the entry clearance application. The certificate acts as confirmation from the sponsor that it wishes to bring the migrant to the UK and that to the best of its knowledge the applicant meets the requirements for the issue of the certificate of sponsorship. The certificate does not guarantee that entry clearance will be given. The ECO will check the application against the requirements of the Immigration Rules, including whether the applicant has enough points.

7.8.3.5 Job or sponsorship ends

What happens if a migrant's employment ends before his limited leave has expired? Or if, during his limited leave, his sponsor does not renew its licence or has it withdrawn? In these circumstances the Home Office will curtail (see **3.7**) the person's leave to 60 days, unless only six months or less is remaining. During that time the person could apply for leave to remain in another category or as a Tier 2 Migrant with another sponsor if he finds one.

7.8.4 Common features: extension

Just before the initial three years' limited leave of a Tier 2 Migrant expires, an application should be made to extend it under para 245GD of the Immigration Rules. Basically, the applicant will have to demonstrate that the original requirements have been met. Note that the migrant must be issued with a further certificate of sponsorship (see **7.8.3.3**) for his continued employment before making the application.

An applicant will fail if his application for an extension is liable to be refused under the general grounds in Part 9 of the Immigration Rules (see **3.5.4**) or he is an illegal entrant (see **10.2.2**), or if he is in the UK in breach of immigration laws, except that any period of overstaying for 28 days or less is ignored.

7.8.5 Common features: change of employment

What if a Tier 2 Migrant changes his employment, either within the same organisation or with a new organisation? He will need to apply for an extension of leave, and this will involve passing the relevant attributes test.

In these circumstances the migrant will automatically receive points for English language ability because he will have shown this for the initial application, although this may not apply to an intra-company transfer migrant (see **7.8.2.4**).

The migrant will also not have to give fresh evidence of maintenance.

7.8.6 Common features: supplementary employment

Can a Tier 2 Migrant work in addition to that for which he was granted leave? Yes, but any supplementary work must be:

(a)   a job on the shortage occupations list (see **7.9.3.1**) or a job in the same profession and at the same professional level as the main employment;

(b)   no more than 20 hours a week; and

(c)   outside of the applicant's normal working hours for which his certificate of sponsorship was issued.

In addition, a migrant may do voluntary work in any sector, provided he is not paid and does not receive any other payment for his work except reasonable expenses.

7.8.7 Common features: limited leave conditions

In each category it will be a condition of a person's limited leave that he does not have recourse to public funds (see **3.3.2**).

A person must also register with the police if this is required by the Immigration Rules, para 326 (see **3.3.3**).

Additionally, it is a condition that the Tier 2 Migrant cannot take up employment except for his sponsor in the employment stated in his certificate, supplementary employment (see **7.8.6**) and voluntary work (see **7.8.6**).

7.8.8 Common features: settlement

Once a Tier 2 Migrant has spent a continuous period of five years in the UK in that category (but including any time as a Tier 1 Entrepreneur or Investor), an application can be made for settlement under para 245GF of the Immigration Rules.

7.8.9 Common features: family members

Who are the family members of a Tier 2 applicant? The answer is the spouse, civil partner, unmarried or same-sex partner, and children under 18.

A family member will have to obtain entry clearance and a subsequent extension. He or she may be able to apply for settlement at the same time as the Tier 2 Migrant. The provisions are exactly the same as for a Tier 1 Migrant family member: see **7.6**.

7.8.10 Switching

Switching to a Tier 2 Migrant category (apart from intra-company transfer) is by way of an application to the Home Office. The applicant must be lawfully in the UK already as a Tier 1 Migrant (see **7.2**), another Tier 2 Migrant, a Tier 4 Migrant (see **Chapter 6**) or a Tier 5 (Temporary Worker) Migrant (see **7.12**).

7.9 TIER 2: GENERAL MIGRANT AND INTRA-COMPANY TRANSFER WORKER

7.9.1 Overview

A general migrant must already have a job offer from a UK-based licensed employer that fills a recognised gap in the UK labour force.

An intra-company transfer worker is an employee of multi-national company who is being transferred by an overseas employer to a skilled job in a related UK entity. There are four sub-categories of intra-company transfer workers:

(a) Long Term Staff – the applicant has been working for the organisation for at least 12 months and is being transferred to a skilled job in the UK to fill a post which cannot be filled by a settled worker for a period of more than 12 calendar months (up to a maximum stay of five years or nine years for any staff earning £152,100 a year or more).

(b) Short Term Staff – the applicant has been working for the organisation for at least 12 months and is being transferred to a skilled job in the UK to fill a post which cannot be filled by a settled worker for a maximum period of 12 months.

(c) Graduate Trainee – the applicant is a recent graduate of a multi-national company who is being transferred to the UK branch of the same organisation as part of a structured graduate training programme, which clearly defines progression towards a managerial or specialist role.

(d) Skills Transfer – the applicant is an overseas employee of a multi-national company who is being transferred to the UK branch of the same organisation in a graduate occupation to learn the skills and knowledge he will need to perform his job overseas, or to impart his specialist skills to the UK workforce.

The certificate of sponsorship (see **7.8.3.4**) must confirm that the job is at NQF level 6 (degree or above) or in a creative sector occupation skilled to NQF level 4 (Certificate of Higher Education), or the job is at NQF level 4 and appears on the list of shortage occupations (see **7.9.3.1**). This does not mean that the applicant must be educated to this level but that the job is at that level.

What is a job at NQF level 4 or 6 or above? If a sponsor has any doubts, the Home Office website reproduces the standard occupational classification codes produced by the Office for National Statistics. This contains nine major groups consisting of managers and senior officials, professional occupations, associate professional and technical occupations, administrative and secretarial occupations, skilled trades occupations, personal service occupations, sales and customer service occupations, process, plant and machine operatives, and elementary occupations. Having identified the appropriate group, the sponsor should check the relevant occupational code of practice in Appendix J to the Immigration Rules. There, occupations skilled to NQF level 6 or above are set out in Table 2 and occupations skilled to NQF level 4 or above are set out in Table 3.

7.9.2 The attributes

Table 7.10   General migrant – attributes points

Certificate of sponsorship	Points
Shortage occupation	30
Job offer passes Resident Labour Market Test	30
Job offer with annual salary of £152,100 or more	30

Appropriate salary	Points
Appropriate annual salary of £20,300 or more	20

To score the required 50 points, the general migrant applicant has to be entitled to a certificate of sponsorship for one of the three possible reasons and also have an appropriate salary.

We shall look at each of these in more detail at **7.9.3.1–7.9.3.4.**

Table 7.11   Intra-company transfer worker – attributes points

	Points
Certificate of sponsorship	30
Appropriate annual salary	20

It can be seen that to score the required 50 points the intra-company applicant will have to be entitled to a certificate of sponsorship and also have an appropriate salary.

We shall look at each of these in more detail at **7.9.3.5–7.9.3.6.**

7.9.3 Attributes: what the requirements mean

7.9.3.1 General migrant: shortage occupations list

For many years the UK has had a shortage of workers in certain occupations – that is to say, there are not enough resident workers to fill available jobs in particular sectors of the UK's economy. Historically this has included various healthcare and teaching jobs.

The Home Office has published a list of shortage occupations in Appendix K to the Immigration Rules.

If an applicant is to be awarded 30 points here, the job must, at the time the certificate of sponsorship was assigned to him, have appeared on the list in Appendix K, and his contracted working hours must be for at least 30 hours a week.

7.9.3.2 General migrant: resident labour market test

The Home Office recognises that it may be necessary for a sponsor to recruit a migrant from outside the UK to fill a particular vacancy that cannot be filled by a settled worker and that is not on the list of shortage occupations list (see **7.9.3.1**). However, this will be possible only if the sponsor can show that no suitably qualified settled worker is available to fill that vacancy.

How does a sponsor satisfy this test? The vacancy must usually be advertised as follows:

(a)   If required by para 2 of Appendix J to the Immigration Rules the job must be advertised in Jobcentre Plus. Details can be found on its website at www.jobcentreplus.gov.uk.

(b)   The sponsor must also advertise the vacancy in accordance with a code of practice specific to the type of sector or job. The codes of practice can be found in Appendix J to the Immigration Rules.

(c)   The vacancy must be advertised to settled workers for a minimum of 28 days during the six-month period immediately before the date the sponsor assigns the certificate of sponsorship to the applicant. See para 78B(c) of the Immigration Rules.

(d)   The sponsor must use the medium of advertising required by para 2 of Appendix J to the Immigration Rules and set out in the relevant code of practice, often a professional journal or the employment section of a national UK newspaper. The advertisement must include the job title; the main duties and responsibilities of the job; the location of the job; an indication of the salary package or salary range or terms on offer; the skills, qualifications and experience required; and the closing date for applications.

Can a sponsor use other recruitment methods? Yes, if allowed by the appropriate code of practice. These may include Internet advertising, as well as the use of a recruitment agency or head-hunters.

If the recruitment process produces no suitable resident workers, the sponsor can recruit from abroad, but any certificate of sponsorship must be issued within six months of the advertisement being placed. Why? Because that will ensure that the results of the advertising reflect the current availability of the skills the sponsor requires.

7.9.3.3 General migrant: job offer with annual salary of £152,100 or more

In order for the applicant to be awarded 30 points here, the applicant's certificate of sponsorship must show that his gross annual salary, including such allowances as are acceptable for this purpose (see **7.9.3.4**), to be paid by his sponsor is £152,100 or more.

7.9.3.4 General migrant: appropriate annual salary of £20,300 or more

In order for the applicant to be awarded 20 points here, the applicant's certificate of sponsorship must show that his gross annual salary, including such allowances as are acceptable, to be paid by his sponsor is £20,300 or more.

So what counts? Paragraph 81E of Appendix A to the Immigration Rules states that Home Office considers the basic gross pay (before tax) plus any allowances, such as London weighting, which would also be paid to a local settled worker in similar circumstances, provided these allowances are part of the applicant's guaranteed salary package.

What is not taken into account? The Home Office will not consider overtime or benefits such as bonus or incentive pay, travel and subsistence (including travel to and from the applicant's home country).

Points are only awarded for up to a maximum of 48 hours a week, even if the applicant will be working more than this. For example, if the applicant will earn £10 per hour, working 60 hours per week, the salary taken into account is £24,960 (£10 x 48 x 52).

No points are awarded for appropriate salary if the salary is less than the appropriate rate for the job as stated in the codes of practice in Appendix J to the Immigration Rules.

7.9.3.5 Intra-company transfer: certificate of sponsorship

Table 7.12   Intra-company transfer worker – 30 points for certificate of sponsorship

Certificate of sponsorship for long term or short term staff
The applicant has been employed by his sponsoring organisation for at least 12 months immediately before the date of the application either outside the UK; and/or in the UK if the applicant has or was last granted leave to work for his sponsoring organisation in the category of Tier 2 (Intra-Company Transfer: Short Term Staff) or Tier 2 (Intra-Company Transfer: Established Staff).
Certificate of sponsorship for graduate trainee
The applicant has been employed outside the UK by his sponsoring organisation as part of a graduate training programme for at least three months immediately before the date of the application.
Certificate of sponsorship for skills transfer
The applicant has been employed outside the UK by his sponsoring organisation immediately before the date of his application. The sole purpose of the transfer to the UK branch of the multi-national company must be for the applicant to learn the skills and knowledge needed to perform his role overseas or to transfer skills and knowledge to the sponsor's UK workforce. The applicant's appointment must be additional to his sponsor's UK staffing requirements; if it were not for the need for skills transfer, the role in the UK would not exist.

7.9.3.6 Intra-company transfer: appropriate salary

Table 7.13   Intra-company transfer worker – 20 points for appropriate annual salary

Long Term Staff	at least £40,600
Short Term Staff, Graduate Trainee or Skills Transfer	at least £24,300

These annual salary figures are the minimum. It is the gross salary that is taken into account and calculated as for a general migrant (**7.9.3.4**). The actual rate of pay must meet the rate set out in the appropriate code of practice.

7.9.4 Tier 2 (General) Migrant monthly limit

From April 2011, the Government introduced a monthly limit on the number of certificates of sponsorship that can be issued for Tier 2 (General) Migrants. Currently, the monthly limit is 1,725 certificates. Note that this does not apply to an applicant filling a vacancy with an annual salary of £152,100 or more, nor to an application to switch into this category.

How does the Home Office apply the limits? For the full and rather complex details, see para 83 of Appendix A to the Immigration Rules.

7.9.5 Tier 4 (General) Student switching to Tier 2 (General) Migrant

What if a Tier 4 (General) Student graduate (see **Chapter 6**) obtains a job offer from a UK-based employer? After graduating, can the student apply to remain in the UK as a Tier 2 (General) Migrant? Yes, provided:

(a)   the Tier 4 (General) Student's leave has not expired;

(b)   the student has lawfully completed and passed a UK Bachelor or postgraduate degree, Postgraduate Certificate in Education or Professional Graduate Diploma of Education, or has completed a minimum of 12 months' study in the UK towards a UK PhD; and

(c)   the course was studied at a UK institution that is a UK recognised or listed body, or which holds a sponsor licence under Tier 4 of the points-based system (see **6.1.1**).

The applicant should apply from within the UK to switch into Tier 2 (General) following graduation. His sponsoring employer does not have to satisfy the resident labour market test (as the applicant is awarded 30 points for sponsorship), but all the other Tier 2 (General) criteria apply.

7.10   TIER 2: MINISTER OF RELIGION

7.10.1   Overview

This category is for a religious worker within a recognised religion and anyone who ministers, whether regularly or occasionally, and/or performs pastoral duties. Pastoral duties include leading worship regularly and on special occasions; providing religious education for children and adults by preaching or teaching; officiating at marriages, funerals and other special services; offering counselling and welfare support to members of the congregation; recruiting, training and co-ordinating the work of any local volunteers and lay preachers.

This category is also for a migrant coming to work in the UK as a missionary, a member of a religious order such as a monastic community of monks or nuns, or a similar religious community which involves permanent commitment.

As to English language, see **7.8.2.4**.

7.10.2   Attributes: sponsorship

The minister must score 50 points by way of sponsorship. This requires the following:

(a)   The minister must be qualified to do the job in question. For example, he must be an ordained minister of religion where ordination is prescribed by a religious faith as the sole means of entering the ministry.

(b)   The minister must intend to be based in the UK for the duration of his limited leave.

(c)   The minister must intend to depart from the UK when his leave expires.

7.10.3   Resident labour market test

What about the resident labour market test (see **7.9.3.2**)? Unless the role is exempt from the test, the sponsor must confirm that the minister will not be displacing or denying an employment opportunity to a suitably qualified member of the resident UK labour force. Either the sponsor must have undertaken an appropriate resident labour market test for the role, or, if that is inappropriate, the migrant must be additional to the sponsor's normal staffing requirements. The minister must not be taking a position that would otherwise need to be filled by a resident UK worker.

7.10.4   Maintenance

As to maintenance, note that the sponsor must provide an undertaking to support the minister through funds and/or accommodation that are sufficient for the minister to maintain himself throughout the duration of the certificate of sponsorship.

7.11   TIER 2: SPORTS PERSON

7.11.1   Overview

This category is for elite sports people and coaches who are internationally established at the highest level, whose employment will make a significant contribution to the development of their sport at the highest level in the UK, and who intend to base themselves in the UK.

7.11.2 Attributes: sponsorship

The sports person must score 50 points by way of sponsorship. This requires the following:

(a)   The sports person must be qualified to do the job in question.

(b)   The sports person must intend to be based in the UK for the duration of his limited leave.

(c)   The sports person must intend to depart from the UK when his leave expires.

All migrants in this category must have the approval of the appropriate governing body for their sport as listed in Appendix M to the Immigration Rules. This is officially known as an endorsement. This endorsement will confirm that the sports person meets the code of practice as agreed between the Home Office and the sporting body, and also confirms that:

(a)   the migrant is internationally established at the highest level;

(b)   the migrant will make a significant contribution to the development of his sport at the highest level in the UK; and

(c)   it is appropriate to fill the post with a migrant who is not settled in the UK. The endorsement therefore replaces the resident labour market test for this category.

As to English language and maintenance, see **7.8.2.4** and **7.8.2.5** respectively.

7.12 TIER 5: TEMPORARY MIGRANTS

This tier covers temporary sponsored workers (and their family members) who can remain in the UK for no longer than 12 months (creative and sporting workers and charity workers) or 24 months (religious workers, Government authorised exchange workers, international agreement workers and workers under a youth mobility scheme), or up to a maximum of 72 months (Government authorised exchange workers). We shall consider each type of worker briefly in turn. Details of sponsorship are given at **7.8.3**.

Note that a Tier 5 Migrant cannot switch into any other immigration category. However, during his limited leave he can do additional work, provided that it is for no longer than 20 hours per week, it is outside his normal working hours, and it is in the same sector and at the same level as the work for which his certificate of sponsorship was issued.

Applicants can find detailed guidance and application forms on the Home Office website (see **1.2.8**).

7.12.1 Creative and sporting worker

7.12.1.1 A profile

This category is for creative artists (performers and entertainers) and sports people who wish to work in the UK for up to 12 months. Entertainers may be individuals, or part of a large touring entourage working in areas such as dance and theatre. Sports people should be internationally established at the highest level in their sport, and/or their employment in the UK should make a significant contribution to the development and operation of that particular sport in this country. A sports coach must be suitably qualified.

7.12.1.2 Sponsorship

In order to gain a licence as a sponsor of creative workers and their entourage, the prospective sponsor must be operating, or intend to operate, in the creative sector. Examples include a national body, event organiser, producer, venue, agent or other similar organisation.

In order to gain a licence as a sponsor of sports people, the prospective sponsor must be a sporting body, sports club, events organiser or other organiser operating, or intending to operate, in the sporting sector. Appendix M to the Immigration Rules contains a list of sports and their respective governing bodies.

7.12.1.3   Resident labour market test

A sponsor of creative artists operating in dance, theatre, film and television must follow the codes of practice for taking into account the needs of the resident labour market in these areas. Otherwise the sponsor must conduct a resident labour market test, unless the migrant falls into one of the following categories that are deemed to be making an additional contribution to the UK creative sector and therefore are not a threat to the resident labour force:

(a)   The migrant is required for continuity in the creative sector. Here the migrant must have worked for a period of one month or more on the same production outside the EEA prior to coming to the UK.

(b)   The migrant is internationally famous in his field.

(c)   The migrant is established at the highest level in his profession within the creative sector, ie he has performed at the highest level and has established a reputation in his profession. This category also includes groups of people.

(d)   The migrant is engaged by a unit company within the creative sector. A unit company is a large group of entertainers who have regularly performed together in their own country and overseas as part of an established production before entering the UK. Home Office guidance is that pop and music groups are not classed as unit companies.

If a Tier 5 sports person does not have the endorsement of his governing body (see **7.11.2**), the resident labour market test must be carried out.

7.12.1.4   The points system

The migrant must score 40 points, as shown in **Table 7.14** below.

Table 7.14   Tier 5 creative and sporting worker – the points system

Criteria	Requirements	Points
Sponsorship	The migrant is seeking entry to the UK to work or perform in the UK in the relevant sector, The migrant is not intending to establish himself in business in the UK, His employment must not threaten the resident labour force, *and* The migrant must comply with the conditions of leave and will depart when his limited leave ends.	30
Maintenance	£900 and £600 for each dependant or the certificate of sponsorship is issued by an A-rated sponsor and the sponsor certifies that the migrant will not claim benefits while in the UK. However, the sponsor cannot certify maintenance for any dependants.	10

7.12.2   Charity worker

7.12.2.1   A profile

This category is for a charity worker undertaking voluntary activity and not paid employment. The migrant should intend to carry out fieldwork directly related to the purpose of the sponsoring organisation.

As the migrant is not taking paid employment, the resident labour market test does not apply.

7.12.2.2   Sponsorship

In order to gain a licence as a sponsor of voluntary workers, the employer must be a registered, excepted or exempt UK charity according to the relevant legislation in force in its part of the UK.

7.12.2.3 The points system

The migrant must score 40 points, as shown in **Table 7.15** below.

Table 7.15   Tier 5 charity worker – the points system

Criteria	Requirements	Points
Sponsorship	The migrant must intend to do voluntary work directly relating to the sponsor's purpose. The migrant must not be paid or otherwise remunerated for his work. The migrant must not take up a permanent position. The migrant must comply with the conditions of leave and depart when his limited leave ends.	30
Maintenance	£900 and £600 for each dependant or the certificate of sponsorship is issued by an A-rated sponsor and the sponsor certifies that the migrant will not claim benefits while in the UK. However, the sponsor cannot certify maintenance for any dependants.	10

7.12.3   Religious worker

7.12.3.1   A profile

This category is for either:

(a)   a religious worker; or

(b)   a visiting religious worker who is employed overseas in the same capacity as that for which he is seeking to come to the UK, although the exact detail of his duties in the UK may differ. This employment should be ongoing, and the time spent in the UK should be consistent with a break from the worker's employment.

In either case the worker may perform religious rites, such as tending to deities or reading scripture aloud to the congregation, but cannot carry out any of the pastoral duties of a Tier 2 minister (see **7.10**).

7.12.3.2   Sponsorship

In order to gain a licence as a sponsor, the employer must be a genuine religious institution, which is a registered, excepted or exempt UK charity according to the relevant charity legislation in force in its part of the UK, or an ecclesiastical corporation (either corporation sole or body corporate) established for charitable purposes.

7.12.3.3   Resident labour market test

When issuing a certificate of sponsorship, the sponsor thereby certifies that the migrant will not be displacing or denying an employment opportunity to a suitably qualified member of the resident labour force.

7.12.3.4   The points system

The migrant must score 40 points, as shown in **Table 7.16** below.

Table 7.16   Tier 5 religious worker – the points system

Criteria	Requirements	Points
Sponsorship	The migrant must be qualified to do the job in question. The migrant must not intend to take employment for the sponsor except as a visiting religious worker or a religious worker. The migrant must not claim benefits while in the UK. The migrant must be filling a genuine vacancy that cannot be filled with a suitable qualified member of the resident labour force. *and* The migrant must comply with the conditions of leave and depart when his limited leave ends.	30
Maintenance	£900 and £600 for each dependant or the certificate of sponsorship is issued by an A-rated sponsor and the sponsor certifies that the migrant will not claim benefits while in the UK. However, the sponsor cannot certify maintenance for any dependants.	10

7.12.4   Government authorised exchange worker

7.12.4.1   A profile

This category is for migrants coming to the UK through approved schemes that aim to share knowledge, experience and best practice. It is for work experience. It cannot be used to fill a job vacancy.

7.12.4.2   Sponsorship

Sponsorship for this category is rather novel. Government policy is that in order to prevent potential abuse of this category and the formation of small individual schemes, employers and organisations cannot sponsor migrants. Instead, there will be an overarching body to administer the exchange scheme. This overarching body will be the sponsor and will need to apply for a licence. The scheme and the body must have the support of a UK government department. The body will issue certificates of sponsorship to migrants who meet the requirements of the scheme. A list of approved schemes can be found in Appendix N to the Immigration Rules.

EXAMPLE

The Law Society is an overarching body that can authorise eligible firms to issue certificates of sponsorship to prospective short-term migrants under internship and secondment programmes.

7.12.4.3   The points system

The migrant must score 40 points, as shown in **Table 7.17** below.

Table 7.17   Tier 5 government authorised exchange worker – the points system

Criteria	Requirements	Points
Sponsorship	The migrant must be taking part in a work experience scheme, The migrant must not be filling a genuine vacancy, The migrant's work must be in addition to the normal staffing needs, The migrant must be undertaking skilled work at S/NVQ level 3 or above, *and* The migrant's work must conform with relevant UK and European legislation.	30
Maintenance	£900 and £600 for each dependant or the certificate of sponsorship is issued by an A-rated sponsor and the sponsor certifies that the migrant will not claim benefits while in the UK. However, the sponsor cannot certify maintenance for any dependants.	10

7.12.5   International agreement worker

This category is for migrants who are coming to the UK under contract to provide a service that is covered under international law, including the General Agreement on Trade in Services; similar agreements between the UK and another country; employees of overseas governments and international organisations; and private servants in diplomatic households.

This is a specialised category the details of which are beyond the scope of this book.

7.12.6   Worker under a youth mobility scheme

7.12.6.1   A profile

This is a novel category, as the sponsors under the youth mobility scheme are the national governments of the Home Office-approved participating countries listed in Appendix G to the Immigration Rules – currently Australia, Canada, Japan, Monaco, Taiwan, South Korea, Hong Kong and New Zealand. Places on the scheme for each of those countries are capped each year by the UK Government. Once the limit is reached, no further applications will be considered that year.

So how young does a national of an approved participating country have to be? The answer is between the ages of 18 and 30 inclusive when his entry clearance is granted.

Anything else? Yes, two matters.

First, an applicant must not previously have been in the UK in this category (or its predecessor, which was known as the 'working holidaymaker scheme').

Secondly, an applicant must not have dependent children, ie children under 18 who either are living with the applicant or for whom he is financially responsible.

What about a spouse or partner? The Home Office guidance is that there is nothing to prevent an applicant who is married or has a partner from participating in the scheme, whether his spouse or partner accompanies him or not. However, spouses and partners of participants under the scheme cannot enter as dependants. They may accompany a participant, or join him in the UK, provided that they qualify and obtain an entry clearance in their own right either under the scheme or in another category.

A young foreign national who has entered the UK in this category may, during his two years' limited leave, do whatever work he likes, except for setting up his own business, professional sport, or working as a doctor in training. An employer is therefore free to employ a youth mobility participant on that basis.

A person can be granted leave in this category only once.

7.12.6.2 The points system

The migrant must score 50 points in three areas, as shown in **Table 7.18** below.

Table 7.18   Tier 5 worker under a youth mobility scheme – the points system

Criteria	Requirements	Points
Sponsorship	Citizen of an approved participating country (currently Australia, Canada, Japan, Monaco and New Zealand) and that country's quota of places has not been exhausted, or a British Overseas Citizen, British Overseas Territories Citizen or British National (Overseas) Citizen (see **2.4**).	30
Age	The applicant must be between 18 and 30 years of age inclusive at the date that his entry clearance becomes valid for use, and under the age of 31 on the date his application was made.	10
Maintenance	The applicant must be able to support himself from the point at which he enters the UK until he begins earning. An applicant will need to demonstrate sufficient funds for the first two months following arrival in the UK in the amount of £1,800 which is held in his personal bank account on the date his application was made.	10

7.13 SOLE REPRESENTATIVE OF AN OVERSEAS FIRM

7.13.1 A profile

If an overseas firm has no branch, subsidiary or representative in the UK, it may wish to send one of its senior employees to the UK to establish a wholly-owned subsidiary or branch in the UK. This is a long-standing category and it is not part of the points system. The requirements are set out in the Immigration Rules, para 144, as follows.

7.13.2 Paragraph 144(i) requirement

The first requirement to be met by a person seeking leave to enter the UK as a sole representative is that the applicant has been recruited and taken on as an employee outside the UK as a representative of a firm which has its headquarters and principal place of business outside the UK and which has no branch, subsidiary or other representative in the UK.

The overseas firm must be a genuine commercial enterprise. This is judged in the round, taking into account the length of time that the company has been established, its turnover, profitability, the number of employees, etc. It must be the intention that the business remains centred abroad. This does not mean, however, that an otherwise sound application is refused because of evidence of an intention to make the branch in the UK flourish so vigorously that it might, at some time in the longer term, overshadow the overseas parent company. Companies which have been trading for less than 12 months are required to justify the need to establish an overseas branch here.

The overseas parent company must be sending the sole representative to the UK in order that he establishes a commercial presence for the company here in the form either of a registered branch or of a wholly-owned subsidiary. A 'branch' is a part of a company which is organised so as to conduct business on behalf of the company. This means that a person is able to deal directly with the branch in the UK, instead of the company overseas. The company setting up a branch in the UK must apply to register with Companies House within one month of having opened the branch. A wholly-owned subsidiary is a separate corporate body and is not subject to these registration requirements, being treated in the same way as any other company incorporated in the UK.

Lastly, note that the branch of the overseas business which is to be established in the UK must be concerned with the same type of business activity as the overseas firm.

7.13.3 Paragraph 144(ii) requirement

The second requirement is that the applicant must seek entry to the UK as a senior employee with full authority to take operational decisions on behalf of the overseas firm for the purpose of representing it in the UK by establishing and operating a registered branch or wholly-owned subsidiary of that overseas firm.

The sole representative must have been recruited outside the UK and joined the parent company abroad. Home Office guidance is that 'he is likely to be someone who has been employed by the parent company for some time and holds a senior position there'. If the sole representative is not an existing employee, or has been employed for a short time only, then he must be able to demonstrate a good track record in the same or in a closely related field, in order to show that the reasons for his appointment are compelling. Sole representatives must, in the first instance, be employed by the overseas firm direct (although they may later be employed by the UK subsidiary). Agents who are hired to market the company's product in the UK are normally self-employed and provide their services for a fee. Such people cannot therefore qualify as sole representatives. Neither can sales representatives or others, such as buyers, who fulfil a single function only. However, senior sales staff who have other responsibilities, such as marketing and distribution, are not debarred from qualifying as sole representatives.

The applicant is required to provide a document detailing the terms and conditions of his employment. The importance of the position should be reflected in the salary and other benefits. The Home Office expects a sole representative to be vested with the authority to take the majority of decisions locally, but accepts that it is unreasonable to expect him to take unilateral decisions on all matters.

7.13.4 Paragraph 144(iii) requirement

The applicant must intend to be employed full time as a representative of that overseas firm.

Sole representatives are expected to base themselves in the UK and to spend a minimum of nine months of the year here. However, applications may be approved from those who intend to spend less time in the UK, provided that the additional absences are essential to the running of the UK business, for example, if the UK office is to be the centre of European operations. Applicants who intend to spend less than four months of the year in the UK are unlikely to satisfy the Home Office that they are making genuine efforts to establish a commercial presence in the UK. Such persons should be advised to apply instead as business visitors (see **5.2**).

7.13.5 Paragraph 144(iv) requirement

The applicant must not be a majority shareholder in the overseas firm.

Majority shareholders in the parent company are not eligible for entry as sole representatives. When the sole representative is a major shareholder in the parent company, Home Office guidance provides that care must be taken to establish that the arrangement is not one devised simply to circumvent the more rigorous requirements of the business rules. As a rule of thumb, shareholdings in excess of 30% should attract detailed scrutiny. If it is evident that the applicant, as well as being a major shareholder, is also the driving force behind the parent company such that his presence in the UK is likely to mean that the centre of operations has shifted to this country, the application should be refused. The factors to be weighed in deciding this include:

(a)   the size of the applicant's shareholding;

(b)   his position within the firm;

(c)   the number of senior employees who will remain abroad; and

(d)   the extent to which the company's success seems linked to the applicant's specific talents and performance.

7.13.6   Paragraph 144(v) requirement

The applicant must not intend to take other employment.

Sole representatives are required to work full time as such, but this is not linked to a set number of hours per week. The main consideration is that the parent firm should be paying a 'full-time' salary sufficient for the sole representative to support and accommodate himself and any dependants without taking other work or resorting to public funds.

7.13.7   Paragraph 144(vi) requirement

The applicant must be able to demonstrate English language skills at a basic user standard. How can he do this?

(a)   he is the national of a Home Office-designated English-speaking country (see the list at **7.4.3.2**);

(b)   he has a Home Office-recognised qualification from a prescribed country (see the details at **7.4.3.3**);

(c)   he has a recognised qualification that was taught or researched in English to a prescribed minimum standard; or

(d)   he passes a prescribed English language test.

7.13.8   Paragraph 144(vii) requirement

The applicant must be able to maintain and accommodate himself and any dependants adequately without recourse to public funds.

Sole representatives may be offered a remuneration package consisting of a basic salary and commission. This is acceptable to the Home Office as long as the salary element is sufficient to support the applicant and his family without recourse to public funds. As this category is not part of the points system, no set amount is prescribed for maintenance. Full details may be found at **8.3.6.9**.

7.13.9   Paragraph 144(viii) requirement

The applicant must hold a valid UK entry clearance for entry in this capacity.

Entry clearance is mandatory for a person who wishes to enter the UK in this category.

It is not possible to switch into this category.

7.13.10   Supporting documentation for entry clearance

The Home Office requires the following documents to support the application:

(a)   a full description of the company's activities with details of the company's assets and accounts, including full details of the company share distribution for the previous year;

(b)   confirmation that the overseas company will establish a wholly-owned subsidiary or register a branch in the UK;

(c)   the applicant's job description, salary and contract of employment;

(d)   confirmation that the applicant is fully familiar with the company's activities and that he has full powers to negotiate and take operational decisions without reference to the parent company;

(e)   a notarised statement from the company that the applicant will be its sole representative and that it has no other branch, subsidiary, or representative in the UK;

(f)   a notarised statement confirming that the company's operations will remain centred overseas;

(g)   a notarised statement that the applicant will not engage in business of his own, neither will he represent any other company's interest.

7.13.11   Extension

Leave is initially given for three years. Towards the end of that time an application may be made to the Home Office for a two-year extension of stay under the Immigration Rules, para 147.

This requires that the sole representative:

(a)   entered the UK with a valid UK entry clearance as a sole representative of an overseas firm;

(b)   can show that the overseas firm still has its headquarters and principal place of business outside the UK;

(c)   is employed full time as a representative of that overseas firm and has established and is in charge of its registered branch or wholly-owned subsidiary;

(d)   is still required for the employment in question, as certified by his employer;

(e)   meets the requirements of para 144(v)–(vii) (see **7.13.6–7.13.8**); and

(f)   must not be in the UK in breach of immigration laws except that any period of overstaying for a period of 28 days or less will be disregarded.

The application should be supported by the following evidence:

(a)   a letter from the parent company stating that it wishes to continue to employ the applicant as previously;

(b)   evidence in the form of accounts of the business generated (this form can be flexible according to the nature of the company's business);

(c)   evidence of the salary paid to the applicant in the first two years of operation and the terms on which the salary will be paid in future;

(d)   evidence that he has established and is in charge of a registered branch or wholly-owned subsidiary of the overseas parent company.

7.13.12   Settlement

When a sole representative has remained in the UK for five years in this capacity, he may be eligible to apply for settlement under the Immigration Rules, para 150.

This requires that the sole representative:

(a)   has spent a continuous period of five years in the UK in this capacity;

(b)   has met the requirements of para 147 (see **7.13.11**) throughout the five-year period;

(c)   is still required for the employment in question, as certified by his employer;

(d)   has sufficient knowledge of the English language and sufficient knowledge about life in the UK (see **3.8.7**);

(e)   does not fall for refusal under the general grounds for refusal (see **3.5.4**); and

(f)   is not in the UK in breach of immigration laws except that any period of overstaying for a period of 28 days or less will be disregarded.

7.13.13 Family members of a sole representative

The spouse, civil partner, same-sex or unmarried partner and children under 18 of an applicant will need to apply for entry clearance (see paras 194 and 197 respectively). They may also subsequently apply for settlement (see paras 196D and 198 respectively). See further **Chapter 8**.

7.14 COMMONWEALTH CITIZEN WITH UK ANCESTRY

7.14.1 A profile

A Commonwealth citizen (see the list at **Appendix 9**), aged 17 or over, who can show that one of his grandparents was born in the UK (and Islands) and who intends to take or seek employment in the UK and support himself without needing public funds, may be granted entry clearance in this category. Entry clearance is compulsory and limited leave is given of five years. Thereafter an application can be made for settlement.

In this category an applicant does not need to meet the requirements of the points system under any of the tiers. The requirements to be met are set out in the Immigration Rules, para 186, as follows.

7.14.2 A Commonwealth citizen

The applicant must satisfy the ECO that he is a citizen of a Commonwealth country.

7.14.3 Aged 17 or over

The applicant must satisfy the ECO that he is or will be at least 17 years of age when entering the UK.

7.14.4 Proof of ancestry

The applicant must be able to provide proof that one of his grandparents was born in the UK and Islands, and that any such grandparent is the applicant's blood grandparent or grandparent by reason of an adoption recognised by the laws of the UK relating to adoption.

As regards proof of birth in the UK and Islands, the applicant must be able to demonstrate that the grandparent on whom the claim is based was born in:

(a)   the UK;

(b)   Channel Islands;

(c)   the Isle of Man; or

(d)   if the grandparent was born before 31 March 1922, what is now the Republic of Ireland.

Home Office guidance is that birth on a British registered ship or aircraft also counts.

The applicant may be related to that grandparent in one of two ways. First, by blood. So a qualifying connection can be made through a legitimate or an illegitimate line. Secondly, by adoption. An applicant who has been adopted, or whose parents were, can qualify if:

(a)   he has been adopted by someone who has a UK-born parent; or

(b)   one of his parents was adopted by a person born in the UK; or

(c)   his natural grandparents were born in the UK.

No claim can be made through step-parents.

What sort of proof of the relationship is required by an ECO? The applicant should produce his own full birth certificate; where appropriate the marriage certificates of his parents and appropriate grandparents (or, if unmarried, evidence of the relationship if the claim is made through the paternal line); if applicable the legal adoption papers of the applicant or his parents; and the full birth certificates of the parent and grandparent through whose ancestry he is making the application.

> **EXAMPLE**
>
> Charles is a Commonwealth citizen, aged 20. His mother, Florence, was not born in the UK. His grandmother, Rose, on his maternal siECOde (ie Florence's mother) was born in the UK. What documents should Charles produce to prove this ancestral link? A minimum of three documents are required to confirm the following details:
>
> (a)   his birth certificate naming Florence as his mother;
>
> (b)   Florence's birth certificate naming Rose as her mother; and
>
> (c)   Rose's UK birth certificate showing she was born in the UK.

7.14.5 Able to work and intends to take or seek employment in the UK

Entry clearance is for the purpose of work in the UK, not to study or visit. The applicant must satisfy the ECO that he has arranged employment in the UK already, or that he genuinely intends to seek employment and has a realistic prospect of securing it. Home Office guidance is that the ECO will consider such factors as the applicant's age and health, eg any medical problems that may prevent the applicant from taking employment.

7.14.6 No recourse to public funds

The applicant must be able to maintain and accommodate himself and any dependants adequately without recourse to public funds (see **3.3.2**).

As this category is not part of the points system, no set amount is prescribed for maintenance. Full details can be found at **8.3.6.9**.

7.14.7 Holds a valid UK entry clearance for entry in this capacity

Entry clearance is mandatory for a person who wishes to enter the UK in this category.

It is not possible to switch into this category.

7.14.8 Settlement

Near to the end of the person's five years' limited leave he should apply for settlement. The requirements are set out in para 192, as follows:

(a)   the applicant meets the requirements of para 186(i)–(v) (see **7.14.2–7.14.7**);

(b)   the applicant has spent a continuous period of five years in the UK in this capacity;

(c)   the applicant has sufficient knowledge of the English language and sufficient knowledge about life in the UK (see **3.8.7**);

(d)   does not fall for refusal under the general grounds for refusal (see **3.5.4**); and

(e)   must not be in the UK in breach of immigration laws except that any period of overstaying for a period of 28 days or less will be disregarded.

Although (b) above requires the applicant to have resided continuously in the UK in this category for five years, there is no requirement that any employment taken must be continuous. Home Office guidance is that if the applicant is in employment at the time of the application then all that is required is a letter from his current employers confirming the employment will continue. If, however, the applicant is not employed then he will need to produce evidence of his employment record throughout the five years and evidence of the attempts made to find employment. If it is clear that the applicant has not been in employment for any length of time over the five years, he will be asked to provide reasons as to why he has failed to obtain employment. Unless there is a very good reason for this, the application will be refused. The Home Office will also make enquiries as to how the applicant has been supporting himself without a regular income.

7.14.9 Family members

The spouse, civil partner, same-sex or unmarried partner and children under 18 of an applicant will need to apply for entry clearance (see paras 194 and 197). They may also subsequently apply for settlement (see paras 196D and 198). See further **Chapter 8**.

7.15 ILLEGAL WORKING IN THE UK

7.15.1 Employer's duties

The law on preventing illegal migrant working in the UK has evolved over time. An employer's legal responsibilities may therefore vary according to when he recruited his existing staff. There is a very useful summary of the previous legal requirements on the Home Office website (see **1.2.8**). The current law may be found in ss 15 to 26 of the IANA 2006 which applies to staff recruited from 1 March 2008. This makes an employer liable to payment of a civil financial penalty of up to £10,000 if he employs a person aged 16 or over who is subject to immigration control and who has no permission to work in the UK, or who works in breach of his conditions of stay in the UK (see **3.3.1**).

Note that it is essential that any appeal against a civil penalty is made promptly as the court has no discretion to extend the time limits laid down in the IANA 2006: see *Massan v Secretary of State for the Home Department* [2011] EWCA Civ 686.

7.15.2 Civil penalty

How can an employer avoid civil liability? This is answered by the Immigration (Restrictions on Employment) Order 2007 (SI 2007/3290, as amended). The employer must obtain from the prospective employee certain original documents that need to be checked in accordance with art 6, for example, if the document contains a date of birth, the employer must be satisfied that this is consistent with the appearance of the prospective employee. The employer must keep a copy of any document for a period of not less than two years after the employment comes to an end. So what documents count? The employer can choose from documents in the Schedule. This consists of two lists: list A, which includes a British or EEA national's passport; and list B, which includes a biometric immigration document issued by the Home Office to the holder which indicates that the person named in it can stay in the UK and is allowed to do the work in question. List A documents only have to be checked once by the employer. However, list B documents must be checked at least once every 12 months.

7.15.3 Criminal offence

An employer commits a criminal offence if he knowingly employs a person aged 16 or over who is subject to immigration control and who has no permission to work in the UK, or who works in breach of his conditions of stay in the UK. What sentence might the employer face? An unlimited fine and/or a maximum two-year prison sentence can be imposed.

FAMILY REUNION

8.1 OVERVIEW

8.1.1 Background

Until July 2012, Part 8 of the Immigration Rules had dealt with most family reunion situations. Now the only significant group left in Part 8 are children seeking to join either a parent, both parents or a relative in the UK for the purposes of settlement (see para 297, detailed at **8.9** below). It is Appendix FM to the Immigration Rules that currently sets out the requirements for a person to enter or remain in the UK on the basis of his family life with a person who is a British citizen (see **2.2**), or settled in the UK (see **3.8**), or in the UK with limited leave as a refugee (see **9.8**) or a person granted humanitarian protection (see **9.10.1**).

Broadly, Appendix FM covers entry clearance, extensions and switching, as well as settlement by partners (see **8.3**), parents (see **8.10**) and adult dependent relatives (see **8.11**). It also provides for entry by a child of a parent already in the UK with limited leave as a partner or parent (see **8.12**).

In this chapter we shall also consider one other category, namely, a person allowed to remain in the UK and ultimately settle on the basis that he has established a private life here under Article 8 ECHR (see **8.13**).

8.1.2 Partners

8.1.2.1 Terminology

The member of the couple who is not a British citizen, nor settled in the UK nor in the UK with limited leave as a refugee or humanitarian protection, is known as the applicant. The applicant's spouse, civil partner, fiancé(e), proposed civil partner or the person with whom he is in a long-term heterosexual or same-sex relationship is known as the applicant's partner (or sometimes as his 'sponsor').

8.1.2.2 Immigration controls for a fiancé(e) or proposed civil partner

There is no provision for a person already in the UK to switch into the category of fiancé(e) or proposed civil partner. So the applicant must be outside the UK and will have to apply for entry clearance. If successful, he will be granted entry clearance for a period not exceeding six months. This will be subject to a condition of no recourse to public funds (see **3.3.2**), a prohibition on employment (see **3.3.1**) and, if appropriate, registration with the police (see **3.3.3**).

The applicant will therefore have six months in the UK for the marriage or civil partnership to take place. He should then apply to the Home Office for leave to remain in the UK as a spouse or civil partner (see **8.1.2.3**).

8.1.2.3 Immigration controls for all other partners

Where the applicant is outside the UK he will have to apply for entry clearance.

If successful, he will be granted entry clearance for an initial period not exceeding 33 months, subject to a condition of no recourse to public funds (see **3.3.2**) and, if appropriate, registration with the police (see **3.3.3**). The applicant will be free to work in the UK. Just before an applicant has completed 30 months with limited leave as a partner, he should make an application for further leave to remain for 30 months. After 60 months' leave in total he will be eligible to apply for indefinite leave to remain. This is known as the 'five-year family route'.

Note that if an applicant cannot meet the usual requirements for an extension of limited leave as a partner, it may be possible to remain by establishing a claim under Article 8 ECHR. In those circumstances the applicant will have a longer route to settlement, namely, 10 years (granted in four periods of limited leave of 30 months, with a fifth application for indefinite leave to remain). This is known as the '10-year family route'.

These five- and 10-year limited leave periods are often called 'probationary periods'.

If a person is already in the UK, it may be possible for him to apply for leave to remain as a partner and so start on a five- or 10-year family route to settlement.

What if the applicant's partner dies before the relevant probationary period is completed? See **8.7**.

What if the couple separate due to domestic violence by the applicant's partner before the relevant probationary period is completed? See **8.8**.

8.1.3 Children

8.1.3.1 Entering for immediate settlement

A child may seek entry clearance and be granted indefinite leave to enter the UK to join one or both parents who are already settled in the UK. Exceptionally he might be joining a relative who is here and settled. See **8.9**.

8.1.3.2 Entering with or to join a parent who has limited leave

Note that if a child's parent has only limited leave to enter or remain in the UK, the child can apply under an associated Immigration Rule to travel with or join that parent during the parent's leave (see, eg, **7.6.1.2** and **8.12**).

8.1.3.3 Entering with limited leave

A child might enter the UK with limited leave in his own right under the Immigration Rules, eg as a student (see **Chapter 6**).

8.1.4 Parents

A parent with sole parental responsibility for, or access rights to, a British citizen child or settled child who is living in the UK, may apply for entry clearance and subsequently leave to remain under Appendix FM to the Immigration Rules.

A parent already in the UK may switch into this category. This most commonly occurs when a person has entered the UK with limited leave as the partner of a British citizen or settled person (see **8.3**) but can no longer remain in the UK in that category as the relationship has broken down. If that person has sole parental responsibility for, or is exercising access rights to, his British or settled child, an application may be made for leave to remain.

Ultimately it may be possible to apply for settlement in this category.

See **8.10**.

8.1.5 Adult dependent relatives entering for immediate settlement

This route allows a non-EEA adult dependent relative of a British citizen in the UK or a person settled in the UK to enter and settle because, as a result of age, illness or disability, he requires a level of long-term personal care that can only be provided in the UK by his relative here. See **8.11**.

8.2 EXEMPT GROUPS

Part 8 of and Appendix FM to the Immigration Rules do not apply to those people who do not need leave, or who are seeking entry under other provisions of the Immigration Rules. For example:

(a)   persons who already have the right of abode in the UK (see **2.2** and **2.3**);

(b)   EEA citizens and family members entering by virtue of EU law (see **4.4.6**);

(c)   family members of a British citizen who has exercised EU Treaty rights (see **4.4.12**);

(d)   persons with settled status re-entering as returning residents (see **3.8.3**);

(e)   persons who are entering in another category under the Rules (eg visitors, etc).

EXAMPLE 1

Ben is a citizen of Canada. He was born in Canada in 1972. Ben's father is Canadian but his mother was born in the UK and she is a British citizen. Ben has recently married Sue, a British citizen. The couple now wish to travel to the UK to set up home together in Manchester, England.

As a British citizen, Sue can freely enter the UK as she is not subject to immigration controls.

Ben is a Commonwealth citizen with right of abode in the UK. So Ben can enter the UK freely as he is not subject to immigration controls and therefore does not need to comply with the provisions in Appendix FM to the Immigration Rules. (Ben will need a 'certificate of entitlement' in his Canadian passport: see **2.3**. A check could also be made to see if he is registered as a British citizen and holds, or is entitled to, a British passport: see **2.2.6.2**.)

EXAMPLE 2

Vlad is a citizen of Russia who is married to Maria, a citizen of Austria. The couple wish to come and live together in the UK.

As an EEA national, Maria can enter the UK. Vlad may enter as her family member (spouse) under EU law with an EEA Family Permit (see **Chapter 4**).

Vlad could not apply to enter the UK under Appendix FM to the Immigration Rules as his partner, Maria, is not a British citizen or settled in the UK, nor in the UK with limited leave as a refugee or humanitarian protection leave.

EXAMPLE 3

Liz is a British citizen. For the last 18 months she has been working in Paris, France (an EEA country). She is thereby exercising her EU Treaty rights. Three months ago she married Bill, an American citizen. The couple now wish to come and live together in the UK.

As a British citizen, Liz can freely enter the UK as she is not subject to immigration controls.

Bill has a choice. He could seek entry clearance to the UK under Appendix FM to the Immigration Rules as Liz's partner (see **8.3**), or he could enter as her family member (spouse) with an EEA Family Permit (see **4.4.12**).

EXAMPLE 4

Carla is a citizen of The Philippines. She married Denis, a British citizen, whilst he was on holiday in The Philippines last month. Denis has just returned to the UK without Carla. She has not yet agreed to join him in the UK. She intends to apply for a visa to enter the UK as a general visitor in order to decide whether she would wish to live in the UK with Denis.

In principle, Carla could obtain a general visitor visa, but she would need to satisfy the ECO that she did intend to leave the UK at the end of her visit (see **5.2.1** at **(b)**).

8.3 ENTRY CLEARANCE AS A PARTNER

8.3.1 Who is a partner?

A partner, for the purposes of Appendix FM (see para GEN 1.2), is:

(a)   the applicant's spouse;

(b)   the applicant's civil partner;

(c)   the applicant's fiancé(e) or proposed civil partner; or

(d)   a person who has been living together with the applicant in a relationship akin to a marriage or civil partnership for at least two years prior to the date of application.

For (a) and (b) the parties must have entered into a valid marriage or valid civil partnership (see **8.3.5.6**).

For (c) the parties must intend to marry or enter into a civil partnership within six months of entering the UK (see **8.3.5.7**).

As to (d), Home Office guidance is that 'living together with' should be applied fairly tightly, in that the couple should show evidence of cohabitation for the preceding two-year period. Short breaks apart may be acceptable for good reasons, such as work commitments or looking after a relative, which take one partner away for a period of up to six months, where it was not possible for the other partner to accompany the first partner and it can be seen that the relationship continued throughout that period by visits, letters, etc. The phrase 'akin to a marriage or civil partnership' is said to refer to a relationship that is similar in its nature to a marriage or a civil partnership, which therefore includes both heterosexual and same-sex relationships. In order to demonstrate a two-year relationship, evidence of cohabitation is needed. In order to show a relationship akin to a marriage or a civil partnership, the Home Office looks for evidence of a committed relationship. The following type of supporting evidence might therefore be useful in this respect:

•   joint commitments (such as joint bank accounts, joint investments, joint tenancy agreement, joint mortgage account, etc);

•   if there are children of the relationship, a full birth or adoption certificate naming the parties as parents;

- correspondence which links them to the same address (eg household bills in joint names, etc); and
- any official records of their address (eg doctors and dentist records, government records, etc).

EXAMPLE 1

Zach and Yvonne are engaged to be married. Zach is a visa national. Yvonne is a British citizen. The couple are living in Zach's home country, but they now wish to travel to the UK to get married and set up home together.

Zach can apply to enter the UK under Appendix FM to the Immigration Rules as Yvonne's partner (fiancé), provided they intend to marry within six months of entering the UK.

EXAMPLE 2

David is a British citizen. He has worked abroad for several years and for the last 18 months has been living in the USA with John, an American citizen. David now wishes to return to the UK and John wishes to travel with him. If John is admitted to the UK he intends to live with David permanently, but the couple do not wish to enter into a civil partnership.

David and John are not civil partners, neither do they intend to enter into a civil partnership. They have not been living in a relationship akin to a civil partnership for at least two years prior to the date of John's wishing to make an application. So the couple's relationship will need to continue for another six months before John can apply under Appendix FM to the Immigration Rules as David's partner.

EXAMPLE 3

Alice and Brian are both citizens of New Zealand. They were both born there and have never been to the UK before. They have recently married and now wish to travel to the UK to set up home together. Whilst they are both Commonwealth citizens, neither has the right of abode in the UK.

Appendix FM to the Immigration Rules does not apply. Whilst the couple are partners (spouses), neither Alice nor Brian is a British citizen or settled in the UK, or in the UK with limited leave as a refugee or person granted humanitarian protection.

8.3.2 An overview of the requirements

The requirements in Appendix FM to be met for entry clearance as a partner (see para EC-P.1.1) are that:

(a) the applicant must be outside the UK;

(b) the applicant must have made a valid application for entry clearance as a partner;

(c) the applicant must not fall for refusal under any of the grounds in Section S-EC: Suitability–entry clearance (see **8.3.3**); and

(d) the applicant must meet all of the requirements of Section E-ECP: Eligibility for entry clearance as a partner (see **8.3.4**).

8.3.3 Suitability requirements in detail

Section S-EC, paras S-EC.1.2 to S-EC.1.7 set out the following mandatory grounds on which an ECO will refuse an application:

S-EC.1.2   The Secretary of State has personally directed that the exclusion of the applicant from the UK is conducive to the public good.

S-EC.1.3   The applicant is at the date of application the subject of a deportation order.

S-EC.1.4   The exclusion of the applicant from the UK is conducive to the public good because they have been convicted of an offence for which they have been sentenced to a period of imprisonment of (a) at least 4 years; or (b) at least 12 months but less than 4 years, unless a period of 10 years has passed since the end of the sentence; or (c) of less than 12 months, unless a period of 5 years has passed since the end of the sentence. Where this paragraph applies, unless refusal would be contrary to the Human Rights Convention or the Convention and Protocol Relating to the Status of Refugees, it will only be in exceptional circumstances that the public interest in maintaining refusal will be outweighed by compelling factors.

S-EC.1.5   The exclusion of the applicant from the UK is conducive to the public good or because, for example, the applicant's conduct (including convictions which do not fall within S-EC.1.4.), character, associations, or other reasons, make it undesirable to grant them entry clearance.

(For each of the above, see further **Chapter 10.**)

S-EC.1.6   The applicant has failed without reasonable excuse to comply with a requirement to –

(a)   attend an interview;

(b)   provide information;

(c)   provide physical data; or

(d)   undergo a medical examination or provide a medical report.

S-EC.1.7   It is undesirable to grant entry clearance to the applicant for medical reasons.

Paragraphs S-EC.2.2 to S-EC.2.5 set out the following discretionary grounds on which an ECO will normally refuse an application:

S-EC.2.2   Whether or not to the applicant's knowledge –

(a)   false information, representations or documents have been submitted in relation to the application (including false information submitted to any person to obtain a document used in support of the application); or

(b)   there has been a failure to disclose material facts in relation to the application.

S-EC.2.3   One or more relevant NHS body has notified the Secretary of State that the applicant has failed to pay charges in accordance with the relevant NHS regulations on charges to overseas visitors and the outstanding charges have a total value of at least £1,000.

S-EC.2.4   A maintenance and accommodation undertaking has been requested or required under paragraph 35 of these Rules or otherwise and has not been provided.

S-EC.2.5   The exclusion of the applicant from the UK is conducive to the public good because (a) within the 12 months preceding the date of the application, the person has been convicted of or admitted an offence for which they received a non-custodial sentence or other out of court disposal that is recorded on their criminal record; or (b) in the view of the Secretary of State (i) the person's offending has caused serious harm; or (ii) the person is a persistent offender who shows a particular disregard for the law.

Note that despite the wording of para S-EC.2.2, Home Office guidance on (b) is that refusal for failure to disclose material facts in relation to the application can be imposed only where the applicant acts with knowledge. An applicant must not therefore be refused on the grounds that he unknowingly failed to disclose material facts in relation to his application.

8.3.4   Eligibility requirements in outline

An applicant must meet all of the eligibility requirements in paras E-ECP.2.1 to E-ECP.4.2. Broadly these are as follows:

(a)   relationship requirements (see **8.3.5**);

(b)   financial requirements (see **8.3.6**);

(c)   accommodation requirements (see **8.3.7**); and

(d)   English language requirement (see **8.3.8**).

8.3.5 Relationship requirements (paras E-ECP.2.1 to E-ECP.2.10)

8.3.5.1 Immigration status of applicant's partner

By para E-ECP.2.1, the applicant's partner must be:

(a)   a British citizen in the UK; or

(b)   present and settled in the UK; or

(c)   in the UK with refugee leave or with humanitarian protection.

For (a) and (b), does this mean that the application will be refused if the British citizen or person settled in the UK is currently living abroad with his partner and will be travelling with the partner to the UK? No, because para GEN.1.3(b) provides that 'references to a person being present and settled in the UK also include a person who is being admitted for settlement on the same occasion as the applicant'. Paragraph 6 of the Immigration Rules also defines 'present and settled' as meaning that the person concerned is settled in the UK and, at the time that an application under the Rules is made, is physically present here or is coming here with or to join the applicant, and intends to make the UK his home with the applicant if the application is successful. In addition, note that para GEN.1.3(c) states that 'references to a British Citizen in the UK also include a British Citizen who is coming to the UK with the applicant as their partner'.

The relationships of fiancé(e) and proposed civil partner are not recognised by EU law (see **4.4.6.6**). So in what circumstances can an EEA national satisfy (b) above? Paragraph 6 of the Immigration Rules provides the answer: it is when an EEA national holds a registration certificate or a document certifying permanent residence issued under the 2006 Regulations (see **4.4.14**).

8.3.5.2 Minimum age

By paras E-ECP.2.2 and E-ECP.2.3, both the applicant and his partner must be aged 18 or over at the date of application.

8.3.5.3 Relationship not within prohibited degree

By para E-ECP.2.4, the applicant and his partner must not be within any prohibited degree of relationship. Three statutory provisions apply, as follows:

(a)   The Marriage Act 1949 prohibits a marriage by a man to any of the persons mentioned in **Table 8.1** below, and prohibits a marriage between a woman and any of the persons mentioned in **Table 8.2** below.

Table 8.1 Prohibited degrees for a man	Table 8.2 Prohibited degrees for a woman
Mother	Father
Daughter	Son
Father's mother	Father's father
Mother's mother	Mother's father
Son's daughter	Son's son
Daughter's daughter	Daughter's son
Sister	Brother
Father's sister	Father's brother
Mother's sister	Mother's brother
Brother's daughter	Brother's son
Sister's daughter	Sister's son

(b)   The Marriage (Prohibited Degrees of Relationship) Act 1986 prohibits a marriage between those listed in **Table 8.3** below until both parties are aged 21 or over, and provided that the younger party has not at any time before attaining the age of 18 been a child of the family in relation to the other party.

Table 8.3 Prohibited degrees

Daughter of former wife
Son of former husband
Former wife of father
Former husband of mother
Former wife of father's father
Former husband of father's mother
Former wife of mother's father
Former husband of mother's mother
Daughter of son of former wife
Son of son of former husband
Daughter of daughter of former wife
Son of daughter of former husband

(c)   The Marriage (Prohibited Degrees of Relationship) Act 1986 also prohibits a marriage between those listed in **Table 8.4** below.

Table 8.4 Prohibited degrees

Mother of former wife, until the death of both the former wife and the father of the former wife
Father of former husband, until after the death of both the former husband and the mother of the former husband
Former wife of son, until after the death of both his son and the mother of his son
Former husband of daughter, until after the death of both her daughter and the father of her daughter

8.3.5.4   The parties have met in person

Paragraph E-ECP.2.5 requires the applicant and his partner to have met in person. What does this mean?

The Home Office guidance, following *Meharban v ECO, Islamabad* [1989] Imm AR 57, is that 'met' requires the parties to have 'made the acquaintance of one another'. This need not have been in the context of marriage or a civil partnership. So if, for example, the parties had originally been childhood friends, perhaps going to the same school for several years, they may be said to have met in person and become acquainted.

'Met' implies a face-to-face meeting which results in the making of mutual acquaintance. There is a requirement of 'at least an appreciation by each party of the other in the sense of, for example, appearance and personality'. Therefore a relationship developed over the Internet by Facebook messages, Skype calls or the like would potentially satisfy this requirement, but only if it includes a personal face-to-face meeting between the couple which itself results in the making of their mutual acquaintance. Evidence of a face-to-face meeting might include travel documents, photographs, statements from witnesses, or relevant email or text message exchanges detailing meetings.

8.3.5.5   The relationship is genuine and subsisting

Paragraph E-ECP.2.6 requires the relationship between the applicant and his partner to be genuine and subsisting. Neither term is defined in the Immigration Rules or the Home Office guidance. However, in *GA ('Subsisting' marriage) Ghana* [2006] UKAIT 00046, the Tribunal held that the requirement that a relationship is subsisting requires more than just double-checking the legal status of that relationship. The nature and quality of the substance of the relationship – therefore including whether or not it is genuine – is under scrutiny. As the Tribunal indicated at para 14, this means that when assessing the subsistence of a relationship, the decision-maker:

> will plainly have to bear in mind the cultural context and the wide differences that exist between individual lifestyles, whether by choice, or by circumstances, or by economic necessity. He will also be able to put the claim into the context of the history of the relationship and to assess whether and to what extent this illuminates the nature of the parties' present relationship and future intentions.

Home Office guidance to its caseworkers is that they must be alert and sensitive to the extent to which religious and cultural practices may shape the factors present or absent in a particular case, particularly at the entry clearance and leave to remain stages. For example, a couple in an arranged marriage may have spent little, if any, time together prior to the marriage. For many faiths and cultures marriage marks the start of a commitment to a lifelong partnership and not the affirmation of a pre-existing partnership. Home Office guidance is that its caseworkers must also take into account normal practices for marriages and family living according to particular religious and cultural traditions. In particular, evidence of pre-marital cohabitation and joint living arrangements can be a factor associated with a genuine relationship; equally, their absence can be too. In some cultures it is traditional for the household accounts, bills, etc to be in the name of the male head of the household (who could be the male partner, or his father or grandfather).

Home Office guidance makes it clear that its caseworkers have discretion to grant or refuse an application based on their overall assessment, regardless of whether one or more of the factors contained in the guidance is, or is not, present in the case. As the guidance stresses, consideration of whether a relationship is genuine and subsisting is not a checklist or tick-box exercise.

It is for the applicant to show the requirement is met on the balance of probabilities: see *Naz (subsisting marriage – standard of proof) Pakistan* [2012] UKUT 00040.

In assessing whether a relationship is genuine and subsisting, Home Office guidance to its caseworkers as to what factors might be taken into account is as follows:

Factors which may be associated with a genuine and subsisting relationship

(i)   The couple are in a current, long-term relationship and are able to provide satisfactory evidence of this.

(ii)   The couple have been or are co-habiting and are able to provide satisfactory evidence of this.

(iii)   The couple have children together (biological, adopted or step-children) and shared responsibility for them.

(iv)   The couple share financial responsibilities, eg a joint mortgage/tenancy agreement, a joint bank account and/or joint savings, utility bills in both their names.

(v)   The partner and/or applicant have visited the other's home country and family and are able to provide evidence of this. (The fact that an applicant has never visited the UK must not be regarded as a negative factor, but it is a requirement of the Immigration Rules that the couple have met in person).

(vi)   The couple, or their families acting on their behalf, have made definite plans concerning the practicalities of the couple living together in the UK. In the case of an arranged marriage, the couple both consent to the marriage and agree with the plans made by their families.

Factors which may be associated with a relationship which is not genuine and subsisting

If a case contains one or more of the factors listed below, this may prompt additional scrutiny of the application but will not necessarily result in a negative decision. Caseworkers must continue to look at the circumstances of the case as a whole.

Even where additional scrutiny has been prompted by any of the following factors, it does not necessarily mean that the relationship is not genuine and subsisting.

The factors which may prompt additional scrutiny of an application include those listed below. Some factors may also, where specifically stated, lead to a refusal of an application without additional scrutiny but again, before deciding, caseworkers must continue to look at the circumstances as a whole:

(i)   If the marriage or civil partnership took place in the UK, a report – of a suspected sham marriage or civil partnership – was made by the registration service under section 24 of the Immigration and Asylum Act 1999.

(ii)   The applicant or partner makes a public statement that their marriage is a sham. An application can be refused on the basis of such a public statement alone.

(iii)   The applicant or partner makes a public statement (not in confidence) that they have been forced into marriage. An application can be refused on the basis of such a public statement alone.

(iv)   A sibling of the partner or applicant has been forced into marriage.

(v)   The applicant, partner or an immediate family member of either is or has been the subject or respondent of a forced marriage protection order under the Forced Marriage (Civil Protection) Act 1997 or the Forced Marriage etc (Protection and Jurisdiction) (Scotland) Act 1999.

An application can be refused on the basis alone of a current order involving the applicant or partner.

(vi)   There is evidence from a reliable third party (eg the Forced Marriage Unit, police, social services, registration service or a minister of religion) which indicates that the marriage is or may be a sham marriage or a forced marriage. (It may not be possible for this information to be used in any refusal notice). The fact that a third party indicates that in their opinion a marriage, partnership or relationship is genuine must not be afforded any weight.

(vii)   The applicant or partner does not appear to have the capacity to consent to the marriage, partnership or relationship, eg owing to learning difficulties, and independent evidence, eg from a social services assessment, has not been provided to confirm that such capacity exists.

(viii) There is evidence of unreasonable restrictions being placed on the applicant or partner, eg being kept at home by their family, being subject to unreasonable financial restrictions, attempts to prevent the police or other agencies having reasonable, unrestricted access to the applicant or partner.

(ix)   Failure by the applicant or partner to attend an interview, without reasonable explanation, where required to do so to discuss the application or their welfare, or seeking to undermine the ability of the [Home Office] to arrange an interview, eg by unreasonable delaying tactics by the couple or a third party.

(x)   The couple are unable to provide any information about their intended living arrangements in the UK or about the practicalities of the applicant moving to the UK.

(xi)   The circumstances of the wedding ceremony or reception, eg no or few guests and/or no significant family members present.

(xii)   The couple are unable to provide accurate personal details about each other (eg name, age, nationality, employment, parent's names and place of residence), provide inconsistent evidence, or do not have a shared understanding of the core facts of their relationship, eg how and where they met for the first time.

(xiii) The couple are unable to communicate with each other in a language understood by them both.

(xiv)   There is evidence of money having been exchanged for the marriage to be contracted (unless this is part of a dowry).

(xv)   There is a lack of appropriate contribution to the responsibilities of the marriage, partnership or relationship, eg a lack of shared financial or other domestic responsibilities.

(xvi)   Matrimonial co-habitation is not maintained (except where one party is working or studying away from home) or there is no evidence that they have ever co-habited since the marriage.

(xvii)   The applicant is a qualified medical practitioner or professional, or has worked as a nurse or carer, and the partner has a mental or physical impairment which currently requires medical assistance or personal care in their own accommodation.

(xviii) The partner has previously sponsored another partner to come to or remain in the UK.

(xix)   The partner has previously been sponsored as a partner to come to or remain in the UK (ie the partner has obtained settlement on this basis) and that marriage, partnership or relationship ended shortly after the partner obtained settlement. This excludes circumstances where the partner is a bereaved partner, or where the partner obtained settlement on the basis of domestic violence perpetrated by their former partner.

(xx)   If the partner was married to or in a partnership with the applicant at an earlier date, married or formed a partnership with another person, and is now sponsoring the original partner to come to or remain in the UK.

(xxi)   The past history of the partner and/or the applicant contains evidence of a previous sham marriage or forced marriage, or of unlawful residence in the UK or elsewhere.

(xxii)   The applicant has applied for leave to enter or remain in the UK in another category and been refused.

In this guidance 'additional scrutiny' means that where a caseworker has doubts that a relationship is genuine and subsisting, they must consider whether further information needs to be obtained, and the application investigated further, before they are able to make a decision on the case.

Also see **4.4.6.2**.

8.3.5.6 Valid marriage or civil partnership

Paragraph E-ECP.2.7 states that if the applicant and partner are married or in a civil partnership, it must be a valid marriage or civil partnership, as specified.

Home Office guidance is that the type of marriage must be recognised in the country in which it took place, it must satisfy the legal requirements of that country and there must not be anything in the law of either party's country of domicile that restricted their freedom to enter into the marriage.

Home Office guidance includes a list of countries where it recognises a civil partnership as valid.

8.3.5.7 Fiancé(e) or proposed civil partner entering UK for marriage or civil partnership

Paragraph E-ECP.2.8 states that if the applicant is a fiancé(e) or proposed civil partner, he must be seeking entry to the UK to enable his marriage or civil partnership to take place. The couple will usually need to produce adequate documentary evidence of the arrangements already made in the UK for the marriage or civil partnership ceremony.

8.3.5.8 Any previous relationship broken down permanently

Paragraph E-ECP.2.9 provides that if the applicant and/or his partner has previously been married or in a civil partnership, the applicant must provide suitable evidence that that relationship has ended (eg decree absolute of divorce, or dissolution order terminating a civil partnership), unless it is a polygamous marriage or civil partnership which falls within para 278(i) of the Immigration Rules. Home Office guidance includes further details.

8.3.5.9 Intention to live together permanently in the UK

By para E-ECP.2.10, the applicant and his partner must intend to live together permanently in the UK. Paragraph 6 of the Immigration Rules defines this as an intention to live together, evidenced by a clear commitment from both parties that they will live together permanently in the UK immediately following the outcome of the application in question or as soon as circumstances permit thereafter.

There is an obvious overlap here with the requirement in para E-ECP.2.6 that the relationship between the applicant and his partner is genuine and subsisting (see **8.3.5.5**), since a relationship that is found to be a sham is a relationship where the parties have no intention of living together at all.

A caseworker may question whether parties meet this requirement if they have lived apart following their marriage or civil partnership. Usually the couple will respond by producing an explanation for the separation, and details of letters sent and telephone calls made during this period, to illustrate their 'intervening devotion'.

In the case of *Amarjit Kaur* [1999] INLP 110, the Immigration Judge had found that the applicant's 'overriding wish was to marry someone from abroad. The letters and phone calls were evidence, not of intervening devotion, but merely of intervening contact'. No further evidence of letters or phone calls was produced to the Tribunal, and although the sponsor had visited his wife in India, the appeal was dismissed. The Immigration Judge had taken a dim view of the fact that the sponsor was a divorcée, 20 years older than the applicant, and that the applicant had turned down Indian-based suitors in order to marry the sponsor. The Tribunal did not demur from that.

Contrast *Amarjit Kaur* with the case of *Goudey (subsisting marriage – evidence) Sudan* [2012] UKUT 00041 (IAC). There the Tribunal concluded that the applicant and her partner were

> the right age for each other, and the [partner] as a young man would undoubtedly be of an age when he would want to have the company of a wife. She appears to have moved homes when the marriage was being arranged. He travelled to Egypt to meet his wife and there is some evidential support for the proposition given in his oral account that the relationship was conducted by telephone. We see no basis on which the judge could dismiss the consistent evidence that they intended to live together as man and wife as lacking in credibility.

The question whether parties intend to live together permanently in the UK is basically one of fact, and decisions often turn on the credibility of the available evidence.

8.3.6 Financial requirements (paras E-ECP.3.1 to 3.3)

8.3.6.1 Overview

When applying for entry clearance (and usually for leave to remain and settlement: see **8.4** and **8.6** respectively) the applicant will have to provide specified documentary evidence that a prescribed minimum gross annual income is available. Home Office guidance is that this sets a benchmark for financial stability and independence on the part of the couple. However, a different test will apply if the applicant's partner is at the time of the application in receipt of certain UK welfare benefits (see **8.3.6.9**).

To satisfy the financial requirement the applicant will have to meet all of the following:

(a)   the level of financial requirement applicable to the application under Appendix FM (see **8.3.6.2**); and

(b)   the requirements specified in Appendix FM and Appendix FM-SE as to:

(i)   the permitted sources of income and savings (see **8.3.6.3** to **8.3.6.7**);

(ii)   the time periods and permitted combinations of sources applicable to each permitted source relied on (see **8.3.6.3** to **8.3.6.7**); and

(iii)   the documentary evidence required for each permitted source relied upon (see **8.3.6.8**).

8.3.6.2 The prescribed minimum gross annual income

Currently, by para E-ECP.3.1, the applicant must provide specified evidence, from the sources listed in para E-ECP.3.2, of a specified gross annual income of at least £18,600.

What if the applicant's child or children will be living with the couple in the UK? An extra £3,800 is required for the first child and a further £2,400 for each additional child.

EXAMPLE

Ivan, a citizen of Russia, has recently married Judith, a British citizen. Ivan and his 8-year-old twin daughters, Olga and Nina, are applying under Appendix FM to the Immigration Rules to enter the UK where they will live with Judith and her 6-year-old son, Mark. What gross annual income must Ivan demonstrate?

The answer is £24,800 (£18,600 for Ivan; £3,800 for Olga; and £2,400 for Nina).

Note that for these purposes a child is defined by para E-ECP.3.1 as a dependent child of the applicant who is:

(a)   under the age of 18 years, or who was under the age of 18 years when first granted entry under this route;

(b)   applying for entry clearance or is in the UK as a dependant of the applicant;

(c)   not a British citizen or settled in the UK; and

(d)   not an EEA national with a right to remain in the UK under the 2006 Regulations.

Note that the set amount of £18,600 was held in *MM (Lebanon) v Secretary of State for the Home Department* [2013] EWHC 1900 (Admin) to disproportionately interfere with the ability of partners to live together contrary to their rights under the Article 8 ECHR. At the time of writing, the Government has indicated that it will appeal the decision.

8.3.6.3   Meeting the prescribed minimum gross annual income

Paragraph E-ECP.3.2 sets out the only financial resources that count, namely:

(a)   income of the partner (and/or the applicant if he is in the UK with permission to work and applying for leave to remain or settlement) from specified employment or self-employment);

(b)   specified pension income of the applicant and partner;

(c)   any specified maternity allowance or bereavement benefit received by the partner in the UK;

(d)   other specified income of the applicant and partner; and

(e)   specified savings of the applicant and partner.

It is clear from the above that certain financial resources on which a couple might wish to rely are excluded. Importantly, para E-ECP.3.2 has the effect of overruling the Supreme Court decision in *Ahmed Mahad (previously referred to as AM) (Ethiopia) v ECO* [2009] UKSC 16, as financial support from a third party, such as relatives or community groups, cannot be counted. If third parties wish to assist a couple, they might do so by gifting them money which can then count towards the couple's savings, provided it is received at least six months before the date of the application (see **Category D** below).

Home Office guidance is that the allowable financial resources can be used to meet the financial requirements in seven different possible ways, which it categorises A to G as follows.

Category A: salaried employment for the last six months

Where the applicant's partner (and/or the applicant if he is in the UK with permission to work and applying for leave to remain or settlement) is in salaried employment at the date of the application and has been with the same employer for at least the last six months, the applicant can count the gross annual salary (at its lowest level in those six months if there has been any increase) towards the financial requirement.

If necessary to meet the level of the financial requirement applicable to the application, the applicant can add to this, as permitted, from Categories C, D and E (see below).

> **EXAMPLE**
>
> The applicant's partner, Alan, is employed in the UK, earning £20,000 gross a year. He has worked for the same firm for over a year. The applicant has no dependent children. Alan should meet the financial requirement under Category A (subject to checking all his salary counts: see **8.3.6.4**).
>
> Note that if Alan had been promoted into his current role within the last six months from a salary of £18,000, he would not fall within Category A. Alan would either have to wait until he had completed six months at his new salary of £20,000, or, if relevant, use income from Categories C, D and E.

But what if the applicant's partner meets the above requirement in respect of salaried employment abroad and is returning with the applicant to the UK to take up employment here? In these circumstances the partner must also have confirmed salaried employment to return to in the UK, starting within three months of their return. This must have an annual starting salary sufficient to meet the financial requirement applicable to the application either alone or in combination with any, or all, of the items in Categories C, D and E as permitted.

For what counts as salaried employment, see **8.3.6.4**.

Category B: salaried employment for less than the last six months

Under Category B, salaried employment at the date of the application with the same employer but for less than the last six months counts in the same way as Category A above, but only if an additional test is met. The couple must also have received in the 12 months prior to the application the level of income required to meet the financial requirement based only on:

(a)   the gross salaried employment income of the applicant's partner (and/or the applicant if he is in the UK with permission to work and applying for leave to remain or settlement);

(b)   the gross amount of any specified non-employment income received by the applicant's partner, the applicant or both jointly;

(c)   the gross amount of any State (UK or foreign) or private pension received by the applicant's partner or the applicant; and/or

(d)   the gross amount of any UK maternity allowance, bereavement allowance, bereavement payment and widowed parent's allowance received by the applicant's partner or the applicant.

> **EXAMPLE**
>
> The applicant's partner, Brenda, is employed in the UK. She started her current employment last month. Her gross annual salary is £32,500. Over the last 12 months she has had two other salaried jobs and earned £28,750 from these in total. The applicant has no dependent children.
>
> Brenda will not qualify under Category A above as she has not been with the same employer for at least six months. However, she will qualify under Category B as she has earned more than £18,600 in the last 12 months from salaried employment and is currently in employment at a salary of at least £18,600. This is subject to checking that all her salary payments count: see **8.3.6.4**.

Category B operates differently where the applicant's partner is abroad and returning with the applicant to the UK to take up employment. The partner does not have to be in employment abroad at the date of application. Instead, the following two tests must be met.

First, the couple returning to the UK must have received in the 12 months prior to the application the level of income required to meet the financial requirement, based only on:

(a)   the gross salaried employment income overseas of the applicant's partner;

(b)   the gross amount of any specified non-employment income received by the applicant's partner, the applicant or both jointly;

(c)   the gross amount of any state (UK or foreign) or private pension received by the applicant's partner or the applicant; and/or

(d)   the gross amount of any UK maternity allowance, bereavement allowance, bereavement payment and widowed parent's allowance received by the applicant's partner or the applicant.

Secondly, the applicant's partner must in addition have confirmed salaried employment to return to in the UK (starting within three months of his return). This must have an annual starting salary sufficient to meet the financial requirement applicable to the application either alone or in combination with any, or all, of the items in Categories C, D and E as permitted.

For what counts as salaried employment, see **8.3.6.4**.

Category C: specified non-employment income

The specified non-employment income (see **8.3.6.5**) (excluding pension and allowances under Category E below) the applicant's partner and/or the applicant have/has received in the 12 months prior to the application can count towards the applicable financial requirement, provided they continue to own the relevant asset (eg property, shares, etc) at the date of application.

This income may also be used in combination with other categories as described.

Category D: cash savings

An amount based on any cash savings above £16,000 held by the applicant's partner, the applicant or both jointly for at least six months prior to the application and under their control, can count towards the applicable financial requirement.

At entry clearance and the leave to remain stages, the amount above £16,000 must be divided by 2.5 (to reflect the 2.5 year or 30-month period before the applicant will have to make a further application) to give the amount which can be used.

On an application for indefinite leave to remain, the whole of the amount above £16,000 can be used.

The amount based on cash savings may also be used in combination with other categories as described.

For further details, see **8.3.6.6**.

Category E: pension and allowances

The gross annual income from any State (UK basic State pension and additional or second State pension, or foreign) or private pension received by the applicant's partner or the applicant can count towards the applicable financial requirement. The annual amount may be counted where the pension has become a source of income at least 28 days prior to the application. This income can also be used in combination with other categories as described.

The gross amount of any State (UK or foreign) or private pension received by the applicant's partner or the applicant in the 12 months prior to the application can be used, alone or in combination with other income, for that period as described.

The gross amount of any UK maternity allowance, bereavement allowance, bereavement payment and widowed parent's allowance received by the applicant's partner or the applicant in the 12 months prior to the application can be used in combination with other income for that period as described.

Only the above UK welfare benefits count. So even if the applicant's partner receives other benefits, such as tax credits, child benefit, etc, these cannot count.

Category F: self-employment (last financial year)

The applicant's partner (and/or the applicant if he is in the UK with permission to work and applying for leave to remain or settlement) must be in self-employment at the date of the application and in the last full financial year received self-employment and other income (salaried, specified non-employment and pension) sufficient to meet the applicable financial requirement.

Note that cash savings cannot be used in combination with Category F.

> **EXAMPLE**
>
> The applicant's partner, Noel, is currently self-employed in the UK and in the last full financial year earned £20,575. The applicant has no dependent children.
>
> Noel will qualify under Category F as he is currently self-employed and in the last full financial year earned at least £18,600.

Category G: self-employment (last two financial years)

The applicant's partner (and/or the applicant if he is in the UK with permission to work and applying for leave to remain or settlement) must be in self-employment at the date of the application and as an average of the last two full financial years received self-employment and other income (salaried, specified non-employment and pension) sufficient to meet the applicable financial requirement.

Note that cash savings cannot be used in combination with Category G.

8.3.6.4 Further details about Categories A and B

For the purposes of Categories A and B, what counts as salaried employment?

Employment may be full-time or part-time. It can also be permanent, a fixed-term contract or with an agency.

Salary, basic pay, plus skills-based allowances and UK location-based allowances, eg London weighting, count as income. But any such allowances must form part of the contracted salary package and, if they exceed 30% of the total salary, only the amount which would correspond to 30% of the total salary will be counted towards the financial requirement. Overtime, commission-based pay and bonuses also count.

United Kingdom and overseas travel, subsistence and accommodation allowances, and allowances relating to the additional cost of living overseas cannot be included.

8.3.6.5 Further details about Category C

What income falls within Category C? The specified sources of non-employment income are:

(a)   dividends or other income from investments, stocks, shares, bonds and trust funds;

(b)   property rental income;

(c)   interest from savings; and

(d)   maintenance payments from a former partner in relation to the applicant and former partner's child or children dependent on and cared for by the applicant.

These sources of income must be in the name of the applicant's partner, the applicant or both jointly.

The relevant asset such as shares, bonds, property, etc must be held by the applicant's partner, the applicant or both jointly at the date of application.

In what circumstances can rent received from a property count? The property, whether in the UK or overseas, must be owned by the applicant's partner, the applicant or both jointly, and must not be their main residence (therefore income from a lodger in that residence cannot be counted). If the applicant's partner or applicant shares ownership of the property with a third party, only income received from the applicant's partner's and/or applicant's share of the property can be counted. Income from property which is rented out for only part of the year, eg a holiday let, can be counted. The equity in a property cannot be used to meet the financial requirement.

> **EXAMPLE**
>
> The applicant's partner, William, has been employed in the UK by the same employer for the last 12 months, earning £16,000 gross a year. He also receives £9,000 a year in rent from a house that he lets out. The house was left to him by his grandfather several years ago. It is in his sole name. The applicant has no dependent children.
>
> William should meet the financial requirement of £18,600 under a combination of Category A income of £16,000 (subject to checking all his salary counts: see **8.3.6.4**) and Category C income of £9,000, so totalling £25,000.

8.3.6.6 Further details about Category D

To be counted, the applicant's partner, the applicant or both jointly must have cash savings of more than £16,000, held by the applicant's partner, the applicant or both jointly (but not with a third party) for at least six months at the date of application and under their control.

Only the amount of cash savings *above* £16,000 can be counted against any shortfall in the £18,600 income threshold (see **8.3.6.2**) or the relevant higher figure where at least one child of the applicant is included (see **8.3.6.2**). How is this done? At the entry clearance and limited leave to remain stages, the amount above £16,000 is divided by 2.5 (to reflect the 2.5 year or 30-month period before the applicant will have to make a further application). On an application for settlement, the whole of the amount above £16,000 can be used.

> **EXAMPLE**
>
> Zach and Yvonne are engaged to be married. Zach is a visa national. Yvonne is a British citizen. The couple are living in Zach's home country but they now wish to travel to the UK to get married and set up home together. Zach has no dependent children.
>
> Zach applies for entry clearance under Appendix FM to the Immigration Rules as Yvonne's partner (fiancé). The couple have no income to count towards the financial requirement, but they do have £70,000 in cash savings which they have held in a joint account for at least the last six months. Will they qualify?
>
> Under Category D, Zach and Yvonne's cash savings exceed £16,000 by £54,000. That figure divided by 2.5 is £21,600. As they require £18,600, they meet the financial requirement, provided they can produce the specified documents for these cash savings.

The level of savings required to meet any shortfall income must be based on the level of employment-related and/or other income at the date of application.

Table 8.5 below sets out some examples of the minimum amount of savings required to meet a shortfall where £18,600 (applicant with no dependent children) is the prescribed minimum gross annual income.

Table 8.5 Minimum amount of savings required to meet shortfall

Income	Entry clearance and leave to enter or remain: minimum amount of savings required
No other relevant income	£62,500 (£16,000 + (shortfall of £18,600 x 2.5))
Other relevant income of £15,000	£25,000 (£16,000 + (shortfall of £3,600 x 2.5))
Other relevant income of £18,000	£17,500 (£16,000 + (shortfall of £600 x 2.5))

8.3.6.7 Further details about Categories F and G

What income from self-employment counts for the purposes of Categories F and G? Where the self-employed person is a sole trader, or is in a partnership or franchise agreement, the income taken into account is the gross taxable profits from that person's share of the business. Allowances or deductible expenses which are not taxed are not counted towards income. What if the self-employed person has set up his own registered company and is listed as a director of that company? The income that counts will then be any salary drawn from the post-tax profits of the company.

8.3.6.8 Specified documents

Full details of the documents that must be produced in order to meet the financial requirement are set out in Appendix FM-SE to the Immigration Rules.

8.3.6.9 When applicant is exempt a maintenance test applies

By para E-ECP.3.3(a), the applicant is exempt from the financial requirement if the applicant's partner is receiving one or more of the following UK welfare benefits:

(a)   disability living allowance or personal independence payment;

(b)   severe disablement allowance;

(c)   industrial injury disablement benefit;

(d)   attendance allowance; or

(e)   carer's allowance.

Para 12 of Appendix FM-SE requires the applicant to produce official documentation from the DfWP confirming the entitlement to the relevant benefit or allowance and the amount received, as well as at least one personal bank statement showing payment of the benefit or allowance into the partner's account.

If the applicant is exempt from the financial requirement then, by para E-ECP.3.3(b), the applicant must provide evidence that his partner is able to maintain and accommodate himself, the applicant and any dependants adequately in the UK without recourse to public funds. As to public funds, see **3.3.2**; and as to accommodation, see **8.3.7**. By para 6 of the Immigration Rules, 'adequately' in relation to this maintenance requirement means that, after income tax, National Insurance contributions and housing costs have been deducted, there must be available to the family the level of income that would be available to them if the family was in receipt of income support.

Home Office guidance to its caseworkers is that the following five steps should be taken:

Step 1   Establish the applicant's partner's (and/or the applicant's if he is in the UK with permission to work and applying for leave to remain or settlement) current income. The gross income should be established and if the income varies, an average should be calculated.

Income from disability benefits can be included as income. Job offers or the prospects of employment are not taken into account.

Promises of third party support are not acceptable as Home Office guidance is that the applicant and his partner must have the required resources under their own control, not somebody else's.

Evidence of employment might include wage slips, a letter from the employer (confirming the employment and annual salary) and bank statements showing where the salary has been paid in.

Evidence of income from benefits received by the applicant's partner, such as disability benefits, may include the notice of award, but the best evidence will be the applicant's partner's bank statement showing where it has been paid into the account (see *Ahmed (benefits: proof of receipt; evidence) Bangladesh* [2013] UKUT 84 (IAC)).

Step 2   Establish the applicant's partner's current housing costs from the evidence provided.

Step 3   Deduct the housing costs from the gross income.

Step 4   Calculate how much the family would receive if they were on income support.

Note that the income support level in 2013/14 was £112.55 a week for a couple and £65.62 a week for a child.

Step 5   The gross income after deduction of housing costs must equal or exceed the income support rate.

Note that if on making any future application for leave or settlement the applicant's partner no longer receives an exempting welfare benefit, the financial requirement (**8.3.6.2**) will apply instead, unless para EX.1 then applies (see **8.5**).

8.3.7   Accommodation requirements (para E-ECP.3.4)

8.3.7.1   Adequate accommodation

By para E-ECP.3.4, the applicant must provide evidence that there will be adequate accommodation, without recourse to public funds, for the family, including other family members who are not included in the application but who live in the same household, which the family own or occupy exclusively.

Accommodation is not regarded as adequate if it is, or will be, overcrowded (or it contravenes public health regulations).

8.3.7.2   Owned or occupied exclusively

The couple will have to provide documentary evidence where the property is either owned or rented by them. This may be in the form of a letter from their mortgagee, if the property was bought with the aid of a mortgage, a copy of the property deeds and, in the case of rented accommodation, a rent book and tenancy agreement.

Where the accommodation is rented from a local authority or housing association, correspondence from the landlord is normally regarded as genuine and sufficient by the Home Office.

Can a third party provide accommodation for the couple? Yes, provided it is a firm arrangement. In *AB (Third-party provision of accommodation)* [2008] UKAIT 00018, the sponsor wife was living in premises provided by a relative. She contributed to the household bills but did not pay any rent. The relative was happy for this arrangement to continue if she was joined by her husband. The Tribunal indicated that the mere mention of a relative or friend who was prepared to accommodate the parties was probably not enough, but a real and stable arrangement for accommodation provided by another might be. In this case the offer of accommodation was a real and stable one. It was credible and practical, and satisfied the requirement. In these circumstances it obviously helps if the third party supplies a statement setting out the accommodation arrangements.

If the accommodation is not owned but shared, para 6 of the Immigration Rules provides that 'occupy exclusively' in relation to accommodation means that part of the property must be for the exclusive use of the family. But what does this mean in practice? In KJ ('Own or occupy exclusively') Jamaica [2008] UKAIT 00006, the Tribunal observed that

> it is clear that it cannot mean either 'alone' nor 'with a legal right to exclude all others' ... it ought not to be enough for an applicant to say that he will be accommodated by a series of friends allowing him to sleep on sofas, or that he has enough money to put up his dependants in hotels from time to time, or that he or they will find space in hostels. What appears to be required is that there is somewhere that the person or people in question can properly, albeit without any legal accuracy, describe as their own home. They may not own it; and they may share it; but it is adequate for them, it is in a defined place, and it is properly regarded as where they live, with the implications of stability that that phrase implies. (per Mr CMG Ockelton, Deputy President, at para 9)

Home Office guidance is that where accommodation is shared with other family members, use of a separate bedroom or bedrooms may suffice.

8.3.7.3 Overcrowding

The Housing Act 1985 (HA 1985), s 324 contains two tests to determine whether or not accommodation is overcrowded. If by coming to live in the property the applicant will cause it to be overcrowded under either test, the application will fail. The relevant law is as follows:

324   Definition of overcrowding

A dwelling is overcrowded for the purposes of this Part when the number of persons sleeping in the dwelling is such as to contravene—

(a)   the standard specified in section 325 (the room standard), or

(b)   the standard specified in section 326 (the space standard).

325   The room standard

(1)   The room standard is contravened when the number of persons sleeping in a dwelling and the number of rooms available as sleeping accommodation is such that two persons of opposite sexes who are not living together as husband and wife must sleep in the same room.

(2)   For this purpose—

(a)   children under the age of ten shall be left out of account, and

(b)   a room is available as sleeping accommodation if it is of a type normally used in the locality either as a bedroom or as a living room.

326   The space standard

(1)   The space standard is contravened when the number of persons sleeping in a dwelling is in excess of the permitted number, having regard to the number and floor area of the rooms of the dwelling available as sleeping accommodation.

(2)   For this purpose—

(a)   no account shall be taken of a child under the age of one and a child aged one or over but under ten shall be reckoned as one-half of a unit, and

(b)   a room is available as sleeping accommodation if it is of a type normally used in the locality either as a living room or as a bedroom.

(3)   The permitted number of persons in relation to a dwelling is the number specified in the following Table but no account shall be taken for the purposes of the Table of a room having a floor area of less than 50 square feet.

Table

Number of rooms	Number of persons
1	2
2	3
3	5
4	7.5
5	10
6 or more	2 persons for each room

As you will have noted, the first test is called 'the room standard'. It means that a property is overcrowded if two people aged 10 or more of the opposite sex, other than the applicant and the applicant's partner, have to sleep in the same room. The second test is 'the space standard'. Basically, this determines whether or not the number of people sleeping in the property exceeds that permitted by the Act. The table sets out the limits. The applicant can meet the accommodation requirement only if both tests are satisfied.

EXAMPLE

Ian, a widower, lives in a house with three rooms that can be used for sleeping. Living with him is his son, Lionel, aged 12, and his daughter, Diane, aged 13. Ian's mother, Mary, also lives with them. Ian recently travelled to Moscow and married Vika, a Russian national. Will the house be overcrowded if she is allowed to join Ian in the UK?

First, apply the room standard and answer the question: who can sleep in each room?

By HA 1985, s 325(1), Ian and Vika, as husband and wife, can share one room.

In light of HA 1985, s 325(1) and (2)(a), Lionel, aged 12, and Diane, aged 13, as two persons of 10 years old or more of the opposite sex, cannot share. So they must be in separate rooms. The house will not be overcrowded, therefore, if Diane shares with Mary (two persons of 10 years old or more but of the same sex) and Lionel has a room of his own.

Secondly, apply the space standard and answer the question: will the permitted number of persons for this property be exceeded?

Here, with three rooms available to sleep in, the limit under HA 1985, s 326(3) is five persons, and that will not be exceeded as there will be only five people in the household if Vika joins them, namely, Ian (an adult counts as one), Vika (an adult counts as one), Lionel (aged 12, so 10 years old or more and counts as one), Diane (aged 12, so 10 years old or more and counts as one) and Mary (an adult counts as one).

A check should be made that each of the three rooms has a floor area of at least 50 square feet for the purposes of HA 1985, s 326(3).

8.3.8 English language requirement (para E-ECP.4.1)

8.3.8.1 Meeting the requirement

By para E-ECP.4.1, the applicant will meet the English language requirement if he provides specified evidence that he:

(a) is a national of a Home Office-designated majority English-speaking country (see **7.4.3.2**);

(b) has an academic qualification recognised by NARIC UK to be equivalent to the standard of a Bachelor's or Master's degree or PhD in the UK, which was taught in English (see **7.4.3.3**);

(c)   has passed an English language test in speaking and listening at a minimum of level A1 of the Common European Framework of Reference for Languages with a provider approved by the Home Office. A list of Home Office-approved tests can be found in Appendix O to the Immigration Rules; or

(d)   is exempt from the English language requirement (see **8.3.8.2**).

The requirement does not breach Article 8 ECHR: see R *(on the application of Bibi) v Secretary of State for the Home Department* [2013] EWCA Civ 322.

8.3.8.2   Exempt from English language requirement

By para E-ECP.4.2, the applicant is exempt from the requirement to provide a suitable English language test certificate if at the date of the application he is is aged 65 or over, or has a disability (physical or mental condition) which prevents him from meeting the requirement, or if there are exceptional compassionate circumstances which prevent him from meeting the requirement prior to entering the UK.

Home Office guidance is that exemption applies only where someone has a physical or mental impairment which prevents him from learning English and/or taking a test. This is not a blanket exemption, as some disabled people are capable of learning English and taking an English test. So the exemption is granted only on production of satisfactory medical evidence from a medical practitioner who is qualified in the appropriate field, which specifies the disability and from which it may be concluded that exemption is justified.

What exceptional compassionate circumstances might lead to exemption? Home Office guidance is that the applicant must demonstrate that as a result of his circumstances he is unable to access facilities for learning English before coming to the UK. Evidence of an inability to attend, prior or previous attendance, or attempts to access learning must be clearly provided. This evidence must be provided by an independent source, eg from an appropriately qualified medical practitioner, or alternatively must be independently verified by a caseworker.

Home Office guidance is that situations which might, subject to receipt of all necessary evidence in support, lead a caseworker to conclude that the applicant can properly claim exceptional compassionate circumstances, include the following:

(a)   if the applicant's partner in the UK is seriously ill and requires immediate support or care from the applicant whilst receiving medical attention in the UK, and there is insufficient time for the applicant to access learning and/or to take a test; and

(b)   where a country or region is affected by conflict or humanitarian disaster, the Home Office will consider whether the situation makes it unreasonable for individuals to learn English and/or to take a test. In such circumstances a caseworker will consider the nature of the situation, including the infrastructure affected, and whether it would be proportionate to expect an applicant to meet the English language requirement.

It will be extremely rare for exceptional circumstances to apply when the applicant is applying in the UK for leave to remain, as applicants already here will have access to a wide variety of facilities for learning English.

Financial reasons, or claims of illiteracy or limited education are not acceptable to the Home Office.

Applicants who are nationals of a country with no test centre and who have made an application for entry clearance from that country are exempt from the requirement.

Note that if an applicant has been granted an exemption due to exceptional compassionate circumstances at entry clearance, he will be required to meet the English language requirement when he applies for further leave to remain after 30 months.

8.3.9 Decision on application

By para D-ECP.1.1, only an applicant who meets the requirements for entry clearance as a partner will be granted entry clearance. This will be for an initial period not exceeding 33 months and subject to a condition of no recourse to public funds. However, if the applicant is a fiancé(e) or proposed civil partner, the applicant will be granted entry clearance for a period not exceeding six months and subject to a condition of no recourse to public funds and a prohibition on employment.

By para D-ECP.1.2, where the applicant does not meet the requirements for entry clearance as a partner the application will be refused.

8.4 LEAVE TO REMAIN IN THE UK AS A PARTNER

8.4.1 Who can apply?

There are six different situations to be considered here, namely:

(a)   where a person entered the UK as a partner under Appendix FM and now seeks an extension of his limited leave for a further 30 months;

(b)   where a person entered the UK as a fiancé(e) or proposed civil partner under Appendix FM and now, following marriage or civil partnership, applies to switch to the category of a partner under Appendix FM;

(c)   where a person is in the UK in a different immigration category has married or entered into a civil partnership and now wishes to switch to the category of a partner under Appendix FM;

(d)   where a person switched in the UK to the category of a partner under Appendix FM and now applies for an extension of his limited leave for a further 30 months;

(e)   where a person wishes to start on the 10-year family route to settlement under Appendix FM (see **8.1.2.3**) by relying on his Article 8 ECHR rights under para EX.1 (see **8.5**). This application might be made, for example, by an overstayer who has married a British citizen or a person settled in the UK, and who otherwise faces administrative removal from the UK (see **10.4**);

(f)   where a person is on the 10-year family route to settlement under Appendix FM and now seeks an extension of his limited leave for a further 30 months.

8.4.2 An overview of the requirements

The requirements in Appendix FM to be met for leave to remain as a partner (see para R-LTRP.1.1) are that:

(a)   the applicant and his partner must be in the UK;

(b)   the applicant must have made a valid application for limited or indefinite leave to remain as a partner; and either

(c)   (i)   the applicant must not fall for refusal under Section S-LTR: Suitability – leave to remain, and

     (ii)   the applicant meets all of the requirements of Section E-LTRP: Eligibility for limited leave to remain as a partner;

    or

(d)   (i)   the applicant must not fall for refusal under Section S-LTR: Suitability – leave to remain, and

     (ii)   the applicant meets the eligibility requirements of paras E-LTRP.1.2–1.12 and E-LTRP.2.1, and

     (iii)   para EX.1 applies.

The suitability requirements are detailed at **8.4.3**, the eligibility requirements at **8.4.4** and para EX.1 at **8.5**.

8.4.3   Suitability requirements

Paragraphs S-LTR.1.2–1.7 and S-LTR.2.2–2.4 set out respectively the mandatory and discretionary grounds on which the Home Office will normally refuse an application. You will see that broadly these are the same as for entry clearance (see **8.3.3**).

S-LTR.1.2   The applicant is at the date of application the subject of a deportation order.

S-LTR.1.3   The presence of the applicant in the UK is not conducive to the public good because he has been convicted of an offence for which he has been sentenced to imprisonment for at least four years.

S-LTR.1.4   The presence of the applicant in the UK is not conducive to the public good because he has been convicted of an offence for which he has been sentenced to imprisonment for less than four years but at least 12 months.

S-LTR.1.5   The presence of the applicant in the UK is not conducive to the public good because, in the view of the Secretary of State, his offending has caused serious harm or he is a persistent offender who shows a particular disregard for the law.

S-LTR.1.6   The presence of the applicant in the UK is not conducive to the public good because his conduct (including convictions which do not fall within paras S-LTR.1.3–1.5), character, associations, or other reasons, make it undesirable to allow him to remain in the UK.

S-LTR.1.7   The applicant has failed without reasonable excuse to comply with a requirement to attend an interview; provide information; provide physical data; or undergo a medical examination or provide a medical report.

S-LTR.2.2   Whether or not to the applicant's knowledge: (a) false information, representations or documents have been submitted in relation to the application (including false information submitted to any person to obtain a document used in support of the application); or (b) there has been a failure to disclose material facts in relation to the application.

S-LTR.2.3   One or more relevant NHS body has notified the Secretary of State that the applicant has failed to pay charges in accordance with the relevant NHS regulations on charges to overseas visitors and the outstanding charges have a total value of at least £1,000.

S-LTR.2.4   A maintenance and accommodation undertaking has been requested under para 35 of the Rules and has not been provided.

Note that when the Secretary of State is considering whether the presence of the applicant in the UK is not conducive to the public good (see S-LTR.1.3–1.6 above), any legal or practical reasons why the applicant cannot presently be removed from the UK must be ignored.

8.4.4   Overview of eligibility requirements

If an applicant meets all of the eligibility requirements in paras E-LTRP.1.2–4.2, he may be granted limited leave to remain and proceed on the five-year family route to settlement. Alternatively, if the applicant can meet the eligibility requirements of paras E-LTRP.1.2–1.12 and E-LTRP.2.1, and also meets para EX.1 (see **8.5** below), he may be granted limited leave to remain and proceed on the 10-year family route to settlement.

The eligibility requirements are as follows:

(a)   relationship requirements (see **8.4.5**);

(b)   immigration requirements (see **8.4.6**);

(c)   financial requirements (see **8.4.7**);

(d)   accommodation requirements (see **8.4.8**); and

(e)   English language requirement (see **8.4.9**).

8.4.5 Relationship requirements

Paras E-LTRP.1.2–1.10 set out the same relationship requirements as for entry clearance (see **8.3.5**). Note that para E-LTRP.1.10 provides, in addition, that the applicant must produce evidence that, since entry clearance as a partner was granted or since the last grant of limited leave to remain as a partner, the applicant and his partner have lived together in the UK, or there is good reason, consistent with a continuing intention to live together permanently in the UK, for any period in which they have not done so.

Note that para E-LTRP.1.11 provides that if the applicant is in the UK with leave as a fiancé(e) or proposed civil partner and the marriage or civil partnership did not take place during that period of leave, there must be good reason why it did not, and evidence must be produced that it will take place within the next six months. In those circumstances any further leave will be for six months only and subject to a condition of no recourse to public finds and a prohibition on employment.

Paragraph E-LTRP.1.12 provides that the applicant's partner cannot be the applicant's fiancé(e) or proposed civil partner, unless the applicant was granted entry clearance as that person's fiancé(e) or proposed civil partner.

8.4.6 Immigration requirements

Paragraph E-LTRP.2.1 excludes certain people already in the UK from switching into this category, namely, a visitor (see **Chapter 5**), or a person with valid leave granted for a period of six months or less, unless that leave is as a fiancé(e) or proposed civil partner, or a person on temporary admission (see **3.5.5**).

By para E-LTRP.2.2, the applicant must not be in the UK in breach of immigration laws (disregarding any period of overstaying for a period of 28 days or less), unless para EX. 1 applies (see **8.5**).

8.4.7 Financial requirements

Generally, by paras E-LTRP.3.1–3.3 the same financial provisions apply as for entry clearance (see **8.3.6**). The key differences to note are as follows:

(a)   Income from specified lawful employment or self-employment (Categories A, B, F and G – see **8.3.6.3**) of the applicant can now be included to meet the financial requirement, provided he is in the UK with permission to work. The only partner prohibited from working is a fiancé(e) or proposed civil partner.

EXAMPLE

Luke is a visa national. Over two years ago he entered the UK as the partner (spouse) of Rachel, a British citizen. He was accompanied by his dependent child, Ambrose. Luke and Ambrose are now applying for leave to remain for a further 30 months under Appendix FM to the Immigration Rules. The financial requirement Luke must meet is a minimum gross annual income of £22,400 (ie £18,600 for himself and £3,800 for Ambrose).

Both Rachel and Luke have had the same jobs for over a year. Luke produces the specified documents evidencing the following financial resources: his annual salary from employment of £11,750, plus Rachel's annual salary from employment of £13,250. Together that totals £25,000 and so the minimum gross annual income is met.

(b)   An applicant does not have to meet the financial requirement, nor the alternative maintenance test (see **8.3.6.9**) if para EX.1 applies (see **8.5**).

8.4.8   Accommodation requirements

By para E-LTRP.3.4, the same accommodation provisions apply as for entry clearance (see **8.3.7**) unless para EX.1 applies (see **8.5**).

8.4.9   English language requirement

If the applicant has not already met this requirement in a previous application for leave as a partner, the applicant must now do so unless para EX.1 applies (see **8.5**). The details are the same as for entry clearance (see **8.3.8**).

8.4.10   Decision on application

If the applicant meets all the requirements he will be granted limited leave to remain for a period not exceeding 30 months and subject to a condition of no recourse to public funds. The applicant will be eligible to apply for settlement after a continuous period of at least 60 months (five years) with such leave (see **8.6**). This includes any period spent in the UK with entry clearance as a partner under para D-ECP1.1, but does not include any period of entry clearance or limited leave as a fiancé(e) or proposed civil partner.

A fiancé(e) or proposed civil partner will be able to work only once he has received notification from the Home Office that his application for leave to remain has been granted.

If the applicant can meet the suitability requirements, the eligibility requirements of paras E-LTRP.1.2–1.12 (the relationship requirements at **8.4.5**) and E-LTRP.2.1 (the first immigration requirement at **8.4.6**), and para EX.1 (see **8.5**) applies, he will be granted leave to remain for a period not exceeding 30 months. This will be subject to a condition of no recourse to public funds (unless there are exceptional circumstances set out in the application which require access to public funds to be granted on grounds of destitution). He will be eligible to apply for settlement after a continuous period of at least 120 months (10 years) with such leave (see **8.6**). This includes any period spent in the UK with entry clearance as a partner under para D-ECP1.1, but does not include any period of entry clearance or limited leave as a fiancé(e) or proposed civil partner.

8.5   PARAGRAPH EX.1

If the applicant can meet the suitability requirements (**8.4.3**) and the eligibility requirements of paras E-LTRP.1.2-1.12 (the relationship requirements at **8.4.5**) and E-LTRP.2.1 (the first immigration requirement at **8.4.6**), the application will be granted if para EX.1 applies. Broadly, this allows an applicant to remain in the UK on the basis of his family life with a child and/or a partner if it would breach Article 8 ECHR to remove the applicant. In these circumstances the applicant will have a longer route to settlement, namely 10 years, granted in four periods of 30 months' limited leave, with a fifth application for indefinite leave to remain.

Note that if the applicant is being deported having committed a criminal offence or criminal offences in the UK, and so does not meet the suitability requirements at **8.4.3**, then different considerations will apply instead of para EX.1: see **10.3.4**.

Further note that if the applicant is liable to being removed from the UK, perhaps as an overstayer, he may still meet the suitability requirements at **8.4.3**, and para EX.1 will then apply: see **10.4.6**.

8.5.1   Family life in UK with a child

Paragraph EX.1 applies if the applicant has a genuine and subsisting parental relationship with a child (under the age of 18 years) who is in the UK, who is a British citizen or who has lived in the UK continuously for at least the seven years immediately preceding the date of application, and it would not be reasonable to expect that child to leave the UK.

8.5.1.1 Genuine and subsisting parental relationship

Home Office guidance to its caseworkers is that when considering whether the relationship is genuine and subsisting, the following questons are likely to be relevant:

(a) Does the applicant have a parental relationship with the child? What is the relationship – biological, adopted, step-child, legal guardian? Is the applicant the child's *de facto* primary carer?

(b) Is it a genuine and subsisting relationship? Does the child live with the person? Where does the applicant live in relation to the child? How regularly do they see one another? Are there any relevant court orders governing access to the child?

(c) Is there any evidence or other relevant information provided within the application, eg the views of the child or other family members, or from social work or other relevant professionals? To what extent is the applicant making an active contribution to the child's life?

Factors which might prompt closer scrutiny include:

(a) that there is little or no contact with the child, or contact is irregular;

(b) any contact is only recent in nature;

(c) support is only financial in nature, there is no contact or emotional or welfare support;

(d) the child is largely independent of the person.

8.5.1.2 Child is a British citizen or been in the UK for a continuous period of seven years

Home Office guidance is that its caseworkers should establish the age and nationality of each child affected by the decision, and where they are foreign nationals their immigration history in the UK, eg how long they have lived in the UK and where they lived before.

In establishing whether a non-British citizen child has been in the UK continuously for more than seven years, the time spent in the UK with and without valid leave can be included. Short periods outside the UK, for example for holidays or family visits, would not count as a break in the seven years required. However, where a child has spent more than six months out of the UK at any one time, this normally should count as a break in continuous residence unless any exceptional factors apply.

8.5.1.3 It would be unreasonable to expect the child to leave the UK

If the child is a British citizen, the applicant is the child's primary carer and there is no other parent, guardian or carer on whom the child is dependent or who could care for the child if the primary carer left the UK, the applicant will have a right of residence under EU law (*Zambrano v Office national de l'emploi* (ONEm) (Case C-34/09) [2011] 2 CMLR 46) (see **4.4.13** and **10.5.2**). In these circumstances the Home Office's European case working team will review the case and, if the claim is established, issue the appropriate documentation.

If the child is a British citizen but *Zambrano* does not apply, the Home Office normally accepts that it would be unreasonable for the child to leave the UK with the applicant where the applicant would be returned to a country outside of the EU. Home Office guidance is that leave to remain may be refused where the conduct of one of the parents gives rise to considerations of such weight as to justify separation, provided the British citizen child could otherwise stay with another parent or primary carer in the UK. The circumstances envisaged by the Home Office include minor criminality falling below the thresholds set out in para 398 of the Immigration Rules (see **10.3.4**) and/or a poor immigration history. In considering whether refusal may be appropriate caseworkers need to consider the impact on the child of any separation.

Where the child is a British citizen, *Zambrano* does not apply and the applicant would be returned to a country in the EU, the Home Office applies the factors at **8.5.1.4** below.

8.5.1.4   Non-British citizen child has been in the UK for more than seven years

The Home Office states that the seven-year threshold recognises that over time children start to put down roots and integrate into life in the UK, to the extent that being required to leave the UK may be unreasonable. It directs its caseworkers to consider whether in the specific circumstances of the case it would be reasonable to expect the child to live in another country. Caseworkers must consider the facts for each child within that family and for the family in the round. They should also engage with any issues explicitly raised by the family, or by or behalf of each child. Relevant considerations are likely to include:

(a) whether there would be a significant risk to the child's health, for example if there is evidence that the child is undergoing a course of treatment for a life- threatening or serious illness and treatment is not likely to be available in the country of return;

(b) whether the child would be leaving with its parent(s). It is generally the case that it is in a child's best interests to remain with its parents. Unless specific factors apply, it will generally not be unreasonable to expect a child to leave the country with its parents, particularly if the parents have no right to remain in the UK;

(c) the extent to which the child is dependent on any wider family members in the UK;

(d) whether the child is likely to be able to (re)integrate readily into life in the country where the parent would be sent. Relevant factors weighing in favour of successful (re)integration include:

(i) whether the parent(s) or child is a citizen of the country and so able to enjoy the full rights of being a citizen in that country,

(ii) whether the parents and/or child have lived in or visited the country before for periods of more than a few weeks. The question here is whether, having visited or lived in the country before, the child would be able to adapt and/or the parents would be able to support the child in adapting to life in the country,

(iii) whether the child or parents have existing family or social ties with the country. A person who has extended family or networks of friends should be able to rely on them for support to help reintegrate on return,

(iv) whether the child or parents have relevant cultural ties to the country Caseworkers should consider any evidence of exposure to and the level of understanding of the cultural norms in the country. For example, a period of time spent living mainly amongst a diaspora from the country may in and of itself give a child an awareness of the culture in the country,

(v) whether the child can speak, read and write in a language of that country, or is likely to achieve this within a reasonable time period. Fluency is not required – an ability to communicate competently with sympathetic interlocutors would normally suffice,

(vi) whether the child has attended school in that country;

(e) any country-specific risks (reference should be made to any relevant country guidance – see **9.7**);

(f) other specific factors raised by, or on behalf of, the child.

Families or children may highlight the differences in quality of education, health and wider public services, and economic or social opportunities between the UK and the country of origin, and argue that these work against the best interests of the child. Home Office guidance is that other than in exceptional circumstances, this would not normally be regarded as a relevant consideration, particularly if the parent(s) or wider family have the means or resources to support the child on return, or the skills, education and training to provide for their family on return.

8.5.1.5 Exceptional factors

If para EX.1 does not apply the application is normally be refused. However, the Home Office accepts that there may be exceptional factors which would make refusal unreasonable. Its caseworkers should consider any other exceptional factors raised in relation to the child's best interests and question whether refusal is still appropriate in light of those factors. In some cases it may be appropriate to grant leave on a short-term temporary basis to enable particular issues relating to the child's welfare to be addressed before return.

Home Office guidance is that whilst all cases are to an extent unique, those unique factors do not generally render them exceptional. Furthermore, a case is not exceptional just because the exceptions to para EX.1 have been missed by a small margin. Rather, the Immigration Rules establish the thresholds as determining when leave would be appropriate bar other factors. However, in assessing exceptionality the matters identified in para EX.1 need to be considered along with all other aspects of the case. The decision maker then needs to determine whether removal would have such severe consequences for the child that exceptionally refusal or return is not appropriate. Finally, the decision maker should be prepared to take into account any order made by the UK Family Court, but that is not determinative of the immigration decision. However, the judgment of the family court, with all the tools at its disposal (including the assistance of the Children and Family Court Advisory and Support Service (CAFCASS) and the opportunity to assess all the adults), could and should inform the decision maker: see *Mohan v Secretary of State for the Home Department* [2012] EWCA Civ 1363.

8.5.2 Family life in UK with a partner

Paragraph EX.1 additionally, or alternatively, applies if the applicant has a genuine and subsisting relationship (see **8.3.5.5**) with a partner who is in the UK and who is a British citizen, settled in the UK, or in the UK with refugee leave or humanitarian protection, and there are insurmountable obstacles to family life with that partner continuing outside the UK.

8.5.2.1 Insurmountable obstacles

In determining whether there are 'insurmountable obstacles', the decision maker should consider the seriousness of the difficulties which the applicant and his partner would face in continuing their family life outside the UK, and whether they entail something that could not, or could not reasonably be expected to, be overcome, even with a degree of hardship for one or more of the individuals concerned.

Home Office guidance is that the decision maker should look at whether there is an inability to live in the country concerned. The focus should also be on the family life which would be enjoyed in the country to which the applicant would be returned, not a comparison to the life they would enjoy were they to remain in the UK.

Lack of knowledge of a language spoken in the country in which the couple would be required to live would not usually amount to an insurmountable obstacle. Why? The Home Office states that it is reasonable to conclude that the couple must have been conversing in a commonly understood language whilst in the UK. Therefore, it is reasonable for that to continue outside the UK, whether or not the partner seeks to learn a – or the – language spoken in the country of proposed return.

The Home Office states that factors which might be relevant to the consideration of whether an insurmountable obstacle exists include, but are not limited to, the following:

(a)   The ability of the family to enter and stay in the country lawfully. The onus is on the applicant to show that this is not possible in order for this to amount to an insurmountable obstacle. A mere wish, desire or preference to live in the UK is not relevant.

(b)   Any cultural and religious barriers to living in the country. This might be relevant in situations where the partner would be so disadvantaged as for it to be unreasonable to expect him to live in that country. The test is a high one. It must be a barrier which either cannot be overcome or is unreasonable to expect a person to overcome.

(c)   The impact of a mental or physical disability. Whether or not either party has a mental or physical disability, a move to another country may involve a normal period of hardship as the person adjusts to his new surroundings. But a physical or mental disability could in some circumstances mean that the degree of hardship which would be experienced by the person would be unreasonable to the extent that it amounts to an insurmountable obstacle.

8.5.2.2   Exceptional circumstances

Where the applicant does not meet the requirements set out above, refusal of the application will be appropriate. However, leave may be granted outside the Rules where exceptional circumstances apply.

The Home Office decision maker needs to determine whether refusal or removal would have such severe consequences for the individual that this would not be proportionate given the nature of his family life, notwithstanding the fact that there are no insurmountable obstacles to family life with the applicant's partner continuing outside the UK. Home Office guidance is that is likely to be the case only very rarely.

In determining whether there are exceptional circumstances, the decision maker must consider all relevant factors, such as the following:

(a)   The circumstances around the applicant's entry to the UK and the proportion of the time he has been in the UK legally as opposed to illegally. Did he form his relationship with his partner at a time when he had no immigration status or this was precarious? Family life which involves the applicant putting down roots in the UK in the full knowledge that his stay here is unlawful or precarious should be given less weight, when balanced against the factors weighing in favour of removal, than family life formed by a person lawfully present in the UK.

(b)   Cumulative factors should be considered. For example, where the applicant has family members in the UK but his family life does not provide a basis for staying and he has a significant private life in the UK. Although under the Rules family life and private life are considered separately, when considering whether there are exceptional circumstances private and family life should be taken into account.

If the application is granted because exceptional circumstances apply, leave outside the Immigration Rules for a period of 30 months is usually given.

8.6   INDEFINITE LEAVE TO REMAIN (SETTLEMENT) AS A PARTNER

8.6.1   Who can apply?

There are two different situations to be considered here, namely:

(a)   where a person has completed the five-year family route to settlement, ie two periods of 30 months' leave in the UK as a partner; and

(b)   where a person has completed the 10-year family route to settlement, ie four periods of 30 months' leave in the UK as a partner.

8.6.2   An overview of the requirements

The requirements in Appendix FM to be met for indefinite leave to remain as a partner (see para R-ILRP.1.1) are that:

(a)   the applicant and his partner must be in the UK;

(b)   the applicant must have made a valid application for indefinite leave to remain as a partner;

(c)   the applicant must not fall for refusal under any of the grounds in Section S-ILR: Suitability – indefinite leave to remain (see **Appendix 16**);

(d)   the applicant must meet all of the requirements of Section E-LTRP: Eligibility for leave to remain as a partner (see **8.4.4**); and

(e)   the applicant must meet all of the requirements of Section E-ILRP: Eligibility for indefinite leave to remain as a partner (see **8.6.3**).

8.6.3   Eligibility requirements for indefinite leave to remain

Note that whilst the applicant must meet all of the requirements of Section E-LTRP: Eligibility for leave to remain as a partner (see **8.4.4**), where the financial requirement applies, any cash savings in Category D that exceed £16,000 are taken into account in full.

Table 8.6 below sets out some examples of the minimum savings required to meet a shortfall where £18,600 (applicant with no dependent children) is the prescribed minimum gross annual income.

Table 8.6 Minimum savings required to meet a shortfall

Income	Indefinite leave to remain: minimum savings required
No other relevant income	£34,600 (£16,000 + shortfall of £18,600)
Other relevant income of £15,000	£19,600 (£16,000 + shortfall of £3,600)
Other relevant income of £18,000	£16,600 (£16,000 + and shortfall of £600)

By para E-ILRP.1.2, the applicant must be in the UK with valid leave to remain as a partner (disregarding any period of overstaying for a period of 28 days or less).

By para E-ILRP.1.3, the applicant must have completed a continuous period of at least 60 months with limited leave as a partner (under para R-LTRP.1.1(a) to (c), or in the UK with entry clearance as a partner under para D-ECP.1.1), or a continuous period of at least 120 months with limited leave as a partner (under para R-LTR.P.1.1(a), (b) and (d), or in the UK with entry clearance as a partner under para D-ECP.1.1) or a continuous period of at least 120 months with limited leave as a partner under a combination of these paragraphs. Note that any period of entry clearance or limited leave as a fiancé(e) or proposed civil partner cannot be included.

By para E-ILRP.1.4, only those periods of limited leave when the applicant's partner is the same person can be taken into account.

By para E-ILRP.1.6, the applicant must have sufficient knowledge of the English language and sufficient knowledge about life in the UK (see **3.8.7** and **8.6.5**).

8.6.4   Absences from the UK

There is no requirement that the entire five- or 10-year leave periods, as appropriate, must be spent in the UK. Home Office guidance is that where an applicant has spent a limited period outside of the UK in connection with his or his partner's employment, this should not count against him. However, if he has spent the majority of the period overseas, there may be reason to doubt that all the requirements of the Immigration Rules have been met, eg that the couple intend to live together permanently in the UK (see **8.3.5.9**). The Home Office states that each case must be judged on its merits, taking into account reasons for travel, length of absence, and whether the applicant and his partner travelled and lived together during the time spent outside the UK. These factors will need to be considered against the relevant requirements of the Immigration Rules.

8.6.5 Decision on the application

By para D-ILRP.1.1, if the applicant meets all of the requirements at **8.6.2** he will be granted indefinite leave to remain unless para EX.1 applies (see **8.5**). Where paragraph EX.1 applies, the applicant will be granted further limited leave to remain as a partner for a period not exceeding 30 months under para D-ILRP.1.2 (see immediately below).

What if the applicant cannot meet all the requirements? Paragraph D-ILRP.1.2 has a limited concession. It provides that if the applicant does not meet the requirements for indefinite leave to remain as a partner only for one or both of the following reasons:

(a)   para S-ILR.1.5 or 1.6 applies; and/or

(b)   the applicant does not have sufficient knowledge of the English language and sufficient knowledge about life in the UK;

then the applicant will be granted further limited leave to remain as a partner for a period not exceeding 30 months and subject to a condition of no recourse to public funds.

Where an applicant is granted further limited leave under para D-ILRP.1.2 he should be advised that should the reason at (a) and/or (b) be overcome, he can make a further application for settlement at any time within the 30-month period.

The application will be refused if the applicant does not meet all the eligibility requirements for indefinite leave to remain as a partner and does not qualify for further leave to remain as a partner under para D-ILRP.1.2.

8.7   INDEFINITE LEAVE TO REMAIN (SETTLEMENT) AS A BEREAVED PARTNER

What if, before the relevant five- or 10-year probationary period is completed, the applicant's partner dies? In these circumstances, if the bereaved partner wishes to remain in the UK permanently, he should apply for settlement.

By para BPILR.1.1, the applicant will have to meet the following requirements:

(a)   the applicant must be in the UK;

(b)   the applicant must have made a valid application for indefinite leave to remain as a bereaved partner;

(c)   the applicant must not fall for refusal under any of the grounds in Section S-ILR: Suitability – indefinite leave to remain (see **8.6.2(c)**); and

(d)   the applicant must meet all of the requirements of Section E-BPILR: Eligibility for indefinite leave to remain as a bereaved partner (see **8.7.1**).

8.7.1 Eligibility requirements

By para E-BPILR.1.2, the applicant's last grant of limited leave must have been as:

(a)   a partner (other than a fiancé(e) or proposed civil partner) of a British citizen or a person settled in the UK; or

(b)   a bereaved partner.

By para E-BPILR.1.3, the person who has died must have been the applicant's partner at the time the applicant was last granted limited leave under Appendix FM.

By para E-BPILR.1.4, at the time of the partner's death the relationship between the applicant and the partner must have been genuine and subsisting (see **8.3.5.5**), and each of the parties must have intended to live permanently with the other in the UK (see **8.3.5.9**).

Home Office guidance is that normally detailed enquiries as to the subsistence of the marriage, civil partnership or relationship will not be made unless there are already doubts expressed on the file. In most cases, provided the eligibility requirements are met, the application will be granted on sight of the partner's death certificate and without further enquiry.

In cases of doubt, for example where there were doubts expressed at the time of granting the initial period of leave to remain, or where allegations have since been made about the genuine and subsisting nature of the relationship, it may be appropriate to refuse the application. However, as the Home Office guidance recognises, it must be borne in mind that the burden of proof on the Secretary of State will be very high in view of the fact that the applicant will no longer be in a position to prove the subsistence of the relationship.

8.7.2   Timeliness of application

Home Office guidance is that this provision is intended to benefit only those whose sponsor has died during the probationary period and who make their application whilst they still have limited leave to enter or remain in the UK.

The provision is also applied where the sponsor dies after an application for settlement has been submitted but before a decision has been reached.

Is the fact that a sponsor dies during the very early stages of the probationary period considered by the Home Office as an adverse factor in reaching a decision? No: Home Office guidance is that where an applicant can meet the requirements, the application is to be granted regardless of how much of the probationary period has been completed.

What if the application is made after the applicant's existing leave has expired? Home Office guidance is that an applicant does not need to comply with the requirement not to have overstayed by more than 28 days (para E-LTRP 2.2 at **8.4.6**), provided that the circumstances of any period of overstaying relates to a period of bereavement and where compassionate circumstances therefore apply. Applications made out of time where all the other requirements are met should be considered sympathetically. An application should not normally be refused solely on the grounds that the applicant is here without leave. Acceptable reasons for the delay in making an application could be that the partner's death only occurred shortly before the application for settlement was due, or that the stress of the situation led the applicant to overlook the need to regularise his immigration status.

8.7.3   Decision on application

If the applicant meets all of the requirements set out at **8.7** above, he will be granted indefinite leave to remain.

But what if the applicant cannot meet all of the requirements? Paragraph D-BPILR.1.2 has a limited concession. It provides that if the only requirement not met is either para S-ILR.1.5 or 1.6, he will be granted further limited leave to remain for a period not exceeding 30 months (subject to a condition of no recourse to public funds). The applicant should be informed that if he is granted a further period of limited leave under para D-BPILR1.2, he can make a further application for settlement at any time within the 30-month period if the requirement is met.

If the applicant does not meet the requirements for indefinite leave to remain as a bereaved partner, or limited leave to remain as a bereaved partner under para D-BPILR.1.2, the application will be refused.

What if the applicant does not wish to settle in the UK but intends to leave the UK, eg to return to his country of origin? In these circumstances, Home Office guidance is that the applicant may be granted further leave to remain for six months, subject to the same conditions, to give him time to sort out his affairs.

8.8 INDEFINITE LEAVE TO REMAIN (SETTLEMENT) AS A PARTNER WHO IS A VICTIM OF DOMESTIC VIOLENCE

What if the couple separate due to domestic violence before the relevant probationary period is completed? In these circumstances, if the applicant wishes to remain in the UK permanently, he should apply for settlement.

By para DVILR.1.1, the applicant will have to meet the following requirements:

(a)   the applicant must be in the UK;

(b)   the applicant must have made a valid application for indefinite leave to remain as a victim of domestic violence;

(c)   the applicant must not fall for refusal under any of the grounds in Section S-ILR: Suitability – indefinite leave to remain (see **8.6.2(c)**); and

(d)   the applicant must meet all of the requirements of Section E-DVILR: Eligibility for indefinite leave to remain as a victim of domestic violence (see **8.8.1**).

8.8.1 Eligibility requirements

By para E-DVILR.1.2, the applicant's last grant of limited leave must have been:

(a)   as a partner (other than a fiancé(e) or proposed civil partner) of a British citizen or a person settled in the UK;

(b)   granted to enable access to public funds pending an application under this provision; or

(c)   granted under para D-DVILR.1.2 (see **8.8.2**).

Paragraph E-DVILR.1.3 provides that the applicant must provide evidence that during the last period of limited leave as a partner, his relationship broke down permanently as a result of domestic violence. Note first that there needs to be a causal link between the infliction of domestic violence on the applicant and the permanent breakdown of the relationship. Secondly, consideration needs to be given as to what evidence might be available. Has the applicant's partner been convicted of assaulting the applicant or formally cautioned by the police? Many victims of domestic violence do not tell anyone. Whatever the circumstances, the detailed guidance issued by the Home Office on this requirement should be consulted.

8.8.2 Decision on application

If the applicant meets all of the requirements set out at **8.8**, he will be granted indefinite leave to remain.

But what if the applicant cannot meet all of the requirements? Paragraph D-DVILR.1.2 has a limited concession. It provides that if the only requirement not met is para S-ILR.1.5 or 1.6, he will be granted further limited leave to remain for a period not exceeding 30 months. The applicant should be informed that if granted a further period of limited leave under para D-DVILR.1.2, he can make a further application for settlement at any time within the 30-month period if the requirement is met.

If the applicant does not meet the requirements for indefinite leave to remain as a victim of domestic violence, or further limited leave to remain under para D-DVILR.1.2, the application will be refused.

8.9 CHILDREN ENTERING FOR IMMEDIATE SETTLEMENT

8.9.1 Who is a child?

A child is a person under the age of 18 at the date he applies for entry clearance. So it is irrelevant if he turns 18 before the ECO decides his application or before travelling to the UK under his visa or entry certificate (see paras 27 and 321(ii) respectively of the Immigration Rules).

This route is only available to a child outside the UK. A child cannot switch into this route whilst in the UK.

8.9.2 Exempt groups

A child will usually need to apply for entry clearance under Part 8 of the Immigration Rules to join a parent, both parents or a relative who is already settled in the UK. The child will need to apply for entry clearance, and if granted can enter the UK for the purposes of immediate settlement. However, those Rules will not apply to the following:

(a)   children who are British citizens (see **Chapter 2**);

(b)   children who have rights of residence in the UK as the family member of an EEA national (see **Chapter 4**).

> **EXAMPLE**
>
> Eva is a German citizen, aged 17. Her father, also German, is working in the UK. She is entitled to enter the UK in her own right (I(EEA) Regs 2006, reg 11). Whether she has any right of residence beyond three months (reg 14) depends on establishing a qualifying status under reg 6. In the alternative, she can enter and reside as the family member of her father who is an EEA national. The Immigration Rules do not apply.

8.9.3 Who is a parent?

The term 'parent', for the purposes of the Immigration Rules, is defined in para 6 and includes:

(a)   the step-father of a child whose father is dead, and the reference to 'step-father' includes a relationship arising through civil partnership;

(b)   the step-mother of a child whose mother is dead, and the reference to 'step-mother' includes a relationship arising through civil partnership;

(c)   the father, as well as the mother, of an illegitimate child where he is proved to be the father;

(d)   an adoptive parent (provided that the child was legally adopted in a country whose adoption orders are recognised by the UK – see **8.9.6**);

(e)   in the case of a child born in the UK who is not a British citizen, a person to whom there has been a genuine transfer of parental responsibility on the ground of the original parent's/parents' inability to care for the child.

8.9.4 Entry clearance requirements

Normally a child will be seeking entry clearance to join one or both parents who are already settled in the UK. Exceptionally, he might be joining a relative who is here and settled. Note that these people are often called the child's 'sponsor'.

The requirements are set out in para 297.

8.9.4.1 Overview of requirements

The starting point is to identify the parent, parents or relative the child is seeking to join in the UK, as listed in para 297(i)(a)–(f). Unless one of those categories is established, the application will fail at this first hurdle.

Then proceed to consider the remaining requirements in para 297(ii)–(v). The main issues normally concern the child's maintenance and accommodation in the UK.

As you would expect, there is a requirement to obtain entry clearance (see para 297(vi)).

8.9.4.2 Parent, parents or relative

There are four straightforward categories of entry for a child. These are listed in para 297(i), as follows:

(a)   both parents are present and settled in the UK; or

(b)   both parents are being admitted on the same occasion with the child for settlement; or

(c)   one parent is present and settled in the UK and the other parent is being admitted on the same occasion with the child for settlement; or

(d)   one parent is present and settled in the UK or being admitted on the same occasion with the child for settlement, and the other parent is dead.

As can be seen, (a)–(c) involve both parents; in (d) one parent is dead.

The remaining two categories impose additional tests. This is because one parent is alive but will *not* be involved in the family reunion. This is likely where the parents have never lived together, or have separated or divorced. On what basis will the child be allowed to join the one parent who is present and settled in the UK? This is provided for in para 297(i), as follows:

(e)   one parent is present and settled in the UK or being admitted on the same occasion with the child for settlement, and has had sole responsibility for the child's upbringing; or

(f)   one parent or a relative is present and settled in the UK or being admitted on the same occasion with the child for settlement, and there are serious and compelling family or other considerations which make exclusion of the child undesirable and suitable arrangements have been made for the child's care.

The sole responsibility test in (e) is discussed at **8.9.4.3**. The serious and compelling reasons test in (f) is examined at **8.9.4.4**.

You will have noted that the only way a child can join a relative other than a parent in the UK is under category (f).

8.9.4.3 Sole responsibility

According to Home Office guidance, the phrase 'sole responsibility' is intended to reflect a situation where parental responsibility for a child, to all intents and purposes, rests chiefly with one parent. Such a situation is in contrast to the ordinary family unit where responsibility for a child's upbringing is shared between the two parents (although not necessarily equally).

In *Suzara Ramos v Immigration Appeal Tribunal* [1989] Imm AR 148, the Court of Appeal (per Dillon LJ) held that

> the words 'sole responsibility' have to carry some form of qualification in that the rule envisages that a parent who is settled in the United Kingdom will or may have had the sole responsibility for the child's upbringing in another country. Obviously there are matters of day-to-day decision in the upbringing of a child which are bound to be decided on the spot by whoever is looking after the child in the absence of the parent settled here, such as getting the child to school safely and on time, or putting the child to bed, or seeing what it has for breakfast, or that it cleans its teeth, or has enough clothing, and so forth. ... The question must be a broad question.
>
> Direction and control of upbringing are ... factors which are part of the total pattern of facts on which the adjudicator had to make his decision. Another matter was of course the extent of contact that the mother had had with the child since the mother went to the United Kingdom ...

A parent claiming to have had 'sole responsibility' for a child must satisfactorily demonstrate that he has, for a period of time, been the chief person exercising parental responsibility. For such an assertion to be accepted by the Home Office, it must be shown that he has had, and still has, the ultimate responsibility for the major decisions relating to the child's upbringing, and provides the child with the majority of the financial and emotional support he requires. It must also be shown that he has had and continues to have care and control of the child.

In the case of *Nmaju v Entry Clearance Officer* (2000) *The Times*, 6 September, the Court of Appeal held that this requirement could be satisfied even where the parent in question had exercised sole responsibility only for a short period of time (namely, about two and a half months on the facts). The Court said that the question posed by the rules was: Had the parent settled in the UK sole responsibility for the upbringing of the child? In this case the Tribunal had found that the mother had had sole responsibility for the upbringing of the appellants. Having concluded that, the Tribunal was not at liberty under the rules to find that the appellants did not qualify for entry merely because that sole responsibility had not been assumed for a period of in excess of much over two months.

In *Nmaju* the Court of Appeal indicated that:

> While legal responsibility under the appropriate legal system will be a relevant consideration, it will not be a conclusive one. One must also look at what has actually been done in relation to the child's upbringing by whom and whether it has been done under the direction of the parent settled here. (per Schiemann LJ)

In *Cenir v Entry Clearance Officer* [2003] EWCA Civ 572 Buxton LJ stated that the following was a useful rule of thumb:

> [A]ll the important decisions in the child's life, questions concerning health and place of abode, schooling and probably going as far as serious questions of behaviour, mode of dress and the like must be under the oversight of the parent claiming sole responsibility or delegated to someone obliged to consult and act upon her instructions. To have responsibility means to be answerable.

Home Office guidance lists the following factors which may be relevant when deciding this issue:

(a)   the period for which the parent in the UK has been separated from the child;

(b)   what the arrangements were for the care of the child before that parent migrated to this country;

(c)   who has been entrusted with day-to-day care and control of the child since the sponsoring parent migrated here;

(d)   who provides, and in what proportion, the financial support for the child's care and upbringing;

(e)   who takes the important decisions about the child's upbringing, such as where and with whom the child lives, the choice of school, religious practice, etc;

(f)   the degree of contact that has been maintained between the child and the parent claiming sole responsibility;

(g)   what part in the child's care and upbringing is played by the parent not in the UK and his relatives.

8.9.4.4   Serious and compelling reasons

Guidance from the Home Office on the meaning of 'serious and compelling reasons' in para 297(i)(f) states:

> [T]he objective of this provision is to allow a child to join a parent or relative in this country only where that child could not be adequately cared for by his parents or relatives in his own country. It has never been the intention of the Rules that a child should be admitted here due to the wish of or for the benefit of other relatives in this country. This approach is entirely consistent with the internationally accepted principle that a child should first and foremost be cared for by his natural parent(s) or, if this is not possible, by his natural relatives in the country in which he lives. Only if the parent(s) or relative(s) in his own country cannot care for him should consideration be given to him joining relatives in another country. It is also consistent with the provisions of the European Convention on Human Rights, and the resolution on the harmonization of family reunification agreed by EU Ministers in June 1993.

The degree to which these considerations should be taken into account, and whether they should relate solely to the child or include the circumstances of the sponsor, is determined by two factors, namely:

(a)   whether the sponsor is a parent or other relative of the child; and

(b)   whether or not the sponsor is settled here.

If the sponsor is not a parent but another relative (eg an aunt or grandparent), the factors which are to be considered relate only to the child and the circumstances in which he lives or lived prior to travelling to the UK. These circumstances should be exceptional in comparison with the ordinary circumstances of other children in his home country. It is not, for instance, sufficient to show he would be better off here by being able to attend a State school.

> The focus needs to be on the circumstances of the child in the light of his or her age, social background and developmental history and will involve inquiry as to whether: (i) there is evidence of neglect or abuse; (ii) there are unmet needs that should be catered for; (iii) there are stable arrangements for the child's physical care. The assessment involves consideration as to whether the combination of circumstances [is] sufficiently serious and compelling to require admission. (per Blake J in *Mundeba* (*s.55 and para 297(i)(f)*) [2013] UKUT 88 (IAC) at [37])

The circumstances relating to the sponsors here (eg the fact that they are elderly or infirm and need caring for) are not taken into account.

If the sponsor in the UK is one of the child's parents, consideration needs to be given to whether or not that parent is settled here or being admitted for settlement. If he is not, the relevant circumstances relate solely to the child (as detailed above). But if the child's sponsor is one of his parents and he is settled here (or being admitted for settlement), the considerations to be taken into account may relate either to the child and his circumstances in the country in which he lives or lived prior to travelling here, or to the parent who is settled here or being admitted for settlement.

The circumstances surrounding the child must be exceptional in relation to those of other children living in that country, but in this case, circumstances relating to the parent here, both of an emotional and of a physical nature, may be taken into account. Such circumstances may include illness or infirmity which requires assistance.

EXAMPLE

Marlene is the mother of Dora, aged 14. Both are citizens of Barbados. Marlene is divorced from Dora's father, who never contacts his daughter. He is still living in Barbados. When Dora was 8 years old, Marlene came to the UK and left Dora in Barbados in the care of her grandmother, who alone has supported her granddaughter financially. Marlene now has indefinite leave to remain in the UK. She wishes to know whether Dora can join her in the UK.

Marlene cannot establish her sole responsibility (see **8.9.4.3**) for Dora, as she has not provided any financial support for her from the UK. She must instead show that there are serious and compelling considerations which make Dora's exclusion undesirable (eg if Dora's grandmother becomes seriously ill and incapable of looking after her). If this requirement is not met, Dora cannot currently be admitted for settlement in the UK.

Marlene may be able to establish sole responsibility (see **8.9.4.3**) over the next few months if she provides all or the majority of Dora's financial and emotional support, and takes responsibility for the major decisions in Dora's life.

8.9.4.5   Age

By para 297(ii), the child must be under the age of 18. See further **8.9.1**.

8.9.4.6 Dependent life-style

By para 297(iii), the child must not be leading an independent life, must be unmarried and not a civil partner, and must not have formed an independent family unit.

Paragraph 6 of the Immigration Rules provides that 'must not be leading an independent life' means that the applicant:

(a)   does not have a partner as defined in Appendix FM (see **8.1.2.1**);

(b)   is living with his parents (except where he is at boarding school, college or university as part of his full-time education);

(c)   is not employed full-time (unless aged 18 years or over);

(d)   is wholly or mainly dependent upon his parents for financial support (unless aged 18 years or over); and

(e)   is wholly or mainly dependent upon his parents for emotional support.

Obviously the above general factors may have to be adapted when applied to the different categories of possible entry in para 297(i): see **8.9.4.2**.

8.9.4.7 Accommodation

By para 297(iv), the child must be accommodated adequately by the parent, parents or relative the child is seeking to join, without recourse to public funds, in accommodation which the parent, parents or relative the child is seeking to join own or occupy exclusively.

The equivalent provision for partners under Appendix FM is detailed at **8.3.7**.

> **EXAMPLE**
>
> In the case of *Loresco* [1999] INLP 18, three teenage children (one girl and two boys) sought to join their mother in the UK. Was her two-bedroomed flat, with a living room that was also available as sleeping accommodation, too small for her, her husband, their 1-year-old child and the three teenagers? The Tribunal said 'Yes'. Three rooms were available to sleep in. There was one room for the sponsor and her husband, one room for the girl over 10, and the third room for the two boys over 10. So the room standard was met.
>
> Under the space standard, with only three available rooms, the permitted number of persons was five. But the child aged 1 year counted as half a unit, and as everyone else was aged 10 or over, that meant the total number of people in the flat would be five and a half persons with the three teenage children. Their application was therefore refused as the flat was overcrowded under the space standard (see **8.3.7.3**).

8.9.4.8 Maintenance

By para 297(v), the child must be maintained adequately by the parent, parents or relative the child is seeking to join, without recourse to public funds. As to public funds, see **3.3.2**.

The equivalent provision for partners under Appendix FM is detailed at **8.3.6.9**.

8.9.4.9 General grounds for refusal

The application must not fall for refusal under the general grounds for refusal (see **3.4.5** and the criminality requirements in **Appendix 8**).

8.9.5 Adopted children

Adopted children are dealt with in paras 309A–316F of the Immigration Rules. The details are beyond the scope of this book.

8.10 PARENT OF A CHILD SETTLED IN THE UK

8.10.1 Who can apply?

A parent with sole parental responsibility for, or access rights to, a British citizen child or settled child who is living in the UK, can apply for entry clearance (see **8.10.2**) and leave to remain (see **8.10.3**) under Appendix FM to the Immigration Rules. Ultimately it may be possible to apply for settlement in this category (see **8.10.4**).

A parent already in the UK may switch into this category. This most commonly occurs when a person has entered the UK with limited leave as the partner of a British citizen or settled person (see **8.3**), but can no longer remain in the UK in that category as the relationship has broken down. If that person has sole parental responsibility for, or is exercising access rights to, his British or settled child, an application may be made for limited leave to remain (see **8.10.3**).

Who is a parent for these purposes? See **8.9.3**.

8.10.2 Entry clearance

By para EC-PT.1.1 of Appendix FM to the Immigration Rules, the requirements to be met for entry clearance as a parent are:

(a)   the applicant must be outside the UK;

(b)   the applicant must have made a valid application for entry clearance as a parent;

(c)   the applicant must not fall for refusal under any of the grounds in Section S-EC: Suitability – entry clearance; and

(d)   the applicant must meet all of the requirements of Section E-ECPT: Eligibility for entry clearance as a parent.

Note that the suitability requirements are the same as for a partner under Appendix FM, and these are detailed at **8.3.3**. As to the eligibility requirements, see **8.10.2.1**.

8.10.2.1 Eligibility requirements in outline

An applicant must meet all of the eligibility requirements in paras E-ECPT.2.1–4.2. Broadly these are as follows:

(a)   relationship requirements (see **8.10.2.2**);

(b)   financial requirements (see **8.10.2.3**)

(c)   accommodation requirements (see **8.10.2.4**); and

(d)   English language requirement (see **8.10.2.5**).

8.10.2.2 Relationship requirements (paras E-ECPT.2.1–2.4)

By para E-ECPT.2.1, the applicant must be aged 18 years or over.

Paragraph E-ECPT.2.2 provides that the child of the applicant must be:

(a)   under the age of 18 years at the date of application;

(b)   living in the UK; and

(c)   a British citizen (see **2.2**) or settled in the UK (see **3.8**).

By para E-ECPT.2.3, either:

(a)   the applicant must have sole parental responsibility for the child (see **8.9.4.3**); or

(b)   the parent or carer with whom the child normally lives must be –

  (i)   a British citizen in the UK or settled in the UK;

  (ii)   not the partner of the applicant; and

(iii)   the applicant must not be eligible to apply for entry clearance as a partner under Appendix FM (see **8.3**).

By para E-ECPT.2.4, the applicant must provide evidence that he has either:

(a)   (i)   sole parental responsibility for the child; or

       (ii)   access rights to the child; and

(b)   the applicant must provide evidence that he is taking, and intends to continue to take, an active role in the child's upbringing.

What evidence is required?

Home Office guidance is that to demonstrate access rights, the applicant will need to produce either a residence or a contact order granted by a court in the UK, or a sworn affidavit from the UK resident parent or carer of the child confirming that the applicant can have access to the child and describing in detail the access arrangements. If the contact with the child is supervised, the supervisor must swear the statement.

How can an applicant show that he is taking, and intends to continue to take, an active role in his child's upbringing? The application form states:

> Please provide details of how you have been involved in the upbringing of your child(ren). You should include information on what role you played in choosing their care arrangements in the UK or which nursery/school they attend. What role have you played in choosing their academic options? How often do you speak to or see your child(ren)? Have you been present for key events in their lives eg religious events, birthdays etc? How do you keep in touch (telephone, email, letters etc)? Please provide any documentary evidence that you have to support your answer.

8.10.2.3 Financial requirements

By para E-ECPT.3.1, the applicant must provide evidence that he will be able to maintain and accommodate himself and any dependants in the UK adequately without recourse to public funds. As to public funds, see **3.3.2.**

The equivalent provision for partners under Appendix FM is detailed at **8.3.6.9.**

8.10.2.4 Accommodation requirements

By para E-ECPT.3.2, the applicant must provide evidence that there will be adequate accommodation in the UK, without recourse to public funds, for the family, including other family members who are not included in the application but who live in the same household, which the family own or occupy exclusively. Accommodation will not be regarded as adequate if:

(a)   it is, or will be, overcrowded; or

(b)   it contravenes public health regulations.

The equivalent provision for partners under Appendix FM is detailed at **8.3.7.**

8.10.2.5 English language requirement

The requirement in para E-ECPT.4.1 is exactly the same as for a partner seeking entry clearance under Appendix FM, and the details are at **8.3.8.**

8.10.2.6 Decision on application

If the applicant meets the requirements for entry clearance as a parent, he will be granted entry clearance for an initial period not exceeding 33 months and subject to a condition of no recourse to public funds.

8.10.3   Leave to remain

8.10.3.1   Who can apply?

There are five different situations to be considered here, namely:

(a)   where an applicant entered the UK as a parent under Appendix FM and now seeks an extension of his limited leave for a further 30 months;

(b)   where a person entered the UK in a different category, often a partner under Appendix FM, and now applies to switch to this category;

(c)   where a person switched in the UK to this category and now wants an extension of his limited leave for a further 30 months;

(d)   where a person seeks to start on the 10-year family route to settlement under Appendix FM by relying on his Article 8 ECHR rights under para EX.1 (see **8.5**). This application might be made, for example, by an overstayer with no partner in the UK but a child, and who otherwise faces administrative removal from the UK (see **10.4**);

(e)   where a person is on the 10-year family route to settlement under Appendix FM and now seeks an extension of his limited leave for a further 30 months.

8.10.3.2   An overview of the requirements

The requirements to be met for limited leave to remain as a parent (see para R-LTRPT.1.1) are that:

(a)   the applicant and the child must be in the UK;

(b)   the applicant must have made a valid application for limited leave to remain as a parent; and either

(c)   (i)   the applicant must not fall for refusal under Section S-LTR: Suitability – leave to remain (see **8.10.3.3**), and

      (ii)   the applicant must meet all of the requirements of Section E-LTRPT: Eligibility for leave to remain as a parent (see **8.10.3.4**), and

      (iii)   para EX.1 (see **8.5**) has not been applied; or

(d)   (i)   the applicant must not fall for refusal under Section S-LTR: Suitability – leave to remain, and

      (ii)   the applicant meets the eligibility requirements of paras E-LTRPT.2.2–2.4 and E-LTRPT.3.1; and

      (iii)   para EX.1 applies.

8.10.3.3   Suitability requirements

Paragraphs S-LTR.1.2–1.7 and S-LTR.2.1–2.4 set out the mandatory and discretionary grounds on which the Home Office will normally refuse an application. These are detailed at **8.4.3**.

8.10.3.4   Overview of eligibility requirements

If an applicant meets all of the eligibility requirements in paras E-LTRPT.1.2–5.2, he may be granted limited leave and proceed on a five-year route to settlement. If he meets the eligibility requirements of paras E-LTRPT.2.2–2.4 and E-LTRPT.3.1, and para EX.1 (see **8.5**) applies, he may be granted limited leave and proceed on a 10-year route to settlement.

The eligibility requirements are as follows:

(a)   relationship requirements (see **8.10.3.5**);

(b)   immigration requirements (see **8.10.3.6**);

(c)   financial requirements (see **8.10.3.7**)

(d)   accommodation requirements (see **8.10.3.8**); and

(e) English language requirement (see **8.10.3.9**).

8.10.3.5 Relationship requirements

Paragraphs E-LTRPT.2.2–2.4 set out virtually the same relationship requirements as for entry clearance (see **8.10.2.2**). However, note that by para E-LTRPT.2.2 the following additional fourth category of child of the applicant is included, namely, where the child has lived in the UK continuously for at least the seven years immediately preceding the date of application and para EX.1 (see **8.5**) applies.

8.10.3.6 Immigration requirements

Paragraph E-LTRPT.3.1 excludes certain people already in the UK from switching into this category, namely, a visitor (see **Chapter 5**), or a person with valid leave granted for a period of six months or less, or a person on temporary admission (see **3.5.5**).

By para E-LTRPT.3.2, the applicant must not be in the UK in breach of immigration laws (disregarding any period of overstaying for a period of 28 days or less), unless para EX. 1 (see **8.5**) applies.

8.10.3.7 Financial requirements

Paragraph E-LTRPT.4.1 set out the same financial requirements as for entry clearance (see **8.10.2.3**), unless para EX. 1 (see **8.5**) applies.

8.10.3.8 Accommodation requirements

Paragraph E-LTRPT.4.2 set out the same accommodation requirements as for entry clearance (see **8.10.2.4**), unless para EX. 1 (see **8.5**) applies.

8.10.3.9 English language requirement

Paragraph E-LTRPT.5.1 set out the same English language requirements as for entry clearance (see **8.10.2.5**), unless para EX. 1 (see **8.5**) applies.

8.10.3.10 Decision on application

If the applicant meets all the requirements for limited leave to remain as a parent, the applicant will be granted limited leave to remain for a period not exceeding 30 months and subject to a condition of no recourse to public funds. The applicant will be eligible to apply for settlement (see **8.10.4**) after a continuous period of at least 60 months with such leave or in the UK with entry clearance as a parent under para D-ECPT.1.1.

If the applicant can meet the suitability requirements, the eligibility requirements of paras E-LTRPT.2.2–2.4 (the relationship requirements at **8.10.3.5**) and E-LTRPT.3.1 (the first immigration requirement at **8.10.3.6**), and para EX.1 (see **8.5**) applies, he will be granted leave to remain for a period not exceeding 30 months. He will be eligible to apply for settlement (see **8.10.4**) after a continuous period of at least 120 months with such leave, with limited leave as a parent under para D-LTRPT.1.1, or in the UK with entry clearance as a parent under para D-ECPT.1.1.

8.10.4 Indefinite leave to remain (settlement) as a parent

8.10.4.1 Who can apply?

There are two different situations to be considered here, namely:

(a) where a person has completed the five-year route to settlement, ie two periods of 30 months' leave as a parent; and

(b) where a person has completed the 10-year route to settlement, ie four periods of 30 months' leave as a parent.

8.10.4.2   An overview of the requirements

The requirements in Appendix FM to be met for indefinite leave to remain as a parent (see para E-ILRPT.1.1) are:

(a)   the applicant must be in the UK;

(b)   the applicant must have made a valid application for indefinite leave to remain as a parent;

(c)   the applicant must not fall for refusal under any of the grounds in Section S-LTR: Suitability – leave to remain (see **8.4.3**);

(d)   the applicant must meet all of the requirements of Section E-LTRPT: Eligibility for leave to remain as a parent **(see 8.10.3.4)**; and

(e)   the applicant must meet all of the requirements of Section E-ILRPT: Eligibility for indefinite leave to remain as a parent (see **8.10.4.3**).

8.10.4.3   Eligibility requirements for indefinite leave to remain

By para E-ILRPT.1.2, the applicant must be in the UK with valid leave to remain as a parent (disregarding any period of overstaying for 28 days or less).

Paragraph E-ILRPT.1.3 provides that the applicant must have completed a continuous period of at least 60 months with limited leave as a parent (under paras R-LTRPT.1.1.(a)–(c) or in the UK with entry clearance as a parent under para D-ECPT.1.1), or a continuous period of at least 120 months with limited leave as a parent (under paras R-LTRPT.1.1(a), (b) and (d) or in the UK with entry clearance as a parent under para D-ECPT.1.1) or a continuous period of at least 120 months with limited leave as a partner under a combination of these paragraphs.

By para E-ILRPT.1.4, the applicant must at the date of application have no unspent convictions (see **Appendix 8** and **8.10.4.4**).

Paragraph E-ILRPT.1.5 requires the applicant to have sufficient knowledge of the English language and sufficient knowledge about life in the UK (see **3.8.7** and **8.10.4.4**).

8.10.4.4   Decision on the application

By para D-ILRPT.1.1, if the applicant meets all of the requirements listed at **8.10.4.2**, he will be granted indefinite leave to remain unless para EX.1 applies. Where para EX.1 applies, the applicant will be granted further limited leave to remain as a parent for a period not exceeding 30 months under para D-ILRPT.1.2 (see immediately below).

But what if the applicant cannot meet all the requirements? Paragraph D-ILRPT.1.2 has a limited concession. It provides that if the applicant does not meet the requirements for indefinite leave to remain as a parent only for one or both of the following reasons:

(a)   the applicant has an unspent conviction; and/or

(b)   the applicant does not have sufficient knowledge of the English language and sufficient knowledge about life in the UK;

then the applicant will be granted further limited leave to remain as a parent for a period not exceeding 30 months and subject to a condition of no recourse to public funds.

Where an applicant is granted further limited leave under para D-ILRPT.1.2, he should be advised that should the reason at (a) and/or (b) be overcome, he can make a further application for settlement at any time within the 30-month period.

The application will be refused if the applicant does not meet the requirements for indefinite leave to remain as a parent, or further leave to remain as a parent under para D-ILRPT.1.2.

8.11   ADULT DEPENDENT RELATIVES ENTERING FOR IMMEDIATE SETTLEMENT

8.11.1   Who can apply?

The purpose of this route is to allow a non-EEA adult dependent relative of a British citizen in the UK, a person settled in the UK, or a person in the UK with refugee leave or humanitarian protection, to enter and settle. On what basis? It must be demonstrated that the applicant, as a result of age, illness or disability, requires a level of long-term personal care that can only be provided in the UK by his relative here and without recourse to public funds.

Note that the applicant's qualifying relative in the UK is known as his 'sponsor'.

Not all relatives can apply. Only the sponsor's parent aged 18 years or over; grandparent; brother or sister aged 18 years or over; and son or daughter aged 18 years or over are able to apply.

Note that this route is available only to an applicant outside the UK. A person cannot switch into this route whilst in the UK.

8.11.2   Entry clearance requirements

By para EC-DR.1.1, the requirements to be met for entry clearance as an adult dependent relative are:

(a)   the applicant must be outside the UK;

(b)   the applicant must have made a valid application for entry clearance as an adult dependent relative;

(c)   the applicant must not fall for refusal under any of the grounds in Section S-EC: Suitability for entry clearance (see **8.3.3**); and

(d)   the applicant must meet all of the requirements of Section E-ECDR: Eligibility for entry clearance as an adult dependent relative (see **8.11.3**).

8.11.3   Eligibility requirements in outline

To meet the eligibility requirements for entry clearance as an adult dependent relative all of the requirements in paras E-ECDR.2.1–3.2 must be met. Broadly these are:

(a)   relationship requirements (see **8.11.4**);

(b)   care needs requirements (see **8.11.5**);

(c)   financial requirements (see **8.11.6**).

8.11.4   Relationship requirements

By para E-ECDR.2.1, the applicant must be related to the sponsor in the UK in one of the following ways:

(a)   a parent aged 18 years or over;

(b)   a grandparent;

(c)   a brother or sister aged 18 years or over; or

(d)   a son or daughter aged 18 years or over.

Note that para E-ECDR.2.2 provides that if the applicant is the sponsor's parent or grandparent, he must not be in a subsisting relationship with a partner unless that partner is also the sponsor's parent or grandparent and is applying for entry clearance at the same time as the applicant.

Evidence of the family relationship should normally take the form of birth or adoption certificates.

By para E-ECDR.2.3, the sponsor must at the date of application be:

(a)   aged 18 years or over; and

(b)   (i)   a British citizen in the UK; or

(ii)   present and settled in the UK; or

(iii) in the UK with refugee leave (see **9.8**) or humanitarian protection (see **9.10.1**).

8.11.5   Care needs requirements

By para E-ECDR.2.4, the applicant (or, if the applicant and his partner are the sponsor's parents or grandparents, the applicant's partner) must, as a result of age, illness or disability, require long-term personal care to perform everyday tasks.

Home Office guidance is that everyday tasks include washing, dressing and cooking. The inability to carry out these tasks may have started recently, eg due to a serious accident resulting in long-term incapacity, or it could be the result of deterioration in the applicant's condition over several years.

By para 34 of Appendix FM-SE, medical evidence that the applicant's physical or mental condition means that he cannot perform everyday tasks must be obtained from a doctor or other health professional. Note that paras 36–39 of the Immigration Rules give the ECO the power to refer the applicant for a medical examination, and to require that this be undertaken by a doctor or other health professional on a list approved by the British Embassy or High Commission.

Paragraph E-ECDR.2.5 provides that the applicant (or, if the applicant and his partner are the sponsor's parents or grandparents, the applicant's partner) must be unable, even with the practical and financial help of the sponsor, to obtain the required level of care in the country where he is living, because:

(a)   it is not available and there is no person in that country who can reasonably provide it; or

(b)   it is not affordable.

As to (a), Home Office guidance is that the ECO should consider whether there is anyone in the country where the applicant is living who can reasonably provide the required level of care. This might be a close family member such as a son, daughter, brother, sister, parent, grandchild or grandparent. But it can include any person who is able to provide care, eg a home-help, housekeeper, nurse, carer, or care or nursing home. If an applicant has more than one close relative in the country where he is living, those relatives may be able to pool resources to provide the required care.

The ECO should bear in mind any relevant cultural factors, such as in countries where women are unlikely to be able to provide support.

Evidence that the required level of care is not, or is no longer, available in the country where the applicant is living could be obtained from a central or local health authority, a local authority, or a doctor or other health professional. If the required care has been provided through a private arrangement, the applicant must provide details of that arrangement and why it is no longer available. See paras 35 and 36 of Appendix FM-SE.

As to (b), if payment was made for arranging care, Home Office guidance is that the ECO should ask to see records and for an explanation of why this payment cannot continue. If financial support has been provided by the sponsor or other close family in the UK, the ECO should ask for an explanation of why this cannot continue or is no longer sufficient to enable the required level of care to be provided (see para 37 of Appendix FM-SE).

8.11.6 Financial requirements

By para E-ECDR.3.1, the applicant must provide evidence that he can be adequately maintained, accommodated and cared for in the UK by the sponsor without recourse to public funds.

The maintenance and accommodation requirements are similar to those for partners under Appendix FM, and are detailed at **8.3.6.9** and **8.3.7** respectively. However, in addition the ECO must be satisfied that the required level of care can and will be met by the sponsor in the UK without recourse to public funds.

Note that by para E-ECDR.3.2, if the applicant's sponsor is a British citizen or settled in the UK, the applicant must provide an undertaking signed by the sponsor confirming that the applicant will have no recourse to public funds, and that the sponsor will be responsible for his maintenance, accommodation and care, for a period of five years from the date the applicant enters the UK if he is granted indefinite leave to enter.

Home Office guidance is that maintenance may be provided by the sponsor, or by any combination of the funds available to the sponsor and the applicant. Promises of third party support will not be accepted, as these are vulnerable to a change in another person's circumstances or in the sponsor's or the applicant's relationship with that party. Cash savings which have originated in a gift (not a loan) from a third party may count towards the required maintenance, but those cash savings must be in an account in the name of the sponsor or the applicant and under that person's control.

What evidence should the sponsor provide? Home Office guidance is:

(a)   original bank statements covering the last six months;

(b)   other evidence of income – such as pay slips, income from savings, shares and bonds – covering the last six months;

(c)   relevant information on outgoings, eg council tax, utilities, etc, and on support for anyone else who is dependent on the sponsor;

(d)   a copy of a mortgage or tenancy agreement showing ownership or occupancy of a property; and

(e)   planned care arrangements for the applicant in the UK (which can involve other family members in the UK) and the cost of these (which must be met by the sponsor, without undertakings of third party support).

8.11.7 Home Office example scenarios taken from guidance

Example 1

A person (aged 25) has a learning disability that means he cannot feed, wash or dress himself. His parents have recently died in an accident and his only surviving close relative is a brother in the UK who has been sending money to the family for some time. The person has been cared for temporarily by family friends since his parents' death, but they are no longer able to do this. The sponsor is unable to meet the costs of full-time residential care, but he and his family have sufficient financial and other means to care for the applicant in their home. **This could meet the criteria if the applicant can demonstrate that he is unable even with the practical and financial help of the sponsor to obtain the required level of care in the country where he is living because it not available and there is no person in that country who can reasonably provide it or it is not affordable and other relevant criteria are met.**

Example 2

A person (aged 30) has lived alone in Sri Lanka for many years. His parents are settled in the UK; other siblings live in the UK and USA. The person has recently been involved in a road accident and as a result has developed a long-term condition which means that he can no longer care for himself. The mother has been visiting Sri Lanka to care for her son, but needs to return to the UK to care for her younger children. **This could meet the criteria if the applicant can demonstrate that he is unable even with the practical and financial help of the sponsor to obtain the required level of care in Sri Lanka where he is living because it not available and there is no person in that country who can reasonably provide it or it is not affordable and other relevant criteria are met.**

Example 3

A husband and wife (both aged 70) live in Pakistan. Their daughter lives in the UK. The wife requires long-term personal care owing to ill health and cannot perform everyday tasks for herself. The husband is in good health, but cannot provide his wife with the level of care she needs. They both want to come and live in the UK. The daughter can care for her mother full time in her home as she does not work whilst her husband provides the family with an income from his employment. Her sister in the UK will also help with care of the mother. The applicant provides the ECO with the planned care arrangements in the UK. **This could meet the criteria if the applicant can demonstrate that she is unable even with the practical and financial help of her sponsor to obtain the required level of care in Pakistan because it not available and there is no person in that country who can reasonably provide it or it is not affordable and other relevant criteria are met.**

8.11.8 Decision on application

By para D-ECDR.1.1, if the applicant meets the requirements for entry clearance as an adult dependent relative of a British citizen or person settled in the UK, he will be granted indefinite leave to enter.

Paragraph D-ECDR.1.2 provides that if the applicant meets the requirements for entry clearance as an adult dependent relative and the sponsor has limited leave as a refugee or with humanitarian protection, the applicant will be granted limited leave of a duration which will expire at the same time as the sponsor's limited leave. This will be subject to a condition of no recourse to public funds. If the sponsor applies for further limited leave, the applicant may apply for further limited leave of the same duration, if the requirements in para EC-DR.1.1(c) and (d) (see **8.11.2**) continue to be met (again subject to no recourse to public funds). In due course an application could be made for settlement – see Section R-ILRDR of Appendix FM.

8.12 CHILD ENTERING WITH OR TO JOIN A PARENT WHO HAS LIMITED LEAVE

8.12.1 Where parent has limited leave as a partner or parent under Appendix FM

8.12.1.1 Entry clearance

By para EC-C.1.1, the requirements to be met for entry clearance as a child are:

(a)   the applicant must be outside the UK;

(b)   the applicant must have made a valid application for entry clearance as a child;

(c)   the applicant must not fall for refusal under any of the grounds in Section S-EC: Suitability for entry clearance; and

(d)   the applicant must meet all of the requirements of Section E-ECC: Eligibility for entry clearance as a child.

Note that the suitability requirements are the same as for a partner under Appendix FM, and these are detailed at **8.3.3**. As to the eligibility requirements, see **8.12.1.2**.

8.12.1.2 Eligibility requirements in outline

To meet the eligibility requirements for entry clearance as a child, all of the requirements of para E-ECC.1.2–2.4 must be met. Broadly these are:

(a)   relationship requirements (see **8.12.1.3**);

(b)   financial requirements (see **8.12.1.4**);

(c)   accommodation requirements (see **8.12.1.5**).

8.12.1.3 Relationship requirements

By para E-ECC.1.2, the applicant must be under the age of 18 at the date of application.

Paragraph E-ECC.1.3 provides that the applicant must not be married or in a civil partnership.

By para E-ECC.1.4, the applicant must not have formed an independent family unit.

Paragraph E-ECC.1.5 provides that the applicant must not be leading an independent life. See further **8.9.4.6**.

By para E-ECC.1.6, one of the applicant's parents must be in the UK with limited leave to enter or remain, or be applying, or have applied, for entry clearance as a partner (see **8.3**) or a parent (see **8.10**) under Appendix FM (the 'applicant's parent') and (a) the applicant's parent's partner is also a parent of the applicant or (b) the applicant's parent has had and continues to have sole responsibility for the child's upbringing (see **8.9.4.3**) or (c) there are serious and compelling family or other considerations which make exclusion of the child undesirable and suitable arrangements have been made for the child's care (see **8.9.4.4**).

8.12.1.4 Financial requirement

The equivalent provision for partners under Appendix FM applies, as detailed at **8.3.6**.

8.12.1.5 Accommodation requirements

The equivalent provision for partners under Appendix FM applies, as detailed at **8.3.6**.

8.12.1.6 Decision on application

If the applicant meets the requirements for entry clearance as a child, he will be granted entry clearance of a duration which will expire at the same time as the leave granted to the applicant's parent and subject to a condition of no recourse to public funds.

8.12.1.7 Leave to remain and settlement

When the applicant's parent applies for further leave to remain and settlement, the applicant should do so as well.

As to leave to remain, see generally Section R-LTRC, para 1.1 of Appendix A. As to settlement, see **8.6** and **8.10.4**.

8.12.2 Other provisions applying to children of parents with limited leave

There are separate requirements applying to children of a parent (or parents) in each of the other categories of limited leave already covered in this book. The relevant provisions are set out in **Table 8.7** below.

Table 8.7 Provisions applying to children of parents with limited leave

Child of	See text	Immigration Rules, paras
Tier 4 General Student	Chapter 6	319F–319K
Tier 1 Migrant	7.6.1.2	319F–319K
Tier 2 Migrant	7.8.9	319F–319K
Sole representative	7.13.13	197–199
Person with UK ancestry	7.14.9	197–199

8.13   PRIVATE LIFE IN THE UK

8.13.1   Limited leave to remain

8.13.1.1   Who can apply?

A person who has lived in the UK for at least 20 years continuously, lawfully or unlawfully, can apply to the Home Office for leave to remain in the UK on the basis of the Article 8 ECHR right to respect for private life. Alternative provisions allow an applicant to be granted limited leave to remain in the UK on the basis of private life after seven years' continuous residence if he is under the age of 18; or if he has spent at least half of his life in the UK if he is aged between 18 and 24; or if the applicant has less than 20 years' continuous residence in the UK but has no ties (including social, cultural or family) with his country of origin.

Most commonly an application will be made as an alternative to an asylum claim (see **Chapter 9**) and when opposing the administrative removal (see **10.4**) of the applicant.

8.13.1.2   Requirements for leave to remain

By para 276ADE(i)–(vi) of the Immigration Rules, the requirements to be met by an applicant for leave to remain on the grounds of private life in the UK are that at the date of application, the applicant:

(a)   does not fall for refusal under any of the grounds in Section S-LTR 1.2 to S- LTR 2.3 and S-LTR.3.1 in Appendix FM (see **8.4.3**); *and*

(b)   has lived continuously in the UK (see **3.8.8.1**) for at least 20 years (discounting any period of imprisonment); *or*

(c)   is under the age of 18 years and has lived continuously in the UK for at least seven years (discounting any period of imprisonment) and it would not be reasonable to expect him to leave the UK; *or*

(d)   is aged 18 years or above and under 25 years, and has spent at least half of his life living continuously in the UK (discounting any period of imprisonment); *or*

(e)   is aged 18 years or above, has lived continuously in the UK for less than 20 years (discounting any period of imprisonment) but has no ties (including social, cultural or family) with the country to which he would have to go if required to leave the UK (see **8.13.1.3**).

How does a caseworker assess the length of time that the applicant has resided in the UK? Home Office guidance is that an applicant needs to provide credible evidence from an independent source, for example letters from a housing trust, local authority, bank, school or doctor. The caseworker must be satisfied that the evidence provided has not been tampered with or otherwise falsified, and that it relates to the person who is making the application. In order to be satisfied that the applicant's residence in the UK was continuous, the caseworker should normally expect to see evidence to cover every 12-month period of the length of continuous residence and travel documents to cover the entire period, unless the caseworker is satisfied on the basis of a credible explanation provided as to why this has not been submitted.

8.13.1.3   The no ties abroad ground

As to the ground in para 276ADE(vi) ((e) in **8.13.1.2** above), how should a caseworker assess this? Home Office guidance is that in determining whether the applicant has no ties, including social, cultural or family ties, the entirety of the applicant's background must be considered. If the applicant has a connection under any of the social, cultural and family headings, this will be sufficient to demonstrate that ties exist. In making the assessment, relevant factors will include, but are not limited to, the following:

(a) *Language* – does the applicant speaks an official language of his country of origin, or a language that is commonly understood in parts of that country? For these purposes fluency is not required, but an ability to communicate competently with sympathetic interlocutors will suffice.

(b) *Cultural background* – is there any evidence of the applicant's exposure to and level of understanding of the cultural norms in the country of origin? Where the person has spent his time in the UK living mainly amongst a diaspora community from his country of origin then it may be reasonable to conclude that he has cultural ties with that country even if he has never lived there, or has been absent from that country for a lengthy period.

(c) *Length of time spent in the country of origin* – if the applicant has spent a considerable period living in the country of origin, it will be difficult for him to demonstrate that he has no ties with that country.

(d) *Family, friends and social network* – an applicant who has extended family in his country of origin should be able to turn to them for support to help him to integrate into society on return. These need not be close blood relatives if the applicant has friends and other contacts to whom he could turn for support. A caseworker must consider whether the applicant or his family has hosted visits in the UK by family and friends from his country of origin.

8.13.1.4 Decision on application

By para 276BE, limited leave to remain on the grounds of private life in the UK may be granted for a period not exceeding 30 months if the requirements in para 276ADE are met (or, in respect of the requirements in para 276ADE(iv) and (v) ((c) and (d) in **8.13.1.2**), were met in a previous application which led to a grant of limited leave to remain under this para). The applicant may be able to apply for further periods of leave in this category and settlement after 120 months (see **8.13.2**).

What if one or more requirement in para 276ADE is not met? Home Office guidance is that the caseworker should consider whether there are any exceptional circumstances (see **8.13.1.5**) which would make refusal and the removal of the applicant from the UK a breach of Article 8 ECHR.

8.13.1.5 Exceptional circumstances

If the requirements in para 276ADE (see **8.13.1.2**) are not met, what exceptional circumstances would make refusal and the requirement for the applicant to leave the UK a breach of Article 8 ECHR? Home Office guidance is that the caseworker should determine whether removal would have such severe consequences for the individual that refusal of the application and his removal from the UK would not be proportionate given the nature of his private life. The Home Office states that this will rarely be the case.

In determining whether a case is exceptional, the decision maker must consider all relevant factors, such as:

(a) the circumstances surrounding the applicant's entry to the UK and proportion of the time he has been in the UK legally as opposed to illegally. Private life which involves the applicant putting down roots in the UK and becoming involved in community life in the full knowledge that his stay here is unlawful or temporary, and therefore precarious, should be given less weight than private life formed by a person lawfully present in the UK;

(b) any exceptional cultural, legal or religious factors which prevent or severely limit the applicant from enjoying private life in his country of origin, for example specific disabilities which would make communication difficult in the country of origin. An inability to speak the language in the country of origin, or lack of fluency in that language, would not normally be considered an exceptional factor where the applicant could reasonably be expected to learn the language;

(c)   cumulative factors. For example, where the applicant has family members in the UK but his family life does not provide a basis to remain, and he also has a significant private life in the UK, for example sibling relationships or an adult child and parent relationship which does not normally qualify as family life under Article 8 ECHR, even where they are particularly close. Although under the Immigration Rules family life and private life are considered separately and are not cumulative, when considering whether there are exceptional circumstances which would make removal from the UK a breach of Article 8 ECHR, both family and private life should be taken into account by the caseworker.

8.13.2   Indefinite leave to remain (settlement)

8.13.2.1   Who can apply?

Once an applicant has been granted four periods of 30 months' limited leave under para 276BE and so spent 10 years in the UK on that basis, he may apply for indefinite leave to remain.

8.13.2.2   Requirements

By para 276DE, the requirements to be met for the grant of indefinite leave to remain on the grounds of private life in the UK are:

(a)   the applicant has been in the UK with continuous leave on the grounds of private life for a period of at least 120 months;

(b)   the applicant meets the requirements of para 276ADE (see **8.13.1.2**);

(c)   the applicant does not fall for refusal under the general grounds for refusal (see **3.5.4**);

(d)   the applicant has sufficient knowledge of the English language and sufficient knowledge about life in the UK by passing the test known as the 'Life in the UK Test' (see **3.8.7 and 8.10.4.4**), unless the applicant is under the age of 18 or aged 65 or over at the time the applicant makes the application; and

(e)   there are no reasons why it would be undesirable to grant the applicant indefinite leave to remain based on the applicant's conduct, character or associations, or because the applicant represents a threat to national security.

8.13.2.3   Decision on the application

By para 276DF, if the applicant meets all of the requirements at **8.13.2.2** he will be granted indefinite leave to remain.

But what if the applicant cannot meet all the requirements? Paragraph 276DG has a limited concession. It provides that if the applicant does not meet the requirements for indefinite leave to remain only for one or both of the following reasons:

(a)   para S-ILR.1.5 or 1.6 applies (see **8.6.2(c)**); and/or

(b)   the applicant does not have sufficient knowledge of the English language and sufficient knowledge about life in the UK;

then the applicant may be granted further limited leave to remain on the grounds of private life in the UK for a period not exceeding 30 months.

Where an applicant is granted further limited leave under para 276DG, he should be advised that should the reason at (a) and/or (b) above be overcome, he can make a further application for settlement at any time within the 30-month period.

The application will be refused if the applicant does not meet the requirements for indefinite leave to remain, or further leave to remain on the grounds of private life in the UK under para 276DG.

CHAPTER 9

ASYLUM-SEEKERS AND REFUGEES

9.1 OVERVIEW

People may flee their own countries for many different reasons – social, economic, political, religious, etc. On arrival in the UK or subsequently, they may state that they do not wish to return to their country of nationality or habitual residence.

An asylum-seeker is a person who flees because of a fear of persecution in his own country and who, as a consequence, is seeking the protection of the UK Government. Such protection is granted if that person is given the immigration status of a refugee. Otherwise, on human rights grounds, he may be granted what is known as humanitarian protection or discretionary leave (see **9.10**).

9.2 LAW AND PROCEDURE

9.2.1 Relevant law

Set out below is a list of the key legal provisions referred to in this chapter:

(a) The United Nations' 1951 Convention and 1967 Protocol Relating to the Status of Refugees (generally known as 'the Geneva Convention').

(b) UNHCR *Handbook on Procedures and Criteria for Determining Refugee Status*.

(c) Parts 11 and 11B of the Immigration Rules.

(d) The Refugee or Person in Need of International Protection (Qualification) Regulations 2006 (SI 2006/2525) ('Qualification Regulations 2006'). A copy is reproduced at **Appendix 14**.

(e) UK and ECHR case law.

(f) Home Office asylum policy instructions and process guidance.

9.2.2 Procedure

Asylum claims are dealt with by the Home Office. This chapter offers only an outline of the procedure involved. Those who wish to have a detailed understanding should consult the Home Office guidance, issued to its asylum staff and published on its website (see **1.2.8**).

Anyone in the UK can make an asylum claim, whatever his immigration status. He may be someone who has arrived without a visa or with forged documents, or someone who has obtained limited leave to enter for a different reason (eg as a visitor), an overstayer, or even an illegal entrant. The claim can be made on entry or after entry to the UK.

The Home Office 'New Asylum Model' (NAM) aims to make a decision on an asylum claim within one month of the claim being made. To act so quickly, the Home Office official responsible for the case, known as 'the case owner', conducts the claim from start to finish to a strict timetable. The case owner should also work closely with the claimant's representative.

On the day a claim is made, the claimant has a screening interview to establish his identity and nationality. At this point fingerprints and photographs are also taken. A few basic questions about the claim are asked. The claim is then transferred to a NAM centre at Glasgow, Cardiff, Leeds, Liverpool, Solihull, Central London or West London. The claimant meets the case owner within three working days. By the tenth working day, the representative should submit the claimant's statement and any supporting evidence. In the following days, the case owner and representative discuss the case to work out what parts of the claim are accepted and what further evidence is needed. On the fifteenth working day, the claimant has an interview. On the Home Office website you will find a protocol and guidance notes for asylum staff conducting an interview, as well as a code of conduct for any interpreter used at an interview. Following any further discussion between the case owner and the representative, the case owner's decision, whether to grant or refuse asylum, is given by the twentieth working day.

In 2013 the Government announced that it would introduce a revised version of NAM known as the Asylum Operating Model. This is intended to speed up decision-making and make it more consistent. At the time of writing (August 2013) the details of the model were not available.

9.3 WHAT IS AN ASYLUM CLAIM?

9.3.1 The Geneva Convention

The Immigration Rules, para 327 defines an applicant for asylum as a person who makes a request to be recognised as a refugee under the Geneva Convention on the basis that it would be contrary to the UK's obligations under that Convention for him to be removed from or required to leave the UK, or otherwise makes a request for international protection.

To be granted asylum, or the status of a refugee, a claimant must meet the following requirements as set out in Article 1A of the Geneva Convention:

> [The claimant,] owing to well-founded fear of being persecuted for reasons of race, religion, nationality, membership of a particular social group or political opinion, is outside the country of his nationality and is unable or, owing to such fear, is unwilling to avail himself of the protection of that country; or who, not having a nationality and being outside the country of his former habitual residence ... is unable, or owing to such fear, is unwilling to return to it.

By para 334 of the Immigration Rules, an asylum applicant will be granted asylum in the UK if the Secretary of State is satisfied that:

(a)   he is in the UK or has arrived at a port of entry in the UK;

(b)   he is a refugee falling within Article 1A (see **9.4**) and not excluded (see **9.5.1**);

(c)   there are no reasonable grounds for regarding him as a danger to the security of the UK (see **9.5.2**);

(d)   he does not, having been convicted by a final judgment of a particularly serious crime, constitute danger to the community of the UK (see **9.5.2**); and

(e)   refusing his application would result in his being required to go (whether immediately or after the time limited by any existing leave to enter or remain) in breach of the Geneva Convention, to a country in which his life or freedom would be threatened on account of his race, religion, nationality, political opinion or membership of a particular social group.

9.3.2   Sources of persecution

Before we look in detail at each requirement of Article 1A, and in particular at what may amount to persecution, we shall consider the possible source of that fear. It might be the government or State itself. Legislation may discriminate against or persecute a certain group, for example, laws may discriminate against women or homosexuals. Or the persecution might come from State bodies, like the police or the army, acting on government orders. Additionally, there may be persecution if the State fails to take steps to protect its citizens from officials who abuse their authority. This might include, for example, a policeman who rapes a woman for his own sexual gratification.

A person may also fear being persecuted by people who have nothing to do with the government. These are known as non-State actors (see further **9.4.1.5**). Common examples concern political or religious intolerance, such as where one section of society does not respect the political or religious beliefs of another. Here we need to remember that part of the Geneva Convention test is that the claimant is unwilling to avail himself of the protection of his country. The question is whether or not the State has a system of criminal law which makes attacks by non-State actors punishable *and* if the State is prepared to take reasonable steps to enforce that law.

9.4   MEETING THE REQUIREMENTS OF THE GENEVA CONVENTION

9.4.1   Well-founded fear of persecution

9.4.1.1   Subjective and objective tests

The claimant must be in fear of persecution, but his claim can be rejected if there is no real risk or reasonable likelihood of persecution (*R v Secretary of State for the Home Department, ex p Sivakumaran and conjoined appeals (UN High Commissioner for Refugees Intervening)* [1988] 1 All ER 193). The main issue will be the credibility of the claimant's testimony (see also **9.6.2**) that he has a genuine fear (the subjective test), but the Home Office may rely on evidence of conditions in the country from which he is fleeing to show that there is insufficient basis for the fear (the objective test). The Home Office Country of Origin Information Service has produced assessments of certain countries that produce a significant number of asylum claims. These are used for background purposes by caseworkers (see further **9.7**).

In some cases applicants may be able to provide some documentary evidence to support their claims, such as newspaper or Internet articles, passports or identity cards, political party membership cards, arrest warrants, photographs and medical reports. Organisations such as Amnesty International and the US Department of State (country reports) may be able to provide helpful evidence. As to medical evidence of torture, an applicant may be able to obtain a report from the charity Medical Foundation for the Care of Victims of Torture (see www.torturecare.org.uk). This organisation provides medical and social care, practical assistance and therapy to survivors of torture. If the applicant is already seeing a doctor or consultant, he may be able to provide a report.

When obtaining medical evidence of a claimant's injuries or scarring, it is important that the expert assesses how they were caused: see *SA (Somalia)* [2006] EWCA Civ 1302 and *RT (medical reports, cause of scarring) Sri Lanka* [2008] UKAIT 00009. Where the expert makes findings that there is a degree of consistency between the injuries or scarring and the claimant's allegations as to how they were caused by his persecutors, the expert should also include any other possible causes (whether many, few or unusually few), and gauge how likely they are, bearing in mind what is known about the individual's life history and experiences. Where possible an expert should be instructed to consider the degree of consistency on the following scale:

(1)   *Not consistent*: the injury or scarring could not have been caused as alleged.

(2)   *Consistent with*: the injury or scarring could have been caused as alleged, but it is non-specific and there are many other possible causes.

(3)   *Highly consistent*: the injury or scarring could have been caused as alleged, and there are few other possible causes.

(4)   *Typical of*: this is an appearance that is usually found with this type of injury or scarring, but there are other possible causes.

(5)   *Diagnostic of*: this appearance could not have been caused in any way other than that alleged.

9.4.1.2   Benefit of the doubt

Obviously, the applicant may find it difficult to provide evidence of events in his home country and many statements may be unsupported. According to the UNHCR *Handbook*, statements should not necessarily be rejected for that reason: 'If the applicant's account appears credible, he should, unless there are good reasons to the contrary, be given the benefit of the doubt' (para 196). Unsupported statements need not, however, be accepted if they are inconsistent with the general account put forward by the applicant (para 197).

9.4.1.3   Acts of persecution

'Persecution' is not defined in the Geneva Convention on refugees. The UNHCR *Handbook* suggests that while it will often involve a threat to life or liberty, it could extend to other threats. Discrimination against a particular group does not of itself amount to persecution; but it may do so if serious, for example if it stops someone practising his religion, or earning a livelihood. 'Persecution' does not mean 'punishment'. A person who fears punishment for commission of a common-law crime will not normally be regarded as a refugee, unless, for example, the law under which he is to be punished is seriously discriminatory.

Further examples of persecution are listed in reg 5(2) of the Qualification Regulations 2006. These include an act of physical or mental violence, including an act of sexual violence; a legal, administrative, police, or judicial measure which in itself is discriminatory, or which is implemented in a discriminatory manner; and prosecution or punishment which is disproportionate or discriminatory.

In R (*Sivakumar*) *v Secretary of State for the Home Department* [2003] 2 All ER 1097, the House of Lords held that it is the severity of the treatment inflicted on the applicant that has a logical bearing on the issues. Excessive or arbitrary punishment can amount to persecution.

Regulation 5(1) of the Qualification Regulations 2006 provides that an act of persecution must be sufficiently serious by its nature or repetition as to constitute a severe violation of a basic human right, in particular a right from which derogation cannot be made under Article 15 ECHR. The basic human rights from which derogation cannot be made under the ECHR include Article 2 (right to life – save that derogation is permitted in respect of deaths resulting from lawful acts of war); Article 3 (prohibition of torture, inhuman or degrading treatment or punishment); Article 4(1) (prohibition of slavery) and Article 7 (no punishment without law). Alternatively, persecution may arise from an accumulation of various measures, including a violation of a human right which is sufficiently severe as to affect an individual in this manner.

A person does not have to be singled out for adverse treatment in order to be said to be persecuted (see R *v Secretary of State for the Home Department, ex p Jeyakumaran (Selladurai)* [1994]

Imm AR 45). Discrimination may amount to persecution – this accords with the Tribunal decision of *Padhu* (12318), concerning the inability to work and deprivation of State benefits due to ethnic origin. What if the persecution feared comes from non-State actors? In the case of *Gashi and Nikshiqi v Secretary of State for the Home Department (United Nations High Commissioner for Refugees Intervening)* [1997] INLR 96, the Tribunal held that persecution includes the failure of a State to protect:

(a)   those rights which are non-derogative even in times of compelling national emergency (the right to life; prohibition against torture and cruel, inhumane or degrading treatment);

(b)   those rights which are derogative during an officially recognised life-threatening public emergency (freedom from arbitrary arrest and detention; fair trial);

(c)   some aspects of those rights which require States to take steps to the maximum of their available resources to realise rights progressively in a non-discriminatory manner (the right to earn a livelihood; the right to a basic education; the right to food, housing and medical care).

9.4.1.4   Current fear and past acts of persecution

Whilst there must be a current fear of persecution for a Convention reason upon return (see *Adan v Secretary of State for the Home Department* [1999] 1 AC 293), persecution suffered in the past is relevant to whether a person has a current, well-founded fear of persecution. This is recognised by para 339K of the Immigration Rules. It provides that the fact that a person has already been subject to persecution, or to direct threats of such persecution, will be regarded as a serious indication of the person's well-founded fear of persecution, unless there are good reasons to consider that such persecution will not be repeated. Equally, whilst a past history of no persecution is not determinative of future risks, unless circumstances in an asylum-seeker's return country have deteriorated or some other special factor is present, it is inevitable that an asylum-seeker will have difficulty in showing future risk in the absence of any finding of past persecution: see *Becerikil v Secretary of State for the Home Department* [2006] EWCA Civ 693.

9.4.1.5   Persecution by non-State actors

The applicable law as to persecution by non-State actors is the House of Lords' decision in *Horvath v Secretary of State for the Home Department* [2001] 1 AC 489. This established that persecution implied a failure by the State to make protection available against the ill-treatment or violence which had been suffered at the hands of the persecutors. In such a case, the failure of the State to provide protection was an essential element, and accordingly the person claiming refugee status had to show that the feared persecution consisted of acts of violence against which the State was unable or unwilling to provide protection. Such a conclusion was consistent with the principle of surrogacy which underpinned the Convention, namely that the protection afforded by the Convention was activated only upon the failure of protection by the home State. Moreover, the application of that principle rested upon the assumption that the home State was not expected to achieve complete protection against random and isolated attacks.

Accordingly, in determining whether the protection afforded by the applicant's home country was sufficient for the purposes of the Convention, the court had to apply a practical standard which took proper account of the duty owed by a State to all its nationals, rather than a standard which eliminated all risk. Thus, the sufficiency of State protection was to be measured not by the existence of a real risk of an abuse of human rights but by the availability of a system for the protection of the citizen and a reasonable willingness to operate that system. This is now reflected in reg 4 of the Qualification Regulations 2006.

9.4.1.6 Attacks on applicant's family members

Can an attack upon an applicant's spouse or close family member amount to persecution of the applicant for the purposes of an asylum claim, even though there was no direct threat to the applicant himself? 'Yes', said the Court of Appeal in *Frantisek Katrinak v Secretary of State for the Home Department* [2001] INLR 499. As Schiemann LJ said:

> If I return with my wife to a country where there is a reasonable degree of likelihood that she will be subjected to further grave physical abuse for racial reasons, that puts me in a situation where there is a reasonable degree of risk that I will be persecuted. It is possible to persecute a husband or a member of a family by what you do to other members of his immediate family. The essential task for the decision taker in these sort of circumstances is to consider what is reasonably likely to happen to the wife and whether that is reasonably likely to affect the husband in such a way as to amount to persecution of him.

9.4.1.7 Should the applicant have to change his behaviour to avoid persecution if returned?

Is a claimant required to take reasonable measures if returned home to avoid persecution? For example, where an applicant claims to have been persecuted as a homosexual, is it relevant to take into account whether it would be reasonable to expect him to behave 'discreetly' if returned? No, held the Supreme Court in *HJ (Iran) v Secretary of State or the Home Department* [2010] UKSC 31. In considering such a claim, the Home Office must address the following issues.

(a)   Is it satisfied on the evidence that the applicant is gay, or that he would be treated as gay by potential persecutors in his country of nationality?

(b)   Is it satisfied on the available evidence that gay people who lived openly would be liable to persecution in the applicant's country of nationality?

(c)   What will the applicant do if returned to that country?

(d)   If he would in fact live openly and thereby be exposed to a real risk of persecution, then he has a well-founded fear of persecution – even if he could avoid the risk by living 'discreetly'.

(e)   If, on the other hand, the applicant would in fact live discreetly and so avoid persecution, the question to be answered is why he would do so.

(f)   If the conclusion is that the applicant would choose to live discreetly simply because that was how he himself would wish to live, or because of social pressures, eg not wanting to distress his parents or embarrass his friends, then his application should be rejected.

(g)   If, on the other hand, the material reason for the applicant living discreetly on his return would be a fear of the persecution which would follow if he were to live openly as a gay man, then, other things being equal, his application should be accepted. Such a person has a well-founded fear of persecution. To reject his application on the ground that he could avoid the persecution by living discreetly would be to defeat the very right which the Convention exists to protect – his right to live freely and openly as a gay man without fear of persecution.

So, equally, as 'a general proposition a person found to have genuine political beliefs cannot be refused refugee status merely because they have declined to hide those beliefs, or to act "discreetly", in order to avoid persecution': per Carnwath LJ in *RT (Zimbabwe) v Secretary of State for the Home Department* [2010] EWCA Civ 1285 at [25].

9.4.1.8 Examples

> **EXAMPLE 1**
>
> Bela has fled from his own country which is engaged in civil war. His farm has been destroyed in a battle, and he has no other means of earning his living.

> The Home Office may argue that Bela is a displaced person rather than a refugee, unless he can show, for example, that he is likely to suffer persecution because he is identified with one of the sides in the civil war.

EXAMPLE 2

Chaka has left his country because high taxes and an economic crisis have caused his business to fail.

The Home Office may argue that he is an economic migrant rather than a refugee, unless he can show, for example, that the tax measures were directed at a particular ethnic group of which he is a member, designed to destroy their economic position.

9.4.2 'For reasons of race, religion, nationality, membership of a particular social group or political opinion'

9.4.2.1 Race

The concept of race includes, for example, colour, descent, or membership of a particular ethnic group. The fact that a claimant belongs to a certain racial group is not normally enough to prove a claim.

9.4.2.2 Religion

As to the meaning of the word 'religion', see *Omoruyi v Secretary of State for the Home Department* [2001] INLR 33. In the case the applicant was a Nigerian Christian persecuted by a group described variously as 'a secret cult ... associated with idol worshipping to the extent of drinking blood', 'a mafia organisation involving criminal acts', and a 'devil cult' carrying out 'rituals', namely 'the sacrificing of animals to a graven image'. The court held that the persecution was not for a Convention reason (ie it was not related to the applicant's beliefs but to the fact that he had failed to comply with certain demands made by the cult) and therefore his application for asylum failed.

Note that reg 6(1)(b) of the Qualification Regulations 2006 provides that the concept of religion includes, for example, the holding of theistic, non-theistic and atheistic beliefs; the participation in, or abstention from, formal worship in private or in public, either alone or in community with others; other religious acts or expressions of view, or forms of personal or communal conduct based on or mandated by any religious belief.

9.4.2.3 Nationality

The term 'nationality' includes citizenship, or the lack of it, as well as membership of a group determined by such matters as its cultural, ethnic, or linguistic identity. Persecution for reasons of nationality may consist of adverse actions and measures against a national, ethnic or linguistic minority, and in certain circumstances the fact of belonging to such a minority may in itself give rise to a well-founded fear of persecution.

Note that nationals of certain countries may have their asylum claims certified by the Secretary of State as unfounded (see **11.15**).

9.4.2.4 Membership of a particular social group

Over recent years, the courts have given much consideration as to what is meant by the expression 'particular social group'. In the joint cases of *Islam (Shahana) v Secretary of State for the Home Department; R v Immigration Appeal Tribunal and Secretary of State for the Home Department, ex p Syeda Shah* [1999] INLR 144, the House of Lords had to decide if two Pakistani women, who had fled Pakistan after false allegations of adultery and violence by their husbands, were part of such a group. The House held that a 'particular social group' consists of a group of persons who share a common, immutable characteristic that either is beyond the power of an individual to change, or is so fundamental to the individual's identity or conscience that he ought not to be required to change it. Thus, as gender is an immutable characteristic that is beyond the power of the individual to change, and as discrimination against women is prevalent in Pakistan, in violation of fundamental rights and freedoms, women in Pakistan constitute a particular social group.

In the *Islam* and *Shah* appeals, Lord Hoffmann asked:

> What is the reason for the persecution which the appellants fear? Here it is important to notice that it is made up of two elements. First, there is the threat of violence to Mrs Islam by her husband and his political friends and to Mrs Shah by her husband. This is a personal affair, directed against them as individuals. Secondly, there is the inability or unwillingness of the State to do anything to protect them. There is nothing personal about this. The evidence was that the State would not assist them because they were women. It denied them a protection against violence which it would have given to men. These two elements have to be combined to constitute persecution within the meaning of the Convention.

See also *RG (Ethiopia) v Secretary of State for the Home Department* [2006] EWCA Civ 339, where it was held that women and girls in Ethiopia constitute a particular social group. The Court found institutionalised discrimination, since the penal law in Ethiopia legitimises the marriage of abducted and raped girls to their violators, which marriage then exempts the latter from punishment. This, and the evidence of a lack of protection of women against sexual abuse and serious discrimination, shows a degree of complicity by the State in the treatment of women in Ethiopia, sufficient to conclude that women constitute a particular social group.

Regulation 6(1)(d) of the Qualification Regulations 2006, as interpreted in *K v Secretary of State for the Home Department; Fornah v Secretary of State for the Home Department* [2006] UKHL 45, [2007] 1 All ER 671, provides two useful guidelines defining a particular social group. First, where members of that group share an innate characteristic, or a common background that cannot be changed, or share a characteristic or belief that is so fundamental to identity or conscience that a person should not be forced to renounce it. Secondly, where the group has a distinct identity in the relevant country, because it is perceived as being different by the surrounding society.

9.4.2.5 Political opinion

To show persecution on grounds of political opinion, it is not enough for the claimant to establish that he holds opinions which his government opposes. He must show that that government will not tolerate his opinions, and that it is aware that he holds them. Where the claimant has committed criminal offences in the course of political opposition, he cannot base a claim to refugee status on fear of his country's normal punishment for that offence.

EXAMPLE

Enrico is a member of a minority linguistic group, and of the political party which represents it. The party is campaigning for language rights, for example in regional schools, and its political activities are permitted. His national government will not concede these rights and pursues discriminatory policies. Enrico has fled the country after setting fire to a school which refused to use the minority language.

The Home Office may argue that Enrico does not fear persecution on grounds of his political opinions, but rather punishment for an ordinary criminal offence. However, he may be able to show that his punishment would be excessive or arbitrary, which would amount to persecution. The discriminatory measures in themselves may not be sufficiently serious to amount to persecution on grounds of nationality.

In what circumstances may a person who objects to carrying out compulsory military service be granted asylum? In *Sepet v Secretary of State for the Home Department* [2003] 3 All ER 304, the House of Lords held that refugee status should be accorded to a person who refuses to undertake compulsory military service on the grounds that such service would or might require him to commit atrocities or gross human rights abuses, or participate in a conflict condemned by the international community, or where refusal to serve would earn grossly excessive or disproportionate punishment.

Even if a claimant does not hold political views which his government opposes, it may well be that the government believes that he does. So a person to whom a political opinion is imputed may qualify for refugee status: see *Sivakumar v Secretary of State for the Home Department* [2002] INLR 310. Imputed political opinion may include those who are perceived to be members or supporters of an opposition party, as well as anyone who is unable to demonstrate support for, or loyalty to, the government regime or ruling political party: see *TM (Zimbabwe) v Secretary of State for the Home Department* [2010] EWCA Civ 916.

> **EXAMPLE**
>
> Alexander has fled from his own country because his brother has been imprisoned for political activities.
>
> The Home Office may argue that Alexander's fear is not well founded, unless he can show that persecution is for an imputed political opinion or extends to the social group associated with the political activity.

9.4.3 'Is outside the country of his nationality'

No one can claim to be a refugee until he has left the country of which he is a citizen. This means that a claimant cannot normally obtain a visa from a UK entry clearance officer in his country, clearing him to enter the UK as a refugee. He must (somehow) find his way to the UK and make the claim on arrival. This may be difficult, as airlines are fined for carrying people without correct travel documents (Immigration (Carriers' Liability) Act 1987).

9.4.3.1 The internal flight alternative or internal relocation

The claimant must be outside his country owing to fear of persecution there. What if the persecution is to be feared in only part of the country? Paragraph 339O of the Immigration Rules provides that the Secretary of State will not grant asylum if in part of the country of origin a person would not have a well-founded fear of being persecuted, and the person can reasonably be expected to stay in that part of the country. So if someone would be safe only if he lived in a remote village, separated from his family, his flight from the country can still be said to be based on a fear of persecution there (see *R v Immigration Appeal Tribunal, ex p Jonah* [1985] Imm AR 7).

The House of Lords, in *Januzi v Secretary of State for the Home Department* [2006] UKHL 5, gave further guidance on this issue. Lord Hope of Craighead said (para 47):

> The question where the issue of internal relocation is raised can, then, be defined quite simply. As Linden JA put it in *Thirunavukkarasu v Canada (Minister of Employment and Immigration)* (1993) 109 DLR (4th) 682, 687, it is whether it would be unduly harsh to expect a claimant who is being persecuted for a Convention reason in one part of his country to move to a less hostile part before seeking refugee status abroad. The words 'unduly harsh' set the standard that must be met for this to be regarded as unreasonable. If the claimant can live a relatively normal life there judged by the standards that prevail in his country of nationality generally, and if he can reach the less hostile part without undue hardship or undue difficulty, it will not be unreasonable to expect him to move there.

9.4.3.2 Safe third country exception (AI(TC)A 2004, Sch 3)

There will be no breach of obligation if the UK returns the refugee to a 'safe country' which itself has an obligation to grant him asylum, and which could be expected to fulfil the requirements of the Geneva Convention on refugees. The general principle operated by governments is that a refugee should seek asylum in the first 'safe country' he reaches.

Under EC Council Regulation 343/2003 ('the Regulation') or the Dublin Convention, the UK may return an asylum seeker to the EU Member State which has responsibility for the asylum claim under the terms of the Geneva Convention on refugees (eg because that State granted him a visa, or he first entered that State as an illegal entrant). The Home Office will not remove the asylum seeker until the State receiving him has accepted its responsibility under the Regulation or the Dublin Convention. Once that has happened, the Home Office will assume that the receiving State will itself consider the claim and grant refugee status if the claim is well founded.

In these cases, it is possible for someone who meets the Geneva Convention on refugees' definition of 'refugee' to claim asylum in the UK, but for his claim, on examination by the Home Office, to fall outside the statutory definition of an asylum claim in the UK. Because return is to a 'safe country', the Home Office may refuse these claims 'without substantive consideration', that is without looking at other aspects of the claimant's case, such as whether he fears persecution in his home country (Immigration Rules, para 345).

Schedule 3 to the AI(TC)A 2004 (which replaced earlier similar provisions) is intended to deal with the fact that many Regulation or Dublin Convention cases were, in the Government's opinion, subject to unnecessary and lengthy delay as a result of judicial review applications which challenged the safety of the transfer. The Schedule sets out in Parts 2 to 5 a graduated approach to the 'safety' of third countries for the purposes of the Geneva Convention on refugees and the ECHR. Broadly, these are as follows.

Part 2 of Sch 3 deals with countries that are deemed safe for Geneva Convention purposes and for claims that onward removal from the State would breach the ECHR. All human rights claims against removal will be certified by the Secretary of State as clearly unfounded unless he is satisfied that they are not. The countries listed at para 2 of Part 2 are those which are subject to or have agreed to be bound by the Dublin Convention, currently the members of the EU (see **Appendix 2** to this book) together with Norway, Switzerland and Iceland. In *Nasser v Secretary of State for the Home Department* [2009] UKHL 23, the claimant challenged the legality of the Part 2, para 2 list. The House of Lords held that whilst the statute creates an irrebuttable presumption that the claimant may be removed from the UK to a country listed at para 2 of Part 2, the presumption does not preclude an inquiry into whether the claimant's Article 3 ECHR rights would be infringed for the different purpose of deciding whether the provision is incompatible with his Convention rights. In this case the Secretary of State accepted that that if removal to the country would infringe those rights then the conclusive presumption would be incompatible.

Paragraph 4 of Part 2 disapplies s 77 of the NIAA 2002 (which prevents removal while an asylum claim is pending) where the Secretary of State certifies that a person is to be removed to a listed State and he is not a national or citizen of that State. Paragraph 5 of Part 2 prevents a person being removed from bringing an appeal within the UK on the basis that the country is not safe for Geneva Convention on refugees' purposes or ECHR purposes in terms of onward removal. Paragraph 5 provides that where a human rights claim made on another basis is certified as clearly unfounded, a person being removed is similarly prevented from bringing an appeal within the UK. Lastly, para 5 provides that any human rights claim against removal (other than on the basis of onward removal) will be certified by the Secretary of State as clearly unfounded unless he is satisfied that it is not.

9.4.3.3 *Sur place* claims

Can a claimant have a well-founded fear of being persecuted or a real risk of suffering serious harm based on events which take place after he leaves his country of origin and/or activities in which he engages since leaving his country of origin? Yes, this provision can be found in the Immigration Rules, para 339P. It will apply, in particular, where it is established that the activities relied upon constitute the expression and continuation of convictions or orientations held in the country of origin by the claimant. The most common example is a claimant who carries on political activities in the UK. However, the provision applies equally to a claimant who was a conformist before leaving his country of origin but who becomes politicised in exile, even if those political activities were designed to create or enhance an asylum claim. As Kay LJ stated in *KS (Burma) v Secretary of State for the Home Department* [2013] EWCA Civ 67 at [32]: 'It is unpalatable that someone may become entitled to refugee status as a result of his cynical manipulation but if, objectively, he has a well-founded fear of persecution by reason of imputed political opinion, that may be the reality.'

In assessing a *sur place* claim, the key question is whether the claimant's activities create a real risk of persecution in his home country. The claim fails if the activities are not likely come to the attention of the authorities of that country or the authorities are likely to ignore them: see *TM (Zimbabwe) v Secretary of State for the Home Department* [2010] EWCA Civ 916.

How should a *sur place* claim be assessed? In *BA (Demonstrators in Britain – risk on return) Iran CG* [2011] UKUT 36 the Tribunal identified the following factors:

(i) *Nature of* sur place *activity*

- Theme of demonstrations – what do the demonstrators want (eg reform of the regime through to its violent overthrow); how will they be characterised by the regime?

- Role in demonstrations and political profile – can the person be described as a leader; mobiliser (eg addressing the crowd); organiser (eg leading the chanting); or simply a member of the crowd; if the latter is he active or passive (eg does he carry a banner); what is his motive, and is this relevant to the profile he will have in the eyes of the regime?

- Extent of participation – has the person attended one or two demonstrations, or is he a regular participant?

- Publicity attracted – has a demonstration attracted media coverage in the United Kingdom or the home country; nature of that publicity (quality of images; outlets where stories appear etc)?

(ii) *Identification risk*

- Surveillance of demonstrators – assuming the regime aims to identify demonstrators against it, how does it do so: through filming them, having agents who mingle in the crowd, reviewing images/recordings of demonstrations etc?

- Regime's capacity to identify individuals – does the regime have advanced technology (eg for facial recognition); does it allocate human resources to fit names to faces in the crowd?

(iii) *Factors triggering inquiry/action on return*

- Profile – is the person known as a committed opponent or someone with a significant political profile; does he fall within a category which the regime regards as especially objectionable?

- Immigration history – how did the person leave the country (illegally; type of visa); where has the person been when abroad; is the timing and method of return more likely to lead to inquiry and/or being detained for more than a short period and ill-treated (overstayer; forced return)?

(iv) Consequences of identification

- Is there differentiation between demonstrators depending on the level of their political profile adverse to the regime?

(v) Identification risk on return

- Matching identification to person – if a person is identified, is that information systematically stored and used; are border posts geared to the task?

9.4.4 'And is unable, or, owing to such fear, is unwilling to avail himself of the protection of that country'

A claimant would be unable to avail himself of his country's protection if, for example, it refused entry to him, or refused to issue him with a passport. A claimant who fears persecution will normally be unwilling to accept his government's protection, and it is inconsistent with his claim to refugee status if, for example, he wishes to retain his national passport.

9.5   EXCLUSION FROM REFUGEE STATUS

Even if an applicant meets the tests under the Geneva Convention, the UK Government will in certain circumstances refuse to grant him refugee status (**9.5.1**) or forcibly remove him (**9.5.2**). However, in either circumstance it must still go on to consider if it is appropriate to award the applicant humanitarian protection or discretionary leave (see **9.10**).

9.5.1   Exclusion under Article 1F

Article 1F of the Geneva Convention excludes the following claimants from asylum because they are considered not to be deserving of international protection. This is because there are serious reasons for considering that they:

(a)   have committed a crime against peace, a war crime or a crime against humanity; or

(b)   have committed a serious non-political crime outside the country of refuge prior to admission into that country; or

(c)   are guilty of acts contrary to the purposes and principles of the United Nations.

The Home Office has set up a War Crimes Team to focus on modern-day war crimes. The team assists in the identification of people who may have committed or been complicit in war crimes, and supports action taken against them.

There is an evidential burden on the Secretary of State to establish serious reasons for considering that a claimant has committed an act under Article 1F (see *JS (Sri Lanka) v Secretary of State for the Home Department* [2010] UKSC 15). However, it does not have to be shown to the criminal standard of proof, ie beyond reasonable doubt (see *Al-Sirri v Secretary of State for the Home Department* [2009] EWCA Civ 222).

So when does Article 1F apply?

> I would hold an accused disqualified under Article 1F if there are serious reasons for considering him voluntarily to have contributed in a significant way to the organisation's ability to pursue its purpose of committing war crimes, aware that his assistance will in fact further that purpose. (per Lord Brown in *R (on the application of JS) (Sri Lanka) v Secretary of State for the Home Department* [2010] UKSC 15 at para 38)

What is a 'crime against humanity' for the purposes of Article 1F(a)? The starting point is the following definition in Article 7(1) of the Rome Statute of the International Criminal Court 2002:

> 1.   ... any of the following acts when committed as part of a widespread or systematic attack directed against any civilian population, with knowledge of the attack:
>
>   (a)   Murder;
>
>   (b)   Extermination;

...

(e)   Imprisonment or other severe deprivation of physical liberty ...;

(f)   Torture;

...

(h)   Persecution ... on political, racial, national, ethnic, cultural, religious, gender ... grounds ...;

(i)   Enforced disappearance of persons;

...

(k)   Other inhumane acts of a similar character intentionally causing great suffering, or serious injury to body or to mental or physical health.

(See *SK (Zimbabwe) v Secretary of State for the Home Department* [2012] 1 WLR 2809.)

Article 25 of the Rome Statute 2002 regulates individual criminal responsibility for a crime against humanity falling within Article 7. Article 25(3) provides that:

3.   In accordance with this Statute, a person shall be criminally responsible and liable for punishment for a crime within the jurisdiction of the Court if that person:

(a)   Commits such a crime, whether as an individual, jointly with another or through another person, regardless of whether that other person is criminally responsible;

(b)   Orders, solicits or induces the commission of such a crime which in fact occurs or is attempted;

(c)   For the purpose of facilitating the commission of such a crime, aids, abets or otherwise assists in its commission or its attempted commission, including providing the means for its commission;

(d)   In any other way contributes to the commission or attempted commission of such a crime by a group of persons acting with a common purpose. Such contribution shall be intentional and shall either:

(i)   Be made with the aim of furthering the criminal activity or criminal purpose of the group, where such activity or purpose involves the commission of a crime within the jurisdiction of the Court; or

(ii)   Be made in the knowledge of the intention of the group to commit the crime.

...

For a detailed discussion of this exclusionary provision, see *AA-R (Iran) v Secretary of State for the Home Department* [2013] EWCA Civ 835.

Note that reg 7(2) of the Qualification Regulations 2006 interprets the meaning of Article 1F(b) as follows:

The reference to 'serious non-political crime' includes a particularly cruel action, even if it is committed with an allegedly political objective. The reference to the crime being committed outside the country of refuge prior to his admission as a refugee shall mean the time up to and including the day on which a residence permit [signifying the grant of refugee status] is issued.

Note that in *AH (Article 1F (b) – 'serious') Algeria* [2013] UKUT 382 it was said: 'The examination of seriousness should be directed at the criminal acts when they were committed, although events in the supervening passage of time may be relevant to whether exclusion is justified: a formal pardon, or subsequent acquittal, or other event illuminating the nature of the activity may be relevant to this assessment.'

Also note that s 54 of the IANA 2006 interprets the meaning of Article 1F(c). It provides that acts of committing, preparing or instigating terrorism, or encouraging or inducing others to do so, are included within the meaning of what constitutes 'acts contrary to the purposes and principles of the United Nations'. See further *AH (Algeria) v Secretary of State for the Home Department* [2012] EWCA Civ 395 and *Al-Sirri v Secretary of State for the Home Department* [2013] 1 AC 745.

The application of Article 1F(c) will be straightforward in the case of an active member of an organisation that promotes its objects only by acts of terrorism. There will almost certainly be serious reasons for considering that he has been guilty of acts contrary to the purposes and principles of the United Nations. However, what if the organisation pursues its political ends in part by acts of terrorism and in part by military action directed against the armed forces of the government? A person may join such an organisation because he agrees with its political objectives, and may be willing to participate in its military actions, but he may not agree with and may not be willing to participate in its terrorist activities. The higher up in the organisation a person is, the more likely will be the inference that he agrees with and promotes all of its activities, including its terrorism.

> **EXAMPLE**
>
> Danilow fled from his country after being imprisoned for distributing political leaflets. In order to finance his escape he commits an armed robbery.
>
> Whether the armed robbery amounts to a serious non-political crime depends on whether it has been committed for political motives, or for personal reasons or gain, and whether the act was proportionate to the alleged objective. The Home Office may well argue that Danilow's criminal character outweighs his character as a bona fide refugee (see T v Secretary of State for the Home Department (1996) The Times, 23 May).

9.5.2 Enforced removal under Article 33(2)

Article 33(2) of the Geneva Convention allows the UK Government to remove a person who is otherwise a refugee where there are reasonable grounds for regarding him as a danger to the security of the UK, or who, having been convicted by a final judgment of a particularly serious crime, constitutes a danger to the community of the UK.

Home Office guidance is that for a person to be a danger to the security of the UK, the actions or anticipated actions of that person need not create a direct threat to the UK's system of government or its people. The interests of national security could be threatened indirectly by activities directed against other States. Thus the definition of a threat to national security is very wide: for example, depending on the specific facts of the case, if someone is believed or known to be a terrorist then, due to the nature of international terrorism, and regardless of the immediate threat of his particular terrorist group, it may be reasonable to regard the person as a threat to the UK's national security.

What is a particularly serious crime such that the person constitutes a danger to the community of the UK? By s 72 of the NIAA 2002, there is a general presumption of this where the person was sentenced to a period of imprisonment of at least two years. Note, however, that in EN (Serbia) v Secretary of State for the Home Department [2009] EWCA Civ 630, the Court of Appeal held that the presumption is rebuttable and that the Nationality, Immigration and Asylum Act 2002 (Specification of Particularly Serious Crimes) Order 2004 (SI 2004/1910), which specifies a large number of offences as offences to which s 72 applies, irrespective of the sentence imposed, is ultra vires and unlawful.

The Court in EN (Serbia) stressed that the second ground for enforced removal under Article 33(2) requires two conditions to be met: first, that the refugee has been convicted by a final judgment of a particularly serious crime; and, secondly, that he constitutes a danger to the community. The presumption that each of these conditions is met is rebuttable. So, for example, if the refugee can demonstrate that he is not a danger to the community, Article 33(2) cannot apply. Note, however, that the Court indicated (at [45] and [46]) that where a person is convicted of a particularly serious crime, and there is a real risk of its repetition or the recurrence of a similar offence, he is likely to constitute a danger to the community. The Court also gave the example of a person convicted of a particularly serious offence of violence whom the Government can establish is a significant drug dealer as being one where removal under Article 33(2) is likely.

9.6 CONSIDERATION OF CASES

9.6.1 The Home Office checklist

Home Office asylum case owners use the following checklist when assessing a claim:

(a) What is the applicant's basis of claim?

(b) Which of the applicant's claims about past events can be accepted?

Are the applicant's claims as to his past experiences consistent with objective country of origin information (see **9.7**) relating to the relevant period, including generally known facts?

Are the applicant's claims consistent with other evidence submitted, eg the evidence of other witnesses, family members or documents specifically referring to the applicant?

Are any of the applicant's claims about his past experiences not able to be corroborated by reference to country of origin information or other evidence? If so, can the benefit of the doubt be given to any of these claims? If not, why not?

After due consideration of the principle of the benefit of the doubt, which of the applicant's material claims can be accepted, and which can be rejected?

(c) Taking into account the applicant's statements and behaviour, does the applicant have a subjective fear of persecution?

(d) Objectively, are there reasonable grounds for believing that the harm feared might in fact occur in the applicant's country of origin?

Who are the actors of persecution? Do the authorities of the home country conduct the persecution, or support persecution committed by others?

How far is the State or organisations controlling the State (including international organisations) able to provide protection from persecution caused by others? What laws are in place and are they enforced effectively?

Has the applicant sought the protection of the authorities? If so, what was the outcome? If not, why not?

Considering the objective country of origin information, the past experiences of the applicant and the attitude of the State authorities, is there a reasonable likelihood that the applicant would experience harm if returned?

(e) Can the applicant return to a part of the country in which he would not be subject to the harm feared (see **9.4.3.1**)?

(f) Is the harm feared a form of persecution (see **9.4.1.3**)?

Is the harm of sufficient gravity to constitute persecution, or is it something less serious?

Does the cumulative effect of lesser prejudicial actions or threats amount to persecution?

If the applicant has a fear of prosecution or punishment for an offence, is the punishment discriminatory or disproportionate? Does this give rise to a fear of persecution?

If the fear of prosecution is due to draft evasion or desertion, special considerations may apply.

(g) If the harm feared is serious enough to constitute persecution, would it be inflicted for one or more of the reasons set out in the Refugee Convention, ie race, religion, nationality, membership of a particular social group or political opinion? See further **9.4.2**.

(h)   In the light of (a)–(g) above, does the applicant satisfy all the criteria of the 1951 Convention?

(i)   Should the applicant be excluded from international protection by operation of the exclusion clauses of the Convention? See further **9.5**.

(j)   If an applicant fails to qualify for asylum, decision makers should consider whether to grant humanitarian protection or discretionary leave (see **9.10**).

9.6.2 Adverse inferences

9.6.2.1 Claimant's duties

The Immigration Rules (paras 339I–339N) list some factors which are taken into account. These start by imposing a duty on the claimant to submit to the Secretary of State, as soon as possible, all material factors needed to substantiate the asylum claim. These material factors include the claimant's statement of the reasons for making an asylum claim; all documentation at the claimant's disposal regarding his age, background, identity, nationality(ies), country(ies) and place(s) of previous residence, previous asylum applications, and travel routes; and identity and travel documents.

It is further the duty of the claimant to substantiate the claim. Paragraph 339L of the Immigration Rules provides that where aspects of the claimant's statements are not supported by documentary or other evidence, those aspects will not need confirmation when *all* of the following conditions are met:

(a)   the claimant has made a genuine effort to substantiate his asylum claim;

(b)   all material factors at the claimant's disposal have been submitted, and a satisfactory explanation regarding any lack of other relevant material has been given;

(c)   the claimant's statements are found to be coherent and plausible, and do not run counter to available specific and general information relevant to his case;

(d)   the claimant has made an asylum claim at the earliest possible time, unless he can demonstrate good reason for not having done so; and

(e)   the general credibility of the claimant has been established.

Paragraph 339M of the Immigration Rules provides that the Secretary of State may consider that a person has not substantiated his asylum claim if he fails, without reasonable explanation, to make a prompt and full disclosure of material facts, either orally or in writing, or otherwise to assist the Secretary of State in establishing the facts of the case. This includes, for example, a failure to attend an interview, failure to report to a designated place to be fingerprinted, failure to complete an asylum questionnaire or failure to comply with a requirement to report to an immigration officer for examination.

9.6.2.2 Statutory adverse inferences

Section 8(1) of the AI(TC)A 2004 includes similar guidelines for assessing the credibility of the claimant. The key provisions are as follows:

(1)   In determining whether to believe a statement made by or on behalf of a person who makes an asylum claim or a human rights claim, a deciding authority shall take account, as damaging the claimant's credibility, of any behaviour to which this section applies.

(2)   This section applies to any behaviour by the claimant that the deciding authority thinks—

    (a)   is designed or likely to conceal information,

    (b)   is designed or likely to mislead, or

    (c)   is designed or likely to obstruct or delay the handling or resolution of the claim or the taking of a decision in relation to the claimant.

(3)   Without prejudice to the generality of subsection (2) the following kinds of behaviour shall be treated as designed or likely to conceal information or to mislead—

(a) failure without reasonable explanation to produce a passport on request to an immigration officer or to the Secretary of State,

(b) the production of a document which is not a valid passport as if it were,

(c) the destruction, alteration or disposal, in each case without reasonable explanation, of a passport,

(d) the destruction, alteration or disposal, in each case without reasonable explanation, of a ticket or other document connected with travel, and

(e) failure without reasonable explanation to answer a question asked by a deciding authority.

(4) This section also applies to failure by the claimant to take advantage of a reasonable opportunity to make an asylum claim or human rights claim while in a safe country.

(5) This section also applies to failure by the claimant to make an asylum claim or human rights claim before being notified of an immigration decision, unless the claim relies wholly on matters arising after the notification.

(6) This section also applies to failure by the claimant to make an asylum claim or human rights claim before being arrested under an immigration provision, unless—

(a) he had no reasonable opportunity to make the claim before the arrest, or

(b) the claim relies wholly on matters arising after the arrest.

9.6.2.3 How adverse?

What is the effect of s 8(1)? In *JT (Cameroon) v Secretary of State for the Home Department* [2008] EWCA Civ 878, the Court of Appeal held that the section lays down a framework of factors that may potentially damage a claimant's credibility. However, it is for the decision maker to decide the extent to which that person's credibility is damaged, if at all, and what weight should be given to any adverse finding of credibility. In this case the claimant had used false papers to enter the UK and false identities whilst in the UK. The Home Office refused the claimant asylum and the Tribunal determined that under s 8 the claimant's conduct had seriously damaged his credibility.

9.6.2.4 Reasonable explanation

What is a reasonable explanation for the purposes of s 8(3)(a) and (c)–(e)? Home Office guidance is that this may include exceptional situations where the applicant could not easily have disobeyed the instructions of an agent who facilitates immigration into the UK; cases where an adult is severely traumatised, or where cultural norms may make it difficult for a person to answer questions at interview or to disobey instructions, including instructions about documents; situations where a person can show that a document was destroyed or disposed of as a direct result of force, threats or intimidation, eg where an individual was forced at knifepoint to give a document to someone else; or where the document has been lost or stolen and the individual can substantiate such a claim, usually with a police report of the loss or theft.

What is a safe country for the purposes of s 8(4)? It is any country listed in Part 2 of Sch 3 to the AI(TC)A 2004 (see **9.4.3.2**). What is a reasonable opportunity to claim asylum in such a country? Home Office guidance is that the claimant could have approached the authorities at the border or internally, as long as there is no reason to think that the claim would not have been received. For example, it might be thought that someone who spent several weeks in France before coming to the UK must have had a reasonable opportunity to claim asylum there; but this would not be reasonable if the applicant was imprisoned by traffickers throughout that time.

As to what is an immigration decision for the purposes of s 8(5), see **11.2**.

As to s 8(6), Home Office guidance is that an applicant's credibility must be treated as damaged if the claim is made after the applicant's arrest under an immigration provision unless there was no reasonable opportunity to make the claim before the arrest, or the claimant relies wholly on matters arising after the arrest. An applicant has had a reasonable opportunity to claim asylum before being arrested if he could have approached the authorities at any time after his arrival in the UK. Each case should be considered on its merits. So, for example, someone who is apprehended by the police soon after getting out of a back of a lorry is less likely to have been able to make a claim before arrest than someone who passed through immigration control when arriving in the UK.

9.7 COUNTRY OF ORIGIN INFORMATION

The Country of Origin Information Service (COI Service) produces key documents that are used by Home Office asylum staff as part of assessing a claim. These include Country of Origin Information Reports, Country of Origin Bulletins and Country of Origin Key Documents.

The Reports provide a brief summary of the general, political and human rights situations in particular countries, and describe common types of claim. There are over 30 country reports.

The Bulletins are issued on an ad hoc basis and aim to provide clear guidance on how to deal with particular country-specific issues arising in asylum and human rights applications.

The Key Documents provide an indexed list of reports, papers and articles produced by a wide range of recognised external information sources, mainly on human rights issues. They do not contain any Home Office opinion or policy.

Full details and the documents can be found at www.homeoffice.gov.uk/rds/country_reports.html.

9.8 REFUGEE STATUS

9.8.1 Five years' limited leave

A refugee is normally granted five years' leave to remain in the UK. Pursuant to para 339Q(i) of the Immigration Rules, the Secretary of State issues what is known as a UK Residence Permit valid for five years. During this time the refugee is free to work and claim all mainstream welfare benefits.

9.8.2 Settlement

After holding limited leave for five years, a refugee may apply for settlement (when the usual criminality requirements will apply by para 339R of the Immigration Rules).

9.8.3 Review of status

A refugee's status is liable to a review which may lead to that status being withdrawn, cancelled or revoked. Such a step does not in itself affect the person's leave but, in practice, it will normally result in curtailment of any limited leave (see **3.7**) or revocation of any indefinite leave, and in action being taken to remove the person from the UK (see **Chapter 10**).

9.8.3.1 Withdrawal of refugee status

Paragraph 339A of the Immigration Rules gives the Secretary of State power to withdraw refugee status from a person where:

(a) he has voluntarily re-availed himself of the protection of the country of nationality;

(b) having lost his nationality, he has voluntarily re-acquired it; or

(c) he has acquired a new nationality, and enjoys the protection of the country of his new nationality;

(d) he has voluntarily re-established himself in the country which he left or outside which he remained owing to a fear of persecution;

(e) he can no longer, because the circumstances in connection with which he has been recognised as a refugee have ceased to exist, continue to refuse to avail himself of the protection of the country of nationality;

(f) being a stateless person with no nationality, he is able, because the circumstances in connection with which he has been recognised a refugee have ceased to exist, to return to the country of former habitual residence.

Note that (a)–(d) are voluntary steps taken by the refugee. In respect of (e) and (f) the Secretary of State must issue a Ministerial Statement announcing that significant and non-temporary changes have occurred in a particular country such that nationals can be expected to return, or that there are exceptional circumstances for that.

9.8.3.2 Cancellation of refugee status

Paragraph 339A of the Immigration Rules gives the Secretary of State power to cancel a person's refugee status where:

(a) he should have been or is excluded from being a refugee in accordance with reg 7 of the Qualification Regulations 2006 (see **9.5.1**);

(b) his misrepresentation or omission of facts, including the use of false documents, was decisive for the grant of asylum;

(c) there are reasonable grounds for regarding him as a danger to the security of the UK (see **9.5.2**);

(d) having been convicted by a final judgment of a particularly serious crime he constitutes danger to the community of the UK (see **9.5.2**).

9.8.3.3 Revocation of refugee status

Home Office guidance is that revocation of refugee status may be appropriate where a refugee's conduct is so serious that it warrants withdrawal of that status. Where there are serious reasons for considering that a person has committed a crime or act that falls within the scope of Article 1F(a) or (c) (see **9.5.1**), subsequent to the grant of asylum, it will be appropriate to revoke a person's refugee status.

9.9 HUMAN RIGHTS ISSUES

A person may claim that he should be allowed to remain in the UK as his removal would be a breach of his human rights and that he cannot reasonably be expected to return voluntarily.

9.9.1 Domestic and foreign cases

The House of Lords in R (*Ullah*) *v Special Adjudicator; Do v Secretary of State for the Home Department* [2004] UKHL 26 distinguished between what it called domestic and foreign cases. A domestic case is where an applicant alleges that the UK has acted in a way which infringes the applicant's enjoyment of a Convention right within the UK. The most common example is where a person claims that his removal would separate him from his family in the UK and so breach Article 8 ECHR.

A foreign case is where a person claims that requiring him to leave the UK will lead to a violation of his Convention rights in the country of return, ie the alleged violation of the Convention right will occur outside the UK. For example, an applicant may allege that on return he will suffer death contrary to Article 2; inhuman or degrading treatment in breach of Article 3; unlawful detention breaching Article 5; an unfair trial contrary to Article 6; or restrictions on his freedom of religion or expression in breach of Articles 9 and 10. Article 8 claims may arise in respect of a claimant's private life. For example, a person may claim that he would be unable to be openly homosexual in the receiving State because of societal prejudice and/or legislation banning homosexuality, and that his removal from the UK would therefore lead to a breach of his right to respect for private life in the receiving country.

9.9.2   Article 2 ECHR

Home Office guidance is that it will not normally seek to return a person to a country where there are substantial grounds for believing that there is a real risk he would be unlawfully killed either by the State, or through the State being unable or unwilling to protect him. In R (Ullah) v Special Adjudicator; Do v Secretary of State for the Home Department (**9.9.1** above) the House of Lords cited the decision of the ECtHR in Dehwari v Netherlands (2000) 29 EHRR CD 74, where the Court doubted whether a real risk was enough to resist removal under Article 2 and suggested that the loss of life must be shown to be a 'near-certainty'.

9.9.3   Article 3 ECHR

A person will not be removed from the UK to a country where there are substantial reasons for believing that he faces a real risk of serious harm or other treatment contrary to Article 3. This includes torture, as well as treatment or punishment that is degrading because it arouses in the victim feelings of fear, anguish or inferiority capable of humiliating and debasing him, and possibly breaking his physical and moral resistance. Severe discrimination based on race, sex or other grounds is also capable of constituting degrading treatment.

Ever since the ECtHR held in D v United Kingdom (1997) 24 EHRR 423 that the expulsion of an AIDS sufferer to St Kitts would breach Article 3 ECHR, the Strasbourg Court has sought to distinguish that case. In the case of D, the court extended the reach of Article 3. The Court noted that Contracting States have the right, as a matter of well-established international law and subject to their treaty obligations including the ECHR, to control the entry, residence and expulsion of aliens. The Court applied Article 3 in what it described as the 'very exceptional circumstances' of that case, namely that the applicant was in the final stage of a terminal illness, AIDS, and had no prospect of medical care or family support on expulsion to St Kitts. In N(FC) v Secretary of State for the Home Department [2005] UKHL 31, [2005] 2 WLR 1124, the House of Lords was not persuaded to extend Article 3 any further. The House held that it must be shown that the applicant's medical condition has reached such a critical state that there are compelling humanitarian grounds for not removing him or her to a place which lacks the medical and social services which he or she would need to prevent acute suffering. This approach was confirmed when the case was appealed to the ECtHR: see N v UK [2008] LTL 28 May (App No 00026565/05).

It can be seen that the case of D v United Kingdom establishes that Article 3 may be engaged where the harm will not result from inhuman and degrading treatment by the receiving authority. For example, in Bensaid v United Kingdom [2001] ECHR 82, the applicant suffered from long-term schizophrenia. He claimed that his condition would seriously deteriorate if he were returned to his home country because of difficulties in obtaining suitable medication there. The Court stated at para 37:

> Deterioration in his already existing mental illness could involve relapse into hallucinations and psychotic delusions involving self-harm and harm to others, as well as restrictions in social functioning (such as withdrawal and lack of motivation). The Court considers that the suffering associated with such a relapse could, in principle, fall within the scope of Article 3.

However, the Court went on to find that Article 3 would not be violated in this case as there were no exceptional circumstances.

9.9.4   Other Convention Articles

When considering a foreign case involving an article other than Articles 2 and 3 ECHR, Home Office guidance is that case owners should assess the likelihood of the alleged treatment or conduct occurring on return and whether that would be a breach of the ECHR; then they should consider whether any breach would be sufficiently serious that it would amount to a flagrant violation of the relevant Convention right.

Where a claim is based on Article 8 ECHR, Home Office guidance is that pursuant to para 326B of the Immigration Rules, it should be considered in line with Appendix FM (family life) (see **8.5**) and para 276ADE to 276DH (see **8.13**). If the claim for asylum (or humanitarian protection) is refused but the claimant qualifies for leave under either of these provisions, he should be granted leave to remain of 30 months, and he may be eligible to apply for settlement after 120 months of such leave.

9.10 HUMANITARIAN PROTECTION AND DISCRETIONARY LEAVE

9.10.1 Humanitarian protection

9.10.1.1 Overlap with asylum claim

The great majority of claims for humanitarian protection are likely to arise in the context of asylum claims. However, where an individual claims that although he is in need of international protection he is not seeking asylum, and the reasons given clearly do not engage the UK Government's obligations under the Refugee Convention (ie the fear of persecution is clearly not for one of the five Convention reasons: see **9.4.2**), then it is accepted as a stand-alone claim for humanitarian protection.

9.10.1.2 Paragraph 339C requirements

A person will be granted humanitarian protection in the UK if the Secretary of State is satisfied that the following requirements of para 339C of the Immigration Rules are met:

(a)   he is in the UK or has arrived at a port of entry in the UK; and

(b)   he does not qualify as a refugee (see **9.1**); and

(c)   substantial grounds have been shown for believing that the person concerned, if he returned to the country of return, would face a real risk of suffering serious harm and is unable, or, owing to such a risk, unwilling to avail himself of the protection of that country; and

(d)   he is not excluded from a grant of humanitarian protection. Exclusion is on the same grounds as that for asylum: see **9.5**.

For the purposes of (c) above, serious harm is defined as:

(a)   the death penalty or execution;

(b)   unlawful killing;

(c)   torture, or inhuman or degrading treatment or punishment of a person in the country of return; or

(d)   serious and individual threat to a civilian's life or person by reason of indiscriminate violence in situations of international or internal armed conflict.

In considering whether there are substantial grounds for believing that a person would face a real risk of suffering serious harm (para 339C(iii)), the standard of proof applied is that of a reasonable degree of likelihood or a real risk.

9.10.1.3 Grant of humanitarian protection

A person granted humanitarian protection is normally granted five years' leave to remain in the UK. Pursuant to para 339Q(i) of the Immigration Rules, the Secretary of State issues what is known as a UK Residence Permit, valid for five years. After holding limited leave for five years an application can be made for settlement. Life a refugee, this status is liable to a review, which may lead to its being withdrawn, cancelled or revoked (see **9.8.3**).

9.10.2   Discretionary leave

9.10.2.1   Overlap with asylum claim

The great majority of claims for discretionary leave are likely to arise in the context of asylum claims. However, a stand-alone human rights claim may also result in a grant of discretionary leave if the qualifying criteria are met.

9.10.2.2   Qualifying criteria for discretionary leave

In exceptional cases a person's medical condition, or severe humanitarian conditions in the country of return, can make his removal contrary to Article 3 ECHR. Home Office guidance is that the fact that the applicant is suffering from a distressing medical condition involving, say, a limited life expectancy or affecting his mental health, may not, in itself, be sufficient. An applicant will need to show exceptional circumstances that prevent return, namely that there are compelling humanitarian considerations, such as the applicant being in the final stages of a terminal illness without prospect of medical care or family support on return.

There may be some extreme, albeit rare, cases where a person would face such poor conditions if returned, like absence of water, food or basic shelter, that removal could be a breach of the UK's Article 3 obligations.

Home Office guidance is that discretionary leave may be appropriate where the breach would not give rise to a grant of humanitarian protection but where return would result in a flagrant denial of an ECHR right in the person's country of origin. However, it cautions that it will be rare for return to breach another Article of the ECHR in this way without also breaching Article 3.

9.10.2.3   Grant of discretionary leave

Where an applicant would have established that he was a refugee under the Geneva Convention (see **9.1**) or eligible for humanitarian protection (see **9.10.1**) but for the fact that he was excluded from that protection (see **9.8.3** and **9.10.1.3**), he is normally granted discretionary leave for six months which is then reviewed. For an example, see R (C) v Secretary of State for the Home Department [2008] LTL, 25 September.

A grant of discretionary leave is otherwise usually made for three years initially. It may then be extended. All applicants need to complete at least six years in total, or at least 10 years in excluded cases, before being eligible to apply for settlement.

Life a refugee and those granted humanitarian protection, this status is liable to a review, which may lead to its being withdrawn, cancelled or revoked (see **9.10.1.3**).

9.10.3   Asylum claims

All asylum claims are treated by the Home Office as containing an implied claim for humanitarian protection on the ground that the applicant will face a real risk of serious harm in the country of return, and/or a claim for discretionary leave on the basis that requiring the applicant to leave the UK will otherwise breach the UK's obligations under Article 3 because of the ill-treatment the applicant alleges he will suffer on return. In other words, all asylum claims should be treated as an implied Article 3 foreign case (see **9.9.1**); and if the asylum claim is refused, consideration should be given to whether return would breach the UK's obligations under Article 3, first by reference to the requirements for humanitarian protection and then by reference to any residual Article 3 issues that may entitle the applicant to discretionary leave.

9.11 CLAIMS CERTIFIED AS BEING UNFOUNDED

Section 94 of the NIAA 2002 allows the Secretary of State to certify that certain asylum or human rights claims are unfounded. The result is that there is no right of appeal in the UK. Further details are given at **11.15**.

9.12 DANGER OF UNSUCCESSFUL CLAIMS

In many cases, an entrant may feel that he has nothing to lose in making an asylum claim. However, his adviser should consider whether he has any other basis for remaining in the UK which might be prejudiced by an unsuccessful claim. If an applicant already has limited leave, the Home Office may, having refused asylum, proceed to consider whether he still meets the requirements of the Rules under which he was admitted to the UK. If he does not, his existing leave can be curtailed (see **3.7**) and he may then be removed from the UK.

> **EXAMPLE**
>
> Manuel was admitted to the UK as a student with 12 months' leave. Three months later he claims asylum. The Home Office refuses the claim. The Home Office may argue that he no longer meets the requirements of para 57 of the Immigration Rules (see **6.2**), for example because he does not intend to leave the UK at the end of his studies. His leave can be curtailed (see **3.7**) so that he is required to leave his course before it ends.

9.13 ASYLUM APPEALS

Any right of appeal is dependent on the outcome of the application.

By s 83 of the NIAA 2002, where an asylum claim is rejected by the Secretary of State but the applicant is granted leave to enter or remain in the UK for a period exceeding one year, an appeal can be made to the First-tier Tribunal (Immigration and Asylum Chamber) against the rejection of the asylum claim. So a person granted humanitarian protection (see **9.10.1**) and discretionary leave (see **9.10.2**) for at least 12 months may use this provision.

A person refused asylum outright will have no right of appeal unless an immigration decision is made at the same time that can be appealed under s 82 of the NIAA 2002 – normally this will be a direction that the person is to be removed from the UK (see **11.2**).

9.14 MAKING A 'FRESH' ASYLUM (OR HUMAN RIGHTS) CLAIM

What can a claimant do if his asylum (or human rights) claim has been refused by the Home Office and all his appeal rights (see **Chapter 11**) have been exhausted?

Successive UK Governments have taken the view that many failed asylum seekers attempt to prolong their stay in the UK by making more than one claim. This has led to two key powers being given to the Secretary of State. First, the ability to certify an asylum (or human rights) claim as clearly unfounded, with the result that no appeal can be made in the UK (see s 94 of the NIAA 2002 at **11.15**). Secondly, another possible bar to an appeal lies in s 96 of the NIAA 2002. This enables the Secretary of State (or an immigration officer) to issue a certificate preventing an appeal when a second asylum (or human rights) claim relies on a matter that should have been raised in an appeal against the first claim (see **11.5**).

Now let us answer the question we posed above. Further submissions in support of an asylum claim can be made to the Home Office. If these are accepted, asylum will be granted. But what if they are rejected? Is there any right of appeal in the UK? Only if the further submissions amount to a 'fresh claim' for the purposes of para 353 of the Immigration Rules. When will the submissions amount to a fresh claim? Only if they are 'significantly different from the material that has previously been considered' because:

(a)   the content has not already been considered; and

(b)   taken together with the previously considered material, the claim has a realistic prospect of success, notwithstanding its rejection.

Note that para 353B of the Immigration Rules provides that where further submissions have been made and the decision maker has established whether or not they amount to a fresh claim under para 353, the decision maker should decide if there are exceptional circumstances which mean that claimant's removal from the UK is no longer appropriate. In doing so the decision maker should take into account the claimant's:

(a)   character, conduct and associations, including any criminal record and the nature of any offence of which the migrant concerned has been convicted;

(b)   compliance with any conditions attached to any previous grant of leave to enter or remain, and compliance with any conditions of temporary admission or immigration bail where applicable; and

(c)   length of time spent in the UK spent for reasons beyond the claimant's control after the human rights or asylum claim has been submitted or refused.

If the Secretary of State concludes that a fresh claim has not been made, this can be challenged by way of judicial review on the traditional *Wednesbury* ground of irrationality: see R (*MN (Tanzania)*) *v Secretary of State for the Home Department* [2011] EWCA Civ 193. This will involve the tribunal answering two questions:

> First, has the Secretary of State asked himself the correct question? The question is not whether the Secretary of State himself thinks that the new claim is a good one or should succeed, but whether there is a realistic prospect of an [immigration judge], applying the rule of anxious scrutiny, thinking that the applicant will be exposed to a real risk of persecution on return … The Secretary of State of course can, and no doubt logically should, treat his own view of the merits as a starting-point for that enquiry; but it is only a starting-point in the consideration of a question that is distinctly different from the exercise of the Secretary of State making up his own mind. Second, in addressing that question, both in respect of the evaluation of the facts and in respect of the legal conclusions to be drawn from those facts, has the Secretary of State satisfied the requirement of anxious scrutiny? If the court cannot be satisfied that the answer to both of those questions is in the affirmative it will have to grant an application for review of the Secretary of State's decision. (per Buxton LJ in *WM (DRC) v Secretary of State for the Home Department* [2006] EWCA Civ 1495)

See also **Chapter 12**.

9.15 ASYLUM CHECKLIST

Consider the following questions when advising an asylum claimant. If a claim is refused, check any appeal rights (see **9.13**).

(a)   Can the applicant return to a part of the country in which he would not be subject to the harm feared (see **9.4.3.1**)?

(b)   Does the safe third country exception apply (see **9.4.3.2**)?

(c)   Is the harm feared a form of persecution (see **9.4.1.3**)? Identify acts of past persecution.

(d)   What ECHR Articles are engaged (see **9.9**)?

(e)   Is that fear of persecution well founded? Taking into account the applicant's statements and behaviour, does the applicant have a subjective fear of persecution (see **9.4.1**)?

(f)   Is that fear of persecution well founded? Objectively, are there reasonable grounds for believing that the harm feared might in fact occur in the applicant's country of origin (see **9.4.1**)?

(g)   What evidence is available or should be obtained (including medical reports)?

(h)   Are any adverse inferences to be drawn (see **9.6.2**)?

(i)   Check any relevant Country of Origin Information Reports, Country of Origin Bulletins and Country of Origin Key Documents (see **9.7**).

(j)   If the harm feared is serious enough to constitute persecution, would it be inflicted for one or more of the reasons set out in the Refugee Convention, ie race, religion, nationality, membership of a particular social group or political opinion (see **9.4.2**)?

(k)   Is the applicant saying he will act discreetly if returned (see **9.4.1.7**)?

(l)   Are there any relevant sur place activities (see **9.4.3.3**)?

(m)   Should the applicant be excluded from international protection by operation of the exclusion clauses of the Convention (see **9.5**)?

(n)   If an applicant fails to qualify for asylum, should he be granted humanitarian protection or discretionary leave (see **9.10**)?

DEPORTATION AND ADMINISTRATIVE REMOVAL

10.1 DEPORTATION

10.1.1 Introduction

Under s 5 of the Immigration Act 1971 (IA 1971), the Secretary of State has a discretionary power to make a deportation order. This requires a person to leave the UK and prohibits him from lawfully re-entering while the order is in force. It also invalidates any existing leave to enter or remain.

British citizens and others with the right of abode in the UK (see **2.2** and **2.3**) cannot be deported. Some Commonwealth and Irish citizens are exempt from deportation (see **10.1.2**). Anyone else, including a person who is settled in the UK (see **3.8** and the example of *Samaroo and Sezek v Secretary of State for the Home Department* [2001] UKHRR 1150), is liable to deportation.

10.1.2 Exemption from deportation

The main exemptions from deportation are dealt with in s 7(1)(b) and (c) of the IA 1971. They apply only to Commonwealth or Irish citizens who had that citizenship at 1 January 1973 and were then ordinarily resident in the UK. Such persons are exempt from deportation on any ground if they have been ordinarily resident in the UK and Islands for five years before the date of the Secretary of State's decision to deport.

The term 'ordinarily resident' is considered in **3.8.2**. However, s 7(2) provides that, for the purpose of this exemption, if a person has at any time become ordinarily resident in the UK, he does not lose that status by remaining in breach of immigration laws. This means that a person who has overstayed, or broken conditions of entry, may nevertheless qualify for exemption.

10.1.3 Grounds for deportation

The Secretary of State may order that a person is to be deported, but only on the alternative grounds specified in s 3(5)(b) and (6) of the IA 1971. These are as follows:

(a) that the Secretary of State considers his deportation to be 'conducive to the public good' (see **10.1.4**);

(b) a person is a member of the family of a deportee (see **10.1.10**);

(c)   a court has recommended deportation, in the case of a person aged 17 or over convicted of an offence punishable with imprisonment (but see the case of *R v Kluxen* at **10.1.5**).

As to the steps the Secretary of State should take to establish any ground, see *DA (Colombia) v Secretary of State for the Home Department* [2009] EWCA Civ 682.

10.1.4   When is deportation conductive to the public good?

In *OH (Serbia)* [2009] INLR 109 (approved by the Court of Appeal in *RU (Bangladesh) v Secretary of State for the Home Department* [2011] EWCA Civ 651) the court identified three important features of the public interest in deportation, namely:

(a)   the risk of re-offending by the person concerned;

(b)   the need to deter foreign nationals from committing serious crimes by leading them to understand that, whatever the other circumstances, one consequence for them may well be their deportation; and

(c)   the role of deportation as an expression of society's revulsion at serious crimes and in building public confidence in the criminal justice system's treatment of foreign citizens who have committed serious crimes.

As to (a), the risk of re-offending is normally addressed in the report prepared for sentencing and commented on by the trial judge when giving reasons for the sentence imposed.

The Secretary of State has traditionally determined that deportation is beneficial for the public good where a person has been convicted either of one serious crime or of a series of lesser offences. The former category has been largely superseded by the fact that foreign nationals sentenced to a period of imprisonment of at least 12 months are invariably deported 'automatically' (see **10.1.5**). But an offender who repeatedly commits minor offences, or a person who commits a single offence involving, for example, the use of false identity documents for which he receives a custodial sentence of less than 12 months, may be deported at the Secretary of State's discretion.

10.1.5   Automatic deportation of foreign criminals

By s 32 of the UK Borders Act 2007, the Secretary of State must, subject to limited exceptions in s 33, make a deportation order in respect of a foreign adult criminal. This is a person who is not a British citizen (see **2.2**), nor a Commonwealth citizen with the right of abode (see **2.3**) or exempt (see **10.1.2**), and who has been convicted in the UK of an offence for which he was sentenced to a period of imprisonment of at least 12 months. Such a person has no right of appeal against an order automatically to deport him. However, he may appeal against the decision that he falls within this provision (see **11.2**).

Moreover, a person may appeal on the ground that his removal from the UK would breach his ECHR rights and/or the UK's obligations under the Refugee Convention (see, eg, *RU (Bangladesh) v Secretary of State for the Home Department* [2011] EWCA Civ 651; *AP (Trinidad & Tobago) v Secretary of State for the Home Department* [2011] EWCA Civ 551; **Chapter 9** and **11.3**).

A person liable to automatic deportation might seek to oppose it by claiming asylum in the UK. However, even if the asylum claim is accepted, the person may still be removed if he had been sentenced to a term of imprisonment of at least two years (see **9.5.2**).

What if the foreign criminal is an EEA citizen? He is an exception to the rule on automatic deportation if removal would breach rights he is exercising under the EU Treaties. He may be removed only on grounds of public policy, public security or public health in accordance with reg 19(3)(b) of the I(EEA) Regs 2006 (see **4.4.14**).

What is the effect of s 32 on a criminal court's power to recommend deportation? The Court of Appeal, in *R v Kluxen* [2010] EWCA Crim 1081, held that:

(a)   in cases to which the 2007 Act applies, it is no longer necessary or appropriate to recommend the deportation of the offender concerned; and

(b)   in cases to which the 2007 Act does not apply (eg the foreign criminal does not receive any single custodial sentence of 12 months or more, or receives a non-custodial sentence), it will rarely be appropriate to recommend the deportation of the offender concerned. Those cases remain within the discretion of the Secretary of State (see **10.1.4**).

10.1.6 Effect

What are the effects of a deportation order? A person may not legally enter the UK whilst an order is in force. By para 320(2) of the Immigration Rules, entry clearance and leave to enter will be refused to such a person.

See **10.1.9** as to revoking an order.

10.1.7 Procedure

The general procedure is described in paras 381, 382 and 384 of the Immigration Rules. Initially, the Home Office takes a decision to deport. Notice of this is then normally given to the deportee. He may then exercise his rights of appeal. If he fails to appeal, or loses his appeal, the Secretary of State may then sign the deportation order. Under Sch 3 to the IA 1971, the deportee may then be removed to the country of which he is a national, or to another country which is likely to receive him.

The deportee may be detained following the decision to deport. The power to detain a person who is subject to deportation action is set out in para 2 of Sch 3 to the IA 1971 and s 36 of the UK Borders Act 2007. This includes those whose deportation has been recommended by a court pending the making of a deportation order, those who have been served with a notice of intention to deport pending the making of a deportation order, those who are being considered for automatic deportation or pending the making of a deportation order as required by the automatic deportation provisions, and those who are the subject of a deportation order pending removal.

Note that a similar power to detain an illegal entrant or a person liable to administrative removal (or someone suspected to be such a person) (see **10.4**) is found in para 16(2) of Sch 2 to the IA 1971.

Rights of appeal against deportation decisions are dealt with in **Chapter 11**.

10.1.8 Voluntary departure

What if a person is subject to enforcement action but a deportation order has not yet been signed? As an order cannot be made against a person who is not in the UK, it is open to the person to leave the UK voluntarily. Enforcement action will cease if it is known that a person has embarked. The advantage is that the person is not subsequently debarred from re-entering the UK, although he must, of course, satisfy the requirements of the Immigration Rules for which he is seeking entry in the normal way.

10.1.9 Revocation of a deportation order

By para 390 of the Immigration Rules, an application may be made for revocation of a deportation order, and this will be considered in the light of all the circumstances, including the following:

(a)   the grounds on which the order was made;

(b)   any representations made in support of revocation;

(c)   the interests of the community, including the maintenance of an effective immigration control; and

(d)   the interests of the applicant, including any compassionate circumstances.

Note that by para 391, if an applicant was deported following conviction for a criminal offence then revocation will not occur:

(a)   in the case of a conviction for an offence for which the person was sentenced to a period of imprisonment of less than 4 years, unless 10 years have elapsed since the making of the deportation order, or

(b)   in the case of a conviction for an offence for which the person was sentenced to a period of imprisonment of at least 4 years, at any time.

In other cases, revocation of the order will not normally be authorised unless the situation has materially altered, either by a change of circumstances since the order was made, or by fresh information coming to light which was not before the appellate authorities or the Secretary of State. The passage of time since the person was deported may also in itself amount to a change of circumstances justifying revocation of the order.

Revocation of a deportation order does not entitle the person concerned to re-enter the UK. It merely renders him eligible to apply for admission under the Immigration Rules.

10.1.10   Family members of deportee

By s 5(4) of the IA 1971, the family members liable to be deported with the deportee are his spouse or civil partner and his or her children under 18. For these purposes an adopted child, whether legally adopted or not, may be treated as the child of the adopter and, if legally adopted, must be regarded as the child only of the adopter. Also an illegitimate child (unless adopted) is regarded as the child of the mother.

Note that no family deportation can be made once eight weeks have elapsed since any other family member was deported (see IA 1971, s 5).

This can be a controversial ground for deportation, as someone who is deported as the family member of the deportee may have committed no breach of immigration law or indeed any other laws. Remember, however, that it cannot be used to deport any family member who has the right of abode in the UK (see **2.2** and **2.3**) or is exempt (see **10.1.2**).

By para 365 of the Immigration Rules, the Secretary of State will not normally decide to deport the spouse or civil partner of a deportee where:

(a)   he has qualified for settlement in his own right; or

(b)   he has been living apart from the deportee.

By para 366 of the Immigration Rules, the Secretary of State will not normally decide to deport the child of a deportee where:

(a)   he and his mother or father are living apart from the deportee; or

(b)   he has left home and established himself on an independent basis; or

(c)   he married or formed a civil partnership before deportation came into prospect.

Note that para 389 of the Immigration Rules provides that a family member of a deportee may be able to seek re-admission to the UK under the Immigration Rules where:

(a)   a child reaches 18 (when he ceases to be subject to the deportation order); or

(b)   in the case of a spouse or civil partner, the marriage or civil partnership comes to an end.

As to arguments opposing deportation based on human rights see **10.2** and **10.3**, and on EU law see **10.5**.

Note that Government policies on marriage and cohabitation known as DP 3/96 and DP 2/93 were withdrawn in April 2008.

10.1.11 Presumption that the public interest requires deportation

Paragraph 396 of the Immigration Rules provides that where a person is liable to deportation, the presumption shall be that the public interest requires deportation.

Paragraph 396 of the Immigration Rules also states that it is in the public interest to deport where the Secretary of State must make a deportation order in accordance with s 32 of the UK Borders Act 2007 (see **10.1.5**).

So in what circumstances is the presumption rebutted? Paragraph 397 provides that a deportation order will not be made if the person's removal pursuant to the order would be contrary to the UK's obligations under the Refugee Convention (see **Chapter 9**) or the Human Rights Convention (see **10.2** and **10.3**). However, it is stressed that where deportation would not be contrary to these obligations, it will be only in exceptional circumstances that the public interest in deportation is outweighed.

10.2 HUMAN RIGHTS CHALLENGES TO DEPORTATION OTHER THAN ARTICLE 8 ECHR

10.2.1 Articles 2 and 3 ECHR

A person will not be expelled from the UK to a country where there are substantial reasons for believing that he faces a real risk of:

(a) being unlawfully killed either by the State, or through the State being unable or unwilling to protect him contrary to Article 2 ECHR; or

(b) suffering serious harm or other treatment contrary to Article 3 ECHR. This includes torture, as well as treatment or punishment that is degrading because it arouses in the victim feelings of fear, anguish or inferiority capable of humiliating and debasing him, and possibly breaking his physical and moral resistance. Severe discrimination based on race, sex or other grounds is also capable of constituting degrading treatment.

Home Office guidance is that Article 3 ECHR may also be engaged where the person has an illness that has reached such a critical stage (ie he is dying) that it would constitute inhuman treatment to deprive him of the care he is currently receiving and send him home to an early death, unless there is care available there to enable him to meet that fate with dignity.

In *Bensaid v United Kingdom* [2001] ECHR 82, the applicant suffered from long-term schizophrenia. He claimed that his condition would seriously deteriorate if he were returned to his home country because of difficulties in obtaining suitable medication there. The Court stated (at para 37):

Deterioration in his already existing mental illness could involve relapse into hallucinations and psychotic delusions involving self-harm and harm to others, as well as restrictions in social functioning (such as withdrawal and lack of motivation). The Court considers that the suffering associated with such a relapse could, in principle, fall within the scope of Article 3.

However, it should be noted that the Court in *Bensaid* went on to find that Article 3 ECHR would not be violated in the case as there were no exceptional circumstances.

Also see **9.9.2** and **9.9.3**.

10.2.2 Articles 5 and 6 ECHR

In resisting expulsion on the ground that his Article 5 ECHR right will be threatened in the country to which he is sent, a person must establish that there are substantial grounds for believing that, if removed, he will face a real risk of a flagrant breach of that Article. In this context, a flagrant breach is a breach the consequences of which are so severe that they override the right of a State to expel an alien from its territory. In describing such a breach of Article 5 in R (*Ullah*) v *Special Adjudicator* [2004] UKHL 26, Lord Steyn (at [43]) gave by way of example the case of intended expulsion to a country in which the rule of law is flagrantly flouted, *habeas corpus* is unavailable and there is a real risk that the individual may face arbitrary detention for many years.

Before the expulsion of a person will be capable of violating Article 6 ECHR, there must be substantial grounds for believing that there is a real risk:

(a) that there will be a fundamental breach of the principles of a fair trial guaranteed by Article 6 ('[w]hat is required is that the deficiency or deficiencies in the trial process should be such as fundamentally to destroy the fairness of the prospective trial', per Lord Phillips in RB (*Algeria*) v *Secretary of State for the Home Department* [2009] UKHL 10 at [136]); and

(b) that this failure will lead to a miscarriage of justice that itself constitutes a flagrant violation of the victim's fundamental rights. This was the situation in RB (*Algeria*), where the appellant had already been tried in his absence and sentenced to life imprisonment. There were substantial grounds for believing that he would not be able to obtain a retrial and would be imprisoned to serve the sentence imposed in his absence.

What is required is a breach of the principles of fair trial guaranteed by Article 6 ECHR which is so fundamental as to amount to a nullification of, or destruction of the very essence of, the right guaranteed by that Article: see *Othman (Abu Qatada)* v *UK* [2012] ECHR 56. Note that in this case the ECtHR held that the applicant's deportation to Jordan would be in violation of Article 6 on account of the real risk that evidence obtained by torturing third persons would be admitted when the applicant was (re-)tried in Jordan.

Article 6 ECHR might also be engaged where the person has an outstanding civil claim in the UK for private law damages, eg a personal injury claim, or is a prospective party to such a civil claim which he actively is pursuing. Home Office guidance is that it may be relevant if the person:

(a) does not have access to communication facilities in the country of return;

(b) needs to undertake a medical examination;

(c) will not have access to funding to pursue his civil claim;

(d) will not be able to have access to interpreters;

(e) wants to represent himself in court;

(f) is required to give evidence in court; and

(g) needs direct personal contact in order to instruct his UK legal representatives.

Other factors may include the complexity of the case; access to telephone and conferencing facilities in the country to which the individual is to be returned; the reliability of postal, email and fax facilities in that country; and whether or not liability has been admitted.

10.3 ARTICLE 8 ECHR CHALLENGES TO DEPORTATION

In July 2012, new Immigration Rules were introduced to:

> reflect the Government's and Parliament's view of how, as a matter of public policy, the balance should be struck between the right to respect for private and family life and the public interest in safeguarding the economic well-being of the UK by controlling immigration and in public safety by protecting the public from foreign criminals. (Home Office, *Statement of Intent: Family Migration*, June 2012, para 33)

In the first case to consider the new provisions, the IAC did not find it easy to regard everything that is said about Article 8 within the new Rules as part of a coherent whole. The tribunal held that even if a decision to refuse an Article 8 claim under the new Rules is found to be correct, judges must still consider whether the decision is in compliance with a person's human rights under s 6 of the HRA 1998 and, in automatic deportation cases, whether removal would breach a person's Convention rights: see MF (*Article 8 – new rules) Nigeria* [2012] UKUT 00393.

10.3.1 Article 8: private life

For the purposes of Article 8 ECHR, what is a person's private life in the UK? The answer is found by establishing the strength of his ties to the UK which he has established here in terms of friends, education, work and leisure activities.

Can a person's contribution to society whilst in the UK, such as voluntary work for a charity, be taken into account as a factor in the balancing exercise necessary to decide whether his expulsion from the UK will breach this right? The Court of Appeal answered this question in the affirmative in *UE (Nigeria) v Secretary of State for the Home Department* [2010] EWCA Civ 975. The Court held that a person's contributions to the community in which he lived would reduce the need to maintain effective immigration control for administrative removal (see **10.4**) purposes, but they would be unlikely to make much difference in a deportation case. However, the greater the person's contribution, the more weight the factor might be given, especially if the person is an essential worker in a company engaged in a successful export business, or a social worker upon whom a local community depends or a scientific research worker engaged on research of public importance.

10.3.2 Article 8: family life

Article 8 ECHR may also be engaged where the person claims that to expel him from the UK will separate him from his family here and would therefore constitute a breach of his right to respect for family life in the UK. Who might form part of a family? Partners in a lawful and genuine marriage or civil partnership, or a relationship akin to such, will normally constitute family life. Home Office guidance is that a relationship between unmarried and same-sex partners of sufficient substance or stability will qualify even if the couple do not meet the usual two years' cohabitation requirement in Appendix FM to the Immigration Rules (see **8.3**). In any event, such relationships would fall within a person's private life. A new or casual relationship will not suffice.

In the case of natural parents and their minor children, there is a general presumption of family life. Further, the relationship between an adoptive parent and an adopted person is in principle the same. The Home Office accepts that family life may exist between a child and his natural parent even if at the time of birth the relationship between the two parents has ended, and even if the child does not live with his parent. However, the fact that a parent has only infrequent contact with his child may be relevant to the question of whether removal would disproportionately interfere with their family life.

Family life may continue between parent and child after the child has attained his majority because it does not suddenly stop when the child reaches 18: see *Secretary of State for the Home Department v HK (Turkey)* [2010] EWCA Civ 583, where Sir Scott Baker said, at [16]:

> [I]t is apparent that the respondent had lived in the same house as his parents since 1994. He reached his majority in September 2005 but continued to live at home. Undoubtedly he had family life while he was growing up and I would not regard it as suddenly cut off when he reached his majority.

Relationships of grandparents and grandchildren, uncles and aunts, nephews and nieces, may fall within the scope of family life, depending upon the strength of the emotional ties. It is rare for relationships between adult siblings or adult children and their parents to count (*Odawey v Entry Clearance Officer* [2011] EWCA Civ 840), unless there are special elements of dependency beyond normal emotional ties (*Kugathas v Secretary of State for the Home Department* [2003] EWCA Civ 31), for example the support of an elder brother for his very sick younger brother in *R (Ahmadi) v Secretary of State for the Home Department* [2005] EWCA Civ 1721.

10.3.3   The traditional five questions

As Article 8 ECHR is a qualified right, traditionally five questions have been posed in determining its role in a person's expulsion:

Question 1: Does the person have a private and/or family life in the UK? See **10.3.1** *and* **10.3.2** *above.*

Question 2: If a private and/or family life exists, will removal interfere with that?

As to family life, the answer depends to some extent on whose family life is being considered – only that of the person being removed, or that of all members of his family unit? The House of Lords, in *Beoku-Betts v Secretary of State for the Home Department* [2008] UKHL 39, held that the effect of expulsion on all members of the person's family unit should be taken into account. Together these members enjoy a single family life, and whether or not the removal would interfere with it has to be looked at by reference to the family unit as a whole and the impact of removal upon each member.

In *Huang v Secretary of State for the Home Department* [2007] UKHL 11, the House of Lords held that the expulsion of the person must prejudice his family life in a manner sufficiently serious to amount to a breach of Article 8 ECHR. However, as Sedley LJ indicated in *AG (Eritrea) v Secretary of State for the Home Department* [2007] EWCA Civ 801, at [28], the threshold of engagement is not a specifically high one. So, for example, in *A (Afghanistan) v Secretary of State for the Home Department* [2009] EWCA Civ 825, the Court held that the interference with family life which would result from not allowing a husband and his heavily pregnant wife in a genuine and subsisting marriage to cohabit, engaged the operation of Article 8 ECHR.

Question 3: If there is interference with a private and/or family life, is it in accordance with the law?

The answer will be yes, provided the decision is in accordance with the relevant statutory provisions, Immigration Rules and the published policies of the Home Office.

Question 4: Is the interference in pursuit of one or more of the permissible aims set out under Article 8(2)?

This may include the maintenance of effective immigration controls by administrative removal (see **10.4**) and public safety, the prevention of crime and disorder, and national security by deportation (see **10.1.4**).

The answer will be yes, provided the decision is in accordance with the stated Government policy.

Question 5: Is the interference proportionate to the permissible aim or aims?

This is normally the key question, and often a difficult one to answer as the assessment of proportionality is a balancing exercise between the individual's private interests and the Government's permissible aims. It is this question that the Immigration Rules seek to address.

10.3.4   Immigration Rules: criminality thresholds

When is it a proportionate step to deport a person for the purposes of Article 8 ECHR? Current government policy, reflected in the Immigration Rules, is that the more serious the nature of the offence, the sentence given or the previous criminal history of the person concerned, the less likely it is that other relevant factors will outweigh automatic deportation or otherwise the presumption of deportation (see **10.1.5** and **10.1.11** respectively). As Richards LJ indicated in *JO (Uganda) v Secretary of State for the Home Department* [2010] EWCA Civ 10, at [27]:

> even if the difficulties do make it unreasonable to expect family members to join the applicant in the country to which he is to be deported, that will not necessarily be a decisive feature in the overall assessment of proportionality. It is plainly an important consideration but it may not be determinative, since it is possible in a case of sufficiently serious offending that the factors in favour of deportation

will be strong enough to render deportation proportionate even if does have the effect of severing established family relationships.

Paragraph 398 of the Immigration Rules addresses the situation where a person claims that his deportation would be contrary to the UK's obligations under Article 8 ECHR.

By sub-para (b), if the person has been convicted of an offence for which he has been sentenced to a period of imprisonment of less than four years but at least 12 months, or under sub-para (c) if, in the view of the Secretary of State, his offending has caused serious harm (see **10.3.5**) or he is a persistent offender who shows a particular disregard for the law (see **10.3.6**), then the Secretary of State may decide not to deport that person but grant him limited leave to remain (see **10.3.10**) should he meet the requirements of paras 399 (see **10.3.7** and **10.3.8**) or 399A (see **10.3.9**); otherwise, it will be only in exceptional circumstances (see **10.3.11**) that the public interest in deportation will be outweighed by other factors.

By sub-para (a) of para 398, if the person has been convicted of an offence for which he has been sentenced to a period of imprisonment of at least four years, it will be only in exceptional circumstances (see **10.3.11**) that the public interest in deportation will be outweighed by other factors.

What does 'sentenced to a period of imprisonment' mean? Home Office guidance is that the determinative factor is the sentence imposed and not the actual time spent in prison. However, this does not include a suspended sentence, unless that sentence is subsequently activated, nor convictions which are subsequently quashed on appeal. Where sentences are subsequently increased or reduced on appeal but the person nevertheless remains convicted of the offence, the revised sentence length applies.

It is important not to confuse consecutive and concurrent sentences of imprisonment in this context. For a consecutive sentence, the period of imprisonment equals the sum of all the sentences. But for a concurrent sentence, the period of imprisonment equals the length of the longest sentence.

10.3.5   Paragraph 398(c): what is meant by 'serious harm'?

Home Office guidance is that references to an 'offence which has caused serious harm' includes, but is not limited to, causing death or serious injury to an individual or group of individuals. A person does not need to be convicted of specifically causing a death or serious injury. Examples might include, but are not limited to, manslaughter; dangerous driving; driving whilst under the influence of drink and/or drugs; and arson.

10.3.6   Paragraph 398(c): who is a persistent offender?

Home Office guidance is that references to a 'persistent offender who, in the view of the Secretary of State, has shown a disregard for the law' involve a case-specific assessment of the nature, extent, seriousness and impact of the person's offending, taking into account the following non-exhaustive list of factors:

(a) *The number of offences committed.* The decision maker must look at how many offences have been committed by the individual. There is no numerical value or limit at which deportation begins to outweigh the person's right to family or private life. But this should be borne in mind when looking at the factors at (b), (c), (d) and (e) below in reaching a decision about persistence and whether the public interest is served by that person's deportation.

(b) *The seriousness of those offences.* The sentence or disposal should be the primary indicator of the seriousness of the offence, but the decision maker should nevertheless consider the nature of any offence(s) of which the person has been convicted and whether there are offences which give rise to the public interest being met.

(c)   *Any escalation in seriousness of the offences.* The decision maker must consider whether the pattern of offending gives particular cause to believe that the public interest would be served by the person's deportation and that it would outweigh that person's right to family or private life. The aim for the decision maker is to identify a pattern of escalating offending and intervene before a very serious offence is committed.

(d)   *The timescale over which the offences were committed.* The decision maker must consider over what timescale the offending has taken place and how recently the last of the offending took place. Less weight might be placed on a series of offences committed over a very short period of time which has long since ceased, particularly if this could be attributed to a particular incident or issue in the person's life which would make deportation now a disproportionate response. But repeated criminality over a lengthy period of time would weigh in favour of deportation. The length of time the person has spent in the UK will be an appropriate consideration. For example, a person who has committed four offences in the 10 years he has spent in the UK might not be viewed as a persistent offender; a person who commits three offences in the course of just six months' residence might be so viewed.

(e)   *The frequency within which they were committed.* Again, the length of time the person has spent in the UK will be an appropriate consideration. The less time a person has spent in the UK relative to the number of offences and level of offending, the more deportation begins to outweigh that person's right to family or private life.

(f)   *Any action taken to address the cause of the offending.* The decision maker should consider any programs or activities aimed at addressing the cause of the offending. Examples might include courses aimed at reduction of alcohol dependency or drug dependency, and anger management. These must demonstrate that they are having the necessary impact, such that the person's offending can be seen to have significantly reduced to the extent that his right to family or private life outweighs the public interest in deporting him.

10.3.7   Paragraph 399: exception based on relationship with a child

What weight should be given to the best interests of children who are affected by the decision to remove one or both of their parents from the UK? The Supreme Court addressed this question in *H (Tanzania) v Secretary of State for the Home Department* [2011] UKSC 4. The Court held that the best interests of the child must be a primary consideration. A decision maker must identify what the best interests of the child require, and then assess whether the strength of any other consideration, or the cumulative effect of other considerations, outweighs the consideration of the best interests of the child.

Home Office guidance is that where a person asserts that he has a family life with a child or children in the UK, the decision maker must ensure that the person can satisfy all of the following requirements of para 399 (emphasis added):

(a)   the person has a genuine and subsisting parental relationship with a child under the age of 18 years who is in the UK [see **8.5.1.1**], *and*

   (i)   the child is a British Citizen [see **2.2**]; *or*

   (ii)   the child has lived in the UK continuously for at least the 7 years immediately preceding the date of the immigration decision [see **8.5.1.2**]; *and in either case*

      (a)   it would not be reasonable to expect the child to leave the UK; *and*

      (b)   there is no other family member who is able to care for the child in the UK ...

10.3.7.1   When is it reasonable to expect a British child to leave the UK?

In what circumstances is it proportionate to remove a parent where the effect will be that a child who is a British citizen will also have to leave? The Supreme Court also addressed this question in *H (Tanzania) v Secretary of State for the Home Department* (see **10.3.7**). The Court stated that whilst nationality is not a 'trump card', it is of particular importance in assessing the best interests of any child. The intrinsic importance of British citizenship should not be played down. As a British citizen, a child has rights which he will not be able to exercise if he moves to another country. He will lose the advantages of growing up and being educated in his own country, his own culture and his own language.

Home Office guidance is that the decision maker needs to consider whether in the specific circumstances of the case it would be reasonable to expect the British citizen child to live in another country. The decision maker needs to consider the facts for each child within the family and for the family in the round. The decision maker should also engage with any issues explicitly raised by the family, or by, or on behalf of, each child. Relevant considerations are likely to include:

(a)   whether there would be a significant risk to the child's health: for example, if there is evidence that the child is undergoing a course of treatment for a life- threatening or serious illness and treatment is not available in the country of return;

(b)   the extent to which the child is dependent on any wider family members in the UK;

(c)   whether the country offers comparable protections and freedoms, access to public services and opportunities to those available in the UK (the answer is likely to be that it does in, say, the case of other EEA countries, the USA, Canada, New Zealand, Australia, etc);

(d)   whether the child is likely to be able to (re)integrate readily into life in another country. Relevant factors weighing in favour of successful (re)integration include:

(i)   whether the parent(s) is a citizen of the country and/or the child has dual nationality,

(ii)   whether the parents and/or child have lived in or visited the country before for periods of more than a few weeks – the question here is whether having visited or lived in the country before, the child would be able to adapt and/or the parents would be able to support the child in adapting to life in the country,

(iii)   whether the child has or parents have existing family or social ties with the country – a person who has extended family or networks of friends should be able to rely on them for support to help reintegrate on return,

(iv)   whether the child has or parents have relevant cultural ties to the country – is there any evidence of exposure to and the level of understanding of the cultural norms in the country? For example, a period of time spent living mainly amongst a diaspora from the country may in and of itself give a child an awareness of the culture in the country,

(v)   whether the child can speak, read and write in a language of that country, or is likely to achieve this within a reasonable time period. Fluency is not required – an ability to communicate competently with sympathetic interlocutors would normally suffice,

(vi)   whether the child has attended school in that country;

(e)   any country-specific risks (reference should be made to any relevant country guidance: see **9.7**);

(f)   other specific factors raised by, or on behalf of, the child (see **10.3.7.4**).

10.3.7.2   When is it reasonable to expect a non-British child to leave the UK?

Where a non-British citizen child has been in the UK for more than seven years, Home Office guidance is that relevant considerations are likely to include:

(a)   whether there would be a significant risk to the child's health: for example, if there is evidence that the child is undergoing a course of treatment for a life threatening or serious illness and treatment is not available in the country of return;

(b)   whether the child would be leaving with its parent(s). It is generally the case that it is in a child's best interests to remain with its parents. Unless specific factors apply, it will generally not be unreasonable to expect a child to leave the country with its parents, particularly if the parents have no right to remain in the UK;

(c)   the extent to which the child is dependent on any wider family members in the UK;

(d)   whether the child is likely to be able to (re)integrate readily into life in another country. Relevant factors weighing in favour of successful (re)integration include:

   (i)   whether the parent(s) or child is a citizen of the country and so able to enjoy the full rights of being a citizen in that country,

   (ii)   whether the parents and/or child have lived in or visited the country before for periods of more than a few weeks – the question here is whether having visited or lived in the country before, the child would be able to adapt and/or the parents would be able to support the child in adapting to life in the country,

   (iii) whether the child has or parents have existing family or social ties with the country – a person who has extended family or networks of friends should be able to rely on them for support to help reintegrate on return,

   (iv)   whether the child has or parents have relevant cultural ties to the country in light of any evidence of exposure to and the level of understanding of the cultural norms in the country. For example, a period of time spent living mainly amongst a diaspora from the country may in of itself give a child an awareness of the culture in the country,

   (v)   whether the child can speak, read and write in a language of that country, or is likely to achieve this within a reasonable time period. Fluency is not required – an ability to communicate competently with sympathetic interlocutors would normally suffice,

   (vi)   whether the child has attended school in that country;

(e)   any country-specific risks (reference should be made to any relevant country guidance: see **9.7**);

(f)   other specific factors raised by, or on behalf of, the child (see **10.3.7.4**).

The Home Office anticipates that families or children may highlight the differences in quality of education, health and wider public services, and economic or social opportunities between the UK and the country of origin, and argue that these work against the best interests of the child. The Home Office response is that other than in exceptional circumstances, this would not normally be regarded as a relevant consideration, particularly if the parent(s) or wider family have the means or resources to support the child on return, or the skills, education and training to provide for their family on return.

10.3.7.3   Is there another family member who is able to care for the child in the UK?

Home Office guidance is that for these purposes a family member is a parent, aunt or uncle, grandparent, adult sibling or legal guardian.

The decision maker should consider whether there is another family member able to care for the child in the UK and the impact on the child's best interests of separation from the person being deported. Relevant factors include:

(a)   the nature of the relationship between the person being deported and the child, eg whether the person is the child's primary carer (ie the person who would normally have day-to-day care and wider welfare and developmental responsibilities for the child, or would have done so if he had not been in prison);

(b)   who has been looking after the child while the parent has been in prison;

(c)   whether both parents and the child are a functioning family unit or the parents are separated;

(d)   any wider support network – whether the wider family are close;

(e)   who would look after the child if the person was removed, and whether that person is able to care for the child. Relevant factors here include:

   (i)   whether that person reasonably could be expected to fulfil the role of primary carer (eg, has he fulfilled that role in the past, is he physically able to care for the child?),

   (ii)   the contact the child has had with the family member before, and the nature of the existing relationship,

   (iii)   any other factors which undermine the ability of that individual to act as the primary carer of the child or that would suggest he is unsuitable (eg previous convictions, immigration status, etc),

   (iv)   how willing the person is to look after the child, and how genuine those views are;

(f)   supporting evidence from other family members and/or social services, etc, and any relevant court orders;

(g)   the views of the child as expressed by the child, or on his behalf (see **10.3.7.4**).

Home Office guidance is that where a child is older or otherwise semi-independent of the parent, and there is evidence that he is being looked after through other arrangements (eg, with local authority or wider community support), it may be possible to remove the parent and allow the child to stay in the UK.

10.3.7.4   Seeking the views of children

In deportation cases where the consequence of the decision may be to separate a child from a parent, the decision maker, when assessing the best interests of the child, must be prepared to discover the views of any affected children. These may already be available or known from information and representations supplied. If not available, and there are no reasons for their non-availability, consideration should be given to obtaining them by means of a request in writing to a parent, legal adviser or other suitable adult (eg social worker or other family member). The decision maker should be prepared to consider hearing the views of the child directly, if requested or deemed necessary.

If there are ongoing proceedings in the UK family courts concerning the child, should the decision to deport be delayed? No, stated the Court of Appeal in *Mohan v Secretary of State for the Home Department* [2012] EWCA Civ 1363, if the material in favour of the applicant lacks substance and the public interest in deportation is overwhelming. But, otherwise, the judgment of the family court, with all the tools at its disposal (including the assistance of the Children and Family Court Advisory and Support Service (CAFCASS) and the opportunity to assess all the adults), can and should inform the decision maker on the issue of the proportionality of deportation in relation to the best interests of the child. See further *RS (immigration/family court liaison: outcome) India* [2013] UKUT 82 (IAC) where the family court held that the child's best interests did not lie with her parents but by being placed in long-term foster care in the UK. The family court regarded it as acceptable for the child to have contact with his parents face-to-face annually by visiting them in India and monthly by means of Skype. On that basis, the deportation of the child's father did not interfere with the child's best interests.

10.3.8   Paragraph 399: exception based on relationship with a partner

Home Office guidance is that where a person asserts that he has a family life with a partner in the UK, the decision maker must ensure that the person can satisfy all of the following requirements of para 399 (emphasis added):

   (b)   the person has a genuine and subsisting relationship [see **8.3.5.5**] with a partner who is in the UK and is a British Citizen [see **2.2**], settled in the UK [see **3.8**], or in the UK with refugee leave [see **9.8**] or humanitarian protection [see **9.10.1**], *and*

(i)   the person has lived in the UK with valid leave continuously for at least the 15 years immediately preceding the date of the immigration decision (discounting any period of imprisonment); *and*

(ii)   there are insurmountable obstacles to family life with that partner continuing outside the UK.

10.3.8.1   'Insurmountable obstacles'

Home Office guidance is that in determining whether there are 'insurmountable obstacles', the decision maker must give this phrase its literal meaning. When assessing the seriousness of the difficulties which the members of the family are likely to face, 'insurmountable' means something that could not, or could not reasonably be expected to, be overcome, even with a degree of hardship for one or more of the individuals concerned.

Home Office guidance is that decision makers should look at whether there is an inability to live in the country concerned. The focus should also be on the family life which would be enjoyed in the country to which the person is being returned, not by comparison to the life he would have enjoyed had he remained in the UK.

The factors which might be relevant to this consideration include, but are not limited to:

(a)   *Language.* In order for this to be a contributory factor, the partner would need to be unable to speak, read and understand a and/or the language in the country to which the person is being deported. However, a lack of knowledge of a language spoken in the country in which the family would be required to live would not necessarily amount to an insurmountable obstacle. It is reasonable to conclude that the family must have been conversing in a commonly understood language whilst in the UK. It could be considered reasonable for that to continue outside of the UK, whether or not the person seeks to learn a and/or the language commonly spoken in the country of destination.

(b)   *Cultural background.* This might be relevant in situations where the partner would be so disadvantaged as for it to be unreasonable, eg a woman required to live in a country with strict laws pertaining to women's rights. However, the test remains high. It must be a barrier which either cannot be overcome, or which is so unreasonable that someone cannot be expected to overcome it.

(c)   *Gaining entry or status in the country outside of the UK.* The decision maker should consider the ability of the partner to regularise his status in the country concerned, ie to be granted a visa and/or admitted entry. The onus is on the individual concerned to show that this was not possible in order for this to amount to an insurmountable obstacle. A mere wish, desire or preference to live in the UK is irrelevant.

(d)   *Means of support, eg education, skills and training.* Where a person being deported will not have the means to support himself and his partner in the other country, decision makers must consider evidence of the partner's education, languages, skills and training, and her profession or occupation in the UK, and determine whether the skills could be transferred to an occupation in that country. It is not appropriate to consider whether the person will be able to undertake the same work overseas; what is important is whether the expectation for her to leave with the partner who is being deported constitutes a barrier that it is unreasonable to expect her to overcome.

10.3.9   Paragraph 399A private life exceptions

Home Office guidance is that where a person asserts that he has a private life in the UK, the decision maker must ensure that the person can satisfy one of the following set of requirements of para 399A:

(a)   the person has lived continuously in the UK for at least 20 years immediately preceding the date of the immigration decision (discounting any period of imprisonment) and he has no ties (including social, cultural or family) with the country to which he would have to go if required to leave the UK; *or*

(b) the person is aged under 25 years, he has spent at least half of his life living continuously in the UK immediately preceding the date of the immigration decision (discounting any period of imprisonment) and he has no ties (including social, cultural or family) with the country to which he would have to go if required to leave the UK.

10.3.9.1 The 'no ties' requirement

In determining whether the person has 'no ties (including social, cultural or family)', the Home Office decision maker should consider whether the person has sufficient knowledge of, or connections to, the country of origin to be able to form an adequate private life in that country. The adequacy of that private life overseas should be determined by reference to norms in that country, not by comparison with the private life the person would have enjoyed had he remained in the UK. The likelihood that the person may find life difficult or challenging upon his return will not of itself render deportation inappropriate.

Home Office guidance is that in making this assessment, decision makers should have regard to the entirety of the person's background and the conditions he is likely to encounter on return to the country of origin. For deportation to be the proper course, a person does not need to have a connection under each of the 'social, cultural and family' headings but his ties to the country need to be looked at in the round. For example, a connection with the culture may suffice where a person has no family contacts whatsoever. In making the assessment, relevant factors will include, but are not limited to, the following:

(a) *Language.* This is likely to be a key factor. If the person speaks an official language of the country of origin, or a language that is commonly understood in parts of that country, it will suggest he could build an adequate private life in that country. For these purposes, fluency is not required – an ability to communicate competently with sympathetic interlocutors will suffice.

(b) *Cultural background.* Decision makers must consider evidence of the person's exposure to and level of understanding of the cultural norms in the country of origin. Where the person has spent his time in the UK living mainly amongst a diaspora from his country of origin then it may well be reasonable to conclude that he will be able to enjoy an adequate private life in that country even if he has never lived there.

(c) *Length of time spent in the country of origin.* Where the person has spent a considerable period living in the country of origin, it will be difficult for him to demonstrate that he cannot enjoy an adequate private life on return. Decision makers should consider the proportion of the person's life spent in that country, and the stage of life at which the person was when living in that country, to determine whether he has had sufficient exposure to that country to be able to form an adequate private life. For example, where a person left his country of origin as an adult or teenager, he will find it difficult to demonstrate that he cannot return, even if he has spent considerably longer than 20 years in the UK. On the other hand, a person with a shorter period of residence in the UK may not be able to return if he left the country at a very young age and has no other ties to that country.

(d) *Family, friends and social network.* A person who has extended family members in his country of origin should be able to rely on them for support to help him to reintegrate into society on return. These need not be close blood relatives if the person has friends and other contacts to whom he could turn for support. Decision makers should have regard to whether the person or his family have hosted visits in the UK by family and friends from their country of origin. These need not be strong familial ties and may include ties that could be strengthened if the person were to return.

(e)   *Means to establish private life, eg education, skills and training.* Where a person has no family or social contacts who could support him in the country of origin, deportation will usually be appropriate where the person has the means to found an adequate private life by the standards of that country. Decision makers must consider evidence of the person's education, languages, skills and training, and his profession or occupation in the UK, and determine whether the skills could be transferred to an occupation in that country. Where a person could find an occupation in his country of origin, he will rarely be able to demonstrate that he would be unable to form an adequate private life.

10.3.10 Grant of limited leave under paras 399 or 399A

By para 399B, where para 399 (see **10.3.7** and **10.3.8**) or 399A (see **10.3.9**) applies, the person may be granted limited leave for a period not exceeding 30 months. Can further periods of limited leave be granted? Yes, the requirements for further leave are that the applicant continues to meet the criteria set out in paras 399 or 399A.

10.3.11 Exceptional circumstances

If a person falls within para 398(a) (he has been convicted of an offence and sentenced to a period of imprisonment of at least four years (see **10.3.4**)), or otherwise does not fall within any of the para 399 (see **10.3.7** and **10.3.8**) or para 399A (see **10.3.9**) exceptions, the person's deportation will be the proper course in all but exceptional cases.

Home Office guidance is that in determining whether a case is exceptional, decision makers must consider all relevant factors that weigh in favour of and against deportation.

Decision makers should be mindful that whilst all cases are to an extent unique, those unique factors do not generally render them exceptional. For these purposes, exceptional cases should be numerically rare. Furthermore, a case is not exceptional just because the exceptions to deportation in paras 399 or 399A have been missed by a small margin. Rather, the Immigration Rules establish those thresholds as determining when deportation would be appropriate bar other factors. However, in assessing exceptionality, the matters identified in paras 399 and 399A need to be considered along with all other aspects of the case. The decision maker then needs to determine whether removal would have such severe consequences for the individual or his family that exceptionally deportation is not appropriate despite the clear articulation of the public interest in para 398 (see **10.3.4**). Home Office guidance is that that is likely to be the case only very rarely indeed.

10.3.12 Future developments

At the time of writing (October 2013) the Upper Tribunal (Immigration and Asylum Chamber) has considered the new Immigration Rules in several cases (see, for example, *Izuazu (Article 8 – new rules)* [2013] UKUT 45, *Ogundimu (Article 8 – new rules) Nigeria* [2013] UKUT 60 and *Green (Article 8 – new rules)* [2013] UKUT 254). Broadly, these have followed *MF (Article 8 – new rules) Nigeria* (2012) (see **10.3**) and the approach was approved in *R (on the application of Nagre) v Secretary of State for the Home Department* [2013] EWHC 720 (Admin) and *MF (Nigeria) v Secretary of State for the Home Department* [2013] EWCA Civ 1192. It appears likely that the Government will introduce legislation in the near future to put the rules on a statutory basis.

10.4 ADMINISTRATIVE REMOVAL

10.4.1 Grounds for removal

Removal from the UK is often described as 'administrative removal', as that is what it is in reality, namely, an administrative step. Under s 10 of the Immigration and Asylum Act 1999 (IAA 1999), the following people may be administratively removed from the UK:

(a)   anyone who has failed to observe the conditions attached to his leave (see **3.3**);

(b)   overstayers (see **3.6.6**);

(c)   anyone who has obtained leave to remain by deception, or who sought to obtain such leave by deception;

(d)   the family members (partner or child) of such people.

The most common grounds for administrative removal are that a person has remained beyond the period specified in his limited leave, or has broken a condition attached to it. For example, a person's leave to enter or remain will often either prohibit or restrict his freedom to take employment, and the person is liable to administrative removal procedures if he is found to be working without authority. Home Office guidance is that there must be firm and recent (within six months) evidence of working in breach. The immigration officer will look for at least an admission by the offender under caution of working in breach; or a statement by the employer; or pay slips or the offender's details on the payroll; or visual observation, by the immigration officer, of the applicant working.

As explained in **3.6.2**, a person who wishes to extend his stay should apply for a variation before his leave expires. He commits a criminal offence under s 24(1)(b) of the IA 1971 if he knowingly overstays or fails to observe a condition of the leave. Note that it is not usual practice for a prosecution to occur. Removal does not require a knowing breach, and so normally the person is removed and not prosecuted.

In addition, illegal entrants (see **10.4.2**) may be removed from the UK in the same way.

10.4.2   Definition of illegal entrant

An illegal entrant is a person who unlawfully enters or seeks to enter in breach of a deportation order or of the immigration laws. This includes a person who has so entered.

Typically, a person might enter the UK without leave clandestinely, eg concealed in a vehicle such as a lorry. Or he might present a forged or false British or EEA passport to an immigration officer.

A person who, contrary to the IA 1971, knowingly enters the UK in breach of a deportation order or without leave commits a criminal offence under s 24(1)(a). However, it is possible to be an illegal entrant without having committed any criminal offence, for instance where a person obtains leave by producing false documents, without knowing them to be false (R v *Immigration Officer, ex p Chan* [1992] 1 WLR 541).

A person will be an illegal entrant if he obtains leave to enter by deception, although mere non-disclosure of material facts will not amount to deception, as the entrant has no positive duty to reveal facts if a relevant question is not asked. It is for the Home Office to prove the deception (R v *Secretary of State for the Home Department, ex p Khawaja* [1984] AC 74).

10.4.3   Procedure

If the Home Office decides not to remove the person, he is normally granted indefinite to leave to remain.

If, after consideration of all the relevant facts, the Home Office decides that administrative removal is the correct course of action, a notice of liability to administrative removal is served. The immigration officer normally serves the notice in person. It still remains open to the person who is subject to enforcement action to leave the UK voluntarily. Otherwise the immigration officer will set removal directions. The costs of complying with removal directions (so far as reasonably incurred) are met by the Secretary of State. Directions for removal of a person given under s 10 of the 1999 Act invalidate any leave to enter or remain in the UK.

There is no right of appeal in the UK against a decision that a person is to be removed from the UK by way of directions under s 10, save on asylum or human rights grounds (see **11.3**).

10.4.4   Effect of administrative removal

Unlike someone who has been deported, a person who is subject to administrative removal does not need to have the decision to remove him rescinded before he may return to the UK, provided that he otherwise qualifies for admission under the Immigration Rules.

10.4.5   Government policy: deportation and administrative removal

It is important to remember that deportation may be automatic (see **10.1.5**), or otherwise there is a presumption of deportation (see **10.1.11**). But administrative removal is never automatic, neither is there a presumption of administrative removal. Why the difference? It is because different government policies are pursued by the use of deportation and administrative removal, as methods to expel a person from the UK.

As we saw at **10.1.4,** there are three important features of the public interest in deportation, namely:

(a)   the risk of re-offending by the person concerned;

(b)   the need to deter foreign nationals from committing serious crimes by leading them to understand that, whatever the other circumstances, one consequence for them may well be their deportation; and

(c)   the role of deportation as an expression of society's revulsion at serious crimes and in building public confidence in the criminal justice system's treatment of foreign citizens who have committed serious crimes.

In *UE (Nigeria) v Secretary of State for the Home Department* [2010] EWCA Civ 975, the Court identified that the main element of public interest in administrative removal is the need for the Government to maintain a firm policy of immigration control.

The difference in aims is important, because it explains why the factors in favour of expulsion are capable of carrying greater weight in a deportation case than in a case of administrative removal. This led Richards LJ, in *JO (Uganda) v Secretary of State for the Home Department* [2010] EWCA Civ 10, to observe (at [29]):

> The maintenance of effective immigration control is an important matter, but the protection of society against serious crime is even more important and can properly be given correspondingly greater weight in the balancing exercise. Thus I think it perfectly possible in principle for a given set of considerations of family life and/or private life to be sufficiently weighty to render expulsion disproportionate in an ordinary removal case, yet insufficient to render expulsion disproportionate in a deportation case because of the additional weight to be given to the criminal offending on which the deportation decision was based.

10.4.6   Human rights challenges to removal

See **10.2** as to challenges based on provisions other than Article 8 ECHR.

As to Article 8 ECHR, para 400 of the Immigration Rules provides that where a person claims that his removal would be contrary to the UK's obligations under Article 8, the Secretary of State may require an application under para 276ADE (private life) or Appendix FM (family life) of the Rules. Where an application is not required, in assessing that claim the Secretary of State or an immigration officer will, subject to para 353 (see **9.14**), consider that claim against the requirements to be met under para 276ADE or Appendix FM, and if appropriate the removal decision will be cancelled.

10.4.6.1   Paragraph 276ADE

A person who has lived in the UK for at least 20 years continuously, lawfully or unlawfully, can apply to the Home Office for leave to remain in the UK on the basis of the Article 8 ECHR right to respect for private life. Alternative provisions allow an applicant to be granted limited leave to remain in the UK on the basis of private life after seven years' continuous residence if he is under the age of 18; or if he has spent at least half of his life in the UK if he is aged between 18 and 24; or if the applicant has less than 20 years' continuous residence in the UK but has no ties (including social, cultural or family) with his country of origin.

Full details are given at **8.13**.

10.4.6.2 Appendix FM (family life)

Under para EX.1 of Appendix FM to the Immigration Rules, an applicant may be allowed to remain in the UK on the basis of his family life with a child and/or a partner if it would breach Article 8 ECHR to remove him.

Paragraph EX.1 applies if the applicant has a genuine and subsisting parental relationship with a child (under the age of 18 years) who is in the UK, who is a British citizen or who has lived in the UK continuously for at least the seven years immediately preceding the date of application, and it would not be reasonable to expect that child to leave the UK. See **8.5.1**.

Paragraph EX.1 additionally, or alternatively, applies if the applicant has a genuine and subsisting relationship with a partner who is in the UK and who is a British citizen, settled in the UK, or in the UK with refugee leave or humanitarian protection, and there are insurmountable obstacles to family life with that partner continuing outside the UK. See **8.5.2**.

10.5 INTERFERENCE WITH EU TREATY RIGHTS BY DEPORTATION OR ADMINISTRATIVE REMOVAL

10.5.1 Partner

What if a British citizen is exercising EU Treaty rights but his non-EEA partner is threatened with expulsion from the UK? In *Carpenter v Secretary of State for the Home Department* [2003] 2 WLR 267, Mrs C was a national of The Philippines. She was given leave to enter the UK as a visitor in September 1994 for six months. She overstayed that leave and failed to apply for any extension of her stay. In May 1996 she married Mr C, a British citizen. Mr C ran a business selling advertising space in medical and scientific journals, and offering various administrative and publishing services to the editors of those journals. A significant proportion of the business was conducted with advertisers established in other Member States of the EU. Mr C travelled to other Member States for the purpose of his business.

In July 1996 Mrs C applied to the Secretary of State for leave to remain in the UK as the spouse of a British citizen. Her application was refused, and the Secretary of State also decided to make an order removing her to The Philippines. Mrs C argued that since her husband's business required him to travel around in other Member States, providing and receiving services, he could do so more easily as she was looking after his children from his first marriage. Therefore, her removal would restrict her husband's right to provide and receive services. It was accepted that Mrs C's marriage was genuine and that she played an important part in the upbringing of her stepchildren. It was also accepted that her husband was a provider of services for the purposes of EU law.

Mrs C accepted that she had no right of her own to reside in any Member State but claimed that her rights derived from those enjoyed by Mr C to provide services and to travel within the EU. Her removal would either require Mr C to go to live with her in The Philippines, or separate the members of the family unit if he remained in the UK. The ECJ agreed that the separation of Mr and Mrs C would be detrimental to their family life and, therefore, to the conditions under which Mr C exercised his fundamental EU Treaty rights. Those rights could not be fully effective if Mr C were deterred from exercising them by obstacles raised by the UK Government to the residence of his spouse.

The ECJ then went on to link the interference with Mr C's EU rights with the interference with his Article 8 ECHR rights. The decision to remove Mrs C did not strike a fair balance between the competing interests, on the one hand, of Mr C to respect for his family life and, on the other hand, the UK Government's removal policy. Although Mrs C had infringed UK immigration laws, her conduct since her arrival in the UK had not been the subject of any other complaint. The Court held that to remove Mrs C constituted an infringement which was not proportionate to the objective pursued of maintaining immigration control. However, in deportation cases where the criminality threshold is reached (see **10.3.4**), it is most likely that the Home Office's position will be that the public interest in deportation (see **10.1.4**) will ordinarily outweigh any right of the non-EEA partner to remain in the EU in these circumstances and that the couple can continue their family life in a country outside the EU.

10.5.2   Child

What if a child is a British citizen and the parent being expelled is not an EEA national? Can the child's EEA rights assist the parent if the child will otherwise be leaving the UK with that parent? In *Zambrano v Office national de l'emploi (ONEm)* (Case C-34/09) [2011] 2 CMLR 46, the applicant and his wife were both Columbian nationals who had sought and been refused refugee status in Belgium. However, the couple were allowed to stay in Belgium temporarily, and had two children who acquired Belgian nationality under national law.

The Court held that Article 20 TFEU (see **4.3**) confers the status of citizen of the EU on every person holding the nationality of a Member State. Since the children of the applicant possessed Belgian nationality under Belgian law, they undeniably enjoyed that status. Further, Article 20 TFEU precludes national measures which have the effect of depriving citizens of the EU of the genuine enjoyment of the substance of the rights conferred by virtue of their status as citizens of the EU. A refusal to grant a right of residence to a third country national with dependent minor children in the Member State where those children were nationals and resided, had such an effect. Such a refusal would lead to a situation where those children, citizens of the EU, would have to leave the territory of the EU in order to accompany their parents. In these circumstances, the children, as citizens of the EU, would, as a result, be unable to exercise the substance of the rights conferred on them by virtue of their status as citizens of the EU.

So if the child is a British citizen, the applicant is the child's primary carer and there is no other parent, guardian or carer on whom the child is dependent or who could care for the child if the primary carer left the UK, the applicant will have a right of residence under the case (see **8.5.1.3**). However, in deportation cases where the criminality threshold is reached (see **10.3.4**), Home Office guidance is that a decision maker considering Article 8 ECHR can use the argument that family life could continue in a country outside the EU because the British citizen child could accompany his primary carer. This is because in such cases the Home Office's position is that the public interest in deportation (see **10.1.4**) will ordinarily outweigh the right of the British citizen child to remain in the EU, and therefore there will be no contradiction between refusing to recognise a right of residence under the case for the primary carer and arguing that the British citizen child can continue his family life in a country outside the EU.

10.6   REMOVAL TO REQUIRE ENTRY CLEARANCE

In *Chikwamba v Secretary of State for the Home Department* [2008] UKHL 40, the House of Lords had to answer this question: When determining an appeal under ss 82 and 84 of the NIAA 2002 (see **Chapter 11**) against the Secretary of State's refusal of leave to remain on the ground that to remove the appellant would interfere disproportionately with his Article 8 right to respect for his family life, when, if ever, is it appropriate to dismiss the appeal on the basis that the appellant should be required to leave the country and seek leave to enter from an entry clearance officer abroad?

The answer was 'comparatively rarely, certainly in family cases involving children, should an Article 8 appeal be dismissed on the basis that it would be proportionate and more appropriate for the appellant to apply for leave from abroad' (per Lord Brown of Eaton-under-Heywood, at [44]).

For an example of an exceptional case justifying removal for an application to be made, see *R (Kotecha) v Secretary of State for the Home Department* [2011] EWHC 2070.

IMMIGRATION APPEALS

11.1 APPEALS: THE GENERAL RULE

The NIAA 2002 sets out a revised system of appeals, including a system for a 'one stop' comprehensive appeal following refusal of leave to enter or remain. It replaces all rights of appeal established in earlier legislation. The Act establishes the principle that there is one right of appeal against any of the listed 'immigration decisions' (see **11.2**). Where multiple decisions would result in multiple rights of appeal, these are subsumed into one appeal. All appealable grounds can and should be raised in an appeal (see **11.5**). Most, but not all, appeal rights can be exercised by the appellant in the UK (see **11.4**). Exceptions and limitations restrict rights of appeal in certain circumstances (see **11.8** onwards).

11.2 DECISIONS AGAINST WHICH THERE IS A RIGHT OF APPEAL

By s 82(2) of the NIAA 2002, an appeal can be made against an 'immigration decision', namely:

(a) refusal of leave to enter the UK;

(b) refusal of entry clearance;

(c) refusal of a certificate of entitlement of the right of abode [see **2.3.3**];

(d) refusal to vary a person's leave to enter or remain in the UK if the result of the refusal is that the person has no leave to enter or remain;

(e) variation of a person's leave to enter or remain in the UK if when the variation takes effect the person has no leave to enter or remain;

(f) revocation of indefinite leave to enter or remain in the UK;

(g)   a decision that a person is to be removed from the UK by way of directions under s 10 of the IAA 1999 [see **10.2.5**];

(h)   a decision that an illegal entrant is to be removed from the UK by way of directions under Sch 2 to the IA 1971 [see **10.2.2**];

(ha)   a decision that a person whose leave has been statutorily extended [see **3.6.2** and **3.7**] is to be removed from the UK;

(i)   a decision to remove a family member of a person refused leave to enter the UK or who is an illegal entrant;

(ia)   a decision to remove a seaman or aircraft crew;

(ib)   a decision to deprive a Commonwealth citizen of right of abode [see **2.3.5**];

(j)   a decision to make a deportation order [see **10.1**]; and

(k)   refusal to revoke a deportation order [see **10.1.8**].

As to (h) above, the appeal is limited to challenging the decision to remove and not the directions made to carry that out: see *MS (Palestinian Territories) v Secretary of State for the Home Department* [2010] UKSC 25.

As to (j) above, a foreign criminal may not appeal against an order to deport him automatically (see **10.1.2.3**). However, he may appeal against the decision that he falls within that provision and additionally, or alternatively, on the ground that removal from the UK would be incompatible with his ECHR rights (see **11.3**).

These rights of appeal are subject to exceptions and limitations (see **11.8** onwards).

11.3 · GROUNDS OF APPEAL

By s 84, an appeal against an immigration decision (see **11.2**) must be brought on one or more of the following grounds:

(a)   that the decision is not in accordance with Immigration Rules (eg a person argues that he meets a particular Rule);

(b)   that the decision is unlawful discrimination by public authorities;

(c)   that the decision is unlawful under s 6 of the Human Rights Act 1998 as being incompatible with the appellant's ECHR rights;

(d)   that the appellant is an EEA national or a member of the family of an EEA national and the decision breaches the appellant's rights under the EU Treaties in respect of entry to or residence in the UK;

(e)   that the decision is otherwise not in accordance with the law (eg a person claims the benefit of a Government policy that is not contained in the Rules);

(f)   that the person taking the decision should have exercised differently a discretion conferred by Immigration Rules (eg a person refused by an exercise of discretion under the Immigration Rules, para 320: see **3.4.5**);

(g)   that removal of the appellant from the UK in consequence of the immigration decision would breach the UK's obligations under the Geneva Convention on refugees, or would be unlawful under s 6 of the Human Rights Act 1998 as being incompatible with the appellant's Convention rights.

Any number of grounds can be set out but such will constitute one appeal (see **11.5**).

11.4 APPEAL RIGHTS EXERCISABLE IN THE UK

By s 92, an appeal right is not exercisable whilst the appellant is in the UK unless:

(a)   the appeal is against an immigration decision of the kind specified in s 82(2)(c), (d), (e), (f), (ha) and (j) (see **11.2**);

(b)   the appeal is against refusal of leave to enter where at the time of the refusal the appellant is in the UK and on his arrival he had entry clearance;

(c)   the appeal is against an immigration decision and the appellant has made an asylum claim, or a human rights claim, while in the UK, or is an EEA national or a member of the family of an EEA national and makes a claim to the Secretary of State that the decision breaches the appellant's rights under the Community Treaties in respect of entry to or residence in the UK.

All other appeal rights can be exercised only from abroad.

Note that by s 113, a 'human rights claim' is defined as a claim made by a person to the Secretary of State at a place designated by the Secretary of State that to remove the person from or require him to leave the UK would be unlawful under s 6 of the Human Rights Act 1998. An 'asylum claim' means a claim made by a person to the Secretary of State at a place designated by the Secretary of State that to remove the person from or require him to leave the UK would breach the UK's obligations under the Geneva Convention on refugees.

11.5   THE 'ONE STOP' PROCESS

11.5.1   Notice of appealable decision

The Immigration (Notices) Regulations 2003 (SI 2003/658) provide that a decision-maker (eg entry clearance officer, immigration officer, Secretary of State) must give written notice to a person of any immigration decision taken in respect of him which is appealable. The notice must include or be accompanied by a statement of the reasons for the decision to which it relates and, if it relates to an immigration decision specified in s 82(2)(a), (g), (h), (ha), (i), (ia) or (j) of the 2002 Act, state the country or territory to which it is proposed to remove the person.

The notice must also include, or be accompanied by, a statement which advises the person of his right of appeal and the statutory provision on which his right of appeal is based; whether or not such an appeal may be brought while in the UK; the grounds on which such an appeal may be brought; and the facilities available for advice and assistance in connection with such an appeal. It must also be accompanied by a notice which indicates the time limit for bringing the appeal (see **11.6.3**), the address to which it should be sent or may be taken by hand and a fax number for service by fax. Where the exercise of the appeal right is restricted by an exception or limitation (see **11.8** onwards), the notice must also include or be accompanied by a statement which refers to the provision limiting or restricting the right of appeal.

Further, by s 120, if a person has made an application to enter or remain in the UK, or an immigration decision (see **11.2**) has been taken or may be taken in respect of him, then the Secretary of State or an immigration officer may by notice in writing require him to state:

(a)   his reasons for wishing to enter or remain in the UK;

(b)   any grounds on which he should be permitted to enter or remain in the UK; and

(c)   any grounds on which he should not be removed from or required to leave the UK.

11.5.2   Consequences of failing to disclose all grounds of appeal

What if a s 120 notice is not answered? Any attempt to raise such grounds later on may lead to certification under s 96, with the effect that there can be no appeal against the decision, or that those grounds cannot be raised in connection with a further appeal.

Before the Secretary of State can lawfully decide to certify, four steps must be taken:

(Step 1)   The Secretary of State must be satisfied that the person was notified of a right of appeal under s 82 against another immigration decision (s 96(1)), or that the person received a notice under s 120 by virtue of an application other than that to which the new decision relates or by virtue of a decision other than the new decision (s 96(2)).

(Step 2)   The Secretary of State must conclude that the claim or application to which the new decision relates relies on a matter that could have been raised in an appeal against the old decision (s 96(1)(b)), or that the new decision relates to an application or claim which relies on a matter that should have been but has not been raised in a statement made in response to that notice (s 96(2)(b)).

(Step 3) The Secretary of State must form the opinion that there is no satisfactory reason for that matter not having been raised in an appeal against the old decision (s 96(1)(c)), or that there is no satisfactory reason for that matter not having been raised in a statement made in response to that notice (s 96(2)(c)).

(Step 4) The Secretary of State must consider whether, having regard to all relevant factors, he should exercise his discretion to certify, and must conclude that it is appropriate to exercise the discretion in favour of certification.

As to the interpretation of the word 'matter' in Steps 2 and 3, see R *(on the application of Khan) v Secretary of State for the Home Department* [2013] LTL, 22 January.

11.5.3 Other certificates under s 96

Certificates can be issued under s 96 otherwise than in relation to s 120 notices (see **11.5.2**).

Note that no appeal can be brought on any ground against an otherwise appealable decision if the Secretary of State or immigration officer certifies that the person was notified of a right of appeal against another decision (whether or not any appeal was lodged or completed) *and* that in his opinion the person made the claim or application in order to delay removal, or the removal of a family member, *and* that in his opinion the person had no other legitimate purpose for making the claim or application. If an appeal has already been brought, the appeal may not be continued if a certificate is issued.

Further s 96 prevents an appeal being brought if the Secretary of State or immigration officer certifies that a new decision relates to a ground which was raised on an earlier appeal or could have been raised at an appeal had the applicant chosen to exercise a right of appeal. If an appeal has already been brought, the appeal may not be continued if a certificate is issued.

Finally, where a further appeal right does arise, the Secretary of State or immigration officer may certify that certain grounds of appeal were already considered in an earlier appeal. The appellant is not then allowed to rely on those grounds.

The certificate may be challenged by way of an application for judicial review: see R *(Adebisi) v Secretary of State for the Home Department* [2011] LTL, 5 May; R *(J) v Secretary of State for the Home Department* [2009] EWHC 705 and **Chapter 12**.

11.6 THE APPEALS SYSTEM

11.6.1 The First-tier Tribunal (Immigration and Asylum Chamber) (IAC)

A right of appeal lies to the IAC, under s 82 of the NIAA 2002, against an immigration decision (see **11.2**); in certain circumstances, against a decision to reject an asylum claim (see **9.1**); and, under s 40A of the BNA 1981, against a decision to make an order depriving a person of a British citizenship status (see **2.2.9**).

The title of the legally-qualified member of the IAC is an Immigration Judge. All IAC appeals are heard in various appeal centres across the UK.

An appeal to the IAC may only be started by giving notice of appeal on a prescribed form in accordance with the Asylum and Immigration Tribunal (Procedure) Rules 2005 (SI 2005/230, as amended). Practitioners must also be familiar with the IAC Practice Directions. Normally there is an initial case management review hearing. This will determine the issues in dispute and the evidence necessary to deal with them. Directions are usually given as to the filing of evidence, etc.

At the appeal hearing the Immigration Judge determines whether or not to uphold the original decision. If it is upheld, appeal lies on a point of law to the Upper Tribunal (Asylum and Immigration Chamber). Permission to appeal is required from the IAC or, failing that, the Upper Tribunal. If both the IAC and Upper Tribunal refuse permission to appeal, that decision can be judicially reviewed, but limited to the grounds that either:

(a)   the proposed appeal would raise some important point of principle or practice; or

(b)   there is some other compelling reason for the court to hear the appeal: see R (Cart) v The Upper Tribunal [2011] UKSC 28.

As to ground (b), note that in PR (Sri Lanka) v Secretary of State for the Home Department [2011] EWCA Civ 988, the Court of Appeal (per Carnwath LJ at [35]) stated that 'compelling means legally compelling, rather than compelling, perhaps, from a political or emotional point of view, although such considerations may exceptionally add weight to the legal arguments.' See also **Chapter 12**.

Appeal on a point of law from the Upper Tribunal lies to the Court of Appeal. It is necessary to obtain that court's permission first.

11.6.2   Appeals to the Court of Appeal

The Court of Appeal has the power to give any decision which might have been given by the IAC. It can also remit the matter for rehearing and determination by the IAC, and then may offer the IAC its opinion and make directions with which the IAC must comply.

11.6.3   The appeals timetable

11.6.3.1   Appealing to the IAC

An appellant appealing in the UK to the IAC must give notice of appeal within five working days of receiving the decision if he is in detention. Otherwise the time limit is 10 working days. However, if the appeal is being made from outside the UK, he must give notice of appeal within 28 calendar days after receiving notice of the decision.

11.6.3.2   Asking the IAC for permission to appeal to the Upper Tribunal

An application for permission to appeal to the Upper Tribunal must be made to the IAC within five working days of receiving the IAC's decision if the appellant is in the UK, but 28 days if he is outside the UK.

11.6.3.3   Asking the Upper Tribunal for its permission to appeal

What are the time limits if the IAC refuses permission? If the appellant is in the UK, the period is seven working days after the date on which notice of the First-tier Tribunal's refusal of permission was sent or five working days if that notice was sent electronically or delivered personally. Where the appellant is outside the UK, the respective periods are 56 and 28 days.

11.6.3.4   Seeking permission of the Court of Appeal

An application for leave to appeal to the Court of Appeal must be made within 12 days of receipt of the Upper Tribunal's determination.

11.6.3.5   Appeals timetable if appellant is detained

Appeals are expedited or 'fast tracked' if the appellant is in detention. For details see the AIT (Fast Track Procedure) Rules 2005 (SI 2005/560, as amended).

11.7   PENDING AND ABANDONED APPEALS

Section 104 sets out when an appeal is pending and when it ends: it clarifies that an appeal ceases to be pending when it is 'abandoned'. An appeal may be treated as abandoned because the appellant leaves the UK, is granted leave to enter or remain, or a deportation order is made against him. However, an appeal continues to be pending so long as a further appeal may be brought and until such further appeal is finally determined.

As a general rule, while an appeal is pending, the leave to which the appeal relates and any conditions subject to which it was granted continue to have effect. Hence, the person has a right to remain in the UK whilst pursuing the appeal. But what does 'the leave to which the appeal relates' mean? It is referring to the leave that the appellant had when he made the application that has been refused. It does not mean the leave for which the appellant applied.

By s 77, while a person's claim for asylum is pending he may not be removed from or required to leave the UK in accordance with a provision of the Immigration Acts.

However, this does not prevent the giving of a direction for the claimant's removal from the UK, the making of a deportation order in respect of the claimant, or the taking of any other interim or preparatory action.

By s 78, while a person's appeal under s 82 is pending he may not be removed from or required to leave the UK in accordance with a provision of the Immigration Acts. However, this does not prevent the giving of a direction for the appellant's removal from the UK, the making of a deportation order in respect of the appellant (subject to s 79: see below), or the taking of any other interim or preparatory action.

Section 78 only applies to an appeal brought while the appellant is in the UK in accordance with s 92 (see **11.4**).

By s 79 a deportation order may not be made in respect of a person while an appeal under s 82 against the decision to make the order could be brought (ignoring any possibility of an appeal out of time with permission), or is pending.

Note that s 99 provides that where a certificate is issued under s 96 (see **11.5.2**) or ss 97 or 98 (see **11.12** and **11.13**) in respect of a pending appeal, then that appeal lapses.

11.8 INELIGIBLE APPEALS

Section 88 applies to an immigration decision of the kind referred to in s 82(2)(a), (b), (d) or (e). These are detailed at **11.2**. A person may not appeal under s 82 against such an immigration decision which is taken on the grounds that he or a person of whom he is a dependant:

(a)   does not satisfy a requirement as to age, nationality or citizenship specified in immigration rules;

(b)   does not have an immigration document of a particular kind (or any immigration document);

(ba)   has failed to supply a medical report or a medical certificate in accordance with a requirement of immigration rules;

(c)   is seeking to be in the UK for a period greater than that permitted in his case by immigration rules; or

(d)   is seeking to enter or remain in the UK for a purpose other than one for which entry or remaining is permitted in accordance with immigration rules.

For the purposes of (b) above, an 'immigration document' means either entry clearance, a passport, a work permit or other immigration employment document, or a document which relates to a national of a country other than the UK and which is designed to serve the same purpose as a passport.

An appeal may nevertheless be brought on asylum, human rights or race discrimination grounds.

11.9 REFUSAL OF ENTRY CLEARANCE TO VISIT UK

Section 88A provides that a person may not appeal under s 82 against refusal of an application for entry clearance as a visitor to the UK. The applicant may re-apply and address the grounds for refusal in the fresh application. An appeal can only be made on human rights or race discrimination grounds.

11.10 REFUSAL OF LEAVE TO ENTER

By s 89, a person may not appeal under s 82 against refusal of leave to enter the UK unless on his arrival in the UK he had entry clearance and the purpose of entry specified in the entry clearance was the same as that specified in his application for leave to enter. However, an appeal may still be brought on asylum, human rights or race discrimination grounds.

11.11 NATIONAL SECURITY AND SIMILAR MATTERS

Section 97 provides that an appeal under s 82 cannot be made or continued where the Secretary of State certifies that a decision was taken to exclude or remove a person from the UK:

(a)   in the interests of national security;

(b)   in the interests of the relationship between the UK and another country; or

(c)   otherwise in the public interest.

However, under the Special Immigration Appeals Commission Act 1997 an appeal can be made to the Special Immigration Appeals Commission (SIAC). This body was set up specifically to deal with appeals where national security and other sensitive matters are a consideration. The proceedings of the SIAC are governed by the Special Immigration Appeals Commission (Procedure) Rules 2003 (SI 2003/1034).

11.12 DEPORTATION ORDER MADE ON NATIONAL SECURITY GROUNDS

Section 97 (see **11.11**) does not apply where the Secretary of State certifies that the decision to make a deportation order (see **10.1**) in respect of a person was taken on the grounds that his removal from the UK would be in the interests of national security. In those circumstances s 97A applies instead, and an appeal can be made only from outside the UK. If the appellant makes a human rights claim the appeal can be brought in country, unless the Secretary of State certifies that removal would not breach the ECHR. Provision is made for an appeal against such a certificate to the SIAC.

11.13 'PUBLIC GOOD' EXCLUSION

Section 98 provides that an appeal cannot be made or continued against a refusal of leave to enter or refusal of entry clearance if the Secretary of State has certified that the person's exclusion from the UK is conducive to the public good, or directed that the person be refused on that ground. However, this does not prevent the person appealing on human rights or race discrimination grounds, or from appealing refusal of leave to enter on asylum grounds.

11.14 EEA NATIONALS

The I(EEA) Regs 2006 give rights of appeal which have been prescribed under EU law for EEA nationals, members of their family and certain non-EEA nationals who are members of a UK national's family (see **4.4**). There are also additional categories of persons who are entitled to similar rights under agreements to which the UK is a party or by which it is bound. The rights of appeal cover decisions relating to admission, residence and the issue or withdrawal of relevant documentation. Appeals against decisions will be heard by the IAC or, where appropriate, by the SIAC. A copy of the Regulations may be found at **Appendix 4** to this book.

11.15 UNFOUNDED HUMAN RIGHTS OR ASYLUM CLAIMS

By s 94(1A), a person may not bring an appeal whilst in the UK against an immigration decision of a kind specified in s 82(2)(c), (d), (e) or (ha) (see **11.2**) in reliance on s 92 (see **11.4**) if the appellant has also made a human rights and/or asylum claim and the Secretary of State certifies that the human rights and/or asylum claim is or are clearly unfounded.

By s 94(2), a person may not bring a human rights and/or asylum appeal whilst in the UK if the Secretary of State certifies that either claim is or both claims are clearly unfounded.

Note that if the Secretary of State is satisfied that an asylum claimant or human rights claimant is entitled to reside in a State listed in s 94(4), he *must* certify the claim unless he is satisfied that it is not clearly unfounded. The s 94(4) States considered to be generally safe in the context of asylum and human rights claims are:

(a)   the Republic of Albania;

(b)   Bosnia-Hertzegovina;

(c)   Jamaica;

(d)   Macedonia;

(e)   the Republic of Moldova;

(f)   India;

(g)   Bolivia;

(h)   Brazil;

(i)   Ecuador;

(j)   South Africa;

(k)   Ukraine;

(l)   Mongolia;

(m)   Ghana (in respect of men);

(n)   Nigeria (in respect of men);

(o)   Gambia (in respect of men);

(p)   Kenya (in respect of men);

(q)   Liberia (in respect of men);

(r)   Malawi (in respect of men);

(s)   Mali (in respect of men);

(t)   Mauritius;

(u)   Montenegro;

(v)   Peru;

(w)   Serbia;

(x)   Sierra Leone (in respect of men);

(y)   Kosovo;

(z)   South Korea

The Home Office gives the following as examples of clearly unfounded claims:

(a)   A claim which raises nothing that could be construed as amounting to an expression of a fear of mistreatment upon return. For example, a person says he is seeking asylum but gives as his reason that he is fleeing poverty or unemployment.

(b)   The claimant expresses a fear of mistreatment, but from the objective evidence it is not arguable that the mistreatment, even if it occurred, would amount to persecution or treatment contrary to Article 3 ECHR.

(c)   The claimant expresses a fear of persecution or Article 3 treatment by non-State actors but the State provides a sufficiency of protection against such actions.

Further, a person may not bring an appeal if the Secretary of State certifies that it is proposed to remove the person to a country of which he is not a national or citizen, and there is no reason to believe that the person's rights under the ECHR will be breached in that country. In determining whether a person in relation to whom such a certificate has been issued may be removed from the UK, the country specified in the certificate is to be regarded as a place where a person's life and liberty is not threatened by reason of his race, religion, nationality, membership of a particular social group, or political opinion, and a place from which a person will not be sent to another country otherwise than in accordance with the Geneva Convention on refugees.

Home Office guidance is that claims should be assessed at their highest and are certified only when they are bound to fail (following R *(Yogathas) v Secretary of State for the Home Department* [2002] UKHL 36).

A certificate may be challenged by way of judicial review.

> It follows that a challenge to the Secretary of State's conclusion that a claim is clearly unfounded is a rationality challenge. There is no way that a court can consider whether her conclusion was rational other than by asking itself the same question that she has considered. If the court concludes that a claim has a realistic prospect of success when the Secretary of State has reached a contrary view, the court will necessarily conclude that the Secretary of State's view was irrational. (per Lord Phillips in ZT *(Kosovo) v Secretary of State for the Home Department* [2009] UKHL 6 at para 23)

How should the Secretary of State set about making the decision? His Lordship explained at para 22 that five steps need to be taken, namely, that the Secretary of State should:

(i)   consider the factual substance and detail of the claim,

(ii)   consider how it stands with the known background data,

(iii)   consider whether in the round it is capable of belief,

(iv)   if not, consider whether some part of it is capable of belief,

(v)   consider whether, if eventually believed in whole or in part, it is capable of coming within the Convention.

> If the answers are such that the claim cannot on any legitimate view succeed, then the claim is clearly unfounded; if not, not.

Where a certificate is issued concerning a national of a country listed in s 94(4), the first challenge may be as to whether the country in question has been properly listed. To succeed, the claimant will have to demonstrate that the evidence clearly establishes that there is a serious risk of persecution in that country that affects a significant number of people: see R *(MD (Gambia)) v Secretary of State for the Home Department* [2011] EWCA Civ 121. It follows that if the listing is lawful, the next question is whether the Secretary of State was obliged to certify the claim on the basis that it was clearly unfounded.

See further **Chapter 12**.

11.16 PERSONS EXCLUDED FROM ASYLUM

Where the Home Office decides that a claimant is excluded from asylum (see **9.5**), the Secretary of State will issue a certificate to that effect. As a result, any appeal made to the IAC or SIAC must start by considering the statements made in the Secretary of State's certificate. By s 55(4) of the IANA 2006, if the Tribunal or Commission agrees with those statements, it must dismiss such part of the appeal as amounts to an asylum claim before considering any other aspect of the case.

11.17 EUROPEAN COMMON LIST OF SAFE COUNTRIES OF ORIGIN

Section 94A allows the Secretary of State by order to prescribe a list of States to be known as the European Common List of Safe Countries of Origin. This is pursuant to EC Council Directive 2005/85, which provides that the Council shall adopt a minimum common list of third countries which shall be regarded by Member States as safe third countries of origin. At the time of writing no order had been made.

If a national of a State which is listed in the European Common List of Safe Countries of Origin, or a Stateless person who was formerly habitually resident in such a State, makes an asylum claim or a human rights claim (or both), the Secretary of State will certify such under s 94 as unfounded unless he is satisfied that there are serious grounds for considering that the State in question is not safe given the particular circumstances of the claimant.

11.18 DEPRIVATION OF CITIZENSHIP ORDERS

By s 40A of the BNA 1981, a person given notice of a decision to make an order depriving him of his British citizenship (see **2.2.9**) has a right of appeal to the IAC. Where, however, the Secretary of State has certified that the decision to deprive was based wholly or partly in reliance on information which he believes should not be made public, the appeal at first instance will instead be heard by the SIAC.

11.19 ADMINISTRATIVE REVIEW

11.19.1 Refusal of entry clearance under points-based system

In **Chapters 6** and **7** we looked at the points-based system for entry to the UK by students, employees, business people and investors. If an applicant for entry clearance is refused, any appeal is limited to grounds (b) and (c) at **11.3** above. Additionally, or alternatively, the applicant may seek administrative review (AR) of any refusal he believes was made in error, including any refusal under the general grounds (see **3.4.5.2**).

11.19.2 What is administrative review?

Administrative review is a non-statutory scheme and the policy is contained solely in the Home Office's guidance notes. It is free of charge. The request for a review must be made to an Entry Clearance Manager (ECM) on the AR Request Notice sent with the entry clearance refusal notice. It must be returned within 28 days, and only in exceptional circumstances will a late application be accepted.

Only one request can be made unless the ECM upholds a refusal on different grounds. The applicant may then request an AR of the new refusal grounds.

Administrative review is normally completed within 28 days. The applicant is notified of the outcome by letter.

11.19.3 The administrative review process

The ECM will consider the areas the applicant has asked to be reviewed and check that points were correctly assessed, documents were properly scrutinised and verification checks appropriately carried out.

11.19.4 Conclusion of the administrative review process

An ECM may recommend that the reason for refusal should be overturned, and issue entry clearance where he finds that the entry clearance officer:

(a)   failed properly to consider evidence submitted with the original application;

(b)   failed correctly to apply the Immigration Rules; or

(c)   made a mistake in processing the application.

11.20 GROUNDS OF APPEAL TO IAC

11.20.1 Asylum appeals

When appealing the refusal of the Secretary of State to grant asylum, the appellant should consider completing, as appropriate, boxes 1 to 7 of Section 3D of the Appeal Form IAFT-1. The form is available on the Ministry of Justice website (see **1.2.8**). The boxes read as follows:

1. If you disagree with the Home Office's interpretation of the situation in your country, please explain why in this box, and give reasons to support your point of view.
2. If the Home Office has suggested that you could live safely in another part of the country of origin, and you disagree, please explain why in this box.
3. If the Home Office has stated that your claim is not credible, and you disagree, please explain why in this box.
4. If the Home Office has stated that you do not qualify as a refugee on grounds of race, religion, nationality, membership of a particular social group or political opinion (under the criteria of the 1951 Geneva Convention), and you disagree, please explain why in this box.
5. If the Home Office has stated that specific articles of the European Convention on Human Rights (ECHR) do not apply to your case, and you disagree, please explain why in this box.
6. If the Home Office has stated that you do not qualify as a person who is eligible for humanitarian protection (under the Refugee or Person in Need of International Protection Regulations 2006), and you disagree, please explain why in this box.
7. If there is anything else that you disagree with in the Home Office letter, please explain why in this box.

11.20.2 Non-asylum appeals

When appealing an immigration decision that does not concern asylum, the appellant should complete box 8 of Section 3D of the Appeal Form IAFT-1. This reads as follows:

8. If your appeal relates to a non-asylum decision with which you disagree, you must give your reasons below and refer to the paragraphs of the refusal letter (you may continue on a separate sheet if necessary).

11.20.3 Appeal against decision of an entry clearance officer

Where an appellant is able to appeal from abroad against the refusal of entry clearance, he should use Appeal Form IAFT-2.

11.21 EXAMPLES OF GROUNDS OF APPEAL

11.21.1 Appeal against deportation or removal order

11.21.1.1 Error in law: Article 8 ECHR

Decision	Grounds of appeal
Family life not established	Family life engaged

CASE LAW EXAMPLE

Kugathas v Secretary of State for the Home Department [2003] EWCA Civ 31 per Sedley LJ at [14]:

Generally, the protection of family life under Article 8 involves cohabiting dependants, such as parents and their dependant minor children. Whether it extends to other relationships depends on the circumstances of the particular case. Relationships between adults, a mother and her 33 year old son in the present case, would not necessarily acquire the protection of Article 8 of the Convention without evidence of further elements of dependency, involving more than the normal emotional ties.

Decision	Grounds of appeal
Deportation or removal is proportionate in the terms of Article 8(2)	Deportation or removal is disproportionate in the terms of Article 8(2)

CASE LAW EXAMPLE

AC (Turkey) v Secretary of State for the Home Department [2009] EWCA Civ 327 per Laws LJ at [14]:

> Clearly the Secretary of State has a particular responsibility to make judgments as to what Judge LJ called 'broad issues of social cohesion and public confidence' within the system of immigration control. The Secretary of State's judgment on those matters must broadly be respected by the [IAC], at least so far as the policy itself is concerned. As Wall LJ stated in *OP (Jamaica) v Secretary of State for the Home Department* [2008] EWCA Civ 440 (paragraph 24), the Secretary of State's assessment of those matters has 'to be taken as a given unless it is palpably wrong'. But then the [IAC] must exercise its own judgment as to whether, in view of that axiom or given, the decision to remove or deport is disproportionate in the terms of Article 8(2) of the Convention. That decision is to be arrived at on the merits and is entirely in the hands of the Tribunal.

11.21.1.2   Error in law: EEA national

Decision	Grounds of appeal
Removal of EEA national justified on public policy grounds	Wrong test applied – by I(EEA) Regs 2006, reg 21(3), as the EEA national had a permanent right of residence, he could be removed only if there were 'serious' grounds of public policy.
Removal of EEA national justified on public security grounds	Wrong test applied – by I(EEA) Regs 2006, reg 21(4), as the EEA national had resided in UK for a continuous period of at least 10 years, he could be removed only if there were 'imperative' grounds of public security.

CASE LAW EXAMPLE

LG (Italy) v Secretary of State for the Home Department [2008] EWCA Civ 190 per Carnwath LJ at [32]:

> The words 'imperative grounds of public security' at the third level are clearly intended to embody a test which is both more stringent and narrower in scope than 'serious grounds of public policy or public security' at the second level ... [L]evel three requires, not simply a serious matter of public policy, but an actual risk to public security, so compelling that it justifies the exceptional course of removing someone who (in the language of the Preamble to the Directive) has become 'integrated' by 'many years' residence in the host state.

JUDICIAL REVIEW PROCEEDINGS

12.1 WHAT IS JUDICIAL REVIEW?

Judicial review involves a challenge to the legal validity of the decision. It does not allow the court of review to examine the evidence with a view to forming its own view about the substantial merits of the case. It may be that the tribunal whose decision is being challenged has done something which it had no lawful authority to do. It may have abused or misused the authority which it had. It may have departed from the procedures which either by statute or at common law as matter of fairness it ought to have observed. As regards the decision itself it may be found to be perverse, or irrational, or grossly disproportionate to what was required. Or the decision may be found to be erroneous in respect of a legal deficiency, as for example, through the absence of evidence, or of sufficient evidence, to support it, or through account being taken of irrelevant matter, or through a failure for any reason to take account of a relevant matter, or through some misconstruction of the terms of the statutory provision which the decision-maker is required to apply. But while the evidence may have to be explored in order to see if the decision is vitiated by such legal deficiencies it is perfectly clear that in a case of review, as distinct from an ordinary appeal, the court may not set about forming its own preferred view of the evidence. (per Lord Clyde in *Reid v Secretary of State for Scotland* [1998] UKHL 43)

12.1.1 Use of judicial review in immigration cases

As we saw at **11.2**, the NIAA 2002 sets out those immigration decisions against which there is a right of appeal. But what about those decisions where there is no right of appeal? Or where all appeal rights have been exhausted? This is where judicial review proceedings may be an appropriate step for the client to take.

Judicial review will be refused if an alternative remedy is more appropriate, such as where an applicant has failed to use a right of appeal, unless he can show that the circumstances are exceptional: see *R v Secretary of State for the Home Department, ex p Swati* [1986] 1 All ER 717. It is not enough to show that the right of appeal is a less convenient remedy, for instance because it must be conducted from abroad: see *Soon Ok Ryoo v Secretary of State for the Home Department* [1992] Imm AR 59. However, if it would be practically impossible to conduct the appeal from abroad, permission may be given: see *R v Chief Immigration Officer, Gatwick Airport, ex p Kharrazi* [1980] 1 WLR 1396 and *R v Secretary of State for the Home Department and Immigration Officer, Waterloo International Station, ex p Canbolat* [1997] INLR 198.

The vast majority of judicial review proceedings concern aspects of asylum and human rights claims, eg when the Secretary of State does not accept that a fresh claim was made (**9.14**), or certifies a claim as no longer appealable (**11.5.2** and **11.5.3**) or unfounded (**11.15**); deportation and removal cases (particularly human rights-based challenges: **Chapter 10**); as well as cases where the Secretary of State refuses to register or naturalise a person as a British citizen (**Chapter 2**).

12.1.2 Grounds for judicial review

The most common grounds for judicial review are set out in the extract from *Reid* at **12.1**.

The usual starting point is to consider if the decision-maker made an error of law, eg did the Secretary of State ask the right question? Otherwise, in many cases the client will be arguing that the decision made was irrational or unreasonable. The test for this was originally laid down by Lord Greene MR in the landmark Court of Appeal case of *Associated Provincial Picture Houses Ltd v Wednesbury Corporation* [1948] 1 KB 223, namely, having regard to relevant considerations only, did the decision-maker come to a conclusion that was so unreasonable that no reasonable authority could ever have come to it? Note that here consideration needs to be given as to whether the Secretary of State took into account factors that were irrelevant and/or omitted to take relevant matters into account. Equally, it should be asked whether the Secretary of State gave undue weight to one or more factors over other relevant factors.

Subsequently, the test of irrationality has been refined. In *CCSU v Minister for Civil Service* [1984] 3 All ER 935, Lord Diplock stated that, to be irrational, a decision needs to be so outrageous in its defiance of logic, or of accepted moral standards, that no sensible person could have arrived at it. In the later case of *R v Ministry of Defence, ex p Smith* [1996] 1 All ER 257, the Court of Appeal found that, to establish irrationality, the decision or policy should be beyond the range of reasonable responses open to the decision-maker.

When making a decision, the Secretary of State or a court must take all relevant considerations into account. This is often known as the 'anxious scrutiny' requirement. In *WM (DRC) v Secretary of State for the Home Department* [2006] EWCA Civ 1495, Buxton LJ stated, at [7], that in an asylum case, for example, 'the consideration of all the decision-makers, the Secretary of State, the [Immigration Judge] and the court, must be informed by the anxious scrutiny of the material that is axiomatic in decisions that if made incorrectly may lead to the Applicant's exposure to persecution.' As Carnwath LJ later explained in *R (YH) v Secretary of State for the Home Department* [2010] EWCA Civ 116, at [24], the requirement has 'by usage acquired special significance as underlining the very special human context in which such cases are brought, and the need for decisions to show by their reasoning that every factor which might tell in favour of an Applicant has been properly taken into account'.

12.1.3 Remedies

The most common remedy sought in an immigration case is for the decision to be quashed, ie declared void. The court may, in addition, remit the case to the Secretary of State for the Home Department, or relevant tribunal, with a direction to reconsider it according to the findings of the court. See further **12.3.6**.

12.2 MAKING A CLAIM: PRE-ACTION STEPS

Before an application is made to the court, the Pre-Action Protocol for Judicial Review should be consulted (there is a copy at **Appendix 15**). The Protocol sets out a code of best practice and contains the steps which parties should normally follow before starting court proceedings. The Protocol will not be appropriate where judicial review is required of a tribunal decision or in urgent cases, for example when directions have been set, or are in force, for the client's removal from the UK.

When following the Protocol, a claimant must always have in mind the fact that any application for judicial review must be filed promptly, and in any event, not later than three months after the grounds to make the claim first arose.

12.2.1 Letter before claim

Where the Protocol applies, the claimant should send a letter before claim to the defendant. This will be the Secretary of State for the Home Department. The relevant address is the

Judicial Review Unit at St Anne's House, 20–26 Wellesley Road, Croydon CR9 2RL. The letter should clearly, succinctly and accurately identify the issues in dispute and seek to establish whether litigation can be avoided. Normally, the suggested standard format for the letter outlined at Annex A should be used, but in addition you should include, where known and appropriate, the client's Home Office, Port, Tribunal and National Asylum Support Service reference numbers. Otherwise, ensure the client's full name, nationality and date of birth are set out.

There is a specimen letter before claim at **12.5**.

12.2.2 Home Office response

Home Office guidance is that if the caseworker decides the representations in the letter before claim have merit then he should try to rectify the problem without the need for court proceedings. If the representations are without merit, the letter of response should fully explain the reasons for that decision and answer any queries the claimant has made. If the caseworker decides that some of the claim has merit but other points do not, the response should comprehensively set out the reasons for this decision, with a full explanation of what is agreed and what steps will be taken to rectify this, and why the other points are not accepted.

12.3 COURT PROCEEDINGS

Judicial review proceedings must be started in the High Court (see the Senior Courts Act 1981, s 31). Claims are dealt with by the Administrative Court (save a challenge to the Secretary of State's refusal to treat submissions as a fresh asylum or human rights claim (**9.14**) as these reviews are normally transferred to the Upper Tribunal under the Senior Courts Act 1981, s 31A).

The judicial review procedure is governed by Part 54 of the Civil Procedure Rules 1998 (SI 1998/3132) (CPR 1998). By r 54.1(2)(a), a 'claim for judicial review' is defined as 'a claim to review the lawfulness of an enactment; or a decision, action or failure to act in relation to the exercise of a public function'.

12.3.1 The two stages of an application

The judicial review procedure has the unusual feature of two separate stages. First, the claimant must start the proceedings by filing a CPR 1998, Part 8 claim form and obtain the court's permission to proceed with it. If permission is granted then, secondly, after the parties have filed various documents, a full judicial review hearing takes place.

12.3.2 The need for a prompt application

An application for permission to apply for judicial review must be made promptly, and in any event within three months from the date when grounds for the application first arose. The time limit cannot be extended by agreement between the parties. The court may extend the period if there is good reason for the delay, but delay may still result in refusal of a remedy at the final hearing (R *(Lichfield Securities Ltd) v Lichfield District Council* (2001) *The Times*, 30 March).

12.3.3 Applying for permission

The claim form and other documents prescribed by CPR 1998, Practice Direction 54A (such as a detailed statement of the grounds for bringing the claim, a statement of the facts relied on, any written evidence relied on and a copy of any order sought to have quashed) must be filed and served on the defendant and any interested party. Where the review is sought of a tribunal decision, the Secretary of State will be an interested party. Rule 6.10 of the CPR 1998 provides that service on a government department must be effected on the solicitor acting for that department, which in the case of the Home Office is the Treasury Solicitor. The address for the Treasury Solicitor can be found in the Annex to Part 66 of the CPR 1998.

The defendant and any interested party have 21 days to acknowledge service of the claim form. Where a party filing an acknowledgment intends to contest the claim, a summary of the grounds on which it will be contested must be included.

12.3.4 Permission hearing

Normally the court determines whether or not to grant permission to proceed without an oral hearing. Permission is granted if the claimant can show on the materials filed a case which is 'arguable' and so requires a full investigation of the substantive merits (see *R v Inland Revenue Commissioners, ex p National Federation of Self-Employed and Small Businesses Ltd* [1982] AC 617).

If permission to proceed is refused or granted subject to conditions and/or on certain grounds only, the claimant may within seven days request an oral hearing for that decision to be reconsidered.

12.3.5 Next steps if permission granted

If permission to proceed is granted, the court will normally give case management directions as to how the parties are to prepare for the final hearing. This normally includes the the filing and service of a detailed response by the defendant and any interested parties, along with their written evidence. The claimant will prepare the trial bundle and each party should file a skeleton argument.

12.3.6 The hearing

The hearing usually takes place before a single judge nominated to hear cases in the Administrative Court. The parties' advocates make their respective submissions on the evidence filed. Only in exceptional cases will any witnesses be called and cross-examined.

What if the key factual evidence submitted to the court is disputed? The court's approach to this issue was summarised by Silber J in *R (McVey) v Secretary of State for Health* [2010] EWHC 437 as follows (at [35]):

(i)   The basic rule is that where there is a dispute on evidence in a judicial review application, then in the absence of cross-examination, the facts in the defendants' evidence must be assumed to be correct;

(ii)   An exception to this rule arises where the documents show that the defendants' evidence cannot be correct; and that

(iii) The proper course for a claimant who wishes to challenge the correctness of an important aspect of the defendant's evidence relating to a factual matter on which the judge will have to make a critical factual finding is to apply to cross-examine the maker of the witness statement on which the defendant relies.

What are the court's powers when making a quashing order? The court will usually remit the matter to the decision-maker, direct it to reconsider the case and reach a decision in accordance with the judgment of the court.

When can the court substitute its own decision? Only if that decision was made by a court or tribunal, the decision is quashed on the ground that there was an error of law, and without that error there would have been only one decision which the court or tribunal could have reached.

12.4 APPEALS FROM JUDICIAL REVIEW DECISIONS

What if permission to proceed is refused at an oral hearing or on reconsideration? The claimant can apply within seven days to the Court of Appeal for permission to appeal that decision. Note that the Court of Appeal is not limited to granting permission to appeal but may grant permission for the judicial review. What if the Court of Appeal refuses permission to appeal? That is the end of the matter. Only if permission to appeal is granted but permission to proceed with the judicial review claim is refused can an appeal be made to the Supreme Court.

What if a party does not agree with the outcome of a judicial review? Permission to appeal can be sought from the court or the Court of Appeal. Any further appeal will be to the Supreme Court.

12.5 SPECIMEN LETTER BEFORE CLAIM

To
The Secretary of State for the Home Department,
Judicial Review Unit,
St Anne's House, 20–26 Wellesley Road,
Croydon, CR9 2RL.

The claimant
Christopher Katongo

Reference details
Home Office reference number [   ].

The details of the matter being challenged
The decision made by the Secretary of State under Section 94 of the Nationality Immigration and Asylum Act 2002 (NIAA 2002) to certify as clearly unfounded the claimant's claim that his removal from the UK would be a disproportionate interference with his right to a family and private life under Article 8 of the European Convention on Human Rights (ECHR).

The issue

1. Date of decision: [   ]

2. Relevant law

A case which is clearly unfounded is one which has no real prospect of success if an appeal was made to the First Tier Tribunal, Immigration and Asylum Chamber.

The Secretary of State was required to give the claim anxious scrutiny. In determining whether the test was met, the Secretary of State had to consider, amongst other matters, the factual substance and detail of the claim; how it stands with the known background data; whether in the round it is capable of belief; if not, whether some part of it is capable of belief; and whether if eventually believed, in whole or in part, it is capable of coming within the ECHR. Only if the answers are such that the claim cannot on any legitimate view succeed is the claim clearly unfounded (*ZT (Kosovo) v Secretary of State for the Home Department* [2009] UKHL 6).

The Secretary of State had to approach the matter by addressing the questions set out by Lord Bingham in paragraph 17 of *R (Razgar) v Secretary of State for the Home Department* [2004] 2 AC 368, as further explained by the subsequent case of *R (Huang) v Secretary of State for the Home Department* [2007] UKHL 11, namely:

(a) Will the proposed removal be an interference by a public authority with the exercise of the applicant's rights to respect for his private or, as the case may be, family life?

(b) If so, will such interference have consequences of such gravity as potentially to engage the operation of Article 8?

(c) If so, is such interference in accordance with law?

(d) If so, is such interference necessary in a democratic society in a number of legitimate interests including, on the established case law, the maintenance of effective immigration control?

(e) If so, is such interference proportionate to the legitimate public ends sought to be achieved?

The relationship of a nephew and his aunt as adults falls within the scope of family life as it started when the nephew was a child and continued after he reached 18 (*Secretary of State for the Home Department v HK (Turkey)* [2010] EWCA Civ 583), and there are special elements of dependency beyond normal emotional ties (*Kugathas v Secretary of State for the Home Department* [2003] EWCA Civ 31 and *Odawey v Entry Clearance Officer* [2011] EWCA Civ 840).

By paragraph 276ADE of the Immigration Rules the Secretary of State had to consider granting the claimant leave to remain on the grounds of his private life in the UK as he is over 18, he has lived continuously in the UK for less than 20 years and has no ties (including social, cultural or family) with the country to which he would have to go if required to leave the UK, namely, Zambia.

As to proportionality, the Supreme Court (then the House of Lords) in *Huang* stated at paragraph 20 that the ultimate question for the appellate authority is whether the refusal of leave to enter or remain, in circumstances where the life of the family cannot reasonably be expected to be enjoyed elsewhere, taking full account of all considerations weighing in favour of the refusal, prejudices the family life of the applicant in a manner that is sufficiently serious to amount to a breach of the fundamental right protected by Article 8.

3. Relevant facts

The claimant is a national of Zambia, aged 22. He was born in Zambia and lived there until he was 15. When he was 5 years old, his mother died. Shortly afterwards his father was diagnosed with a terminal illness. The claimant was an only child. He was cared for, together with his father, by his paternal grandmother. His father died when he was 10. The claimant's grandmother died when he was 15. It was at this point that the claimant was invited by his aunt, Mrs Francis, to visit her and her family in Huddersfield, England. Mrs Francis is a British citizen and the claimant's only living relative.

The claimant entered the UK as a minor. His passport was stamped with a 6-month visitor's visa but he stayed on in the UK when that period expired. His case, supported by Mrs Francis, is that Mrs Francis decided the claimant should stay with her family in the UK permanently but she overlooked applying for the appropriate permissions for the claimant from the immigration authorities.

The claimant had no formal education in Zambia. He can speak little English. He cannot speak Bemba which is spoken nationwide in Zambia. He has no understanding of the cultural norms in Zambia. Mrs Francis describes him as very slow in his learning. She says that he is not capable of looking after himself as an adult. The claimant is dependent on her both financially and emotionally. This is supported by a doctor's report. The report also confirms that the claimant has suffered from time to time with depression and that he has mentioned on occasions that he was thinking of committing suicide because he is very lonely and, in particular, because he misses his father.

4. Why the decision is wrong

The claimant has established a family and private life in the UK. He entered as a child and has been here for approximately 7 years. During that time he has been staying with and has been both financially and emotionally dependent on his aunt, Mrs Francis. The Secretary of State failed to give sufficient weight to the significant relationship that the claimant has with, and his dependency on, Mrs Francis. He is dependent upon her for his day to day health and wellbeing. He has no family, friends or social network to turn to for support in Zambia.

To remove the claimant from the UK is a disproportionate interference with that established family life. The Secretary of State's conclusion that the claimant entered the UK by deception is erroneous. It is the claimant's case that when he arrived in the UK he told the Immigration Officer that he was coming to stay with his aunt in Huddersfield and his visa was stamped. It is Mrs Francis' evidence that she had given the claimant a letter to hand to the immigration authorities confirming this. It was only after the claimant had lived with the family in Huddersfield for several months that it was decided the claimant should remain here permanently with them. This is not a case where the claimant chose to enter or remain in the UK unlawfully. Nor is it a case where the claimant has developed a private and family life in flagrant disregard of orders requiring him to leave the UK.

The claimant is a depressed young man who is suffering from the loss of all of his immediate family members. He was brought up in a family environment and this has continued for the last 7 years in the UK. To separate him from Mrs Francis' family unit, will, as the medical report states, significantly contribute to his state of alienation and depression.

In all these circumstances the Secretary of State's conclusion that the claimant would be able to establish and maintain a private life in his own right on his return to Zambia is irrational.

The claimant has a realistic prospect of persuading an appeal tribunal that to remove him from the UK would be a disproportionate interference with the family life that he has established here.

The details of the action that the defendant is expected to take
The Secretary of State is asked to review the decision and revoke the certificate.

The details of the legal advisers dealing with this claim and the claimant's address for reply and service of court documents
The details of the claimant's legal advisers and his address for service are as follows:

XYZ Lawyers LLP
1 The Avenue
Nowhere
Mythshire
MY11 1AB
Tel: 012345678
Ref: 123/ABC/CK

The details of any interested parties
n/a

Information sought and documents that are considered relevant and necessary
If the Secretary of State intends to rely on additional information and/or documents, please ensure that full details and copies are enclosed with the reply to this letter.

Proposed reply date
Please ensure that a reply is given within 14 days.

APPENDICES

APPENDIX 1

Immigration Rules

The Immigration Rules were last updated in October 2013

	Paragraph number
Introduction	
Implementation and transitional provisions	4
Application	5
Interpretation	6
Public funds clarification	6A–6C
Part 1: General provisions regarding leave to enter or remain in the United Kingdom	
Leave to enter the United Kingdom	7–9
Exercise of the power to refuse leave to enter the United Kingdom	10
Suspension of leave to enter or remain in the United Kingdom	10A
Cancellation of leave to enter or remain in the United Kingdom	10B
Requirement for persons arriving in the United Kingdom or seeking entry through the Channel Tunnel to produce evidence of identity and nationality	11
Requirement for a person not requiring leave to enter the United Kingdom to prove that he has the right of abode	12–14
Common Travel Area	15
Admission for certain British passport holders	16–17
Persons outside the United Kingdom	17A–17B
Returning residents	18–20
Non-lapsing leave	20A
Holders of restricted travel documents and passports	21–23
Leave to enter granted on arrival in the United Kingdom	23A–23B
Entry clearance	24–30C
Variation of leave to enter or remain in the United Kingdom	31–33A
Specified forms and procedures for applications or claims in connection with immigration	A34–34D
Variation of applications or claims for leave to remain	34E–34F
Determination of the date of an application or claim (or variation of an application or claim) in connection with immigration	34G–34I
Withdrawn applications or claims for leave to remain in the United Kingdom	34J–34K
Undertakings	35
Medical	36–39
Students	39A
Specified documents	39B
Part 2: Persons seeking to enter or remain in the United Kingdom for visits	
Visitors	40–46X
Visitors in transit	47–50
Visitors seeking to enter or remain for private medical treatment	51–56
Parent of a child at school	56A–56C

	Paragraph number
Visitors seeking to enter for the purposes of marriage or to enter into a civil partnership	56D–56F
Visitors seeking leave to enter under the Approved Destinations Status (ADS) agreement with China	56G–56J
Student visitors	56K–56M
Prospective entrepreneurs	56N–56Q
Visitors undertaking permitted paid engagements	56X–56Z
Commonwealth Games Family Member Visitor	56ZA–56ZH
Part 3: Persons seeking to enter or remain in the United Kingdom for studies	
Postgraduate doctors and dentists	70–75M
Spouses or civil partners of students or prospective students granted leave under this part of the Rules	76–78
Children of students or prospective students granted leave under this part of the Rules	79–81
Prospective students	A82–87
Part 4: Persons seeking to enter or remain in the United Kingdom in an 'au pair' placement, as a working holidaymaker or for training or work experience	
Spouses of persons with limited leave to enter or remain under paragraphs 110–121	122–124
Children of persons with limited leave to enter or remain under paragraphs 110–121	125–127
Part 5: Persons seeking to enter or remain in the United Kingdom for employment.	
Work permit employment	128A–135
Highly skilled migrants	135A–135HA
Representatives of overseas newspapers, news agencies and broadcasting organisations	136–143
Representatives of Overseas Business	144–151
Private servants in diplomatic households	152–159
Domestic workers in private households	159A–159H
Overseas government employees	160–169
Ministers of religion, missionaries and members of religious orders	170–177
Airport based operational ground staff of overseas-owned airlines	178–185
Persons with United Kingdom ancestry	186–193
Partners of persons who have or have had leave to enter or remain under paragraphs 128–193 (but not paragraphs 135I–135K)	193A–196F
Children of persons with limited leave to enter or remain under paragraphs 128–193 (but not paragraphs 135I–135K)	196G–199B
Part 6: Persons seeking to enter or remain in the United Kingdom as a businessman, self-employed person, investor, writer, composer or artist	
Part 6A: Points-Based System	
General requirements for indefinite leave to remain	245AAA
Documents not submitted with applications	245AA
Specified documents for students previously sponsored by an overseas government or international scholarship agency	245A
Tier 1 (Exceptional Talent) Migrants	245B–245BF
Tier 1 (General) Migrants	245C–245CE
Tier 1 (Entrepreneur) Migrants	245D–245DF
Tier 1 (Investor) Migrants	245E–245EF

	Paragraph number
Part 9 – General grounds for the refusal of entry clearance, leave to enter, leave to remain, variation of leave to enter or remain and curtailment of leave in the United Kingdom	
Refusal of entry clearance or leave to enter the United Kingdom	A320
Refusal of leave to enter in relation to a person in possession of an entry clearance	321
Refusal of variation of leave to enter or remain or curtailment of leave	322–323C
Crew members	324
Part 10: Registration with the police	325–326
Part 11: Asylum	326A–352G
Part 11A: Temporary Protection	354–356B
Part 11B: Asylum	357–361
Part 12: Procedure and Rights of appeal	353–352A
Part 13: Deportation	A362–400
Part 14: Stateless persons	401–416
Appendix 1: Visa requirements for the United Kingdom	
Appendix 2: Countries or territories whose nationals or citizens are relevant foreign nationals for the purposes of Part 10 of these Rules	
Appendix 3: DELETED	
Appendix 4: DELETED	
Appendix 5: DELETED	
Appendix 6: Disciplines for which an Academic Technology Approval Scheme certificate from the Counter-Proliferation Department of the Foreign and Commonwealth Office is required for the purposes of Tier 4 of the Points Based System	
Appendix 7 – Statement of Written Terms and Conditions of employment required in paragraphs 159A (v), 159D(iv) and 159EA(iii)	
Appendix A: Attributes	
Appendix B: English language – English language	
Appendix C: Maintenance (funds)	
Appendix D: Immigration rules for leave to remain as a Highly Skilled Migrant as at 28 February 2008	
Appendix E: Maintenance (funds) for the family of Relevant Points Based Systems Migrants	
Appendix F: Archived Immigration Rules	
Appendix FM: Family members	
Appendix FM-SE: Family members – specified evidence	
Appendix G: Countries and territories participating in the Tier 5 Youth mobility scheme and annual allocations of places for 2013	
Appendix H: Applicants who are subject to different documentary requirements under Tier 4 of the Points Based System	
Appendix I: Pay requirements which the Secretary of State intends to apply to applications for indefinite leave to remain from Tier 2 (General) and Tier 2 (Sportspersons) migrants made on or after 6 April 2016	
Appendix J: Codes of practice for Tier 2 sponsors, Tier 5 sponsors and employers of work permit holders	
Appendix K: Shortage occupation list	
Appendix KoLL	

	Paragraph number
Appendix L: Designated competent body criteria for Tier 1 (Exceptional talent) applications	
Appendix M: Sports governing bodies for Tier 2 (Sportsperson) and Tier 5 (Temporary worker – creative and sporting) applications	
Appendix N: Approved Tier 5 Government authorised exchange schemes	
Appendix O: List of English Language tests that have been assessed as meeting the UK Border Agency's requirements	
Appendix P: Lists of financial institutions that do not satisfactorily verify financial statements, or whose financial statements are accepted	
Appendix Q: Statement of written terms and conditions of employment required in paragraph 245ZO(f)(ii) and paragraph 245 ZQ (e)(ii)	
Appendix R: List of recognised festivals for which entry by amateur and professional entertainer visitors is permitted	
Appendix S: Highly Skilled Migrants Programme (HSMP) – qualifying for indefinite leave to remain after four years' continuous residence	
Appendix T: Tuberculosis screening	

Introduction

The Home Secretary has made changes in the Rules laid down by him as to the practice to be followed in the administration of the Immigration Acts for regulating entry into and the stay of persons in the United Kingdom and contained in the statement laid before Parliament on 23 March 1990 (HC 251) (as amended). This statement contains the Rules as changed and replaces the provisions of HC 251 (as amended).

2. Immigration Officers, Entry Clearance Officers and all staff of the Home Office Immigration and Nationality Directorate will carry out their duties without regard to the race, colour or religion of persons seeking to enter or remain in the United Kingdom and in compliance with the provisions of the Human Rights Act 1998.

3. In these Rules words importing the masculine gender include the feminine unless the contrary intention appears.

Implementation and transitional provisions

4. These Rules come into effect on 1 October 1994 and will apply to all decisions taken on or after that date save that any application made before 1 October 1994 for entry clearance, leave to enter or remain or variation of leave to enter or remain other than an application for leave by a person seeking asylum shall be decided under the provisions of HC 251, as amended, as if these Rules had not been made.

Application

5. Save where expressly indicated, these Rules do not apply to those persons who are entitled to enter or remain in the United Kingdom by virtue of the provisions of the 2006 EEA Regulations. But any person who is not entitled to rely on the provisions of those Regulations is covered by these Rules.

Interpretation

6. In these Rules the following interpretations apply:

'the **Immigration Acts**' has the same meaning as it has in the Interpretation Act 1978.

'**the 1993 Act**' is the Asylum and Immigration Appeals Act 1993.

'**the 1996 Act**' is the Asylum and Immigration Act 1996

'**the 2006 EEA Regulations**' means the Immigration (European Economic Area) Regulations 2006

'**adoption**' unless the contrary intention appears, includes a de facto adoption in accordance with the requirements of paragraph 309A of these Rules, and 'adopted' and 'adoptive parent' should be construed accordingly.

In Appendix FM references to '**application for leave to remain**' include an application for variation of leave to enter or remain of a person in the UK.

'**Approved Destination Status Agreement with China**' means the Memorandum of Understanding on visa and related issues concerning tourist groups from the People's Republic of China to the United Kingdom as a approved destination, signed on 21 January 2005.

'**a bona fide private education institution**' is a private education institution which:

(a)   maintains satisfactory records of enrolment and attendance of students, and supplies these to the Border and Immigration Agency when requested;

(b)   provides courses which involve a minimum of 15 hours organised daytime study per week;

(c)   ensures a suitably qualified tutor is present during the hours of study to offer teaching and instruction to the students;

(d)   offers courses leading to qualifications recognised by the appropriate accreditation bodies;

(e)   mploys suitably qualified staff to provide teaching, guidance and support to the students;

(f)   provides adequate accommodation, facilities, staffing levels and equipment to support the numbers of students enrolled at the institution; and

(g)   if it offers tuition support to external students at degree level, ensures that such students are registered with the UK degree awarding body.

'**Business day**' means any day other than Saturday or Sunday, a day which is a bank holiday under the Banking and Financial Dealings Act 1971 in the part of the United Kingdom to which the notice is sent, Christmas Day or Good Friday.

'**civil partner**' means a civil partnership which exists under or by virtue of the Civil Partnership Act 2004 (and any reference to a civil partner is to be read accordingly);

'**conviction**' means conviction for a criminal offence in the UK or any other country.

'**degree level study**' means a course which leads to a recognised United Kingdom degree at bachelor's level or above, or an equivalent qualification at level 6 or above of the revised National Qualifications Framework, or levels 9 or above of the Scottish Credit and Qualifications Framework.

Under Part 8 of these Rules, '**post-graduate level study**' means a course at level 7 or above of the revised National Qualifications Framework or Qualifications and Credit Framework, or level 11 or above of the Scottish Credit and Qualifications Framework, which leads to a recognised United Kingdom postgraduate degree at Master's level or above, or an equivalent qualification at the same level.

'**foundation degree**' means a programme of study which leads to a qualification awarded by an English higher education institution with degree awarding powers which is at a minimum of level 5 on the revised National Qualifications Framework, or awarded on a directly equivalent basis in the devolved administrations.

'**primary degree**' means a qualification obtained from a course of degree level study, which did not feature as an entry requirement a previous qualification obtained from degree level study. An undergraduate degree is a primary degree. A Masters degree that has a Bachelor degree as an entry requirement is not a primary degree.

A '**UK recognised body**' is an institution that has been granted degree awarding powers by either a Royal Charter, an Act of Parliament or the Privy Council. For the purposes of these Rules we will consider the Foundation Programme Office, South London Local Education and Training Board and the Yorkshire and Humber Strategic Health Authority as equivalent to UK Recognised Bodies.

A '**UK listed body**' is an institution that is not a UK recognised body but which provides full courses that lead to the award of a degree by a UK recognised body.

'**EEA national**' has the meaning given in regulation 2(1) of the 2006 EEA Regulations.

'**an external student**' is a student studying for a degree from a UK degree awarding body without any requirement to attend the UK degree awarding body's premises or a UK Listed Body's premises for lectures and tutorials.

'**United Kingdom passport**' bears the meaning it has in the Immigration Act 1971.

'**a UK Bachelors degree**' means

(a)   A programme of study or research which leads to the award, by or on behalf of a university, college or other body which is authorised by Royal Charter or by or under an Act of Parliament to grant degrees, of a qualification designated by the awarding institution to be of Bachelors degree level; or

(b)   A programme of study or research, which leads to a recognised award for the purposes of section 214(2)(c) of the Education Reform Act 1988, of a qualification designated by the awarding institution to be of Bachelors degree level.

'**Immigration Officer**' includes a Customs Officer acting as an Immigration Officer.

'**Multiple Entry work permit employment**' is work permit employment where the person concerned does not intend to spend a continuous period in the United Kingdom in work permit employment.

'**public funds**' means

(a)   housing under Part VI or VII of the Housing Act 1996 and under Part II of the Housing Act 1985, Part I or II of the Housing (Scotland) Act 1987, Part II of the Housing (Northern Ireland) Order 1981 or Part II of the Housing (Northern Ireland) Order 1988;

(b)   attendance allowance, severe disablement allowance, carer's allowance and disability living allowance under Part III of the Social Security Contribution and Benefits Act 1992;, income support, council tax benefit and housing benefit under Part VII of that Act; a social fund payment under Part VIII of that Act; child benefit under Part IX of that Act; income based jobseeker's allowance under the Jobseekers Act 1995, income related allowance under Part 1 of the Welfare Reform Act 2007 (employment and support allowance) state pension credit under the State Pension Credit Act 2002; or child tax credit and working tax credit under Part 1 of the Tax Credits Act 2002;

(c)   attendance allowance, severe disablement allowance, carer's allowance and disability living allowance under Part III of the Social Security Contribution and Benefits (Northern Ireland) Act 1992;, income support, council tax benefit and, housing benefit under Part VII of that Act; a social fund payment under Part VIII of that Act; child benefit under Part IX of that Act; income based jobseeker's allowance under the Jobseekers (Northern Ireland) Order 1995 or income related allowance under Part 1 of the Welfare Reform Act (Northern Ireland) 2007;

(d)   Universal Credit under Part 1 of the Welfare Reform Act 2012 or Personal Independence Payment under Part 4 of that Act;

(e)   Universal Credit, Personal Independence Payment or any domestic rate relief under the Northern Ireland Welfare Reform Act 2013;

(f)   a council tax reduction under a council tax reduction scheme made under section 13A of the Local Government Finance Act 1992 in relation to England or Wales or a council tax reduction pursuant to the Council Tax Reduction (Scotland) Regulations 2012 or the Council Tax Reduction (State Pension Credit) (Scotland) Regulations 2012.

'**settled in the United Kingdom**' means that the person concerned:

(a)   is free from any restriction on the period for which he may remain save that a person entitled to an exemption under Section 8 of the Immigration Act 1971 (otherwise than as a member of the home forces) is not to be regarded as settled in the United Kingdom except in so far as Section 8(5A) so provides; and

(b)   is either:

(i)   ordinarily resident in the United Kingdom without having entered or remained in breach of the immigration laws; or

(ii)   despite having entered or remained in breach of the immigration laws, has subsequently entered lawfully or has been granted leave to remain and is ordinarily resident.

'**a parent**' includes

(a)   the stepfather of a child whose father is dead and the reference to stepfather includes a relationship arising through civil partnership;

(b)   the stepmother of a child whose mother is dead and the reference to stepmother includes a relationship arising through civil partnership and;

(c)   the father as well as the mother of an illegitimate child where he is proved to be the father;

(d)   an adoptive parent, where a child was adopted in accordance with a decision taken by the competent administrative authority or court in a country whose adoption orders are recognised by the United Kingdom or where a child is the subject of a de facto adoption in accordance with the requirements of paragraph 309A of these Rules (except that an adopted child or a child who is the subject of a de facto adoption may not make an application for leave to enter or remain in order to accompany, join or remain with an adoptive parent under paragraphs 297303);

(e)   in the case of a child born in the United Kingdom who is not a British citizen, a person to whom there has been a genuine transfer of parental responsibility on the ground of the original parent(s)' inability to care for the child.

'**date of application**' means the date of application determined in accordance with paragraph 30 or 34G of these rules as appropriate.

'**a valid application**' means an application made in accordance with the requirements of Part 1 of these Rules.

'**refugee leave**' means limited leave granted pursuant to paragraph 334 or 335 of these rules and has not been revoked pursuant to paragraph 339A or 339B of these rules.

'**humanitarian protection**' means limited leave granted pursuant to paragraph 339C of these rules and has not been revoked pursuant to paragraph 339G or 339H of these rules.

'**a period of imprisonment**' referred to in these rules has the same meaning as set out in section 38(2) of the UK Borders Act 2007.

'**Overstayed**' or '**Overstaying**' means the applicant has stayed in the UK beyond the latest of:

(i)   the time limit attached to the last period of leave granted, or

(ii)   beyond the period that his leave was extended under sections 3C or 3D of the Immigration Act 1971, or

(iii)   the date that an applicant receives the notice of invalidity declaring that an
application for leave to remain is not a valid application, provided the application was submitted before the time limit attached to the last period of
leave expired.

'**intention to live permanently with the other**' and intend to live together permanently means an intention to live together, evidenced by a clear commitment from both parties that they will live together permanently in the United Kingdom immediately following the outcome of the application in question or as soon as circumstances permit thereafter.

'**present and settled**' means that the person concerned is settled in the United Kingdom, and, at the time that an application under these Rules is made, is physically present here or is coming here with or to join the applicant and intends to make the United Kingdom their home with the applicant if their application is successful.

For the purposes of Appendix FM a member of HM Forces serving overseas, or a permanent member of HM Diplomatic Service, or a comparable UK-based staff member of the British Council on a tour of duty abroad, or a staff member of the Department for International Development or the Home Office, who is a British Citizen or settled in the UK, is to be regarded as present and settled in the UK.

'**sponsor**' means the person in relation to whom an applicant is seeking leave to enter or remain as their spouse, fiance, civil partner, proposed civil partner, unmarried partner, same-sex partner or dependent relative, as the case may be, under paragraphs 277 to 295O or 317 to 319 or the person in relation to whom an applicant is seeking entry clearance or leave as their partner or dependent relative under Appendix FM.

'**overcrowded**' means overcrowded within the meaning of the Housing Act 1985, the Housing (Scotland) Act 1987 or the Housing (Northern Ireland) Order 1988 (as appropriate).

'**working illegally**' means working in breach of conditions of leave or working when in the UK without valid leave where such leave is required.

'**in breach of immigration laws**' means without valid leave where such leave is required, or in breach of the conditions of leave.

''**adequate**' and '**adequately**' in relation to a maintenance and accommodation requirement shall mean that, after income tax, national insurance contributions and housing costs have been deducted, there must be available to the family the level of income that would be available to them if the family was in receipt of income support.'

'**occupy exclusively**' in relation to accommodation shall mean that part of the accommodation must be for the exclusive use of the family.

'**must not be leading an independent life**' means that the applicant does not have a partner as defined in Appendix FM; is living with their parents (except where they are at boarding school, college or university as part of their full-time education); is not employed full-time (unless aged 18 years or over); is wholly or mainly dependent upon their parents for financial support (unless aged 18 years or over); and is wholly or mainly dependent upon their parents for emotional support.

'**prohibited degree of relationship**' has the same meaning as in the Marriage Act 1949, the Marriage (Prohibited Degrees of Relationship) Act 1986 and the Civil Partnership Act 2004.

'**visa nationals**' are the persons specified in Appendix 1 to these Rules who need a visa for the United Kingdom.

'**non-visa nationals**' are persons who are not specified in Appendix 1 to these Rules.

'**specified national**' is a person specified in Appendix 3 to these Rules who seeks leave to enter the United Kingdom for a period of more than 6 months.

'**employment**' unless the contrary intention appears, includes paid and unpaid employment, paid and unpaid work placements undertaken as part of a course or period of study, self employment and engaging in business or any professional activity.

'**the Human Rights Convention**' means the Convention for the Protection of Human Rights and Fundamental Freedoms, agreed by the Council of Europe at Rome on 4th November 1950 as it has effect for the time being in relation to the United Kingdom.

'**immigration employment document**' means a work permit or any other document which relates to employment and is issued for the purpose of these Rules or in connection with leave to enter or remain in the United Kingdom.

'**Employment as a Doctor in Training**' means employment in a medical post or training programme which has been approved by the Postgraduate Medical Education and Training Board, or employment in a postgraduate training programme in dentistry.

'**these Rules**' means these immigration rules (HC 395) made under section 3(2) of the Immigration Act 1971.

A '**refugee**' is a refugee as defined in regulation 2 of The Refugee or Person in Need of International Protection (Qualification) Regulation 2006.

In part 6A of these Rules, 'relevant grant allocation period' means a specified period of time, which will be published by the Secretary of State on the UK Border Agency website, during which applications for entry clearance or leave to enter in respect of a particular route may be granted subject to the grant allocation for that period;

In part 6A of these Rules, 'grant allocation' means a limit, details of which will be published by the Secretary of State on the UK Border Agency website, on the number of grants of entry clearance or leave to enter which may be granted in respect of a particular route during the relevant grant allocation period;

Under Part 6A of these Rules, '**Highly Skilled Migrant**' means a migrant granted leave under paragraphs 135A to 135G of the Rules in force before 30th June 2008.

Under Part 6A of these Rules, '**Highly Skilled Migrant Programme Approval Letter**' means a letter issued by the Home Office confirming that the applicant meets the criteria specified by the Secretary of State for entry to or stay in the UK under the Highly Skilled Migrant Programme.

Under Part 6A of these Rules, '**Innovator**' means a migrant granted leave under paragraphs 210A to 210F of the Rules in force before 30th June 2008.

Under Part 6A of these Rules, '**Participant in the Fresh Talent Working in Scotland Scheme**' means a migrant granted leave under paragraphs 143A to 143F of the Rules in force before 30th June 2008.

Under Part 6A of these Rules, '**Participant in the International Graduates Scheme**' means a migrant granted leave under paragraphs 135O to 135T of the Rules in force before 30th June 2008.

Under Part 6A of these Rules, '**Postgraduate Doctor or Dentist**' means a migrant who is granted leave under paragraphs 70 to 75 of these Rules.

Under Part 6A of these Rules, '**Self-Employed**' means an applicant is registered as self-employed with HM Revenue & Customs, or is employed by a company of which the applicant is a controlling shareholder.

Under Part 6A of these Rules, '**Student**' means a migrant who is granted leave under paragraphs 57 to 62 of these Rules.

Under Part 6A of these Rules, '**Student Nurse**' means a migrant who is granted leave under paragraphs 63 to 69 of these Rules.

Under Part 6A of these Rules, '**Student Re-Sitting an Examination**' means a migrant who is granted leave under paragraphs 69A to 69F of these Rules.

Under Part 6A of these Rules, '**Student Writing-Up a Thesis**' means a migrant who is granted leave under paragraphs 69G to 69L of these Rules.

Under Part 6A of these Rules, '**Work Permit Holder**' means a migrant who is granted leave under paragraphs 128 to 133 of these Rules.

Under Part 6A of these Rules, '**Prospective Student**' means a migrant who is granted leave under paragraphs 82 to 87 of these rules.

Under Part 6A of these Rules, an '**A-rated Sponsor**' is a Sponsor which is recorded as being 'A-rated' on the register of licensed Sponsors maintained by the United Kingdom Border Agency.

Under Part 6A and Appendix A of these Rules, a '**B-Rated Sponsor**' is a sponsor which is recorded as being 'B-Rated' on the register of licensed sponsors maintained by the United Kingdom Border Agency.

Under Part 6A of these Rules, **'Highly Trusted Sponsor'** means a sponsor which is recorded as being 'Highly Trusted' on the register of licensed sponsors maintained by the United Kingdom Border Agency.

Under paragraph 34K of these Rules, a 'Premium Sponsor' is a Sponsor which is recorded as holding Premium status on the register of licensed Sponsors maintained by the United Kingdom Border Agency.

Under Part 6A of these Rules, **'Certificate of Sponsorship'** means an authorisation issued by the Secretary of State to a Sponsor in respect of one or more applications, or potential applications, for entry clearance, leave to enter or remain as a Tier 2 migrant or a Tier 5 migrant in accordance with these Rules.

Under Part 6A and Appendix A of these Rules, **'Confirmation of Acceptance for Studies'** means a unique reference number electronically issued by a sponsor via the Sponsor Management System to an applicant for entry clearance, leave to enter or remain as a Tier 4 Migrant in accordance with these Rules.

Under Part 6A of these Rules, **'Certificate of Sponsorship Checking Service'** means a computerised interface with the Points Based System computer database which allows a United Kingdom Border Agency caseworker or entry clearance officer assessing a migrant's application for entry clearance, leave to enter or leave to remain to access and review details of the migrant's Certificate of Sponsorship, including details of the migrant's Sponsor, together with details of the job and other details associated with the circumstances in which the Certificate of Sponsorship was issued.

Under Part 6A and Appendix A of these Rules, **'length of the period of engagement'** is the period beginning with the employment start date as recorded on the Certificate of Sponsorship Checking service entry which relates to the Certificate of Sponsorship reference number for which the migrant was awarded points under Appendix A and ending on the employment end date as recorded in the same entry.

Under Part 6A and Appendix A of these Rules, **'working for the same employer'** includes working for the business or concern in respect of which employment the earlier grant of leave was granted where that business or concern has, since that date, merged with, or been taken over by, another entity.

Under Part 6A and Appendix A of these Rules, **'Designated Competent Body'** means an organisation which has been approved by the UK Border Agency to endorse applicants as a Tier 1 (Exceptional Talent) Migrant.

Under Part 6A and Appendix A of these Rules, **'Tier 1 (Exceptional Talent) Unique Reference Number'** means a unique reference number issued for the purposes of managing the Tier 1 (Exceptional Talent) Limit and provided by the UK Border Agency to an applicant prior to making his application as a Tier 1 (Exceptional Talent) Migrant.

For the purpose of para 320(7B) of these Rules 'Removal Decision' means (a) a decision to remove in accordance with section 10 of the Immigration and Asylum Act 1999; (b) a decision to remove an illegal entrant by way of directions under paragraphs 8 to 10 of Schedule 2 to the Immigration Act 1971 or (c) a decision to remove in accordance with section 47 of the Immigration, Asylum and Nationality Act 2006. Pending appeal has the same meaning as in section 104 of the nationality, immigration and asylum act 2002.

Under Part 6A of these Rules, **'Confirmation of Acceptance for Studies Checking Service'** means a computerised interface with the Points Based System computer database which allows a United Kingdom Border Agency caseworker or entry clearance officer assessing a migrant's application for entry clearance, leave to enter or leave to remain as a Tier 4 migrant under these Rules to access and review details of the migrant's Confirmation of Acceptance for Studies, including details of the migrant's Sponsor, together with details of the course of study and other details associated with the circumstances in which the Confirmation of Acceptance for Studies was issued.

Under Part 6A of these Rules, **'Established Entertainer'** means an applicant who is applying for leave to remain as a Tier 2 (General) Migrant or a Tier 2 (Intra-Company Transfer) Migrant in respect of whom the following conditions are satisfied:

(a)   the Certificate of Sponsorship Checking Service entry to which the applicant's Certificate of Sponsorship reference number relates, records that the applicant is being sponsored in an occupation which is defined in the United Kingdom Border Agency's Transitional Guidance as being a job in the entertainment sector,

(b)   the applicant has, or has previously had, entry clearance, leave to enter or leave to remain in the UK as a Work Permit Holder, and the work permit that led to that grant was issued in the sports and entertainment category to enable him to work in the occupation in which he is, at the date of the application for leave to remain, currently being sponsored,

(c)   the applicant's last grant of leave was:

(i)   as a Work Permit Holder in the sports and entertainment category, provided the work permit on the basis of which that leave was granted was issued in the sports and entertainment category to enable him to work either in the occupation in which he is, at the date of the current application for leave to remain, currently being sponsored, or in another occupation which is defined in the UK Border Agency's Transitional Guidance as being a job in the entertainment sector, or

(ii) leave to remain as a Tier 2 (General) Migrant or a Tier 2 (Intra-Company Transfer) Migrant, provided (in either case):

(1) he previously had leave as a Work Permit Holder in the sports and entertainment category to work as described in (i) above,

(2) he has not been granted entry clearance in this or any other route since his last grant of leave as a Work Permit Holder, and

(3) his last grant of leave was made to enable him to work either in the occupation in which he is, at the date of the current application for leave to remain, currently being sponsored or in another occupation which is defined in the UK Border Agency's Transitional Guidance as being a job in the entertainment sector,

(d) the Certificate of Sponsorship Checking Service entry to which the applicant's Certificate of Sponsorship reference number relates records:

(i) that the applicant will be paid a salary for the job that is at or above the appropriate entertainments industry rate, as listed in the United Kingdom Border Agency's Transitional Guidance; and

(ii) that before agreeing to employ the applicant, the Sponsor consulted with such bodies as the United Kingdom Border Agency's Transitional Guidance indicates that it should consult with before employing someone in this capacity, and

(e) the applicant has not spent a period of 5 years or more in the UK, beginning with the last grant of entry clearance, as a Qualifying Work Permit Holder, Tier 2 (General) Migrant or Tier 2 (Intra-Company Transfer) Migrant, or in any combination of these.

Under Part 6A of these Rules, '**Qualifying Work Permit Holder**' means a Work Permit Holder who was issued a work permit in the business and commercial or sports and entertainment work permit categories.

Under Part 6A of these Rules, '**Senior Care Worker**' means an applicant who is applying for leave to remain as a Tier 2 (General) Migrant or a Tier 2 (Intra-Company Transfer) Migrant in respect of whom the following conditions are satisfied:

(a) the Certificate of Sponsorship Checking Service entry to which the applicant's Certificate of Sponsorship reference number relates, records that the applicant is being sponsored in an occupation which is defined in the codes of practice for Tier 2 sponsors published by the UK Border Agency as being a Senior Care Worker role,

(b) the applicant's last grant of leave was:

(i) as a Qualifying Work Permit Holder, or

(ii) leave to remain as a Tier 2 (General) Migrant or a Tier 2 (Intra-Company Transfer) Migrant, provided (in either case):

(1) he previously had leave as a Qualifying Work Permit Holder, and

(2) he has not been granted entry clearance in this or any other route since his last grant of leave as a Qualifying Work Permit Holder.

(c) the work permit or Certificate of Sponsorship that led to the last grant of leave was issued to enable the applicant to work as a senior care worker, and

(d) the applicant has not spent a period of 5 years or more in the UK, beginning with the last grant of entry clearance, as a Qualifying Work Permit Holder, Tier 2 (General) Migrant or Tier 2 (Intra-Company Transfer) Migrant, or in any combination of these.

Under Part 6A of these Rules, '**Sponsor**' means the person or Government that the Certificate of Sponsorship Checking Service or Confirmation of Acceptance for Studies Checking Service records as being the Sponsor for a migrant.

Under Part 6A of these Rules, a reference to a '**sponsor licence**' means a licence granted by the Secretary of State to a person who, by virtue of such a grant, is licensed as a Sponsor under Tiers 2, 4 or 5 of the Points Based System.

'In Part 6A and Appendices A and J of these Rules, '**settled worker**' means a person who:

(i) is a national of the UK,

(ii) is a person with a right of residence in accordance with the Immigration (European Economic Area) Regulations 2006 or, except where that person is subject to worker authorisation, the regulations made under section 2 of the European Union (Accessions) Act 2006 in combination with section 2(2) of the European Communities Act 1972 or the regulations made under section 4 of the European Union (Croatian Accession and Irish Protocol) Act 2013,

(iii) is a British overseas territories citizen, except those from Sovereign Base Areas in Cyprus,

(iv) is a Commonwealth citizen with leave to enter or remain granted on the basis of UK Ancestry (paragraphs 186 to 193 of these Rules), or

(v) has settled status in the UK within the meaning of the Immigration Act 1971, as amended by the Immigration and Asylum Act 1999, and the Nationality, Immigration and Asylum Act 2002.'

Under Part 6A of these Rules, '**supplementary employment**' means other employment in a job which appears on the Shortage Occupation List in Appendix K, or in the same profession and at the same professional level as that which the migrant is being sponsored to do provided that:

(a) the migrant remains working for the Sponsor in the employment that the Certificate of Sponsorship Checking Service records that the migrant is being sponsored to do,

(b) the other employment does not exceed 20 hours per week and takes place outside of the hours when the migrant is contracted to work for the Sponsor in the employment the migrant is being sponsored to do.

Under part 6A and Appendix A of these Rules, '**overseas higher education institution**' means an institution which holds overseas accreditation confirmed by UK NARIC as offering degree programmes which are equivalent to UK degree level qualifications, and which teach no more than half of a degree programme in the UK as a study abroad programme.

'Business person' means a migrant granted leave under paragraphs 200 to 208 of the Rules in force before 30th June 2008.

'Investor' means a migrant granted leave under paragraphs 224 to 229 of the Rules in force before 30th June 2008.

'Self-employed Lawyer' means a migrant granted entry clearance, or leave to enter or remain, outside the Rules under the concession for Self-employed lawyers that formerly appeared in Chapter 6, Section 1 Annex D of the Immigration Directorate instructions.

'**Points Based System Migrant**' means a migrant applying for or granted leave as a Tier 1 Migrant, a Tier 2 Migrant, a Tier 4 Migrant or a Tier 5 Migrant.

'**Tier 1 Migrant**' means a migrant who is granted leave as a Tier 1 (Exceptional Talent) Migrant, a Tier 1 (General) Migrant, a Tier 1 (Entrepreneur) Migrant, a Tier 1 (Investor) Migrant, a Tier 1 (Graduate Entrepreneur) Migrant or a Tier 1 (Post-Study Work) Migrant.

'**Tier 1 (Exceptional Talent) Migrant**' means a migrant who is granted leave under paragraphs 245B to 245BF of these Rules.

'**Tier 1 (General) Migrant**' means a migrant who is granted leave under paragraphs 245C to 245CE of these Rules.

'**Tier 1 (Entrepreneur) Migrant**' means a migrant who is granted leave under paragraphs 245D to 245DF of these Rules.

'**Tier 1 (Investor) Migrant**' means a migrant who is granted leave under paragraphs 245E to 245EF of these Rules.

'**Tier 1 (Graduate Entrepreneur) Migrant**' means a migrant who is granted leave under paragraphs 245F to 245FB of these Rules in place on or after 6 April 2012.

'**Tier 1 (Post-Study Work) Migrant**' means a migrant who is granted leave under paragraphs 245F to 245FE of the Rules in place before 6 April 2012.

'**Tier 2 Migrant**' means a migrant who is granted leave as a Tier 2 (Intra-Company Transfer) Migrant, a Tier 2 (General) Migrant, a Tier 2 (Minister of Religion) Migrant or a Tier 2 (Sportsperson) Migrant.

Tier 2 (Intra-Company Transfer) Migrant' means a migrant granted leave under paragraphs 245G to 245GF of these Rules.

'**Tier 2 (General) Migrant**' means a migrant granted leave under paragraphs 245H to 245HF of these Rules and who obtains points under paragraphs 76 to 84A of Appendix A.

'**Tier 2 (Minister of Religion) Migrant**' means a migrant granted leave under paragraphs 245H to 245HF of these Rules and who obtains points under paragraphs 85 to 92 of Appendix A.

'**Tier 2 (Sportsperson) Migrant**' means a migrant granted leave under paragraphs 245H to 245HF of these Rules and who obtains points under paragraphs 93 to 100 of Appendix A.'

'Tier 4 (General) Student' means a migrant granted leave under paragraphs 245ZT to 245ZY of these Rules.

'Tier 4 (Child) Student' means a migrant granted leave under paragraphs 245ZZ to 245ZZD of these Rules.

'Tier 4 Migrant' means a Tier 4 (General) Student or a Tier 4 (Child) Student.

'expected end date of a course leading to the award of a PhD' means the date the PhD is expected to be formally confirmed, by the sponsor, as completed to the standard required for the award of a PhD and recorded on the confirmation of acceptance for studies accompanying the application for leave to remain as a Tier 4 (General) Student on the doctorate extension scheme.

'Tier 5 (Youth Mobility) Temporary Migrant' means a migrant granted leave under paragraphs 245ZI to 245ZL of these Rules.

'Tier 5 (Temporary Worker) Migrant' means a migrant granted leave under paragraphs 245ZM to 245ZS of these Rules.

'Deemed sponsorship status' means that the country or territory is not required to issue its nationals or passport holders with a Certificate of Sponsorship in order to enable a successful application under the Tier 5 Youth Mobility Scheme and is held by a country or territory listed as such at Appendix G of these Rules.

'Tier 5 Migrant' means a migrant who is either a Tier 5 (Temporary Worker) Migrant or a Tier 5 (Youth Mobility) Temporary Migrant.

Under Part 6A of these Rules '**Government Authorised Exchange Scheme**' means a scheme under the Tier 5 (Temporary Worker) Government Authorised Exchange sub-category which is endorsed by a Government Department in support of Government objectives and provides temporary work in an occupation which appears on the list of occupations skilled to National Qualifications Framework level 3, as stated in the codes of practice for Tier 2 Sponsors published by the UK Border Agency, and where the migrant will be supernumerary.

Under Part 6A of these Rules '**Work Experience Programme**' means work experience including volunteering and job-shadowing, internships and work exchange programmes under a Government Authorised Exchange Scheme.

Under Part 6A of these Rules '**Research Programme**' means research programmes and fellowships under a Government Authorised Exchange Scheme where the migrant is working on a scientific, academic, medical, or government research project/s at either a UK Higher Education Institution or another research institution operating under the authority and/or financial sponsorship of a relevant Government Department.'

Under Part 6A of these Rules '**Training Programme**' means a training programme under a Government Authorised Exchange Scheme where the migrant either receives formal, practical training in the fields of science and / or medicine or will be trained by HM Armed Forces or by UK emergency services, or meets the requirements of paragraph 245ZQ(b)(vi)(2) to(4).

Under Part 6A of these Rules, '**Temporary Engagement as a Sports Broadcaster**' means providing guest expert commentary on a particular sporting event.'

'**Contractual Service Supplier**' means a migrant who is granted entry clearance, leave to enter or leave to remain under paragraphs 245ZP(e) and 245ZR(b)(ii)(3) of these Rules on the basis that the circumstances in which such leave is sought engage the United Kingdom's commitments in respect of contractual service suppliers under the relevant provisions of one of the agreements specified in paragraph 111(f)(i) of Appendix A of these Rules.

'**Independent Professional**' means a migrant who is granted entry clearance, leave to enter or leave to remain under paragraphs 245ZP(e) and 245ZR(b)(ii)(3) of these Rules on the basis that the circumstances in which such leave is sought engage the United Kingdom's commitments in respect of independent professionals under the relevant provisions of one of the agreements specified in paragraph 111(f)(i) of Appendix A of these Rules.

'Jewish Agency Employee' means a migrant granted leave outside of these Rules under the concession that formerly appeared in Chapter 17 Section 5 Part 2 of the Immigration Directorate Instructions.

'Member of the Operational Ground Staff of an Overseas-owned Airline' means a migrant granted leave under paragraphs 178 to 185 of the Rules in force before 27 November 2008.

'Minister of Religion, Missionary or Member of a Religious Order' means a migrant granted leave under paragraphs 170 to 177A of the Rules in force before 27 November 2008.

'Overseas Qualified Nurse or Midwife' means a migrant granted leave under paragraphs 69M to 69R of the Rules in force before 27 November 2008.

'Participant in the Science and Engineering Graduates Scheme' means a migrant granted leave under paragraphs 135O to 135T of the Rules in force before 1 May 2007.

'Representative of an Overseas Newspaper, News Agency or Broadcasting Organisation' means a migrant granted leave under paragraphs 136 to 143 of the Rules in force before 27 November 2008.

'**Student Union Sabbatical Officer**' means a migrant granted leave under paragraphs 87A to 87F of the Rules in force before 27 November 2008.

'**Working Holidaymaker**' means a migrant granted leave under paragraphs 95 to 97 of the Rules in force before 27 November 2008.

A '**visitor**' is a person granted leave to enter or remain in the UK under paragraphs 40–56Z, 75A–M or 82–87 of these Rules.

A '**Business Visitor**' is a person granted leave to enter or remain in the UK under paragraphs 46G–46L, 75A–F or 75G–M of these Rules.

An '**Academic Visitor**' is a person who is from an overseas academic institution or who is highly qualified within his own field of expertise seeking leave to enter the UK to carry out research and associated activities for his own purposes.

A '**Visiting Professor**' is a person who is seeking leave to enter the UK as an academic professor to accompany students who are studying here on Study Abroad Programmes.

A '**Sports Visitor**' is a person granted leave to enter or remain in the UK under paragraphs 46M–46R of these Rules.

An '**Amateur**' is a person who engages in a sport or creative activity solely for personal enjoyment and who is not seeking to derive a living from the activity.

A '**Series of events**' is two or more linked events, such as a tour, or rounds of a competition, which do not add up to a league or a season.

An '**Entertainer Visitor**' is a person granted leave to enter or remain in the UK under paragraphs 46S–46X of these Rules.

A '**Special Visitor**' is a person granted leave for a short-term visit in the following circumstances:

'A visitor undertaking permitted paid engagements' is someone who is granted leave to enter under paragraphs 56X–56Z of these Rules.

(a)   A person granted leave to enter or remain in the UK as a visitor for private medical treatment under paragraphs 51–56 of these Rules

(b)   A person granted leave to enter or remain in the UK for the purpose of marriage or to enter into civil partnership under paragraphs 56D–56F of these Rules

(c)   A person granted leave to enter or remain in the UK as a Parent of a child at school under paragraphs 56A–56C of these Rules

(d)   A person granted leave to enter or remain in the UK as a Child Visitor under paragraphs 46A–46F of these Rules

(e)   A person granted leave to enter or remain in the UK as a Student Visitor under paragraphs 56K–56M of these Rules

(f)   A person granted leave to enter or remain in the UK as a Prospective Student under paragraphs 82–87 of these Rules

(g)   A person granted leave to enter the UK as a Visitor in transit under paragraphs 47–50 of these Rules, or

(h)   A person granted entry clearance, leave to enter or leave to remain in the UK as a Prospective Entrepreneur under paragraphs 56n–56Q of these Rules.

'**Writer, Composer or Artist**' means a migrant granted leave under paragraphs 232 to 237 of the Rules in force before 30th June 2008.

In paragraph 320(7B) and paragraph 320(11) of these Rules:

'**Deception**' means making false representations or submitting false documents (whether or not material to the application), or failing to disclose material facts.

'**Illegal Entrant**' has the same definition as in section 33(1) of the Immigration Act 1971.

In paragraph 320(22) and 322(12) of these Rules, and in paragraphs S-EC.2.3., S-LTR.2.3. and S-ILR.2.3. of Appendix FM to these Rules.

'**relevant NHS body**' means

(a)   in relation to England–

        (i)   a National Health Service Trust established under section 25 of the National Health Service Act 2006,

        (ii)   a NHS foundation trust.

(b)   in relation to Wales–

        (i)   a Local Health Board established under section 11 of the National Health Service (Wales) Act 2006,

        (ii)   a National Health Service Trust established under section 18 of the National Health Service (Wales) Act 2006,

        (iii)   a Special Health Authority established under 22 of the National Health Service (Wales) Act 2006.

(c)   in relation to Scotland–

        (i)   a Health Board or Special Health Board established under section 2 of the National Health Service (Scotland) Act 1978 (c. 29),

        (ii)   the Common Services Agency for the Scottish Health Service established under section 10 of that Act,

        (iii)   Healthcare Improvement Scotland established under section 10A of that Act.

(d)   in relation to Northern Ireland–

        (i)   the Regional Health and Social Care Board established under the Health and Social Care (Reform) Act (Northern Ireland) 2009,

        (ii)   a Health and Social Care trust established under the Health and Personal Social Services (Northern Ireland) Order 1991 (S.I. 1991/194 (N.I. 1)) and renamed under the Health and Social Care (Reform) Act (Northern Ireland) 2009.

'**relevant NHS regulations**' means

(i)   The National Health Service (Charges to Overseas Visitors) (Amendment) (Wales) Regulations 2004 (2004 No 1433);

(ii)   The National Health Service (Charges to Overseas Visitors) (Scotland) Regulations 1989 as amended (1989 No 364);

(iii)   The Health and Personal Social Services (Provision of Health Services to Persons not Ordinarily Resident) Regulations (Northern Ireland) 2005 (2005 No 551); or

(iv)   The National Health Service (Charges to Overseas Visitors) Regulations (2011 No 1556).

6A.   For the purpose of these Rules, a person (P) is not to be regarded as having (or potentially having) recourse to public funds merely because P is (or will be) reliant in whole or in part on public funds provided to P's sponsor unless, as a result of P's presence in the United Kingdom, the sponsor is (or would be) entitled to increased or additional public funds (save where such entitlement to increased or additional public funds is by virtue of P and the sponsor's joint entitlement to benefits under the regulations referred to in paragraph 6B).

6B.   Subject to paragraph 6C, a person (P) shall not be regarded as having recourse to public funds if P is entitled to benefits specified under section 115 of the Immigration and Asylum Act 1999 by virtue of regulations made under sub-sections (3) and (4) of that section or section 42 of the Tax Credits Act 2002.

6C.   A person (P) making an application from outside the United Kingdom will be regarded as having recourse to public funds where P relies upon the future entitlement to any public funds that would be payable to P or to P's sponsor as a result of P's presence in the United Kingdom, (including those benefits to which P or the sponsor would be entitled as a result of P's presence in the United Kingdom under the regulations referred to in to paragraph 6B)'.

'For the purposes of an application as a fiancé(e) or proposed civil partner under Appendix FM, an EEA national who holds a registration certificate or a document certifying permanent residence issued under the 2006 EEA Regulations (including an EEA national who holds a residence permit issued under the Immigration (European Economic Area) Regulations 2000 which is treated as if it were such a certificate or document by virtue of Schedule 4 to the 2006 EEA Regulations) is to be regarded as present and settled in the United Kingdom.'.

Part 1 – General provisions regarding leave to enter or remain in the United Kingdom

Leave to enter the United Kingdom

7. A person who is neither a British citizen nor a Commonwealth citizen with the right of abode nor a person who is entitled to enter or remain in the United Kingdom by virtue of the provisions of the 2006 EEA Regulations requires leave to enter the United Kingdom.

8. Under Sections 3 and 4 of the Immigration Act 1971 an Immigration Officer when admitting to the United Kingdom a person subject to immigration control under that Act may give leave to enter for a limited period and, if he does, may impose all or any of the following conditions:

    (i)   a condition restricting employment or occupation in the United Kingdom;

    (ii)   a condition requiring the person to maintain and accommodate himself, and any dependants of his, without recourse to public funds; and

    (iii) a condition requiring the person to register with the police.

    He may also require him to report to the appropriate Medical Officer of Environmental Health. Under Section 24 of the 1971 Act it is an offence knowingly to remain beyond the time limit or fail to comply with such a condition or requirement.

9. The time limit and any conditions attached will be made known to the person concerned either:

    (i)   by written notice given to him or endorsed by the Immigration Officer in his passport or travel document; or

    (ii)   in any other manner permitted by the Immigration (Leave to Enter and Remain) Order 2000.

Exercise of the power to refuse leave to enter the United Kingdom or to cancel leave to enter or remain which is in force

10. The power to refuse leave to enter the United Kingdom or to cancel leave to enter or remain which is already in force is not to be exercised by an Immigration Officer acting on his own. The authority of a Chief Immigration Officer or of an Immigration Inspector must always be obtained.

Suspension of leave to enter or remain in the United Kingdom

10A. Where a person has arrived in the United Kingdom with leave to enter or remain which is in force but which was given to him before his arrival he may be examined by an Immigration Officer under paragraph 2A of Schedule 2 to the Immigration Act 1971. An Immigration Officer examining a person under paragraph 2A may suspend that person's leave to enter or remain in the United Kingdom until the examination is completed.

Cancellation of leave to enter or remain in the United Kingdom

10B. Where a person arrives in the United Kingdom with leave to enter or remain in the United Kingdom which is already in force, an Immigration Officer may cancel that leave.

Requirement for persons arriving in the United Kingdom or seeking entry through the Channel Tunnel to produce evidence of identity and nationality

11. A person must, on arrival in the United Kingdom or when seeking entry through the Channel Tunnel, produce on request by the Immigration Officer:

    (i)   a valid national passport or other document satisfactorily establishing his identity and nationality; and

    (ii)   such information as may be required to establish whether he requires leave to enter the United Kingdom and, if so, whether and on what terms leave to enter should be given.

Requirement for a person not requiring leave to enter the United Kingdom to prove that he has the right of abode

12. A person claiming to be a British citizen must prove that he has the right of abode in the United Kingdom by producing either:

    (i)   a United Kingdom passport describing him as a British citizen or as a citizen of the United Kingdom and Colonies having the right of abode in the United Kingdom; or

    (ii)   a certificate of entitlement duly issued by or on behalf of the Government of the United Kingdom certifying that he has the right of abode.

13. A person claiming to be a Commonwealth citizen with the right of abode in the United Kingdom must prove that he has the right of abode by producing a certificate of entitlement duly issued to him by or on behalf of the Government of the United Kingdom certifying that he has the right of abode.

14. A Commonwealth citizen who has been given limited leave to enter the United Kingdom may later claim to have the right of abode. The time limit on his stay may be removed if he is able to establish a claim to the right of abode, for example by showing that:

   (i)   immediately before the commencement of the British Nationality Act 1981 he was a Commonwealth citizen born to or legally adopted by a parent who at the time of the birth had citizenship of the United Kingdom and Colonies by his birth in the United Kingdom or any of the Islands; and

   (ii)   he has not ceased to be a Commonwealth citizen in the meanwhile.

Common Travel Area

15. The United Kingdom, the Channel Islands, the Isle of Man and the Republic of Ireland collectively form a common travel area. A person who has been examined for the purpose of immigration control at the point at which he entered the area does not normally require leave to enter any other part of it. However certain persons subject to the Immigration (Control of Entry through the Republic of Ireland) Order 1972 (as amended) who enter the United Kingdom through the Republic of Ireland do require leave to enter. This includes:

   (i)   those who merely passed through the Republic of Ireland;

   (ii)   persons requiring visas;

   (iii) persons who entered the Republic of Ireland unlawfully;

   (iv)   persons who are subject to directions given by the Secretary of State for their exclusion from the United Kingdom on the ground that their exclusion is conducive to the public good;

   (v)   persons who entered the Republic from the United Kingdom and Islands after entering there unlawfully or overstaying their leave.

Admission of certain British passport holders

16. A person in any of the following categories may be admitted freely to the United Kingdom on production of a United Kingdom passport issued in the United Kingdom and Islands or the Republic of Ireland prior to 1 January 1973, unless his passport has been endorsed to show that he was subject to immigration control:

   (i)   a British Dependent Territories citizen;

   (ii)   a British National (Overseas);

   (iii) a British Overseas citizen;

   (iv)   a British protected person;

   (v)   a British subject by virtue of Section 30(a) of the British Nationality Act 1981, (who, immediately before the commencement of the 1981 Act would have been a British subject not possessing citizenship of the United Kingdom and Colonies or the citizenship of any other Commonwealth country or territory).

17. British Overseas citizens who hold United Kingdom passports wherever issued and who satisfy the Immigration Officer that they have, since 1 March 1968, been given indefinite leave to enter or remain in the United Kingdom may be given indefinite leave to enter.

Persons outside the United Kingdom

17A. Where a person is outside the United Kingdom but wishes to travel to the United Kingdom an Immigration Officer may give or refuse him leave to enter. An Immigration Officer may exercise these powers whether or not he is, himself, in the United Kingdom. However, an Immigration Officer is not obliged to consider an application for leave to enter from a person outside the United Kingdom.

17B. Where a person having left the common travel area, has leave to enter the United Kingdom which remains in force under article 13 of the Immigration (Leave to Enter and Remain) Order 2000, an Immigration Officer may cancel that leave. An Immigration Officer may exercise these powers whether or not he is, himself, in the United Kingdom. If a person outside the United Kingdom has leave to remain in the United Kingdom which is in force in this way, the Secretary of State may cancel that leave.

Returning Residents

18. A person seeking leave to enter the United Kingdom as a returning resident may be admitted for settlement provided the Immigration Officer is satisfied that the person concerned:

> (i)   had indefinite leave to enter or remain in the United Kingdom when he last left; and
>
> (ii)   has not been away from the United Kingdom for more than 2 years; and
>
> (iii)   did not receive assistance from public funds towards the cost of leaving the United Kingdom; and
>
> (iv)   now seeks admission for the purpose of settlement.

19.   A person who does not benefit from the preceding paragraph by reason only of having been away from the United Kingdom too long may nevertheless be admitted as a returning resident if, for example, he has lived here for most of his life.

19A.   Where a person who has indefinite leave to enter or remain in the United Kingdom accompanies, on a tour of duty abroad, a spouse, civil partner, unmarried partner or same-sex partner who is a member of HM Forces serving overseas, or a permanent member of HM Diplomatic Service, or a comparable United Kingdom-based staff member of the British Council, or a staff member of the Department for International Development who is a British Citizen or is settled in the United Kingdom, sub-paragraphs (ii) and (iii) of paragraph 18 shall not apply.

20.   The leave of a person whose stay in the United Kingdom is subject to a time limit lapses on his going to a country or territory outside the common travel area if the leave was given for a period of six months or less or conferred by a visit visa. In other cases, leave lapses on the holder remaining outside the United Kingdom for a continuous period of more than two years. A person whose leave has lapsed and who returns after a temporary absence abroad within the period of this earlier leave has no claim to admission as a returning resident. His application to re-enter the United Kingdom should be considered in the light of all the relevant circumstances. The same time limit and any conditions attached will normally be reimposed if he meets the requirements of these Rules, unless he is seeking admission in a different capacity from the one in which he was last given leave to enter or remain.

Non-lapsing leave

20A.   Leave to enter or remain in the United Kingdom will usually lapse on the holder going to a country or territory outside the common travel area. However, under article 13 of the Immigration (Leave to Enter and Remain) Order 2000 such leave will not lapse where it was given for a period exceeding six months or where it was conferred by means of an entry clearance (other than a visit visa).

Holders of restricted travel documents and passports

21.   The leave to enter or remain in the United Kingdom of the holder of a passport or travel document whose permission to enter another country has to be exercised before a given date may be restricted so as to terminate at least 2 months before that date.

22.   If his passport or travel document is endorsed with a restriction on the period for which he may remain outside his country of normal residence, his leave to enter or remain in the United Kingdom may be limited so as not to extend beyond the period of authorised absence.

23.   The holder of a travel document issued by the Home Office should not be given leave to enter or remain for a period extending beyond the validity of that document. This paragraph and paragraphs 21–22 do not apply to a person who is eligible for admission for settlement or to a spouse or civil partner who is eligible for admission under paragraph 282 or to a person who qualifies for the removal of the time limit on his stay.

Leave to enter granted on arrival in the United Kingdom

23A.   A person who is not a visa national and who is seeking leave to enter on arrival in the United Kingdom for a period not exceeding 6 months for a purpose for which prior entry clearance is not required under these Rules may be granted such leave, for a period not exceeding 6 months. This paragraph does not apply where the person is a British National (Overseas), a British overseas territories citizen, a British Overseas citizen, a British protected person, or a person who under the British Nationality Act 1981 is a British subject.

23B.   A person who is a British National (Overseas), a British overseas territories citizen, a British Overseas citizen, a British protected person, or a person who under the British Nationality Act 1981 is a British subject, and who is seeking leave to enter on arrival in the United Kingdom for a purpose for which prior entry clearance is not required under these Rules may be granted such leave, irrespective of the period of time for which he seeks entry, for a period not exceeding 6 months.

Entry clearance

24.   The following must produce to the Immigration Officer a valid passport or other identity document endorsed with a United Kingdom entry clearance issued to him for the purpose for which he seeks entry:

(i)   a visa national;

(ii)   any other person (other than British Nationals (Overseas), a British overseas territories citizen, a British Overseas citizen, a British protected person or a person who under the British Nationality Act 1981 is a British subject) who is seeking entry for a period exceeding six months or is seeking entry for a purpose for which prior entry clearance is required under these Rules.

Such a person will be refused leave to enter if he has no such current entry clearance. Any other person who wishes to ascertain in advance whether he is eligible for admission to the United Kingdom may apply for the issue of an entry clearance.

25.   Entry clearance takes the form of a visa (for visa nationals) or an entry certificate (for non visa nationals). These documents are to be taken as evidence of the holder's eligibility for entry into the United Kingdom, and accordingly accepted as 'entry clearances' within the meaning of the Immigration Act 1971.

25A.   An entry clearance which satisfies the requirements set out in article 3 of the Immigration (Leave to Enter and Remain) Order 2000 will have effect as leave to enter the United Kingdom. The requirements are that the entry clearance must specify the purpose for which the holder wishes to enter the United Kingdom and should be endorsed with the conditions to which it is subject or wish a statement that it has effect as indefinite leave to enter the United Kingdom. The holder of such an entry clearance will not require leave to enter on arrival in the United Kingdom and, for the purposes of these Rules, will be treated as a person who has arrived in the United Kingdom with leave to enter the United Kingdom which is in force but which was given to him before his arrival.

26.   An application for entry clearance will be considered in accordance with the provisions in these Rules governing the grant or refusal of leave to enter. Where appropriate, the term 'Entry Clearance Officer' should be substituted for 'Immigration Officer'.

27.   An application for entry clearance is to be decided in the light of the circumstances existing at the time of the decision, except that an applicant will not be refused an entry clearance where entry is sought in one of the categories contained in paragraphs 296–316 *or paragraph EC-C of Appendix FM* solely on account of his attaining the age of 18 years between receipt of his application and the date of the decision on it.

28.   An applicant for an entry clearance must be outside the United Kingdom and Islands at the time of the application. An applicant for an entry clearance who is seeking entry as a visitor must apply to a post designated by the Secretary of State to accept applications for entry clearance for that purpose and from that category of applicant. Subject to paragrapgh 28A, any other application must be made to the post in the country or territory where the applicant is living which has been designated by the Secretary of State to accept applications for entry clearance for that purpose and from that category of applicant. Where there is no such post the applicant must apply to the appropriate designated post outside the country or territory where he is living.

28A.   (a)   An application for entry clearance as a Tier 5 (Temporary Worker) Migrant in the creative and sporting sub-category of Tier 5 may also be made at the post in the country or territory where the applicant is situated at the time of the application, provided that:

          (i)   the post has been designated by the Secretary of State to accept applications for entry clearance for that purpose and from that category of applicant,

          (ii)   the applicant is in that country or territory for a similar purpose to the activity he proposes to undertake in the UK, and

          (iii) the applicant is able to demonstrate to the Entry Clearance Officer that he has authority to be living in that country or territory in accordance with its immigration laws. Those applicants who are known to the authorities of that country or territory but who have not been given permission to live in that country or territory will not be eligible to make an application.

       (b)   An application for entry clearance as a Tier 5 (Youth Mobility Scheme) Temporary Migrant may also be made at the post in the country or territory where the applicant is situated at the time of the application, provided that:

          (i)   the post has been designated by the Secretary of State to accept applications for entry clearance for that purpose and from that category of applicant, and

          (ii)   the applicant is able to demonstrate to the Entry Clearance Officer that he has authority to be living in that country or territory in accordance with its immigration laws and that when he was given authority to live in that country or territory he was given authority to live in that country or territory for a period of more than 6 months. Those applicants who are known to the authorities of that country or territory but who have not been given permission to live in that country or territory will not be eligible to make an application.

29. For the purposes of paragraph 28 'post' means a British Diplomatic Mission, British Consular post or the office of any person outside the United Kingdom and Islands who has been authorised by the Secretary of State to accept applications for entry clearance. A list of designated posts is published by the Foreign and Commonwealth Office.

30. An application for an entry clearance is not made until any fee required to be paid under the Consular Fees Act 1980 (including any Regulations or Orders made under that Act) has been paid.

30A. An entry clearance may be revoked if the Entry Clearance Officer is satisfied that:

(i) whether or not to the holder's knowledge, false representations were employed or material facts were not disclosed, either in writing or orally, for the purpose of obtaining the entry clearance; or

(ii) a change of circumstances since the entry clearance was issued has removed the basis of the holder's claim to be admitted to the United Kingdom, except where the change of circumstances amounts solely to his exceeding the age for entry in one of the categories contained in paragraphs 296–316 of these Rules since the issue of the entry clearance; or

(iii) the holder's exclusion from the United Kingdom would be conducive to the public good.

30B. An entry clearance shall cease to have effect where the entry clearance has effect as leave to enter and an Immigration Officer cancels that leave in accordance with paragraph 2A(8) of Schedule 2 to the Immigration Act 1971.

30C. An Immigration Officer may cancel an entry clearance which is capable of having effect as leave to enter if the holder arrives in the United Kingdom before the day on which the entry clearance becomes effective or if the holder seeks to enter the United Kingdom for a purpose other than the purpose specified in the entry clearance.

Variation of leave to enter or remain in the United Kingdom

31. Under Section 3(3) of the 1971 Act a limited leave to enter or remain in the United Kingdom may be varied by extending or restricting its duration, by adding, varying or revoking conditions or by removing the time limit (where upon any condition attached to the leave ceases to apply). When leave to enter or remain is varied an entry is to be made in the applicant's passport or travel document (and his registration certificate where appropriate) or the decision may be made known in writing in some other appropriate way.

31A. Where a person has arrived in the United Kingdom with leave to enter or remain in the United Kingdom which is in force but was given to him before his arrival, he may apply, on arrival at the port of entry in the United Kingdom, for variation of that leave. An Immigration Officer acting on behalf of the Secretary of State may vary the leave at the port of entry but is not obliged to consider an application for variation made at the port of entry. If an Immigration Officer acting on behalf of the Secretary of State has declined to consider an application for variation of leave at a port of entry but the leave has not been cancelled under paragraph 2A(8) of Schedule 2 to the Immigration Act 1971, the person seeking variation should apply to the Home office under paragraph 32.

32. DELETED

33. DELETED

33A. Where a person having left the common travel area, has leave to enter or remain in the United Kingdom which remains in force under article 13 of the Immigration (Leave to Enter and Remain) Order 2000., his leave may be varied (including any condition to which it is subject in such form and manner as permitted for the giving of leave to enter. However, the Secretary of State is not obliged to consider an application for variation of leave to enter or remain from a person outside the United Kingdom.

33B.–33G. DELETED

Specified forms and procedures for applications or claims in connection with immigration

A34. An application for leave to remain in the United Kingdom under these Rules must be made either by completing the relevant online application process in accordance with paragraph A34 (iii) or by using the specified application form in accordance with paragraphs 34A to 34D.

(i) 'The relevant online application process' means the application process accessible via the website of the United Kingdom Border Agency and identified there as relevant for applications for leave to remain for the immigration category under which the applicant wishes to apply.

(ii)   'Specified' in relation to the relevant online application process means specified in the online guidance accompanying that process.

(iii)   When the application is made via the relevant online application process:

(a)   any specified fee in connection with the application must be paid in accordance with the method specified;

(b)   if the online application process requires the applicant to provide biometric information that information must be provided as specified;

(c)   if the online application process requires supporting documents to be submitted by post then any such documents specified as mandatory must be submitted in the specified manner within 15 working days of submission of the online application;

(d)   if the online application process requires the applicant to make an appointment to attend a public enquiry office of the United Kingdom Border Agency the applicant must, within 45 working days of submission of the online application, make and attend that appointment; and comply with any specified requirements in relation to the provision of biometric information and documents specified as mandatory.

(iv)   Where an application for leave to remain in the United Kingdom is made by completing the relevant online application process, the application will be invalid if it does not comply with the requirements of paragraph A34(iii) and will not be considered.

Notice of invalidity will be given in writing and deemed to be received on the date it is given, except where it is sent by post, in which case it will be deemed to be received on the second day after it was posted excluding any day which is not a business day.

34.   An application form is specified when:

(i)   it is posted on the website of the United Kingdom Border Agency of the Home Office,

(ii)   it is marked on the form that it is a specified form for the purpose of the immigration rules,

(iii) it comes into force on the date specified on the form and/or in any accompanying announcement.

34A.   Where an application form is specified, the application or claim must also comply with the following requirements:

(i)   Subject to paragraph A34 the application or claim must be made using the specified form,

(ii)   any specified fee in connection with the application or claim must be paid in accordance with the method specified in the application form, separate payment form and/or related guidance notes, as applicable,

(iii) any section of the form which is designated as mandatory in the application form and/or related guidance notes must be completed as specified,

(iv)   if the application form and/or related guidance notes require the applicant to provide biographical information, such information must be provided as specified,

(v)   an appointment for the purposes stated in subparagraph (iv) must be made and must take place by the dates specified in any subsequent notification by the Secretary of State following receipt of the application, or as agreed by the Secretary of State,

(vi)   where the application or claim is made by post or courier, or submitted in person:

(a)   the application or claim must be accompanied by the photographs and documents specified as mandatory in the application form and/or related guidance notes,

(ab)   those photographs must be in the same format specified as mandatory in the application form and/or related guidance notes, and

(b)   the form must be signed by the applicant, and where applicable, the applicant's spouse, civil partner, same-sex partner or unmarried partner, save that where the applicant is under the age of eighteen, the form may be signed by the parent or legal guardian of the applicant on his behalf,

34B.   Where an application form is specified, it must be sent by prepaid post to the United Kingdom Border Agency of the Home Office, or submitted in person at a public enquiry office of the United Kingdom Border Agency of the Home Office, save for the following exceptions:

(i)   an application may not be submitted at a public enquiry office of the United Kingdom Border Agency of the Home Office if it is an application for:

(a)   limited or indefinite leave to remain as a sole representative or retired person of independent means (ba)   limited or indefinite leave to remain as a Tier 1 (Exceptional Talent) Migrant, Tier 1 (Entrepreneur) Migrant, Tier 1 (Investor) Migrant or Tier 1 (Graduate Entrepreneur) Migrant,

(b)   indefinite leave to remain as a victim of domestic violence,

(c)   a certificate of approval for a marriage or civil partnership,

(d)   a Tier 2, Tier 4 or Tier 5 (Temporary Worker) sponsorship licence,

(e)   Indefinite leave to remain as a businessperson, investor or innovator,

(f)   an extension of stay or indefinite leave to remain on the basis of long residence in the United Kingdom, or

(g)   a Designated Competent Body endorsement under the Tier 1 (Exceptional Talent) category.

(ii)   an application may be sent by courier to the United Kingdom Border Agency of the Home Office if it is an application for:

(a)   limited or indefinite leave to remain as a sole representative, retired person of independent means or as a Tier 1 Migrant or Tier 2 Migrant;

(b)   limited leave to remain for work permit employment, as a seasonal agricultural worker, for the purpose of employment under the Sectors-Based Scheme.

(c)   Indefinite leave to remain as a businessperson, investor or innovator, or

(d)   limited leave to remain as a Tier 5 (Temporary Worker) Migrant.

(iii)   an applicant may submit an application online where this option is available on the United Kingdom Border Agency's website

(iv)   an application may not be sent by pre-paid post, and must be made online, if it is an application for a Tier 2, Tier 4 or Tier 5 (Temporary Worker) sponsorship licence.

34C.   Where an application or claim in connection with immigration for which an application form is specified does not comply with the requirements in paragraph 34A, such application or claim will be invalid and will not be considered.

Notice of invalidity will be given in writing and deemed to be received on the date it is given, except where it is sent by post, in which case it will be deemed to be received on the second day after it was posted excluding any day which is not a business day.

34D.   Where the main applicant wishes to include applications or claims by any members of his family as his dependants on his own application form, the applications or claims of the dependants must meet the following requirements or they will be invalid and will not be considered:

(i)   the application form must expressly permit the applications or claims of dependants to be included, and

(ii)   such dependants must be the spouse, civil partner, unmarried or same-sex partner and/or children under the age of 18 of the main applicant.

Variation of Applications or Claims for Leave to Remain

34E.   If a person wishes to vary the purpose of an application or claim for leave to remain in the United Kingdom and an application form is specified for such new purpose or paragraph A34 applies, the variation must comply with the requirements of paragraph 34A or paragraph A34 (as they apply at the date the variation is made) as if the variation were a new application or claim, or the variation will be invalid and will not be considered.

34F.   Any valid variation of a leave to remain application will be decided in accordance with the immigration rules in force at the date such variation is made.

Determination of the date of an application or claim (or variation of an application or claim) in connection with immigration

34G.   For the purposes of these rules, the date on which an application or claim (or a variation in accordance with paragraph 34E) is made is as follows:

(i)   where the application form is sent by post, the date of posting,

(ii)   where the application form is submitted in person, the date on which it is accepted by a public enquiry office of the United Kingdom Border Agency of the Home Office,

(iii)   where the application form is sent by courier, the date on which it is delivered to the United Kingdom Border Agency of the Home Office, or

(iv)   where the application is made via the online application process, on the date on which the online application is submitted.

34H.   Applications or claims for leave to remain made before 29 February 2008 for which a form was prescribed prior to 29 February 2008 shall be subject to the forms and procedures as in force on the date on which the application or claim was made.

34I.   Where an application or claim is made no more than 21 days after the date on which a form is specified under the immigration rules and on a form that was permitted for such application or claim immediately prior to the date of such specification, the application or claim shall be deemed to have been made on the specified form.

Withdrawn applications or claims for leave to remain in the United Kingdom

34J.   Where a person whose application or claim for leave to remain is being considered requests the return of his passport for the purpose of travel outside the common travel area, the application for leave shall, provided it has not already been determined, be treated as withdrawn as soon as the passport is returned in response to that request.

34K.   Paragraph 34J does not apply to an applicant who is applying as a Tier 2 Migrant or a Tier 5 Migrant and whose application is supported by a Certificate of Sponsorship from a Premium Sponsor.

Undertakings

35.   A sponsor of a person seeking leave to enter or remain in the United Kingdom may be asked to give an undertaking in writing to be responsible for that person's maintenance, accommodation and (as appropriate) personal care for the period of any leave granted, including any further variation or for a period of 5 years from date of grant where indefinite leave to enter or remain is granted. Under the Social Security Administration Act 1992 and the Social Security Administration (Northern Ireland) Act 1992, the Department of Social Security or, as the case may be, the Department of Health and Social Services in Northern Ireland, may seek to recover from the person giving such an undertaking any income support paid to meet the needs of the person in respect of whom the undertaking has been given. Under the Immigration and Asylum Act 1999 the Home Office may seek to recover from the person giving such an undertaking amounts attributable to any support provided under section 95 of the Immigration and Asylum Act 1999 (support for asylum seekers) to, or in respect of, the person in respect of whom the undertaking has been given. Failure by the sponsor to maintain that person in accordance with the undertaking, may also be an offence under section 105 of the Social Security Administration Act 1992 and/or under section 108 of the Immigration and Asylum Act 1999 if, as a consequence, asylum support and/or income support is provided to, or in respect of, that person.

Medical

36.   A person who intends to remain in the United Kingdom for more than 6 months should normally be referred to the Medical Inspector for examination. If he produces a medical certificate he should be advised to hand it to the Medical Inspector. Any person seeking entry who mentions health or medical treatment as a reason for his visit, or who appears not to be in good mental or physical health, should also be referred to the Medical Inspector; and the Immigration Officer has discretion, which should be exercised sparingly, to refer for examination in any other case.

37.   Where the Medical Inspector advises that a person seeking entry is suffering from a specified disease or condition which may interfere with his ability to support himself or his dependants, the Immigration Officer should take account of this, in conjunction with other factors, in deciding whether to admit that person. The Immigration Officer should also take account of the Medical Inspector's assessment of the likely course of treatment in deciding whether a person seeking entry for private medical treatment has sufficient means at his disposal.

38.   A returning resident should not be refused leave to enter or have existing leave to enter or remain cancelled on medical grounds. But where a person would be refused leave to enter or have existing leave to enter or remain cancelled on medical grounds if he were not a returning resident or in any case where it is decided on compassionate grounds not to exercise the power to refuse leave to enter or to cancel existing leave to enter or remain, or in any other case where the Medical Inspector so recommends, the Immigration Officer should give the person concerned a notice requiring him to report to the Medical Officer of Environmental Health designated by the Medical Inspector with a view to further examination and any necessary treatment.

A39.   Any person from a country listed in Appendix T Part 1 making an application for entry clearance to come to the UK for more than six months or as a fiance(e) or proposed civil partner applying for leave to enter under Section EC-P:Entry clearance as a partner under Appendix FM or leave to enter under paragraphs 290–291 in

Part 8 of these Rules, must present, at the time of application, a valid medical certificate issued by a medical practitioner listed in Appendix T Part 2 confirming that they have undergone screening for active pulmonary tuberculosis and that this tuberculosis is not present in the applicant.

B39.　Applicants seeking leave to enter as a returning resident under paragraph 19 of these rules, having been absent from the United Kingdom for more than two years are also subject to the requirements in paragraph A39.

39.　The Entry Clearance Officer has the same discretion as an Immigration Officer to refer applicants for entry clearance for medical examination and the same principles will apply to the decision whether or not to issue an entry clearance.

Students

39A.　An application for a variation of leave to enter or remain made by a student who is sponsored by a government or international sponsorship agency may be refused if the sponsor has not given written consent to the proposed variation.

Specified documents

39B.　(a)　Where these Rules state that specified documents must be provided, that means documents specified in these Rules as being specified documents for the route under which the applicant is applying. If the specified documents are not provided, the applicant will not meet the requirement for which the specified documents are required as evidence.

(b)　Where these Rules specify documents that are to be provided, those documents are considered to be specified documents, whether or not they are named as such, and as such are subject to the requirements in (c) to (f) below.

(c)　If the Entry Clearance Officer or Secretary of State has reasonable cause to doubt the genuineness of any document submitted by an applicant which is, or which purports to be, a specified document under these Rules, and having taken reasonable steps to verify the document is unable to verify that it is genuine, the document will be discounted for the purposes of this application.

(d)　Specified documents must be originals, not copies, except where stated otherwise.

(e)　Specified documents must contain, or the applicant must provide, full contact details to allow each document to be verified.

(f)　Where any specified documents provided are not in English or Welsh, the applicant must provide the original and a full translation that can be independently verified by the Entry Clearance Officer, Immigration Officer or the Secretary of State. The translation must be dated and include:

(i)　confirmation that it is an accurate translation of the original document;

(ii)　the full name and original signature of the translator or an authorised official of the translation company;

(iii)　the translator or translation company's contact details; and

(iv)　if the applicant is applying for leave to remain or indefinite leave to remain, certification by a qualified translator and details of the translator or translation company's credentials.

Part 2 – Persons seeking to enter or remain in the United Kingdom for visits

Visitors

Requirements for leave to enter as a general visitor

40.　For the purposes of paragraphs 41–46 a general visitor includes a person living and working outside the United Kingdom who comes to the United Kingdom as a tourist. A person seeking leave to enter the United Kingdom as a Business Visitor, which includes Academic Visitors, must meet the requirements of paragraph 46G. A person seeking entry as a Sports Visitor must meet the requirements of paragraph 46M. A person seeking entry as an Entertainer Visitor must meet the requirements of paragraph 46S. A visitor seeking leave to enter for the purposes of marriage or to enter into a civil partnership must meet the requirements of paragraph 56D. A person seeking entry to study as a student visitor must meet the requirements of paragraph 56K.

41.　The requirements to be met by a person seeking leave to enter the United Kingdom as a general visitor are that he:

(i)   is genuinely seeking entry as a general visitor for a limited period as stated by him, not exceeding 6 months or not exceeding 12 months in the case of a person seeking entry to accompany an academic visitor, provided in the latter case the visitor accompanying the academic visitor has entry clearance; and

(ii) intends to leave the United Kingdom at the end of the period of the visit as stated by him; and does not intend to live for extended periods in the United Kingdom through frequent or successive visits; and

(iii) does not intend to take employment in the United Kingdom; and

(iv) does not intend to produce goods or provide services within the United Kingdom, including the selling of goods or services direct to members of the public; and

(v)   Save to the extent provided by paragraph 43A, does not intend to undertake a course of study; and

(vi) will maintain and accommodate himself and any dependants adequately out of resources available to him without recourse to public funds or taking employment; or will, with any dependants, be maintained and/or accommodated adequately by relatives or friends who can demonstrate they are able and intend to do so, and are legally present in the United Kingdom, or will be at the time of their visit; and

(vii) can meet the cost of the return or onward journey; and

(viii) is not a child under the age of 18.

(ix) does not intend to do any of the activities provided for in paragraphs 46G (iii), 46M (iii) or 46S (iii); and

(x)   does not, during his visit, intend to marry or form a civil partnership, or to give notice of marriage or civil partnership; and

(xi) does not intend to receive private medical treatment during his visit; and

(xii) is not in transit to a country outside the common travel area.

(xiii) where he is seeking leave to enter as a general visitor to take part in archaeological excavations, provides a letter from the director or organiser of the excavation stating the length of their visit and, where appropriate, what arrangements have been made for their accommodation and maintenance..

Leave to enter as a general visitor

42. A person seeking leave to enter to the United Kingdom as a general visitor may be admitted for a period not exceeding 6 months, or not exceeding 12 months in the case of a person accompanying an academic visitor, subject to a condition prohibiting employment and recourse to public funds, provided the Immigration Officer is satisfied that each of the requirements of paragraph 41 is met.

Refusal of leave to enter as a general visitor

43. Leave to enter as a general visitor is to be refused if the Immigration Officer is not satisfied that each of the requirements of paragraph 41 is met.

Permitted study as a general visitor

43A. (1) A person who has been granted leave to enter the United Kingdom under paragraph 42 may undertake a course of study to the extent permitted by this paragraph.

(2) A course of study is permitted under this paragraph if it–

(a) does not exceed 30 days in duration (either alone or taken together with any other course and whether continuous or otherwise); and

(b) is a recreational course; but

(c) is not an English language course.

(3) A course of study is also permitted under this paragraph if it–

(a) does not exceed 30 days in duration (either alone or taken together with any other course and whether continuous or otherwise); and

(b) is provided by an institution which is–

(i)   the holder of a Sponsor licence for Tier 4 of the Points-Based System,

(ii) the holder of valid accreditation from Accreditation UK, the Accreditation Body for Language Services (ABLS), the British Accreditation Council (BAC), or the Accreditation Service for International Colleges (ASIC),

(iii) the holder of a valid and satisfactory full institutional inspection, review or audit by the Bridge Schools Inspectorate, the Education and Training Inspectorate, Estyn, Education

Scotland, the Independent Schools Inspectorate, Office for Standards in Education, the Quality Assurance Agency for Higher Education, the Schools Inspection Service or the Education and Training Inspectorate Northern Ireland, or

    (iv)   an overseas higher education institution offering only part of its programmes in the United Kingdom, holding its own national accreditation and offering programmes that are an equivalent level to a United Kingdom degree.

(4)   For the purposes of this paragraph a 'recreational course' is one which a person undertakes purely for leisure purposes.

Requirements for an extension of stay as a general visitor

44.   Six months is the maximum permitted leave which may be granted to a general visitor. The requirements for an extension of stay as a general visitor are that the applicant:

    (i)   meets the requirements of paragraph 41 (ii)–(vii) and (ix)–(xii); and

    (ii)   has not already spent, or would not as a result of an extension of stay spend, more than 6 months in total in the United Kingdom or not more than 12 months in the case of a person accompanying an academic visitor as a general visitor. Any periods spent as a child visitor are to be counted as a period spent as a general visitor; and

    (iii)   has, or was last granted, entry clearance, leave to enter or leave to remain as a general visitor or as a child visitor; and

    (iv)   must not be in the UK in breach of immigration laws except that any period of overstaying for a period of 28 days or less will be disregarded.

Extension of stay as a general visitor

45.   An extension of stay as a general visitor may be granted, subject to a condition prohibiting employment and recourse to public funds, provided the Secretary of State is satisfied that each of the requirements of paragraph 44 is met.

Refusal of extension of stay as a general visitor

46.   An extension of stay as a general visitor is to be refused if the Secretary of State is not satisfied that each of the requirements of paragraph 44 is met.

Child visitors

Requirements for leave to enter as a child visitor

46A.   The requirements to be met by a person seeking leave to enter the United Kingdom as a child visitor are that the applicant:

    (i)   is genuinely seeking entry as a child visitor for a limited period as stated, not exceeding 6 months or not exceeding 12 months to accompany an academic visitor, provided in the latter case the applicant has entry clearance; and

    (ii)   meets the requirements of paragraph 41 (ii)–(iv), (vi)–(vii) and (x)–(xii); and

    (iii)   is under the age of 18; and

    (iv)   can demonstrate that suitable arrangements have been made for their travel to, and reception and care in the United Kingdom; and;

    (v)   has a parent or guardian in their home country or country of habitual residence who is responsible for their care and who confirms that they consent to the arrangements for the applicant's travel, reception and care in the United Kingdom; and

    (vi)   if a visa national:

        (a)   the applicant holds a valid United Kingdom entry clearance for entry as an accompanied child visitor and is travelling in the company of the adult identified on the entry clearance, who is on the same occasion being admitted to the United Kingdom; or

        (b)   the applicant holds a valid United Kingdom entry clearance for entry as an unaccompanied child visitor; and

    (vii)   if the applicant has been accepted for a course of study, this is to be provided by an institution which is outside the maintained sector and is:

        (a)   the holder of a Sponsor Licence for Tier 4 of the Points Based System, or

(b)   the holder of valid accreditation from Accreditation UK; the Accreditation Body for Language Services (ABLS); the British Accreditation Council (BAC) or the Accreditation Service for International Colleges (ASIC), or

(c)   the holder of a valid and satisfactory full institutional inspection, review or audit by one of the following bodies: the Bridge Schools Inspectorate; the Education and Training Inspectorate; Estyn; Education Scotland; the Independent Schools Inspectorate; Office for Standards in Education; the Schools Inspection Service or the Education and Training Inspectorate Northern Ireland.

(viii)   if the applicant is undertaking an exchange or educational visit only, this is to be provided by one of the following schools:

(a)   For England and Wales, maintained schools as defined under section 20(7) of the School Standards and Framework Act 1998; non-maintained special schools approved under section 342 of the Education Act 1996; independent schools as defined under section 463 of the Education Act 1996 and registered independent schools entered on the register of independent schools maintained under section 158 of the Education Act 2002; academies as defined in section 1(10) of the Academies Act 2010; city technology colleges and city colleges for technology of the arts as established under the Education Act 1996 and treated as academies under section 15(4) of the Academies Act.

(b)   For Scotland, state-maintained schools, grant-aided schools and independent fee paying schools as defined under Section 135 of the Education (Scotland) Act 1980.

(c)   For Northern Ireland, grant-aided schools as defined under Articles 10 and 11 of and Schedules 4 to 7 to the Education and Libraries (NI) Order in Council 1986; grant maintained integrated schools as defined under Article 69 of and Schedule 5 to the Education Reform (NI) Order 1989; independent fee paying schools as defined under Article 38 of the Education and Libraries (NI) Order 1986.

Leave to enter as a child visitor

46B.   An applicant seeking leave to enter the United Kingdom as a child visitor may be admitted for a period not exceeding 6 months, or not exceeding 12 months in the case of a child visitor accompanying an academic visitor subject to a condition prohibiting employment and recourse to public funds, providing that the Immigration Officer is satisfied that each of the requirements of paragraph 46A is met.

Refusal of leave to enter as a child visitor

46C.   Leave to enter as a child visitor is to be refused if the Immigration Officer is not satisfied that each of the requirements of paragraph 46A is met.

Requirements for an extension of stay as a child visitor

46D.   Six months is the maximum permitted leave which may be granted to a child visitor. The requirements for an extension of stay as a child visitor are that the applicant:

(i)   meets the requirements of paragraph 41 (ii)–(vii) and (x) –(xii); and

(ii)   is under the age of 18; and

(iii)   can demonstrate that there are suitable arrangements for his care in the United Kingdom; and

(iv)   has a parent or guardian in his home country or country of habitual residence who is responsible for his care, and who confirms that they consent to the arrangements for the applicant's travel, reception and care in the United Kingdom; and

(v)   has not already spent, or would not as a result of an extension of stay spend, more than 6 months in total in the United Kingdom, or not more than 12 months in the case of a child visitor accompanying an academic visitor, as a child visitor; and

(vi)   has, or was last granted, entry clearance, leave to enter or leave to remain as a child visitor; and

(vii)   must not be in the UK in breach of immigration laws except that any period of overstaying for a period of 28 days or less will be disregarded.

Extension of stay as a child visitor

46E.   An extension of stay as a child visitor may be granted, subject to a condition prohibiting employment and recourse to public funds, provided the Secretary of State is satisfied that each of the requirements of paragraph 46D is met.

Refusal of extension of stay as a child visitor

46F.   An extension of stay as a child visitor is to be refused if the Secretary of State is not satisfied that each of the requirements of paragraph 46D is met.

Business Visitors

Requirements for leave to enter as a Business Visitor

46G.   The requirements to be met by a person seeking leave to enter the United Kingdom as a business visitor are that he:

(i)   is genuinely seeking entry as a Business Visitor for a limited period as stated by him:

    (a)   not exceeding 6 months; or

    (b)   not exceeding 12 months if seeking entry as an Academic Visitor

(ii)   meets the requirements of paragraphs 41 (ii)–(iv), subject to paragraph 46HA, (v), (vi)–(viii) and (x)–(xii);

(iii)   intends to do one or more of the following during his visit:

    (a)   to carry out one of the following activities;

        (i)   to attend meetings, conferences and interviews, provided they were arranged before arrival in the UK and, if the applicant is a board-level director attending board meetings in the UK, provided they are not employed by a UK company (although they may be paid a fee for attending the meeting);

        (ii)   to attend trade fairs for promotional work only, provided they are not directly selling;

        (iii)   to arrange deals, or negotiating or signing trade agreements or contracts;

        (iv)   to carry out fact-finding missions;

        (v)   to conduct site visits;

        (vi)   to work as a driver on a genuine international route delivering goods or passengers from abroad;

        (vii)   to work as a tour group courier, providing the applicant is contracted to a firm with headquarters outside the UK, is seeking entry to accompany a tour group, and will depart with that tour, or another tour organised by the same company;

        (viii)   to speak at a one-off conference which is not organised as a commercial concern, and is not making a profit for the organiser;

        (ix)   to represent a foreign manufacturer by:

            (i)   carrying out installing, debugging or enhancing work for computer software companies,

            (ii)   servicing or repairing the manufacturer's products within the initial guarantee period, or

            (iii)   being briefed on the requirements of a UK customer, provided this is limited to briefing and does not include work involving use of the applicant's expertise to make a detailed assessment of a potential customer's requirements;

        (x)   to represent a foreign machine manufacturer, as part of the contract of purchase and supply, in erecting and installing machinery too heavy to be delivered in one piece;

        (xi)   to act as an interpreter or translator for visiting business people, provided they are all employed by, and doing the business of, the same overseas company;

        (xii)   to erect, dismantle, install, service, repair or advise on the development of foreign-made machinery, provided they will only do so in the UK for up to six months;

    (b)   to take part in a location shoot as a member of a film crew meaning he is a film actor, producer, director or technician paid or employed by an overseas firm other than one established in the UK and is coming to the UK for location sequences only for an overseas film;

    (c)   to represent overseas news media including as a journalist, correspondent, producer or cameraman provided he is employed or paid by an overseas company and is gathering information for an overseas publication;

    (d)   to act as an Academic Visitor but only if

        (1)   he is an academic who is:

(a) on sabbatical leave from an overseas academic institution to carry out research;

(b) taking part in formal exchange arrangements with UK counterparts (including doctors);

(c) coming to share knowledge or experience, or to hold informal discussions with their UK counterparts, or

(d) taking part in a single conference or seminar that is not a commercial or non-profit venture;

(e) an eminent senior doctor or dentist taking part in research, teaching or clinical practice; and

(2) he has been working as an academic in an institution of higher education overseas or in the field of their academic expertise immediately prior to seeking entry;

(e) to act as a Visiting Professor; subject to undertaking only a small amount of teaching for the institution hosting the students he is supervising, being employed and paid by the overseas academic institution and not intending to base himself or seek employment in the UK.

(f) to be a secondee to a UK company which is directly contracted with the visitor's overseas company, with which it has no corporate relationship, to provide goods or services, provided the secondee remains employed and paid by the overseas company throughout the secondee's visit;

(g) to undertake some preaching or pastoral work as a religious worker, provided his base is abroad and he is not taking up an office, post or appointment;

(h) To act as an adviser, consultant, trainer, internal auditor or trouble shooter, to the UK branch of the same group of companies as the visitor's overseas company, provided the visitor remains employed and paid by the overseas company and does not undertake work, paid or unpaid with the UK company's clients;

(i) To receive specific, one-off training on techniques and work practices used in the UK where:

(a) the training is to be delivered by the UK branch of the same group of companies to which the individual's employer belongs; or

(b) the training is to be provided by a UK company contracted to provide goods or services to the overseas company; or

(c) a UK company is contracted to provide training facilities only, to an overseas company; or

(d) the training is corporate training which is being delivered by an outside provider to overseas and UK employees of the same group of companies; or

(e) the training is corporate training provided for the purposes of the person's employment overseas and delivered by a UK company that is neither part of the person's employer's corporate group nor whose main activity is the provision of training.

Leave to enter as a Business Visitor

46H. A person seeking leave to enter to the United Kingdom as a Business Visitor may be admitted for a period not exceeding 6 months, subject to a condition prohibiting employment and recourse to public funds, provided the Immigration Officer is satisfied that each of the requirements of paragraph 46G is met. A person seeking leave to enter the United Kingdom as an Academic Visitor who does not have entry clearance may, if otherwise eligible, be admitted for a period not exceeding 6 months, subject to a condition prohibiting employment, provided the Immigration Officer is satisfied that each of the requirements of paragraph 46G are met. An Academic Visitor who has entry clearance may be admitted for up to 12 months subject to a condition prohibiting employment.

Permitted study as a business visitor

46HA. A person granted leave to enter under paragraph 46H may undertake a course of study to the same extent permitted by paragraph 43A.

Refusal of leave to enter as a Business Visitor

46I. Leave to enter as a Business Visitor is to be refused if the Immigration Officer is not satisfied that each of the requirements of paragraph 46G are met.

Requirements for an extension of stay as a Business Visitor

46J.   Twelve months is the maximum permitted leave which may be granted to an Academic Visitor and six months is the maximum that may be granted to any other form of Business Visitor. The requirements for an extension of stay as a Business Visitor are that the applicant:

(i)   meets the requirements of paragraph 46G(ii)–(iii); and

(ii)   if he is a Business Visitor other than an Academic Visitor, has not already spent, or would not as a result of an extension of stay spend, more than 6 months in total in the United Kingdom as a Business Visitor; and

(iii)   if he is an Academic Visitor, has not already spent, or would not as a result of an extension of stay spend, more than 12 months in total in the United Kingdom as a Business Visitor; and

(iv)   has, or was last granted, entry clearance, leave to enter or leave to remain as a Business Visitor; and

(v)   must not be in the UK in breach of immigration laws except that any period of overstaying for a period of 28 days or less will be disregarded.

Extension of stay as a Business Visitor

46K.   An extension of stay as a Business Visitor may be granted, subject to a condition prohibiting employment and recourse to public funds, provided the Secretary of State is satisfied that each of the requirements of paragraph 46J is met.

Refusal of extension of stay as a Business Visitor

46L.   An extension of stay as a Business Visitor is to be refused if the Secretary of State is not satisfied that each of the requirements of paragraph 46J is met.

Sports Visitors

Requirements for leave to enter as a Sports Visitor

46M.   The requirements to be met by a person seeking leave to enter the United Kingdom as a Sports Visitor are that he:

(i)   is genuinely seeking entry as a Sports Visitor for a limited period as stated by him, not exceeding six months; and

(ii)   meets the requirements of paragraphs 41(ii)–(viii) and (x)–(xii) (except that the requirement in paragraph 41(v) is to be read as if it were not qualified by paragraph 43A); and

(iii)   intends to do one or more of the following during his visit:

(a)   to take part in a sports tournament, a particular sporting event or series of sporting events in which the applicant is either:

(i)   taking part, either as an individual or as part of a team;

(ii)   making personal appearances and promotions, such as book signings, television interviews, guest commentaries, negotiating contracts, or to discuss sponsorship deals;

(iii)   taking part in 'trials', providing it is not in front of an audience, either paying or non-paying;

(iv)   undertaking short periods of training, either as an individual or as part of a team, providing the applicant is not intending to settle in the UK, being paid by a UK sporting body, or joining a UK team where they are involved in friendly or exhibition matches.

(b)   To take part in a specific one off charity sporting event, provided no payment is received other than for travelling and other expenses;

(c)   To join, as an Amateur, a wholly or predominantly amateur team provided no payment is received other than for board and lodging and reasonable expenses;

(d)   To serve as a member of the technical or personal staff, or as an official, attending the same event as a visiting sportsperson coming for one or more of the purposes listed in (a), (b) or (c) or attending the same event as a sports-person carrying out permitted paid engagements as a visitor.

Leave to enter as a Sports Visitor

46N. A person seeking leave to enter to the United Kingdom as a Sports Visitor may be admitted for a period not exceeding 6 months, subject to a condition prohibiting employment, study and recourse to public funds, provided the Immigration Officer is satisfied that each of the requirements of paragraph 46M is met.

Refusal of leave to enter as a Sports Visitor

46O. Leave to enter as a Sports Visitor is to be refused if the Immigration Officer is not satisfied that each of the requirements of paragraph 46M is met.

Requirements for an extension of stay as a Sports Visitor

46P. Six months is the maximum permitted leave which may be granted to a Sports Visitor. The requirements for an extension of stay as a sports visitor are that the applicant:

    (i)   meets the requirements of paragraph 46M(ii)–(iii); and

    (ii)   has not already spent, or would not as a result of an extension of stay spend, more than 6 months in total in the United Kingdom as a Sports Visitor; and

    (iii)   has, or was last granted, entry clearance, leave to enter or leave to remain as a Sports Visitor; and

    (iv)   must not be in the UK in breach of immigration laws except that any period of overstaying for a period of 28 days or less will be disregarded.

Extension of stay as a Sports Visitor

46Q. An extension of stay as a Sports Visitor may be granted, subject to a condition prohibiting employment, study and recourse to public funds, provided the Secretary of State is satisfied that each of the requirements of paragraph 46P is met.

Refusal of extension of stay as a Sports Visitor

46R. An extension of stay as a Sports Visitor is to be refused if the Secretary of State is not satisfied that each of the requirements of paragraph 46P is met.

Entertainer Visitors

Requirements for leave to enter as an Entertainer Visitor

46S. The requirements to be met by a person seeking leave to enter the United Kingdom as an Entertainer Visitor are that he:

    (i)   is genuinely seeking entry as an Entertainer Visitor for a limited period as stated by him, not exceeding six months and

    (ii)   meets the requirements of paragraphs 41(ii)–(viii) and (x)–(xii) (except that the requirement in paragraph 41(v) is to be read as if it were not qualified by paragraph 43A) and

    (iii)   intends to do one or more of the following during his visit:

        (a)   to take part as a professional entertainer in one or more music competitions; and/or

        (b)   to fulfil one or more specific engagements as either an individual Amateur entertainer or as an Amateur group; and/or

        (c)   to take part, as an amateur or professional entertainer, in one or more cultural events or festivals on the list of permit free festivals at Appendix R to these Rules.

        (d)   serve as a member of the technical or personal staff, or of the production team, of an entertainer coming for one or more of the purposes listed in (a), (b), or (c), or attending the same event as an entertainer carrying out permitted paid engagements as a visitor

Leave to enter as an Entertainer Visitor

46T. A person seeking leave to enter to the United Kingdom as an Entertainer Visitor may be admitted for a period not exceeding 6 months, subject to a condition prohibiting employment, study and recourse to public funds, provided the Immigration Officer is satisfied that each of the requirements of paragraph 46S is met.

Refusal of leave to enter as an Entertainer Visitor

46U. Leave to enter as an Entertainer Visitor is to be refused if the Immigration Officer is not satisfied that each of the requirements of paragraph 46S is met.

Requirements for an extension of stay as an Entertainer Visitor

46V. Six months is the maximum permitted leave which may be granted to an Entertainer Visitor. The requirements for an extension of stay as an Entertainer Visitor are that the applicant:

(i)   meets the requirements of paragraph 46S(ii)–(iii); and

(ii)   has not already spent, or would not as a result of an extension of stay spend, more than 6 months in total in the United Kingdom as an Entertainer Visitor; and

(iii)   has, or was last granted, entry clearance, leave to enter or leave to remain as an Entertainer Visitor; and

(iv)   must not be in the UK in breach of immigration laws except that any period of overstaying for a period of 28 days or less will be disregarded.

Extension of stay as an Entertainer Visitor

46W. An extension of stay as an Entertainer Visitor may be granted, subject to a condition prohibiting employment, study and recourse to public funds, provided the Secretary of State is satisfied that each of the requirements of paragraph 46V is met.

Refusal of extension of stay as an Entertainer Visitor

46X. An extension of stay as an Entertainer Visitor is to be refused if the Secretary of State is not satisfied that each of the requirements of paragraph 46V is met.

Visitors in transit

Requirements for admission as a visitor in transit to another country

47.   The requirements to be met by a person (not being a member of the crew of a ship, aircraft, hovercraft, hydrofoil or train) seeking leave to enter the United Kingdom as a visitor in transit to another country are that he:

(i)   is in transit to a country outside the common travel area; and

(ii)   has both the means and the intention of proceeding at once to another country; and

(iii)   is assured of entry there; and

(iv)   intends and is able to leave the United Kingdom within 48 hours.

Leave to enter as a visitor in transit

48.   A person seeking leave to enter the United Kingdom as a visitor in transit may be admitted for a period not exceeding 48 hours with a prohibition on employment, study and recourse to public funds, provided the Immigration Officer is satisfied that each of the requirements of paragraph 47 is met.

Refusal of leave to enter as a visitor in transit

49.   Leave to enter as a visitor in transit is to be refused if the Immigration Officer is not satisfied that each of the requirements of paragraph 47 is met.

Extension of stay as a visitor in transit

50.   The maximum permitted leave which may be granted to a visitor in transit is 48 hours. An application for an extension of stay beyond 48 hours from a person admitted in this category is to be refused.

Visitors seeking to enter or remain for private medical treatment

Requirements for leave to enter as a visitor for private medical treatment

51.   The requirements to be met by a person seeking leave to enter the United Kingdom as a visitor for private medical treatment are that he:

(i)   meets the requirements set out in paragraph 41 (iii)–(vii), (ix)–(x) and (xii) (except that the requirement in paragraph 41(v) is to be read as if it were not qualified by paragraph 43A) for entry as a general visitor; and

(ii)   in the case of a person suffering from a communicable disease, has satisfied the Medical Inspector that there is no danger to public health; and

(iii)   can show, if required to do so, that any proposed course of treatment is of finite duration; and

(iv)   intends to leave the United Kingdom at the end of his treatment; and

(v)   can produce satisfactory evidence, if required to do so, of:

(a)   the medical condition requiring consultation or treatment; and

(b)   satisfactory arrangements for the necessary consultation or treatment at his own expense; and

(c)   the estimated costs of such consultation or treatment; and

(d)   the likely duration of his visit; and

(e)   sufficient funds available to him in the United Kingdom to meet the estimated costs and his undertaking to do so.

Leave to enter as a visitor for private medical treatment

52.   A person seeking leave to enter the United Kingdom as a visitor for private medical treatment may be admitted for a period not exceeding 6 months, subject to a condition prohibiting employment, study and recourse to public funds, provided the Immigration Officer is satisfied that each of the requirements of paragraph 51 is met.

Refusal of leave to enter as a visitor for private medical treatment

53.   Leave to enter as a visitor for private medical treatment is to be refused if the Immigration Officer is not satisfied that each of the requirements of paragraph 51 is met.

Requirements for an extension of stay as a visitor for private medical treatment

54.   The requirements for an extension of stay as a visitor to undergo or continue private medical treatment are that the applicant:

(i)   meets the requirements set out in paragraph 41(iii)–(vii), (ix)–(x) and (xii) and paragraph 51 (ii)–(v); and

(ii)   has produced evidence in the form of a letter on headed notepaper giving a private practice or hospital address from a registered medical practitioner who holds an NHS consultant post or who appears in the Specialist Register of the General Medical Council that provides full details of the:

(a)   nature of the illness;

(b)   proposed or continuing treatment;

(c)   frequency of consultations;

(d)   probable duration of the treatment:

(e)   details of the cost of treatment and confirmation that all expenses are being met; and

(f)   where treatment amounts to private visits to a consultant for a relatively minor ailment, details of the progress being made and;

(iii) has provided evidence that he has met, out of the resources available to him, any costs and expenses incurred in relation to his treatment in the United Kingdom; and

(iv)   has provided evidence that he has sufficient funds available to him in the United Kingdom or if relying on funds from abroad has provided evidence that those funds are fully transferable to the United Kingdom, to meet the likely costs of his treatment and intends to meet those costs; and

(v)   was not last admitted to the United Kingdom under the Approved Destination Status Agreement with China; and

(vi)   must not be in the UK in breach of immigration laws except that any period of overstaying for a period of 28 days or less will be disregarded.

Extension of stay as a visitor for private medical treatment

55.   An extension of stay to undergo or continue private medical treatment may be granted, with a prohibition on employment, study and recourse to public funds, provided the Secretary of State is satisfied that each of the requirements of paragraph 54 is met.

Refusal of extension of stay as a visitor for private medical treatment

56.   An extension of stay as a visitor to undergo or continue private medical treatment is to be refused if the Secretary of State is not satisfied that each of the requirements of paragraph 54 is met.

Parent of a child at school

Requirements for leave to enter or remain as the parent of a child at school

56A. The requirements to be met by a person seeking leave to enter or remain in the United Kingdom as the parent of a child at school are that:

(i)   the parent meets the requirements set out in paragraph 41 (ii)–(xii) (except that the requirement in paragraph 41(v) is to be read as if it were not qualified by paragraph 43A); and

(ii)   (1)   if the child has leave under paragraphs 57 to 62 of these Rules, the child is attending an independent fee paying day school and meets the requirements set out in paragraph 57(i) to (ix), or

        (2)   if the child is a Tier 4 (Child) Student, the child is attending an independent fee paying day school and meets the requirements set out in paragraph 245ZZA (if seeking leave to enter) or 245ZZC (if seeking leave to remain); and

(iii)   the child is under 12 years of age; and

(iv)   the parent can provide satisfactory evidence of adequate and reliable funds for maintaining a second home in the United Kingdom; and

(v)   the parent is not seeking to make the United Kingdom his main home; and

(vi)   the parent was not last admitted to the United Kingdom under the Approved Destination Status Agreement with China; and

(vii)   if seeking leave to remain must not be in the UK in breach of immigration laws except that any period of overstaying for a period of 28 days or less will be disregarded.

Leave to enter or remain as the parent of a child at school

56B.   A person seeking leave to enter or remain in the United Kingdom as the parent of a child at school may be admitted or allowed to remain for a period not exceeding 12 months, subject to a condition prohibiting employment, study and recourse to public funds, provided the Immigration Officer or, in the case of an application for limited leave to remain, the Secretary of State is satisfied that each of the requirements of paragraph 56A is met.

Refusal of leave to enter or remain as the parent of a child at school

56C.   Leave to enter or remain in the United Kingdom as the parent of a child at school is to be refused if the Immigration Officer or, in the case of an application for limited leave to remain, the Secretary of State is not satisfied that each of the requirements of paragraph 56A is met.

Visitors seeking to enter for the purposes of marriage or to enter a civil partnership

Requirements for leave to enter as a visitor for marriage or to enter a civil partnership

56D.   The requirements to be met by a person seeking leave to enter the United Kingdom as a visitor for marriage or civil partnership are that he:

(i)   meets the requirements set out in paragraph 41 (i)–(ix) and (xi)–(xii) (except that the requirement in paragraph 41(v) is to be read as if it were not qualified by paragraph 43A); and

(ii)   can show that he intends to give notice of marriage or civil partnership, or marry or form a civil partnership, in the United Kingdom within the period for which entry is sought; and

(iii)   can produce satisfactory evidence, if required to do so, of the arrangements for giving notice of marriage or civil partnership, or for his wedding or civil partnership to take place, in the United Kingdom during the period for which entry is sought; and

(iv)   holds a valid United Kingdom entry clearance for entry in this capacity.

Leave to enter as a visitor for marriage or civil partnership

56E.   A person seeking leave to enter the United Kingdom as a visitor for marriage or civil partnership may be admitted for a period not exceeding 6 months, subject to a condition prohibiting employment, study and recourse to public funds, provided the Immigration Officer is satisfied that each of the requirements of paragraph 56D is met.

Refusal of leave to enter as a visitor for marriage or civil partnership

56F.   Leave to enter as a visitor for marriage or civil partnership is to be refused if the Immigration Officer is not satisfied that each of the requirements of paragraph 56D is met.

Visitors seeking leave to enter under the Approved Destinations Status (ADS) agreement with China

Requirements for leave to enter as a visitor under the Approved Destination Status Agreement with China ('ADS Agreement')

56G.   The requirements to be met by a person seeking leave to enter the United Kingdom as a visitor under the ADS agreement with China are that he:

  (i)   meets the requirements set out in paragraph 41(ii)–(xii) (except that the requirement in paragraph 41(v) is to be read as if it were not qualified by paragraph 43A); and

  (ii)   is a national of the People's Republic of China; and

  (iii) is genuinely seeking entry as a visitor for a limited period as stated by him, not exceeding 30 days; and

  (iv)   intends to enter, leave and travel within the territory of the United Kingdom as a member of a tourist group under the ADS agreement; and

  (v)   holds a valid ADS agreement visit visa.

Leave to enter as a visitor under the ADS agreement with China

56H.   A person seeking leave to enter the United Kingdom as a visitor under the ADS Agreement may be admitted for a period not exceeding 30 days, subject to a condition prohibiting employment, study and recourse to public funds, provided they hold an ADS Agreement visit visa.

Refusal of leave to enter as a visitor under the ADS agreement with China

56I.   Leave to enter as a visitor under the ADS agreement with China is to be refused if the person does not hold an ADS Agreement visit visa.

Extension of stay as a visitor under the ADS agreement with China

56J.   Any application for an extension of stay as a visitor under the ADS Agreement with China is to be refused.

Student visitors

Requirements for leave to enter as a student visitor

56K.   (1)   The requirements to be met by a person seeking leave to enter the United Kingdom as a student visitor are that he:

  (i)   is genuinely seeking entry as a student visitor for a limited period as stated by him, not exceeding six months; and

  (ii)   has been accepted on a course of study which is to be provided by an institution which is:

  (a)   the holder of a Sponsor licence for Tier 4 of the Points Based System, or

  (b)   the holder of valid accreditation from Accreditation UK, the Accreditation Body for Language Services (ABLS), the British Accreditation Council (BAC) or the Accreditation Service for International Colleges (ASIC), or

  (c)   the holder of a valid and satisfactory full institutional inspection, review or audit by one of the following bodies: Bridge Schools Inspectorate; the Education and Training Inspectorate; Estyn; Education Scotland; the Independent Schools Inspectorate; Office for Standards in Education; the Quality Assurance Agency for Higher Education; the Schools Inspection Service or the Education and Training Inspectorate Northern Ireland, or

  (d)   an overseas Higher Education Institution offering only part of their programmes in the United Kingdom, holding its own national accreditation and offering programmes that are an equivalent level to a United Kingdom degree, or

  (iia)   (a)   is enrolled on a course of study abroad equivalent to at least UK degree level study, and

  (b)   has been accepted by a UK recognised body or a body in receipt of public funding as a higher education institution from the Department for Employment and Learning in Northern Ireland, the Higher Education Funding Council for England, the Higher Education Funding Council for Wales or the Scottish Funding Council to undertake research or research tuition at the UK institution, providing that–

  (c)   the overseas course provider confirms that the research or research tuition is part of or relevant to the course of study mentioned in sub-paragraph (a) above, and

(d)   the student is not to be employed as a sponsored researcher under the relevant Tier 5 Government Authorised Exchange scheme, or under Tier 2 of the Points-Based System, at the UK institution; and

(iii)   intends to leave the United Kingdom at the end of his visit as stated by him; and

(iv)   does not intend to take employment in the United Kingdom; and

(v)   does not intend to engage in business, to produce goods or provide services within the United Kingdom, including the selling of goods or services direct to members of the public; and

(vi)   does not intend to study at a maintained school; and

(vii)   will maintain and accommodate himself and any dependants adequately out of resources available to him without recourse to public funds or taking employment; or will, with any dependants, be maintained and accommodated adequately by relatives or friends; and

(viii)   can meet the cost of the return or onward journey; and

(ix)   is not a child under the age of 18; and

(x)   meets the requirements set out in paragraph 41 (ix)–(xii).

(2)   In sub-paragraph (1) (iia) 'research tuition' means tuition given to the applicant about how to conduct research.

Leave to enter as a student visitor

56L.   A person seeking leave to enter to the United Kingdom as a student visitor may be admitted for a period not exceeding 6 months, subject to a condition prohibiting employment, and recourse to public funds, provided the Immigration Officer is satisfied that each of the requirements of paragraph 56K is met.

Refusal of leave to enter as a student visitor

56M.   Leave to enter as a student visitor is to be refused if the Immigration Officer is not satisfied that each of the requirements of paragraph 56K is met.

Prospective Entrepreneurs

Purpose

56N.   This Special Visitor route is to enable individuals who are at the time of applying for leave under this route in discussions with:

(i)   one or more registered venture capitalist firms regulated by the Financial Conduct Authority, and/or

(ii)   one or more UK entrepreneurial seed funding competitions which is listed as endorsed on the UK Trade & Investment website, and/or

(iii)   one or more UK Government Departments,

to secure funding in order to join, set up or take over, and be actively involved in the running of, a business in the UK.

Requirements for leave to enter as a Prospective Entrepreneur

56O.   The requirements to be met by a person seeking leave to enter the United Kingdom as a Prospective Entrepreneur are that:

(a)   The applicant must provide an original, letter on headed paper signed by an authorised official of that institution supporting the application from:

(i)   one or more registered venture capitalist firms regulated by the financial conduct authority,

(ii)   one or more UK entrepreneurial seed funding competitions which is listed as endorsed on the UK Trade & Investment website, or

(iii)   one or more UK Government Departments;

(b)   The letter referred to in (a) must be dated no earlier than three months before the date of the application, be signed by an authorised official, and contain:

(i)   a description of the nature of the individual(s) and/or organisation(s) supporting the application;

(ii)   a description of the background and nature of the proposed business;

(iii)   a description of the applicant's suitability to be involved with the proposed business;

(iv)   a commitment by the individual(s) and/or organisation(s) supporting the applicant to make a decision whether to make a decision whether to provide a minimum of £50,000 funding for the proposed business within 6 months of the applicant entering the UK. (if more than one individual and/or organisation is supporting the applicant, each amount proposed may be less than £50k, provided that the total amount is a minimum of £50k);

(v)   a commitment by the individual(s) or organisation(s) supporting the applicant that the proposed business will be set up and run from the UK;

(vi)   details of a contact name, telephone number and e-mail address for the individual(s) and/or organisation(s) supporting the applicant; and

(vii) confirmation that the individual(s) and/or organisation(s) supporting the applicant is content to be contacted about the applicant;

(c)   The applicant's primary intention in applying as a Prospective Entrepreneur is to secure funding in order to join, set up or take over, and be actively involved in the running of a business in the UK;

(d)   The applicant intends to carry out one of the activities as listed in paragraph 56O(d)(i), specifying the activities that a Prospective Entrepreneur may undertake during a visit to the UK;

56O(d)(i) The permitted activities are:

(1)   attending meetings, including meetings arranged while in the UK, interviews arranged before arriving in the UK and conferences;

(2)   attending trade fairs provided this is restricted to promotional work and does not involve selling directly to members of the public;

(3)   arranging deals and negotiating or signing trade agreements and contracts;

(4)   conducting site visits;

(5)   speaking at a one-off conference which is not organised as a commercial concern;

(6)   undertaking fact finding missions;

(7)   purchasing, checking the details of or examining goods;

(8)   recruiting staff for the proposed business activity which is the object of the visa

(e)   The applicant intends to leave the United Kingdom at the end of the period of the visit as stated by him, unless he makes a successful application for leave to remain as a Tier 1 (Entrepreneur) Migrant before the end of the period of the visit;

(f)   The applicant will maintain and accommodate himself and any dependants adequately out of resources available to him without recourse to public funds or taking employment; or will, with any dependants, be maintained and accommodated adequately by relatives or friends;

(g)   The applicant does not intend during his visit to:

(i)   take employment in the United Kingdom;

(ii)   produce goods or provide services within the United Kingdom, including the selling of goods or services direct to members of the public;

(iii) undertake a course of study;

(iv) marry or form a civil partnership, or to give notice of marriage or civil partnership; or

(v)   receive private medical treatment.

(h)   The applicant is not under the age of 18;

(i)   The applicant is not in transit to a country outside the common travel area; and

(j)   The applicant holds a valid United Kingdom entry clearance for entry in this capacity.

Leave to enter as a Prospective Entrepreneur

56P.   a person seeking leave to enter to the United Kingdom as a Prospective Entrepreneur may be admitted for a period not exceeding 6 months, subject to a condition prohibiting employment, study and recourse to public funds, provided the secretary of state is satisfied that each of the requirements of paragraph 56O is met.

Refusal of leave to enter as a Prospective Entrepreneur

56Q.   Leave to enter as a Prospective Entrepreneur is to be refused if the secretary of state is not satisfied that each of the requirements of paragraph 56O is met.

Rules 56R to 56W DELETED.

Visitors undertaking permitted paid engagements

Requirements for leave to enter as a visitor undertaking permitted paid engagements

56X.   The requirements to be met by a person seeking leave to enter the United Kingdom as a visitor undertaking permitted paid engagements are that the applicant:

(i)   is genuinely seeking entry as a visitor undertaking a permitted paid engagement for a limited period, not exceeding one month; and

(ii)   meets the requirements of paragraphs 41(ii), (v), (vii), (viii), (x)–(xii) (except that the requirement in paragraph 41(v) is to be read as if it were not qualified by paragraph 43A); and

(iii)   intends to do one of the following pre-arranged permitted paid engagements which can be evidenced by a formal invitation, and can show that the engagement relates to his or her area of expertise and/or qualifications, and full time occupation overseas:

(a)   examine students and/or participate in or chair selection panels as a visiting academic, who is highly qualified within his or her own field of expertise, invited by a United Kingdom Higher Education Institution or a United Kingdom based research or arts organisation as part of that institution or organisation's quality assurance processes;

(b)   give one or more lectures in his or her field of expertise as a visiting lecturer, invited by a United Kingdom Higher Education Institution or a United Kingdom based research or arts organisation provided this is not in a formal teaching role;

(c)   as an overseas designated pilot examiner, assess United Kingdom based pilots to ensure they meet the national aviation regulatory requirements of other countries, by invitation of an approved training organisation based in the United Kingdom that is regulated by the United Kingdom Civil Aviation Authority for that purpose;

(d)   provide advocacy in a particular area of law as a qualified lawyer for the purposes of a court or tribunal hearing, arbitration or other form of alternative dispute resolution for legal proceedings within the United Kingdom, at the invitation of a client in the United Kingdom or foreign based client;

(e)   undertake an activity relating to the arts, entertainment or sporting professions, by invitation of an arts or sports organisation or broadcaster based in the United Kingdom; and

(iv)   does not intend to take employment, produce goods or provide services within the United Kingdom, including the selling of goods or services direct to members of the public other than as permitted for by the pre-arranged paid engagement; and

(v)   will maintain and accommodate him or herself adequately out of resources available to the applicant without recourse to public funds or taking employment; or will be maintained and accommodated adequately by relatives or friends.

Leave to enter as a visitor undertaking permitted paid engagements

56Y.   A person seeking leave to enter the United Kingdom as a visitor undertaking permitted paid engagements may be admitted for a single entry and for a period not exceeding 1 month, with a condition prohibiting study and recourse to public funds provided the Immigration Officer is satisfied that each of the requirements of paragraph 56X are met.

Refusal of leave to enter as a visitor undertaking permitted paid engagements

56Z.   Leave to enter as a visitor undertaking permitted paid engagements is to be refused if the Immigration Officer is not satisfied that each of the requirements at paragraph 56X are met.

56ZA.–56ZH.   OMITTED

Part 3 – Persons seeking to enter or remain in the United Kingdom for studies

57.–75.   DELETED.

Requirements for leave to enter the United Kingdom to take the PLAB Test

75A.   The requirements to be met by a person seeking leave to enter in order to take the PLAB Test are that the applicant:

(i)   is a graduate from a medical school and intends to take the PLAB Test in the United Kingdom; and

(ii)   can provide documentary evidence of a confirmed test date or of his eligibility to take the PLAB Test by way of a letter or email from the General Medical Council or a test admission card; and

(iii)   meets the requirements of paragraph 41 (iii)–(vii) for entry as a visitor; and

(iv)   intends to leave the United Kingdom at the end of the leave granted under this paragraph unless he is successful in the PLAB Test and granted leave to remain to undertake a clinical attachment in accordance with paragraphs 75G to 75M of these Rules.

Leave to enter to take the PLAB Test

75B.   A person seeking leave to enter the United Kingdom to take the PLAB Test may be admitted for a period not exceeding 6 months subject to a condition prohibiting employment, study and recourse to public funds, provided the Immigration Officer is satisfied that each of the requirements of paragraph 75A is met.

Refusal of leave to enter to take the PLAB Test

75C.   Leave to enter the United Kingdom to take the PLAB Test is to be refused if the Immigration Officer is not satisfied that each of the requirements of paragraph 75A is met.

Requirements for an extension of stay in order to take the PLAB Test

75D.   The requirements for an extension of stay in the United Kingdom in order to take the PLAB Test are that the applicant:

(i)   was given leave to enter the United Kingdom for the purposes of taking the PLAB Test in accordance with paragraph 75B of these Rules; and

(ii)   intends to take the PLAB Test and can provide documentary evidence of a confirmed test date, by way of a letter or email from the General Medical Council or a test admission card; and

(iii)   meets the requirements set out in paragraph 41 (iii)–(vii); and

(iv)   intends to leave the United Kingdom at the end of the leave granted under this paragraph unless he is successful in the PLAB Test and granted leave to remain to undertake a clinical attachment in accordance with paragraphs 75G to 75M of these Rules; and

(v)   would not as a result of an extension of stay spend more than 18 months in the United Kingdom for the purpose of taking the PLAB Test; and

(vi)   must not be in the UK in breach of immigration laws except that any period of overstaying for a period of 28 days or less will be disregarded.

Extension of stay to take the PLAB Test

75E.   A person seeking leave to remain in the United Kingdom to take the PLAB Test may be granted an extension of stay for a period not exceeding 6 months, subject to a condition prohibiting employment, study and recourse to public funds, provided the Secretary of State is satisfied that each of the requirements of paragraph 75D is met.

Refusal of extension of stay to take the PLAB Test

75F.   Leave to remain in the United Kingdom to take the PLAB Test is to be refused if the Secretary of State is not satisfied that each of the requirements of paragraph 75D is met.

Requirements for leave to enter to undertake a clinical attachment or dental observer post

75G.   The requirements to be met by a person seeking leave to enter to undertake a clinical attachment or dental observer post are that the applicant:

(i)   is a graduate from a medical or dental school and intends to undertake a clinical attachment or dental observer post in the United Kingdom; and

(ii)   can provide documentary evidence of the clinical attachment or dental observer post which will:

(a)   be unpaid; and

(b)   only involve observation, not treatment, of patients; and

(iii)   meets the requirements of paragraph 41 (iii)–(vii) of these Rules; and

(iv)   intends to leave the United Kingdom at the end of the leave granted under this paragraph;

(v)   if he has previously been granted leave in this category, is not seeking leave to enter which, when amalgamated with those previous periods of leave, would total more than 6 months.

Leave to enter to undertake a clinical attachment or dental observer post

75H.   A person seeking leave to enter the United Kingdom to undertake a clinical attachment or dental observer post may be admitted for the period of the clinical attachment or dental observer post, up to a maximum of 3 months at a time, or 6 months in total in this category, subject to a condition prohibiting employment, study and recourse to public funds, provided the Immigration Officer is satisfied that each of the requirements of paragraph 75G is met.

Refusal of leave to enter to undertake a clinical attachment or dental observer post

75J.   Leave to enter the United Kingdom to undertake a clinical attachment or dental observer post is to be refused if the Immigration Officer is not satisfied that each of the requirements of paragraph 75G is met.

Requirements for an extension of stay in order to undertake a clinical attachment or dental observer post

75K.   The requirements to be met by a person seeking an extension of stay to undertake a clinical attachment or dental observer post are that the applicant:

(i)   was given leave to enter or remain in the United Kingdom to undertake a clinical attachment or dental observer post or:

(a)   for the purposes of taking the PLAB Test in accordance with paragraphs 75A to 75F and has passed both parts of the PLAB Test;

(b)   as a postgraduate doctor, dentist or trainee general practitioner in accordance with paragraphs 70 to 75; or

(c)   as a work permit holder for employment in the UK as a doctor or dentist in accordance with paragraphs 128 to 135; and

(ii)   is a graduate from a medical or dental school and intends to undertake a clinical attachment or dental observer post in the United Kingdom; and

(iii)   can provide documentary evidence of the clinical attachment or dental observer post which will:

(a)   be unpaid; and

(b)   only involve observation, not treatment, of patients; and

(iv)   intends to leave the United Kingdom at the end of the leave granted under this paragraph; and

(v)   meets the requirements of paragraph 41 (iii)–(vii) of these Rules; and

(vi)   if he has previously been granted leave in this category, is not seeking an extension of stay which, when amalgamated with those previous periods of leave, would total more than 6 months; and

(vii)   must not be in the UK in breach of immigration laws except that any period of overstaying for a period of 28 days or less will be disregarded.

Extension of stay to undertake a clinical attachment or dental observer post

75L.   A person seeking leave to remain in the United Kingdom to undertake a clinical attachment or dental observer post up to a maximum of 3 months at a time or 6 months in total in this category, subject to a condition prohibiting employment, study and recourse to public funds, may be granted an extension of stay for the period of their clinical attachment or dental observer post, provided that the Secretary of State is satisfied that each of the requirements of paragraph 75K is met.

Refusal of extension of stay to undertake a clinical attachment or dental observer post

75M.   Leave to remain in the United Kingdom to undertake a clinical attachment or dental observer post is to be refused if the Secretary of State is not satisfied that each of the requirements of paragraph 75K is met.

Spouses or civil partners of students or prospective students granted leave under this part of the Rules

Requirements for leave to enter or remain as the spouse or civil partner of a student and for leave to remain as the spouse or civil partner of a prospective student

76.   The requirements to be met by a person seeking leave to enter or remain in the United Kingdom as the spouse or civil partner of a student or leave to remain as the spouse or civil partner of a prospective student are that:

(i)   the applicant is married to or the civil partner of a person admitted to or allowed to remain in the United Kingdom under paragraphs 57–75 or 82–87F; and

(ii) each of the parties intends to live with the other as his or her spouse or civil partner during the applicant's stay and the marriage or the civil partner of is subsisting; and

(iii) there will be adequate accommodation for the parties and any dependants without recourse to public funds; and

(iv) the parties will be able to maintain themselves and any dependants adequately without recourse to public funds; and

(v) the applicant does not intend to take employment except as permitted under paragraph 77 below; and

(vi) the applicant intends to leave the United Kingdom at the end of any period of leave granted to him; and

(vii) if seeking leave to remain must not be in the UK in breach of immigration laws except that any period of overstaying for a period of 28 days or less will be disregarded.

Leave to enter or remain as the spouse or civil partner of a student or leave to remain as the spouse or civil partner of a prospective student

77. A person seeking leave to enter or remain in the United Kingdom as the spouse or civil partner of a student or leave to remain as the spouse or civil partner of a prospective student may be admitted or allowed to remain for a period not in excess of that granted to the student or prospective student provided the Immigration Officer or, in the case of an application for limited leave to remain, the Secretary of State is satisfied that each of the requirements of paragraph 76 is met. Employment may be permitted where the period of leave granted to the student or prospective student is, or was, 12 months or more.

Refusal of leave to enter or remain as the spouse or civil partner of a student or leave to remain as the spouse or civil partner of a prospective student

78. Leave to enter or remain as the spouse or civil partner of a student or leave to remain as the spouse or civil partner of a prospective student is to be refused if the Immigration Officer or, in the case of an application for limited leave to remain, the Secretary of State is not satisfied that each of the requirements of paragraph 76 is met.

Children of students or prospective students granted leave under this part of the Rules

Requirements for leave to enter or remain as the child of a student and for leave to remain as the child of a prospective student

79. The requirements to be met by a person seeking leave to enter or remain in the United Kingdom as the child of a student or leave to remain as the child of a prospective student are that he:

(i) is the child of a parent admitted to or allowed to remain in the United Kingdom as a student or prospective student under paragraphs 57–75 or 82–87F; and

(ii) is under the age of 18 or has current leave to enter or remain in this capacity; and

(iii) is not married or in a civil partnership, has not formed an independent family unit and is not leading an independent life; and

(iv) can, and will, be maintained and accommodated adequately without recourse to public funds; and

(v) will not stay in the United Kingdom beyond any period of leave granted to his parent; and

(vi) meets the requirements of paragraph 79A; and

(vii) if seeking leave to remain must not be in the UK in breach of immigration laws except that any period of overstaying for a period of 28 days or less will be disregarded.

79A. Both of the applicant's parents must either be lawfully present in the UK, or being granted entry clearance or leave to remain at the same time as the applicant or one parent must be lawfully present in the UK and the other being granted entry clearance or leave to remain at the same time as the applicant, unless:

(i) The student or prospective student is the applicant's sole surviving parent, or

(ii) The student or prospective student parent has and has had sole responsibility for the applicant's upbringing, or

(iii) there are serious or compelling family or other considerations which would make it desirable not to refuse the application and suitable arrangements have been made in the UK for the applicant's care.

Leave to enter or remain as the child of a student or leave to remain as the child of a prospective student

80.   A person seeking leave to enter or remain in the United Kingdom as the child of a student or leave to remain as the child of a prospective student may be admitted or allowed to remain for a period not in excess of that granted to the student or prospective student provided the Immigration Officer or, in the case of an application for limited leave to remain, the Secretary of State is satisfied that each of the requirements of paragraph 79 is met. Employment may be permitted where the period of leave granted to the student or prospective student is, or was, 12 months or more.

Refusal of leave to enter or remain as the child of a student or prospective student

81.   Leave to enter or remain in the United Kingdom as the child of a student or leave to remain as the child of a prospective student is to be refused if the Immigration Officer or, in the case of an application for limited leave to remain, the Secretary of State, is not satisfied that each of the requirements of paragraph 79 is met.

Prospective students

A82.   In this Part 'prospective student' means a person who was granted leave to enter as a prospective student under paragraph 83 as it was at 30 September 2013 (and see further Part 5 of Appendix F to these Rules).

82–84.   DELETED.

Requirements for extension of stay as a prospective student

85.   Six months is the maximum permitted leave which may be granted to a prospective student. The requirements for an extension of stay as a prospective student are that the applicant:

    (i)   was admitted to the United Kingdom with a valid prospective student entry clearance; and

    (ii)   meets the requirements of paragraph 82; and

    (iii)   would not, as a result of an extension of stay, spend more than 6 months in the United Kingdom; and

    (iv)   must not be in the UK in breach of immigration laws except that any period of overstaying for a period of 28 days or less will be disregarded.

Extension of stay as a prospective student

86.   An extension of stay as a prospective student may be granted, with a prohibition on employment, provided the Secretary of State is satisfied that each of the requirements of paragraph 85 is met.

Refusal of extension of stay as a prospective student

87.   An extension of stay as a prospective student is to be refused if the Secretary of State is not satisfied that each of the requirements of paragraph 85 is met.

87A.–87F.   DELETED.

Part 4 – OMITTED

Part 5 – Persons seeking to enter or remain in the United Kingdom for employment

128A.–143F.   OMITTED

Representatives of overseas businesses

Requirements for leave to enter as a representative of an overseas business

144.   The requirements to be met by a person seeking leave to enter the United Kingdom as a representative of an overseas business are that he:

    (i)   has been recruited and taken on as an employee outside the United Kingdom of a business which has its headquarters and principal place of business outside the United Kingdom; and

    (ii)   is seeking entry to the United Kingdom:

        (a)   as a senior employee of an overseas business which has no branch, subsidiary or other representative in the United Kingdom with full authority to take operational decisions on behalf of the overseas business for the purpose of representing it in the United Kingdom by establishing and operating a registered branch or wholly owned subsidiary of that overseas business, the branch or subsidiary of which will be concerned with same type of business activity as the overseas business; or

    (b)   as an employee of an overseas newspaper, news agency or broadcasting organisation being posted on a long-term assignment as a representative of their overseas employer.

(iii)   where entry is sought under (ii)(a), the person:

    (a)   will be the sole representative of the employer present in the United Kingdom under the terms of this paragraph;

    (b)   intends to be employed full time as a representative of that overseas business; and

    (c)   is not a majority shareholder in that overseas business.

(iv)   where entry is sought under (ii)(b), the person intends to work full-time as a representative of their overseas employer.

(v)   does not intend to take employment except within the terms of this paragraph; and

(vi)   has competence in the English language to the required standard on the basis that

    (a)   the applicant is a national of one of the following countries: Antigua and Barbuda; Australia; the Bahamas; Barbados; Belize; Canada; Dominica; Grenada; Guyana; Jamaica; New Zealand; St Kitts and Nevis; St Lucia; St Vincent and the Grenadines; Trinidad and Tobago; United States of America; and provides the specified documents in paragraph 144-SD(a) or

    (b)   the applicant has a knowledge of English equivalent to level A1 or above of the Council of Europe's Common European Framework for Language Learning, and

        (1)   provides the specified documents from an English language test provider approved by the Secretary of State for these purposes, as listed in Appendix O, which clearly show the applicant's name, the qualification obtained (which must meet or exceed the standard described above) and the date of the award, or

        (2)   has obtained an academic qualification (not a professional or vocational qualification) which is deemed by UK NARIC to meet the recognised standard of a Bachelor's degree in the UK, and

            (i)   provides the specified documents in paragraph 144-SD(b) to show he has the qualification, and

            (ii)   UK NARIC has confirmed that the qualification was taught or researched in English to level C1 of the Council of Europe's Common European Framework for Language learning or above, or

        (3)   has obtained an academic qualification (not a professional or vocational qualification) which is deemed by UK NARIC to meet or exceed the recognised standard of a Bachelor's or Master's degree in the UK, and provides the specified documents in paragraph 144-SD(c) to show that:

            (i)   he has the qualification, and

            (ii)   the qualification was taught or researched in English, or

        (4)   has obtained an academic qualification (not a professional or vocational qualification), which is deemed by UK NARIC to meet the recognised standard of a Bachelor's or Master's degree or PhD in the UK, from an educational establishment in one of the following countries: Antigua and Barbuda; Australia; The Bahamas; Barbados; Belize; Dominica; Grenada; Guyana; Ireland; Jamaica; New Zealand; St Kitts and Nevis; St Lucia; St Vincent and The Grenadines; Trinidad and Tobago; the UK; the USA; and provides the specified documents in paragraph 144-SD(b).

(vii)   can maintain and accommodate himself and any dependants adequately without recourse to public funds; and

(viii)   holds a valid United Kingdom entry clearance for entry in this capacity.

Specified documents

144-SD.   (a)   The specified documents in paragraph 144(vi)(a) as evidence of nationality are the applicant's current valid original passport or travel document. If the applicant is unable to provide these, the UK Border Agency may exceptionally consider this requirement to have been met where the applicant provides full reasons in the passport section of the application form, and either:

(1)   a current national identity document, or

(2)   an original letter from his home government or embassy, on the letter-headed paper of the government or embassy, which has been issued by an authorised official of that institution and confirms the applicant's full name, date of birth and nationality.

(b)   The specified documents in paragraph 144(vi)(b)(2)(i) and paragraph 144(vi)(4) as evidence of qualifications taught in English are:

(1)   the original certificate of the award, or

(2)   if the applicant is awaiting graduation having successfully completed the qualification, or no longer has the certificate and the awarding institution is unable to provide a replacement, an academic transcript (or original letter in the case of a PhD qualification) from the awarding institution on its official headed paper, which clearly shows:

(a)   the applicant's name,

(b)   the name of the awarding institution,

(c)   the title of the award,

(d)   confirmation that the qualification has been or will be awarded, and

(e)   the date that the certificate will be issued (if the applicant has not yet graduated) or confirmation that the institution is unable to reissue the original certificate or award.

(c)   The specified documents in paragraph 144(vi)(b)(3)(i) as evidence of qualifications taught in English are:

(1)   the specified documents in (b) above, and

(2)   an original letter from the awarding institution on its official headed paper, which clearly shows:

(a)   the applicant's name,

(b)   the name of the awarding institution,

(c)   the title of the award,

(d)   the date of the award, and

(e)   confirmation that the qualification was taught in English.

Leave to enter as a representative of an overseas business

145.   A person seeking leave to enter the United Kingdom as a representative of an overseas business may be admitted for a period not exceeding 3 years provided he is able to produce to the Immigration Officer, on arrival, a valid United Kingdom entry clearance for entry in this capacity, and his leave may be subject to the following conditions:

(i)   no recourse to public funds,

(ii)   registration with the police, if this is required by paragraph 326 of these Rules, and

(iii)   no employment other than working for the business which the applicant has been admitted to represent.

Refusal of leave to enter as a representative of an overseas business

146.   Leave to enter as a representative of an overseas business is to be refused if a valid United Kingdom entry clearance for entry in this capacity is not produced to the Immigration Officer on arrival.

Requirements for an extension of stay as a representative of an overseas business

147.   The requirements for an extension of stay as a representative of an overseas business are that the applicant:

(i)   entered the United Kingdom with a valid United Kingdom entry clearance as:

(a)   a sole representative of an overseas business, including entry under the rules providing for the admission of sole representatives in force prior to 1 October 2009; or

(b)   a representative of an overseas newspaper, news agency or broadcasting organisation;

(ii)   the person was admitted in accordance with paragraph 144(ii)(a) and can show that:

(a)   the overseas business still has its headquarters and principal place of business outside the United Kingdom; and

(b)   he is employed full time as a representative of that overseas business and has established and is in charge of its registered branch or wholly owned subsidiary; and

      (c)   he is still required for the employment in question, as certified by his employer;

(iii)   the person was admitted in accordance with paragraph 144(ii)(b) and can show that:

      (a)   he is still engaged in the employment for which the entry clearance was granted; and

      (b)   he is still required for the employment in question, as certified by his employer.

(iv)   does not intend to take employment except within the terms of this paragraph; and

(v)   can maintain and accommodate himself and any dependants adequately without recourse to public funds; and

(vi)   must not be in the UK in breach of immigration laws except that any period of overstaying for a period of 28 days or less will be disregarded.

Extension of stay as a representative of an overseas business

148.   An extension of stay as a representative of an overseas business may be granted provided the Secretary of State is satisfied that each of the requirements of paragraph 147 is met. The extension of stay will be granted for:

(i)   a period not exceeding 2 years, unless paragraph (ii) applies.

(ii)   a period not exceeding 3 years, if the applicant was last granted leave prior to 1 October 2009, and will be subject to the following conditions:

      (i)   no recourse to public funds,

      (ii)   registration with the police, if this is required by paragraph 326 of these Rules, and

      (iii)   no employment other than working for the business which the applicant has been admitted to represent.

Refusal of extension of stay as a representative of an overseas business

149.   An extension of stay as a representative of an overseas business is to be refused if the Secretary of State is not satisfied that each of the requirements of paragraph 147 is met.

Indefinite leave to remain for a representative of an overseas business

150.   Indefinite leave to remain may be granted, on application, to a representative of an overseas business provided the applicant:

(i)   has spent a continuous period of 5 years lawfully in the United Kingdom in this capacity; and

(ii)   has met the requirements of paragraph 147 throughout the 5 year period; and

(iii)   is still required for the employment in question, as certified by the employer; and

(iv)   has demonstrated sufficient knowledge of the English language and sufficient knowledge about life in the United Kingdom, in accordance with Appendix KoLL, and

(v)   does not fall for refusal under the general grounds for refusal; and

(vi)   is not in the UK in breach of immigration laws except that any period of overstaying for a period of 28 days or less will be disregarded; and

(vii)   provides the specified documents in paragraph 150-SD to evidence the reason for the absences set out in paragraph 128A.

Specified documents

150-SD.   The specified documents referred to in paragraph 150(vii) are:

(a)   A letter from the employer detailing the purpose and period of absences in connection with the employment, including periods of annual leave.

(b)   Where the absence was due to a serious or compelling reason, a personal letter from the applicant which includes full details of the reason for the absences and all original supporting documents in relation to those reasons – e.g. medical certificates, birth/death certificates, information about the reasons which led to the absence from the UK.

Refusal of indefinite leave to remain for a sole representative of an overseas business

151.   Indefinite leave to remain in the United Kingdom for a representative of an overseas business is to be refused if the Secretary of State is not satisfied that each of the requirements of paragraph 150 is met.

152–185.   OMITTED

Persons with United Kingdom ancestry

Requirements for leave to enter on the grounds of United Kingdom ancestry

186.   The requirements to be met by a person seeking leave to enter the United Kingdom on the grounds of his United Kingdom ancestry are that he:

(i)   is a Commonwealth citizen; and

(ii)   is aged 17 or over; and

(iii)   is able to provide proof that one of his grandparents was born in the United Kingdom and Islands and that any such grandparent is the applicant's blood grandparent or grandparent by reason of an adoption recognised by the laws of the United Kingdom relating to adoption; and

(iv)   is able to work and intends to take or seek employment in the United Kingdom; and

(v)   will be able to maintain and accommodate himself and any dependants adequately without recourse to public funds; and

(vi)   holds a valid United Kingdom entry clearance for entry in this capacity.

Leave to enter the United Kingdom on the grounds of United Kingdom ancestry

187.   A person seeking leave to enter the United Kingdom on the grounds of his United Kingdom ancestry may be given leave to enter for a period not exceeding 5 years provided he is able to produce to the Immigration Officer, on arrival, a valid United Kingdom entry clearance for entry in this capacity.

Refusal of leave to enter on the grounds of United Kingdom ancestry

188.   Leave to enter the United Kingdom on the grounds of United Kingdom ancestry is to be refused if a valid United Kingdom entry clearance for entry in this capacity is not produced to the Immigration Officer on arrival.

Requirements for an extension of stay on the grounds of United Kingdom ancestry

189.   The requirements to be met by a person seeking an extension of stay on the grounds of United Kingdom ancestry are that:

(i)   he is able to meet each of the requirements of paragraph 186 (i)–(v); and

(ii)   he was admitted to the United Kingdom on the grounds of United Kingdom ancestry in accordance with paragraphs 186 to 188 or has been granted an extension of stay in this capacity; and

(iii)   he is not in the UK in breach of immigration laws except that any period of overstaying for a period of 28 days or less will be disregarded.

Extension of stay on the grounds of United Kingdom ancestry

190.   An extension of stay on the grounds of United Kingdom ancestry may be granted for a period not exceeding 5 years provided the Secretary of State is satisfied that each of the requirements of paragraph 189 is met.

Refusal of extension of stay on the grounds of United Kingdom ancestry

191.   An extension of stay on the grounds of United Kingdom ancestry is to be refused if the Secretary of State is not satisfied that each of the requirements of paragraph 189 is met.

Indefinite leave to remain on the grounds of United Kingdom ancestry

192.   Indefinite leave to remain may be granted, on application, to a Commonwealth citizen with a United Kingdom born grandparent provided the applicant:

(i)   meets the requirements of paragraph 186 (i)–(v); and

(ii)   has spent a continuous period of 5 years lawfully in the United Kingdom in this capacity; and

(iii)   has demonstrated sufficient knowledge of the English language and sufficient knowledge about life in the United Kingdom, in accordance with Appendix KoLL; and

(iv)   does not fall for refusal under the general grounds for refusal; and

(v)   is not in the UK in breach of immigration laws except that any period of overstaying for a period of 28 days or less will be disregarded; and

(vi)   provides the specified documents in paragraph 192-SD to evidence the reason for the absences set out in paragraph 128A, where the absence was due to a serious or compelling reason.

Specified documents

192-SD.   The specified documents referred to in paragraph 192(vi) are:

A personal letter from the applicant which includes full details of the reason for the absences and all original supporting documents in relation to those reasons e.g. medical certificates, birth/death certificates, information about the reasons which led to the absence from the UK.

Refusal of indefinite leave to remain on the grounds of United Kingdom ancestry

193.   Indefinite leave to remain in the United Kingdom on the grounds of a United Kingdom born grandparent is to be refused if the Secretary of State is not satisfied that each of the requirements of paragraph 192 is met.

Partners of persons who have or have had leave to enter or remain under paragraphs 128–193 (but not paragraphs 135I–135K)

193A.   Nothing in paragraphs 194–196F is to be construed as allowing a person to be granted entry clearance, leave to enter, leave to remain or variation of leave as a partner of a person granted entry clearance or leave to enter under Paragraph 159A where that entry clearance or leave to enter was granted under 159A on or after 6 April 2012.

Requirements for leave to enter as the partner of a person with limited leave to enter or remain in the United Kingdom under paragraphs 128–193 (but not paragraphs 135I–135K)

194.   The requirements to be met by a person seeking leave to enter the United Kingdom as the partner of a person with limited leave to enter or remain in the United Kingdom under paragraphs 128–193 (but not paragraphs 135I–135K) are that:

(i)   the applicant is the spouse, civil partner, unmarried or same-sex partner of a person with limited leave to enter in the United Kingdom under paragraphs 128–193 (but not paragraphs 135I–135K); and

(ii)   if an unmarried or same-sex partner:

(1)   any previous marriage or civil partnership (or similar relationship) by either partner has permanently broken down; and

(2)   the parties are not involved in a consanguineous relationship with one another; and

(3)   the parties have been living together in a relationship akin to marriage or civil partnership which has subsisted for 2 years or more; and

(iii)   each of the parties intends to live with the other as his or her partner during the applicant's stay and the relationship is subsisting; and

(iv)   there will be adequate accommodation for the parties and any dependants without recourse to public funds in accommodation which they own or occupy exclusively; and

(v)   the parties will be able to maintain themselves and any dependants adequately without recourse to public funds; and

(vi)   the applicant does not intend to stay in the United Kingdom beyond any period of leave granted to his partner; and

(vii)   the applicant does not fall for refusal under the general grounds for refusal; and

(viii)   the applicant holds a valid United Kingdom entry clearance for entry in this capacity.

Leave to enter as the partner of a person with limited leave to enter or remain in the United Kingdom under paragraphs 128–193 (but not paragraphs 135I–135K)

195.   A person seeking leave to enter the United Kingdom as the partner of a person with limited leave to enter or remain in the United Kingdom under paragraphs 128–193 (but not paragraphs 135I–135K) may be given leave to enter for a period not in excess of that granted to the person with limited leave to enter or remain under paragraphs 128–193 (but not paragraphs 135I–135K) provided the Immigration Officer is satisfied that each of the requirements of paragraph 194 is met. If the person is seeking leave to enter as the partner of a Highly Skilled Migrant, leave which is granted will be subject to a condition prohibiting Employment as a Doctor or Dentist in Training, unless the applicant has obtained a degree in medicine or dentistry at bachelor's level or above from a UK institution that is a UK recognised or listed body, or which holds a sponsor licence under Tier 4 of the Points Based System and provides evidence of this degree.

Refusal of leave to enter as the partner of a person with limited leave to enter or remain in the United Kingdom under paragraphs 128–193 (but not paragraphs 135I–135K)

196.   Leave to enter the United Kingdom as the partner of a person with limited leave to enter or remain in the United Kingdom under paragraphs 128–193 (but not paragraphs 135I–135K) is to be refused if the Immigration Officer is not satisfied that each of the requirements of paragraph 194 is met.

Requirements for extension of stay as the partner of a person who has or has had leave to enter or remain in the United Kingdom under paragraphs 128–193 (but not paragraphs 135I–135K)

196A.   The requirements to be met by a person seeking an extension of stay in the United Kingdom as the partner of a person who has or has had leave to enter or remain in the United Kingdom under paragraphs 128–193 (but not paragraphs 135I–135K) are that the applicant:

    (i)   is the spouse, civil partner, unmarried or same sex partner of a person who:

        (1)   has limited leave to enter or remain in the United Kingdom under paragraphs 128–193 (but not paragraphs 135I–135K); or

        (2)   has indefinite leave to remain in the United Kingdom or has become a British citizen, and who had limited leave to enter or remain in the United Kingdom under paragraphs 128–193 (but not paragraphs 135I–135K) immediately before being granted indefinite leave to remain; and

    (ii)   meets the requirements of paragraph 194(ii)–(vii); and

    (iii)   was not last granted:

        (1)   entry clearance or leave as a visitor,

        (2)   temporary admission, or

        (3)   temporary release; and

    (iv)   must not be in the UK in breach of immigration laws except that any period of overstaying for a period of 28 days or less will be disregarded.

Extension of stay as the partner of a person who has or has had leave to enter or remain in the United Kingdom under paragraphs 128–193 (but not paragraphs 135I–135K)

196B.   An extension of stay in the United Kingdom as:

    (i)   the partner of a person who has limited leave to enter or remain under paragraphs 128–193 (but not paragraphs 135I–135K) may be granted for a period not in excess of that granted to the person with limited leave to enter or remain; or

    (ii)   the partner of a person who is being admitted at the same time for settlement, or the partner of a person who has indefinite leave to remain or has become a British citizen, may be granted for a period not exceeding 2 years, in both instances, provided the Secretary of State is satisfied that each of the requirements of paragraph 196A is met.

If the person is seeking an extension of stay as the partner, of a Highly Skilled Migrant, leave which is granted will be subject to a condition prohibiting Employment as a Doctor or Dentist in Training, unless the applicant:

    (1)   has obtained a primary degree in medicine or dentistry at bachelor's level or above from a UK institution that is a UK recognised or listed body, or which holds a sponsor licence under Tier 4 of the Points Based System; or

    (2)   has, or has last been granted, entry clearance, leave to enter or leave to remain that was not subject to any condition restricting him from taking employment as a Doctor in Training, and has been employed during that leave as a Doctor in Training; or

    (3)   has, or has last been granted, entry clearance, leave to enter or leave to remain that was not subject to any condition restricting him from taking employment as a Dentist in Training, and has been employed during that leave as a Dentist in Training.

Refusal of extension of stay as the partner of a person who has or has had leave to enter or remain in the United Kingdom under paragraphs 128–193 (but not paragraphs 135I–135K)

196C.   An extension of stay in the United Kingdom as the partner of a person who has or has had leave to enter or remain in the United Kingdom under paragraphs 128–193 (but not paragraphs 135I–135K) is to be refused if the Secretary of State is not satisfied that each of the requirements of paragraph 196A is met.

Requirements for indefinite leave to remain for the partner of a person who has or has had leave to enter or remain in the United Kingdom under paragraphs 128–193 (but not paragraphs 135I–135K)

196D.　The requirements to be met by a person seeking indefinite leave to remain in the United Kingdom as the partner of a person who has or has had leave to enter or remain in the United Kingdom under paragraphs 128–193 (but not paragraphs 135I–135K) are that the applicant:

(i)　is the spouse, civil partner, unmarried or same-sex partner of a person who:

    (1)　has limited leave to enter or remain in the United Kingdom under paragraphs 128–193 (but not paragraphs 135I–135K) and who is being granted indefinite leave to remain at the same time; or

    (2)　is the spouse, civil partner, unmarried or same-sex partner of a person who has indefinite leave to remain in the United Kingdom or has become a British citizen, and who had limited leave to enter or remain in the United Kingdom under paragraphs 128–193 (but not paragraphs 135I–135K) immediately before being granted indefinite leave to remain; and

(ii)　meets the requirements of paragraph 194(ii)–(vii); and

(iii)　has demonstrated sufficient knowledge of the English language and sufficient knowledge about life in the United Kingdom, in accordance with Appendix KoLL; and

(iv)　was not last granted:

    (1)　entry clearance or leave as a visitor,

    (2)　temporary admission, or

    (3)　temporary release; and

(v)　must not be in the UK in breach of immigration laws except that any period of overstaying for a period of 28 days or less will be disregarded.

Indefinite leave to remain as the partner of a person who has or has had leave to enter or remain in the United Kingdom under paragraphs 128–193 (but not paragraphs 135I–135K)

196E.　Indefinite leave to remain in the United Kingdom as the partner of a person who has or has had leave to enter or remain in the United Kingdom under paragraphs 128–193 (but not paragraphs 135I–135K) may be granted provided the Secretary of State is satisfied that each of the requirements of paragraph 196D is met.

Refusal of indefinite leave to remain as the partner of a person who has or has had leave to enter or remain in the United Kingdom under paragraphs 128–193 (but not paragraphs 135I–135K)

196F.　Indefinite leave to remain in the United Kingdom as the partner of a person who has or has had limited leave to enter or remain in the United Kingdom under paragraphs 128–193 (but not paragraphs 135I–135K) is to be refused if the Secretary of State is not satisfied that each of the requirements of paragraph 196D is met.

Children of persons with limited leave to enter or remain in the United Kingdom under paragraphs 128–193 (but not paragraphs 135i–135k)

196G.　Nothing in paragraphs 197–199 is to be construed as allowing a person to be granted entry clearance, leave to enter, leave to remain or variation of leave as the child of a person granted entry clearance or leave to enter under Paragraph 159A where that entry clearance or leave to enter was granted under 159A on or after 6 April 2012.

Requirements for leave to enter or remain as the child of a person with limited leave to enter or remain in the United Kingdom under paragraphs 128–193 (but not paragraphs 135I–135K)

197.　The requirements to be met by a person seeking leave to enter or remain in the United Kingdom as a child of a person with limited leave to enter or remain in the United Kingdom under paragraphs 128–193 (but not paragraphs 135I–135K) are that:

(i)　he is the child of a parent with limited leave to enter or remain in the United Kingdom under paragraphs 128–193 (but not paragraphs 135I–135K) or, in respect of applications for leave to remain only, of a parent who has indefinite leave to remain in the UK but who immediately before that grant had limited leave to enter or remain under those paragraphs; and

(ii)　he is under the age of 18 or has current leave to enter or remain in this capacity; and

(iii)   he is unmarried and is not a civil partner, has not formed an independent family unit and is not leading an independent life; and

(iv)   he can and will be maintained and accommodated adequately without recourse to public funds in accommodation which his parent(s) own or occupy exclusively; and

(v)   he will not stay in the United Kingdom beyond any period of leave granted to his parent(s); and

(vi)   both parents are being or have been admitted to or allowed to remain in the United Kingdom save where:

    (a)   the parent he is accompanying or joining is his sole surviving parent; or

    (b)   the parent he is accompanying or joining has had sole responsibility for his upbringing; or

    (c)   there are serious and compelling family or other considerations which make exclusion from the United Kingdom undesirable and suitable arrangements have been made for his care; and

(vii) if seeking leave to enter, he holds a valid United Kingdom entry clearance for entry in this capacity or, if seeking leave to remain, he was not last granted:

    (1)   entry clearance or leave as a visitor,

    (2)   temporary admission, or

    (3)   temporary release; and

(viii) if seeking leave to remain, must not be in the UK in breach of immigration laws except that any period of overstaying for a period of 28 days or less will be disregarded.

Leave to enter or remain as the child of a person with limited leave to enter or remain in the United Kingdom under paragraphs 128–193 (but not paragraphs 135I–135K)

198.   (a)   A person seeking leave to enter or remain in the United Kingdom as the child of a person with limited leave to enter or remain in the United Kingdom under paragraphs 128–193 (but not paragraphs 135I–135K) may be given leave to enter or remain in the United Kingdom for a period of leave not in excess of that granted to the person with limited leave to enter or remain under paragraphs 128–193 (but not paragraphs 135I–135K) provided that:

    (i)   in relation to an application for leave to enter, he is able to produce to the Immigration Officer, on arrival, a valid United Kingdom entry clearance for entry in this capacity; or

    (ii)   in the case of an application for limited leave to remain, he was not last granted:

        (1)   entry clearance or leave as a visitor,

        (2)   temporary admission, or

        (3)   temporary release,

    and is able to satisfy the Secretary of State that each of the requirements of paragraph 197(i)–(vi) and (viii) is met.

    (b)   A person seeking leave to remain as the child of a parent who has indefinite leave to remain in the UK and who had limited leave under paragraphs 128 – 193 (but not paragraphs 135l–135K) immediately before being granted indefinite leave may be given leave to remain in the UK for a period of 30 months provided he is in the UK with valid leave under paragraph 198 and is able to satisfy the Secretary of State that each of the requirements of paragraph 197(i) and 197 (ii)–(vi) and (viii) is met.

Refusal of leave to enter or remain as the child of a person with limited leave to enter or remain in the United Kingdom under paragraphs 128–193 (but not paragraphs 135I–135K)

198A. Leave to enter or remain in the United Kingdom as the child of a person with limited leave to enter or remain in the United Kingdom under paragraphs 128–193 (but not paragraphs 135I–135K) is to be refused if:

    (i)   in relation to an application for leave to enter, a valid United Kingdom entry clearance for entry in this capacity is not produced to the Immigration Officer on arrival; or

    (ii)   in the case of an application for limited leave to remain, if the applicant was last granted:

        (1)   entry clearance or leave as a visitor,

        (2)   temporary admission, or

        (3)   temporary release,

    or is unable to satisfy the Secretary of State that each of the requirements of paragraph 197(i)–(vi) and (viii) is met.

Requirements for indefinite leave to remain as the child of a person who has or has had leave to enter or remain in the United Kingdom under paragraphs 128–193 (but not paragraphs 135I–135K)

199.   The requirements to be met by a person seeking indefinite leave to remain in the United Kingdom as the child of a person who has or has had leave to enter or remain in the United Kingdom under paragraphs 128–193 (but not paragraphs 135I–135K) are that the applicant:

(i)   is the child of a person who:

(1)   has limited leave to enter or remain in the United Kingdom under paragraphs 128–193 (but not paragraphs 135I–135K) and who is being granted indefinite leave to remain at the same time; or

(2)   has indefinite leave to remain in the United Kingdom and who had limited leave to enter or remain in the United Kingdom under paragraphs 128–193 (but not paragraphs 135I–135K) immediately before being granted indefinite leave to remain; and

(ii)   meets the requirements of paragraph 197(i)–(vi) and (viii); and

(iii)   was not last granted:

(1)   entry clearance or leave as a visitor,

(2)   temporary admission, or

(3)   temporary release; and

(iv)   does not fall for refusal under the general grounds for refusal; and

(v)   must not be in the UK in breach of immigration laws except that any period of overstaying for a period of 28 days or less will be disregarded; and

(vi)   has demonstrated sufficient knowledge of the English language and sufficient knowledge about life in the United Kingdom, in accordance with Appendix KoLL, unless he is under the age of 18 at the date on which the application is made.

Indefinite leave to remain as the child of a person who has or has had leave to enter or remain in the United Kingdom under paragraphs 128–193 (but not paragraphs 135I–135K)

199A.   Indefinite leave to remain in the United Kingdom as the child of a person who has or has had leave to enter or remain in the United Kingdom under paragraphs 128–193 (but not paragraphs 135I–135K) may be granted provided the Secretary of State is satisfied that each of the requirements of paragraph 199 is met.

Refusal of indefinite leave to remain as the child of a person who has or has had leave to enter or remain in the United Kingdom under paragraphs 128–193 (but not paragraphs 135I–135K)

199B.   Indefinite leave to remain in the United Kingdom as the child of a person who has or has had limited leave to enter or remain in the United Kingdom under paragraphs 128–193 (but not paragraphs 135I–135K) is to be refused if the Secretary of State is not satisfied that each of the requirements of paragraph 199 is met.

Part 6 – OMITTED

Part 6A – Points-based system

General requirements for indefinite leave to remain

245AAA.   For the purposes of references in this Part to requirements for indefinite leave to remain, except for those in paragraphs 245BF, 245DF and 245EF:

(a)   'continuous period of 5 years lawfully in the UK' means, subject to paragraphs 245CD, 245GF and 245HF, residence in the United Kingdom for an unbroken period with valid leave, and for these purposes a period shall not be considered to have been broken where:

(i)   the applicant has been absent from the UK for a period of 180 days or less in any of the five consecutive 12 month periods preceding the date of the application for leave to remain;

(ii)   the applicant has existing limited leave to enter or remain upon their departure and return except that where that leave expired no more than 28 days prior to a further application for entry clearance, that period and any period pending the determination of an application made within that 28 day period shall be disregarded; and

(iii) the applicant has any period of overstaying between periods of entry clearance, leave to enter or leave to remain of up to 28 days and any period of overstaying pending the determination of an application made within that 28 day period disregarded.

(b) Except for periods when the applicant had leave as a Tier 1 (General) Migrant, a Tier 1 (Investor) Migrant, a Tier 1 (Entrepreneur) Migrant, a Tier 1 (Exceptional Talent) Migrant, a highly skilled migrant, a Businessperson, an Innovator, an Investor, a self-employed lawyer or a writer, composer or artist, the applicant must have been employed in the UK continuously throughout the five years, under the terms of their Certificate of Sponsorship, work permit or in the employment for which they were given leave to enter or remain, except that any breaks in employment in which they applied for leave as a Tier 2 Migrant, or, under Tier 5 Temporary Worker (International Agreement) Migrant as a private servant in a diplomatic household, where in the latter case they applied to enter the UK before 6 April 2012, to work for a new employer shall be disregarded, provided this is within 60 days of the end of their employment with their previous employer or Sponsor.

(c) Except for periods where the applicant had leave as a Tier 1(Investor) Migrant, a Tier 1(Entrepreneur) Migrant, a Tier 1(Exceptional Talent) Migrant or a highly skilled migrant, any absences from the UK during the five years must have been for a purpose that is consistent with the applicant's basis of stay here, including paid annual leave, or for serious or compelling reasons.

Documents not submitted with applications

245AA. (a) Where Part 6A or any appendices referred to in Part 6A state that specified documents must be provided, the Entry Clearance Officer, Immigration Officer or the Secretary of State will only consider documents that have been submitted with the application, and will only consider documents submitted after the application where they are submitted in accordance with subparagraph (b).

(b) If the applicant has submitted specified documents in which:

(i) Some of the documents in a sequence have been omitted (for example, if one bank statement from a series is missing);

(ii) A document is in the wrong format (for example, if a letter is not on letterhead paper as specified); or

(iii) A document is a copy and not an original document; or

(iv) A document does not contain all of the specified information;

the Entry Clearance Officer, Immigration Officer or the Secretary of State may contact the applicant or his representative in writing, and request the correct documents. The requested documents must be received at the address specified in the request within 7 working days of the date of the request.

(c) Documents will not be requested where a specified document has not been submitted (for example an English language certificate is missing), or where the Entry Clearance Officer, Immigration Officer or the Secretary of State does not anticipate that addressing the omission or error referred to in subparagraph (b) will lead to a grant because the application will be refused for other reasons.

(d) If the applicant has submitted a specified document:

(i) in the wrong format; or

(ii) which is a copy and not an original document; or

(iii) which does not contain all of the specified information, but the missing information is verifiable from:

(1) other documents submitted with the application,

(2) the website of the organisation which issued the document, or

(3) the website of the appropriate regulatory body;

the application may be granted exceptionally, providing the Entry Clearance Officer, Immigration Officer or the Secretary of State is satisfied that the specified documents are genuine and the applicant meets all the other requirements. The Entry Clearance Officer, Immigration Officer or the Secretary of State reserves the right to request the specified original documents in the correct format in all cases where (b) applies, and to refuse applications if these documents are not provided as set out in (b).

Specified documents for students previously sponsored by an overseas government or international scholarship agency

245A. Where Part 6A of these Rules state that specified documents must be provided to show that a sponsoring government or international scholarship agency has provided its unconditional written consent to the application, the specified documents are original letters, on the official letter-headed paper or stationery of the organisation(s), bearing the official stamp of that organisation and issued by an authorised official of that organisation. The documents must confirm that the organisation gives the applicant unconditional consent to remain in or re-enter the UK for an unlimited time.

Tier 1 (Exceptional Talent) Migrants

Purpose

245B. This route is for exceptionally talented individuals in the fields of science, humanities, engineering and the arts, who wish to work in the UK. These individuals are those who are already internationally recognised at the highest level as world leaders in their particular field, or who have already demonstrated exceptional promise and are likely to become world leaders in their particular area.

Entry to the UK

245BA. All migrants arriving in the UK and wishing to enter as a Tier 1 (Exceptional Talent) Migrant must have a valid entry clearance for entry under this route. If they do not have a valid entry clearance, entry will be refused.

Requirements for entry clearance

245BB. To qualify for entry clearance as a Tier 1 (Exceptional Talent) Migrant, an applicant must meet the requirements listed below. If the applicant meets these requirements, entry clearance will be granted. If the applicant does not meet these requirements, the application will be refused.

Requirements:

(a) The applicant must not fall for refusal under the general grounds for refusal.

(c) The applicant must have a minimum of 75 points under paragraphs 1 to 6 of Appendix A.

(d) an applicant who has, or was last granted, leave as a student or a Postgraduate Doctor or Dentist, a Student Nurse, a Student Writing-Up a Thesis, a Student Re-Sitting an Examination or as a Tier 4 Migrant and:

(i) is currently being sponsored by a government or international scholarship agency, or

(ii) was being sponsored by a government or international scholarship agency, and that sponsorship came to an end 12 months ago or less,

must provide the unconditional written consent of the sponsoring Government or agency to the application and must provide the specified documents as set out in paragraph 245A above to show that this requirement has been met.

Period and conditions of grant

245BC. Entry clearance will be granted for a period of 3 years and 4 months and will be subject to the following conditions:

(i) no recourse to public funds,

(ii) registration with the police, if this is required by paragraph 326,

(iii) no employment as a Doctor or Dentist in Training, and

(iv) no employment as a professional sportsperson (including as a sports coach).

Requirements for leave to remain

245BD. To qualify for leave to remain as a Tier 1 (Exceptional Talent) Migrant, an applicant must meet the requirements listed below. If the applicant meets these requirements, leave to remain will be granted. If the applicant does not meet these requirements, the application will be refused.

Requirements:

(a) The applicant must not fall for refusal under the general grounds for refusal, and must not be an illegal entrant.

(b) The applicant must have a minimum of 75 points under paragraphs 1 to 6 of Appendix A.

(c) If the applicant has, or was last granted, leave as a Tier 1 (Exceptional Talent) Migrant, the applicant must have a minimum of 10 points under paragraphs 1 to 15 of Appendix B.

(d) The applicant must have, or have last been granted, entry clearance, leave to enter or remain as:

(i) a Tier 1 (Exceptional Talent) Migrant,

(ii) a Tier 2 Migrant, or

(iii)   as a Tier 5 (Temporary Worker) Migrant, sponsored in the Government Authorised Exchange sub-category in an exchange scheme for sponsoredresearchers.

(e)   The applicant must not be in the UK in breach of immigration laws except that any period of overstaying for a period of 28 days or less will be disregarded.

Period and conditions of grant

245BE.   (a)   Leave to remain will be granted:

(i)   for a period of 2 years, to an applicant who has, or was last granted, leave as a Tier 1 (Exceptional Talent) Migrant, or

(ii)   for a period of 3 years, to any other applicant.

(b)   Leave to remain under this route will be subject to the following conditions:

(i)   no recourse to public funds,

(ii)   registration with the police, if this is required by paragraph 326,

(iii)   no employment as a Doctor or Dentist in Training, and

(iv)   no employment as a professional sportsperson (including as a sports coach).

Requirements for indefinite leave to remain

245BF.   To qualify for indefinite leave to remain, a Tier 1 (Exceptional Talent) Migrant must meet the requirements listed below. If the applicant meets these requirements, indefinite leave to remain will be granted. If the applicant does not meet these requirements, the application will be refused.

Requirements:

(a)   DELETED

(b)   The applicant must not fall for refusal under the general grounds for refusal, and must not be an illegal entrant.

(c)   The applicant must have spent a continuous period of 5 years lawfully in the UK, with absences from the UK of no more than 180 days in any 12 calendar months during that period, with leave as a Tier 1 (Exceptional Talent) Migrant.

(d)   The applicant must have a minimum of 75 points under paragraphs 1 to 6 of Appendix A.

(e)   The applicant must have demonstrated sufficient knowledge of the English language and sufficient knowledge about life in the United Kingdom, in accordance with Appendix KoLL.

(f)   The applicant must not be in the UK in breach of immigration laws except that any period of overstaying for a period of 28 days or less will be disregarded.

Tier 1 (General) Migrants

Purpose

245C.   This route is for highly skilled migrants who wish to work, or become self-employed, to extend their stay in the UK.

Requirements for leave to remain

245CA.   To qualify for leave to remain as a Tier 1 (General) Migrant, an applicant must meet the requirements listed below. If the applicant meets these requirements, leave to remain will be granted. If the applicant does not meet these requirements, the application will be refused.

Requirements:

(a)   The applicant must not fall for refusal under the general grounds for refusal, and must not be an illegal entrant.

(b)   if the applicant has, or has had, leave as a Highly Skilled Migrant, as a Writer, Composer or Artist, Self-Employed Lawyer, or as a Tier 1 (General) Migrant under the Rules in place before 19 July 2010, and has not been granted leave in any categories other than these under the Rules in place since 19 July 2010, the applicant must have 75 points under paragraphs 7 to 34 of Appendix A.

(c)   in all cases other than those referred to in (b) above, the applicant must have 80 points under paragraphs 7 to 34 of Appendix A.

(d)   The applicant must have 10 points under paragraphs 1 to 15 of Appendix B.

(e)   The applicant must have 10 points under paragraphs 1 to 3 of appendix C.

(f)   The applicant must have, or have last been granted, entry clearance, leave to enter or remain:

    (i)   as a Tier 1 (General) Migrant,

    (ii)   as a Highly Skilled Migrant,

    (iii)   as a Writer, Composer or Artist, or

    (iv)   as a self-employed lawyer.

(g)   The applicant must not be in the UK in breach of immigration laws except that any period of overstaying for a period of 28 days or less will be disregarded.

Period and conditions of grant

245CB. (a)   Leave to remain will be granted for a period of 2 years, to an applicant who has, or was last granted, leave as a Tier 1 (General) Migrant under the Rules in place before 6 April 2010.

    (b)   in all other cases, leave to remain will be granted for a period of 3 years.

    (c)   leave to remain under this route will be subject to the following conditions:

        (i)   no recourse to public funds,

        (ii)   registration with the police, if this is required by paragraph 326, and

        (iii)   no Employment as a Doctor or Dentist in Training, unless the applicant:

            (1)   has obtained a primary degree in medicine or dentistry at bachelor's level or above from a UK institution that is a UK recognised or listed body, or which holds a sponsor licence under Tier 4 of the Points Based System, and provides evidence of this degree; or

            (2)   has, or has last been granted, entry clearance, leave to enter or leave to remain that was not subject to any condition restricting him from taking employment as a Doctor in Training, has been employed during that leave as a Doctor in Training, and provides a letter from the Postgraduate Deanery or NHS Trust employing them which confirms that they have been working in a post or programme that has been approved by the General Medical Council as a training programme or post; or

            (3)   has, or has last been granted, entry clearance, leave to enter or leave to remain that was not subject to any condition restricting him from taking employment as a Dentist in Training, has been employed during that leave as a Dentist in Training, and provides a letter from the Postgraduate Deanery or NHS Trust employing them which confirms that they have been working in a post or programme that has been approved by the Joint Committee for Postgraduate Training in Dentistry as a training programme or post.

                (1)   has obtained a primary degree in medicine or dentistry at bachelor's level or above from a UK institution that is a UK recognised or listed body, or which holds a sponsor licence under Tier 4 of the Points Based system;

                (2)   has, or has last been granted, entry clearance, leave to enter or leave to remain that was not subject to any condition restricting him from taking employment as a Doctor in Training, and has been employed during that leave as a Doctor in Training; or

                (3)   has, or has last been granted, entry clearance, leave to enter or leave to remain that was not subject to any condition restricting him from taking employment as a dentist in Training, and has been employed during that leave as a Dentist in Training,

        (iv)   no employment as a professional sportsperson (including as a sports coach).

Requirements for indefinite leave to remain

245CD. To qualify for indefinite leave to remain, a Tier 1 (General) Migrant must meet the requirements listed below. If the applicant meets these requirements, indefinite leave to remain will be granted. If the applicant does not meet these requirements, the application will be refused.

Requirements:

(a)   DELETED

(b)   The applicant must not fall for refusal under the general grounds for refusal, and must not be an illegal entrant.

(c)   Unless the application is being made under the terms set out in Appendix S, the applicant must have spent a continuous period of 5 years lawfully in the UK, of which the most recent period must have been spent with leave as a Tier 1 (General) Migrant, in any combination of the following categories:

(i)   as a Tier 1 (General) Migrant,

(ii)   as a Highly Skilled Migrant,

(iii)   as a Work Permit Holder,

(iv)   as an innovator,

(v)   as a Self-Employed Lawyer,

(vi)   as a Writer, Composer or Artist,

(vii)   as a Tier 2 (General) Migrant, a Tier 2 (Minister of Religion) Migrant or a Tier 2 (Sportsperson) Migrant, or

(viii)   as a Tier 2 (Intra-Company Transfer) Migrant, provided the continuous period of 5 years spent lawfully in the UK includes a period of leave as a Tier 2 (Intra-Company Transfer) Migrant granted under the Rules in place before 6 April 2010, or as a Work Permit Holder where the work permit was granted because the applicant was the subject of an Intra-Company Transfer.

(d)   if the applicant has or has had leave as a Highly skilled Migrant, a Writer, Composer or artist, a self-employed lawyer or as a Tier 1 (General) Migrant under the Rules in place before 19 July 2010, and has not been granted leave in any categories other than these under the Rules in place since 19 July 2010, the applicant must have 75 points under paragraphs 7 to 34 of Appendix A.

(e)   Where the application is being made under the terms set out in Appendix S, the applicant must have a continuous period of 4 years lawful leave in the UK, or 5 years lawful leave in the UK if the applicant applied to the HSMP between 3 April 2006 and 7 November 2006, received an approval letter and came to or stayed in the United Kingdom on the basis of that letter, of which the most recent must have been spent with leave as a Tier 1 (General) Migrant, in any combination of the following categories:

(i)   as a Tier 1 (General) Migrant;

(ii)   as a Highly Skilled Migrant;

(iii)   as a Work Permit Holder; or

(iv)   as an innovator.

(f)   Where the application is being made under the terms set out in Appendix S, the applicant must be economically active in the UK, in employment or self-employment or both.

(g)   in all other cases than those referred to in (d) or (e) above, the applicant must have 80 points under paragraphs 7 to 34 of Appendix A.

(h)   The applicant must have sufficient knowledge of the English language and sufficient knowledge about life in the United Kingdom, in accordance with Appendix KoLL of these Rules unless the applicant is applying under the terms set out in Appendix S.

(i)   The applicant must not be in the UK in breach of immigration laws except that any period of overstaying for a period of 28 days or less will be disregarded.

(j)   The applicant must provide the specified documents in paragraph 245CD-SD to evidence the reason for the absences set out in paragraph 245AAA.

(k)   For the purposes of sub-paragraph (c), time spent with valid leave in the Bailiwick of Guernsey, the Bailiwick of Jersey or the Isle of Man in a category equivalent to those set out in (c)(i) to (viii) may be included in the continuous period of 5 years lawful residence in the UK, provided that:

(i)   the most recent period of leave was granted in the UK as a Tier 1 (General) Migrant; and

(ii)   any period of leave granted in the Bailiwick of Guernsey, the Bailiwick of Jersey or the Isle of Man as a work permit holder or a Tier 2 Migrant was for employment:

(a)   in a job which appears on the list of occupations skilled to National Qualifications Framework level 3 or above (or from 6 April 2011, National Qualifications Framework level 4 or above or from 14 June 2012, National Qualifications Framework level 6 or above), as stated in the Codes of Practice in Appendix J, or

(b)   in a job which appears in the Creative Sector Codes of Practice in Appendix J, or

(c)   as a professional sportsperson (including as a sports coach).

(iii)   In any such case, references to the 'UK' in paragraph 245AAA shall include a reference to the Bailiwick of Guernsey, Bailiwick of Jersey or the Isle of Man, as the case may be.

(l)   For the purposes of paragraph (e), time spent with valid leave in the Bailiwick of Guernsey, the Bailiwick of Jersey and the Isle of Man in a category equivalent to those set out in (e)(i) to (iv) may be included in the continuous period of 4 years (or 5 years as the case may be) lawful residence in the UK, provided that:

    (i)   the most recent period of leave was granted in the UK as a Tier 1 (General) Migrant; and

    (ii)   any period of leave granted in the Bailiwick of Guernsey, the Bailiwick of Jersey or the Isle of Man as a work permit holder or a Tier 2 Migrant was for employment:

        (a)   in a job which appears on the list of occupations skilled to National Qualifications Framework level 3 or above (or from 6 April 2011, National Qualifications Framework level 4 or above or from 14 June 2012, National Qualifications Framework level 6 or above), as stated in the Codes of Practice in Appendix J, or

        (b)   in a job which appears in the Creative Sector Codes of Practice in Appendix J, or

        (c)   as a professional sportsperson (including as a sports coach).

    (iii)   In any such case, references to the 'UK' in paragraph 245AAA shall include a reference to the Bailiwick of Guernsey, Bailiwick of Jersey or the Isle of Man, as the case may be.

Specified documents

245CD-SD.   The specified documents referred to in paragraph 245CD(j) are:

(a)   For periods where the applicant was in employment in the UK, a letter from the employer detailing the purpose and period of absences in connection with the employment, including periods of annual leave.

(b)   For periods where the applicant was self-employed or in business in the UK, or looking for work or setting up in business in the UK, a personal letter from the applicant detailing the purpose and period of absences in relation to those activities.

(c)   A personal letter from the applicant which includes full details of the reason for the absences and all original supporting documents in relation to those reasons – e.g. medical certificates, birth/death certificates, information about the reasons which led to the absence from the UK.

Transitional arrangements

245CE.   This paragraph makes special provision for applicants who on 29 February 2008 are in the UK, or on 1 April 2008 are in India, and who are in the process of applying to become a Highly Skilled Migrant. It will also be relevant to applicants who have, or have last been granted, leave to remain as a Highly Skilled Migrant, and who fall within subparagraph (c) below.

(a)   If an applicant has made an application for entry clearance in India as a Highly Skilled Migrant before 1 April 2008, and the application has not been decided before that date, it will be decided in accordance with the Rules in force on 31 March 2008 as set out in Appendix D.

(b)   If an applicant has made an application for limited leave to remain as a Highly Skilled Migrant before 29 February 2008, and the application has not been decided before that date, it will be decided in accordance with these Rules in force on 28 February 2008 as set out in Appendix D.

(c)   If an applicant has made an application in India for entry clearance on or after 1 April 2008, or has made an application in the UK for limited leave to remain on or after 29 February 2008, and has submitted with that application a valid Highly Skilled Migrant Programme Approval Letter, the applicant will be automatically awarded 75 points under Appendix A and 10 points under Appendix B. The applicant must separately score 10 points under Appendix C.

(ca)   If an applicant has made an application other than in India for entry clearance on or after 30th June 2008, and has submitted with that application a valid Highly Skilled Migrant Programme Approval Letter, the applicant will be automatically awarded 75 points under Appendix A and 10 points under Appendix B. The applicant must separately score 10 points under Appendix C.

(d)   The applicant must not fall for refusal under the general grounds for refusal, and must not be an illegal entrant.

(da)   The applicant must not be in the UK in breach of immigration laws except that any period of overstaying for a period of 28 days or less will be disregarded.

(e)   If the requirements are met, leave to remain as a Tier 1 (General) Migrant will be granted for a period of 3 years, subject to the conditions in paragraph 245CB(c) above.

Tier 1 (Entrepreneur) Migrants

Purpose of this route and meaning of business

245D.   (a)   This route is for migrants who wish to establish, join or take over one or more businesses in the UK.

(b)   For the purpose of paragraphs 245D to 245DF and paragraphs 35 to 53 of Appendix A 'business' means an enterprise as:

(i)   a sole trader,

(ii)   a partnership, or

(iii)   a company registered in the UK.

Entry to the UK

245DA.   All migrants arriving in the UK and wishing to enter as a Tier 1 (Entrepreneur) Migrant must have a valid entry clearance for entry under this route. If they do not have a valid entry clearance, entry will be refused.

Requirements for entry clearance

245DB.   To qualify for entry clearance as a Tier 1 (Entrepreneur) Migrant, an applicant must meet the requirements listed below. If the applicant meets those requirements, entry clearance will be granted. If the applicant does not meet these requirements, the application will be refused.

Requirements:

(a)   The applicant must not fall for refusal under the general grounds for refusal.

(b)   The applicant must have a minimum of 75 points under paragraphs 35 to 53 of Appendix A.

(c)   The applicant must have a minimum of 10 points under paragraph 1 to 15 of Appendix B.

(d)   The applicant must have a minimum of 10 points under paragraph 1 to 2 of Appendix C.

(e)   An applicant who has, or was last granted, leave as a Student or a Postgraduate Doctor or Dentist, a Student Nurse, a Student Writing-Up a Thesis, a Student Re-Sitting an Examination or as a Tier 4 Migrant and:

(i)   is currently being sponsored by a government or international scholarship agency, or

(ii)   was being sponsored by a government or international scholarship agency, and that sponsorship came to an end 12 months ago or less,

must provide the unconditional written consent of the sponsoring Government or agency to the application and must provide the specified documents as set out in paragraph 245A above, to show that this requirement has been met.

(f)   Except where the applicant has had entry clearance, leave to enter or leave to remain as a Tier 1 (Entrepreneur) Migrant, a Businessperson or an Innovator in the 12 months immediately before the date of application and is being assessed under Table 5 of Appendix A, the Entry Clearance Officer must be satisfied that:

(i)   the applicant genuinely intends and is able to establish, take over or become a director of one or more businesses in the UK within the next six months;

(ii)   the applicant genuinely intends to invest the money referred to in Table 4 of Appendix A in the business or businesses referred to in (i);

(iii)   that the money referred to in Table 4 of Appendix A is genuinely available to the applicant, and will remain available to him until such time as it is spent by his business or businesses. 'Available to him' means that the funds are:

(1)   in his own possession,

(2)   in the financial accounts of a UK incorporated business of which he is the director, or

(3)   available from the third party or parties named in the application under the terms of the declaration(s) referred to in paragraph 41-SD(b) of Appendix A;

(iv)   that the applicant does not intend to take employment in the United Kingdom other than under the terms of paragraph 245DC;

(g)   In making the assessment in (f), the Entry Clearance Officer will assess the balance of probabilities. The Entry Clearance Officer may take into account the following factors:

(i)   the evidence the applicant has submitted;

(ii)   the viability and credibility of the source of the money referred to in Table 4 of Appendix A;

(iii)   the viability and credibility of the applicant's business plans and market research into their chosen business sector;

(iv)   the applicant's previous educational and business experience (or lack thereof); (v) the applicant's immigration history and previous activity in the UK; and

(vi)   any other relevant information.

(h)   The Entry Clearance Officer reserves the right to request additional information and evidence to support the assessment in (f), and to refuse the application if the information or evidence is not provided. Any requested documents must be received by the UK Border Agency at the address specified in the request within 28 working days of the date of the request.

(i)   If the Entry Clearance Officer is not satisfied with the genuineness of the application in relation to a points-scoring requirement in Appendix A, those points will not be awarded.

(j)   The Entry Clearance Officer may decide not to carry out the assessment in (f) if the application already falls for refusal on other grounds, but reserves the right to carry out this assessment in any reconsideration of the decision.

Period and conditions of grant

245DC.   (a)   Entry clearance will be granted for a period of 3 years and four months and will be subject to the following conditions:

(i)   no recourse to public funds,

(ii)   registration with the police, if this is required by paragraph 326 of these Rules, and

(iii)   no employment other than working for the business(es) the applicant has established, joined or taken over, and

(iv)   no employment as a professional sportsperson (including as a sports coach).

Requirements for leave to remain

245DD.   To qualify for leave to remain as a Tier 1 (Entrepreneur) Migrant under this rule, an applicant must meet the requirements listed below. If the applicant meets these requirements, leave to remain will be granted. If the applicant does not meet these requirements, the application will be refused.

Requirements:

(a)   The applicant must not fall for refusal under the general grounds for refusal, except that paragraph 322(10) shall not apply, and must not be an illegal entrant.

(b)   The applicant must have a minimum of 75 points under paragraphs 35 to 53 of Appendix A.

(c)   The applicant must have a minimum of 10 points under paragraphs 1 to 15 of Appendix B.

(d)   The applicant must have a minimum of 10 points under paragraphs 1 to 2 of Appendix C.

(e)   The applicant who is applying for leave to remain must have, or have last been granted, entry clearance, leave to enter or remain:

(i)   as a Highly Skilled Migrant,

(ii)   as a Tier 1 (General) Migrant,

(iii)   as a Tier 1 (Entrepreneur) Migrant,

(iv)   as a Tier 1 (Investor) Migrant,

(v)   as a Tier 1 (Graduate Entrepreneur) Migrant

(vi)   as a Tier 1 (Post-Study Work) Migrant,

(vii)   as a Businessperson,

(viii)   as an Innovator,

(ix)   as an Investor,

(x)   as a Participant in the Fresh Talent: Working in Scotland Scheme,

(xi)   as a Participant in the International Graduates Scheme (or its predecessor, the Science and Engineering Graduates Scheme),

(xii)   as a Postgraduate Doctor or Dentist,

(xiii)   as a Self-employed Lawyer,

(xiv)   as a Student,

(xv)   as a Student Nurse,

       (xvi)   as a Student Re-sitting an Examination,

       (xvii)   as a Student Writing Up a Thesis,

       (xviii) as a Work Permit Holder,

       (xix)   as a Writer, Composer or Artist,

       (xx)   as a Tier 2 Migrant

       (xxi)   as a Tier 4 Migrant, or

       (xxii)   as a Prospective Entrepreneur

(f)   An applicant who has, or was last granted, leave as a Student or a Postgraduate Doctor or Dentist, Student Nurse, Student Re-Sitting an Examination, a Student Writing-Up a Thesis or as a Tier 4 Migrant and:

       (i)   is currently being sponsored by a government or international scholarship agency, or

       (ii)   was being sponsored by a government or international scholarship agency, and that sponsorship came to an end 12 months ago or less,

    must provide the unconditional written consent of the sponsoring Government or agency to the application and must provide the specified documents as set out in paragraph 245A above, to show that this requirement has been met.

(g)   The applicant must not be in the UK in breach of immigration laws except that any period of overstaying for a period of 28 days or less will be disregarded.

(h)   Except where the applicant has, or was last granted, leave as a Tier 1 (Entrepreneur) Migrant, a Businessperson or an Innovator and is being assessed under Table 5 of Appendix A, the Secretary of State must be satisfied that:

       (i)   the applicant genuinely:

            (1)   intends and is able to establish, take over or become a director of one or more businesses in the UK within the next six months, or

            (2)   has established, taken over or become a director of one or more businesses in the UK and continues to operate that business or businesses; and

       (ii)   the applicant genuinely intends to invest the money referred to in Table 4 of Appendix A in the business or businesses referred to in (i);

       (iii)   that the money referred to in Table 4 of Appendix A is genuinely available to the applicant, and will remain available to him until such time as it is spent by his business or businesses. 'Available to him' means that the funds are:

            (1)   in his own possession,

            (2)   in the financial accounts of a UK incorporated business of which he is the director, or

            (3)   available from the third party or parties named in the application under the terms of the declaration(s) referred to in paragraph 41-SD(b) of Appendix A;

       (iv)   that the applicant does not intend to take employment in the United Kingdom other than under the terms of paragraph 245DE.

(i)   In making the assessment in (h), the Secretary of State will assess the balance of probabilities. The Secretary of State may take into account the following factors:

       (i)   the evidence the applicant has submitted;

       (ii)   the viability and credibility of the source of the money referred to in Table 4 of Appendix A;

       (iii)   the viability and credibility of the applicant's business plans and market research into their chosen business sector;

       (iv)   the applicant's previous educational and business experience (or lack thereof);

       (v)   the applicant's immigration history and previous activity in the UK;

       (vi)   where the applicant has already registered in the UK as self-employed or as the director of a business, and the nature of the business requires mandatory accreditation, registration and/or insurance, whether that accreditation, registration and/or insurance has been obtained; and

       (vii)   any other relevant information.

(j)   The Secretary of State reserves the right to request additional information and evidence to support the assessment in (h), and to refuse the application if the information or evidence is not provided. Any requested documents must be received by the Secretary of State at the address specified in the request within 28 working days of the date of the request.

(k) If the Secretary of State is not satisfied with the genuineness of the application in relation to a points-scoring requirement in Appendix A, those points will not be awarded.

(l) The Secretary of State may decide not to carry out the assessment in (h) if the application already falls for refusal on other grounds, but reserves the right to carry out this assessment in any reconsideration of the decision.

(m) The applicant must, unless he provides a reasonable explanation, comply with any request made by the Secretary of State to attend for interview.

Period, conditions and curtailment of grant

245DE. (a) Leave to remain will be granted:

    (i) for a period of 2 years, to an applicant who has, or was last granted, leave as a Tier 1 (Entrepreneur) Migrant,

    (ii) for a period of 3 years, to any other applicant.

(b) Leave to remain under this route will be subject to the following conditions:

    (i) no recourse to public funds,

    (ii) registration with the police, if this is required by paragraph 326 of these Rules, and

    (iii) no employment, other than working for the business or businesses which he has established, joined or taken over, and

    (iv) no employment as a professional sportsperson (including as a sports coach).

(c) Without prejudice to the grounds for curtailment in paragraph 323 of these Rules, leave to enter or remain granted to a Tier 1 (Entrepreneur) Migrant may be curtailed if:

    (i) within 6 months of the date specified in paragraph (d), the applicant has not done one or more of the following things:

        (1) registered with HM Revenue and Customs as self-employed,

        (2) registered a new business in which he is a director, or

        (3) registered as a director of an existing business, or

    (ii) the funds referred to in the relevant sections of Appendix A cease to be available to him, except where they have been spent in the establishment or running of his business or businesses. 'Spent' excludes spending on the applicant's own remuneration. 'Available to him' means that the funds are:

        (1) in his own possession,

        (2) in the financial accounts of a UK incorporated business of which he is the director, or

        (3) available from the third party or parties named in the application under the terms of the declaration(s) referred to in paragraph 41-SD(b) of Appendix A.

(d) The date referred to in paragraph (c) is:

    (i) the date of the applicant's entry to the UK, in the case of an applicant granted entry clearance as a Tier 1 (Entrepreneur) Migrant where there is evidence to establish the applicant's date of entry to the UK,

    (ii) the date of the grant of entry clearance to the applicant, in the case of an applicant granted entry clearance as a Tier 1 (Entrepreneur) Migrant where there is no evidence to establish the applicant's date of entry to the UK, or

    (iii) the date of the grant of leave to remain to the applicant, in any other case.

(e) Paragraph 245DE(c) does not apply where the applicant's last grant of leave prior to the grant of the leave that he currently has was as a Tier 1 (Entrepreneur) Migrant, a Businessperson or an Innovator.

Requirements for indefinite leave to remain

245DF. To qualify for indefinite leave to remain as a Tier 1 (Entrepreneur) Migrant, an applicant must meet the requirements listed below. If the applicant meets these requirements, indefinite leave to remain will be granted. If the applicant does not meet these requirements, the application will be refused.

Requirements:

(a) DELETED

(b) The applicant must not fall for refusal under the general grounds for refusal, and must not be an illegal entrant.

(c)   The applicant must have a minimum of 75 points under paragraphs 35 to 53 of Appendix A.

(d)   The applicant must have demonstrated sufficient knowledge of the English language and sufficient knowledge about life in the United Kingdom, in accordance with Appendix KoLL.

(e)   The applicant must not be in the UK in breach of immigration laws except that any period of overstaying for a period of 28 days or less will be disregarded.

Tier 1 (Investor) Migrants

Purpose

245E.   This route is for high net worth individuals making a substantial financial investment to the UK.

Entry to the UK

245EA.   All migrants arriving in the UK and wishing to enter as a Tier 1 (Investor) Migrant must have a valid entry clearance for entry under this route. If they do not have a valid entry clearance, entry will be refused.

Requirements for entry clearance

245EB.   To qualify for entry clearance or leave to remain as a Tier 1 (Investor) Migrant, an applicant must meet the requirements listed below. If the applicant meets these requirements, entry clearance will be granted. If the applicant does not meet these requirements, the application will be refused.

Requirements:

(a)   The applicant must not fall for refusal under the general grounds for refusal.

(b)   The applicant must have a minimum of 75 points under paragraphs 54 to 65 of Appendix A.

(c)   An applicant who has, or was last granted, leave as a Student or a Postgraduate Doctor or Dentist, a Student Nurse, a Student Re-Sitting an Examination, a Student Writing-Up a Thesis or as a Tier 4 Migrant and:

(i)   is currently being sponsored by a government or international scholarship agency, or

(ii)   was being sponsored by a government or international scholarship agency, and that sponsorship came to an end 12 months ago or less

must provide the unconditional written consent of the sponsoring Government or agency to the application and must provide the specified documents to as set out in paragraph 245A above, show that this requirement has been met.

Period and conditions of grant

245EC.   (a)   Entry clearance will be granted for a period of 3 years and four months and will be subject to the following conditions:

(i)   no recourse to public funds,

(ii)   registration with the police, if this is required by paragraph 326 of these Rules,

(iii)   no Employment as a Doctor or Dentist in Training, unless the applicant has obtained a primary degree in medicine or dentistry at bachelor's level or above from a UK institution that is a UK recognised or listed body, or which holds a sponsor licence under Tier 4 of the Points Based System, and

(iv)   no employment as a professional sportsperson (including as a sports coach).

Requirements for leave to remain

245ED.   To qualify for leave to remain as a Tier 1 (Investor) Migrant, an applicant must meet the requirements listed below. If the applicant meets these requirements, leave to remain will be granted. If the applicant does not meet these requirements, the application will be refused.

Requirements:

(a)   The applicant must not fall for refusal under the general grounds for refusal, and must not be an illegal entrant.

(b)   The applicant must have a minimum of 75 points under paragraphs 54 to 65 of Appendix A.

(c)   The applicant must have, or have last been granted, entry clearance, leave to enter or remain:

(i)   as a Highly Skilled Migrant,

(ii)   as a Tier 1 (General) Migrant,

(iii)   as a Tier 1 (Entrepreneur) Migrant,

(iv)   as a Tier 1 (Investor) Migrant,

(v)   as a Tier 1 (Post-Study Work) Migrant,

(vi)   as a Businessperson,

(vii)   as an Innovator,

(viii)   as an Investor,

(ix)   as a Student,

(x)   as a Student Nurse,

(xi)   as a Student Re-Sitting an Examination,

(xii)   as a Student Writing Up a Thesis,

(xiii)   as a Work Permit Holder,

(xiv)   as a Writer, Composer or Artist,

(xv)   as a Tier 2 Migrant, or

(xvi)   as a Tier 4 Migrant.

(d)   An applicant who has, or was last granted, leave as a Student Nurse, Student Re-Sitting an Examination, Student Writing-Up a Thesis or as a Tier 4 Migrant and:

(i)   is currently being sponsored by a government or international scholarship agency, or

(ii)   was being sponsored by a government or international scholarship agency, and that sponsorship came to an end 12 months ago or less,

must provide the unconditional written consent of the sponsoring Government or agency to the application and must provide the specified documents as set out in paragraph 245A above, to show that this requirement has been met.

(e)   The applicant must not be in the UK in breach of immigration laws except that any period of overstaying for a period of 28 days or less will be disregarded.

Period, conditions and curtailment of grant

245EE.   (a)   Leave to remain will be granted:

(i)   for a period of 2 years, to an applicant who has, or was last granted, leave as a Tier 1 (Investor) Migrant,

(ii)   for a period of 3 years, to any other applicant.

(b)   Leave to remain under this route will be subject to the following conditions:

(i)   no recourse to public funds,

(ii)   registration with the police, if this is required by paragraph 326 of these Rules,

(iii)   no Employment as a Doctor or Dentist in Training, unless the applicant:

(1)   has obtained a primary degree in medicine or dentistry at bachelor's level or above from a UK institution that is a UK recognised or listed body, or which holds a sponsor licence under Tier 4 of the Points Based System, and provides evidence of this degree; or

(2)   has, or has last been granted, entry clearance, leave to enter or leave to remain that was not subject to any condition restricting him from taking employment as a Doctor in Training, has been employed during that leave as a Doctor in Training, and provides a letter from the Postgraduate Deanery or NHS Trust employing them which confirms that they have been working in a post or programme that has been approved by the General Medical Council as a training programme or post; or

(3)   has, or has last been granted, entry clearance, leave to enter or leave to remain that was not subject to any condition restricting him from taking employment as a Dentist in Training, has been employed during that leave as a Dentist in Training, and provides a letter from the Postgraduate Deanery or NHS Trust employing them which confirms that they have been working in a post or programme that has been approved by the Joint Committee for Postgraduate Training in Dentistry as a training programme or post, and

(iv)   no employment as a professional sportsperson (including as a sports coach).

(c)   Without prejudice to the grounds for curtailment in paragraph 323 of these Rules, leave to enter or remain as a Tier 1 (Investor) Migrant may be curtailed if:

          (i)   within 3 months of the date specified in paragraph (d), the applicant has not invested, or had invested on his behalf, at least £750,000 of his capital in the UK by way of UK Government bonds, share capital or loan capital in active and trading UK registered companies other than those principally engaged in property investment, or

          (ii)   the applicant does not maintain the investment in (i) throughout the remaining period of his leave.

(d)   The date referred to in paragraph (c) is:

          (i)   the date of the applicant's entry to the UK, in the case of an applicant granted entry clearance as a Tier 1 (Investor) Migrant where there is evidence to establish the applicant's date of entry to the UK,

          (ii)   the date of the grant of entry clearance to the applicant, in the case of an applicant granted entry clearance as a Tier 1 (Investor) Migrant where there is no evidence to establish the applicant's date of entry to the UK, or

          (iii)   the date of the grant of leave to remain to the applicant, in any other case.

(e)   Paragraph 245EE(c) does not apply where the applicant's last grant of leave prior to the grant of the leave that he currently has was as a Tier 1 (Investor) Migrant or as an Investor.

Requirements for indefinite leave to remain

245EF.   To qualify for indefinite leave to remain, a Tier 1 (Investor) Migrant must meet the requirements listed below. if the applicant meets these requirements, indefinite leave to remain will be granted. if the applicant does not meet these requirements, the application will be refused.

Requirements:

(a)   DELETED

(b)   The applicant must not fall for refusal under the general grounds for refusal, and must not be an illegal entrant.

(c)   The applicant must have a minimum of 75 points under paragraphs 54 to 65 of Appendix A

(d)   The applicant must have demonstrated sufficient knowledge of the English language and sufficient knowledge about life in the United Kingdom, in accordance with Appendix KoLL.

(e)   The applicant must not be in the UK in breach of immigration laws except that any period of overstaying for a period of 28 days or less will be disregarded.

Tier 1 (Graduate Entrepreneur) Migrants

Purpose of the route and meaning of business

245F.   (a)   This route is for MBA and other UK graduates who have been identified by Higher Education Institutions as having developed genuine and credible business ideas and entrepreneurial skills to extend their stay in the UK after graduation to establish one or more businesses in the UK. It is also for overseas graduates who have been identified by UK Trade and Investment as elite global graduate entrepreneurs to establish one or more businesses in the UK.

        (b)   For the purpose of paragraphs 245F to 245FC and paragraphs 66 to 72 of Appendix A 'business' means an enterprise as:

          (i)   a sole trader,

          (ii)   a partnership, or

          (iii)   a company registered in the UK.

Entry to the UK

245FA.   All migrants arriving in the UK and wishing to enter as a Tier 1 (Graduate Entrepreneur) Migrant must have a valid entry clearance for entry under this route. If they do not have a valid entry clearance, entry will be refused.

Requirements for entry clearance or leave to remain

245FB.   To qualify for entry clearance or leave to remain as a Tier 1 (Graduate Entrepreneur) Migrant, an applicant must meet the requirements listed below. If the applicant meets these requirements, entry clearance or leave to remain will be granted. If the applicant does not meet these requirements, the application will be refused.

Requirements:

(a)   The applicant must not fall for refusal under the general grounds for refusal, and must not be an illegal entrant.

(b)   The applicant must have a minimum of 75 points under paragraphs 66 to 72 of Appendix A.

(c)   The applicant must have a minimum of 10 points under paragraphs 1 to 15 of Appendix B.

(d)   The applicant must have a minimum of 10 points under paragraphs 1 to 2 of Appendix C. 11

(e)   If applying for leave to remain, the applicant must have, or have last been granted, entry clearance, leave to enter or remain:

    (i)   as a Tier 4 Migrant,

    (ii)   as a Student,

    (iii)   as a Student Nurse,

    (iv)   as a Student Re-sitting an Examination,

    (v)   as a Student Writing Up a Thesis,

    (vi)   as a Postgraduate Doctor or Dentist,

    (vii)   as a Tier 1 (Graduate Entrepreneur) Migrant, or

    (viii) as a Tier 2 (General) Migrant.

(f)   An applicant who has, or was last granted, entry clearance or leave to remain as a Tier 2 (General) Migrant must score points from paragraph (b) in the second row of Table 10 of Appendix A.

(g)   The applicant must not have previously been granted entry clearance, leave to enter or remain as a Tier 1 (Post-Study Work) Migrant, a Participant in the Fresh Talent: Working in Scotland Scheme, or a Participant in the International Graduates Scheme (or its predecessor, the Science and Engineering Graduates Scheme).

(h)   The applicant must not previously have been granted leave as a Tier 1 (Graduate Entrepreneur) Migrant on more than 1 occasion.

(i)   An applicant who does not have, or was not last granted, leave to remain as a Tier 1 (Graduate Entrepreneur) Migrant and:

    (i)   is currently being sponsored in his studies by a government or international scholarship agency, or

    (ii)   was being sponsored in his studies by a government or international scholarship agency, and that sponsorship came to an end 12 months ago or less,

must provide the unconditional written consent of the sponsoring government or agency to the application and must provide the specified documents as set out in paragraph 245A above, to show that this requirement has been met.

(j)   The applicant must not be in the UK in breach of immigration laws except that any period of overstaying for a period of 28 days or less will be disregarded.

Period and conditions of grant

245FC.   Entry clearance or leave to remain will be granted for a period of 1 year and will be subject to the following conditions:

    (i)   no recourse to public funds,

    (ii)   registration with the police, if this is required by paragraph 326 of these Rules,

    (iii)   no employment as a Doctor or Dentist in Training, and

    (iv)   no employment as a professional sportsperson (including as a sports coach).

Tier 2 Migrants

Tier 2 (Intra-Company Transfer) Migrants

Purpose of this route and definitions

245G.   This route enables multinational employers to transfer their existing employees from outside the EEA to their UK branch for training purposes or to fill a specific vacancy that cannot be filled by a British or EEA worker. There are four sub-categories in this route:

(i)   Short Term staff: for established employees of multi-national companies who are being transferred to a skilled job in the UK for 12 months or less that could not be carried out by a new recruit from the resident workforce;

(ii)   Long Term staff: for established employees of multi-national companies who are being transferred to a skilled job in the UK which will, or may, last for more than 12 months and could not be carried out by a new recruit from the resident workforce;

(iii)   Graduate Trainee: for recent graduate recruits of multi-national companies who are being transferred to the UK branch of the same organisation as part of a structured graduate training programme, which clearly defines progression towards a managerial or specialist role;

(iv)   Skills Transfer: for overseas employees of multi-national companies who are being transferred to the UK branch of the same organisation in a graduate occupation to learn the skills and knowledge they will need to perform their jobs overseas, or to impart their specialist skills to the UK workforce.

Entry clearance

245GA.   All migrants arriving in the UK and wishing to enter as a Tier 2 (Intra-Company Transfer) Migrant must have a valid entry clearance for entry under this route. If they do not have a valid entry clearance, entry will be refused.

Requirements for entry clearance

245GB.   To qualify for entry clearance as a Tier 2 (Intra-Company Transfer) Migrant, an applicant must meet the requirements listed below. If the applicant meets these requirements, entry clearance will be granted. if the applicant does not meet these requirements, the application will be refused.

Requirements:

(a)   The applicant must not fall for refusal under the general grounds for refusal.

(b)   The applicant must have a minimum of 50 points under paragraphs 73 to 75E of Appendix A.

(c)   The applicant must have a minimum of 10 points under paragraphs 4 to 5 of Appendix C.

(d)   The applicant must not have had entry clearance or leave to remain as a Tier 2 Migrant at any time during the 12 months immediately before the date of the application, unless paragraph (e) below applies.

(e)   Paragraph (d) above does not apply to an applicant who:

    (i)   was not in the UK with leave as a Tier 2 migrant at any time during the above 12-month period, and provides evidence to show this,

    (ii)   is applying under the Long Term Staff sub-category and who has, or last had entry clearance or leave to remain as a Tier 2 (Intra-Company Transfer) Migrant in the Short Term staff, Graduate Trainee or Skills Transfer sub-categories, or under the Rules in place before 6 April 2011, or

    (iii)   will be paid a gross annual salary (as recorded by the Certificate of Sponsorship Checking Service entry, and including such allowances as are specified as acceptable for this purpose in paragraph 75 of Appendix A) of £152,100 or higher.

(f)   an applicant who has, or was last granted, leave as a Student, a Student Nurse, a Student Re-Sitting an Examination, a Student Writing-Up a Thesis, a Postgraduate Doctor or Dentist or a Tier 4 Migrant and:

    (i)   is currently being sponsored by a government or international scholarship agency, or

    (ii)   was being sponsored by a government or international scholarship agency, and that sponsorship came to an end 12 months ago or less,

must provide the unconditional written consent of the sponsoring Government or agency to the application and must provide the specified documents as set out in paragraph 245A above, to show that this requirement has been met.

(g)   The applicant must be at least 16 years old.

(h)   Where the applicant is under 18 years of age, the application must be supported by the applicant's parents or legal guardian, or by one parent if that parent has sole legal responsibility for the child.

(i)   Where the applicant is under 18 years of age, the applicant's parents or legal guardian, or just one parent if that parent has sole responsibility for the child, must confirm that they consent to the arrangements for the applicant's travel to, and reception and care in, the UK.

Period and conditions of grant

245GC. (a) if the applicant is applying as a Tier 2 (Intra-Company Transfer) Migrant in either of the short Term staff or Graduate Trainee sub-categories, entry clearance will be granted for:

    (i) a period equal to the length of the period of engagement plus 1 month, or

    (ii) a period of 1 year, whichever is the shorter.

  (b) if the applicant is applying as a Tier 2 (Intra-Company Transfer) Migrant in the Skills Transfer sub-category, entry clearance will be granted for:

    (i) a period equal to the length of the period of engagement plus 1 month, or

    (ii) a period of 6 months, whichever is the shorter.

  (c) if the applicant is applying as a Tier 2 (Intra-Company Transfer) Migrant in the Long Term Staff sub-category, entry clearance will be granted for:

    (i) a period equal to the length of the period of engagement plus 1 month, or

    (ii) a period of 3 years and 1 month, whichever is the shorter.

  (d) entry clearance will be granted with effect from 14 days before the date that the Certificate of Sponsorship Checking Service records as the start date for the applicant's employment in the UK, unless entry clearance is being granted less than 14 days before that date, in which case it will be granted with immediate effect.

  (e) Entry clearance will be subject to the following conditions:

    (i) no recourse to public funds,

    (ii) registration with the police, if this is required by paragraph 326, and

    (iii) no employment except:

      (1) working for the sponsor in the employment that the Certificate of Sponsorship Checking Service records that the migrant is being sponsored to do, subject to any notification of a change to the details of that employment, other than prohibited changes as defined in paragraph 323AA,

      (2) supplementary employment, and

      (3) voluntary work.

Requirements for leave to remain

245GD. To qualify for leave to remain as a Tier 2 (Intra-Company Transfer) Migrant under this rule, an applicant must meet the requirements listed below. If the applicant meets these requirements, leave to remain will be granted. If the applicant does not meet these requirements, the application will be refused.

Requirements:

  (a) The applicant must not fall for refusal under the general grounds for refusal, and must not be an illegal entrant.

  (b) if the applicant is applying for leave to remain as a Tier 2 (Intra-Company Transfer) Migrant in the Long Term Staff sub-category:

    (i) the applicant must have, or have last been granted, entry clearance, leave to enter or leave to remain as either:

      (1) a Tier 2 (Intra-Company Transfer) Migrant in the Long Term Staff sub-category, or

      (2) a Tier 2 (Intra-Company Transfer) Migrant in the established Staff sub-category under the Rules in place before 6 April 2011, or

      (3) a Tier 2 (Intra-Company Transfer) Migrant granted under the Rules in place before 6 April 2010, or

      (4) a Qualifying Work Permit Holder, provided that the work permit was granted because the applicant was the subject of an Intra-Company Transfer, or

      (5) as a representative of an overseas Business, and

    (ii) the applicant must still be working for the same employer as he was at the time of that earlier grant of leave.

  (c) if the applicant is applying for leave to remain as a Tier 2 (Intra-Company Transfer) Migrant in the Short Term Staff sub-category:

(i)   the applicant must have, or have last been granted, entry clearance, leave to enter or leave to remain as a Tier 2 (Intra-Company Transfer) Migrant in the Short Term Staff sub-category, and

(ii)   the applicant must still be working for the same employer as he was at the time of that earlier grant of leave.

(d)   if the applicant is applying for leave to remain as a Tier 2 (Intra-Company Transfer) Migrant in the Graduate Trainee sub-category:

(i)   the applicant must have, or have last been granted, entry clearance, leave to enter or leave to remain as a Tier 2 (Intra-Company Transfer) Migrant in the Graduate Trainee sub-category, and

(ii)   the applicant must still be working for the same employer as he was at the time of that earlier grant of leave.

(e)   if the applicant is applying for leave to remain as a Tier 2 (Intra-Company Transfer) Migrant in the Skills Transfer sub-category:

(i)   the applicant must have, or have last been granted, entry clearance, leave to enter or leave to remain as a Tier 2 (Intra-Company Transfer) Migrant in the skills Transfer sub-category, and

(ii)   the applicant must still be working for the same employer as he was at the time of that earlier grant of leave.

(f)   in all cases the applicant must have a minimum of 50 points under paragraphs 73 to 75E of Appendix A.

(g)   DELETED.

(h)   The applicant must have a minimum of 10 points under paragraphs 4 to 5 of Appendix C.

(i)   The applicant must be at least 16 years old.

(j)   Where the applicant is under 18 years of age, the application must be supported by the applicant's parents or legal guardian or by one parent if that parent has sole legal responsibility for the child.

(k)   Where the applicant is under 18 years of age, the applicant's parents or legal guardian, or one parent if that parent has sole legal responsibility for the child, must confirm that they consent to the arrangements for the applicant's care in the UK.

(l)   The applicant must not be in the UK in breach of immigration laws except that any period of overstaying for a period of 28 days or less will be disregarded.

Period and conditions of grant

245GE.   (a)   if the applicant is applying for leave to remain as a Tier 2 (Intra-Company Transfer) Migrant in either the Short Term Staff or Graduate Trainee sub-categories, leave to remain will be granted for:

(i)   the length of the period of engagement plus 14 days, or

(ii)   the difference between the period of leave that the applicant has already been granted, beginning with his last grant of entry clearance as a Tier 2 (Intra-Company Transfer) Migrant, and 12 months,

whichever is the shorter. If the calculation of period of leave comes to zero or a negative number, leave to remain will be refused.

(b)   if the applicant is applying for leave to remain as a Tier 2 (Intra-Company Transfer) Migrant in the Skills Transfer sub-category, leave to remain will be granted for:

(i)   the length of the period of engagement plus 14 days, or

(ii)   the difference between the period of leave that the applicant has already been granted, beginning with his last grant of entry clearance as a Tier 2 (Intra-Company Transfer) Migrant, and 6 months,

whichever is the shorter. If the calculation of period of leave comes to zero or a negative number, leave to remain will be refused.

(c)   in the cases set out in paragraph (d) below, leave to remain will be granted for:

(i)   a period equal to the length of the period of engagement plus 14 days, or

(ii)   a period of 3 years plus 14 days,

whichever is the shorter.

(d)   The cases referred to in paragraph (c) are those where the applicant is applying for leave to remain as a Tier 2 (Intra-Company Transfer) Migrant in the Long Term Staff sub-category, and was last granted:

(i)   entry clearance, leave to enter or leave to remain as a Qualifying Work Permit Holder, or

(ii) leave to remain as a Tier 2 (Intra-Company Transfer) Migrant, provided:

(1) he previously had leave as a Qualifying Work Permit Holder,

(2) at some time during that period of leave as a Qualifying Work Permit Holder he was granted leave to remain as a Tier 2 (Intra-Company Transfer) Migrant,

(3) he has not been granted entry clearance in this or any other route since his last grant of leave as a Qualifying Work Permit Holder, and

(4) he is still working for the same employer named on the Work Permit document which led to his last grant of leave as a Qualifying Work Permit Holder.

(e) in the cases set out in paragraph (f) below, leave to remain will be granted for:

(i) a period equal to the length of the period of engagement plus 14 days, or

(ii) a period of 2 years,

whichever is the shorter.

(f) The cases referred to in paragraph (e) are those where:

(i) the applicant is applying for leave to remain as a Tier 2 (Intra-Company Transfer) Migrant in the Long Term Staff sub-category, and

(ii) the applicant previously had leave as a Tier 2 (Intra-Company Transfer)Migrant under the Rules in place before 6 April 2011; and

(iii) the applicant has not been granted entry clearance in this or any other route since the grant of leave referred to in (ii) above; and

(iv) paragraphs (c) to (d) do not apply.

(g) in the cases set out in paragraph (h) below, leave to remain will be granted for:

(i) a period equal to the length of the period of engagement plus 14 days, or

(ii) a period of 2 years, or

(iii) the difference between 9 years and the continuous period immediately before the date of application during which the applicant has had leave as a Tier 2 (Intra-Company Transfer) Migrant, or been in the UK without leave,

whichever is the shorter.

(h) The cases referred to in paragraph (g) are those where:

(i) the applicant is applying for leave to remain as a Tier 2 (Intra-Company Transfer) Migrant in the Long Term Staff sub-category, and

(ii) the Certificate of Sponsorship Checking Service entry records that the applicant's gross annual salary (including such allowances as are specified as acceptable for this purpose in paragraph 75 of Appendix A) to be paid by the Sponsor is £152,100 or higher, and

(iii) paragraphs (c) to (f) do not apply.

(i) if the applicant is applying for leave to remain as a Tier 2 (Intra-Company Transfer) Migrant in the Long Term Staff sub-category and paragraphs (c) to (h) do not apply, leave to remain will be granted for:

(i) a period equal to the length of the period of engagement plus 14 days, or

(ii) a period of 2 years,

(iii) the difference between the period that the applicant has already spent in the UK since his last grant of entry clearance as a Tier 2 (Intra-Company Transfer) Migrant and 5 years, whichever is the shorter. If the calculation of period of leave comes to zero or a negative number, leave to remain will be refused.

(j) in addition to the periods in paragraphs (a) to (i), leave to remain will be granted for the period between the date that the application is decided and the date that the Certificate of Sponsorship Checking Service records as the start date of employment in the UK, provided this is not a negative value.

(i) leave to remain will be granted subject to the following conditions:

(i) no recourse to public funds,

(ii) registration with the police, if this is required by paragraph 326, and

(iii) no employment except:

(1) working for the sponsor in the employment that the Certificate of Sponsorship Checking Service records that the migrant is being sponsored to do, subject to any

notification of a change to the details of that employment, other than prohibited changes as defined in paragraph 323AA,

(2)   supplementary employment, and

(3)   voluntary work.

Requirements for indefinite leave to remain

245GF.   To qualify for indefinite leave to remain as a Tier 2 (Intra-Company Transfer) Migrant, an applicant must meet the requirements listed below. If the applicant meets these requirements, indefinite leave to remain will be granted. if the applicant does not meet these requirements, the application will be refused.

Requirements:

(a)   DELETED

(b)   The applicant must not fall for refusal under the general grounds for refusal, and must not be an illegal entrant.

(c)   The applicant must have spent a continuous period of 5 years lawfully in the UK, of which the most recent period must have been spent with leave as a Tier 2 (Intra-Company Transfer) Migrant, in any combination of the following categories:

(i)   as a Tier 2 (Intra-Company Transfer) Migrant,

(ii)   as a Qualifying Work Permit Holder, or

(iii)   as a representative of an overseas Business.

(d)   The continuous period of 5 years referred to in paragraph (c) must include a period of leave as:

(i)   a Tier 2 (Intra-Company Transfer) Migrant granted under the Rules in place before 6 April 2010, or

(ii)   a Qualifying Work Permit Holder, provided that the work permit was granted because the applicant was the subject of an Intra-Company Transfer.

(e)   The Sponsor that issued the Certificate of Sponsorship that led to the applicant's last grant of leave must:

(i)   still hold, or have applied for a renewal of, a Tier 2 (Intra-Company Transfer) Sponsor licence; and

(ii)   certify in writing that:

(1)   he still requires the applicant for the employment in question, and

(2)   the applicant is paid at or above the appropriate rate for the job as stated in the Codes of Practice in Appendix J, or where the applicant is not paid at that rate only due to maternity, paternity or adoption leave, the date that leave started and that the applicant was paid at the appropriate rate immediately before the leave.

(f)   The applicant provides the specified documents in paragraph 245GF-SD to evidence the sponsor's certification in subsection (e) (ii) and to evidence the reason for the absences set out in paragraph 245AAA.

(g)   The applicant must have sufficient knowledge of the English language and sufficient knowledge about life in the United Kingdom, in accordance with Appendix KoLL.

(h)   The applicant must not be in the UK in breach of immigration laws except that any period of overstaying for a period of 28 days or less will be disregarded.

(i)   For the purposes of sub-paragraph (c), time spent with valid leave in the Bailiwick of Guernsey, the Bailiwick of Jersey or the Isle of Man in a category equivalent to the categories set out in (c)(i) to (iii) above, may be included in the continuous period of 5 years lawful residence, provided that:

(i)   the continuous period of 5 years includes a period of leave as a Tier 2 (Intra-Company Transfer) Migrant granted before 6 April 2010, or a Qualifying Work Permit Holder (provided the work permit was granted because the applicant was the subject of an Intra-Company Transfer); and

(ii)   any period of leave granted in the Bailiwick of Guernsey, the Bailiwick of Jersey or the Isle of Man as a work permit holder or as a Tier 2 Migrant was for employment:

(a)   in a job which appears on the list of occupations skilled to National Qualifications Framework level 3 or above (or from 6 April 2011, National Qualifications Framework level 4 or above or from 14 June 2012, National Qualifications Framework level 6 or above), as stated in the Codes of Practice in Appendix J, or

        (b)   in a job which appears in the Creative Sector Codes of Practice in Appendix J, or

        (c)   as a professional sportsperson (including as a sports coach); and

    (iii)   the most recent period of leave was granted in the UK as a Tier 2 (Intra-Company Transfer) Migrant.

In such cases, references to the 'UK' in paragraph 245AAA shall include a reference to the Bailiwick of Guernsey, Bailiwick of Jersey or the Isle of Man, as the case may be.

Specified documents

245GF-SD.   The specified documents referred to in paragraph 245GF(f) are set out in A, B and C below:

    A.   Either a payslip and a personal bank or building society statement, or a payslip and a building society pass book.

        (a)   Payslips must be:

            (i)   the applicant's most recent payslip,

            (ii)   dated no earlier than one calendar month before the date of the application, and

            (iii)   either:

                (1)   an original payslip,

                (2)   on company-headed paper, or

                (3)   accompanied by a letter from the applicant's Sponsor, on company headed paper and signed by a senior official, confirming the payslip is authentic.

        (b)   Personal bank or building society statements must:

            (i)   be the applicant's most recent statement,

            (ii)   be dated no earlier than one calendar month before the date of the application,

            (iii)   clearly show:

                (1)   the applicant's name,

                (2)   the applicant's account number,

                (3)   the date of the statement,

                (4)   the financial institution's name,

                (5)   the financial institution's logo, and

                (6)   transactions by the Sponsor covering the period no earlier than one calendar month before the date of the application, including the amount shown on the specified payslip as at 245GF-SD A.(a)

            (iv)   be either:

                (1)   printed on the bank's or building society's letterhead,

                (2)   electronic bank or building society statements, accompanied by a supporting letter from the bank or building society, on company headed paper, confirming the statement provided is authentic, or

                (3)   electronic bank or building society statements, bearing the official stamp of the bank or building society on every page,

        and

            (v)   not be mini-statements from automatic teller machines (ATMs).

        (c)   Building society pass books must

            (i)   clearly show:

                (1)   the applicant's name,

                (2)   the applicant's account number,

                (3)   the financial institution's name,

                (4)   the financial institution's logo, and

                (5)   transactions by the sponsor covering the period no earlier than one calendar month before the date of the application, including the amount shown on the specified payslip as at 245GF-SD A.(a)

        and

            (ii)   be either:

                (1)   the original pass book, or

(2)   a photocopy of the pass book which has been certified by the issuing building society on company headed paper, confirming the statement provided is authentic.

B.   A letter from the employer detailing the purpose and period of absences in connection with the employment, including periods of annual leave. Where the absence was due to a serious or compelling reason, a personal letter from the applicant which includes full details of the reason for the absences and all original supporting documents in relation to those reasons – e.g. medical certificates, birth/death certificates, information about the reasons which led to the absence from the UK.

C.   Where the applicant is not being paid the appropriate rate in Appendix J due to maternity, paternity or adoption leave:

(a)   Payslips must be:

(i)   the applicant's payslip from the month immediately preceding the leave,

(ii)   the applicant's payslips for each month of the period of the leave,

(iii)   as set out in A(a)(iii) above.

(b)   Bank or building society statements must be:

(i)   the applicant's statement from the month immediately preceding the leave,

(ii)   the applicant's statement for each month of the period of the leave,

(iii)   as set out in A(b)(iii) above.

Tier 2 (General) Migrants, Tier 2 (Minister of Religion) Migrants and Tier 2 (Sportsperson) Migrants

Purpose of these routes and definitions

245H.   These routes enable UK employers to recruit workers from outside the EEA to fill a particular vacancy that cannot be filled by a British or EEA worker.

Entry clearance

245HA.   All Migrants arriving in the UK and wishing to enter as a Tier 2 (General) Migrant, Tier 2 (Minister of Religion) Migrant or Tier 2 (Sportsperson) Migrant must have a valid entry clearance for entry under the relevant one of these routes. If they do not have a valid entry clearance, entry will be refused.

Requirements for entry clearance

245HB.   To qualify for entry clearance as a Tier 2 (General) Migrant, Tier 2 (Minister of Religion) Migrant or Tier 2 (Sportsperson) Migrant, an applicant must meet the requirements listed below. If the applicant meets these requirements, entry clearance will be granted. if the applicant does not meet these requirements, the application will be refused.

Requirements:

(a)   The applicant must not fall for refusal under the general grounds for refusal.

(b)   If applying as a Tier 2 (General) Migrant, the applicant must have a minimum of 50 points under paragraphs 76 to 84A of Appendix A.

(c)   If applying as a Tier 2 (Minister of religion) Migrant, the applicant must have a minimum of 50 points under paragraphs 85 to 92A of Appendix A.

(d)   If applying as a Tier 2 (sportsperson) Migrant, the applicant must have a minimum of 50 points under paragraphs 93 to 100 of Appendix A.

(e)   The applicant must have a minimum of 10 points under paragraphs 1 to 18 of Appendix B.

(f)   The applicant must have a minimum of 10 points under paragraphs 4 to 5 of Appendix C.

(g)   The applicant must not have had entry clearance or leave to remain as a Tier 2 Migrant at any time during the 12 months immediately before the date of the application, unless the applicant:

(i)   was not in the UK with leave as a Tier 2 Migrant during this period, and provides evidence to show this, or

(ii)   will be paid a gross annual salary (as recorded by the Certificate of Sponsorship Checking Service entry, and including such allowances as are specified as acceptable for this purpose in paragraph 79 of Appendix A) of £152,100 or higher.

(h) An applicant who has, or was last granted, leave as a Student, a Student Nurse, a Student Re-Sitting an Examination, a Student Writing-Up a Thesis, a Postgraduate Doctor or Dentist or a Tier 4 Migrant and:

    (i) is currently being sponsored by a government or international scholarship agency, or

    (ii) was being sponsored by a government or international scholarship agency, and that sponsorship came to an end 12 months ago or less

must provide the unconditional written consent of the sponsoring Government or agency to the application and must provide the specified documents as set out in paragraph 245A above, to show that this requirement has been met.

(i) The applicant must be at least 16 years old.

(j) Where the applicant is under 18 years of age, the application must be supported by the applicant's parents or legal guardian, or by one parent if that parent has sole legal responsibility for the child.

(k) Where the applicant is under 18 years of age, the applicant's parents or legal guardian, or one parent if that parent has sole responsibility for the child, must confirm that they consent to the arrangements for the applicant's travel to, and reception and care in, the UK.

(l) If the Sponsor is a limited company, the applicant must not own more than 10% of its shares, unless the gross annual salary (as recorded by the Certificate of Sponsorship Checking Service entry, and including such allowances as are specified as acceptable for this purpose in paragraph 79 of Appendix A) is £152,100 or higher.

(m) If the applicant is applying as a Tier 2 (Minister of Religion) Migrant, the Entry Clearance Officer must be satisfied that the applicant:

    (i) genuinely intends to undertake, and is capable of undertaking, the role recorded by the Certificate of Sponsorship Checking Service; and

    (ii) will not undertake employment in the United Kingdom other than under the terms of paragraph 245HC(e)(iii).

(n) To support the assessment in paragraph 245HB(m), the Entry Clearance Officer may:

    (i) request additional information and evidence, and refuse the application if the information or evidence is not provided. Any requested documents must be received by the Home Office at the address specified in the request within 28 working days of the date the request is sent, and

    (ii) request the applicant attends an interview, and refuse the application if the applicant fails to comply with any such request without providing a reasonable explanation.

(o) If the Entry Clearance Officer is not satisfied following the assessment in paragraph 245HB(m), no points will be awarded under paragraphs 85 to 92A of Appendix A.

(p) The Entry Clearance Officer may decide not to carry out the assessment in paragraph 245HB(m) if the application already falls for refusal on other grounds, but reserves the right to carry out this assessment in any reconsideration of the decision.

Period and conditions of grant

245HC. (a) Entry clearance will be granted for:

    (i) a period equal to the length of the period of engagement plus 1 month, or

    (ii) a period of 3 years and 1 month,

whichever is the shorter.

(d) Entry clearance will be granted with effect from 14 days before the date that the Certificate of Sponsorship Checking Service records as the start date for the applicant's employment in the UK, unless entry clearance is being granted less than 14 days before that date, in which case it will be granted with immediate effect.

(e) Entry clearance will be subject to the following conditions:

    (i) no recourse to public funds,

    (ii) registration with the police, if this is required by paragraph 326 of these Rules, and

    (iii) no employment except:

        (1) working for the sponsor in the employment that the Certificate of Sponsorship Checking Service records that the migrant is being sponsored to do, subject to any notification of a change to the details of that employment, other than prohibited changes as defined in paragraph 323AA,

        (2) supplementary employment,

(3)   voluntary work, and

(4)   if the applicant is applying as a Tier 2 (Sportsperson) Migrant, employment as a sportsperson for his national team while his national team is in the UK.

(f)   (i)   Applicants who meet the requirements for entry clearance and who obtain points under paragraphs 76 to 79D of Appendix A shall be granted entry clearance as a Tier 2 (General) Migrant.

(ii)   Applicants who meet the requirements for entry clearance and who obtain points under paragraphs 85 to 92 of Appendix A shall be granted entry clearance as a Tier 2 (Minister of Religion) Migrant.

(iii)   Applicants who meet the requirements for entry clearance and who obtain points under paragraphs 93 to 100 of Appendix A shall be granted entry clearance as a Tier 2 (Sportsperson) Migrant.

Requirements for leave to remain

245HD.   To qualify for leave to remain as a Tier 2 (General) Migrant, Tier 2 (Minister of Religion Migrant or Tier 2 (Sportsperson) Migrant under this rule, an applicant must meet the requirements listed below. if the applicant meets these requirements, leave to remain will be granted. if the applicant does not meet these requirements, the application will be refused.

Requirements:

(a)   The applicant must not fall for refusal under the general grounds for refusal, and must not be an illegal entrant.

(b)   the applicant must:

(i)   have, or have last been granted, entry clearance, leave to enter or leave to remain as:

(1)   a Tier 1 Migrant,

(2)   a Tier 2 Migrant,

(3)   a Highly Skilled Migrant,

(4)   an Innovator,

(5)   a Jewish Agency Employee,

(6)   a Member of the Operational Ground Staff of an Overseas-owned Airline,

(7)   a Minister of Religion, Missionary or Member of a Religious Order,

(8)   a Participant in the Fresh Talent: Working in Scotland Scheme,

(9)   a Participant in the International Graduates Scheme (or its predecessor, the Science and Engineering Graduates Scheme),

(10)   a Qualifying Work Permit Holder,

(11)   a Representative of an Overseas Business,

(12)   a Representative of an Overseas Newspaper, News Agency or Broadcasting Organisation,

(13)   a Tier 5 (Temporary Worker) Migrant, or

(14)   the partner of a Relevant Points Based System Migrant if the relevant Points Based System Migrant is a Tier 4 Migrant,

or

(ii)   have, or have last been granted, entry clearance, leave to enter or leave to remain as:

(1)   a Tier 4 Migrant,

(2)   a Student,

(3)   a Student Nurse,

(4)   a Student Re-Sitting an Examination,

(5)   a Person Writing Up a Thesis,

(6)   an Overseas Qualified Nurse or Midwife,

(7)   a Postgraduate Doctor or Dentist, or

(8)   a Student Union Sabbatical Officer.

(c)   An applicant who has, or was last granted leave as a Tier 2 (Intra-Company Transfer) Migrant must:

(i) have previously had leave as a Tier 2 (Intra-Company Transfer) Migrant under the Rules in place before 6 April 2010, or in the Established Staff sub-category under the Rules in place before 6 April 2011,

(ii) not have been granted entry clearance in this or any other route since the grant of leave referred to in (i) above; and

(iii) not be applying to work for the same Sponsor as sponsored him when he was last granted leave.

(d) An applicant under the provisions in (b)(ii) above must meet the following requirements:

(i) The applicant must have completed and passed:

(1) a UK recognised bachelor's or master's degree (not a qualification of equivalent level which is not a degree),

(2) a UK Postgraduate Certificate in Education or Professional Graduate Diploma of Education (not a qualification of equivalent level),

or the applicant must have completed a minimum of 12 months study in the UK towards a UK PhD.

(ii) The applicant must have studied for the course in (d)(i) at a UK institution that is a UK recognised or listed body, or which holds a sponsor licence under Tier 4 of the Points Based System.

(iii) The applicant must have studied the course referred to in (d)(i) during:

(1) his last grant of leave, or

(2) a period of continuous leave which includes his last grant of leave, (for these purposes continuous leave will not be considered to have been broken if any of the circumstances set out in paragraphs 245AAA(a)(i) to (iii) of these Rules apply.).

(iv) The applicant's periods of UK study and/or research towards the course in (i) must have been undertaken whilst he had entry clearance, leave to enter or leave to remain in the UK that was not subject to a restriction preventing him from undertaking that course of study and/or research.

(v) If the institution studied at is removed from the Tier 4 Sponsor Register, the applicant's qualification must not have been obtained on or after the date of removal from the Sponsor Register.

(vi) If the applicant:

(1) is currently being sponsored by a government or international scholarship agency, or

(2) was being sponsored by a government or international scholarship agency, and that sponsorship came to an end 12 months ago or less,

the applicant must provide the unconditional written consent of the sponsoring Government or agency to the application and must provide the specified documents as set out in paragraph 245A above, to show that this requirement has been met.

(vii) The applicant must provide an original degree certificate, academic transcript or an academic reference on official headed paper of the institution, which clearly shows:

(1) The applicant's name,

(2) the course title/award,

(3) the course duration (except in the case of a degree certificate), and

(4) unless the course is a PhD course, the date of course completion and pass (or the date of award in the case of a degree certificate).

(e) an applicant who was last granted leave as a Tier 5 (Temporary Worker) Migrant must have been granted such leave in the Creative and Sporting sub-category of Tier 5 in order to allow the applicant to work as a professional footballer, and the applicant must be applying for leave to remain as a Tier 2 (Sportsperson) Migrant.

(f) If applying as a Tier 2 (General) Migrant, the applicant must have a minimum of 50 points under paragraphs 76 to 79D of Appendix A.

(g) If applying as a Tier 2 (Minister of Religion) Migrant, the applicant must have a minimum of 50 points under paragraphs 85 to 92A of Appendix A.

(h) If applying as a Tier 2 (Sportsperson) Migrant, the applicant must have a minimum of 50 points under paragraphs 93 to 100 of Appendix A.

(i)   The applicant must have a minimum of 10 points under paragraphs 1 to 16 of Appendix B.

(j)   The applicant must have a minimum of 10 points under paragraphs 4 to 5 of Appendix C.

(k)   The applicant must not have had entry clearance or leave to remain as a Tier 2 Migrant at any time during the 12 months immediately before the date of the application, unless:

    (i)   the applicant's last grant of leave was as a Tier 2 Migrant,

    (ii)   the applicant was not in the UK with leave as a Tier 2 Migrant during this period, and provides evidence to show this, or

    (iii) the applicant will be paid a gross annual salary (as recorded by the Certificate of Sponsorship Checking Service entry, and including such allowances as are specified as acceptable for this purpose in paragraph 79 of Appendix A) of £152,100 or higher.

(l)   The applicant must be at least 16 years old.

(m)   Where the applicant is under 18 years of age, the application must be supported by the applicant's parents or legal guardian, or by just one parent if that parent has sole legal responsibility for the child.

(n)   Where the applicant is under 18 years of age, the applicant's parents or legal guardian, or just one parent if that parent has sole legal responsibility for the child, must confirm that they consent to the arrangements for the applicant's care in the UK.

(o)   if the sponsor is a limited company, the applicant must not own more than 10% of its shares, unless the gross annual salary (as recorded by the Certificate of Sponsorship Checking Service entry, and including such allowances as are specified as acceptable for this purpose in paragraph 79 of Appendix A) is £152,100 or higher.

(p)   The applicant must not be in the UK in breach of immigration laws except that any period of overstaying for a period of 28 days or less will be disregarded.

(q)   If the applicant is applying as a Tier 2 (Minister of Religion) Migrant, the Secretary of State must be satisfied that the applicant:

    (i)   genuinely intends to undertake, and is capable of undertaking, the role recorded by the Certificate of Sponsorship Checking Service; and

    (ii)   will not undertake employment in the United Kingdom other than under the terms of paragraph 245HE(g)(iii).

(r)   To support the assessment in paragraph 245HD(q), the Secretary of State may:

    (i)   request additional information and evidence, and refuse the application if the information or evidence is not provided. Any requested documents must be received by the Home Office at the address specified in the request within 28 working days of the date the request is sent, and

    (ii)   request the applicant attends an interview, and refuse the application if the applicant fails to comply with any such request without providing a reasonable explanation.

(s)   If the Secretary of State is not satisfied following the assessment in paragraph 245HD(q), no points will be awarded under paragraphs 85 to 92A of Appendix A.

(t)   The Secretary of State may decide not to carry out the assessment in paragraph 245HD(q) if the application already falls for refusal on other grounds, but reserves the right to carry out this assessment in any reconsideration of the decision.

Period and conditions of grant

245HE. (a)   If the applicant:

    (i)   previously had leave under the Rules in place before 6 April 2011 as:

        (1)   a Tier 2 (General) Migrant,

        (2)   a Tier 2 (Minister of Religion) Migrant,

        (3)   a Tier 2 (Sportsperson) Migrant,

        (4)   a Jewish Agency Employee,

        (5)   a Member of the Operational Ground Staff of an Overseas-owned Airline,

        (6)   a Minister of Religion, Missionary or Member of a Religious Order,

        (7)   a Qualifying Work Permit Holder, or

        (8)   a Representative of an Overseas Newspaper, News Agency or Broadcasting Organisation,

    and

(ii)   has not been granted entry clearance as a Tier 2 (General) Migrant, Tier 2 (Minister of Religion) Migrant or Tier 2 (Sportsperson) Migrant under the Rules in place from 6 April 2011, and

(iii)   has not been granted entry clearance, leave to enter or leave to remain in any other category since the grant of leave referred to in (i) above,

leave to remain will be granted as set out in paragraph (d) below.

(b)   In all other cases, leave to remain will be granted as set out in paragraph (e) below.

(c)   In paragraph (e) below, X refers to the continuous period of time, during which the applicant:

(i)   has had entry clearance, leave to enter or leave to remain as a Tier 2 (General) Migrant, Tier 2 (Minister of Religion) Migrant or Tier 2 (Sportsperson) Migrant; or

(ii)   has been in the UK without leave following leave in one of these categories.

(d)   in the cases set out in paragraph (a) above, leave to remain will be granted for:

(i)   the length of the period of engagement plus 14 days, or

(ii)   a period of 3 years plus 14 days,

whichever is the shorter.

(e)   If paragraph (a) does not apply, leave to remain will be granted for:

(i)   the length of the period of engagement plus 14 days,

(ii)   a period of 3 years plus 14 days, or

(iii)   a period equal to 6 years less X,

whichever is the shorter. If the calculation of the period of leave comes to zero or a negative number, leave to remain will be refused.

(f)   in addition to the periods in paragraphs (d) and (e), leave to remain will be granted for the period between the date that the application is decided and the date that the Certificate of Sponsorship Checking Service records as the start date of employment in the UK, provided this is not a negative value.

(g)   leave to remain will be granted subject to the following conditions:

(i)   no recourse to public funds,

(ii)   registration with the police, if this is required by paragraph 326 of these Rules, and

(iii)   no employment except:

(1)   working for the sponsor in the employment that the Certificate of Sponsorship Checking Service records that the migrant is being sponsored to do, subject to any notification of a change to the details of that employment, other than prohibited changes as defined in paragraph 323AA,

(2)   supplementary employment,

(3)   voluntary work,

(4)   until the start date of the period of engagement, any employment which the applicant was lawfully engaged in on the date of his application, and

(5)   if the applicant is applying as a Tier 2 (Sportsperson) Migrant, employment as a sportsperson for his national team while his national team is in the UK.

(h)   (i)   Applicants who meet the requirements for leave to remain and who obtain points under paragraphs 76 to 79D of Appendix A shall be granted leave to remain as a Tier 2 (General) Migrant.

(ii)   Applicants who meet the requirements for leave to remain and who obtain points under paragraphs 85 to 92 of Appendix A shall be granted leave to remain as a Tier 2 (Minister of Religion) Migrant.

(iii)   Applicants who meet the requirements for leave to remain and who obtain points under paragraphs 93 to 100 of Appendix A shall be granted leave to remain as a Tier 2 (Sportsperson) Migrant.

Requirements for indefinite leave to remain

245HF.   To qualify for indefinite leave to remain as a Tier 2 (General) Migrant, Tier 2 (Minister of Religion) Migrant or Tier 2 (Sportsperson) Migrant, an applicant must meet the requirements listed below. If the applicant meets these requirements, indefinite leave to remain will be granted. If the applicant does not meet these requirements, the application will be refused.

Requirements:

(a)   DELETED.

(b)   The applicant must not fall for refusal under the general grounds for refusal, and must not be an illegal entrant.

(c)   The applicant must have spent a continuous period of 5 years lawfully in the UK, of which the most recent period must have been spent with leave as a Tier 2 Migrant, in any combination of the following categories:

   (i)   as a Member of the Operational Ground Staff of an Overseas-owned Airline,

   (ii)   as a Minister of Religion, Missionary or Member of a Religious Order,

   (iii)   as a Qualifying Work Permit Holder,

   (iv)   as a Representative of an Overseas Business,

   (v)   as a Representative of an Overseas Newspaper, News Agency or Broadcasting Organisation,

   (vi)   as a Tier 1 Migrant, other than a Tier 1 (Post Study Work) Migrant,

   (vii)   as a Highly Skilled Migrant,

   (viii)   as an innovator,

   (ix)   as a Tier 2 (General) Migrant, a Tier 2 (Minister of Religion) Migrant or a Tier 2 (Sportsperson) Migrant, or

   (x)   as a Tier 2 (Intra-Company Transfer) Migrant, provided the continuous period of 5 years spent lawfully in the UK includes a period of leave as:

      (1)   a Tier 2 (Intra-Company Transfer) Migrant granted under the Rules in place before 6 April 2010, or

      (2)   a Qualifying Work Permit Holder, provided that the work permit was granted because the applicant was the subject of an Intra-Company Transfer.

(d)   The Sponsor that issued the Certificate of Sponsorship that led to the applicant's last grant of leave must:

   (i)   still hold, or have applied for a renewal of, a Tier 2 Sponsor licence in the relevant category; and

   (ii)   certify in writing that:

      (1)   he still requires the applicant for the employment in question, and

      (2)   in the case of a Tier 2 (General) Migrant applying for settlement, the applicant is paid at or above the appropriate rate for the job as stated in the Codes of Practice in Appendix J, or where the applicant is not paid at that rate only due to maternity, paternity or adoption leave, the date that leave started and that the applicant was paid at the appropriate rate immediately before the leave.

(e)   The applicant provides the specified documents in paragraph 245HF-SD to evidence the sponsor's certification in subsection (d)(ii) and to evidence the reason for the absences set out in paragraph 245AAA.

(f)   The applicant must have sufficient knowledge of the English language and sufficient knowledge about life in the United Kingdom, in accordance with Appendix KoLL.

(g)   The applicant must not be in the UK in breach of immigration laws except that any period of overstaying for a period of 28 days or less will be disregarded.

(h)   For the purposes of sub-paragraph (c), time spent with valid leave in the Bailiwick of Guernsey, the Bailiwick of Jersey or the Isle of Man in a category equivalent to any of the categories set out in (c)(i) to (x), may be included in the continuous period of 5 years lawful residence, provided that:

   (i)   where the leave is in category (x), the continuous period of 5 years includes a period of leave as a Tier 2 (Intra-Company Transfer) Migrant granted before 6 April 2010, or a Qualifying Work Permit Holder (provided the work permit was granted because the applicant was the subject of an Intra-Company Transfer); and

   (ii)   any period of leave granted in the Bailiwick of Guernsey, the Bailiwick of Jersey or the Isle of Man as a work permit holder or as a Tier 2 Migrant was for employment:

      (a)   in a job which appears on the list of occupations skilled to National Qualifications Framework level 3 or above (or from 6 April 2011, National Qualifications Framework level 4 or above or from 14 June 2012, National Qualifications Framework level 6 or above), as stated in the Codes of Practice in Appendix J, or

(b)   in a job which appears in the Creative Sector Codes of Practice in Appendix J, or

(c)   as a professional sportsperson (including as a sports coach); and

(iii)   the most recent period of leave was granted in the UK as a Tier 2 Migrant.

In any such case, references to the 'UK' in paragraph 245AAA shall include a reference to the Bailiwick of Guernsey, Bailiwick of Jersey or the Isle of Man, as the case may be.

Specified documents

245HF-SD.

The specified documents referred to in paragraph 245HF(e) are set out in A, B and C below:

A.   Either a payslip and a personal bank or building society statement, or a payslip and a building society pass book.

(a)   Payslips must be:

(i)   the applicant's most recent payslip,

(ii)   dated no earlier than one calendar month before the date of the application, and

(iii)   either:

(1)   an original payslip,

(2)   on company-headed paper, or

(3)   accompanied by a letter from the applicant's Sponsor, on company headed paper and signed by a senior official, confirming the payslip is authentic.

(b)   Personal bank or building society statements must:

(i)   be the applicant's most recent statement,

(ii)   be dated no earlier than one calendar month before the date of the application,

(iii)   clearly show:

(1)   the applicant's name,

(2)   the applicant's account number,

(3)   the date of the statement,

(4)   the financial institution's name,

(5)   the financial institution's logo, and

(6)   transactions by the Sponsor covering the period no earlier than one calendar month before the date of the application, including the amount shown on the specified payslip as at 245HF-SD A.(a)

(iv)   be either:

(1)   printed on the bank's or building society's letterhead,

(2)   electronic bank or building society statements, accompanied by a supporting letter from the bank or building society, on company headed paper, confirming the statement provided is authentic, or

(3)   electronic bank or building society statements, bearing the official stamp of the bank or building society on every page,

and

(v)   not be mini-statements from automatic teller machines (ATMs).

(c)   Building society pass books must

(i)   clearly show:

(1)   the applicant's name,

(2)   the applicant's account number,

(3)   the financial institution's name,

(4)   the financial institution's logo, and

(5)   transactions by the sponsor covering the period no earlier than one calendar month before the date of the application, including the amount shown on the specified payslip as at 245HF-SD A.(a)

and

(ii)   be either:

(1)   the original pass book, or

(2)   a photocopy of the pass book which has been certified by the issuing building society on company headed paper, confirming the statement provided is authentic.

B.   A letter from the employer detailing the purpose and period of absences in connection with the employment, including periods of annual leave. Where the absence was due to a serious or compelling reason, a personal letter from the applicant which includes full details of the reason for the absences and all original supporting documents in relation to those reasons – e.g. medical certificates, birth/ death certificates, information about the reasons which led to the absence from the UK.

C.   Where the applicant is not being paid the appropriate rate in Appendix J due to maternity, paternity or adoption leave:

(a)   Payslips must be:

(i)   the applicant's payslip from the month immediately preceding the leave,

(ii)   the applicant's payslips for each month of the period of the leave,

(iii)   as set out in A(a)(iii) above.

(b)   Bank or building society statements must be:

(i)   the applicant's statement from the month immediately preceding the leave,

(ii)   the applicant's statements for each month of the period of the leave,

(iii)   as set out in A(b)(iii) above.

245ZI.–245ZS.   OMITTED

Tier 4 (General) Student

Purpose of this route

245ZT.   This route is for migrants aged 16 or over who wish to study in the UK.

Entry clearance

245ZU.   All migrants arriving in the UK and wishing to enter as a Tier 4 (General) Student must have a valid entry clearance for entry under this route. If they do not have a valid entry clearance, entry will be refused.

Requirements for entry clearance

245ZV.   To qualify for entry clearance as a Tier 4 (General) Student, an applicant must meet the requirements listed below. If the applicant meets these requirements, entry clearance will be granted. If the applicant does not meet these requirements, the application will be refused.

Requirements:

(a)   The applicant must not fall for refusal under the General Grounds for Refusal.

(b)   The applicant must have a minimum of 30 points under paragraphs 113 to 120 of Appendix A.

(c)   The applicant must have a minimum of 10 points under paragraphs 10 to 14 of Appendix C.

(ca)   The applicant must, if required to do so on examination or interview, be able to demonstrate without the assistance of an interpreter English language proficiency of a standard to be expected from an individual who has reached the standard specified in a Confirmation of Acceptance for Studies assigned in accordance with Appendix A paragraph 118(b) (for the avoidance of doubt, the applicant will not be subject to a test at the standard set out in Appendix A, paragraph 118(b).

(da)   if the applicant wishes to undertake a course:

(i)   undergraduate or postgraduate studies leading to a Doctorate or Masters degree by research in one of the disciplines listed in paragraph 1 of Appendix 6 of these Rules, or

(ii)   undergraduate or postgraduate studies leading to a taught Masters degree or other postgraduate qualification in one of the disciplines listed in paragraph 2 of Appendix 6 of these Rules, or

(iii)   a period of study or research in excess of 6 months in one of the disciplines listed in paragraphs 1 or 2 of Appendix 6 of these Rules at an institution of higher education where this forms part of an overseas postgraduate qualification

the applicant must hold a valid Academic Technology Approval Scheme clearance certificate from the Counter-Proliferation Department of the Foreign and Commonwealth Office which relates to the course, or area of research, that the applicant will be taking and at the institution at which the applicant wishes to undertake it and must provide a print-out of his Academic Technology Approval Scheme clearance certificate to show that these requirements have been met.

(e)   If the applicant wishes to be a postgraduate doctor or dentist on a recognised Foundation Programme:

    (i)   the applicant must have successfully completed a recognised UK degree in medicine or dentistry from:

        (1)   an institution with a Tier 4 General Sponsor Licence,

        (2)   a UK publicly funded institution of further or higher education or

        (3)   a UK bona fide private education institution which maintains satisfactory records of enrolment and attendance,

    (ii)   the applicant must have previously been granted leave:

        (1)   as a Tier 4 (General) Student, or as a Student, for the final academic year of the studies referred to in paragraph (i) above, and

        (2)   as a Tier 4 (General) Student, or as a Student, for at least one other academic year (aside from the final year) of the studies referred to in paragraph (i) above,

    (iii)   if the applicant has previously been granted leave as a Postgraduate Doctor or Dentist, the applicant must not be seeking entry clearance or leave to enter or remain to a date beyond 3 years from the date on which he was first granted leave to enter or remain in that category, and

    (iv)   if the applicant has previously been granted leave as a Tier 4 (General) Student to undertake a course as a postgraduate doctor or dentist, the applicant must not be seeking entry clearance or leave to enter or remain to a date beyond 3 years from the date on which the applicant was first granted leave to undertake such a course.

(f)   If the applicant is currently being sponsored by a Government or international scholarship agency, or within the last 12 months has come to the end of such a period of sponsorship, the applicant must provide the written consent of the sponsoring Government or agency to the application and must provide the specified documents as set out in paragraph 245A above, to show that this requirement has been met.

(g)   If the course is below degree level the grant of entry clearance the applicant is seeking must not lead to the applicant having spent more than 3 years in the UK as a Tier 4 Migrant since the age of 18 studying courses that did not consist of degree level study.

(ga)   If the course is at degree level or above, the grant of entry clearance the applicant is seeking must not lead to the applicant having spent more than 5 years in the UK as a Tier 4 (General) Migrant, or as a Student, studying courses at degree level or above unless:

    (i)   the applicant has successfully completed a course at degree level in the UK of a minimum duration of 4 academic years, and will follow a course of study at Master's degree level sponsored by a Sponsor that is a Recognised Body or a body in receipt of public funding as a higher education institution from the Department of Employment and Learning in Northern Ireland, the Higher Education Funding Council for England, the Higher Education Funding Council for Wales or the Scottish Funding Council, and the grant of entry clearance must not lead to the applicant having spent more than 6 years in the UK as a Tier 4 (General) Migrant, or as a Student, studying courses at degree level or above; or

    (ii)   the grant of entry clearance is to follow a course leading to the award of a PhD, and the applicant is sponsored by a Sponsor that is a Recognised Body or a body in receipt of public funding as a higher education institution from the Department of Employment and Learning in Northern Ireland, the Higher Education Funding Council for England, the Higher Education Funding Council for Wales or the Scottish Funding Council; or

    (iii)   the applicant is following a course of study in;

        (1)   Architecture;

        (2)   Medicine;

        (3)   Dentistry;

        (4)   Law, where the applicant has completed a course at degree level in the UK and is progressing to:

            a.   a law conversion course validated by the Joint Academic Stage Board in England and Wales, a Masters in Legal Science (MLegSc) in Northern Ireland, or an accelerated graduate LLB in Scotland; or

b.   the Legal Practice Course in England and Wales, the Solicitors Course in Northern Ireland, or a Diploma in Professional Legal Practice in Scotland; or

c.   the Bar Professional Training Course in England and Wales, or the Bar Course in Northern Ireland.

(5)   Veterinary Medicine & Science; or

(6)   Music at a music college that is a member of Conservatoires UK (CUK).

(gb)   If the applicant has completed a course leading to the award of a PhD in the UK, the grant of entry clearance the applicant is seeking must not lead to the applicant having spent more than 8 years in the UK as a Tier 4 (General) Migrant, or as a Student.

(h)   The applicant must be at least 16 years old.

(i)   Where the applicant is under 18 years of age, the application must be supported by the applicant's parents or legal guardian, or by just one parent if that parent has sole legal responsibility for the child.

(j)   Where the applicant is under 18 years of age, the applicant's parents or legal guardian, or just one parent if that parent has sole responsibility for the child, must confirm that they consent to the arrangements for the applicant's travel to, and reception and care in, the UK.

(k)   The Entry Clearance Officer must be satisfied that the applicant is a genuine student. 245ZV(k) will not be applied to a national or the rightful holder of a qualifying passport issued by one of the relevant competent authorities listed in Appendix H.

Period and conditions of grant

245ZW.   (a)   Subject to paragraph (b), entry clearance will be granted for the duration of the course.

(b)   In addition to the period of entry clearance granted in accordance with paragraph (a), entry clearance will also be granted for the periods set out in the following table. Notes to accompany the table appear below the table.

Type of course	Period of entry clearance to be granted before the course starts	Period of entry clearance to be granted after the course ends
12 months or more	1 month	4 months
6 months or more but less than 12 months	1 month	2 months
Pre-sessional course of less than 6 months	1 month	1 month
Course of less than 6 months that is not a pre-sessional course	7 days	7 days
Postgraduate doctor or dentist	1 month	1 month

Notes

(i)   If the grant of entry clearance is made less than 1 month or, in the case of a course of less than 6 months that is not a pre-sessional course, less than 7 days before the start of the course, entry clearance will be granted with immediate effect.

(ii)   A pre-sessional course is a course which prepares a student for the student's main course of study in the UK.

(iii)   The additional periods of entry clearance granted further to the table above will be disregarded for the purposes of calculating whether a migrant has exceeded the limits specified at 245ZV(g) to 245ZV(gb).

(c)   Entry clearance will be granted subject to the following conditions:

(i)   no recourse to public funds,

(ii)   registration with the police, if this is required by paragraph 326 of these Rules,

(iii)   no employment except:

(1)   employment during term time of no more than 20 hours per week and employment (of any duration) during vacations, where the student is following a course of degree level study and is either:

(a)   sponsored by a Sponsor that is a Recognised Body or a body in receipt of public funding as a higher education institution from the Department of Employment and Learning in Northern Ireland, the Higher Education Funding Council for

England, the Higher Education Funding Council for Wales or the Scottish Funding Council; or

(b) sponsored by an overseas higher education institution to undertake a short-term Study Abroad Programme in the United Kingdom.

(2) employment during term time of no more than 10 hours per week and employment (of any duration) during vacations, where the student is following a course of below degree level study and is sponsored by a Sponsor that is a Recognised Body or a body in receipt of public funding as a higher education institution from the Department of Employment and Learning in Northern Ireland, the Higher Education Funding Council for England, the Higher Education Funding Council for Wales or the Scottish Funding Council,

(3) employment during term time of no more than 10 hours per week and employment (of any duration) during vacations, where the student is following a course of study at any academic level and is sponsored by a Sponsor that is a publicly funded further education college,

(4) employment as part of a course-related work placement which forms an assessed part of the applicant's course and provided that any period that the applicant spends on that placement does not exceed one third of the total length of the course undertaken in the UK except:

(i) where it is a United Kingdom statutory requirement that the placement should exceed one third of the total length of the course; or

(ii) where the placement does not exceed one half of the total length of the course undertaken in the UK and the student is following a course of degree level study and is either:

(a) sponsored by a Sponsor that is a Recognised Body or a body in receipt of public funding as a higher education institution from the Department of Employment and Learning in Northern Ireland, the Higher Education Funding Council for England, the Higher Education Funding Council for Wales or the Scottish Funding Council; or

(b) sponsored by an overseas higher education institution to undertake a short-term Study Abroad Programme in the United Kingdom.

(5) employment as a Student Union Sabbatical Officer, for up to 2 years, provided the post is elective and is at the institution which is the applicant's Sponsor or they must be elected to a national National Union of Students (NUS) position.

(6) employment as a postgraduate doctor or dentist on a recognised Foundation Programme

(7) until such time as a decision is received from the UK Border Agency on an application which is supported by a Certificate of Sponsorship assigned by a licensed Tier 2 Sponsor and which is made following successful completion of course at degree level or above at a Sponsor that is a Recognised Body or a body in receipt of public funding as a higher education institution from the Department of Employment and Learning in Northern Ireland, the Higher Education Funding Council for England, the Higher Education Funding Council for Wales or the Scottish Funding Council and while the applicant has extant leave, and any appeal against that decision has been determined, employment with the Tier 2 Sponsor, in the role for which they assigned the Certificate of Sponsorship to the Tier 4 migrant,

(8) self-employment, providing the migrant has made an application for leave to remain as a Tier 1 (Graduate Entrepreneur) Migrant which:

(_a) is supported by an endorsement from a qualifying Higher Education Institution,

(_b) is made following successful completion of a UK recognised Bachelor degree, Masters degree or PhD (not a qualification of equivalent level which is not a degree) course at a Sponsor that is a Recognised Body or a body in receipt of public funding as a higher education institution from the Department of Employment and Learning in Northern Ireland, the Higher Education Funding Council for England, the Higher Education Funding Council for Wales or the Scottish Funding Council, and

(_c) is made while the applicant has extant leave,

until such time as a decision is received from the UK Border Agency on that application and any appeal against that decision has been determined,

provided that the migrant is not self-employed other than under the conditions of (8) above, or employed as a Doctor or Dentist in Training other than under the conditions of (v) below, professional sportsperson (including a sports coach) or an entertainer, and provided that the migrant's employment would not fill a permanent full time vacancy other than under the conditions of (7) above, or a vacancy on a recognised Foundation Programme or as a sabbatical officer; and

(iv)   no study except:

(1)   study at the institution that the Confirmation of Acceptance for Studies Checking Service records as the migrant's Sponsor, or where the migrant was awarded points for a visa letter, study at the institution which issued that visa letter unless the migrant is studying at an institution which is a partner institution of the migrant's Sponsor.

(2)   until such time as a decision is received from the UK Border Agency on an application which is supported by a Confirmation of Acceptance for Studies assigned by a Highly Trusted Sponsor and which is made while the applicant has extant leave, and any appeal against that decision has been determined, study at the Highly Trusted Sponsor institution which the Confirmation of Acceptance for Studies Checking Service records as having assigned a Confirmation of Acceptance for Studies to the Tier 4 migrant;

(3)   supplementary study,

(4)   study at the same or a higher level of course as that stated on the confirmation of acceptance for studies, or at a lower level where the same requirements or conditions of leave would have applied if the application had been to study at that lower level.

(v)   no employment as a Doctor or Dentist in Training unless:

(1)   the course that the migrant is being sponsored to do (as recorded by the Confirmation of Acceptance for Studies Checking Service) is a recognised Foundation Programme, or

(2)   the migrant has made an application as a Tier 4 (General) Student which is supported by a Confirmation of Acceptance for Studies assigned by a Highly Trusted Sponsor to sponsor the applicant to do a recognised Foundation Programme, and this study satisfies the requirements of (iv)(2) above, or

(3)   the migrant has made an application as a Tier 2 (General) Migrant which is supported by a Certificate of Sponsorship assigned by a licensed Tier 2 Sponsor to sponsor the applicant to work as a Doctor or Dentist in Training, and this employment satisfies the conditions of (iii)(7) above.

Requirements for leave to remain

245ZX.   To qualify for leave to remain as a Tier 4 (General) Student under this rule, an applicant must meet the requirements listed below. If the applicant meets these requirements, leave to remain will be granted. If the applicant does not meet these requirements, the applicant will be refused.

Requirements:

(a)   The applicant must not fall for refusal under the general grounds for refusal and must not be an illegal entrant.

(b)   The applicant must have, or have last been granted, entry clearance, leave to enter or leave to remain:

(i)   as a Tier 4 (General) Student,

(ii)   as a Tier 4 (Child) Student,

(iii)   as a Tier 1 (Post-study Work) Migrant,

(iv)   as a Tier 2 Migrant,

(v)   as a Participant in the International Graduates Scheme (or its predecessor, the Science and Engineering Graduates Scheme),

(vi)   as a Participant in the Fresh Talent: Working in Scotland Scheme,

(vii)   as a Postgraduate Doctor or Dentist,

(viii)   as a Prospective Student,

(ix)   as a Student,

(x)   as a Student Nurse,

(xi)   as a Student Re-sitting an Examination,

(xii)   as a Student Writing-Up a Thesis,

(xiii)   as a Student Union Sabbatical Officer, or

(xiv)   as a Work Permit Holder.

(c)   The applicant must have a minimum of 30 points under paragraphs 113 to 120 of Appendix A.

(d)   The applicant must have a minimum of 10 points under paragraphs 10 to 14 of Appendix C.

(da)   The applicant must, if required to do so on examination or interview, be able to demonstrate without the assistance of an interpreter English language proficiency of a standard to be expected from an individual who has reached the standard specified in a Confirmation of Acceptance for Studies assigned in accordance with Appendix A paragraph 118(b) (for the avoidance of doubt, the applicant will not be subject to a test at the standard set out in Appendix A, paragraph 118(b)).

(ea)   if the applicant wishes to undertake a course:

(i)   undergraduate or postgraduate studies leading to a Doctorate or Masters degree by research in one of the disciplines listed in paragraph 1 of Appendix 6 of these Rules, or

(ii)   undergraduate or postgraduate studies leading to a taught Masters degree or other postgraduate qualification in one of the disciplines listed in paragraph 2 of Appendix 6 of these Rules, or

(iii)   a period of study or research in excess of 6 months in one of the disciplines listed in paragraphs 1 or 2 of Appendix 6 of these Rules at an institution of higher education where this forms part of an overseas postgraduate qualification

the applicant must hold a valid Academic Technology Approval Scheme clearance certificate from the Counter-Proliferation Department of the Foreign and Commonwealth Office which relates to the course, or area of research, that the applicant will be taking and at the institution at which the applicant wishes to undertake it and must provide a print-out of his Academic Technology Approval Scheme clearance certificate to show that these requirements have been met.

(f)   If the applicant wishes to be a postgraduate doctor or dentist on a recognised Foundation Programme:

(i)   the applicant must have successfully completed a recognised UK degree in medicine or dentistry from:

(1)   an institution with a Tier 4 General Sponsor Licence,

(2)   a UK publicly funded institution of further or higher education or

(3)   a UK bona fide private education institution which maintains satisfactory records of enrolment and attendance,

(ii)   the applicant must have previously been granted leave:

(1)   as a Tier 4 (General) Student, or as a Student, for the final academic year of the studies referred to in paragraph (i) above, and

(2)   as a Tier 4 (General) Student, or as a Student, for at least one other academic year (aside from the final year) of the studies referred to in paragraph (i) above,

(iii)   if the applicant has previously been granted leave as a Postgraduate Doctor or Dentist the applicant must not be seeking entry clearance or leave to enter or remain to a date beyond 3 years from the date on which he was first granted leave to enter or remain in that category, and

(iv)   if the applicant has previously been granted leave as a Tier 4 (General) Student to undertake a course as a postgraduate doctor or dentist, the applicant must not be seeking entry clearance or leave to enter or remain to a date beyond 3 years from the date on which he was first granted leave to undertake such a course.

(g)   If the applicant is currently being sponsored by a Government or international scholarship agency, or within the last 12 months has come to the end of such a period of sponsorship, the applicant must provide the unconditional written consent of the sponsoring Government or agency to the application and must provide the specified documents as set out in paragraph 245A above, to show that this requirement has been met.

(h)   If the course is below degree level the grant of leave to remain the applicant is seeking must not lead to the applicant having spent more than 3 years in the UK as a Tier 4 Migrant since the age of 18 studying courses that did not consist of degree level study.

(ha)   If the course is at degree level or above, the grant of leave to remain the applicant is seeking must not lead to the applicant having spent more than 5 years in the UK as a Tier 4 (General) Migrant, or as a Student, studying courses at degree level or above unless:

(i)   the applicant has successfully completed a course at degree level in the UK of a minimum duration of 4 academic years, and will follow a course of study at Master's degree level sponsored by a Sponsor that is a Recognised Body or a body in receipt of public funding as a higher education institution from the Department of Employment and Learning in Northern Ireland, the Higher Education Funding Council for England, the Higher Education Funding Council for Wales or the Scottish Funding Council, and the grant of leave to remain must not lead to the applicant having spent more than 6 years in the UK as a Tier 4 (General) Migrant, or as a Student, studying courses at degree level or above; or

(ii)   the grant of leave to remain is to follow a course leading to the award of a PhD and the applicant is sponsored by a Sponsor that is a Recognised Body or a body in receipt of public funding as a higher education institution from the Department of Employment and Learning in Northern Ireland, the Higher Education Funding Council for England, the Higher Education Funding Council for Wales or the Scottish Funding Council; or

(iii)   the applicant is following a course of study in;

    (1)   Architecture;

    (2)   Medicine;

    (3)   Dentistry;

    (4)   Law, where the applicant has completed a course at degree level in the UK and is progressing to:

        a.   a law conversion course validated by the Joint Academic Stage Board in England and Wales, a Masters in Legal Science (MLegSc) in Northern Ireland, or an accelerated graduate LLB in Scotland; or

        b.   the Legal Practice Course in England and Wales, the Solicitors Course in Northern Ireland, or a Diploma in Professional Legal Practice in Scotland; or

        c.   the Bar Professional Training Course in England and Wales, or the Bar Course in Northern Ireland.

    (5)   Veterinary Medicine & Science; or

    (6)   Music at a music college that is a member of Conservatoires UK (CUK).

(hb)   If the applicant has completed a course leading to the award of a PhD in the UK, the grant of leave to remain the applicant is seeking must not lead to the applicant having spent more than 8 years in the UK as a Tier 4 (General) Migrant, or as a Student.

(i)   The applicant must be at least 16 years old.

(j)   Where the applicant is under 18 years of age, the application must be supported by the applicant's parents or legal guardian, or by just one parent if that parent has sole legal responsibility for the child.

(k)   Where the applicant is under 18 years of age, the applicant's parents or legal guardian, or just one parent if that parent has sole legal responsibility for the child, must confirm that they consent to the arrangements for the applicant's care in the UK.

(l)   Unless applying for leave to remain as a Tier 4 (General) Student on the doctorate extension scheme, the applicant must be applying for leave to remain for the purpose of studies which commence within 28 days of the expiry of the applicant's current leave to enter or remain or, where the applicant has overstayed, within 28 days of when that period of overstaying began.

(m)   The applicant must not be in the UK in breach of immigration laws except that any period of overstaying for a period of 28 days or less will be disregarded.

(n)   Where the applicant is applying for leave to remain as a Tier 4 (General) Student on the doctorate extension scheme:

    (i)   leave to remain as a Tier 4 (General) Student on the doctorate extension scheme must not have previously been granted;

    (ii)   the applicant must be following a course leading to the award of a PhD;

    (iii)   the applicant must be sponsored by a Sponsor that is a Recognised Body or a body in receipt of public funding as a higher education institution from the Department of Employment and Learning in Northern Ireland, the Higher Education Funding Council for England, the Higher Education Funding Council for Wales or the Scottish Funding Council and that sponsor will be the sponsor awarding the PhD; and

(iv) the date of the application must be within 60 days of the expected end date of a course leading to the award of a PhD.

(o) the Secretary of State must be satisfied that the applicant is a genuine student. 245ZX(o) will not be applied to a national or the rightful holder of a qualifying passport issued by one of the relevant competent authorities listed in Appendix H.

Period and conditions of grant

245ZY. (a) Subject to paragraphs (b), (ba) and (c) below, leave to remain will be granted for the duration of the course.

(b) In addition to the period of leave to remain granted in accordance with paragraph (a), leave to remain will also be granted for the periods set out in the following table. Notes to accompany the table appear below the table.

Type of course	Period of leave to remain to be granted before the course starts	Period of leave to remain to be granted after the course ends
12 months or more	1 month	4 months
6 months or more but less than 12 months	1 month	2 months
Pre-sessional course of less than 6 months	1 month	1 month
Course of less than 6 months that is not a pre-sessional course	7 days	7 days
Postgraduate doctor or dentist	1 month	1 month

Notes

(i) If the grant of leave to remain is being made less than 1 month or, in the case of a course of less than 6 months that is not a pre-sessional course, less than 7 days before the start of the course, leave to remain will be granted with immediate effect.

(ii) A pre-sessional course is a course which prepares a student for the student's main course of study in the UK.

(iii) The additional periods of leave to remain granted further to the table above will be disregarded for the purposes of calculating whether a migrant has exceeded the limits specified at 245ZX(h) to 245ZX(hb).

(ba) Leave to remain as a Tier 4 (General) Student on the doctorate extension scheme will be granted for 12 months, commencing on the expected end date of a course leading to the award of a PhD.

(bb) Leave to remain as a Tier 4 (General) Student on the doctorate extension scheme will not be subject to the conditions on the limited time that can be spent as a Tier 4 (General) Student or as a student, specified at 245ZX (hb).

(c) Leave to remain will be granted subject to the following conditions:

(i) no recourse to public funds,

(ii) registration with the police, if this is required by paragraph 326 of these Rules,

(iii) no employment except:

(1) employment during term time of no more than 20 hours per week and employment (of any duration) during vacations, where the student is following a course of degree level study and is either:

(a) sponsored by a Sponsor that is a Recognised Body or a body in receipt of public funding as a higher education institution from the Department of Employment and Learning in Northern Ireland, the Higher Education Funding Council for England, the Higher Education Funding Council for Wales or the Scottish Funding Council; or

(b) sponsored by an overseas higher education institution to undertake a short-term Study Abroad Programme in the United Kingdom.

(2) employment during term time of no more than 10 hours per week and employment (of any duration) during vacations, where the student is following a course of below degree level study and is sponsored by a Sponsor that is a Recognised Body or a body in receipt of public funding as a higher education institution from the Department of Employment

and Learning in Northern Ireland, the Higher Education Funding Council for England, the Higher Education Funding Council for Wales or the Scottish Funding Council,

(3)   employment during term time of no more than 10 hours per week and employment (of any duration) during vacations, where the student is following a course of study at any academic level and is sponsored by a Sponsor that is a publicly funded further education college,

(4)   employment as part of a course-related work placement which forms an assessed part of the applicant's course and provided that any period that the applicant spends on that placement does not exceed one third of the total length of the course undertaken in the UK except:

(i)   where it is a United Kingdom statutory requirement that the placement should exceed one third of the total length of the course; or

(ii)   where the placement does not exceed one half of the total length of the course undertaken in the UK and the student is following a course of degree level study and is either:

(a)   sponsored by a Sponsor that is a Recognised Body or a body in receipt of public funding as a higher education institution from the Department of Employment and Learning in Northern Ireland, the Higher Education Funding Council for England, the Higher Education Funding Council for Wales or the Scottish Funding Council; or

(b)   sponsored by an overseas higher education institution to undertake a short-term Study Abroad Programme in the United Kingdom.

(5)   employment as a Student Union Sabbatical Officer for up to 2 years provided the post is elective and is at the institution which is the applicant's Sponsor or they must be elected to a national National Union of Students (NUS) position,

(6)   employment as a postgraduate doctor or dentist on a recognised Foundation Programme

(7)   until such time as a decision is received from the UK Border Agency on an application which is supported by a Certificate of Sponsorship assigned by a licensed Tier 2 Sponsor and which is made following successful completion of course at degree level or above at a Sponsor that is a Recognised Body or a body in receipt of public funding as a higher education institution from the Department of Employment and Learning in Northern Ireland, the Higher Education Funding Council for England, the Higher Education Funding Council for Wales or the Scottish Funding Council and while the applicant has extant leave, and any appeal against that decision has been determined, employment with the Tier 2 Sponsor institution, in the role for which they assigned the Certificate of Sponsorship to the Tier 4 migrant,

(8)   self-employment, providing the migrant has made an application for leave to remain as a Tier 1 (Graduate Entrepreneur) Migrant which is supported by an endorsement from a qualifying Higher Education Institution and which is made following successful completion of a course at degree level or above at a Sponsor that is a Recognised Body or a body in receipt of public funding as a higher education institution from the Department of Employment and Learning in Northern Ireland, the Higher Education Funding Council for England, the Higher Education Funding Council for Wales or the Scottish Funding Council and while the applicant has extant leave, until such time as a decision is received from the UK Border Agency on an application and any appeal against that decision has been determined,

provided that the migrant is not self-employed other than under the conditions of (8) above, or employed as a Doctor or Dentist in Training other than under the conditions of (v) below, a professional sportsperson (including a sports coach) or an entertainer, and provided that the migrant's employment would not fill a permanent full time vacancy other than under the conditions of (7) above, or a vacancy on a recognised Foundation Programme or as a sabbatical officer.

(9)   where, during the current period of leave, the migrant has successfully completed a PhD at a Sponsor that is a Recognised Body or a body in receipt of public funding as a higher education institution from the Department of Employment and Learning in Northern Ireland, the Higher Education Funding Council for England, the Higher Education

Funding Council for Wales or the Scottish Funding Council, and has been granted leave to remain as a Tier 4 (General) Student on the doctorate extension scheme or has made a valid application for leave to remain as a Tier 4 (General) Student on the doctorate extension scheme but has not yet received a decision from the UK Border Agency on that application, there will be no limitation on the type of employment that may be taken, except for:

- (a) no employment as a Doctor or Dentist in Training other than under the conditions of (v) below;
- (b) no employment as a professional sportsperson (including a sports coach).

(iv) no study except:

- (1) study at the institution that the Confirmation of Acceptance for Studies Checking Service records as the migrant's Sponsor, or where the migrant was awarded points for a visa letter, study at the institution which issued that visa letter unless the migrant is studying at an institution which is a partner institution of the migrant's Sponsor,

- (2) until such time as a decision is received from the UK Border Agency on an application which is supported by a Confirmation of Acceptance for Studies assigned by a Highly Trusted Sponsor and which is made while the applicant has extant leave, and any appeal against that decision has been determined, study at the Highly Trusted Sponsor institution which the Confirmation of Acceptance for Studies Checking Service records as having assigned a Confirmation of Acceptance for Studies to the Tier 4 migrant,

- (3) supplementary study;

- (4) study at the same or a higher level of course as that stated on the confirmation of acceptance for studies, or at a lower level where the same requirements or conditions of leave would have applied if the application had been to study at that lower level.'

(v) no employment as a Doctor or Dentist in Training unless:

- (1) the course that the migrant is being sponsored to do (as recorded by the Confirmation of Acceptance for Studies Checking Service) is a recognised Foundation Programme, or

- (2) the migrant has made an application as a Tier 4 (General) Student which is supported by a Confirmation of Acceptance for Studies assigned by a Highly Trusted Sponsor to sponsor the applicant to do a recognised Foundation Programme, and this study satisfies the requirements of (iv)(2) above, or

- (3) the migrant has made an application as a Tier 2 (General) Migrant which is supported by a Certificate of Sponsorship assigned by a licensed Tier 2 Sponsor to sponsor the applicant to work as a Doctor or Dentist in Training, and this employment satisfies the conditions of (iii)(7) above.

245ZZ.–245ZZE.   OMITTED

Part 7 – Other Categories

Requirements for leave to enter the United Kingdom as a person exercising rights of access to a child resident in the United Kingdom

A246.   Paragraphs 246 to 248F apply only to a person who has made an application before 9 July 2012 for leave to enter or remain or indefinite leave to remain as a person exercising rights of access to a child resident in the UK, or who before 9 July 2012 has been granted leave to enter or remain as a person exercising rights of access to a child resident in the UK.

AB246.   Where an application for leave to enter or remain is made on or after 9 July 2012 as a person exercising rights of access to a child resident in the UK Appendix FM will apply.

246.   The requirements to be met by a person seeking leave to enter the United Kingdom to exercise access rights to a child resident in the United Kingdom are that:

(i)   the applicant is the parent of a child who is resident in the United Kingdom; and

(ii)   the parent or carer with whom the child permanently resides is resident in the United Kingdom; and

(iii)   the applicant produces evidence that he has access rights to the child in the form of:

(a)   a Residence Order or a Contact Order granted by a Court in the United Kingdom; or

        (b)   a certificate issued by a district judge confirming the applicant's intention to maintain contact with the child; and

    (iv)   the applicant intends to take an active role in the child's upbringing; and

    (v)   the child is under the age of 18; and

    (vi)   there will be adequate accommodation for the applicant and any dependants without recourse to public funds in accommodation which the applicant owns or occupies exclusively; and

    (vii) the applicant will be able to maintain himself and any dependants adequately without recourse to public funds; and

    (viii) the applicant holds a valid United Kingdom entry clearance for entry in this capacity.

Leave to enter the United Kingdom as a person exercising rights of access to a child resident in the United Kingdom

247.   Leave to enter as a person exercising access rights to a child resident in the United Kingdom may be granted for 12 months in the first instance, provided that a valid United Kingdom entry clearance for entry in this capacity is produced to the Immigration Officer on arrival.

Refusal of leave to enter the United Kingdom as a person exercising rights of access to a child resident in the United Kingdom

248.   Leave to enter as a person exercising rights of access to a child resident in the United Kingdom is to be refused if a valid United Kingdom entry clearance for entry in this capacity is not produced to the Immigration Officer on arrival.

Requirements for leave to remain in the United Kingdom as a person exercising rights of access to a child resident in the United Kingdom

248A.   The requirements to be met by a person seeking leave to remain in the United Kingdom to exercise access rights to a child resident in the United Kingdom are that:

    (i)   the applicant is the parent of a child who is resident in the United Kingdom; and

    (ii)   the parent or carer with whom the child permanently resides is resident in the United Kingdom; and

    (iii) the applicant produces evidence that he has access rights to the child in the form of:

        (a)   a Residence Order or a Contact Order granted by a Court in the United Kingdom; or

        (b)   a certificate issued by a district judge confirming the applicant's intention to maintain contact with the child; or

        (c)   a statement from the child's other parent (or, if contact is supervised, from the supervisor) that the applicant is maintaining contact with the child; and

    (iv)   the applicant takes and intends to continue to take an active role in the child's upbringing; and

    (v)   the child visits or stays with the applicant on a frequent and regular basis and the applicant intends this to continue; and

    (vi)   the child is under the age of 18; and

    (vii) the applicant has limited leave to remain in the United Kingdom as the spouse, civil partner, unmarried partner or same-sex partner of a person present and settled in the United Kingdom who is the other parent of the child; and

    (viii) the applicant has not remained in breach of the immigration laws; and

    (ix)   there will be adequate accommodation for the applicant and any dependants without recourse to public funds in accommodation which the applicant owns or occupies exclusively; and

    (x)   the applicant will be able to maintain himself and any dependants adequately without recourse to public funds.

Leave to remain in the United Kingdom as a person exercising rights of access to a child resident in the United Kingdom

248B.   Leave to remain as a person exercising access rights to a child resident in the United Kingdom may be granted for 12 months in the first instance, provided the Secretary of State is satisfied that each of the requirements of paragraph 248A is met.

Refusal of leave to remain in the United Kingdom as a person exercising rights of access to a child resident in the United Kingdom

248C.   Leave to remain as a person exercising rights of access to a child resident in the United Kingdom is to be refused if the Secretary of State is not satisfied that each of the requirements of paragraph 248A is met.

Indefinite leave to remain in the United Kingdom as a person exercising rights of access to a child resident in the United Kingdom

248D.   The requirements for indefinite leave to remain in the United Kingdom as a person exercising rights of access to a child resident in the United Kingdom are that:

    (i)   the applicant was admitted to the United Kingdom or granted leave to remain in the United Kingdom for a period of 12 months as a person exercising rights of access to a child and has completed a period of 12 months as a person exercising rights of access to a child; and

    (ii)   the applicant takes and intends to continue to take an active role in the child's upbringing; and

    (iii)   the child visits or stays with the applicant on a frequent and regular basis and the applicant intends this to continue; and

    (iv)   there will be adequate accommodation for the applicant and any dependants without recourse to public funds in accommodation which the applicant owns or occupies exclusively; and

    (v)   the applicant will be able to maintain himself and any dependants adequately without recourse to public funds; and

    (vi)   the child is under 18 years of age; and

    (vii)   The applicant must have demonstrated sufficient knowledge of the English language and sufficient knowledge about life in the United Kingdom, in accordance with Appendix KoLL; and

    (viii)   the applicant does not fall for refusal under the general grounds for refusal.

Indefinite leave to remain as a person exercising rights of access to a child resident in the United Kingdom

248E.   Indefinite leave to remain as a person exercising rights of access to a child may be granted provided the Secretary of State is satisfied that each of the requirements of paragraph 248D is met.

Refusal of indefinite leave to remain in the United Kingdom as a person exercising rights of access to a child resident in the United Kingdom

248F.   Indefinite leave to remain as a person exercising rights of access to a child is to be refused if the Secretary of State is not satisfied that each of the requirements of paragraph 248D is met.

249.–265.   DELETED

266–276.   OMITTED

Long residence

Long residence in the United Kingdom

276A.   For the purposes of paragraphs 276B to 276D and 276ADE and 399A.

    (a)   'continuous residence' means residence in the United Kingdom for an unbroken period, and for these purposes a period shall not be considered to have been broken where an applicant is absent from the United Kingdom for a period of 6 months or less at any one time, provided that the applicant in question has existing limited leave to enter or remain upon their departure and return, but shall be considered to have been broken if the applicant:

        (i)   has been removed under Schedule 2 of the 1971 Act, section 10 of the 1999 Act, has been deported or has left the United Kingdom having been refused leave to enter or remain here; or

        (ii)   has left the United Kingdom and, on doing so, evidenced a clear intention not to return; or

        (iii)   left the United Kingdom in circumstances in which he could have had no reasonable expectation at the time of leaving that he would lawfully be able to return; or

        (iv)   has been convicted of an offence and was sentenced to a period of imprisonment or was directed to be detained in an institution other than a prison (including, in particular, a hospital or an institution for young offenders), provided that the sentence in question was not a suspended sentence; or

        (v)   has spent a total of more than 18 months absent from the United Kingdom during the period in question.

    (b)   'lawful residence' means residence which is continuous residence pursuant to:

        (i)   existing leave to enter or remain; or

        (ii)   temporary admission within section 11 of the 1971 Act where leave to enter or remain is subsequently granted; or

        (iii)   an exemption from immigration control, including where an exemption ceases to apply if it is immediately followed by a grant of leave to enter or remain.

    (c)   'lived continuously' and 'living continuously' mean 'continuous residence', except that paragraph 276A(a)(iv) shall not apply.

276A0. For the purposes of paragraph 276ADE the requirement to make a valid application will not apply when the Article 8 claim is raised:

    (i)   as part of an asylum claim, or as part of a further submission in person after an asylum claim has been refused;

    (ii)   where a migrant is in immigration detention;

    (iii)   where removal directions have been set pending an imminent removal;

    (iv)   in an appeal; or

    (v)   in response to a (one stop) notice issued under section 120 of the Nationality, Immigration and Asylum Act 2002.

Requirements for an extension of stay on the ground of long residence in the United Kingdom

276A1. The requirement to be met by a person seeking an extension of stay on the ground of long residence in the United Kingdom is that the applicant meets each of the requirements in paragraph 276B(i)–(ii) and (v).

Extension of stay on the ground of long residence in the United Kingdom

276A2. An extension of stay on the ground of long residence in the United Kingdom may be granted for a period not exceeding 2 years provided that the Secretary of State is satisfied that the requirement in paragraph 276A1 is met, and a person granted such an extension of stay following an application made before 9 July 2012 will remain subject to the rules in force on 8 July 2012.

Conditions to be attached to extension of stay on the ground of long residence in the United Kingdom

276A3. Where an extension of stay is granted under paragraph 276A2:

    (i)   if the applicant has spent less than 20 years in the UK, the grant of leave should be subject to the same conditions attached to his last period of lawful leave, or

    (ii)   if the applicant has spent 20 years or more in the UK, the grant of leave should not contain any restriction on employment.

Refusal of extension of stay on the ground of long residence in the United Kingdom

276A4. An extension of stay on the ground of long residence in the United Kingdom is to be refused if the Secretary of State is not satisfied that the requirement in paragraph 276A1 is met.

Requirements for indefinite leave to remain on the ground of long residence in the United Kingdom

276B. The requirements to be met by an applicant for indefinite leave to remain on the ground of long residence in the United Kingdom are that:

    (i)   (a)   he has had at least 10 years continuous lawful residence in the United Kingdom.

    (ii)   having regard to the public interest there are no reasons why it would be undesirable for him to be given indefinite leave to remain on the ground of long residence, taking into account his:

        (a)   age; and

        (b)   strength of connections in the United Kingdom; and

        (c)   personal history, including character, conduct, associations and employment record; and

        (d)   domestic circumstances; and

        (e)   compassionate circumstances; and

(f)   any representations received on the person's behalf; and

(iii)   the applicant does not fall for refusal under the general grounds for refusal.

(iv)   the applicant has demonstrated sufficient knowledge of the English language and sufficient knowledge about life in the United Kingdom, in accordance with Appendix KoLL.

(v)   the applicant must not be in the UK in breach of immigration laws except that any period of overstaying for a period of 28 days or less will be disregarded, as will any period of overstaying between periods of entry clearance, leave to enter or leave to remain of up to 28 days and any period of overstaying pending the determination of an application made within that 28 day period.

Indefinite leave to remain on the ground of long residence in the United Kingdom

276C.   Indefinite leave to remain on the ground of long residence in the United Kingdom may be granted provided that the Secretary of State is satisfied that each of the requirements of paragraph 276B is met.

Refusal of indefinite leave to remain on the ground of long residence in the United Kingdom

276D.   Indefinite leave to remain on the ground of long residence in the United Kingdom is to be refused if the Secretary of State is not satisfied that each of the requirements of paragraph 276B is met.

Private life

Requirements to be met by an applicant for leave to remain on the grounds of private life

276ADE.   The requirements to be met by an applicant for leave to remain on the grounds of private life in the UK are that at the date of application, the applicant:

(i)   does not fall for refusal under any of the grounds in Section S-LTR 1.2 to S-LTR 2.3. and S-LTR.3.1. in Appendix FM; and

(ii)   has made a valid application for leave to remain on the grounds of private life in the UK; and

(iii)   has lived continuously in the UK for at least 20 years (discounting any period of imprisonment); or

(iv)   is under the age of 18 years and has lived continuously in the UK for at least 7 years (discounting any period of imprisonment) and it would not be reasonable to expect the applicant to leave the UK; or

(v)   is aged 18 years or above and under 25 years and has spent at least half of his life living continuously in the UK (discounting any period of imprisonment); or

(vi)   is aged 18 years or above, has lived continuously in the UK for less than 20 years (discounting any period of imprisonment) but has no ties (including social, cultural or family) with the country to which he would have to go if required to leave the UK.

Leave to remain on the grounds of private life in the UK

276BE.   Limited leave to remain on the grounds of private life in the UK may be granted for a period not exceeding 30 months provided that the Secretary of State is satisfied that the requirements in paragraph 276ADE are met or, in respect of the requirements in paragraph 276ADE(iv) and (v), were met in a previous application which led to a grant of limited leave to remain under paragraph 276BE. Such leave shall be given subject to such conditions as the Secretary of State deems appropriate.

Refusal of limited leave to remain on the grounds of private life in the UK

276CE.   Limited leave to remain on the grounds of private life in the UK is to be refused if the Secretary of State is not satisfied that the requirements in paragraph 276ADE are met.

Requirements for indefinite leave to remain on the grounds of private life in the UK

276DE.   The requirements to be met for the grant of indefinite leave to remain on the grounds of private life in the UK are that:

(a)   the applicant has been in the UK with continuous leave on the grounds of private life for a period of at least 120 months.This continuous leave will disregard any period of overstaying between periods of leave on the grounds of private life where the application was made no later than 28 days after the expiry of the previous leave. Any period pending the determination of the application will also be disregarded;

(b)   the applicant meets the requirements of paragraph 276ADE or, in respect of the requirements in paragraph 276ADE(iv) and (v), the applicant met the requirements in a previous application which led to a grant of limited leave to remain under paragraph 276BE;

(c)   the applicant does not fall for refusal under any of the grounds in Section S-ILR: Suitability-indefinite leave to remain in Appendix FM;

(d)   the applicant has demonstrated sufficient knowledge of the English language and sufficient knowledge about life in the United Kingdom, in accordance with Appendix KoLL; and

(e)   there are no reasons why it would be undesirable to grant the applicant indefinite leave to remain based on the applicant's conduct, character or associations or because the applicant represents a threat to national security.

Indefinite leave to remain on the grounds of private life in the UK

276DF.   Indefinite leave to remain on the grounds of private life in the UK may be granted provided that the Secretary of State is satisfied that each of the requirements of paragraph 276DE is met.

276DG.   If the applicant does not meet the requirements for indefinite leave to remain on the grounds of private life in the UK only for one or both of the following reasons–

(a)   paragraph S-ILR.1.5. or S-ILR.1.6. in Appendix FM applies;

(b)   the applicant has not met the requirements of paragraphs 33B to 33G of these Rules,

the applicant may be granted further limited leave to remain on the grounds of private life in the UK for a period not exceeding 30 months, and subject to such conditions as the Secretary of State deems appropriate.

Refusal of indefinite leave to remain on the grounds of private life in the UK

276DH.   Indefinite leave to remain on the grounds of private life in the UK is to be refused if the Secretary of State is not satisfied that each of the requirements of paragraph 276DE is met, subject to paragraph 276DG.

276E–276BS1.   OMITTED

Part 8 – Family members

A277–A295O.   OMITTED

Children

296.   Nothing in these Rules shall be construed as permitting a child to be granted entry clearance, leave to enter or remain, or variation of leave where his parent is party to a polygamous marriage or civil partnership and any application by that parent for admission or leave to remain for settlement or with a view to settlement would be refused pursuant to paragraphs 278 or 278A.

Leave to enter or remain in the United Kingdom as the child of a parent, parents or a relative present and settled or being admitted for settlement in the United Kingdom

Requirements for indefinite leave to enter the United Kingdom as the child of a parent, parents or a relative present and settled or being admitted for settlement in the United Kingdom

297.   The requirements to be met by a person seeking indefinite leave to enter the United Kingdom as the child of a parent, parents or a relative present and settled or being admitted for settlement in the United Kingdom are that he:

(i)   is seeking leave to enter to accompany or join a parent, parents or a relative in one of the following circumstances:

(a)   both parents are present and settled in the United Kingdom; or

(b)   both parents are being admitted on the same occasion for settlement; or

(c)   one parent is present and settled in the United Kingdom and the other is being admitted on the same occasion for settlement; or

(d)   one parent is present and settled in the United Kingdom or being admitted on the same occasion for settlement and the other parent is dead; or

(e)   one parent is present and settled in the United Kingdom or being admitted on the same occasion for settlement and has had sole responsibility for the child's upbringing; or

(f)   one parent or a relative is present and settled in the United Kingdom or being admitted on the same occasion for settlement and there are serious and compelling family or other considerations which make exclusion of the child undesirable and suitable arrangements have been made for the child's care; and

(ii)   is under the age of 18; and

(iii) is not leading an independent life, is unmarried and is not a civil partner, and has not formed an independent family unit; and

(iv)   can, and will, be accommodated adequately by the parent, parents or relative the child is seeking to join without recourse to public funds in accommodation which the parent, parents or relative the child is seeking to join, own or occupy exclusively; and

(v)   can, and will, be maintained adequately by the parent, parents, or relative the child is seeking to join, without recourse to public funds; and

(vi)   holds a valid United Kingdom entry clearance for entry in this capacity; and

(vii) does not fall for refusal under the general grounds for refusal.

Requirements for indefinite leave to remain in the United Kingdom as the child of a parent, parents or a relative present and settled or being admitted for settlement in the United Kingdom

298. The requirements to be met by a person seeking indefinite leave to remain in the United Kingdom as the child of a parent, parents or a relative present and settled in the United Kingdom are that he:

(i)   is seeking to remain with a parent, parents or a relative in one of the following circumstances:

    (a)   both parents are present and settled in the United Kingdom; or

    (b)   one parent is present and settled in the United Kingdom and the other parent is dead; or

    (c)   one parent is present and settled in the United Kingdom and has had sole responsibility for the child's upbringing or the child normally lives with this parent and not their other parent; or

    (d)   one parent or a relative is present and settled in the United Kingdom and there are serious and compelling family or other considerations which make exclusion of the child undesirable and suitable arrangements have been made for the child's care; and

(ii)   has or has had limited leave to enter or remain in the United Kingdom, and

    (a)   is under the age of 18; or

    (b)   was given leave to enter or remain with a view to settlement under paragraph 302 or Appendix FM; or

    (c)   was admitted into the UK in accordance with paragraph 319R and has completed a period of 2 years limited leave as the child of a refugee or beneficiary of humanitarian protection who is now present and settled in the UK or as the child of a former refugee or beneficiary of humanitarian protection who is now a British Citizen, or

    (d)   the applicant *has limited leave to enter or remain in* the United Kingdom in accordance with paragraph 319X, as the child of a relative with limited leave to remain as a refugee or beneficiary of humanitarian protection in the United Kingdom and who is now present and settled here.

(iii) is not leading an independent life, is unmarried, and has not formed an independent family unit; and

(iv)   can, and will, be accommodated adequately by the parent, parents or relative the child was admitted to join, without recourse to public funds in accommodation which the parent, parents or relative the child was admitted to join, own or occupy exclusively; and

(v)   can, and will, be maintained adequately by the parent, parents or relative the child was admitted to join, without recourse to public funds; and

(vi)   does not have fall for refusal under the general grounds for refusal;

(vii) if aged 18 or over, was admitted to the United Kingdom under paragraph 302, or Appendix FM, or 319R or 319X and has demonstrated sufficient knowledge of the English language and sufficient knowledge about life in the United Kingdom in accordance with Appendix KoLL.

Indefinite leave to enter or remain in the United Kingdom as the child of a parent, parents or a relative present and settled or being admitted for settlement in the United Kingdom

299. Indefinite leave to enter the United Kingdom as the child of a parent, parents or a relative present and settled or being admitted for settlement in the United Kingdom may be granted provided a valid United Kingdom entry clearance for entry in this capacity is produced to the Immigration Officer on arrival. Indefinite leave to remain in the United Kingdom as the child of a parent, parents or a relative present and settled in the United

Kingdom may be granted provided the Secretary of State is satisfied that each of the requirements of paragraph 298 is met.

Refusal of indefinite leave to enter or remain in the United Kingdom as the child of a parent, parents or a relative present and settled or being admitted for settlement in the United Kingdom

300.   Indefinite leave to enter the United Kingdom as the child of a parent, parents or a relative present and settled or being admitted for settlement in the United Kingdom is to be refused if a valid United Kingdom entry clearance for entry in this capacity is not produced to the Immigration Officer on arrival. Indefinite leave to remain in the United Kingdom as the child of a parent, parents or a relative present and settled in the United Kingdom is to be refused if the Secretary of State is not satisfied that each of the requirements of paragraph 298 is met.

Requirements for limited leave to enter or remain in the United Kingdom with a view to settlement as the child of a parent or parents given limited leave to enter or remain in the United Kingdom with a view to settlement

301.   The requirements to be met by a person seeking limited leave to enter or remain in the United Kingdom with a view to settlement as the child of a parent or parents given limited leave to enter or remain in the United Kingdom with a view to settlement are that he:

(i)   is seeking leave to enter to accompany or join or remain with a parent or parents in one of the following circumstances:

    (a)   one parent is present and settled in the United Kingdom or being admitted on the same occasion for settlement and the other parent is being or has been given limited leave to enter or remain in the United Kingdom with a view to settlement; or

    (b)   one parent is being or has been given limited leave to enter or remain in the United Kingdom with a view to settlement and has had sole responsibility for the child's upbringing; or

    (c)   one parent is being or has been given limited leave to enter or remain in the United Kingdom with a view to settlement and there are serious and compelling family or other considerations which make exclusion of the child undesirable and suitable arrangements have been made for the child's care; and

(ii)   is under the age of 18; and

(iii)   is not leading an independent life, is unmarried and is not a civil partner, and has not formed an independent family unit; and

(iv)   can, and will, be accommodated adequately without recourse to public funds, in accommodation which the parent or parents own or occupy exclusively; and

(iva)   can, and will, be maintained adequately by the parent or parents without recourse to public funds; and

(ivb)   does not qualify for limited leave to enter as a child of a parent or parents given limited leave to enter or remain as a refugee or beneficiary of humanitarian protection under paragraph 319R; and

(v)   (where an application is made for limited leave to remain with a view to settlement) has limited leave to enter or remain in the United Kingdom; and

(vi)   if seeking leave to enter, holds a valid United Kingdom entry clearance for entry in this capacity.

Limited leave to enter or remain in the United Kingdom with a view to settlement as the child of a parent or parents given limited leave to enter or remain in the United Kingdom with a view to settlement

302.   A person seeking limited leave to enter the United Kingdom with a view to settlement as the child of a parent or parents given limited leave to enter or remain in the United Kingdom with a view to settlement may be admitted for a period not exceeding 27 months provided he is able, on arrival, to produce to the Immigration Officer a valid United Kingdom entry clearance for entry in this capacity. A person seeking limited leave to remain in the United Kingdom with a view to settlement as the child of a parent or parents given limited leave to enter or remain in the United Kingdom with a view to settlement may be given limited leave to remain for a period not exceeding 27 months provided the Secretary of State is satisfied that each of the requirements of paragraph 301 (i)–(v) is met.

Refusal of limited leave to enter or remain in the United Kingdom with a view to settlement as the child of a parent or parents given limited leave to enter or remain in the United Kingdom with a view to settlement

303. Limited leave to enter the United Kingdom with a view to settlement as the child of a parent or parents given limited leave to enter or remain in the United Kingdom with a view to settlement is to be refused if a valid United Kingdom entry clearance for entry in this capacity is not produced to the Immigration Officer on arrival. Limited leave to remain in the United Kingdom with a view to settlement as the child of a parent or parents given limited leave to enter or remain in the United Kingdom with a view to settlement is to be refused if the Secretary of State is not satisfied that each of the requirements of paragraph 301 (i)–(v) is met.

Leave to enter and extension of stay in the United Kingdom as the child of a parent who is being, or has been admitted to the united kingdom as a fiance(e) or proposed civil partner

Requirements for limited leave to enter the United Kingdom as the child of a fiance(e) or proposed civil partner

303A. The requirements to be met by a person seeking limited leave to enter the United Kingdom as the child of a fiance(e) or proposed civil partner, are that:

(i)   he is seeking to accompany or join a parent who is, on the same occasion that the child seeks admission, being admitted as a fiance(e) or proposed civil partner , or who has been admitted as a fiance(e) or proposed civil partner; and

(ii)   he is under the age of 18; and

(iii) he is not leading an independent life, is unmarried and is not a civil partner, and has not formed an independent family unit; and

(iv)   he can and will be maintained and accommodated adequately without recourse to public funds with the parent admitted or being admitted as a fiance(e) or proposed civil partner; and

(v)   there are serious and compelling family or other considerations which make the child's exclusion undesirable, that suitable arrangements have been made for his care in the United Kingdom, and there is no other person outside the United Kingdom who could reasonably be expected to care for him; and

(vi)   he holds a valid United Kingdom entry clearance for entry in this capacity.

Limited leave to enter the United Kingdom as the child of a parent who is being, or has been admitted to the United Kingdom as a fiance(e) or proposed civil partner

303B. A person seeking limited leave to enter the United Kingdom as the child of a fiance(e) or proposed civil partner, may be granted limited leave to enter the United Kingdom for a period not in excess of that granted to the fiance(e) or proposed civil partner, provided that a valid United Kingdom entry clearance for entry in this capacity is produced to the Immigration Officer on arrival. Where the period of limited leave granted to a fiance(e) will expire in more than 6 months, a person seeking limited leave to enter as the child of the fiance(e) or proposed civil partner should be granted leave for a period not exceeding six months.

Refusal of limited leave to enter the United Kingdom as the child of a parent who is being, or has been admitted to the United Kingdom as a fiance(e) or proposed civil partner

303C. Limited leave to enter the United Kingdom as the child of a fiance(e) or proposed civil partner, is to be refused if a valid United Kingdom entry clearance for entry in this capacity is not produced to the Immigration Officer on arrival.

Requirements for an extension of stay in the United Kingdom as the child of a fiance(e) or proposed civil partner

303D. The requirements to be met by a person seeking an extension of stay in the United Kingdom as the child of a fiance(e) or proposed civil partner are that:

(i)   the applicant was admitted with a valid United Kingdom entry clearance as the child of a fiance(e) or proposed civil partner; and

(ii)   the applicant is the child of a parent who has been granted limited leave to enter, or an extension of stay, as a fiance(e) or proposed civil partner; and

(iii) the requirements of paragraph 303A (ii)–(v) are met.

Extension of stay in the United Kingdom as the child of a fiance(e) or proposed civil partner

303E.   An extension of stay as the child of a fiance(e) or proposed civil partner may be granted provided that the Secretary of State is satisfied that each of the requirements of paragraph 303D is met.

Refusal of an extension of stay in the United Kingdom as the child of a fiance(e) or proposed civil partner

303F.   An extension of stay as the child of a fiance(e) or proposed civil partner is to be refused if the Secretary of State is not satisfied that each of the requirements of paragraph 303D is met.

Children born in the United Kingdom who are not British citizens

304.   This paragraph and paragraphs 305–309 apply only to dependent children under 18 years of age who are unmarried and are not civil partners and who were born in the United Kingdom on or after 1 January 1983 (when the British Nationality Act 1981 came into force) but who, because neither of their parents was a British Citizen or settled in the United Kingdom at the time of their birth, are not British Citizens and are therefore subject to immigration control. Such a child requires leave to enter where admission to the United Kingdom is sought, and leave to remain where permission is sought for the child to be allowed to stay in the United Kingdom. If he qualifies for entry clearance, leave to enter or leave to remain under any other part of these Rules, a child who was born in the United Kingdom but is not a British Citizen may be granted entry clearance, leave to enter or leave to remain in accordance with the provisions of that other part.

Requirements for leave to enter or remain in the United Kingdom as the child of a parent or parents given leave to enter or remain in the United Kingdom

305.   The requirements to be met by a child born in the United Kingdom who is not a British Citizen who seeks leave to enter or remain in the United Kingdom as the child of a parent or parents given leave to enter or remain in the United Kingdom are that he:

(i)   (a)   is accompanying or seeking to join or remain with a parent or parents who have, or are given, leave to enter or remain in the United Kingdom; or

(b)   is accompanying or seeking to join or remain with a parent or parents one of whom is a British Citizen or has the right of abode in the United Kingdom; or

(c)   is a child in respect of whom the parental rights and duties are vested solely in a local authority; and

(ii)   is under the age of 18; and

(iii)   was born in the United Kingdom; and

(iv)   is not leading an independent life, is unmarried and is not a civil partner, and has not formed an independent family unit; and

(v)   (where an application is made for leave to enter) has not been away from the United Kingdom for more than 2 years.

Leave to enter or remain in the United Kingdom

306.   A child born in the United Kingdom who is not a British Citizen and who requires leave to enter or remain in the circumstances set out in paragraph 304 may be given leave to enter for the same period as his parent or parents where paragraph 305 (i)(a) applies, provided the Immigration Officer is satisfied that each of the requirements of paragraph 305 (ii)–(v) is met. Where leave to remain is sought, the child may be granted leave to remain for the same period as his parent or parents where paragraph 305 (i)(a) applies, provided the Secretary of State is satisfied that each of the requirements of paragraph 305 (ii)–(iv) is met. Where the parent or parents have or are given periods of leave of different duration, the child may be given leave to whichever period is longer except that if the parents are living apart the child should be given leave for the same period as the parent who has day to day responsibility for him.

307.   If a child does not qualify for leave to enter or remain because neither of his parents has a current leave, (and neither of them is a British Citizen or has the right of abode), he will normally be refused leave to enter or remain, even if each of the requirements of paragraph 305 (ii)–(v) has been satisfied. However, he may be granted leave to enter or remain for a period not exceeding 3 months if both of his parents are in the United Kingdom and it appears unlikely that they will be removed in the immediate future, and there is no other person outside the United Kingdom who could reasonably be expected to care for him.

308.   A child born in the United Kingdom who is not a British Citizen and who requires leave to enter or remain in the United Kingdom in the circumstances set out in paragraph 304 may be given indefinite leave to enter

where paragraph 305 (i)(b) or (i)(c) applies provided the Immigration Officer is satisfied that each of the requirements of paragraph 305 (ii)–(v) is met. Where an application is for leave to remain, such a child may be granted indefinite leave to remain where paragraph 305 (i)(b) or (i)(c) applies, provided the Secretary of State is satisfied that each of the requirements of paragraph 305 (ii)–(iv) is met.

Refusal of leave to enter or remain in the United Kingdom

309.   Leave to enter the United Kingdom where the circumstances set out in paragraph 304 apply is to be refused if the Immigration Officer is not satisfied that each of the requirements of paragraph 305 is met. Leave to remain for such a child is to be refused if the Secretary of State is not satisfied that each of the requirements of paragraph 305 (i)–(iv) is met.

309A.–319.   OMITTED

Family members of relevant points-based system migrants

Partners of relevant points-based system migrants

319AA.   In paragraphs 319A to 319K and Appendix E, 'Relevant Points Based System Migrant' means a migrant granted to leave as a Tier 1 Migrant, a Tier 2 Migrant, a Tier 4 (General) Student or a Tier 5 (Temporary Worker) Migrant.

Purpose

319A.   This route is for the spouse, civil partner, unmarried or same-sex partner of a Relevant Points Based System Migrant (Partner of a Relevant Points Based System Migrant). Paragraphs 277 to 280 of these Rules apply to spouses or civil partners of Relevant Points Based System Migrant; paragraph 277 of these Rules applies to civil partners of Relevant Points Based System Migrant; and paragraph 295AA of these Rules applies to unmarried and same-sex partners of Relevant Points Based System Migrant

Entry to the UK

319B.   (a)   Subject to paragraph (b), all migrants wishing to enter as the Partner of a relevant Points Based System Migrant must have a valid entry clearance for entry under this route. If they do not have a valid entry clearance, entry will be refused.

(b)   A Migrant arriving in the UK and wishing to enter as a partner of a Tier 5 (Temporary Worker) Migrant, who does not have a valid entry clearance will not be refused entry if the following conditions are met:

(i)   the migrant wishing to enter as partner is not a visa national,

(ii)   the migrant wishing to enter as a Partner is accompanying an applicant who at the same time is being granted leave to enter under paragraph 245ZN(b), and

(iii)   the migrant wishing to enter as a Partner meets the requirements of entry clearance in paragraph 319C.

Requirements for entry clearance or leave to remain

319C.   To qualify for entry clearance or leave to remain as the Partner of a Relevant Points Based System Migrant, an applicant must meet the requirements listed below. If the applicant meets these requirements, entry clearance or leave to remain will be granted. If the applicant does not meet these requirements, the application will be refused.

Requirements:

(a)   The applicant must not fall for refusal under the general grounds for refusal, and if applying for leave to remain, must not be an illegal entrant.

(b)   The applicant must be the spouse or civil partner, unmarried or same-sex partner of a person who:

(i)   has valid leave to enter or remain as a Relevant Points Based System Migrant, or

(ii)   is, at the same time, being granted entry clearance or leave to remain as a Relevant Points Based System Migrant, or

(iii)   has indefinite leave to remain as a Relevant Points Based System Migrant, or is, at the same time being granted indefinite leave to remain as a Relevant Points Based System Migrant, where the applicant is applying for further leave to remain and was last granted leave:

(1)   as the partner of that same Relevant Points Based System Migrant: or

(2)   as the spouse or civil partner, unmarried or same-sex partner of that person at a time when that person had leave under another category of these Rules; or

(iv) has become a British Citizen where prior to that they held indefinite leave to Remain as a Relevant Points Based System Migrant and where the applicant is applying for further leave to remain and was last granted leave:

   (1)   as the partner of that same Relevant Points Based System Migrant, or

   (2)   as the spouse or civil partner, unmarried or same-sex partner of that person at a time when that person had leave under another category of these Rules.

(c) An applicant who is the unmarried or same-sex partner of a Relevant Points Based System Migrant must also meet the following requirements:

   (i)   any previous marriage or civil partnership or similar relationship by the applicant or the Relevant Points Based System Migrant with another person must have permanently broken down,

   (ii)   the applicant and the Relevant Points Based System Migrant must not be so closely related that they would be prohibited from marrying each other in the UK, and

   (iii)   the applicant and the Relevant Points Based System Migrant must have been living together in a relationship similar to marriage or civil partnership for a period of at least 2 years.

(d) The marriage or civil partnership, or relationship similar to marriage or civil partnership, must be subsisting at the time the application is made.

(e) The applicant and the Relevant Points Based System Migrant must intend to live with the other as their spouse or civil partner, unmarried or same-sex partner throughout the applicants stay in the UK.

(f) The applicant must not intend to stay in the UK beyond any period of leave granted to the Relevant Points Based System Migrant .

(g) Unless the Relevant Points Based System Migrant is a Tier 1 (Investor) Migrant or a Tier 1 (Exceptional Talent) Migrant, there must be a sufficient level of funds available to the applicant, as set out in Appendix E.

(h) An applicant who is applying for leave to remain must not have last been granted:

   (i)   entry clearance or leave as a visitor, unless the Relevant Points Based System Migrant has, or is being granted, leave to remain as a Tier 5 (Temporary Worker) Migrant in the creative and sporting subcategory on the basis of having met the requirement at paragraph 245ZQ(b)(ii);

   (ii)   temporary admission; or

   (iii)   temporary release.

(i) Where the relevant Points Based System Migrant is applying for, or has been granted, entry clearance, leave to enter, or leave to remain in the United Kingdom as a Tier 4 (General) Student either:

   (i)   the relevant Points Based System Migrant must be a government sponsored student who is applying for, or who has been granted, entry clearance or leave to remain to undertake a course of study longer than six months;

   (ii)   the relevant Points Based System Migrant must:

      (1)   be applying for, or have been granted entry clearance or leave to remain in order to undertake a course of study at post-graduate level that is 12 months or longer in duration; and

      (2)   be sponsored by a sponsor who is a Recognised Body or a body in receipt of funding as a higher education institution from either:

         (a)   the Department for Employment and Learning in Northern Ireland;

         (b)   the Higher Education Funding Council for England;

         (c)   the Higher Education Funding Council for Wales; or

         (d)   the Scottish Funding Council;

   (iii)   the relevant Points Based System Migrant must be applying for, or have been granted leave to remain as a Tier 4 (General) Student on the doctorate extension scheme; or

   (iv)   the following conditions must be met:

      (1)   the relevant Points Based System Migrant must be applying for entry clearance, leave to enter, or leave to remain, to undertake a course of study that is longer than six months and either:

         (a)   have entry clearance, leave to enter, or leave to remain as a Tier 4 (General) Student or as a student to undertake a course of study longer than six months; or

        (b)   have last had entry clearance, leave to enter, or leave to remain within the three months preceding the application as a Tier 4 (General) Student or as a student to undertake a course of study longer than six months; and

    (2)   the Partner must either:

        (a)   have entry clearance, leave to enter, or leave to remain as the Partner of a Tier 4 (General) Student or a student with entry clearance, leave to enter, or leave to remain, to undertake a course of study longer than six months; or

        (b)   have last had entry clearance, leave to enter, or leave to remain within the three months preceding the application as the Partner of a Tier 4 (General) Student or as a student to undertake a course of study longer than six months; and

    (3)   the relevant Points Based System Migrant and the Partner must be applying at the same time.

(j)   The applicant must not be in the UK in breach of immigration laws except that any period of overstaying for a period of 28 days will be disregarded.

Period and conditions of grant

319D. (a) (i)   Entry clearance or limited leave to remain will be granted for a period which expires on the same day as the leave granted to the Relevant Points Based System Migrant, or

        (ii)   If the Relevant Points-Based System Migrant has indefinite leave to remain as a Relevant Points Based System Migrant, or is, at the same time being granted indefinite leave to remain as a Relevant Points Based System Migrant, or where the Relevant Points-Based System Migrant has since become a British Citizen, leave to remain will be granted to the applicant for a period of 3 years.

    (b)   Entry clearance and leave to remain under this route will be subject to the following conditions:

        (i)   no recourse to public funds,

        (ii)   registration with the police, if this is required under paragraph 326 of these Rules,

        (iii)   no Employment as a Doctor or Dentist in Training, unless the applicant:

            (1)   has obtained a primary degree in medicine or dentistry at bachelor's level or above from a UK institution that is a UK recognised or listed body, or which holds a sponsor licence under Tier 4 of the Points Based System, and provides evidence of this degree; or

            (2)   is applying for leave to remain and has, or has last been granted, entry clearance, leave to enter or leave to remain that was not subject to any condition restricting him from taking employment as a Doctor in Training, has been employed during that leave as a Doctor in Training, and provides a letter from the Postgraduate Deanery or NHS Trust employing them which confirms that they have been working in a post or programme that has been approved by the General Medical Council as a training programme or post; or

            (3)   is applying for leave to remain and has, or has last been granted, entry clearance, leave to enter or leave to remain that was not subject to any condition restricting him from taking employment as a Dentist in Training, has been employed during that leave as a Dentist in Training, and provides a letter from the Postgraduate Deanery or NHS Trust employing them which confirms that they have been working in a post or programme that has been approved by the Joint Committee for Postgraduate Training in Dentistry as a training programme or post.

        (iv)   if the Relevant Points Based System Migrant is a Tier 4 (General) Student and the Partner meets the requirements of paragraphs 319C(i)(iv)(1),(2) and (3) and:

            (1)   the Relevant Points Based System Migrant is a Tier 4 (General) Student applying for leave for less than 12 months, no employment, or

            (2)   the Relevant Points Based System Migrant is a Tier 4 (General) Student who is following a course of below degree level study, no employment.

Requirements for indefinite leave to remain

319E. To qualify for indefinite leave to remain as the Partner of a Relevant Points Based System Migrant, an applicant must meet the requirements listed below. If the applicant meets these requirements, indefinite leave to remain will be granted. If the applicant does not meet these requirements, the application will be refused.

Requirements:

(a)   The applicant must not fall for refusal under the general grounds for refusal, and must not be an illegal entrant.

(b)   The applicant must be the spouse or civil partner, unmarried or same-sex partner of a person who:

    (i)   has indefinite leave to remain as a Relevant Points Based System Migrant; or

    (ii)   is, at the same time being granted indefinite leave to remain as a Relevant Points Based System Migrant, or

    (iii)   has become a British Citizen where prior to that they held indefinite leave to remain as a Relevant Points Based System Migrant.

(c)   The applicant must have, or have last been granted, leave as the partner of the Relevant Points Based System Migrant who:

    (i)   has indefinite leave to remain as a Relevant Points Based System Migrant; or

    (ii)   is, at the same time being granted indefinite leave to remain as a Relevant Points Based System Migrant, or

    (iii)   has become a British Citizen where prior to that they held indefinite leave to remain as a Relevant Points Based System Migrant.

(d)   The applicant and the Relevant Points Based System Migrant must have been living together in the UK in a marriage or civil partnership, or in a relationship similar to marriage or civil partnership, for at least the period specified in (i) or (ii):

    (i)   If the applicant was granted leave as:

        (a)   the Partner of that Relevant Points Based System Migrant, or

        (b)   the spouse or civil partner, unmarried or same-sex partner of that person at a time when that person had leave under another category of these Rules under the Rules in place before 9 July 2012, and since then has had continuous leave as the Partner of that Relevant Points based System Migrant, the specified period is 2 years

    (ii)   If (i) does not apply, the specified period is a continuous period of 5 years, during which the applicant must:

        (a)   have been in a relationship with the same Relevant Points Based System Migrant for this entire period,

        (b)   have spent the most recent part of the 5 year period with leave as the Partner of that Relevant Points Based System Migrant, and during that part of the period have met all of the requirements of paragraph 319C(a) to (e), and

        (c)   have spent the remainder of the 5 year period, where applicable, with leave as the spouse or civil partner, unmarried or same-sex partner of that person at a time when that person had leave under another category of these Rules.

(e)   The marriage or civil partnership, or relationship similar to marriage or civil partnership, must be subsisting at the time the application is made.

(f)   The applicant and the Relevant Points Based System Migrant must intend to live permanently with the other as their spouse or civil partner, unmarried or same-sex partner.

(g)   The applicant has demonstrated sufficient knowledge of the English language and sufficient knowledge about life in the United Kingdom, in accordance with Appendix KoLL.

(h)   DELETED

(i)   The applicant must not be in the UK in breach of immigration laws except that any period of overstaying for a period of 28 days will be disregarded.

Children of relevant points-based system migrants

Purpose

319F.   This route is for the children of a Relevant Points Based System Migrant who are under the age of 18 when they apply to enter under this route. Paragraph 296 of these Rules applies to children of a Relevant Points Based System Migrants.

Entry to the UK

319G. (a)   Subject to paragraph (b), all migrants wishing to enter as the Child of a relevant Points Based System Migrant must have a valid entry clearance for entry under this route. If they do not have a valid entry clearance, entry will be refused.

(b)   A Migrant arriving in the UK and wishing to enter as a child of a Tier 5 (Temporary Worker) Migrant, who does not have a valid entry clearance will not be refused entry if the following conditions are met:

(i)   the migrant wishing to enter as a child is not a visa national,

(ii)   the migrant wishing to enter as a child is accompanying an applicant who at the same time is being granted leave to enter under paragraph 245ZN(b), and

(iii)   the migrant wishing to enter as a Child meets the requirements of entry clearance in paragraph 319H.

Requirements for entry clearance or leave to remain

319H. To qualify for entry clearance or leave to remain under this route, an applicant must meet the requirements listed below. If the applicant meets these requirements, entry clearance or leave to remain will be granted. If the applicant does not meet these requirements, the application will be refused.

Requirements:

(a)   The applicant must not fall for refusal under the general grounds for refusal, and if applying for leave to remain, must not be an illegal entrant.

(b)   The applicant must be the child of a parent who has, or is at the same time being granted, valid entry clearance, leave to enter or remain as:

(i)   a Relevant Points Based System Migrant, or

(ii)   the partner of a Relevant Points Based System Migrant.

(c)   The applicant must be under the age of 18 on the date the application is made, or if over 18 and applying for leave to remain, must have, or have last been granted, leave as the child of a **Relevant Points Based System Migrant** or as the child of the parent who had leave under another category of these Rules and who has since been granted, or, is at the same time being granted, leave to remain as a Relevant Points Based System Migrant.

(d)   The applicant must not be married or in a civil partnership, must not have formed an independent family unit, and must not be leading an independent life and, if he is over the age of 16 on the date the application is made, he must provide the specified documents and information in paragraph 319H-SD to show that this requirement is met.

(e)   The applicant must not intend to stay in the UK beyond any period of leave granted to the Relevant Points Based System Migrant parent.

(f)   Both of the applicant's parents must either be lawfully present in the UK, or being granted entry clearance or leave to remain at the same time as the applicant or one parent must be lawfully present in the UK and the other is being granted entry clearance or leave to remain at the same time as the applicant, unless:

(i)   The Relevant Points Based System Migrant is the applicant's sole surviving parent, or

(ii)   The Relevant Points Based System Migrant parent has and has had sole responsibility for the applicant's upbringing, or

(iii)   there are serious or compelling family or other considerations which would make it desirable not to refuse the application and suitable arrangements have been made in the UK for the applicant's care.

(g)   Unless the Relevant Points Based System Migrant is a Tier 1 (Investor) Migrant or a Tier 1 (Exceptional Talent) Migrant, there must be a sufficient level of funds available to the applicant, as set out in Appendix E.

(h)   An applicant who is applying for leave to remain must not have last been granted:

(i)   entry clearance or leave as a visitor, unless the Relevant Points Based System Migrant has, or is being granted, leave to remain as a Tier 5 (Temporary Worker) Migrant in the creative and sporting subcategory on the basis of having met the requirement at paragraph 245ZQ(b)(ii);

(ii)   temporary admission; or

(iii)   temporary release.

(i)   Where the relevant Points Based System Migrant is applying for, or has been granted, entry clearance, leave to enter, or leave to remain in the United Kingdom as a Tier 4 (General) Student either:

    (i)   the relevant Points Based System Migrant must be a government sponsored student who is applying for, or who has been granted, entry clearance or leave to remain to undertake a course of study longer than six months;

    (ii)   the relevant Points Based System Migrant must:

        (1)   be applying for, or have been granted entry clearance or leave to remain in order to undertake a course of study at post-graduate level that is 12 months or longer in duration; and

        (2)   be sponsored by a sponsor who is a Recognised Body or a body in receipt of funding as a higher education institution from either:

            (a)   the Department for Employment and Learning in Northern Ireland;

            (b)   the Higher Education Funding Council for England;

            (c)   the Higher Education Funding Council for Wales; or

            (d)   the Scottish Funding Council;

    (iii)   the relevant Points Based System Migrant must be applying for, or have been granted leave to remain as a Tier 4 (General) Student on the doctorate extension scheme; or

    (iv)   the following conditions must be met:

        (1)   the relevant Points Based System Migrant must be applying for entry clearance, leave to enter, or leave to remain, to undertake a course of study that is longer than six months and either:

            (a)   have entry clearance, leave to enter, or leave to remain as a Tier 4 (General) Student or as a student to undertake a course of study longer than six months; or

            (b)   have last had entry clearance, leave to enter, or leave to remain within the three months preceding the application as a Tier 4 (General) Student or as a student to undertake a course of study longer than six months; and

        (2)   the Child must either:

            (a)   have entry clearance, leave to enter, or leave to remain as the Child of a Tier 4 (General) Student or a student with entry clearance, leave to enter, or leave to remain, to undertake a course of study longer than six months; or

            (b)   have last had entry clearance, leave to enter, or leave to remain within the three months preceding the application as the Child of a Tier 4 (General) Student or as a student to undertake a course of study longer than six months; and

        (3)   the relevant Points Based System Migrant and the Child must be applying at the same time.

(j)   A Child whose parent is a Relevant Points Based System Migrant, who is a Tier 4 (General) Student or Student, and who does not otherwise meet the requirements of paragraph 319H(i):

    (1)   must have been born during the Relevant Points Based System Migrant's most recent grant of entry clearance, leave to enter or leave to remain as a Tier 4 (General) Student or Student with leave for a course of more than six months duration; or

    (2)   where the Relevant Points Based System Migrant's most recent grant of entry clearance, leave to enter or leave to remain was to re-sit examinations or repeat a module of a course, must either have been born during a period of leave granted for the purposes of re-sitting examinations or repeating a module of a course or during the Relevant Points Based System Migrant's grant of leave for a course of more than six months, where that course is the same as the one for which the most recent grant of leave was to re-sit examinations or repeat a module; or

    (3)   must have been born no more than three months after the expiry of that most recent grant of leave; and

    (4)   must be applying for entry clearance.

(k)   If the applicant is a child born in the UK to a Relevant Points Based System migrant and their partner, the applicant must provide a full UK birth certificate showing the names of both parents.

(l)   All arrangements for the child's care and accommodation in the UK must comply with relevant UK legislation and regulations.

(m)   The applicant must not be in the UK in breach of immigration laws except that any period of overstaying for a period of 28 days will be disregarded.

Specified documents and information

319H-SD.   Applicants who are over the age of 16 on the date the application is made must provide the following specified documents and information:

(a)   The applicant must provide two items from the list below confirming his residential address:

    (i)   bank statements,

    (ii)   credit card bills,

    (iii)   driving licence,

    (iv)   NHS Registration document,

    (v)   letter from his current school, college or university, on official headed paper and bearing the official stamp of that organisation, and issued by an authorised official of that organisation.

(b)   The documents submitted must be from two separate sources and dated no more than one calendar month before the date of the application.

(c)   If the applicant pays rent or board, he must provide details of how much this amounts to each calendar month.

(d)   If the applicant is residing separately from the Relevant Points Based System Migrant, he must provide:

    (i)   reasons for residing away from the family home. Where this is due to academic endeavours he must provide confirmation from his university or college confirming his enrolment and attendance on the specific course, on official headed paper and bearing the official stamp of that organisation, and issued by an authorised official of that organisation,

    (ii)   the following evidence that he has been supported financially by his parents whilst residing away from the family home:

        (1)   bank statements for the applicant covering the three months before the date of the application clearly showing the origin of the deposits; and

        (2)   bank statements for the applicant's parent covering the three months before the date of the application also showing corroborating payments out of their account.

Period and conditions of grant

319I.   (a)   Entry clearance and leave to remain will be granted for a period which expires on the same day as the leave granted to the Relevant Points Based System Migrant parent or, where paragraph 319H (b) (ii) applies, for a period which expires on the same day as the leave granted to the parent who has valid leave to enter or remain as the partner of a person who has either limited leave to enter or remain as a Relevant Points Based System Migrant, indefinite leave to remain as a Relevant Points Based System Migrant, or who has become a British Citizen where prior to that they held indefinite leave to remain as a Relevant Points Based System Migrant.

(b)   Entry clearance and leave to remain under this route will be subject to the following conditions:

    (i)   no recourse to public funds,

    (ii)   registration with the police, if this is required under paragraph 326 of these Rules, and

    (iii)   if the Relevant Points Based System Migrant is a Tier 4 (General) Student and the Child meets the requirements of paragraphs 319H(i)(iv)(1), (2) and (3) or 319H(j) and:

        (1)   the Relevant Points Based System Migrant is a Tier 4 (General) Student applying for leave for less than 12 months, no employment, or

        (2)   the Relevant Points Based System Migrant is a Tier 4 (General) Student who is following a course of below degree level study, no employment.

Requirements for indefinite leave to remain

319J.   To qualify for indefinite leave to remain under this route, an applicant must meet the requirements listed below. If the applicant meets these requirements, indefinite leave to remain will be granted. If the applicant does not meet these requirements, the application will be refused.

Requirements:

(a)   The applicant must not fall for refusal under the general grounds for refusal, and must not be an illegal entrant.

(b)   The applicant must be the child of a parent who has, or is at the same time being granted, indefinite leave to remain as:

    (i)   a Relevant Points Based System Migrant, or

    (ii)   the partner of a Relevant Points Based System Migrant.

(c)   The applicant must have, or have last been granted, leave as the child of or have been born in the United Kingdom to, the Points Based System Migrant, or the partner of a Points Based System migrant who is being granted indefinite leave to remain.

(d)   The applicant must not be married or in a civil partnership, must not have formed an independent family unit, and must not be leading an independent life, and if he is over the age of 16 on the date the application is made, he must provide the specified documents and information in paragraph 319H-SD to show that this requirement is met.

(e)   Both of an applicant's parents must either be lawfully settled in the UK, or being granted indefinite leave to remain at the same time as the applicant, unless:

    (i)   The Points Based System Migrant is the applicant's sole surviving parent, or

    (ii)   The Points Based System Migrant parent has and has had sole responsibility for the applicant's upbringing, or

    (iii)   there are serious and compelling family or other considerations which would make it desirable not to refuse the application and suitable arrangements have been made for the applicant's care, or

    (iv)   One parent is, at the same time, being granted indefinite leave to remain as a Relevant Points Based System Migrant, the other parent is lawfully present in the UK or being granted leave at the same time as the applicant, and the applicant was granted leave as the child of a Relevant Points Based System Migrant under the Rules in place before 9 July 2012.

(f)   The applicant has demonstrated sufficient knowledge of the English language and sufficient knowledge about life in the United Kingdom, in accordance with Appendix KoLL, unless he is under the age of 18 at the date on which the application is made.

(g)   If the applicant is a child born in the UK to a Relevant Points Based System migrant and their partner, the applicant must provide a full UK birth certificate showing the names of both parents.

(h)   All arrangements for the child's care and accommodation in the UK must comply with relevant UK legislation and regulations.

(i)   The applicant must not be in the UK in breach of immigration laws except that any period of overstaying for a period of 28 days will be disregarded.

Please note in the printed version of CM5829 these points appear in error numbered as an alternative version of 316D (iii) and (iv).

319L.–319Y.   OMITTED

Part 9 – General grounds for the refusal of entry clearance, leave to enter or variation of leave to enter or remain in the United Kingdom

Refusal of entry clearance or leave to enter the United Kingdom

A320.   Paragraphs 320 (except subparagraph (3), (10) and (11)) and 322 do not apply to an application for entry clearance, leave to enter or leave to remain as a Family Member under Appendix FM, and Part 9 (except for paragraph 322(1)) does not apply to an application for leave to remain on the grounds of private life under paragraphs 276ADE–276DH.

320.   In addition to the grounds of refusal of entry clearance or leave to enter set out in Parts 2–8 of these Rules, and subject to paragraph 321 below, the following grounds for the refusal of entry clearance or leave to enter apply:

Grounds on which entry clearance or leave to enter the United Kingdom is to be refused

(1)   the fact that entry is being sought for a purpose not covered by these Rules;

(2)   320(2) the fact that the person seeking entry to the United Kingdom:

    (a)   is currently the subject of a deportation order; or

    (b)   has been convicted of an offence for which they have been sentenced to a period of imprisonment of at least 4 years; or

(c)   has been convicted of an offence for which they have been sentenced to a period of imprisonment of at least 12 months but less than 4 years, unless a period of 10 years has passed since the end of the sentence; or

(d)   has been convicted of an offence for which they have been sentenced to a period of imprisonment of less than 12 months, unless a period of 5 years has passed since the end of the sentence.

Where this paragraph applies, unless refusal would be contrary to the Human Rights Convention or the Convention and Protocol Relating to the Status of Refugees, it will only be in exceptional circumstances that the public interest in maintaining refusal will be outweighed by compelling factors.

(3)   failure by the person seeking entry to the United Kingdom to produce to the Immigration Officer a valid national passport or other document satisfactorily establishing his identity and nationality;

(4)   failure to satisfy the Immigration Officer, in the case of a person arriving in the United Kingdom or seeking entry through the Channel Tunnel with the intention of entering any other part of the common travel area, that he is acceptable to the immigration authorities there;

(5)   failure, in the case of a visa national, to produce to the Immigration Officer a passport or other identity document endorsed with a valid and current United Kingdom entry clearance issued for the purpose for which entry is sought;

(6)   where the Secretary of State has personally directed that the exclusion of a person from the United Kingdom is conducive to the public good;

(7)   save in relation to a person settled in the United Kingdom or where the Immigration Officer is satisfied that there are strong compassionate reasons justifying admission, confirmation from the Medical Inspector that, for medical reasons, it is undesirable to admit a person seeking leave to enter the United Kingdom.

(7A)   where false representations have been made or false documents or information have been submitted (whether or not material to the application, and whether or not to the applicant's knowledge), or material facts have not been disclosed, in relation to the application or in order to obtain documents from the Secretary of State or a third party required in support of the application.

(7B)   where the applicant has previously breached the UK's immigration laws (and was 18 or over at the time of his most recent breach) by:

(a)   Overstaying;

(b)   breaching a condition attached to his leave;

(c)   being an Illegal Entrant;

(d)   using Deception in an application for entry clearance, leave to enter or remain, or in order to obtain documents from the Secretary of State or a third party required in support of the application (whether successful or not);

unless the applicant:

(i)   Overstayed for 90 days or less and left the UK voluntarily, not at the expense (directly or indirectly) of the Secretary of State;

(ii)   used Deception in an application for entry clearance more than 10 years ago;

(iii)   left the UK voluntarily, not at the expense (directly or indirectly) of the Secretary of State, more than 12 months ago;

(iv)   left the UK voluntarily, at the expense (directly or indirectly) of the Secretary of State, more than 2 years ago; and the date the person left the UK was no more than 6 months after the date on which the person was given notice of the removal decision, or no more than 6 months after the date on which the person no longer had a pending appeal; whichever is the later;

(v)   left the UK voluntarily, at the expense (directly or indirectly) of the Secretary of State, more than 5 years ago;

(vi)   was removed or deported from the UK more than 10 years ago or;

(vii)   left or was removed from the UK as a condition of a caution issued in accordance with s.134 Legal Aid, Sentencing and Punishment of Offenders Act 2012 more than 5 years ago.

Where more than one breach of the UK's immigration laws has occurred, only the breach which leads to the longest period of absence from the UK will be relevant under this paragraph.

(7D)   failure, without providing a reasonable explanation, to comply with a request made on behalf of the Entry Clearance Officer to attend for interview.

Grounds on which entry clearance or leave to enter the United Kingdom should normally be refused

(8)   failure by a person arriving in the United Kingdom to furnish the Immigration Officer with such information as may be required for the purpose of deciding whether he requires leave to enter and, if so, whether and on what terms leave should be given;

(8A)   where the person seeking leave is outside the United Kingdom, failure by him to supply any information, documents, copy documents or medical report requested by an Immigration Officer;

(9)   failure by a person seeking leave to enter as a returning resident to satisfy the Immigration Officer that he meets the requirements of paragraph 18 of these Rules, or that he seeks leave to enter for the same purpose as that for which his earlier leave was granted;

(10)   production by the person seeking leave to enter the United Kingdom of a national passport or travel document issued by a territorial entity or authority which is not recognised by Her Majesty's Government as a state or is not dealt with as a government by them, or which does not accept valid United Kingdom passports for the purpose of its own immigration control; or a passport or travel document which does not comply with international passport practice;

(11)   where the applicant has previously contrived in a significant way to frustrate the intentions of the Rules by:

    (i)   overstaying; or

    (ii)   breaching a condition attached to his leave; or

    (iii)   being an illegal entrant; or

    (iv)   using deception in an application for entry clearance, leave to enter or remain or in order to obtain documents from the Secretary of State or a third party required in support of the application (whether successful or not);

and there are other aggravating circumstances, such as absconding, not meeting temporary admission/reporting restrictions or bail conditions, using an assumed identity or multiple identities, switching nationality, making frivolous applications or not complying with the re-documentation process.

(12)   DELETED

(13)   failure, except by a person eligible for admission to the United Kingdom for settlement, to satisfy the Immigration Officer that he will be admitted to another country after a stay in the United Kingdom;

(14)   refusal by a sponsor of a person seeking leave to enter the United Kingdom to give, if requested to do so, an undertaking in writing to be responsible for that person's maintenance and accommodation for the period of any leave granted;

(16)   failure, in the case of a child under the age of 18 years seeking leave to enter the United Kingdom otherwise than in conjunction with an application made by his parent(s) or legal guardian to provide the Immigration Officer, if required to do so, with written consent to the application from his parent(s) or legal guardian; save that the requirement as to written consent does not apply in the case of a child seeking admission to the United Kingdom as an asylum seeker;

(17)   save in relation to a person settled in the United Kingdom, refusal to undergo a medical examination when required to do so by the Immigration Officer;

(18)   DELETED

(18A)   within the 12 months preceding the date of the application, the person has been convicted of or admitted an offence for which they received a non-custodial sentence or other out of court disposal that is recorded on their criminal record;

(18B)   in the view of the Secretary of State:

    (a)   the person's offending has caused serious harm; or

    (b)   the person is a persistent offender who shows a particular disregard for the law.

(19)   The immigration officer deems the exclusion of the person from the United Kingdom to be conducive to the public good. For example, because the person's conduct (including convictions which do not fall within paragraph 320(2)), character, associations, or other reasons, make it undesirable to grant them leave to enter.

(20) failure by a person seeking entry into the United Kingdom to comply with a requirement relating to the provision of physical data to which he is subject by regulations made under section 126 of the Nationality, Immigration and Asylum Act 2002.

(21) DELETED

(22) where one or more relevant NHS body has notified the Secretary of State that the person seeking entry or leave to enter has failed to pay a charge or charges with a total value of at least £1000 in accordance with the relevant NHS regulations on charges to overseas visitors.

Refusal of leave to enter in relation to a person in possession of an entry clearance

321. A person seeking leave to enter the United Kingdom who holds an entry clearance which was duly issued to him and is still current may be refused leave to enter only where the Immigration Officer is satisfied that:

(i) False representations were made or false documents or information were submitted (whether or not material to the application, and whether or not to the holder's knowledge), or material facts were not disclosed, in relation to the application for entry clearance; or in order to obtain documents from the Secretary of State or a third party required in support of the application.

(ii) a change of circumstances since it was issued has removed the basis of the holder's claim to admission, except where the change of circumstances amounts solely to the person becoming over age for entry in one of the categories contained in paragraphs 296–316 of these Rules since the issue of the entry clearance; or

(iii) on grounds which would have led to a refusal under paragraphs 320(2), 320(6), 320(18A), 320(18B) or 320(19).

Grounds on which leave to enter or remain which is in force is to be cancelled at port or while the holder is outside the United Kingdom

321A. The following grounds for the cancellation of a person's leave to enter or remain which is in force on his arrival in, or whilst he is outside, the United Kingdom apply;

(1) there has been such a change in the circumstances of that person's case since the leave was given, that it should be cancelled; or

(2) false representations were made or false documents were submitted (whether or not material to the application, and whether or not to the holder's knowledge), or material facts were not disclosed, in relation to the application for leave; or in order to obtain documents from the Secretary of State or a third party required in support of the application or,

(3) save in relation to a person settled in the United Kingdom or where the Immigration Officer or the Secretary of State is satisfied that there are strong compassionate reasons justifying admission, where it is apparent that, for medical reasons, it is undesirable to admit that person to the United Kingdom; or

(4) where the Secretary of State has personally directed that the exclusion of that person from the United Kingdom is conducive to the public good; or

(4A) Grounds which would have led to a refusal under paragraphs 320(2), 320(6), 320(18A), 320(18B) or 320(19) if the person concerned were making a new application for leave to enter or remain; or

(5) The Immigration Officer or the Secretary of State deems the exclusion of the person from the United Kingdom to be conducive to the public good. For example, because the person's conduct (including convictions which do not fall within paragraph 320(2)), character, associations, or other reasons, make it undesirable to grant them leave to enter the United Kingdom; or

(6) where that person is outside the United Kingdom, failure by that person to supply any information, documents, copy documents or medical report requested by an Immigration Officer or the Secretary of State.

Refusal of leave to remain, variation of leave to enter or remain or curtailment of leave

322. In addition to the grounds for refusal of extension of stay set out in Parts 2–8 of these Rules, the following provisions apply in relation to the refusal of an application for leave to remain, variation of leave to enter or remain or, where appropriate, the curtailment of leave:

Grounds on which leave to remain and variation of leave to enter or remain in the United Kingdom are to be refused

(1) the fact that variation of leave to enter or remain is being sought for a purpose not covered by these Rules.

(1A) where false representations have been made or false documents or information have been submitted (whether or not material to the application, and whether or not to the applicant's knowledge), or material facts have not been disclosed, in relation to the application or in order to obtain documents from the Secretary of State or a third party required in support of the application.

(1B) the applicant is, at the date of application, the subject of a deportation order or a decision to make a deportation order;

(1C) where the person is seeking indefinite leave to enter or remain:

    (i) they have been convicted of an offence for which they have been sentenced to imprisonment for at least 4 years; or

    (ii) they have been convicted of an offence for which they have been sentenced to imprisonment for at least 12 months but less than 4 years, unless a period of 15 years has passed since the end of the sentence; or

    (iii) they have been convicted of an offence for which they have been sentenced to imprisonment for less than 12 months, unless a period of 7 years has passed since the end of the sentence; or

    (iv) they have, within the 24 months preceding the date of the application, been convicted of or admitted an offence for which they have received a non-custodial sentence or other out of court disposal that is recorded on their criminal record.

(1D) DELETED.

Grounds on which leave to remain and variation of leave to enter or remain in the United Kingdom should normally be refused

(2) the making of false representations or the failure to disclose any material fact for the purpose of obtaining leave to enter or a previous variation of leave or in order to obtain documents from the Secretary of State or a third party required in support of the application for leave to enter or a previous variation of leave.

(3) failure to comply with any conditions attached to the grant of leave to enter or remain;

(4) failure by the person concerned to maintain or accommodate himself and any dependants without recourse to public funds;

(5) the undesirability of permitting the person concerned to remain in the United Kingdom in the light of his conduct (including convictions which do not fall within paragraph 322(1C), character or associations or the fact that he represents a threat to national security;

(5A) it is undesirable to permit the person concerned to enter or remain in the United Kingdom because, in the view of the Secretary of State:

    (a) their offending has caused serious harm; or

    (b) they are a persistent offender who shows a particular disregard for the law;

(6) refusal by a sponsor of the person concerned to give, if requested to do so, an undertaking in writing to be responsible for his maintenance and accommodation in the United Kingdom or failure to honour such an undertaking once given;

(7) failure by the person concerned to honour any declaration or undertaking given orally or in writing as to the intended duration and/or purpose of his stay;

(8) failure, except by a person who qualifies for settlement in the United Kingdom or by the spouse or civil partner of a person settled in the United Kingdom, to satisfy the Secretary of State that he will be returnable to another country if allowed to remain in the United Kingdom for a further period;

(9) failure by an applicant to produce within a reasonable time information, documents or other evidence required by the Secretary of State to establish his claim to remain under these Rules;

(10) failure, without providing a reasonable explanation, to comply with a request made on behalf of the Secretary of State to attend for interview;

(11) failure, in the case of a child under the age of 18 years seeking a variation of his leave to enter or remain in the United Kingdom otherwise than in conjunction with an application by his parent(s) or legal guardian, to provide the Secretary of State, if required to do so, with written consent to the application

from his parent(s) or legal guardian; save that the requirement as to written consent does not apply in the case of a child who has been admitted to the United Kingdom as an asylum seeker.

(12) where one or more relevant NHS body has notified the Secretary of State that the person seeking leave to remain or a variation of leave to enter or remain has failed to pay a charge or charges with a total value of at least £1000 in accordance with the relevant NHS regulations on charges to overseas visitors.

Grounds on which leave to enter or remain may be curtailed

323. A person's leave to enter or remain may be curtailed:

(i) on any of the grounds set out in paragraph 322(2)–(5A) above; or

(ii) if he ceases to meet the requirements of the Rules under which his leave to enter or remain was granted; or

(iii) if he is the dependant, or is seeking leave to remain as the dependant, of an asylum applicant whose claim has been refused and whose leave has been curtailed under section 7 of the1993 Act, and he does not qualify for leave to remain in his own right, or

(iv) on any of the grounds set out in paragraph 339A (i)–(vi) and paragraph 339G (i)–(vi), or

(v) where a person has, within the first 6 months of being granted leave to enter, committed an offence for which they are subsequently sentenced to a period of imprisonment.

Curtailment of leave or alteration of duration of leave in relation to a Tier 2 Migrant, a Tier 5 Migrant or a Tier 4 Migrant

323A. In addition to the grounds specified in paragraph 323, the leave to enter or remain of a Tier 2 Migrant, a Tier 4 Migrant or a Tier 5 Migrant:

(a) is to be curtailed, or its duration varied, if:

(i) in the case of a Tier 2 Migrant or a Tier 5 Migrant:

(1) the migrant fails to commence working for the Sponsor, or

(2) the migrant ceases to be employed by the Sponsor.

(ii) in the case of a Tier 4 Migrant:

(1) the migrant fails to commence studying with the Sponsor, or

(2) the migrant has been excluded or withdrawn from the course of studies, or

(3) the Sponsor withdraws their sponsorship of a migrant on the doctorate extension scheme, or

(4) the Sponsor withdraws their sponsorship of a migrant who, having completed a pre-sessional course as provided in paragraph 120(b) (i) of Appendix A, does not have a knowledge of English equivalent to level B2 of the Council of Europe's Common European Framework for Language Learning in all four components (reading, writing, speaking and listening) or above.

(b) may be curtailed, or its duration varied, if:

(i) the migrant's Sponsor ceases to have a sponsor licence (for whatever reason); or

(ii) the migrant's Sponsor transfers the business for which the migrant works, or at which the migrant is studying, to another person; and

(1) that person does not have a sponsor licence; and

(2) fails to apply for a sponsor licence within 28 days of the date of the transfer of the business; or

(3) applies for a sponsor licence but is refused; or

(4) makes a successful application for a sponsor licence, but the Sponsor licence granted is not in a category that would allow the Sponsor to issue a Certificate of Sponsorship to the migrant;

(iii) in the case of a Tier 2 Migrant or a Tier 5 Migrant, if the employment that the Certificate of Sponsorship Checking Service records that the migrant is being sponsored to do undergoes a prohibited change as specified in paragraph 323AA;

(iv) paragraph (a) above applies but:

(1) the migrant is under the age of 18;

(2) the migrant has a dependant child under the age of 18;

(3)   leave is to be varied such that when the variation takes effect the migrant will have leave to enter or remain and the migrant has less than 60 days extant leave remaining;

(4)   the migrant has been granted leave to enter or remain with another Sponsor or under another immigration category; or

(5)   the migrant has a pending application for leave to remain, or variation of leave, with the UK Border Agency, or has a pending appeal under Section 82 of the Nationality, Immigration and Asylum Act 2002.

Prohibited changes to employment for Tier 2 Migrants and Tier 5 Migrants

323AA.   The following are prohibited changes, unless a further application for leave to remain is granted which expressly permits the changes:

(a)   The migrant is absent from work without pay for one calendar month or more in total (whether over a single period or more than one period), during anycalendar year (1 January to 31 December), unless the absence from work is due solely to:

(i)   maternity leave,

(ii)   paternity leave,

(iii) adoption leave, or

(iv)   long term sick leave of one calendar month or more during any one period.

(b)   The employment changes such that the migrant is working for a different employer or Sponsor, unless:

(i)   the migrant is a Tier 5 (Temporary Worker) Migrant in the Government Authorised Exchange sub-category and the change of employer is authorised by the Sponsor and under the terms of the work, volunteering or job shadowing that the Certificate of Sponsorship Checking Service records that the migrant is being sponsored to do, or

(ii)   the migrant is working for a different Sponsor under arrangements covered by the Transfer of Undertakings (Protection of Employment) Regulations 2006 or similar protection to continue in the same job.

(c)   The employment changes to a job in a different Standard Occupational Classification (SOC) code to that recorded by the Certificate of Sponsorship Checking Service.

(d)   If the migrant is a Tier 2 (Intra-Company Transfer) Migrant or a Tier 2 (General) Migrant, the employment changes to a different job in the same Standard Occupational Classification code to that recorded by the Certificate of Sponsorship Checking Service, and the gross annual salary (including such allowances as are specified as acceptable for this purpose in Appendix A) is below the appropriate salary rate for that new job as specified in the Codes of Practice in Appendix J.

(e)   If the migrant was required to be Sponsored for a job at a minimum National Qualification Framework level in the application which led to his last grant of entry clearance or leave to remain, the employment changes to a job which the Codes of Practice in Appendix J record as being at a lower level.

(f)   If the migrant is a Tier 2 (General) Migrant and scored points from the shortage occupation provisions of Appendix A, the employment changes to a job which does not appear in the Shortage Occupation List in Appendix K.

(g)   Except where (h) applies, the gross annual salary (including such allowances as are specified as acceptable for this purpose in Appendix A) reduces below:

(i)   any minimum salary threshold specified in Appendix A of these Rules, where the applicant was subject to or relied on that threshold in the application which led to his current grant of entry clearance or leave to remain, or

(ii)   the appropriate salary rate for the job as specified in the Codes of Practice in Appendix J, or

(iii) in cases where there is no applicable threshold in Appendix A and no applicable salary rate in Appendix J, the salary recorded by the Certificate of Sponsorship Checking Service.

(h)   Other reductions in salary are permitted if the reduction coincides with a period of:

(i)   maternity leave,

(ii)   paternity leave,

(iii) adoption leave,

(iv)   long term sick leave of one calendar month or more, or

(v)   reduced working hours for a temporary period, where:

(1)   the reduced working hours are part of a company-wide policy to avoid redundancies,

(2)   under this policy, the Sponsor is not treating the migrant more, or less, favourably than settled workers,

(3)   the migrant's pay and working hours do not reduce by more than 30%,

(4)   the reduction in pay is proportionate to the reduction in working hours,

(5)   the arrangements will not be in place for more than one year, and

(6)   the migrant's pay will return to at least the level it was before these arrangements were in place, immediately after the arrangements end.

Curtailment of leave in relation to a Tier 1 (Exceptional Talent) Migrant

323B.   In addition to the grounds specified in paragraph 323, the leave to enter or remain of a Tier 1 (Exceptional Talent) Migrant may be curtailed if the Designated Competent Body that endorsed the application which led to the migrant's current grant of leave withdraws its endorsement of the migrant.

Curtailment of leave in relation to a Tier 1 (Graduate Entrepreneur) Migrant

323C.   In addition to the grounds specified in paragraph 323, the leave to enter or remain of a Tier 1 (Graduate Entrepreneur) Migrant may be curtailed if the endorsing body that endorsed the application which led to the migrant's current grant of leave:

(a)   loses its status as an endorsing institution for Tier 1 (Graduate Entrepreneur) Migrants,

(b)   loses its status as a Highly Trusted Sponsor under Tier 4 of the Points-Based System (for whatever reason),

(c)   ceases to be an A-rated Sponsor under Tier 2 or Tier 5 of the Points-Based System because its Tier 2 or Tier 5 Sponsor licence is downgraded or revoked by the UK Border Agency, or

(d)   withdraws its endorsement of the migrant.

Crew members

324.   A person who has been given leave to enter to join a ship, aircraft, hovercraft, hydrofoil or international train service as a member of its crew, or a crew member who has been given leave to enter for hospital treatment, repatriation or transfer to another ship, aircraft, hovercraft, hydrofoil or international train service in the United Kingdom, is to be refused leave to remain unless an extension of stay is necessary to fulfil the purpose for which he was given leave to enter or unless he meets the requirements for an extension of stay as a spouse or civil partner in paragraph 284.

Part 10 – Registration with the police

For the purposes of paragraph 326, a 'relevant foreign national' is a person aged 16 or over who is:

325.   (i)   a national or citizen of a country or territory listed in Appendix 2 to these Rules;

(ii)   a stateless person; or

(iii)   a person holding a non-national travel document.

326.   (1)   Subject to sub-paragraph (2) below, a condition requiring registration with the police should normally be imposed on any relevant foreign national who is:

(i)   given limited leave to enter the United Kingdom for longer than six months; or

(ii)   given limited leave to remain which has the effect of allowing him to remain in the United Kingdom for longer than six months, reckoned from the date of his arrival (whether or not such a condition was imposed when he arrived).

(2)   Such a condition should not normally be imposed where the leave is given:

(i)   as a seasonal agricultural worker;

(ii)   as a Tier 5 (Temporary Worker) Migrant, provided the Certificate of Sponsorship Checking System refrence for which points were awarded records that the applicant is being sponsored as an overseas goverment employee or a private servant is a diplomatic household;

(iii)   as a Tier 2 (Minister of Religion) Migrant;

(iv)   on the basis of marriage to or civil partnership with a person settled in the United Kingdom or as the unmarried or same-sex partner of a person settled in the United Kingdom

(v)   as a person exercising access rights to a child resident in the United Kingdom;

(vi)   as the parent of a child at school; or

(vii)   following the grant of asylum.

(3)   Such a condition should also be imposed on any foreign national given limited leave to enter the United Kingdom where, exceptionally, the Immigration Officer considers it necessary to ensure that he complies with the terms of the leave.

Part 11 – Asylum

Procedure

326A.   The procedures set out in these Rules shall apply to the consideration of asylum and humanitarian protection.

326B.   Where the Secretary of State is considering a claim for asylum or humanitarian protection under this Part, she will consider any Article 8 elements of that claim in line with the provisions of Appendix FM (family life) which are relevant to those elements and in line with paragraphs 276ADE to 276DH (private life) of these Rules.

Definition of asylum applicant

327.   Under the Rules an asylum applicant is a person who either;

(a)   makes a request to be recognised as a refugee under the Geneva Convention on the basis that it would be contrary to the United Kingdom's obligations under the Geneva Convention for him to be removed from or required to leave the United Kingdom, or

(b)   otherwise makes a request for international protection. 'Application for asylum' shall be construed accordingly.

327A.   Every person has the right to make an application for asylum on his own behalf.

Applications for asylum

328.   All asylum applications will be determined by the Secretary of State in accordance with the Geneva Convention. Every asylum application made by a person at a port or airport in the United Kingdom will be referred by the Immigration Officer for determination by the Secretary of State in accordance with these Rules.

328A.   The Secretary of State shall ensure that authorities which are likely to be addressed by someone who wishes to make an application for asylum are able to advise that person how and where such an application may be made.

329.   Until an asylum application has been determined by the Secretary of State or the Secretary of State has issued a certificate under Part 2, 3, 4 or 5 of Schedule 3 to the Asylum and Immigration (Treatment of Claimants, etc.) Act 2004 no action will be taken to require the departure of the asylum applicant or his dependants from the United Kingdom.

330.   If the Secretary of State decides to grant asylum and the person has not yet been given leave to enter, the Immigration Officer will grant limited leave to enter.

331.   If a person seeking leave to enter is refused asylum or their application for asylum is withdrawn or treated as withdrawn under paragraph 333C of these Rules, the Immigration Officer will consider whether or not he is in a position to decide to give or refuse leave to enter without interviewing the person further. If the Immigration Officer decides that a further interview is not required he may serve the notice giving or refusing leave to enter by post. If the Immigration Officer decides that a further interview is required, he will then resume his examination to determine whether or not to grant the person leave to enter under any other provision of these Rules. If the person fails at any time to comply with a requirement to report to an Immigration Officer for examination, the Immigration Officer may direct that the person's examination shall be treated as concluded at that time. The Immigration Officer will then consider any outstanding applications for entry on the basis of any evidence before him.

332.   If a person who has been refused leave to enter applies for asylum and that application is refused or withdrawn or treated as withdrawn under paragraph 333C of these Rules, leave to enter will again be refused unless the applicant qualifies for admission under any other provision of these Rules.

333.   Written notice of decisions on applications for asylum shall be given in reasonable time. Where the applicant is legally represented, notice may instead be given to the representative. Where the applicant has no legal representative and free legal assistance is not available, he shall be informed of the decision on the application

for asylum and, if the application is rejected, how to challenge the decision, in a language that he may reasonably be supposed to understand.

333A. The Secretary of State shall ensure that a decision is taken by him on each application for asylum as soon as possible, without prejudice to an adequate and complete examination.

Where a decision on an application for asylum cannot be taken within six months of the date it was recorded, the Secretary of State shall either:

(a) inform the applicant of the delay; or

(b) if the applicant has made a specific written request for it, provide information on the timeframe within which the decision on his application is to be expected. The provision of such information shall not oblige the Secretary of State to take a decision within the stipulated time-frame.

333B. Applicants for asylum shall be allowed an effective opportunity to consult, at their own expense or at public expense in accordance with provision made for this by the Legal Services Commission or otherwise, a person who is authorised under Part V of the Immigration and Asylum Act 1999 to give immigration advice. This paragraph shall also apply where the Secretary of State is considering revoking a person's refugee status in accordance with these Rules.

Withdrawal of applications

333C. If an application for asylum is withdrawn either explicitly or implicitly, consideration of it may be discontinued. An application will be treated as explicitly withdrawn if the applicant signs the relevant form provided by the Secretary of State. An application may be treated as impliedly withdrawn if an applicant fails to attend the personal interview as provided in paragraph 339NA of these Rules unless the applicant demonstrates within a reasonable time that that failure was due to circumstances beyond his or her control. The Secretary of State will indicate on the applicant's asylum file that the application for asylum has been withdrawn and consideration of it has been discontinued.

Grant of asylum

334. An asylum applicant will be granted asylum in the United Kingdom if the Secretary of State is satisfied that:

(i) he is in the United Kingdom or has arrived at a port of entry in the United Kingdom;

(ii) he is a refugee, as defined in regulation 2 of The Refugee or Person in Need of International Protection (Qualification) Regulations 2006;

(iii) there are no reasonable grounds for regarding him as a danger to the security of the United Kingdom;

(iv) he does not, having been convicted by a final judgment of a particularly serious crime, he does not constitute danger to the community of the United Kingdom; and

(v) refusing his application would result in him being required to go (whether immediately or after the time limited by any existing leave to enter or remain) in breach of the Geneva Convention, to a country in which his life or freedom would threatened on account of his race, religion, nationality, political opinion or membership of a particular social group.

335. If the Secretary of State decides to grant asylum to a person who has been given leave to enter (whether or not the leave has expired) or to a person who has entered without leave, the Secretary of State will vary the existing leave or grant limited leave to remain.

Refusal of asylum

336. An application which does not meet the criteria set out in paragraph 334 will be refused. Where an application for asylum is refused, the reasons in fact and law shall be stated in the decision and information provided in writing on how to challenge the decision.

337. DELETED

338. When a person in the United Kingdom is notified that asylum has been refused he may, if he is liable to removal as an illegal entrant , removal under section 10 of the Immigration and Asylum Act 1999 or to deportation, at the same time be notified of removal directions, served with a notice of intention to make a deportation order, or served with a deportation order, as appropriate.

339. DELETED

Revocation or refusal to renew a grant of asylum

339A. A person's grant of asylum under paragraph 334 will be revoked or not renewed if the Secretary of State is satisfied that:

(i) he has voluntarily re-availed himself of the protection of the country of nationality;

(ii)   having lost his nationality, he has voluntarily re-acquired it; or

(iii)   he has acquired a new nationality, and enjoys the protection of the country of his new nationality;

(iv)   he has voluntarily re-established himself in the country which he left or outside which he remained owing to a fear of persecution;

(v)   he can no longer, because the circumstances in connection with which he has been recognised as a refugee have ceased to exist, continue to refuse to avail himself of the protection of the country of nationality;

(vi)   being a stateless person with no nationality, he is able, because the circumstances in connection with which he has been recognised a refugee have ceased to exist, to return to the country of former habitual residence;

(vii)   he should have been or is excluded from being a refugee in accordance with regulation 7 of The Refugee or Person in Need of International Protection (Qualification) Regulations 2006;

(viii) his misrepresentation or omission or facts, including the use of false documents, were decisive for the grant of asylum;

(ix)   there are reasonable grounds for regarding him as a danger to the security of the United Kingdom; or

(x)   having been convicted by a final judgment of a particularly serious crime he constitutes danger to the community of the United Kingdom.

In considering (v) and (vi), the Secretary of State shall have regard to whether the change of circumstances is of such a significant and non-temporary nature that the refugee's fear of persecution can no longer be regarded as well-founded.

Where an application for asylum was made on or after the 21st October 2004, the Secretary of State will revoke or refuse to renew a person's grant of asylum where he is satisfied that at least one of the provisions in sub-paragraph (i)–(vi) apply.

339B.   When a person's grant of asylum is revoked or not renewed any limited leave which they have may be curtailed.

339BA.   Where the Secretary of State is considering revoking refugee status in accordance with these Rules, the person concerned shall be informed in writing that the Secretary of State is reconsidering his qualification for refugee status and the reasons for the reconsideration. That person shall be given the opportunity to submit, in a personal interview or in a written statement, reasons as to why his refugee status should not be revoked. If there is a personal interview, it shall be subject to the safeguards set out in these Rules. However, where a person acquires British citizenship status, his refugee status is automatically revoked in accordance with paragraph 339A (iii) upon acquisition of that status without the need to follow the procedure set out above.

Grant of humanitarian protection

339C.   A person will be granted humanitarian protection in the United Kingdom if the Secretary of State is satisfied that:

(i)   he is in the United Kingdom or has arrived at a port of entry in the United Kingdom;

(ii)   he does not qualify as a refugee as defined in regulation 2 of The Refugee or Person in Need of International Protection (Qualification) Regulations 2006;

(iii)   substantial grounds have been shown for believing that the person concerned, if he returned to the country of return, would face a real risk of suffering serious harm and is unable, or, owing to such risk, unwilling to avail himself of the protection of that country; and

(iv)   he is not excluded from a grant of humanitarian protection.

Serious harm consists of:

(i)   the death penalty or execution;

(ii)   unlawful killing;

(iii)   torture or inhuman or degrading treatment or punishment of a person in the country of return; or

(iv)   serious and individual threat to a civilian's life or person by reason of indiscriminate violence in situations of international or internal armed conflict.

Exclusion from humanitarian protection

339D.   A person is excluded from a grant of humanitarian protection under paragraph 339C (iv) where the Secretary of State is satisfied that:

(i)   there are serious reasons for considering that he has committed a crime against peace, a war crime, a crime against humanity, or any other serious crime or instigated or otherwise participated in such crimes;

(ii)   there are serious reasons for considering that he is guilty of acts contrary to the purposes and principles of the United Nations or has committed, prepared or instigated such acts or encouraged or induced others to commit, prepare or instigate instigated such acts;

(iii)   there are serious reasons for considering that he constitutes a danger to the community or to the security of the United Kingdom; or

(iv)   prior to his admission to the United Kingdom the person committed a crime outside the scope of (i) and (ii) that would be punishable by imprisonment were it committed in the United Kingdom and the person left his country of origin solely in order to avoid sanctions resulting from the crime.

339E.   If the Secretary of State decides to grant humanitarian protection and the person has not yet been given leave to enter, the Secretary of State or an Immigration Officer will grant limited leave to enter. If the Secretary of State decides to grant humanitarian protection to a person who has been given limited leave to enter (whether or not that leave has expired) or a person who has entered without leave, the Secretary of State will vary the existing leave or grant limited leave to remain.

Refusal of humanitarian protection

339F.   Where the criteria set out in paragraph 339C is not met humanitarian protection will be refused.

Revocation of humanitarian protection

339G.   A person's humanitarian protection granted under paragraph 339C will be revoked or not renewed if the Secretary of State is satisfied that at least one of the following applies:

(i)   the circumstances which led to the grant of humanitarian protection have ceased to exist or have changed to such a degree that such protection is no longer required;

(ii)   the person granted humanitarian protection should have been or is excluded from humanitarian protection because there are serious reasons for considering that he has committed a crime against peace, a war crime, a crime against humanity, or any other serious crime or instigated or otherwise participated in such crimes;

(iii)   the person granted humanitarian protection should have been or is excluded from humanitarian protection because there are serious reasons for considering that he is guilty of acts contrary to the purposes and principles of the United Nations or has committed, prepared or instigated such acts or encouraged or induced others to commit, prepare or instigate such acts;

(iv)   the person granted humanitarian protection should have been or is excluded from humanitarian protection because there are serious reasons for considering that he constitutes a danger to the community or to the security of the United Kingdom;

(v)   the person granted humanitarian protection misrepresented or omitted facts, including the use of false documents, which were decisive to the grant of humanitarian protection; or

(vi)   the person granted humanitarian protection should have been or is excluded from humanitarian protection because prior to his admission to the United Kingdom the person committed a crime outside the scope of (ii) and (iii) that would be punishable by imprisonment had it been committed in the United Kingdom and the person left his country of origin solely in order to avoid sanctions resulting from the crime.

In applying (i) the Secretary of State shall have regard to whether the change of circumstances is of such a significant and non-temporary nature that the person no longer faces a real risk of serious harm;

339H.   When a person's humanitarian protection is revoked or not renewed any limited leave which they have may be curtailed.

Consideration of applications

339HA.   The Secretary of State shall ensure that the personnel examining applications for asylum and taking decisions on his behalf have the knowledge with respect to relevant standards applicable in the field of asylum and refugee law.

339I.   When the Secretary of State considers a person's asylum claim, eligibility for a grant of humanitarian protection or human rights claim it is the duty of the person to submit to the Secretary of State as soon as possible all material factors needed to substantiate the asylum claim or establish that he is a person eligible for humanitarian protection or substantiate the human rights claim, which the Secretary of State shall assess in cooperation with the person.

The material factors include:

(i)   the person's statement on the reasons for making an asylum claim or on eligibility for a grant of humanitarian protection or for making a human rights claim;

(ii)   all documentation at the person's disposal regarding the person's age, background (including background details of relevant relatives), identity, nationality(ies), country(ies) and place(s) of previous residence, previous asylum applications, travel routes; and

(iii)   identity and travel documents.

339IA. For the purposes of examining individual applications for asylum

(i)   information provided in support of an application and the fact that an application has been made shall not be disclosed to the alleged actor(s) of persecution of the applicant, and

(ii)   information shall not be obtained from the alleged actor(s) of persecution that would result in their being directly informed that an application for asylum has been made by the applicant in question and would jeopardise the physical integrity of the applicant and his dependants, or the liberty and security of his family members still living in the country of origin.

This paragraph shall also apply where the Secretary of State is considering revoking a person's refugee status in accordance with these Rules.

339J.   The assessment by the Secretary of State of an asylum claim, eligibility for a grant of humanitarian protection or a human rights claim will be carried out on an individual, objective and impartial basis. This will include taking into account in particular:

(i)   all relevant facts as they relate to the country of origin or country of return at the time of taking a decision on the grant; including laws and regulations of the country of origin or country of return and the manner in which they are applied;

(ii)   relevant statements and documentation presented by the person including information on whether the person has been or may be subject to persecution or serious harm;

(iii)   the individual position and personal circumstances of the person, including factors such as background, gender and age, so as to assess whether, on the basis of the person's personal circumstances, the acts to which the person has been or could be exposed would amount to persecution or serious harm;

(iv)   whether the person's activities since leaving the country of origin or country of return were engaged in for the sole or main purpose of creating the necessary conditions for making an asylum claim or establishing that he is a person eligible for humanitarian protection or a human rights claim, so as to assess whether these activities will expose the person to persecution or serious harm if he returned to that country; and

(v)   whether the person could reasonably be expected to avail himself of the protection of another country where he could assert citizenship.

339JA. Reliable and up-to-date information shall be obtained from various sources as to the general situation prevailing in the countries of origin of applicants for asylum and, where necessary, in countries through which they have transited. Such information shall be made available to the personnel responsible for examining applications and taking decisions and may be provided to them in the form of a consolidated country information report.

This paragraph shall also apply where the Secretary of State is considering revoking a person's refugee status in accordance with these Rules.

339K.   The fact that a person has already been subject to persecution or serious harm, or to direct threats of such persecution or such harm, will be regarded as a serious indication of the person's well-founded fear of persecution or real risk of suffering serious harm, unless there are good reasons to consider that such persecution or serious harm will not be repeated.

339L.   It is the duty of the person to substantiate the asylum claim or establish that he is a person eligible humanitarian protection or substantiate his human rights claim. Where aspects of the person's statements are not supported by documentary or other evidence, those aspects will not need confirmation when all of the following conditions are met:

(i)   the person has made a genuine effort to substantiate his asylum claim or establish that he is a person eligible humanitarian protection or substantiate his human rights claim;

(ii)   all material factors at the person's disposal have been submitted, and a satisfactory explanation regarding any lack of other relevant material has been given;

(iii)   the person's statements are found to be coherent and plausible and do not run counter to available specific and general information relevant to the person's case;

(iv)   the person has made an asylum claim or sought to establish that he is a person eligible for humanitarian protection or made a human rights claim at the earliest possible time, unless the person can demonstrate good reason for not having done so; and

(v)   the general credibility of the person has been established.

339M.   The Secretary of State may consider that a person has not substantiated his asylum claim or established that he is a person eligible for humanitarian protection or substantiated his human rights claim, and thereby reject his application for asylum, determine that he is not eligible for humanitarian protection or reject his human rights claim, if he fails, without reasonable explanation, to make a prompt and full disclosure of material facts, either orally or in writing, or otherwise to assist the Secretary of State in establishing the facts of the case; this includes, for example, failure to report to a designated place to be fingerprinted, failure to complete an asylum questionnaire or failure to comply with a requirement to report to an immigration officer for examination.

339MA.   Applications for asylum shall be neither rejected nor excluded from examination on the sole ground that they have not been made as soon as possible.

339N.   In determining whether the general credibility of the person has been established the Secretary of State will apply the provisions in s.8 of the Asylum and Immigration (Treatment of Claimants, etc.) Act 2004.

Personal interview

339NA.   Before a decision is taken on the application for asylum, the applicant shall be given the opportunity of a personal interview on his application for asylum with a representative of the Secretary of State who is legally competent to conduct such an interview.

The personal interview may be omitted where:

(i)   the Secretary of State is able to take a positive decision on the basis of evidence available;

(ii)   the Secretary of State has already had a meeting with the applicant for the purpose of assisting him with completing his application and submitting the essential information regarding the application;

(iii)   the applicant, in submitting his application and presenting the facts, has only raised issues that are not relevant or of minimal relevance to the examination of whether he is a refugee, as defined in regulation 2 of the Refugee or Person in Need of International Protection (Qualification) Regulations 2006;

(iv)   the applicant has made inconsistent, contradictory, improbable or insufficient representations which make his claim clearly unconvincing in relation to his having been the object of persecution;

(v)   the applicant has submitted a subsequent application which does not raise any relevant new elements with respect to his particular circumstances or to the situation in his country of origin;

(vi)   the applicant is making an application merely in order to delay or frustrate the enforcement of an earlier or imminent decision which would result in his removal; and

(vii)   it is not reasonably practicable, in particular where the Secretary of State is of the opinion that the applicant is unfit or unable to be interviewed owing to enduring circumstances beyond his control.

The omission of a personal interview shall not prevent the Secretary of State from taking a decision on the application.

Where the personal interview is omitted, the applicant and dependants shall be given a reasonable opportunity to submit further information.

339NB.

(i)   The personal interview mentioned in paragraph 339NA above shall normally take place without the presence of the applicant's family members unless the Secretary of State considers it necessary for an appropriate examination to have other family members present.

(ii)   The personal interview shall take place under conditions which ensure appropriate confidentiality.

339NC.   (i)   A written report shall be made of every personal interview containing at least the essential information regarding the asylum application as presented by the applicant in accordance with paragraph 339I of these Rules.

(ii)   The Secretary of State shall ensure that the applicant has timely access to the report of the personal interview and that access is possible as soon as necessary for allowing an appeal to be prepared and lodged in due time.

339ND.   The Secretary of State shall provide at public expense an interpreter for the purpose of allowing the applicant to submit his case, wherever necessary. The Secretary of State shall select an interpreter who can ensure appropriate communication between the applicant and the representative of the Secretary of State who conducts the interview.

Internal relocation

339O.

(i)   The Secretary of State will not make:

(a)   a grant of asylum if in part of the country of origin a person would not have a well founded fear of being persecuted, and the person can reasonably be expected to stay in that part of the country; or

(b)   a grant of humanitarian protection if in part of the country of return a person would not face a real risk of suffering serious harm, and the person can reasonably be expected to stay in that part of the country.

(ii)   In examining whether a part of the country of origin or country of return meets the requirements in (i) the Secretary of State, when making his decision on whether to grant asylum or humanitarian protection, will have regard to the general circumstances prevailing in that part of the country and to the personal circumstances of the person.

(iii)   (i) applies notwithstanding technical obstacles to return to the country of origin or country of return

Sur place claims

339P.   A person may have a well-founded fear of being persecuted or a real risk of suffering serious harm based on events which have taken place since the person left the country of origin or country of return and/or activates which have been engaged in by a person since he left he country of origin or country of return, in particular where it is established that the activities relied upon constitute the expression and continuation of convictions or orientations held in the country of origin or country of return.

Residence Permits

339Q.   (i)   The Secretary of State will issue to a person granted asylum in the United Kingdom a United Kingdom Residence Permit (UKRP) as soon as possible after the grant of asylum. The UKRP will be valid for five years and renewable, unless compelling reasons of national security or public order otherwise require or where there are reasonable grounds for considering that the applicant is a danger to the security of the UK or having been convicted by a final judgment of a particularly serious crime, the applicant constitutes a danger to the community of the UK.

(ii)   The Secretary of State will issue to a person granted humanitarian protection in the United Kingdom a UKRP as soon as possible after the grant of humanitarian protection. The UKRP will be valid for five years and renewable, unless compelling reasons of national security or public order otherwise require or where there are reasonable grounds for considering that the person granted humanitarian protection is a danger to the security of the UK or having been convicted by a final judgment of a serious crime, this person constitutes a danger to the community of the UK.

(iii)   The Secretary of State will issue a UKRP to a family member of a person granted asylum or humanitarian protection where the family member does not qualify for such status. A UKRP will be granted for a period of five years. The UKRP is renewable on the terms set out in (i) and (ii) respectively. 'Family member' for the purposes of this sub-paragraph refers only to those who are treated as dependants for the purposes of paragraph 349.

(iv)   The Secretary of State may revoke or refuse to renew a person's UKRP where their grant of asylum or humanitarian protection is revoked under the provisions in the immigration rules.

Requirements for indefinite leave to remain for persons granted asylum or humanitarian protection

339R.   The requirements for indefinite leave to remain for a person granted asylum or humanitarian protection, or their dependants granted asylum or humanitarian protection in line with the main applicant, are that:

(i)   the applicant has held a UK Residence Permit (UKRP) issued under paragraph 339Q for a continuous period of five years in the UK; and

(ii)   the applicant's UKRP has not been revoked or not renewed under paragraphs 339A or 339G of the immigration rules; and

(iii)   the applicant has not:

    (a)   been convicted of an offence for which they have been sentenced to imprisonment for at least 4 years; or

    (b)   been convicted of an offence for which they have been sentenced to imprisonment for at least 12 months but less than 4 years, unless a period of 15 years has passed since the end of the sentence; or

    (c)   been convicted of an offence for which they have been sentenced to imprisonment for less than 12 months, unless a period of 7 years has passed since the end of the sentence; or

    (d)   been convicted of an offence for which they have received a non-custodial sentence or other out of court disposal that is recorded on their criminal record, unless a period of 24 months has passed since they received their sentence; or

    (e)   in the view of the Secretary of State persistently offended and shown a particular disregard for the law, unless a period of seven years has passed since the most recent sentence was received.

Indefinite leave to remain for a person granted asylum or humanitarian protection

339S.   Indefinite leave to remain for a person granted asylum or humanitarian protection will be granted where each of the requirements in paragraph 339R is met.

Refusal of indefinite leave to remain for a person granted asylum or humanitarian protection

339T.   (i)   Indefinite leave to remain for a person granted asylum or humanitarian protection is to be refused if any of the requirements of paragraph 339R is not met.

    (ii)   An applicant refused indefinite leave to remain under paragraph 339T(i) may apply to have their UK Residence Permit extended in accordance with paragraph 339Q.

Consideration of asylum applications and human rights claims

340.   DELETED

341.   DELETED

342.   The actions of anyone acting as an agent of the asylum applicant or human rights claimant may also be taken into account in regard to the matters set out in paragraphs 340 and 341.

343.   DELETED

344.   DELETED

Travel documents

344A.   (i)   After having received a complete application for a travel document, the Secretary of State will issue to a person granted asylum in the United Kingdom and their family members travel documents, in the form set out in the Schedule to the Geneva Convention, for the purpose of travel outside the United Kingdom, unless compelling reasons of national security or public order otherwise require.

    (ii)   After having received a complete application for a travel document, the Secretary of State will issue travel documents to a person granted humanitarian protection in the United Kingdom where that person is unable to obtain a national passport or other identity documents which enable him to travel, unless compelling reasons of national security or public order otherwise require.

    (iii)   Where the person referred to in (ii) can obtain a national passport or identity documents but has not done so, the Secretary of State will issue that person with a travel document where he can show that he has made reasonable attempts to obtain a national passport or identity document and there are serious humanitarian reasons for travel.

Access to Employment

344B.   The Secretary of State will not impose conditions restricting the employment or occupation in the United Kingdom of a person granted asylum or humanitarian protection.

Information

344C. A person who is granted asylum or humanitarian protection will be provided with access to information in a language that they may reasonably be supposed to understand which sets out the rights and obligations relating to that status. The Secretary of State will provide the information as soon as possible after the grant of asylum or humanitarian protection.

Third country cases

345. (1) In a case where the Secretary of State is satisfied that the conditions set out in Paragraphs 4 and 5(1), 9 and 10(1), 14 and 15(1) or 17 of Schedule 3 to the Asylum and Immigration (Treatment of Claimants, etc.) Act 2004 are fulfilled, he will normally decline to examine the asylum application substantively and issue a certificate under Part 2, 3, 4 or 5 of Schedule 3 to the Asylum and Immigration (Treatment of Claimants, etc.) Act 2004 as appropriate.

   (2) The Secretary of State shall not issue a certificate under Part 2, 3, 4 or 5 of Schedule 3 to the Asylum and Immigration (Treatment of Claimants, etc.) Act 2004 unless:

   (i) the asylum applicant has not arrived in the United Kingdom directly from the country in which he claims to fear persecution and has had an opportunity at the border or within the third country or territory to make contact with the authorities of that third country or territory in order to seek their protection; or

   (ii) there is other clear evidence of his admissibility to a third country or territory.

   Provided that he is satisfied that a case meets these criteria, the Secretary of State is under no obligation to consult the authorities of the third country or territory before the removal of an asylum applicant to that country or territory.

   (2A) Where a certificate is issued under Part 2, 3, 4 or 5 of Schedule 3 to the Asylum and Immigration (Treatment of Claimants, etc.) Act 2004 the asylum applicant shall:

   (i) be informed in a language that he may reasonably be expected to understand regarding his removal to a safe third country;

   (ii) be provided with a document informing the authorities of the safe third country, in the language of that country, that the asylum application has not been examined in substance by the authorities in the United Kingdom;

   (iii) sub-paragraph 345(2A)(ii) shall not apply if removal takes place with reference to the arrangements set out in Regulation (EC) No. 343/2003 (the Dublin Regulation); and

   (iv) if an asylum applicant removed under this paragraph is not admitted to the safe third country (not being a country to which the Dublin Regulation applies as specified in paragraph 345(2A)(iii)), subject to determining and resolving the reasons for his nonadmission, the asylum applicant shall be admitted to the asylum procedure in the United Kingdom.

   (3) Where a certificate is issued under Part 2, 3, 4 or 5 of Schedule 3 to the Asylum and Immigration (Treatment of Claimants, etc.) Act 2004 in relation to the asylum claim and the person is seeking leave to enter the Immigration Officer will consider whether or not he is in a position to decide to give or refuse leave to enter without interviewing the person further. If the Immigration Officer decides that a further interview is not required he may serve the notice giving or refusing leave to enter by post. If the Immigration Officer decides that a further interview is required, he will then resume his examination to determine whether or not to grant the person leave to enter under any other provision of these Rules. If the person fails at any time to comply with a requirement to report to an Immigration Officer for examination, the Immigration Officer may direct that the person's examination shall be treated as concluded at that time. The Immigration Officer will then consider any outstanding applications for entry on the basis of any evidence before him.

   (4) Where a certificate is issued under Part 2, 3, 4 or 5 of Schedule 3 to the Asylum and Immigration (Treatment of Claimants, etc.) Act 2004 the person may, if liable to removal as an illegal entrant, or removal under section 10 of the Immigration and Asylum Act 1999 or to deportation, at the same time be notified of removal directions, served with a notice of intention to make a deportation order, or served with a deportation order, as appropriate.

Previously rejected applications

346. DELETED

347. DELETED

Rights of appeal

348. DELETED

Dependants

349. A spouse, civil partner, unmarried or same-sex partner, or minor child accompanying a principal applicant may be included in his application for asylum as his dependant, provided, in the case of an adult dependant with legal capacity, the dependant consents to being treated as such at the time the application is lodged. A spouse, civil partner, unmarried or same-sex partner or minor child may also claim asylum in his own right. If the principal applicant is granted asylum or humanitarian protection and leave to enter or remain any spouse, civil partner, unmarried or same-sex partner or minor child will be granted leave to enter or remain for the same duration. The case of any dependant who claims asylum in his own right will be also considered individually in accordance with paragraph 334 above. An applicant under this paragraph, including an accompanied child, may be interviewed where he makes a claim as a dependant or in his own right.

If the spouse, civil partner, unmarried or same-sex partner, or minor child in question has a claim in his own right, that claim should be made at the earliest opportunity. Any failure to do so will be taken into account and may damage credibility if no reasonable explanation for it is given. Where an asylum or humanitarian protection application is unsuccessful, at the same time that asylum or humanitarian protection is refused the applicant may be notified of removal directions or served with a notice of the Secretary of State's intention to deport him, as appropriate. In this paragraph and paragraphs 350–352 a child means a person who is under 18 years of age or who, in the absence of documentary evidence establishing age, appears to be under that age. An unmarried or same sex partner for the purposes of this paragraph, is a person who has been living together with the principal applicant in a subsisting relationship akin to marriage or a civil partnership for two years or more.

Unaccompanied children

350. Unaccompanied children may also apply for asylum and, in view of their potential vulnerability, particular priority and care is to be given to the handling of their cases.

351. A person of any age may qualify for refugee status under the Convention and the criteria in paragraph 334 apply to all cases. However, account should be taken of the applicant's maturity and in assessing the claim of a child more weight should be given to objective indications of risk than to the child's state of mind and understanding of his situation. An asylum application made on behalf of a child should not be refused solely because the child is too young to understand his situation or to have formed a well founded fear of persecution. Close attention should be given to the welfare of the child at all times.

352. Any child over the age of 12 who has claimed asylum in his own right shall be interviewed about the substance of his claim unless the child is unfit or unable to be interviewed. When an interview takes place it shall be conducted in the presence of a parent, guardian, representative or another adult independent of the Secretary of State who has responsibility for the child. The interviewer shall have specialist training in the interviewing of children and have particular regard to the possibility that a child will feel inhibited or alarmed. The child shall be allowed to express himself in his own way and at his own speed. If he appears tired or distressed, the interview will be suspended. The interviewer should then consider whether it would be appropriate for the interview to be resumed the same day or on another day.

352ZA. The Secretary of State shall as soon as possible after an unaccompanied child makes an application for asylum take measures to ensure that a representative represents and/or assists the unaccompanied child with respect to the examination of the application and ensure that the representative is given the opportunity to inform the unaccompanied child about the meaning and possible consequences of the interview and, where appropriate, how to prepare himself for the interview. The representative shall have the right to be present at the interview and ask questions and make comments in the interview, within the framework set by the interviewer.

352ZB. The decision on the application for asylum shall be taken by a person who is trained to deal with asylum claims from children.

Requirements for limited leave to remain as an unaccompanied asylum seeking child.

352ZC. The requirements to be met in order for a grant of limited leave to remain to be made in relation to an unaccompanied asylum seeking child under paragraph 352ZE are:

(a) the applicant is an unaccompanied asylum seeking child under the age of 17 ½ years throughout the duration of leave to be granted in this capacity;

(b)   the applicant must have applied for asylum and been refused Refugee Leave and Humanitarian Protection;

(c)   there are no adequate reception arrangements in the country to which they would be returned if leave to remain was not granted;

(d)   the applicant must not be excluded from a grant of asylum under Regulation 7 of the Refugee or Person in Need of International Protection (Qualification) Regulations 2006 or excluded from a grant of Humanitarian Protection under paragraph 339D or both;

(e)   there are no reasonable grounds for regarding the applicant as a danger to the security of the United Kingdom;

(f)   the applicant has not been convicted by a final judgment of a particularly serious crime, and the applicant does not constitute a danger to the community of the United Kingdom; and

(g)   the applicant is not, at the date of their application, the subject of a deportation order or a decision to make a deportation order.

352ZD.   An unaccompanied asylum seeking child is a person who:

(a)   is under 18 years of age when the asylum application is submitted.

(b)   is applying for asylum in their own right; and

(c)   is separated from both parents and is not being cared for by an adult who in law or by custom has responsibility to do so.

352ZE.   Limited leave to remain should be granted for a period of 30 months or until the child is 17 ½ years of age whichever is shorter, provided that the Secretary of State is satisfied that the requirements in paragraph 352ZC are met.

352ZF.   Limited leave granted under this provision will cease if

(a)   any one or more of the requirements listed in paragraph 352ZC cease to be met, or

(b)   a misrepresentation or omission of facts, including the use of false documents, were decisive for the grant of leave under 352ZE.

352A.   The requirements to be met by a person seeking leave to enter or remain in the United Kingdom as the spouse civil partner of a refugee are that:

(i)   the applicant is married to or the civil partner of a person who is currently a refugee granted status as such under the immigration rules in the United Kingdom ; and

(ii)   the marriage or civil partnership did not take place after the person granted asylum left the country of his former habitual residence in order to seek asylum; an

(iii)   the applicant would not be excluded from protection by virtue of article 1F of the United Nations Convention and Protocol relating to the Status of Refugees if he were to seek asylum in his own right; and

(iv)   each of the parties intends to live permanently with the other as his or her spouse civil partner and the marriage is subsisting; and

(v)   if seeking leave to enter, the applicant holds a valid United Kingdom entry clearance for entry in this capacity.

352AA.   The requirements to be met by a person seeking leave to enter or remain in the United Kingdom as the unmarried or the same-sex partner of a refugee are that:

(i)   the applicant is the unmarried or same-sex partner of a person who is currently a refugee granted status as such under the immigration rules in the United Kingdom and was granted that status in the UK on or after 9th October 2006; and

(ii)   the parties have been living together in a relationship akin to either a marriage or a civil partnership which has subsisted for two years or more; and

(iii)   the relationship existed before the person granted asylum left the country of his former habitual residence in order to seek asylum; and

(iv)   the applicant would not be excluded from protection by virtue of paragraph 334(iii) or

(v)   of these Rules or article 1F of the Geneva Convention if he were to seek asylum in his own right; and

(vi)   each of the parties intends to live permanently with the other as his or her unmarried or same-sex partner and the relationship is subsisting; and

(vii)   if seeking leave to enter, the applicant holds a valid United Kingdom entry clearance for entry in this capacity.

          (viii)   the parties are not involved in a consanguineous relationship with one another; and

352B. Limited leave to enter the United Kingdom as the spouse civil partner of a refugee may be granted provided a valid United Kingdom entry clearance for entry in this capacity is produced to the Immigration Officer on arrival. Limited leave to remain in the United Kingdom as the spouse of a refugee may be granted provided the Secretary of State is satisfied that each of the requirements of paragraph 352A (i)–(v) are met.

352BA. Limited leave to enter the United Kingdom as the unmarried or same-sex partner of a refugee may be granted provided a valid United Kingdom entry clearance for entry in this capacity is produced to the Immigration Officer on arrival. Limited leave to remain in the United Kingdom as the unmarried or same sex partner of a refugee may be granted provided the Secretary of State is satisfied that each of the requirements of paragraph 352AA (i)–(vii) are met.

352C. Limited leave to enter the United Kingdom as the spouse civil partner of a refugee is to be refused if a valid United Kingdom entry clearance for entry in this capacity is not produced to the Immigration Officer on arrival. Limited leave to remain as the spouse civil partner of a refugee is to be refused if the Secretary of State is not satisfied that each of the requirements of paragraph 352A (i)–(v) are met.

352CA. Limited leave to enter the United Kingdom as the unmarried or same-sex partner of a refugee is to be refused if a valid United Kingdom entry clearance for entry in this capacity is not produced to the Immigration Officer on arrival. Limited leave to remain as the unmarried or same sex partner of a refugee is to be refused if the Secretary of State is not satisfied that each of the requirements of paragraph 352AA (i)–(vi) are met.

352D. The requirements to be met by a person seeking leave to enter or remain in the United Kingdom in order to join or remain with the parent who is currently a refugee granted status as such under the immigration rules in the United Kingdom are that the applicant:

          (i)   is the child of a parent who is currently a refugee granted status as such under the immigration rules in the United Kingdom; and

          (ii)   is under the age of 18, and

          (iii)   is not leading an independent life, is unmarried and is not a civil partner, and has not formed an independent family unit; and

          (iv)   was part of the family unit of the person granted asylum at the time that the person granted asylum left the country of his habitual residence in order to seek asylum; and

          (v)   would not be excluded from protection by virtue of article 1F of the United Nations Convention and Protocol relating to the Status of Refugees if he were to seek asylum in his own right; and

          (vi)   if seeking leave to enter, holds a valid United Kingdom entry clearance for entry in this capacity.

352E. Limited leave to enter the United Kingdom as the child of a refugee may be granted provided a valid United Kingdom entry clearance for entry in this capacity is produced to the Immigration Officer on arrival. Limited leave to remain in the United Kingdom as the child of a refugee may be granted provided the Secretary of State is satisfied that each of the requirements of paragraph 352D (i)–(v) are met.

352F. Limited leave to enter the United Kingdom as the child of a refugee is to be refused if a valid United Kingdom entry clearance for entry in this capacity is not produced to the Immigration Officer on arrival. Limited leave to remain as the child of a refugee is to be refused if the Secretary of State is not satisfied that each of the requirements of paragraph 352D (i)–(v) are met.

352FA. The requirements to be met by a person seeking leave to enter or remain in the United Kingdom as the spouse or civil partner of a person who is currently a beneficiary of humanitarian protection granted under the immigration rules in the United Kingdom and was granted that status on or after 30 August 2005 are that:

          (i)   the applicant is married to or the civil partner of a person who is currently a beneficiary of humanitarian protection granted under the immigration rules and was granted that status on or after 30 August 2005; and

          (ii)   the marriage or civil partnership did not take place after the person granted humanitarian protection left the country of his former habitual residence in order to seek asylum in the UK; and

          (iii)   the applicant would not be excluded from a grant of humanitarian protection for any of the reasons in paragraph 339D; and

          (iv)   each of the parties intend to live permanently with the other as his or her spouse or civil partner and the marriage or civil partnership is subsisting; and

          (v)   if seeking leave to enter, the applicant holds a valid United Kingdom entry clearance for entry in this capacity.

352FB.   Limited leave to enter the United Kingdom as the spouse or civil partner of a person granted humanitarian protection may be granted provided a valid United Kingdom entry clearance for entry in this capacity is produced to the Immigration Officer on arrival. Limited leave to remain in the United Kingdom as the spouse or civil partner of a person granted humanitarian protection may be granted provided the Secretary of State is satisfied that each of the requirements in sub paragraphs 352FA(i)–(iv) are met.

352FC.   Limited leave to enter the United Kingdom as the spouse or civil partner of a person granted humanitarian protection is to be refused if a valid United Kingdom entry clearance for entry in this capacity is not produced to the Immigration Officer on arrival. Limited leave to remain as the spouse or civil partner of a person granted humanitarian protection is to be refused if the Secretary of State is not satisfied that each of the requirements in sub paragraphs 352FA (i)–(iv) are met.

352FD.   The requirements to be met by a person seeking leave to enter or remain in the United Kingdom as the unmarried or same-sex partner of a person who is currently a beneficiary of humanitarian protection granted under the immigration rules in the United Kingdom are that:

(i)   the applicant is the unmarried or same-sex partner of a person who is currently a beneficiary of humanitarian protection granted under the immigration rules and was granted that status on or after 9th October 2006; and

(ii)   the parties have been living together in a relationship akin to either a marriage or a civil partnership which has subsisted for two years or more; and

(iii)   the relationship existed before the person granted humanitarian protection left the country of his former habitual residence in order to seek asylum; and

(iv)   the applicant would not be excluded from a grant of humanitarian protection for any of the reasons in paragraph 339D; and

(v)   each of the parties intends to live permanently with the other as his or her unmarried or same-sex partner and the relationship is subsisting; and

(vi)   the parties are not involved in a consanguineous relationship with one another; and

(vii)   if seeking leave to enter, the applicant holds a valid United Kingdom entry clearance for entry in this capacity.

352FE.   Limited leave to enter the United Kingdom as the unmarried or same-sex partner of a person granted humanitarian protection may be granted provided a valid United Kingdom entry clearance for entry in this capacity is produced to the Immigration Officer on arrival. Limited leave to remain in the United Kingdom as the unmarried or same sex partner of a person granted humanitarian protection may be granted provided the Secretary of State is satisfied that each of the requirements in subparagraphs 352FD (i)–(vi) are met.

352FF.   Limited leave to enter the United Kingdom as the unmarried or same-sex partner of a person granted humanitarian protection is to be refused if a valid United Kingdom entry clearance for entry in this capacity is not produced to the Immigration Officer on arrival. Limited leave to remain as the unmarried or same sex partner of a person granted humanitarian protection is to be refused if the Secretary of State is not satisfied that each of the requirements in sub paragraphs 352FD(i)–(vi) are met.

352FG.   The requirements to be met by a person seeking leave to enter or remain in the United Kingdom in order to join or remain with their parent who is currently a beneficiary of humanitarian protection granted under the immigration rules in the United Kingdom and was granted that status on or after 30 August 2005 are that the applicant:

(i)   is the child of a parent who is currently a beneficiary of humanitarian protection granted under the immigration rules in the United Kingdom and was granted that status on or after 30 August 2005; and

(ii)   is under the age of 18, and

(iii)   is not leading an independent life, is unmarried or is not in a civil partnership, and has not formed an independent family unit; and

(iv)   was part of the family unit of the person granted humanitarian protection at the time that the person granted humanitarian protection left the country of his habitual residence in order to seek asylum in the UK; and

(v)   would not be excluded from a grant of humanitarian protection for any of the reasons in paragraph 339D; and

(vi)   if seeking leave to enter, holds a valid United Kingdom entry clearance for entry in this capacity.

352FH.   Limited leave to enter the United Kingdom as the child of a person granted humanitarian protection may be granted provided a valid United Kingdom entry clearance for entry in this capacity is produced to the Immigration Officer on arrival. Limited leave to remain in the United Kingdom as the child of a person granted humanitarian protection may be granted provided the Secretary of State is satisfied that each of the requirements in sub paragraphs 352FG (i)–(v) are met.

352FI. Limited leave to enter the United Kingdom as the child of a person granted humanitarian protection is to be refused if a valid United Kingdom entry clearance for entry in this capacity is not produced to the Immigration Officer on arrival. Limited leave to remain as the child of a person granted humanitarian protection is to be refused if the Secretary of State is not satisfied that each of the requirements in sub paragraphs 352FG (i)–(v) are met.

352FJ. Nothing in paragraphs 352A–352FI shall allow a person to be granted leave to enter or remain in the United Kingdom as the spouse or civil partner, unmarried or same sex partner or child of a refugee, or of a person granted humanitarian protection under the immigration rules in the United Kingdom on or after 30 August 2005, if the refugee or, as the case may be, person granted humanitarian protection, is a British Citizen.

Interpretation

352G. For the purposes of this Part:

(a) 'Geneva Convention' means the United Nations Convention and Protocol relating to the Status of Refugees;

(b) 'Country of return' means a country or territory listed in paragraph 8(c) of Schedule 2 of the Immigration Act 1971;

(c) 'Country of origin' means the country or countries of nationality or, for a stateless person, or former habitual residence.

Part 11A – Temporary Protection

Definition of Temporary Protection Directive

354. For the purposes of paragraphs 355 to 356B, 'Temporary Protection Directive' means Council Directive 2001/55/EC of 20 July 2001 regarding the giving of temporary protection by Member States in the event of a mass influx of displaced persons.

Grant of temporary protection

355. An applicant for temporary protection will be granted temporary protection if the Secretary of State is satisfied that:

(i) the applicant is in the United Kingdom or has arrived at a port of entry in the United Kingdom; and

(ii) the applicant is a person entitled to temporary protection as defined by, and in accordance with, the Temporary Protection Directive; and

(iii) the applicant does not hold an extant grant of temporary protection entitling him to reside in another Member State of the European Union. This requirement is subject to the provisions relating to dependants set out in paragraphs 356 to 356B and to any agreement to the contrary with the Member State in question; and

(iv) the applicant is not excluded from temporary protection under the provisions in paragraph 355A.

355A. An applicant or a dependant may be excluded from temporary protection if:

(i) there are serious reasons for considering that:

(a) he has committed a crime against peace, a war crime, or a crime against humanity, as defined in the international instruments drawn up to make provision in respect of such crimes; or

(b) he has committed a serious non-political crime outside the United Kingdom prior to his application for temporary protection; or

(c) he has committed acts contrary to the purposes and principles of the United Nations, or

(ii) there are reasonable grounds for regarding the applicant as a danger to the security of the United Kingdom or, having been convicted by a final judgment of a particularly serious crime, to be a danger to the community of the United Kingdom.

Consideration under this paragraph shall be based solely on the personal conduct of the applicant concerned. Exclusion decisions or measures shall be based on the principle of proportionality.

355B. If temporary protection is granted to a person who has been given leave to enter or remain (whether or not the leave has expired) or to a person who has entered without leave, the Secretary of State will vary the existing leave or grant limited leave to remain.

355C.   A person to whom temporary protection is granted will be granted limited leave to enter or remain, which is not to be subject to a condition prohibiting employment, for a period not exceeding 12 months. On the expiry of this period, he will be entitled to apply for an extension of this limited leave for successive periods of 6 months thereafter.

355D.   A person to whom temporary protection is granted will be permitted to return to the United Kingdom from another Member State of the European Union during the period of a mass influx of displaced persons as established by the Council of the European Union pursuant to Article 5 of the Temporary Protection Directive.

355E.   A person to whom temporary protection is granted will be provided with a document in a language likely to be understood by him in which the provisions relating to temporary protection and which are relevant to him are set out. A person with temporary protection will also be provided with a document setting out his temporary protection status.

355F.   The Secretary of State will establish and maintain a register of those granted temporary protection. The register will record the name, nationality, date and place of birth and marital status of those granted temporary protection and their family relationship to any other person who has been granted temporary protection.

355G.   If a person who makes an asylum application is also eligible for temporary protection, the Secretary of State may decide not to consider the asylum application until the applicant ceases to be entitled to temporary protection.

Dependants

356.   In this part:

'dependant' means a family member or a close relative.

'family member' means:

(i)   the spouse or civil partner of an applicant for, or a person who has been granted, temporary protection; or

(ii)   the unmarried or same-sex partner of an applicant for, or a person who has been granted, temporary protection where the parties have been living together in a relationship akin to marriage which has subsisted for 2 years or more; or

(iii)   the minor child (who is unmarried and not a civil partner); of an applicant for, or a person who has been granted, temporary protection or his spouse,

who lived with the principal applicant as part of the family unit in the country of origin immediately prior to the mass influx.

'close relative' means:

(i)   the adult child (who is unmarried and not a civil partner), parent or grandparent of an applicant for, or person who has been granted, temporary protection; or

(ii)   sibling (who is unmarried and not a civil partner or the uncle or aunt of an applicant for, or person who has been granted, temporary protection, who lived with the principal applicant as part of the family unit in the country of origin immediately prior to the mass influx and was wholly or mainly dependent upon the principal applicant at that time, and would face extreme hardship if reunification with the principal applicant did not take place.

356A.   A dependant may apply for temporary protection. Where the dependant falls within paragraph 356 and does not fall to be excluded under paragraph 355A, he will be granted temporary protection for the same duration and under the same conditions as the principal applicant.

356B.   When considering any application by a dependant child, the Secretary of State shall take into consideration the best interests of that child.

Part 11B – Asylum

Reception Conditions for non-EU asylum applicants

357.   Part 11B only applies to asylum applicants (within the meaning of these Rules) who are not nationals of a member State.

Information to be provided to asylum applicants

357A.   The Secretary of State shall inform asylum applicants in a language they may reasonably be supposed to understand and within a reasonable time after their claim for asylum has been recorded of the procedure to be followed, their rights and obligations during the procedure, and the possible consequences of non-compliance and non-co-operation. They shall be informed of the likely timeframe for consideration of the application and the means at their disposal for submitting all relevant information.

358. The Secretary of State shall inform asylum applicants within a reasonable time not exceeding fifteen days after their claim for asylum has been recorded of the benefits and services that they may be eligible to receive and of the rules and procedures with which they must comply relating to them. The Secretary of State shall also provide information on non-governmental organisations and persons that provide legal assistance to asylum applicants and which may be able to help asylum applicants or provide information on available benefits and services.

358A. The Secretary of State shall ensure that the information referred to in paragraph 358 is available in writing and, to the extent possible, will provide the information in a language that asylum applicants may reasonably be supposed to understand. Where appropriate, the Secretary of State may also arrange for this information to be supplied orally.

Information to be provided by asylum applicants

358B. An asylum applicant must notify the Secretary of State of his current address and of any change to his address or residential status. If not notified beforehand, any change must be notified to the Secretary of State without delay after it occurs.

The United Nations High Commissioner for Refugees

358C. A representative of the United Nations High Commissioner for Refugees (UNHCR) or an organisation working in the United Kingdom on behalf of the UNHCR pursuant to an agreement with the government shall:

(a) have access to applicants for asylum, including those in detention;

(b) have access to information on individual applications for asylum, on the course of the procedure and on the decisions taken on applications for asylum, provided that the applicant for asylum agrees thereto;

(c) be entitled to present his views, in the exercise of his supervisory responsibilities under Article 35 of the Geneva Convention, to the Secretary of State regarding individual applications for asylum at any stage of the procedure.

This paragraph shall also apply where the Secretary of State is considering revoking a person's refugee status in accordance with these Rules.

Documentation

359. The Secretary of State shall ensure that, within three working days of recording an asylum application, a document is made available to that asylum applicant, issued in his own name, certifying his status as an asylum applicant or testifying that he is allowed to remain in the United Kingdom while his asylum application is pending. For the avoidance of doubt, in cases where the Secretary of State declines to examine an application it will no longer be pending for the purposes of this rule.

359A. The obligation in paragraph 359 above shall not apply where the asylum applicant is detained under the Immigration Acts, the Immigration and Asylum Act 1999 or the Nationality, Immigration and Asylum Act 2002.

359B. A document issued to an asylum applicant under paragraph 359 does not constitute evidence of the asylum applicant's identity.

359C. In specific cases the Secretary of State or an Immigration Officer may provide an asylum applicant with evidence equivalent to that provided under rule 359. This might be, for example, in circumstances in which it is only possible or desirable to issue a time-limited document.

Right to request permission to take up employment

360. An asylum applicant may apply to the Secretary of State for permission to take up employment if a decision at first instance has not been taken on the applicant's asylum application within one year of the date on which it was recorded. The Secretary of State shall only consider such an application if, in the Secretary of State's opinion, any delay in reaching a decision at first instance cannot be attributed to the applicant.

360A. If permission to take up employment is granted under paragraph 360, that permission will be subject to the following restrictions:

(i)   employment may only be taken up in a post which is, at the time an offer of employment is accepted, included on the list of shortage occupations published by the United Kingdom Border Agency (as that list is amended from time to time);

(ii)   no work in a self-employed capacity; and

(iii)   no engagement in setting up a business.

360B.   If an asylum applicant is granted permission to take up employment under paragraph 360 this shall only be until such time as his asylum application has been finally determined.

360C.   Where an individual makes further submissions which raise asylum grounds and which fall to be considered under paragraph 353 of these Rules, that individual may apply to the Secretary of State for permission to take up employment if a decision pursuant to paragaph 353 of these Rules has not been taken on the further submissions within one year of the date on which they were recorded. The Secretary of State shall only consider such an application if, in the Secretary of State's opinion, any delay in reaching a decision pursuant to paragraph 353 of these Rules cannot be attributed to the individual.

360D.   If permission to take up employment is granted under paragraph 360C, that permission will be subject to the following restrictions:

(i)   employment may only be taken up in a post which is, at the time an offer of employment is accepted, included on the list of shortage occupations published by the United Kingdom Border Agency (as that list is amended from time to time);

(ii)   no work in a self-employed capacity; and

(iii)   no engagement in setting up a business.

360E.   Where permission to take up employment is granted pursuant to paragraph 360C, this shall only be until such time as:

(i)   a decision has been taken pursuant to paragraph 353 that the further submissions do not amount to a fresh claim; or

(ii)   where the further submissions are considered to amount to a fresh claim for asylum pursuant to paragraph 353, all rights of appeal from the immigration decision made in consequence of the rejection of the further submissions have been exhausted.

Interpretation

361.   For the purposes of this Part–

(a)   'working day' means any day other than a Saturday or Sunday, a bank holiday, Christmas day or Good Friday;

(b)   'member State' has the same meaning as in Schedule 1 to the European Communities Act 1972.

Part 12 – Procedure and rights of appeal

Fresh Claims

353.   When a human rights or asylum claim has been refused or withdrawn or treated as withdrawn under paragraph 333C of these Rules and any appeal relating to that claim is no longer pending, the decision maker will consider any further submissions and, if rejected, will then determine whether they amount to a fresh claim. The submissions will amount to a fresh claim if they are significantly different from the material that has previously been considered. The submissions will only be significantly different if the content:

(i)   had not already been considered; and

(ii)   taken together with the previously considered material, created a realistic prospect of success, notwithstanding its rejection.

This paragraph does not apply to claims made overseas.

353A.   Consideration of further submissions shall be subject to the procedures set out in these Rules. An applicant who has made further submissions shall not be removed before the Secretary of State has considered the submissions under paragraph 353 or otherwise.

Exceptional Circumstances

353B.   Where further submissions have been made and the decision maker has established whether or not they amount to a fresh claim under paragraph 353 of these Rules, or in cases with no outstanding further submissions whose appeal rights have been exhausted and which are subject to a review, the decision maker will also have regard to the migrant's:

(i) character, conduct and associations including any criminal record and the nature of any offence of which the migrant concerned has been convicted;

(ii) compliance with any conditions attached to any previous grant of leave to enter or remain and compliance with any conditions of temporary admission or immigration bail where applicable;

(iii) length of time spent in the United Kingdom spent for reasons beyond the migrant's control after the human rights or asylum claim has been submitted or refused; in deciding whether there are exceptional circumstances which mean that removal from the United Kingdom is no longer appropriate.

This paragraph does not apply to submissions made overseas.

This paragraph does not apply where the person is liable to deportation.

Part 13 – Deportation

A deportation order

A362. Where Article 8 is raised in the context of deportation under Part 13 of these Rules, the claim under Article 8 will only succeed where the requirements of these rules as at 9 July 2012 are met, regardless of when the notice of intention to deport or the deportation order, as appropriate, was served.

362. A deportation order requires the subject to leave the United Kingdom and authorises his detention until he is removed. It also prohibits him from re-entering the country for as long as it is in force and invalidates any leave to enter or remain in the United Kingdom given him before the Order is made or while it is in force.

363. The circumstances in which a person is liable to deportation include:

(i) where the Secretary of State deems the person's deportation to be conducive to the public good;

(ii) where the person is the spouse or civil partner or child under 18 of a person ordered to be deported; and

(iii) where a court recommends deportation in the case of a person over the age of 17 who has been convicted of an offence punishable with imprisonment.

363A. Prior to 2 October 2000, a person would have been liable to deportation in certain circumstances in which he is now liable to administrative removal. However, such a person remains liable to deportation, rather than administrative removal where:

(i) a decision to make a deportation order against him was taken before 2 October 2000; or

(ii) the person has made a valid application under the Immigration (Regularisation Period for Overstayers) Regulations 2000.

Deportation of family members

364. DELETED

364A. DELETED

365. Section 5 of the Immigration Act 1971 gives the Secretary of State power in certain circumstances to make a deportation order against the spouse, civil partner or child of a person against whom a deportation order has been made. The Secretary of State will not normally decide to deport the spouse or civil partner of a deportee where:

(i) he has qualified for settlement in his own right; or

(ii) he has been living apart from the deportee.

366. The Secretary of State will not normally decide to deport the child of a deportee where:

(i) he and his mother or father are living apart from the deportee; or

(ii) he has left home and established himself on an independent basis; or

(iii) he married or formed a civil partnership before deportation came into prospect.

367. DELETED

368. Where the Secretary of State decides that it would be appropriate to deport a member of a family as such, the decision, and the right of appeal, will be notified and it will at the same time be explained that it is open to the member of the family to leave the country voluntarily if he does not wish to appeal or if he appeals and his appeal is dismissed.

369.–375.   DELETED

Hearing of appeals

376., 377.   DELETED

378.   A deportation order may not be made while it is still open to the person to appeal against the Secretary of State's decision, or while an appeal is pending except where the Secretary of State is required to make the deportation order in respect of a foreign criminal under section 32(5) of the UK Borders Act 2007. There is no appeal within the immigration appeal system against the making of a deportation order on the recommendation of a court; but there is a right of appeal to a higher court against the recommendation itself. A deportation order may not be made while it is still open to the person to appeal against the relevant conviction, sentence or recommendation, or while such an appeal is pending.

379.–380.   DELETED

Procedure

381.   When a decision to make a deportation order has been taken (otherwise than on the recommendation of a court) a notice will be given to the person concerned informing him of the decision and of his right of appeal.

382.   Following the issue of such a notice the Secretary of State may authorise detention or make an order restricting a person as to residence, employment or occupation and requiring him to report to the police, pending the making of a deportation order.

383.   DELETED

384.   If a notice of appeal is given within the period allowed, a summary of the facts of the case on the basis of which the decision was taken will be sent to the appropriate appellate authorities, who will notify the appellant of the arrangements for the appeal to be heard.

Arrangements for removal

385.   A person against whom a deportation order has been made will normally be removed from the United Kingdom. The power is to be exercised so as to secure the person's return to the country of which he is a national, or which has most recently provided him with a travel document, unless he can show that another country will receive him. In considering any departure from the normal arrangements, regard will be had to the public interest generally, and to any additional expense that may fall on public funds.

386.   The person will not be removed as the subject of a deportation order while an appeal may be brought against the removal directions or such an appeal is pending.

Supervised departure

387.   DELETED

Returned deportees

388.   Where a person returns to this country when a deportation order is in force against him, he may be deported under the original order. The Secretary of State will consider every such case in the light of all the relevant circumstances before deciding whether to enforce the order.

Returned family members

389.   Persons deported in the circumstances set out in paragraphs 365–368 above (deportation of family members) may be able to seek re-admission to the United Kingdom under the Immigration Rules where:

(i)   a child reaches 18 (when he ceases to be subject to the deportation order); or

(ii)   in the case of a spouse or civil partner, the marriage or civil partnership comes to an end.

Revocation of deportation order

390.   An application for revocation of a deportation order will be considered in the light of all the circumstances including the following:

(i)   the grounds on which the order was made;

(ii)   any representations made in support of revocation;

(iii)   the interests of the community, including the maintenance of an effective immigration control;

(iv)   the interests of the applicant, including any compassionate circumstances.

390A.   Where paragraph 398 applies the Secretary of State will consider whether paragraph 399 or 399A applies and, if it does not, it will only be in exceptional circumstances that the public interest in maintaining the deportation order will be outweighed by other factors.

391.   In the case of a person who has been deported following conviction for a criminal offence, the continuation of a deportation order against that person will be the proper course:

(a)   in the case of a conviction for an offence for which the person was sentenced to a period of imprisonment of less than 4 years, unless 10 years have elapsed since the making of the deportation order, or

(b)   in the case of a conviction for an offence for which the person was sentenced to a period of imprisonment of at least 4 years, at any time,

Unless, in either case, the continuation would be contrary to the Human Rights Convention or the Convention and Protocol Relating to the Status of Refugees, or there are other exceptional circumstances that mean the continuation is outweighed by compelling factors.

391A.   In other cases, revocation of the order will not normally be authorised unless the situation has been materially altered, either by a change of circumstances since the order was made, or by fresh information coming to light which was not before the appellate authorities or the Secretary of State. The passage of time since the person was deported may also in itself amount to such a change of circumstances as to warrant revocation of the order.

392.   Revocation of a deportation order does not entitle the person concerned to re-enter the United Kingdom; it renders him eligible to apply for admission under the Immigration Rules. Application for revocation of the order may be made to the Entry Clearance Officer or direct to the Home Office.

Rights of appeal in relation to a decision not to revoke a deportation order

393., 394.   DELETED

395.   There may be a right of appeal against refusal to revoke a deportation order. Where an appeal does lie the right of appeal will be notified at the same time as the decision to refuse to revoke the order.

396.   Where a person is liable to deportation the presumption shall be that the public interest requires deportation. It is in the public interest to deport where the Secretary of State must make a deportation order in accordance with section 32 of the UK Borders Act 2007.

397.   A deportation order will not be made if the person's removal pursuant to the order would be contrary to the UK's obligations under the Refugee Convention or the Human Rights Convention. Where deportation would not be contrary to these obligations, it will only be in exceptional circumstances that the public interest in deportation is outweighed.

Deportation and Article 8

398.   Where a person claims that their deportation would be contrary to the UK's obligations under Article 8 of the Human Rights Convention, and

(a)   the deportation of the person from the UK is conducive to the public good because they have been convicted of an offence for which they have been sentenced to a period of imprisonment of at least 4 years;

(b)   the deportation of the person from the UK is conducive to the public good because they have been convicted of an offence for which they have been sentenced to a period of imprisonment of less than 4 years but at least 12 months; or

(c)   the deportation of the person from the UK is conducive to the public good because, in the view of the Secretary of State, their offending has caused serious harm or they are a persistent offender who shows a particular disregard for the law,

the Secretary of State in assessing that claim will consider whether paragraph 399 or 399A applies and, if it does not, it will only be in exceptional circumstances that the public interest in deportation will be outweighed by other factors.

399.   This paragraph applies where paragraph 398 (b) or (c) applies if –

(a)   the person has a genuine and subsisting parental relationship with a child under the age of 18 years who is in the UK, and

(i)   the child is a British Citizen; or

(ii)   the child has lived in the UK continuously for at least the 7 years immediately preceding the date of the immigration decision; and in either case

(a)   it would not be reasonable to expect the child to leave the UK; and

(b)   there is no other family member who is able to care for the child in the UK; or

(b)   the person has a genuine and subsisting relationship with a partner who is in the UK and is a British Citizen, settled in the UK, or in the UK with refugee leave or humanitarian protection, and

    (i)   the person has lived in the UK with valid leave continuously for at least the 15 years immediately preceding the date of the immigration decision (discounting any period of imprisonment); and

    (ii)   there are insurmountable obstacles to family life with that partner continuing outside the UK.

399A.   This paragraph applies where paragraph 398(b) or (c) applies if –

(a)   the person has lived continuously in the UK for at least 20 years immediately preceding the date of the immigration decision (discounting any period of imprisonment) and he has no ties (including social, cultural or family) with the country to which he would have to go if required to leave the UK; or

(b)   the person is aged under 25 years, he has spent at least half of his life living continuously in the UK immediately preceding the date of the immigration decision (discounting any period of imprisonment) and he has no ties (including social, cultural or family) with the country to which he would have to go if required to leave the UK.

399B.   Where paragraph 399 or 399A applies limited leave may be granted for periods not exceeding 30 months. Such leave shall be given subject to such conditions as the Secretary of State deems appropriate. Where a person who has previously been granted a period of leave under paragraph 399B would not fall for refusal under paragraph 322(1C), indefinite leave to remain may be granted.

399C.   DELETED

400.   Where a person claims that their removal under paragraphs 8 to 10 of Schedule 2 to the Immigration Act 1971, section 10 of the Immigration and Asylum Act 1999 or section 47 of the Immigration, Asylum and Nationality Act 2006 would be contrary to the UK's obligations under Article 8 of the Human Rights Convention, the Secretary of State may require an application under paragraph 276ADE (private life) or Appendix FM (family life) of these rules. Where an application is not required, in assessing that claim the Secretary of State or an immigration officer will, subject to paragraph 353, consider that claim against the requirements to be met under paragraph 276ADE or Appendix FM and if appropriate the removal decision will be cancelled.

Part 14 – OMITTED

Appendix 1 – Visa requirements for the United Kingdom

1.   Subject to paragraph 2 below, the following persons need a visa for the United Kingdom:

(a)   Nationals or citizens of the following countries or territorial entities:
Afghanistan
Albania
Algeria
Angola
Armenia
Azerbaijan
Bahrain
Bangladesh
Belarus
Benin
Bhutan
Bolivia
Bosnia Herzegovina
Burkina Faso
Burma
Burundi
Cambodia
Cameroon
Cape Verde
Central African Republic

Chad

People's Republic of China (except those referred to in sub-paragraphs 2(d) and (e) of this Appendix)

Colombia

Comoros

Congo

Cuba

Democratic Republic of the Congo

Djibouti

Dominican Republic

Ecuador

Egypt

Equatorial Guinea

Eritrea

Ethiopia

Fiji

Gabon

Gambia

Georgia

Ghana

Guinea

Guinea Bissau

Guyana

Haiti

India

Indonesia

Iran

Iraq

Ivory Coast

Jamaica

Jordan

Kazakhstan

Kenya

Korea (North)

Kuwait (except those referred to in sub-paragraph 2(r) of this Appendix)

Kyrgyzstan

Laos

Lebanon

Lesotho

Liberia

Libya

Macedonia

Madagascar

Malawi

Mali

Mauritania

Moldova

Mongolia

Morocco

Mozambique

Nepal

Niger

Nigeria

Oman (except those referred to in sub-paragraph 2(j) of this Appendix)

Pakistan

Peru

Philippines

Qatar (except those referred to in sub-paragraph 2(k) of this Appendix)

Russia

Rwanda
Sao Tome e Principe
Saudi Arabia
Senegal
Serbia
Sierra Leone
Somalia
South Africa
South Sudan
Sri Lanka
Sudan
Surinam
Swaziland
Syria
Taiwan (except those referred to in sub-paragraph 2(h) of this Appendix)
Tajikistan
Tanzania
Thailand
Togo
Tunisia
Turkey (except those referred to in sub-paragraph 2(q) of this Appendix)
Turkmenistan
Uganda
Ukraine
United Arab Emirates (except those referred to in sub-paragraph 2(1) of this Appendix)
Uzbekistan
Venezuela (except those referred to in sub-paragraph 2(i) of this Appendix)
Vietnam
Yemen
Zambia
Zimbabwe
The territories formerly comprising the socialist Federal Republic of Yugoslavia

   (b)   Persons who hold passports or travel documents issued by the former Soviet Union or by the former Socialist Federal Republic of Yugoslavia.

   (c)   Stateless persons.

   (d)   Persons who hold non-national documents.

2.   The following persons do not need a visa for the United Kingdom:

   (a)   those who qualify for admission to the United Kingdom as returning residents in accordance with paragraph 18;

   (b)   those who seek leave to enter the United Kingdom within the period of their earlier leave and for the same purpose as that for which that leave was granted, unless it

       (i)   was for a period of six months or less; or

       (ii)   was extended by statutory instrument or by section 3C of the Immigration Act 1971 (inserted by section 3 of the Immigration and Asylum Act 1999);

   (c)   DELETED

   (d)   those nationals or citizens of the People's Republic of China holding passports issued by Hong Kong Special Administrative Region;

   (e)   those nationals or citizens of the People's Republic of China holding passports issued by Macao Special Administrative Region;

   (f)   those who arrive in the United Kingdom with leave to enter which is in force but which was given before arrival, so long as those in question arrive within the period of their earlier leave and for the same purpose as that for which leave was granted, unless that leave–

       (i)   was for a period of six months or less, or

       (ii)   was extended by statutory instrument or by section 3C of the Immigration Act 1971 (inserted by section 3 of the Immigration and Asylum Act 1999);

(g) DELETED

(h) those nationals or citizens of Taiwan who hold a passport by Taiwan that includes the number of the identification card issued by the competent authority in Taiwan in it.

(i) those nationals or citizens of Venezuela who hold a passport issued by the Republic of Venezuela that contains biometric information held in an electronic chip.

(j) those nationals or citizens of Oman, who hold diplomatic and special passports issued by oman when travelling to the UK for the purpose of a general visit in accordance with paragraph 41,

(k) those nationals or citizens of Qatar who hold diplomatic and special passports issued by Qatar when travelling to the UK for the purpose of a general visit in accordance with paragraph 41,

(l) those nationals or citizens of the United arab emirates who hold diplomatic and special passports issued by the United arab emirates when travelling to the UK for the purpose of a general visit in accordance with paragraph 41.

(m) DELETED.

(n) DELETED.

(o) DELETED.

(p) DELETED.

(q) those nationals or citizens of Turkey, who hold diplomatic passports issued by Turkey when travelling to the UK for the purpose of a general visit in accordance with paragraph 41.

(r) those nationals of Kuwait who hold diplomatic and special passports issued by Kuwait when travelling to the UK for the purpose of a general visit in accordance with paragraph 41.

(r) for the period beginning with 4 March 2014 and ending with 3 August 2014, nationals or citizens of the countries or territorial entities listed in paragraph 1 who hold a XX (20th) Commonwealth Games Identity and Accreditation Card issued by the Organising Committee of the Commonwealth Games (Glasgow 2014 Ltd) save for those who are accredited under (and whose card indicates accreditation under) category code WKF or S,

(s) for the period beginning with 4 August 2014 and ending with 3 September 2014 nationals or citizens of the countries or territorial entities listed in paragraph 1 who hold a Commonwealth Games Identity and Accreditation Card issued by Glasgow 2014 Ltd unless

   (i) the holder is accredited under (and the card indicates accreditation under) category code WKF or S; or

   (ii) the holder had not had leave to enter, leave to remain or entry clearance under paragraph 56ZC or 56ZF at any time during the period beginning with 4 March 2014 and ending with 3 August 2014

Appendix 2 – Countries or territories whose nationals or citizens are relevant foreign nationals for the purposes of Part 10 of these Rules

Registration with the police

Afghanistan
Algeria
Argentina
Armenia
Azerbaijan
Bahrain
Belarus
Bolivia
Brazil
China
Colombia
Cuba
Egypt
Georgia
Iran
Iraq

Israel
Jordan
Kazakhstan
Kuwait
Kyrgyzstan
Lebanon
Libya
Moldova
Morocco
North Korea
Oman
Palestine
Peru
Qatar
Russia
Saudi Arabia
Sudan
Syria
Tajikistan
Tunisia
Turkey
Turkmenistan
United Arab Emirates
Ukraine
Uzbekistan
Yemen

Appendix 3–5 – DELETED

Appendix 6, 7 – OMITTED

Appendix A – Attributes

Attributes for Tier 1 (Exceptional Talent) Migrants

1. An applicant applying for entry clearance, leave to remain or indefinite leave to remain as a Tier 1 (Exceptional Talent) Migrant must score 75 points for attributes.

2. Available points are shown in Table 1.

3. Notes to accompany the table are shown below the table.

Table 1

All applications for entry clearance and applications for leave to remain where the applicant has, or last had leave that was not leave as a Tier 1 Exceptional Talent) Migrant

Criterion	Points
Endorsed by Designated Competent Body according to that Body's criteria as set out in Appendix L.	75

All other applications for leave to remain and applications for indefinite leave to remain

Criterion		Points
(i)	During his most recent period of leave as a Tier 1 (Exceptional Talent) Migrant, the applicant has earned money in the UK as a result of employment or self-employment in his expert field as previously endorsed by a Designated Competent Body; and	75
(ii)	That Designated Competent Body has not withdrawn its endorsement of the applicant.	

Notes

Tier 1 (Exceptional Talent) Limit

4. (a) The Secretary of State shall be entitled to limit the total number of Tier 1 (Exceptional Talent) endorsements Designated Competent Bodies may make in support of successful applications, for entry clearance and leave to remain in a particular period, to be referred to as the Tier 1 (Exceptional Talent) Limit.

   (b) The Tier 1 (Exceptional Talent) Limit is 1,000 endorsements in total per year (beginning on 6 April and ending on 5 April) which will be allocated to the Designated Competent Bodies as follows:

      (i) 300 endorsements to The Arts Council for the purpose of endorsing applicants with exceptional talent in the fields of arts and culture;

      (ii) 300 endorsements to The Royal Society for the purpose of endorsing applicants with exceptional talent in the fields of natural sciences and medical science research;

      (iii) 200 endorsements to The Royal Academy of Engineering for the purpose of endorsing applicants with exceptional talent in the field of engineering; and

      (iv) 200 endorsements to The British Academy for the purpose of endorsing applicants with exceptional talent in the fields of humanities and social sciences.

   (c) The Tier 1 (Exceptional Talent) Limit will be operated according to the practice set out in paragraph 5 below.

   (d) If a Designated Competent Body chooses to transfer part of its unused allocation of endorsements to another Designated Competent Body by mutual agreement of both bodies and the Secretary of State, the allocations of both bodies will be adjusted accordingly and the adjusted allocations will be published on the UK Border Agency website.

5. (a) Before an applicant applies for entry clearance or leave to remain (unless he has, or last had, leave as a Tier 1 (Exceptional Talent) Migrant), he must make an application for a Designated Competent Body endorsement, and this application must:

      (i) be made to the UK Border Agency using the specified form,

      (ii) state which Designated Competent Body he wishes to endorse his application, and

      (iii) provide the specified evidence set out in Appendix L.

   (b) A number of endorsements will be made available for each Designated Competent Body, as follows:

      (i) From 6 April to 30 September each year, half that body's allocated endorsements under paragraph 4 above.

      (ii) From 1 October to 5 April each year, that body's remaining unused allocated endorsements under paragraph 4 above.

   (c) Unused endorsements will not be carried over from one year to the next.

   (d) If a Designated Competent Body endorses an application for an endorsement, the applicant subsequently uses that endorsement to make an application for entry clearance or leave to remain which is refused, and that refusal is not subsequently overturned, the used endorsement will be returned to the number of endorsements available for the relevant Designated Competent Body, providing the end of the period (6 April to 5 April) to which it relates has not yet passed.

   (e) An application for a Designated Competent Body endorsement will be refused if the Designated Competent Body has reached or exceeded the number of endorsements available to it.

   (f) The number of endorsements available for each Designated Competent Body to endorse Tier 1 (Exceptional Talent) applicants in a particular period, will be reduced by one for each Croatian national that body endorses in that period for the purposes of applying to be deemed a highly skilled person under the Accession of Croatia (Immigration and Worker Authorisation) Regulations 2013.

Endorsement by the relevant Designated Competent Body

6. Points will only be awarded in an application for entry clearance or leave to remain (except where the applicant has, or last had, leave as a Tier 1 (Exceptional Talent) Migrant) for an endorsement from the relevant Designated Competent Body if:

   (a) the applicant provides a valid approval letter from the UK Border Agency for a Designated Competent Body endorsement, which was granted to him no more than three months before the date of the application for entry clearance or leave to remain, and

(b)   the endorsement has not been withdrawn by the relevant Designated Competent Body at the time the application is considered by the UK Border Agency.

Money earned in the UK

6A.   Points will only be awarded for money earned in the UK if the applicant provides the following specified documents:

(a)   If the applicant is a salaried employee, the specified documents are at least one of the following:

   (i)   payslips confirming his earnings, which must be either:

   (1)   original formal payslips issued by the employer and showing the employer's name, or

   (2)   accompanied by a letter from the applicant's employer, on company headed paper and signed by a senior official, confirming the payslips are authentic;

   or

   (ii)   personal bank statements on official bank stationery, showing the payments made to the applicant; or

   (iii)   electronic bank statements, which either:

   (1)   are accompanied by a supporting letter from the bank on company headed paper confirming that the documents are authentic, or

   (2)   bear the official stamp of the issuing bank on every page of the document;

   or

   (iv)   an official tax document produced by HM Revenue & Customs or the applicant's employer, which shows earnings on which tax has been paid or will be paid in a tax year, and is either:

   (1)   a document produced by HM Revenue & Customs that shows details of declarable taxable income on which tax has been paid or will be paid in a tax year, such as a tax refund letter or tax demand,

   (2)   a P60 document produced by an employer as an official return to HM Revenue & Customs, showing details of earnings on which tax has been paid in a tax year, or

   (3)   a document produced by a person, business, or company as an official return to HM Revenue & Customs, showing details of earnings on which tax has been paid or will be paid in a tax year, and which has been approved, registered, or stamped by HM Revenue & Customs;

   or

   (v)   Dividend vouchers, confirming the gross and net dividend paid by a company to the applicant, normally from its profits. The applicant must provide a separate dividend voucher or payment advice slip for each dividend payment.

(b)   If the applicant has worked in a self-employed capacity, the specified documents are at least one of the following:

   (i)   A letter from the applicant's accountant (who must be either a fully qualified chartered accountant or a certified accountant who is a member of a registered body in the UK), on headed paper, which shows a breakdown of the gross and net earnings. The letter should give a breakdown of salary, dividends, profits, tax credits and dates of net payments earned. If the applicant's earnings are a share of the net profit of the company, the letter should also explain this; or

   (ii)   Company or business accounts that meet statutory requirements and clearly show:

   (1)   the net profit of the company or business made over the earnings period to be assessed,

   (2)   both a profit and loss account (or income and expenditure account if the organisation is not trading for profit), and

   (3)   a balance sheet signed by a director;

   or

   (iii)   If the applicant has worked as a sponsored researcher, a letter on official headed paper to the applicant from the institution providing the funding, which confirms:

   (1)   the applicant's name,

   (2)   the name of the sponsoring institution providing the funding,

   (3)   the name of the host institution where the applicant's sponsored research is based,

(4)   the title of the post, and

(5)   details of the funding provided.

(c)   All applicants must also provide at least one of the following specified documents:

   (i)   A contract of service or work between the applicant and a UK employer or UK institution which indicates the field of work he has undertaken; or

   (ii)   A letter from a UK employer or UK institution on its official headed paper, confirming that the applicant has earned money in his expert field.

7–34-SD.   OMITTED

Attributes for Tier 1 (Entrepreneur) Migrants

35.   An applicant applying for entry clearance, leave to remain or indefinite leave to remain as a Tier 1 (Entrepreneur) Migrant must score 75 points for attributes.

36.   Subject to paragraph 37, available points for applications for entry clearance or leave to remain are shown in Table 4.

36A.   An applicant who is applying for leave to remain and has, or was last granted, entry clearance, leave to enter or leave to remain as:

(i)   a Tier 4 Migrant,

(ii)   a Student,

(iii)   a Student Nurse,

(iv)   a Student Re-sitting an Examination, or

(v)   a Student Writing Up a Thesis,

will only be awarded points under the provisions in (b) in Table 4.

37.   Available points are shown in Table 5 for an applicant who:

(a)   has had entry clearance, leave to enter or leave to remain as a Tier 1 (Entrepreneur) Migrant, a Businessperson or an Innovator in the 12 months immediately before the date of application, or

(b)   is applying for leave to remain and has, or was last granted, entry clearance, leave to enter or leave to remain as a Tier 1 (Entrepreneur) Migrant, a Businessperson or an Innovator.

38.   Available points for applications for indefinite leave to remain are shown in Table 6.

39.   (a)   Notes to accompany Table 4 appear below Table 4.

   (b)   Notes to accompany Tables 4, 5 and 6 appear below Table 6.

40.   In all cases, an applicant cannot use the same funds to score points for attributes under this Appendix and to score points for maintenance funds for himself or his dependants under Appendices C or E.

Table 4: Applications for entry clearance or leave to remain referred to in paragraph 36

Investment and business activity			Points
(a)	The applicant has access to not less than £200,000, or		25
(b)	The applicant has access to not less than £50,000 from:		
	(i)	one or more registered venture capitalist firms regulated by the Financial Conduct Authority (FCA),	
	(ii)	one or more UK Entrepreneurial seed funding competitions which is listed as endorsed on the UK Trade & Investment website, or	
	(iii)	one or more UK Government Departments, or Devolved Government Departments in Scotland, Wales or Northern Ireland, and made available by the Department(s) for the specific purpose of establishing or expanding a UK business, or	
(c)	The applicant:		
	(i)	is applying for leave to remain,	
	(ii)	has, or was last granted, leave as a Tier 1 (Graduate Entrepreneur) Migrant, and	
	(iii)	has access to not less than £50,000, or	

Investment and business activity	Points

(d)   The applicant:
 	
    (i)   is applying for leave to remain,
 	
    (ii)   has, or was lasted granted, leave as a Tier 1 (Post-Study Work) Migrant,
 	
    (iii)   was, on a date falling within the three months immediately prior to the date of application,
 	
        (1)   registered with HM Revenue and Customs as self-employed, or
 	
        (2)   registered as a new business in which he is a director, or
 	
        (3)   registered as a director of an existing business,
 	
    (iv)   is working in an occupation which appears on the list of occupations skilled to National Qualifications Framework level 4 or above, as stated in the Codes of Practice in Appendix J, and provides the specified evidence in paragraph 41-SD. 'Working' in this context means that the core service his business provides to its customers or clients involves the business delivering a service in an occupation at this level. It excludes any work involved in administration, marketing or website functions for the business, and
 	
    (v) has access to not less than £50,000.	

The money is held in one or more regulated financial institutions	25
The money is disposable in the UK	25

Investment: notes

41.   An applicant will only be considered to have access to funds if:

    (a)   The specified documents in paragraph 41-SD are provided to show cash money to the amount required (this must not be in the form of assets);

    (b)   The specified documents in paragraph 41-SD are provided to show that the applicant has permission to use the money to invest in a business in the UK;

    (c)   The money is either held in a UK regulated financial institution or is transferable to the UK; and

    (d)   The money will remain available to the applicant until such time as it is spent in the establishment or running of the applicant's business or businesses. 'Spent' excludes spending on the applicant's own remuneration. The UK Border Agency reserves the right to request further evidence or otherwise verify that the money will remain available, and to refuse the application if this evidence is not provided or it is unable to satisfactorily verify. 'Available to him' means that the funds are:

        (1)   in his own possession,

        (2)   in the financial accounts of a UK incorporated business of which he is the director, or

        (3)   available from the third party or parties named in the application under the terms of the declaration(s) referred to in paragraph 41-SD(b) of Appendix A.

41-SD.   The specified documents in Table 4 and paragraph 41, and associated definitions, are as follows:

    (a)   Where this paragraph refers to funding being available, unless stated otherwise, this means funding available to:

    (i)   the applicant;

    (ii)   the entrepreneurial team, if the applicant is applying under the provisions in paragraph 52 of this Appendix; or

    (iii)   the applicant's business.

    (b)   Where this paragraph refers to the applicant's business, the applicant must be registered as a director of that business in the UK, and provide a Companies House document showing the address of the registered office in the UK, or head office in the UK if it has no registered office, and the applicant's name, as it appears on the application form, as a director.

    (c)   The specified documents to show evidence of the funding available to invest are one or more of the following specified documents:

    (i)   A letter from each financial institution holding the funds, to confirm the amount of money available. Each letter must:

        (1)   be an original document and not a copy,

(2)   be on the institution's headed paper,

(3)   have been issued by an authorised official of that institution,

(4)   have been produced within the three months immediately before the date of application,

(5)   confirm that the institution is regulated by the appropriate body,

(6)   state the applicant's name, and his team partner's name where relevant,

(7)   show the account number and,

(8)   state the date of the document,

(9)   confirm the amount of money available from the applicant's own funds (if applicable) that are held in that institution,

(10)   confirm the amount of money available from any third party (if applicable) that is held in that institution,

(11)   confirm the name of each third party and their contact details, including their full address including postal code, and where available landline phone number and any email address, and

(12)   confirm that if the money is not in an institution regulated by the Financial Conduct Authority (FCA) and the Prudential Regulation Authority (PRA), the money can be transferred into the UK; or

(ii)   For money held in the UK only, a recent personal bank or building society statement from each UK financial institution holding the funds, which confirms the amount of money available. Each statement must satisfy the following requirements:

(1)   the statements must be original documents and not copies;

(2)   the bank or building society holding the money must be based in the UK and regulated by the Financial Conduct Authority (FCA) and the Prudential Regulation Authority (PRA);

(3)   the money must be in cash in the account, not Individual Savings Accounts or assets such as stocks and shares;

(4)   the account must be in the applicant's own name only (or both names for an entrepreneurial team), not in the name of a business or third party;

(5)   each statement must be on the institution's official stationery showing the institution's name and logo, and confirm the applicant's name (and, where relevant, the applicant's entrepreneurial team partner's name), the account number and the date of the statement;

(6)   each statement must have been issued by an authorised official of that institution and produced within the three months immediately before the date of the application; and

(7)   if the statements are printouts of electronic statements, they must either be accompanied by a supporting letter from the bank, on the bank's headed paper, confirming the authenticity of the statements, or bear the official stamp of the bank in question on each page of the statement; or

(iii)   For £50,000 from a Venture Capital firm, Seed Funding Competition or UK Government Department only, a recent letter from an accountant, who is a member of a recognised UK supervisory body, or other authorised official in the case of a UK Government Department, confirming the amount of money made available. Each letter must:

(1)   be an original document and not a copy,

(2)   be on the institution's official headed paper,

(3)   have been issued by an accountant engaged by the Venture Capital firm, Seed Funding Competition or UK Government Department or other official of the UK Government Department authorised to provide the information,

(4)   have been produced within the three months immediately before the date of the application,

(5)   state the applicant's name, and his team partner's name where relevant, or the name of the applicant's business,

(6)   state the date of the document,

(7)   confirm the amount of money available to the applicant, the entrepreneurial team or the applicant's business from the Venture Capital firm, Seed funding competition or UK Government Department, and

(8)   confirm the name of the Venture Capital firm, Seed funding competition or UK Government Department and the contact details of an official of that organisation, including their full address, postal code and, where available, landline phone number and any email address,

(d)   If the applicant is applying using money from a third party, he must provide all of the following specified documents:

(i)   An original written declaration from every third party that they have made the money available to invest in a business in the United Kingdom, containing:

(1)   the names of the third party and the applicant (and his team partner's name where relevant), or the name of the applicant's business,

(2)   the date of the declaration,

(3)   the applicant's signature and the signature of the third party (and the signature of the applicant's team partner where relevant),

(4)   the amount of money available in pounds sterling,

(5)   the relationship(s) of the third party to the applicant,

(6)   if the third party is a venture capitalist firm, confirmation of whether this body is regulated by the Financial Conduct Authority (FCA) and is listed as permitted to operate as a Venture Capital firm,

(7)   if the third party is a UK Seed Funding Competition, confirmation that the applicant, the entrepreneurial team or the applicant's business has been awarded money and that the competition is listed as endorsed on the UK Trade & Investment website, together with the amount of the award and naming the applicant, the entrepreneurial team or the applicant's business as a winner,

(8)   if the third party is a UK Government Department, confirmation that it has made money available for the specific purpose of establishing or expanding a UK business, and the amount, and

(9)   confirmation that the money will remain available until such time as it is transferred to the applicant, the entrepreneurial team or the applicant's business.

and

(ii)   A letter from a legal representative confirming the validity of signatures on each third-party declaration provided, which confirms that the declaration(s) from the third party or parties contains the signatures of the people stated. It can be a single letter covering all third-party permissions, or several letters from several legal representatives. It must be an original letter and not a copy, and it must be from a legal representative permitted to practise in the country where the third party or the money is. The letter must clearly show the following:

(1)   the name of the legal representative confirming the details,

(2)   the registration or authority of the legal representative to practise legally in the country in which the permission or permissions was or were given,

(3)   the date of the confirmation letter,

(4)   the applicant's name (and the name of the applicant's team partner's name where relevant) and, where (b) applies, that the applicant is a director of the business named in each third-party declaration,

(5)   the third party's name,

(6)   that the declaration from the third party is signed and valid, and

(7)   if the third party is not a Venture Capitalist Firm, Seed Funding Competition or UK Government Department, the number of the third party or their authorised representative's identity document (such as a passport or national identity card), the place of issue and dates of issue and expiry.

(e)   If the applicant is applying under the provisions in (d) in Table 4, he must also provide:

(i)   his job title,

(ii)   the Standard Occupational Classification (SOC) code of the occupation that the applicant is working in, which must appear on the list of occupations skilled to National Qualifications Framework level 4 or above, as stated in the Codes of Practice in Appendix J,

(iii)   one or more of the following specified documents:

       (1)   advertising or marketing material, including printouts of online advertising, that has been published locally or nationally, showing the applicant's name (and the name of the business if applicable) together with the business activity or, where his business is trading online, confirmation of his ownership of the domain name of the business's website,

       (2)   article(s) or online links to article(s) in a newspaper or other publication showing the applicant's name (and the name of the business if applicable) together with the business activity,

       (3)   information from a trade fair, at which the applicant has had a stand or given a presentation to market his business, showing the applicant's name (and the name of the business if applicable) together with the business activity, or

       (4)   personal registration with a UK trade body linked to the applicant's occupation; and

   (iv)   one or more of the following documents showing trading:

       (1)   a contract. If a contract is not an original the applicant must sign each page. The contract must show:

           (a)   the applicant's name and the name of the business,

           (b)   the service provided by the applicant's business; and

           (c)   the name of the other party or parties involved in the contract and their contact details, including their full address, postal code and, where available, landline phone number and any email address; or

       (2)   an original letter from a UK-regulated financial institution with which the applicant has a business bank account, on the institution's headed paper, confirming that the business is trading; and

    (v)   if:

       (1)   claiming points for being self-employed, the following specified documents to show that he is paying Class 2 National Insurance contributions:

           (a)   the original bill from the billing period immediately before the application, if his Class 2 National Insurance is paid by quarterly bill;

           (b)   the most recent bank statement issued before the date of application, showing the direct debit payment of National Insurance to HM Revenue & Customs, if his National Insurance is paid by direct debit;

           (c)   an original small earnings exception certificate issued by HM Revenue & Customs for the most recent return date, if he has low earnings; or

           (d)   the original, dated welcome letter from HM Revenue & Customs containing the applicant's unique taxpayer reference number, if he has not yet received the documents in (a) to (c); or

       (2)   if claiming points for being a director of a UK company, a printout of a Current Appointment Report from Companies House, dated no earlier than three months before the date of the application, listing the applicant as a director of the company, and confirming the date of his appointment. The company must be actively trading and not struck-off, or dissolved or in liquidation. Directors who are on the list of disqualified Directors provided by Companies House will not be awarded points.

42.   Points will only be awarded to an applicant to whom Table 4, paragraph (b) applies if the total sum of those funds derives from one or more of the sources listed in (b)(i) to (iii) in Table 4.

43.   A regulated financial institution is one, which is regulated by the appropriate regulatory body for the country in which the financial institution operates.

44.   Money is disposable in the UK if all of the money is held in a UK based financial institution or if the money is freely transferable to the UK and convertible to sterling. Funds in a foreign currency will be converted to pounds sterling (£) using the spot exchange rate which appeared on www.oanda.com* on the date on which the application was made.

45.   If the applicant has invested the money referred to in Table 4 in the UK before the date of the application, points will be awarded for funds available as if the applicant had not yet invested the funds, providing the investment was made no more than 12 months before the date of the application and the specified documents in paragraph 46-SD are provided.

45A.   No points will be awarded where the specified documents show that the funds are held in a financial institution listed in Appendix P as being an institution with which the UK Border Agency is unable to make satisfactory verification checks.

Table 5: Applications for entry clearance or leave to remain referred to in paragraph 37

Investment and business activity	Points
The applicant has invested, or had invested on his behalf, not less than £200,000 (or £50,000 if, in his last grant of leave, he was awarded points for funds of £50,000 as set out in Table 4 above in cash directly into one or more businesses in the UK.	20
The applicant has: (a) registered with HM revenue and Customs as self-employed, or (b) registered a new business in which he is a director, or (c) registered as a director of an existing business. Where the applicant's last grant of entry clearance, leave to enter or leave to remain was as a Tier 1 (Entrepreneur) Migrant, the above condition must have been met within 6 months of his entry to the UK (if he was granted entry clearance as a Tier 1 (Entrepreneur) Migrant and there is evidence to establish his date of arrival to the UK), or, in any other case, the date of the grant of leave to remain.	20
On a date no earlier than three months prior to the date of application, the applicant was: (a) registered with HM revenue and Customs as self-employed, or (b) registered a new business in which he is a director, or (c) registered as a director of an existing business.	15
The applicant has: (a) established a new business or businesses that has or have created the equivalent of at least two new full time jobs for persons settled in the UK, or (b) taken over or invested in an existing business or businesses and his services or investment have resulted in a net increase in the employment provided by the business or businesses for persons settled in the UK by creating the equivalent of at least two new full time jobs. Where the applicant's last grant of entry clearance or leave to enter or remain was as a Tier 1 (Entrepreneur) Migrant, the jobs must have existed for at least 12 months of the period for which the previous leave was granted.	20

Table 6: Applications for indefinite leave to remain as referred to in paragraph 38

Row	Investment and business activity	Points
1.	On a date no earlier than three months prior to the date of application, the applicant was: (a) registered with HM Revenue and Customs as self-employed, or (b) registered a new business in which he is a director, or (c) registered as a director of an existing business.	20
2.	The applicant has: (a) established a new UK business or businesses that has or have created the equivalent of X new full time jobs for persons settled in the UK, or (b) taken over or invested in an existing UK business or businesses and his services or investment have resulted in a net increase in the employment provided by the business or businesses for persons settled in the UK by creating the equivalent of X new full time jobs where X is at least 2. Where the applicant's last grant of entry clearance or leave to enter or remain was as a Tier 1 (Entrepreneur) Migrant, the jobs must have existed for at least 12 months of the period for which the previous leave was granted.	20

Row	Investment and business activity	Points
3.	The applicant has spent the specified continuous period lawfully in the UK, with absences from the UK of no more than 180 days in any 12 calendar months during that period. The specified period must have been spent with leave as a Tier 1 (Entrepreneur) Migrant, as a Businessperson and/or as an Innovator, of which the most recent period must have been spent with leave as a Tier (1) (Entrepreneur) Migrant. The specified continuous period is: (a) 3 years if the number of new full time jobs, X, referred to in row 2 above is at least 10, or (b) 3 years if the applicant has: (i) established a new UK business that has had an income from business activity of at least £5 million during a 3 year period in which the applicant has had leave as a Tier 1 (Entrepreneur) Migrant, or (ii) taken over or invested in an existing UK business and his services or investment have resulted in a net increase in income from business activity to that business of £5 million during a 3 year period in which the applicant has had leave as a Tier 1 (Entrepreneur) Migrant, when compared to the immediately preceding 3 year period, or (c) 5 years in all other cases. Time spent with valid leave in the Bailiwick of Guernsey, the Bailiwick of Jersey or the Isle of Man in a category equivalent to the categories set out above may be included in the continuous period of lawful residence, provided the most recent period of leave was as a Tier 1 (Entrepreneur) Migrant in the UK. In any such case, the applicant must have absences from the Bailiwick of Guernsey, the Bailiwick of Jersey or the Isle of Man (as the case may be) of no more than 180 days in any 12 calendar months during the specified continuous period.	35

Investment and business activity: notes

46.   Documentary evidence must be provided in all cases. The specified documents in paragraph 46-SD must be provided as evidence of any investment and business activity that took place when the applicant had leave as a Tier 1 (Entrepreneur) Migrant or a Tier 1 (Post-Study Work) Migrant, and any investment made no more than 12 months before the date of the application for which the applicant is claiming points.

46-SD.   The specified documents in paragraphs 45 and 46 are as follows:

(a)   The applicant must provide all the appropriate specified documents needed to establish the amount of money he has invested from the following list:

    (i)   If the applicant's business is a registered company that is required to produce audited accounts, the audited accounts must be provided;

    (ii)   If the applicant's business is not required to produce audited accounts, unaudited accounts and an accountant's certificate of confirmation, from an accountant who is a member of a UK Recognised Supervisory Body (as defined in the Companies Act 2006), must be provided;

    (iii)   If the applicant has made the investment in the form of a director's loan, it must be shown in the relevant set of accounts provided, and the applicant must also provide a legal agreement, between the applicant (in the name that appears on his application) and the company, showing:

        (1)   the terms of the loan,

        (2)   any interest that is payable,

        (3)   the period of the loan, and

        (4)   that the loan is unsecured and subordinated in favour of third-party creditors.

(b)   Audited or unaudited accounts must show the investment in money made directly by the applicant, in his own name or on his behalf (and showing his name). If he has invested by way of share capital the business accounts must show the shareholders, the amount and value of the shares (on the date of purchase) in the applicant's name as it appears on his application. If the value of the applicant's share capital is not shown in the accounts, then share certificates must be submitted as documentary evidence. The accounts must clearly show the name of the accountant, the date the accounts were produced, and how much the applicant has invested in the business.

(c)   The applicant must provide the following specified documents to show that he has established a UK business:

(i)   Evidence that the business has business premises in the United Kingdom:

(1)   If the applicant is self employed, his registration with HM Revenue and Customs to show that the business is based in the UK, or

(2)   If the applicant is a director, printout of a Companies House document showing the address of the registered office in the UK, or head office in the UK if it has no registered office, and the applicant's name, as it appears on the application form, as a director,

and

(ii)   Evidence that the business has a UK bank account:

(1)   If the applicant is self employed, a personal bank statement showing transactions for his business, or a business bank statement, or a letter from a UK bank confirming that he has a business and acts through that bank, or

(2)   If the applicant is a director, a company bank statement showing that the company has a UK account, or a letter from a UK bank confirming that the company has a bank account,

and

(iii)   Evidence that the business is subject to UK taxation:

(1)   If the applicant is self-employed, he must be registered as self-employed for National Insurance assessment and provide either the welcome letter from HM Revenue & Customs, the Small Earnings Exception certificate, a copy of the National Insurance bill from HM Revenue & Customs, or the applicant's bank statement showing that National Insurance is taken by HM Revenue & Customs by direct debit, or

(2)   If the applicant is a director of a business, the business must be registered for corporation tax and the applicant must provide documentation from HM Revenue & Customs which confirms this.

(d)   If the applicant has bought property that includes residential accommodation the value of this part of the property will not be counted towards the amount of the business investment. The applicant must provide an estimate of the value of the living accommodation if it is part of the premises also used for the business, from a surveyor who is a member of the Royal Institution of Chartered Surveyors. This valuation must be produced in the three months prior to the date of application.

(e)   If some of the money has been invested into a business in the UK, the balance of funds must be held in a regulated financial institution and disposable in the UK, and the applicant must provide the specified documents required in paragraph 41-SD for the previous investment of money together with the specified documents required in paragraph 41-SD required for his access to the balance of sufficient funds.

(f)   Where Table 5 applies and the applicant's last grant of entry clearance, leave to enter or leave to remain was as a Tier 1 (Entrepreneur) Migrant, he must provide the following specified documents as evidence of his registration as self-employed or as a director within the 6 months after the specified date in the relevant table:

(i)   If the applicant was self-employed, he must provide one of the following:

(1)   an original, dated welcome letter from HM Revenue & Customs containing the applicant's unique taxpayer reference number, dated no more than 8 months from the specified date in the relevant table,

(2)   an original Exception Certificate from HM Revenue & Customs, dated no more than 8 months from the specified date in the relevant table,

(3)   an original National Insurance bill from the HM Revenue & Customs dated during the 6 months after the specified date in the relevant table, or

(4)   a bank statement dated in the 6 months after the specified date in the relevant table, showing the direct debit payment of National Insurance to HM Revenue & Customs.

(ii)   If the applicant was a director of a new or existing company, he must provide a Current Appointment Report from Companies House, listing the applicant as the Director of the company and the date of his appointment, which must be no more than 8 months after the specified date in the relevant table.

(g) The applicant must provide the following specified documents as evidence of his current registration as self-employed or as a director:

(i) If the applicant is claiming points for being currently self-employed, he must provide the following specified documents to show that he is paying Class 2 National Insurance contributions:

(1) the original bill from the billing period immediately before the application, if his Class 2 National Insurance is paid by quarterly bill,

(2) the most recent bank statement issued before the application, showing the direct debit payment of National Insurance to HM Revenue & Customs, if his National Insurance is paid by direct debit,

(3) an original small earnings exception certificate issued by HM Revenue & Customs for the most recent return date, if he has low earnings, or

(4) the original, dated welcome letter from HM Revenue & Customs containing the applicant's unique taxpayer reference number, if he has not yet received the documents in (1) to (3).

(ii) If the applicant is claiming points for currently being a director of a UK company, he must provide a printout of a Current Appointment Report from Companies House, dated no earlier than three months before the date of the application, listing the applicant as a director of the company, and confirming the date of his appointment. The company must be actively trading and not struck-off, or dissolved or in liquidation on the date that the printout was produced. Directors who are on the list of disqualified Directors provided by Companies House will not be awarded points.

(h) If the applicant is required to score points for creating the net increase in employment in Table 5 or Table 6, he must provide the following information and specified documents:

(i) A HM Revenue & Customs Employee Payment Record, showing details of the earnings for the settled worker for each week that he worked for the applicant, and signed and dated by the applicant;

(ii) If the date of the start of the employment is not shown in the Employee Payment Record, an original HM Revenue & Customs form P45 or form P46 (also called a Full Payment Submission) for the settled worker, showing the starting date of the employment;

(iii) If the employer is taking part in the Real Time Initiative pilot, printouts of the Full Payment Submission, sent to HM Revenue & Customs, which include the start date of the settled worker and are initialled by the applicant;

(iv) Duplicate payslips or wage slips for each settled worker for whom points are being claimed, covering the full period of the employment for which points are being claimed;

(v) Confirmation of the hourly rate for each settled worker used to claim points, including any changes in the hourly rate and the dates of the changes, enabling calculation of the hours of work created for each settled worker;

(vi) Documents which show that the employment was created for settled workers, such as the passport pages from a UK passport that contain the employee's personal details, and the page containing the UK Government stamp or endorsement, if appropriate, or the worker's full birth certificate, showing the name of at least one parent;

(vii) If the applicant was a director of a company, the information from the Companies House Current Appointment Report to confirm that he was a Director of the company that employed the settled worker at the time that he was employed;

(viii) If the applicant was self-employed, the specified documents in (c) above showing the dates that the applicant became self-employed, the names on the Employee Payment Record and bank account, and the address of the business;

(ix) If the applicant took over or joined a business that employed workers before he joined it, he must also provide one of the following types of payroll documentation:

(1) a duplicate HM Revenue & Customs Full Payment Submission for the year before the jobs were created and the year that the jobs were created, showing the net increase in employment, and signed and dated by the applicant (If the posts were created too

recently for a Full Payment Submission to have been produced, the applicant must provide a draft copy), or

    (2)   a printout of the information sent to HM Revenue & Customs, initialled by the applicant, if the employer is taking part in the Real Time Initiative pilot;

  (x)   If the applicant took over or joined a business that employed workers before he joined it, he must also provide an original accountant's letter verifying the net increase in employment and confirming the number of posts. The accountant must be a member of the Institute of Chartered Accountants in England and Wales, the Institute of Chartered Accountants in Scotland, the Institute of Chartered Accountants in Ireland, the Association of Chartered Certified Accountants, or the Association of Authorised Public Accountants. The letter must contain:

    (1)   the name and contact details of the business,

    (2)   the applicant's status in the business,

    (3)   the number of posts created in the business and the hours worked,

    (4)   the dates of the employment created,

    (5)   the registration or permission of the accountant to operate in the United Kingdom,

    (6)   the date that the accountant created the letter on the applicant's behalf, and

    (7)   that the accountant will confirm the content of the letter to the UK Border Agency on request.

47.   For the purposes of tables 4, 5 and 6, 'investment' does not include the value of any residential accommodation, property development or property management and must not be in the form of a director's loan, unless it is unsecured and subordinated in favour of the business.

48.   Points will only be awarded in respect of a UK business or businesses. a business will be considered to be in the UK if:

  (i)   it is trading within the UK economy, and

  (ii)   it has a registered office in the UK, except where the applicant is registered with HM revenue & Customs as self-employed and does not have a business office, and

  (iii)   it has a UK bank account, and

  (iv)   it is subject to UK taxation.

Multinational companies that are registered as UK companies with either a registered office or head office in the UK are considered to be UK businesses for the purposes of tables 4, 5 and 6.

49.   A full time job is one involving at least 30 hours of work a week. Two or more part time jobs that add up to 30 hours a week will count as one full time job but one full time job of more than 30 hours work a week will not count as more than one full time job.

50.   Where the applicant's last grant of entry clearance or leave was as a Tier (Entrepreneur) Migrant, the jobs must have existed for a total of at least 12 months during the period in which the migrant had leave in that category. This need not consist of 12 consecutive months and the jobs need not exist at the date of application, provided they existed for at least 12 months during the period in which the migrant had leave as a Tier 1 (Entrepreneur) Migrant.

51.   The jobs must comply with all relevant UK legislation including, but not limited to, the national Minimum Wage and the Working Time Directive.

Entrepreneurial teams: Notes

52.   Two applicants, and no more than two applicants, may claim points for the same investment and business activity in Tables 4, 5 or 6 providing the following requirements are met.

Requirements:

  (a)   The applicants have equal level of control over the funds and/or the business or businesses in question;

  (b)   The applicants are both shown by name in each other's applications and in the specified evidence required in the relevant table; and

  (c)   Neither applicant has previously been granted leave as a Tier 1 (Entrepreneur) Migrant on the basis of investment and/or business activity linked in this way with any applicant other than each other if the same funds are being relied on as in a previous application.

53. No points will be awarded for funds that are made available to any individual other than the applicant, except under the terms of paragraph 52 above.

Attributes for Tier 1 (Investor) Migrants

54. An applicant applying for entry clearance, leave to remain or indefinite leave to remain as a Tier 1 (Investor) Migrant must score 75 points for attributes.

55. Subject to paragraph 56, available points for applications for entry clearance or leave to remain are shown in Table 7.

56. Available points are shown in Table 8 for an applicant who:

    (a) has had entry clearance, leave to enter or leave to remain as a Tier 1 (Investor) Migrant or an Investor in the 12 months immediately before the date of application, or

    (b) is applying for leave to remain and has, or was last granted, entry clearance, leave to enter or leave to remain as a Tier 1 (Investor) Migrant or an Investor.

57. Available points for applications for indefinite leave to remain are shown in Table 9.

58. Notes to accompany Table 7, Table 8 and Table 9 appear below Table 9.

Table 7: applications for entry clearance or leave to remain referred to in paragraph 55

Assets	Points
The applicant: (a) has money of his own under his control held in a regulated financial institution and disposable in the UK amounting to not less than £1 million; or (b) (i) owns personal assets which, taking into account any liabilities to which they are subject, have a value of at least £2 million, and (ii) has money under his control held in a regulated financial institution and disposable in the UK amounting to not less than £1 million which has been loaned to him by a UK regulated financial institution.	75

Table 8: Applications for entry clearance or leave to remain referred to in paragraph 56

Assests and investment	Points
The applicant: (a) has money of his own under his control in the UK amounting to not less than £1 million, or (b) (i) owns personal assets which, taking into account any liabilities to which they are subject, have a value of not less than £2 million, and (ii) has money under his control and disposable in the UK amounting to not less than £1 million which has been loaned to him by a UK regulated financial institution.	30
The applicant has invested not less than £750,000 of his capital in the UK by way of UK Government bonds, share capital or loan capital in active and trading UK registered companies, subject to the restrictions set out in paragraph 65 below and has invested the remaining balance of £1,000,000 in the UK by the purchase of assets or by maintaining the money on deposit in a UK regulated financial institution.	30
The investment referred to above was made: (1) within 3 months of the applicant's entry to the UK, if he was granted entry clearance as a Tier 1 (Investor) Migrant and there is evidence to establish his date of entry to the UK, (2) within 3 months of the date of the grant of entry clearance or leave to remain as a Tier 1 (Investor) Migrant, or (3) no earlier than 12 months before the date of the application which led to the first grant of leave as a Tier 1 (Investor) Migrant, and in each case the investment has been maintained for the whole of the remaining period of that leave; or The migrant has, or was last granted, entry clearance, leave to enter or leave to remain as an Investor.	15

Table 9: applications for indefinite leave to remain

Row	Assesst and investment	Points
1.	The applicant: (a) (i) has money of his own under his control in the UK amounting to not less than £10 million, or (ii) (1) owns personal assets which, taking into account any liabilities to which they are subject, have a value of not less than £20 million, and (2) has money under his control and disposable in the UK amounting to not less than £10 million which has been loaned to him by a UK regulated financial institution, or (b) (i) has money of his own under his control in the UK amounting to not less than £5 million, or (ii) (1) owns personal assets which, taking into account any liabilities to which they are subject, have a value of not less than £10 million, and (2) has money under his control and disposable in the UK amounting to not less than £5 million which has been loaned to him by a UK regulated financial institution, or (c) (i) has money of his own under his control in the UK amounting to not less than £1 million, or (ii) (1) owns personal assets which, taking into account any liabilities to which they are subject, have a value of not less than £2 million, and (2) has money under his control and disposable in the UK amounting to not less than £1 million which has been loaned to him by a UK regulated financial institution,	20
2.	The applicant has invested not less than 75% of the specified invested amount of his capital in the UK by way of UK Government bonds, share capital or loan capital in active and trading UK registered companies, subject to the restrictions set out in paragraph 65 below, and has invested the remaining balance of the specified invested amount in the UK by the purchase of assets or by maintaining the money on deposit in a UK regulated financial institution. The specified invested amount is: (a) £10,000,000 if the applicant scores points from row 1(a) above, (b) £5,000,000 if the applicant scores points from row 1(b) above, or (c) £1,000,000 if the applicant scores points from row 1(c) above.	20
3.	The applicant has spent the specified continuous period lawfully in the UK, with absences from the UK of no more than 180 days in any 12 calendar months during that period. The specified continuous period must have been spent with leave as a Tier 1 (Investor) Migrant and/or as an Investor, of which the most recent period must have been spent with leave as a Tier 1 (Investor) Migrant. The specified continuous period is: (a) 2 years if the applicant scores points from row 1(a) above, (b) 3 years if the applicant scores points from row 1(b) above, or (c) 5 years if the applicant scores points from row 1(c) above.	20

Row	Assests and investment	Points
	Time spent with valid leave in the Bailiwick of Guernsey, the Bailiwick of Jersey or the Isle of Man in a category equivalent to the categories set out above may be included in the continuous period of lawful residence, provided the most recent period of leave was as a Tier 1 (Investor) Migrant in the UK. In any such case, the applicant must have absences from the Bailiwick of Guernsey, the Bailiwick of Jersey or the Isle of Man (as the case may be) of no more than 180 days in any 12 calendar months during the specified continuous period.	
4.	The investment referred to above was made no earlier than 12 months before the date of the application which led to the first grant of leave as a Tier 1 (Investor) Migrant. The applicant has maintained the full specified invested amount referred to in the relevant part of row 2 throughout the time spent with leave as a Tier 1 (Investor) Migrant in the UK in the relevant specified continuous period referred to in row 3, other than in the first 3 months of that period with leave as a Tier 1 (Investor) Migrant in the UK. In relation to time spent with leave as a Tier 1 (Investor) Migrant in the UK, the applicant has provided specified documents to show that this requirement has been met. When calculating the specified continuous period, the first day of that period will be taken to be the later of: (a) the date the applicant first entered the UK as a Tier 1 (Investor) Migrant (or the date entry clearance was granted, if this was within three months of the date of entry), or the date the applicant first entered the Bailiwick of Guernsey, the Bailiwick of Jersey or the Isle of Man with leave in a category equivalent to Tier 1 (Investor) if this is earlier, or (b) the date 3 months before the full specified amount was invested in the UK, or before the full required amount in an equivalent category was invested in the Bailiwick of Guernsey, the Bailiwick of Jersey or the Isle of Man.	15

Assets and investment: notes

59. DELETED.

60. Money is disposable in the UK if all of the money is held in a UK based financial institution or if the money is freely transferable to the UK and convertible to sterling. funds in a foreign currency will be converted to pounds sterling (£) using the spot exchange rate which appeared on www.oanda.com* on the date on which the application was made.

61. 'Money of his own', 'personal assets' and 'his capital' include money or assets belonging to the applicant's spouse, civil partner or unmarried or same-sex partner, provided that:

    (a) the applicant's spouse, civil partner or unmarried or same-sex partner meets the requirements of paragraphs 319C(c) and (d) of these rules, and the specified documents in paragraph 61-SD are provided, and

    (b) specified documents in paragraph 61-SD are provided to show that the money or assets are under the applicant's control and that he is free to invest them.

61A. In Tables 7, 8 and 9, 'money of his own under his control' and 'money under his control' exclude money that a loan has been secured against, where another party would have a claim on the money if loan repayments were not met, except where:

    (i) the applicant made an application before 13 December 2012 which is undecided or which led to a grant of entry clearance or leave to remain as an Investor or a Tier 1 (Investor) migrant,

    (ii) the applicant has not been granted entry clearance, leave to enter or leave to remain in any other category since the grant referred to in (i), and

    (iii) the money is under the applicant's control, except for the fact that the loan referred to in paragraph (b) in Table 7, paragraph (b) in Table 8 or row 1 of Table 9 has been secured against it.

61-SD. The specified documents in paragraph 61, as evidence of the relationship and to show that the money or assets are under the applicant's control and that he is free to invest them, are as follows:

    (a) The applicant must provide:

        (i) The original certificate of marriage or civil partnership, to confirm the relationship, which includes the name of the applicant and the husband, wife or civil partner, or

(ii)   At least three of the following types of specified documents to demonstrate a relationship similar in nature to marriage or civil partnership, including unmarried and same-sex relationships, covering a full two-year period immediately before the date of the application:

    (1)   a bank statement or letter from a bank confirming a joint bank account held in both names,

    (2)   an official document such as a mortgage agreement showing a joint mortgage,

    (3)   official documents such as deeds of ownership or a mortgage agreement showing a joint investment, such as in property or business,

    (4)   a joint rent (tenancy) agreement,

    (5)   any other official correspondence linking both partners to the same address, such as example bills for council tax or utilities,

    (6)   a life insurance policy naming the other partner as beneficiary,

    (7)   birth certificates of any children of the relationship, showing both partners as parents, or

    (8)   any other evidence that adequately demonstrates the couple's long-term commitment to one another.

(b)   The applicant must provide an original declaration from the applicant's husband, wife, civil partner, or unmarried or same-sex partner that he will permit all joint or personal money used to claim points for the application to be under the control of the applicant in the UK, known as a gift of beneficial ownership of the money while retaining the legal title, which clearly shows:

    (1)   the names of husband, wife, civil partner, or unmarried or same-sex partner and the applicant,

    (2)   the date of the declaration,

    (3)   the signatures of the husband, wife, civil partner, or unmarried or same-sex partner and applicant,

    (4)   the amount of money available, and

    (5)   a statement that the husband, wife, civil partner, or unmarried or same-sex partner agrees that the applicant has sole control over the money.

(c)   The applicant must provide a letter, from a legal adviser who is permitted to practise in the country where the declaration was made, confirming that the declaration is valid and which clearly shows:

    (1)   the name of the legal adviser confirming that the declaration is valid,

    (2)   the registration or authority of the legal adviser to practise legally in the country in which the document was drawn up,

    (3)   the date of the confirmation of the declaration,

    (4)   the names of the applicant and husband, wife, civil partner, or unmarried or same-sex partner, and

    (5)   that the declaration is signed and valid according to the laws of the country in which it was made.

62.   'Regulated financial institution' is defined in paragraph 43, Appendix A.

62A.   'Active and trading UK registered companies' means companies which:

(a)   have a registered office or head office in the UK;

(b)   have a UK bank account showing current business transactions; and

(c)   are subject to UK taxation.

63.   In the case of an application where Table 7 applies, where the money or assets referred to in Table 7 have already been invested in the UK before the date of application, points will only be awarded if they were invested in the UK no more than 12 months before the date of application.

64.   In the case of an application where Table 7 applies, points will only be awarded if the applicant:

(a)   has had the money or assets referred to in Table 7 for a consecutive 90-day period of time, ending no earlier than one calendar month before the date of application, and provides the specified documents in paragraph 64-SD; or

(b)   provides the additional specified documents in paragraph 64A-SD of the source of the money or assets.

64-SD.   The specified document requirements in paragraph 64(a), as evidence of having held the money or assets for the specified 90-day period, are as follows:

(a)   If the applicant is claiming points from (a) in the first row of Table 7, he must provide:

(i)   A portfolio report produced by a UK regulated financial institution, or a breakdown of investments in an original letter produced by a UK regulated financial institution, on the official letter-headed paper of the institution, issued by an authorised official of that institution. The portfolio report or letter must cover the three consecutive months before the date of application. The report must be no more than one calendar month old at the time of application. The portfolio report or letter must confirm all the following:

(1)   the amount of the money held in the investments,

(2)   the beneficial owner of the funds,

(3)   the date of the investment period covered,

(4)   that the institution is a UK regulated financial institution, with the details of the registration shown on the documentation, and

(5)   that the money can be transferred into the UK should the application be successful, if it is held abroad, or that the money has already been invested in the UK in the form of UK Government bonds, share capital or loan capital in active and trading UK registered companies, and the dates of these investments;

(ii)   If the applicant manages his own investments, or has a portfolio manager who does not operate in the UK and is not therefore regulated by the Financial Conduct Authority (FCA) (and the Prudential Regulation Authority (PRA) where applicable), he must provide one or more of the documents from the list below, as relevant to their type of investments, covering the three consecutive months in the period immediately before the date of application:

(1)   certified copies of bond documents showing the value of the bonds, the date of purchase and the owner;

(2)   share documents showing the value of the shares, the date of purchase and the owner,

(3)   the latest audited annual accounts of the organisation in which the investment has been made, clearly showing the amount of money held in the investments, the name of the applicant (or applicant and/or husband, wife, civil partner, or unmarried or same-sex partner), and the date of investment, or, if no accounts have been produced, a certificate from an accountant showing the amount of money held in the investments, and

(4)   original trust fund documents from a legal adviser showing the amount of money in the fund, the date that the money is available and the beneficial owner, and including the name and contact details of the legal adviser and at least one of the trustees;

(iii) Original personal bank statements on the official bank stationery from a bank that is regulated by the official regulatory body for the country in which the institution operates and the funds are located, showing the amount of money available in the name of the applicant (or applicant and/or husband, wife, civil partner, or unmarried or same-sex partner), covering the three full consecutive months before the date of application. The most recent statement must be no more than one calendar month old at the date of application. Electronic bank statements must be accompanied by a supporting letter from the bank on the institution's official headed paper, issued by an authorising official of that institution, confirming the content and that the document is genuine;

(iv)   If the applicant cannot provide bank statements, an original letter from a bank that is regulated by the official regulatory body for the country in which the institution operates and the funds are located, on the institution's official headed paper, issued by an authorised official of that institution, stating that the account has held the required amount of money on the day the letter was produced and for the three full consecutive months immediately before the date of the letter. The letter must be dated no more than one calendar month before the date of application. The letter must confirm:

(1)   the name of the applicant (or applicant and/or husband, wife, civil partner, or unmarried or same-sex partner), and that the money is available in their name(s),

(2)   that the bank is regulated by the official regulatory body for the country in which the institution operates and the funds are located,

(3)   the dates of the period covered, including both the day the letter was produced and three full consecutive months immediately before the date of the letter, and

(4)   the balance of the account to cover the amount claimed as a credit balance on the date of the letter and the three full consecutive months before the date of the letter;

(v) If the funds are not held in the UK, the applicant must provide an original letter from a bank or financial institution that is regulated by the official regulatory body for the country in which the institution operates and the funds are located, on the institution's official headed paper, issued by an authorised official of that institution, which confirms:

    (1) the name of the beneficial owner, which should be the applicant (or applicant and/or husband, wife, civil partner, or unmarried or same-sex partner),

    (2) the date of the letter,

    (3) the amount of money to be transferred,

    (4) that the money can be transferred to the UK if the application is successful, and

    (5) that the institution will confirm the content of the letter to the UK Border Agency on request.

(b) If the applicant is claiming points from (b) in the first row of Table 7, he must provide an original letter of confirmation produced by a UK regulated financial institution, on the official letter-headed paper of the institution, issued by an authorised official of that institution, which confirms:

    (1) that not less than £1 million are available for the applicant to borrow,

    (2) that the money is available on the date that the letter is issued,

    (3) that the institution is a UK regulated financial institution,

    (4) that the applicant has personal assets with a net value of at least £2 million, and

    (5) that the institution will confirm the content of the letter to the UK Border Agency on request.

(c) If specified documents are provided from accountants, the accountant must:

    (i) if based in the UK, be a member of the Institute of Chartered Accountants in England and Wales, the Institute of Chartered Accountants in Scotland, the Institute of Chartered Accountants in Ireland, the Association of Chartered Certified Accountants, or the Association of Authorised Public Accountants, or

    (ii) if not based in the UK, be a member of an equivalent, appropriate supervisory or regulatory body in the country in which they operate.

64A-SD. Where paragraph 64(b) states that specified documents are required as evidence that the money or assets are under the applicant's control and that he is free to invest them, the applicant must provide all the specified documents from the following list, with contact details that enable verification:

(a) Original documents in the form of:

    (i) Money given to the applicant (or applicant and/or husband, wife, civil partner, or unmarried or same-sex partner) within the three months immediately before the application must be shown in an irrevocable memorandum of gift, which clearly shows:

        (1) the name and signature of the person receiving the gift,

        (2) the name and signature of the person giving the gift,

        (3) the date of the memorandum,

        (4) the amount of money being given,

        (5) a statement that the legal ownership of the gift is transferred and that the document is the memorandum of transfer,

        (6) a clear description of the gift, and

        (7) a statement that the gift is irrevocable;

    (ii) If a memorandum of gift in (i) is provided, it must be accompanied by an original confirmation letter from a legal adviser permitted to practise in the country where the gift was made, which clearly shows:

        (1) the name of the legal adviser who is confirming the details,

        (2) the registration or authority of the legal adviser to practise legally in the country in which the gift was made,

        (3) the date of the confirmation of the memorandum,

        (4) the names of the person giving the gift and the person receiving it,

        (5) the amount of money given,

        (6) the date that the money was transferred to the applicant, or to the husband, wife, civil partner, or unmarried partner or same-sex partner of the applicant,

(7)   that the memorandum is signed and valid,

(8)   that the gift is irrevocable, and

(9)   that the memorandum is binding according to the laws of the country in which it was made;

(iii)   Deeds of sale of assets such as business or property, if the applicant has generated these funds within the three months immediately before the date of application, which meet the relevant legal requirements of the country of sale and clearly show:

(1)   the name of the applicant (or applicant and/or husband, wife, civil partner, or unmarried or same-sex partner),

(2)   the amount of money raised, and

(3)   the date of the sale;

(iv)   If a deed of sale in (iii) is provided, it must be accompanied by an original confirmation letter from a legal adviser permitted to practise in the country where the sale was made, which clearly shows:

(1)   the name of the legal adviser confirming the details,

(2)   the registration or authority of the legal adviser to practise legally in the country in which the sale was made,

(3)   the date of the sale,

(4)   the date of production of the letter confirming the sale,

(5)   the details of what was sold and the amount of money received from the sale,

(6)   the name of the person receiving the money from the sale,

(7)   the date that the money was transferred, and

(8)   that the sale was valid according to the laws of the country in which it was made;

(v)   If the funds are currently held in the applicant's business (or the business of the applicant and/or the applicant's husband, wife, civil partner, or unmarried or same-sex partner), the applicant must provide business accounts, which:

(1)   are profit and loss accounts (or income and expenditure accounts if the organisation is not trading for profit),

(2)   are prepared and signed off in accordance with statutory requirements, and

(3)   clearly show the amount of money available for investment;

(vi)   If business accounts in (v) are provided, they must be accompanied by an original letter from a legal adviser who is permitted to practise in the country where business was operating, confirming that the applicant (or applicant and/or husband, wife, civil partner, or unmarried or same-sex partner) can lawfully extract the money from the business, which clearly shows:

(1)   the name of the legal adviser who is confirming the details,

(2)   the registration or authority of the legal adviser to practise legally in the country in which the business is operating,

(3)   the date on which the details are confirmed, and

(4)   that the applicant (or applicant and/or husband, wife, civil partner, or unmarried or same-sex partner) can lawfully extract the money from the business in question;

(vii)   If the applicant (or applicant and/or husband, wife, civil partner, or unmarried or same sex partner) has been the beneficiary of a will within the three months before making the application, and has received money as a result, the applicant must provide a notarised copy of the will. If the applicant (or applicant and/or husband, wife, civil partner, or unmarried or same-sex partner) has received possessions or assets, rather than money, then the applicant (or applicant and/or husband, wife, civil partner, or unmarried or same-sex partner) may not use estimates of the value of the items as evidence of funds for investment. The notarised copy of the will must clearly show:

(1)   the date of the will,

(2)   the beneficiary of the will (this should be the applicant or applicant and/or husband, wife, civil partner, or unmarried or same-sex partner),

(3)   the amount of money that the applicant (or applicant and/or husband, wife, civil partner, or unmarried or same-sex partner) has inherited, and

(4)   the names of any executors, plus any codicils (additions) to the will that affect the amount of money that was received;

(viii)   If a notarised copy of a will in (vii) is provided, it must be accompanied by an original confirmation letter from a legal adviser who is permitted to practise in the country where will was made, confirming the validity of the will, which clearly shows:

   (1)   the name of the legal adviser confirming the details,

   (2)   the registration or authority of the legal adviser to practise legally in the country in which the will was made,

   (3)   the date of the document produced by the legal adviser confirming the will,

   (4)   the date that the applicant received the money as a result of the settlement of the will,

   (5)   the names of the person making the will and the beneficiary,

   (6)   confirmation of the amount of money received by the applicant (or applicant and/or husband, wife, civil partner, or unmarried or same-sex partner).

   (7)   that the will is signed and valid, and

   (8)   that the will is valid according to the laws of the country in which it was made;

(ix)   If the applicant (or applicant and/or husband, wife, civil partner, or unmarried or same-sex partner) has obtained money as a result of a divorce settlement within the three months immediately before the date of application, the applicant must provide a notarised copy of a financial agreement following a divorce. If the applicant (or applicant and/or husband, wife, civil partner, or unmarried or same-sex partner) has received possessions or assets, rather than money, estimates of the value of the items will not be accepted as evidence of money for investment.

(x)   If a divorce settlement in (ix) is provided, it must be accompanied by an original confirmation letter from a legal adviser who is permitted to practise in the country where the divorce took place, which clearly shows:

   (1)   the name of the legal adviser confirming the details,

   (2)   the registration or authority of the legal adviser to practise legally in the country in which the divorce took place,

   (3)   the date of the document produced by the legal adviser confirming the divorce settlement,

   (4)   the date that the applicant received the money as a result of the settlement,

   (5)   the names of the persons who are divorced,

   (6)   confirmation of the amount of money received by the applicant (or applicant and/or husband, wife, civil partner, or unmarried or same-sex partner,

   (7)   that the divorce settlement is complete and valid, and

   (8)   that the divorce settlement is valid according to the laws of the country in which it was made;

(xi)   If the applicant is relying on a financial award or winnings as a source of funds, he must provide an original letter from the organisation issuing the financial award or winnings, which clearly shows:

   (1)   the name of the applicant (or applicant and/or husband, wife, civil partner, or unmarried or same-sex partner),

   (2)   the date of the award,

   (3)   the amount of money won,

   (4)   the winnings are genuine, and

   (5)   the contact details for the organisation issuing the award or winnings;

(xii)   If a letter showing a financial award or winnings in (xi) is provided, it must be accompanied by an original confirmation letter from a legal adviser who is permitted to practise in the country where the award was made, which clearly shows:

   (1)   the name of the legal adviser confirming the details,

   (2)   the registration or authority of the legal adviser to practise legally in the country in which the award was made,

   (3)   the date of the letter of confirmation,

     (4) the date of the award,

     (5) the name of the recipient of the award,

     (6) the amount of the winnings,

     (7) the source of the winnings, and

     (8) the date that the money was transferred to the applicant, or husband, wife, civil partner, or unmarried or same-sex partner;

   (xiii) If the applicant (or applicant and/or husband, wife, civil partner, or unmarried or same-sex partner) has received money from a source not listed above, the applicant must provide relevant original documentation as evidence of the source of the money, together with independent supporting evidence, which both clearly confirm:

     (1) the amount of money received,

     (2) the date that the money was received,

     (3) the source of the money, and

     (4) that the applicant (or applicant and/or husband, wife, civil partner, or unmarried or same-sex partner) was the legal recipient of the money.

64B-SD. In the case of an application where Table 9, row 1 (a) or (b) applies, points will only be awarded if the applicant:

 (a) (i) has had the additional money or assets that he was not awarded points for in his previous grant of leave for a consecutive 90-day period of time, ending no earlier than one calendar month before the date(s) this additional capital was invested (as set out in Table 9, row 2), and

   (ii) provides the specified documents in paragraph 64-SD (with the difference that references to 'date of application' in that paragraph are taken to read 'date of investment'); or

 (b) provides the additional specified documents in paragraph 64A-SD of the source of the additional money or assets (with the difference that references to 'date of application' in that paragraph are taken to read 'date of investment').

65. Investment excludes investment by the applicant by way of:

 (a) an offshore company or trust, or investments that are held in offshore custody except that investments held in offshore custody shall not be excluded where the applicant made an application before 13 December 2012 which is undecided or which led to a grant of entry clearance or leave to remain as an Investor or a Tier 1 (Investor) migrant and has not since been granted entry clearance, leave to enter or leave to remain in any other category,

 (b) Open-ended investment companies, investment trust companies or pooled investment vehicles,

 (c) Companies mainly engaged in property investment, property management or property development,

 (d) Deposits with a bank, building society or other enterprise whose normal course of business includes the acceptance of deposits,

 (e) ISAs, premium bonds and saving certificates issued by the National Savings and Investment Agency (NS&I), for an applicant who has, or last had leave as a Tier 1 (Investor) Migrant, or

 (f) Leveraged investment funds, except where the leverage in question is the security against the loan referred to in paragraph (b) in Table 7, paragraph (b) in Table 8 or row 1 of Table 9 (as appropriate), and paragraph 61A(i)–(iii) apply.

65A. No points will be awarded where the specified documents show that the funds are held in a financial institution listed in Appendix P as being an institution with which the UK Border Agency is unable to make satisfactory verification checks.

65-SD. The following specified documents must be provided as evidence of investment:

 (a) The applicant must provide a portfolio of investments certified as correct by a UK regulated financial institution, which must:

   (i) Cover the required period, beginning no later than the end of the 3 month timescale specified in the third row of Table 8;

   (ii) Continue to the last reporting date of the most recent billing period of the year directly before the date of the application;

   (iii) Include the value of the investments;

   (iv) Show that any shortfall in investments below the specified investment amount was made up by the next reporting period;

(v)   Show the dates that the investments were made;

(vi)   Show the destination of the investments;

(vii)   Include, for investments made as loan funds to companies, audited accounts or unaudited accounts with an accountant's certificate for the investments made, giving the full details of the applicant's investment. The accountant must be a member of the Institute of Chartered Accountants in England and Wales, the Institute of Chartered Accountants in Scotland, the Institute of Chartered Accountants in Ireland, the Association of Chartered Certified Accountants, or the Association of Authorised Public Accountants;

(viii) Show the name and contact details of the financial institution that has certified the portfolio as correct, and confirmation that this institution is regulated by the Financial Conduct Authority (FCA) (and the Prudential Regulation Authority (PRA) where applicable);

(ix)   Show that the investments were made in the applicant's name and/or that of his spouse, civil partner, unmarried or same-sex partner and not in the name of an offshore company or trust even if this is wholly owned by the applicant;

(x)   include the date that the portfolio was certified by the financial institution; and

(xi)   state that the institution will confirm the content of the letter to the UK Border Agency on request.

(b)   Where the applicant previously had leave as an Investor and is unable to provide the evidence listed above because he manages his own investments, or has a portfolio manager who does not operate in the UK and is therefore not regulated by the Financial Conduct Authority (FCA) (and the Prudential Regulation Authority (PRA) where applicable), the applicant must provide the following specified documents showing his holdings used to claim points, as relevant to the type of investment:

(i)   Certified copies of bond documents showing the value of the bonds, the date of purchase and the owner;

(ii)   Share documents showing the value of the shares, the date of purchase and the owner;

(iii)   The latest audited annual accounts of the organisation in which the investment has been made, which clearly show:

(1)   the amount of money held in the investments,

(2)   the name of the applicant (or applicant and/or husband, wife, civil partner, or unmarried or same-sex partner), and

(3)   the date of investment.

(iv)   If the organisation in (iii) is not required to produce accounts, the applicant must provide a certificate showing the amount of money held in the investments, from an accountant who is a member of the Institute of Chartered Accountants in England and Wales, the Institute of Chartered Accountants in Scotland, the Institute of Chartered Accountants in Ireland, the Association of Chartered Certified Accountants, or the Association of Authorised Public Accountants.

(c)   Where the applicant has invested at least 75% of the specified investment amount but less than 100%, he must provide one or more of the following specified documents as evidence of the balance of the funds required to bring his total investment in the UK up to the specified investment amount:

(i)   Documents confirming the purchase of assets in the UK, showing the assets purchased, the value of these assets and the dates of purchase. When using property only the unmortgaged portion of the applicant's own home can be considered and the valuation must be provided on a report issued by a surveyor (who is a member of the Royal Institution of Chartered Surveyors) in the six months prior to the date of application;

(ii)   If the applicant maintained money on deposit in the UK, a statement or statements of account on the official stationery of the institution that holds the funds. These statements must be in the name of the applicant (or applicant and/or the husband, wife, civil partner, or unmarried or same-sex partner of the applicant) and confirm the dates and amount of money held. The applicant must ensure that the institution will confirm the content of the statement to the UK Border Agency on request;

(iii)   An original letter from the financial institution that holds the cash on deposit, on the institution's official headed paper, issued by an authorised official of that institution, which confirms the dates and amount of money held and that the institution will confirm the content of the letter to the UK Border Agency on request.

(d) If the applicant wishes the start of the 3 month timescale specified in the third row of Table 8 to be taken as the date he entered the UK, he must provide evidence which proves this date, such as a stamp in the applicant's passport, or an aircraft boarding card.

(e) Evidence of the investment having been maintained, from the date that the funds were invested for the full period of remaining leave, will be determined using the portfolio provided in (a).

Attributes for Tier 1 (Graduate Entrepreneur) Migrants

66. An applicant applying for leave to remain as a Tier 1 (Graduate Entrepreneur) Migrant must score 75 points for attributes.

67. Available points are shown in Table 10.

68. Notes to accompany the table appear below the table.

Table 10

Criterion	Points
The applicant has been endorsed by UK Trade and Investment or by a UK Higher Education Institution which: (a) has Highly Trusted Sponsor status under Tier 4 of the Points-Based System, (b) is an A-rated Sponsor under Tier 2 of the Points-Based System if a Tier 2 licence is held, (c) is an A-rated Sponsor under Tier 5 of the Points-Based System if a Tier 5 licence is held, (d) has degree-awarding powers, and (e) has established processes and competence for identifying, nurturing and developing entrepreneurs among its undergraduate and postgraduate population.	25

(a) If the applicant's previous grant of leave was not as a Tier 1 (Graduate Entrepreneur) Migrant, within the 12 months immediately before the date of the endorsement, the applicant has been awarded a qualification as follows:
   (i) If the applicant has a General Endorsement (see paragraph 69 below), the endorsing institution has awarded the applicant a UK recognised Bachelor degree, Masters degree or PhD (not a qualification of equivalent level which is not a degree),
   (ii) If the applicant has a MBA Endorsement (see paragraph 69 below), the endorsing institution has awarded the applicant a UK recognised Master of Business Administration degree (not a qualification of equivalent level), or
   (iii) If the applicant has a Global Endorsement (see paragraph 69 below), the applicant has been awarded a degree qualification (not a qualification of equivalent level which is not a degree) which is deemed by UK NARIC to meet or exceed the recognised standard of a Bachelor's degree in the UK,
(b) If the applicant's previous grant of leave was as a Tier 2 (General) Migrant to work as a post-doctoral researcher:
   (i) the applicant has a General Endorsement from the same body that was his Sponsor on the application which led to that previous grant of leave, and
   (ii) the applicant has, at any time before the date of endorsement, been awarded a UK recognised Bachelor degree, Masters degree or PhD (not a qualification of equivalent level which is not a degree) from a UK Higher Education Institution,
   or
(c) If the applicant's previous grant of leave was as a Tier 1 (Graduate Entrepreneur) Migrant, the endorsement is from the same body which provided the endorsement for that previous grant of leave.
	25

The endorsement must confirm that the endorsing body has assessed the applicant and considers that: (a) the applicant has a genuine and credible business idea, and (b) the applicant will spend the majority of his working time on developing business ventures, and (c) if the applicant's previous grant of leave was as a Tier 1 (Graduate Entrepreneur), he has made satisfactory progress in developing his business since that leave was granted.	25

Notes Tier 1 (Graduate Entrepreneur) Limit

69. (a) The Secretary of State shall be entitled to limit the total number of Tier 1 (Graduate Entrepreneur) endorsements qualifying endorsing bodies may make in support of successful applications in a particular period, to be referred to as the Tier 1 (Graduate Entrepreneur) Limit.

(b) The Tier 1 (Graduate Entrepreneur) Limit is 2,000 places per year (beginning on 6 April and ending on 5 April), which will be allocated as follows:

(i) 900 places will be allocated to qualifying Higher Education Institutions for the purpose of endorsing graduates in any subject, referred to as General Endorsements;

(ii) 1,000 places will be allocated to qualifying Higher Education Institutions for the purpose of endorsing MBA graduates, referred to as MBA Endorsements; and

(iii) 100 places will be allocated to UK Trade and Investment for the purpose of endorsing overseas graduates, referred to as Global Endorsements.

(c) Places for qualifying Higher Education Institutions will be allocated as follows:

(i) The UK Border Agency will, on an annual basis, invite all UK Higher Education Institutions which meet the requirements in (a) to (c) in the first row of Table 10 to take part as endorsing institutions, with responses required by 5 April for the year beginning the next day;

(ii) The endorsements will be allocated between all invited institutions who confirm that:

(1) they wish to take part,

(2) they meet the requirement in (d) in the first row of Table 10 above, and

(3) in the case of MBA Endorsements, that they award MBA qualifications;

(iii) Each qualifying institution in (ii) will be allocated the smallest of:

(1) The number of each type of endorsements it has requested,

(2) Its equal share of the number of each type of endorsements available (If the result is not an integer it will be rounded down to the next lowest integer), or

(3) 10 of each type of endorsements

(iv) If the result of (i) to (iii) is that there are fewer than 880 General Endorsements or 980 MBA Endorsements allocated for the year, the UK Border Agency will invite all UK Higher Education Institutions which meet the requirements in (a) to (c) in the first row of Table 10 to request the remaining endorsements for the year ending 5 April, with responses required by 30 September;

(v) The remaining endorsements will be allocated between all invited institutions who meet the criteria in (ii), regardless of whether they were previously allocated endorsements for the year;

(vi) Each qualifying institution in (v) will be allocated the smaller of:

(1) The number of each type of endorsements it has requested, or

(2) Its equal share of the number of each type of endorsements available (If the result is not an integer it will be rounded down to the next lowest integer);

(vii) If the result of (iv) to (vi) is that there are still fewer than 900 General Endorsements or 1,000 MBA Endorsements allocated for the year, the remaining places in the Tier 1 (Graduate Entrepreneur) Limit will not be allocated.

(d) If:

(i) an applicant does not make a valid application within 3 months of the date of his endorsement, or

(ii) an application is refused, and that refusal is not subsequently overturned,

the endorsement used in that application will be cancelled and the relevant endorsing body's unused allocation of endorsements will be increased by one, providing the end of the period (6 April to 5 April) to which it relates has not yet passed.

(e) The Tier 1 (Graduate Entrepreneur) limit will not apply to applications for leave to remain where the applicant has, or last had, leave to remain as a Tier 1 (Graduate Entrepreneur).

(f) Endorsements which have not been used by endorsing bodies cannot be carried over from one year (beginning on 6 April and ending on 5 April) to the next.

Endorsement

70. Points will only be awarded for an endorsement if:

(a) the endorsement was issued to the applicant no more than 3 months before the date of application,

(b)   the endorsement has not been withdrawn by the relevant endorsing body at the time the application is considered by the UK Border Agency, and

(c)   the applicant provides an original endorsement from the relevant endorsing body, which shows:

    (i)   the endorsement reference number,

    (ii)   the date of issue (including a statement on how long the letter is valid for),

    (iii)   the applicant's name,

    (iv)   the applicant's date of birth,

    (v)   the applicant's nationality,

    (vi)   the applicant's current passport number,

    (vii)   details of any dependants of the applicant who are already in the UK or who the applicant intends to bring to the UK,

    (viii)   the name of the endorsing body,

    (ix)   the name and contact details of the authorising official of the endorsing body,

    (x)   the name, level and date of award of the applicant's qualification, unless the endorsement is a Global endorsement or the applicant was last granted leave as a Tier 1 (Graduate Entrepreneur) Migrant,

    (xi)   the applicant's intended business sector or business intention,

    (xii)   what has led the endorsing body to endorse the application, and

    (xiii)   if the applicant was last granted leave as a Tier 1 (Graduate Entrepreneur) Migrant, confirmation that the endorsing body is satisfied that he has made satisfactory progress.

Qualifications

71.   Points will only be awarded for a qualification awarded by a UK Higher Education Institution if the endorsement in paragraph 70(c) contains the specified details of the qualification, as set out in paragraph 70(c).

72.   (a)   Points will only be awarded for an overseas qualification if the applicant has a Global Endorsement and provides the following specified documents:

    (i)   The original certificate of award of the qualification, which clearly shows the:

        (1)   applicant's name,

        (2)   title of the award,

        (3)   date of the award, and

        (4)   name of the awarding institution,

        or

    (ii)   if:

        (1)   the applicant is awaiting graduation having successfully completed his degree, or

        (2)   the applicant no longer has the certificate and the institution who issued the certificate is unable to produce a replacement, an original academic reference from the institution that is awarding, or has awarded, the degree together with an original academic transcript, unless (d) applies.

(b)   The academic reference referred to in (a)(ii) must be on the official headed paper of the institution and clearly show the:

    (1)   applicant's name,

    (2)   title of award,

    (3)   date of award, confirming that it has been or will be awarded, and

    (4)   either the date that the certificate will be issued (if the applicant has not yet graduated) or confirmation that the institution is unable to re-issue the original certificate or award.

(c)   The academic transcript referred to in (a)(ii) must be on the institution's official paper and must show the:

    (1)   applicant's name,

    (2)   name of the academic institution,

    (3)   course title, and

    (4)   confirmation of the award.

(d)   If the applicant cannot provide his original certificate for one of the reasons given in (a)(ii) and is claiming points for a qualification with a significant research bias, such as a doctorate, an academic transcript is not required, providing the applicant provides an academic reference which includes all the information detailed in (b) above.

(e)   Where an applicant cannot find details of his qualification on the points based calculator on the UK Border Agency website, he must, in addition to the document or documents in (a), provide an original letter or certificate from UK NARIC confirming the equivalency of the level of his qualification.

Attributes for Tier 2 (Intra-Company Transfer) Migrants

73.   An applicant applying for entry or leave to remain as a Tier 2 (Intra-Company Transfer) Migrant must score 50 points for attributes.

73A.   Available points for entry clearance or leave to remain are shown in Table 11.

73B.   Notes to accompany Table 11 appear below the table.

Table 11

Criterion	Points
Certificate of Sponsorship	30
Appropriate salary	20

Notes

Certificate of Sponsorship

74.   In order to obtain points for a Certificate of Sponsorship, the applicant must provide a valid Certificate of Sponsorship reference number.

74A.   A Certificate of Sponsorship reference number will only be considered to be valid if:

(a)   the number supplied links to a Certificate of Sponsorship Checking Service entry that names the applicant as the migrant and confirms that the Sponsor is Sponsoring him as a Tier 2 (Intra-Company Transfer) Migrant and specifies the sub-category of Tier 2 (Intra-Company Transfer) under which he is applying,

(b)   the Sponsor assigned the Certificate of Sponsorship reference number to the migrant no more than 3 months before the application for entry clearance or leave to remain is made,

(c)   the application for entry clearance or leave to remain is made no more than 3 months before the start of the employment as stated on the Certificate of Sponsorship,

(d)   The migrant must not previously have applied for entry clearance, leave to enter or leave to remain using the same Certificate of Sponsorship reference number, if that application was either approved or refused (not rejected as an invalid application declared void or withdrawn),

(e)   that reference number must not have been withdrawn or cancelled by the Sponsor or by the UK Border Agency since it was assigned, including where it has been cancelled by the UK Border Agency due to having been used in a previous application, and

(f)   the Sponsor is an A-rated Sponsor, unless the application is for leave to remain and the applicant has, or was last granted, leave as a Tier 2 (Intra-Company) Migrant or a Qualifying Work Permit Holder.

74B.   No points will be awarded for a Certificate of Sponsorship unless:

(a)   the job that the Certificate of Sponsorship Checking Service entry records that the person is being sponsored to do appears on:

(i)   the list of occupations skilled to National Qualifications Framework level 6 or above, as stated in the codes of practice in Appendix J, or

(ii)   one of the following creative sector occupations skilled to National Qualifications Framework level 4 or above:

(1)   3411 Artists,

(2)   3412 Authors, writers and translators,

(3)   3413 Actors, entertainers and presenters,

(4)   3414 Dancers and choreographers, or

(5)   3422 Product, clothing and related designers,

or

(b)   (i)   the applicant is applying for leave to remain,

    (ii)   the applicant previously had leave as a Tier 2 (Intra-Company Transfer) Migrant under the Rules in place between 6 April 2011 and 13 June 2012, and has not since been granted leave to remain in any other route, or entry clearance or leave to enter in any route, and

    (iii)   the job that the Certificate of Sponsorship Checking Service entry records that the person is being sponsored to do appears on the list of occupations skilled to National Qualifications Framework level 4 or above, as stated in the codes of practice in Appendix J, or

(c)   (i)   the applicant is applying for leave to remain as a Tier 2 (Intra-Company Transfer) Migrant in the Long Term Staff sub-category,

    (ii)   the applicant previously had leave as:

      (1)   a Tier 2 (Intra-Company Transfer) Migrant under the rules in place before 6 April 2011, or

      (2)   a Qualifying Work Permit Holder,

     and has not since been granted leave to remain in any other route, or entry clearance or leave to enter in any route, and

    (iii)   the job that the Certificate of Sponsorship Checking Service entry records that the person is being sponsored to do appears on the list of occupations skilled to National Qualifications Framework level 3 or above, as stated in the codes of practice in Appendix J, or the applicant is a Senior Care Worker or an Established Entertainer as defined in paragraph 6 of these Rules.

(d)   (i)   the applicant was last granted entry clearance or leave as a Tier 2 (Intra-Company Transfer) Migrant,

    (ii)   the applicant is applying for leave to remain to work in the same occupation for the same Sponsor as in the application which led to his previous grant of leave,

    (iii)   the Certificate of Sponsorship used in support of the applicant's previous application was assigned by the Sponsor before 6 April 2013, and

    (iv)   the occupation fails to meet the required skill level in (a) to (c) above solely due to reclassification from the SOC 2000 system to the SOC 2010 system.

74C. (a)   if the applicant is applying as a Tier 2 (Intra-Company Transfer) Migrant in either the Short Term Staff or Long Term Staff sub-categories, no points will be awarded for a Certificate of Sponsorship unless:

    (i)   the Certificate of Sponsorship Checking Service entry confirms that the applicant has been working for the Sponsor for the specified period in paragraph (b) below,

    (ii)   the applicant has been working for the Sponsor outside the UK and/or in the UK, provided he had leave to work for the Sponsor as:

      (1)   a Tier 2 (Intra-Company Transfer) Migrant in either of the Short Term Staff or Long Term Staff sub-categories,

      (2)   a Tier 2 (Intra-Company Transfer) Migrant in the established staff sub-category under the rules in place before 6 April 2011,

      (3)   a Tier 2 (Intra-Company Transfer) Migrant under the rules in place before 6 April 2010,

      (4)   a Qualifying Work Permit Holder (provided that the work permit was granted because the holder was the subject of an Intra-Company Transfer), and/or

      (5)   as a representative of an Overseas Business, and

    (iii)   the applicant provides, if requested to do so, the specified documents as set out in paragraph 74C-SD(a) below, unless he was last granted leave to work for the same Sponsor in the same sub-category as he is currently applying under. The application may be granted without these specified documents, but the UK Border Agency reserves the right to request the specified documents, and to refuse applications if these documents are not received at the address specified in the request within 7 working days of the date of the request.

(b)   The specified period referred to in paragraph (a)(i) above is:

    (i)   a continuous period of 12 months immediately prior to the date of application, or

    (ii)   if at some point within the 12 months preceding the date of application, the applicant has been:

      (1)   on maternity, paternity or adoption leave,

      (2)   on long-term sick leave lasting one month or longer, or

(3)   working for the Sponsor in the UK as a Tier 2 (Intra-Company Transfer) Migrant in either of the Graduate Trainee or Skills Transfer sub-categories,

and if requested to provide the specified documents set out in paragraph 74C-SD(a) below, also provides, at the same time, the specified documents as set out in paragraph 74C-SD(c) below, an aggregated period of at least 12 months within the 24 month period immediately prior to the date of application.

74C-SD.   (a)   The specified documents in paragraph 74C(a) are:

(i)   Original formal payslips issued by the employer and showing the employer's name covering the full specified period (The most recent payslip must be dated no earlier than 31 days before the date of the application);

(ii)   Other payslips covering the full specified period (The most recent payslip must be dated no earlier than 31 days before the date of the application), accompanied by a letter from the Sponsor, on company headed paper and signed by a senior official, confirming the authenticity of the payslips;

(iii)   Personal bank or building society statements covering the full specified period, which clearly show:

(1)   the applicant's name,

(2)   the account number,

(3)   the date of the statement (The most recent statement must be dated no earlier than 31 days before the date of the application),

(4)   the financial institution's name and logo, and

(5)   transactions by the Sponsor covering the full specified period; or

(iv)   A building society pass book, which clearly shows:

(1)   the applicant's name,

(2)   the account number,

(3)   the financial institution's name and logo, and

(4)   transactions by the Sponsor covering the full specified period.

(b)   If the applicant provides the bank or building society statements in (a)(iii):

(i)   The statements must:

(1)   be printed on paper bearing the bank or building society's letterhead,

(2)   bear the official stamp of the bank on every page, or

(3)   be accompanied by a supporting letter from the issuing bank or building society, on company headed paper, confirming the authenticity of the statements provided;

(ii)   The statements must not be mini-statements obtained from an Automated Teller Machine.

(c)   The specified documents as evidence of periods of maternity, paternity or adoption leave, as required in paragraph 74C(b), are:

(i)   The original full birth certificate or original full certificate of adoption (as appropriate) containing the names of the parents or adoptive parents of the child for whom the leave was taken, if this is available; and

(ii)   At least one (or both, if the document in (i) is unavailable) of the following, if they are available:

(1)   An original letter from the applicant and his sponsor, on company headed paper, confirming the start and end dates of the applicant's leave,

(2)   One of the types of documents set out in (a) above, covering the entire period of leave, and showing the maternity, paternity or adoption payments.

and

(iii)   If the applicant cannot provide two of the types of specified document in (i) and (ii), at least one of the types of specified documents in either (i) or (ii), a full explanation of why the other documents cannot be provided, and at least one of the following specified documents, from an official source and which is independently verifiable:

(1)   official adoption papers issued by the relevant authority,

(2)   any relevant medical documents, or

(3)   a relevant extract from a register of birth which is accompanied by an original letter from the issuing authority.

(d)   The specified documents as evidence of periods of long term sick leave, as required in paragraph 74C(b), are:

    (i)   An original letter from the applicant's Sponsor, on company headed paper, confirming the start and end dates of the applicant's leave, if this is available;

    (ii)   One of the types of documents set out in (a) above, covering the entire period of leave, and showing the statutory sick pay and/or sick pay from health insurance, if these documents are available; and

    (iii)   If the applicant cannot provide the specified documents in both (i) and (ii), the specified documents in either (i) or (ii), a full explanation of why the other documents cannot be provided, and any relevant medical documents, from an official source and which are independently verifiable.

74D.   if the applicant is applying as a Tier 2 (Intra-Company Transfer) Migrant in the Graduate Trainee sub-category, no points will be awarded for a Certificate of Sponsorship unless:

(a)   the job that the Certificate of Sponsorship Checking Service entry records that the person is being Sponsored to do is part of a structured graduate training programme, with clearly defined progression towards a managerial or specialist role within the organisation,

(b)   the Sponsor has assigned Certificates of Sponsorship to 5 applicants or fewer, including the applicant in question, under the Graduate Trainee sub-category in the current year, beginning 6 April and ending 5 April each year, and

(c)   the Certificate of Sponsorship Checking Service entry confirms that the applicant has been working for the Sponsor outside the UK for a continuous period of 3 months immediately prior to the date of application and, if requested to do so, the applicant provides the specified documents in paragraph 74C-SD(a) above to prove this. The application may be granted without these specified documents, but the UK Border Agency reserves the right to request the specified documents, and to refuse applications if these documents are not received at the address specified in the request within 7 working days of the date of the request.

74E.   If the applicant is applying as a Tier 2 (Intra-Company Transfer) Migrant in the Skills Transfer subcategory, no points will be awarded for a Certificate of Sponsorship unless the job that the Certificate of Sponsorship Checking Service entry records that the person is being Sponsored to do is for the sole purpose of transferring skills to or from the Sponsor's UK work environment. The appointment must be additional to staffing requirements that is the role in the UK would not exist but for the need for skills transfer.

74F.   An applicant cannot score points for a Certificate of Sponsorship from Table 11 if the job that the Certificate of Sponsorship Checking Service entry records that he is being Sponsored to do is as a sports person or a Minister of Religion.

Appropriate salary

75.   The points awarded for appropriate salary will be based on the applicant's gross annual salary to be paid by the Sponsor, subject to the following conditions:

(i)   Points will be awarded based on basic pay (excluding overtime);

(ii)   Allowances will be included in the salary for the awarding of points where they are part of the guaranteed salary package and:

    (1)   would be paid to a local settled worker in similar circumstances, or

    (2)   are paid to cover the additional cost of living in the UK;

(iii)   Where allowances are made available solely for the purpose of accommodation, they will only be included up to a value of:

    (1)   40% of the total salary package for which points are being awarded, if the applicant is applying in either the Short Term Staff, Graduate Trainee or Skills Transfer sub-categories, or

    (2)   30% of the total salary package for which points are being awarded, if the applicant is applying in the Long Term Staff sub-category;

(iv)   Other allowances and benefits, such as bonus or incentive pay, employer pension contributions, and allowances to cover business expenses, including (but not limited to) travel to and from the sending country, will not be included;

(v)   If the applicant has exchanged some of his UK employment rights for shares as an employee-owner, the value of those shares will not be included.

75A. No points will be awarded if the salary referred to in paragraph 75 above is less than £40,600 per year where the applicant is applying in the Long Term Staff sub-category, unless the applicant is applying for leave to remain and previously had leave as:

(i) a Qualifying Work Permit Holder, or

(ii) a Tier 2 (Intra-Company Transfer) Migrant under the rules in place before 6 April 2011,

and has not been granted entry clearance in this or any other route since that grant of leave.

75B. No points will be awarded if the salary referred to in paragraph 75 above is less than £24,300 per year where the applicant is applying in the Short Term Staff, Graduate Trainee or Skills Transfer sub-categories, unless the applicant is applying for leave to remain and has, or last had entry clearance, leave to enter or leave to remain as a Tier 2 (Intra-Company Transfer) Migrant under the rules in place before 6 April 2011.

75C. No points will be awarded if the salary referred to in paragraph 75 above is less than the appropriate rate for the job as stated in the codes of practice in Appendix J, unless the applicant is an established entertainer as defined in paragraph 6 of these Rules.

75D. Where the applicant is paid hourly, the appropriate salary consideration will be based on earnings up to a maximum of 48 hours a week, even if the applicant works for longer than this. For example, an applicant who works 60 hours a week for £8 per hour be considered to have a salary of £19,968 (8x48x52) and not £25,960 (8x60x52), and will therefore not be awarded points for appropriate salary.

75E. No points will be awarded for appropriate salary if the applicant does not provide a valid Certificate of Sponsorship reference number with his application.

Attributes for Tier 2 (General) Migrants

76. An applicant applying for entry or leave to remain as a Tier 2 (General) Migrant must score 50 points for attributes.

76A. Available points for entry clearance or leave to remain are shown in Table 11A.

76B. Notes to accompany Table 11A appear below the table.

Table 11A

Certificate of Sponsorship	Points	Appropriate salary	Points
Job offer passes Resident Labour Market Test	30	Appropriate salary	20
Resident Labour Market Test exemption applies	30		
Continuing to work in the same occupation for the same Sponsor	30		

Notes

Certificate of Sponsorship

77. Points may only be scored for one entry in the Certificate of Sponsorship column.

77A. In order to obtain points for a Certificate of Sponsorship, the applicant must provide a valid Certificate of Sponsorship reference number.

77B. The only Certificates of Sponsorship to be allocated to Sponsors for applicants to be Sponsored as Tier 2 (General) Migrants are:

(a) Certificates of Sponsorship to be assigned to applicants as a Tier 2 (General) Migrant, as allocated to Sponsors under the Tier 2 (General) limit, which is set out in paragraphs 80 to 84A below.

(b) Certificates of Sponsorship to be assigned to specified applicants for leave to remain as a Tier 2 (General) Migrant, as set out in paragraph 77D of Appendix A,

(c) Certificates of Sponsorship to be assigned to an applicant to do a job for which the gross annual salary (including such allowances as are specified as acceptable for this purpose in paragraph 79 of this Appendix) is £152,100 (or £150,000, if the recruitment took place before 6 April 2013) or higher,

and

77C. A Certificate of Sponsorship reference number will only be considered to be valid if:

(a) the number supplied links to a Certificate of Sponsorship Checking Service entry that names the applicant as the migrant and confirms that the Sponsor is Sponsoring him as a Tier 2 (General) Migrant,

(b)   the Sponsor assigned that reference number to the migrant no more than 3 months after the Sponsor was allocated the Certificate of Sponsorship, if the Certificate of Sponsorship was allocated to the Sponsor under the Tier 2 (General) limit,

(c)   the Sponsor assigned that reference number to the migrant no more than 3 months before the application for entry clearance or leave to remain is made,

(d)   the application for entry clearance or leave to remain is made no more than 3 months before the start of the employment as stated on the Certificate of Sponsorship,

(e)   The migrant must not previously have applied for entry clearance, leave to enter or leave to remain using the same Certificate of Sponsorship reference number, if that application was either approved or refused (not rejected as an invalid application, declared void or withdrawn),

(f)   that reference number must not have been withdrawn or cancelled by the Sponsor or by the UK Border Agency since it was assigned, including where it has been cancelled by the UK Border Agency due to having been used in a previous application, and

(g)   the Sponsor is an A-rated Sponsor, unless:

    (1)   the application is for leave to remain, and

    (2)   the applicant has, or was last granted, leave as a Tier 2 (General) Migrant, a Jewish Agency Employee, a Member of the Operational Ground Staff of an Overseas-owned Airline, a Representative of an Overseas Newspaper, News Agency or Broadcasting Organisation, or a Qualifying Work Permit Holder, and

    (3)   the applicant is applying to work for the same employer named on the Certificate of Sponsorship or Work Permit document which led to his last grant of leave or, in the case of an applicant whose last grant of leave was as a Jewish Agency Employee, a Member of the Operational Ground Staff of an Overseas-owned Airline, a Representative of an Overseas Newspaper, News Agency or Broadcasting Organisation, the same employer for whom the applicant was working or stated he was intending to work when last granted leave.

77D.   No points will be awarded for a Certificate of Sponsorship unless:

(a)   in the case of a Certificate of Sponsorship which was allocated to the Sponsor under the Tier 2 (General) limit, the number supplied links to a Certificate of Sponsorship Checking Service entry which contains the same job and at least the same salary details as stated in the Sponsor's application for that Certificate of Sponsorship,

(b)   in the case of a Certificate of Sponsorship which was not allocated to the Sponsor under the Tier 2 (General) limit:

    (i)   the applicant is applying for leave to remain unless the applicant has, or was last granted entry clearance, leave to enter or leave to remain as the partner of a Relevant Points Based System Migrant, or

    (ii)   the number supplied links to a Certificate of Sponsorship Checking Service entry which shows that the applicant's gross annual salary (including such allowances as are specified as acceptable for this purpose in paragraph 79 of this appendix) to be paid by the Sponsor is £152,100 (or £150,000, if the recruitment took place before 6 April 2013) or higher.

77E.   No points will be awarded for a Certificate of Sponsorship unless:

(a)   the job that the Certificate of Sponsorship Checking Service entry records that the person is being sponsored to do appears on:

    (i)   the list of occupations skilled to National Qualifications Framework level 6 or above, as stated in the codes of practice in Appendix J, or

    (ii)   one of the following creative sector occupations skilled to National Qualifications Framework level 4 or above:

        (1)   3411 Artists,

        (2)   3412 Authors, writers and translators,

        (3)   3413 Actors, entertainers and presenters,

        (4)   3414 Dancers and choreographers, or

        (5)   3422 Product, clothing and related designers,

        or

    (b)   the job that the Certificate of Sponsorship Checking Service entry records that the person is being sponsored to do is skilled to National Qualifications Framework level 4 or above, and appears on the shortage occupation list in Appendix K,

or

    (c)   (i)   the applicant is applying for leave to remain,

             (ii)   the applicant previously had leave as a Tier 2 (General) Migrant or a Qualifying Work Permit Holder, and has not since been granted leave to remain in any other route, or entry clearance or leave to enter in any route,

             (iii)   at the time a Certificate of Sponsorship or Work Permit which led to a grant of leave in (ii) was issued, the job referred to in that Certificate of Sponsorship or Work Permit appeared on the shortage occupation list in Appendix K, and

             (iv)   the job that the Certificate of Sponsorship Checking service entry records that the person is being sponsored to do in his current application is the same as the job referred to in (iii), for either the same or a different employer,

or

    (d)   (i)   the applicant is applying for leave to remain,

             (ii)   the applicant previously had leave as a Tier 2 (General) Migrant under the Rules in place between 6 April 2011 and 13 June 2012, and has not since been granted leave to remain in any other route, or entry clearance or leave to enter in any route, and

             (iii)   the job that the Certificate of Sponsorship Checking Service entry records that the person is being sponsored to do appears on the list of occupations skilled to National Qualifications Framework level 4 or above, as stated in the codes of practice in Appendix J,

or

    (e)   (i)   the applicant is applying for leave to remain,

             (ii)   the applicant previously had leave as:

                    (1)   a Tier 2 (General) Migrant under the rules in place before 6 April 2011,

                    (2)   a Qualifying Work Permit Holder,

                    (3)   a Representative of an Overseas Newspaper, News Agency or Broadcasting Organisation,

                    (4)   a Member of the Operational Ground Staff of an Overseas-owned Airline

                    (5)   a Jewish Agency Employee,

                and has not since been granted leave to remain in any other route, or entry clearance or leave to enter in any route, and

             (iii)   the job that the Certificate of Sponsorship Checking Service entry records that the person is being sponsored to do appears on the list of occupations skilled to National Qualifications Framework level 3 or above, as stated in the codes of practice in Appendix J, or the applicant is a Senior Care Worker or an Established Entertainer as defined in paragraph 6 of these Rules.

    (f)   (i)   the applicant was last granted as a Tier 2 (General) Migrant,

             (ii)   the applicant is applying for leave to remain to work in the same occupation for the same Sponsor as in the application which led to his previous grant of leave,

             (iii)   the Certificate of Sponsorship used in support of the applicant's previous application was assigned by the Sponsor before 6 April 2013, and

             (iv)   the occupation fails to meet the required skill level in (a) to (e) above solely due to reclassification from the SOC 2000 system to the SOC 2010 system.

77F.   An applicant cannot score points for a Certificate of Sponsorship from Table 11A if the job that the Certificate of Sponsorship Checking Service entry records that he is being sponsored to do is as a sports person or a Minister of Religion.

Job offer passes Resident Labour Market Test

78.   Points will only be awarded for a job offer that passes the Resident Labour Market Test if:

    (a)   the Sponsor has advertised (or had advertised on its behalf) the job as set out in Tables 11B and 11C below; and

    (b)   The advertisements have stated:

             (i)   the job title,

(ii)   the main duties and responsibilities of the job (job description),

(iii)   the location of the job,

(iv)   an indication of the salary package or salary range or terms on offer,

(v)   the skills, qualifications and experience required for the job, and

(vi)   the closing date for applications, unless it is part of the Sponsor's rolling recruitment programme, in which case the advertisement should show the period of the recruitment programme;

and

(c)   The advertisements were published in English (or Welsh if the job is based in Wales); and

(d)   The Sponsor can show that no suitable settled worker is available to fill the job unless the job is in a PhD-level occupation listed in Appendix J. Settled workers will not be considered unsuitable on the basis that they lack qualifications, experience or skills (including language skills) that were not specifically requested in the job advertisement; and

(e)   The Certificate of Sponsorship Checking Service entry contains full details of when and where the job was advertised, and any advertisement reference numbers, including the Universal Jobmatch (or other Jobcentre Plus online service) or JobCentre Online vacancy reference number where relevant.

Table 11B: Advertising methods and duration which satisfy the Resident Labour Market Test

Type of job	Methods of advertising / recruitment	Duration / timing of advertising
New graduate jobs or internships	• University milkround visits to at least 3 UK universities (or all UK universities which provide the relevant course, whichever is the lower number), • At least one of the following websites: • – www.jobs.ac.uk, – www.milkround.com, – www.prospects.ac.uk, or – www.targetjobs.co.uk • and • At least one other medium listed in Table 11C	At least 28 days within the **4 years** immediately before the Sponsor assigned the Certificate of Sponsorship to the applicant
Pupillages for trainee barristers	• At least two media (or one medium if the job was advertised before 6 April 2013) listed in Table 11C	At least 28 days within the **2 years** immediately before the Sponsor assigned the Certificate of Sponsorship to the applicant
Jobs in PhD-level occupations as listed in Appendix J	• At least two media (or one medium if the job was advertised before 6 April 2013) listed in Table 11C	At least 28 days within the **1 year** immediately before the Sponsor assigned the Certificate of Sponsorship to the applicant
Jobs where the appropriate salary, as determined by paragraphs 79 to 79D of Appendix A, is at least £71,000 per year (or £70,000 per year if the job was advertised before 6 April 2013) or there is a stock exchange disclosure requirement	• At least two media (or one medium if the job was advertised before 6 April 2013) listed in Table 11C	At least 28 days within the **6 months** immediately before the Sponsor assigned the Certificate of Sponsorship to the applicant
Creative sector jobs covered by Table 9 of Appendix J	• As set out in Table 9 of Appendix J	As set out in Table 9 of Appendix J

Type of job	Methods of advertising / recruitment	Duration / timing of advertising
Orchestral musicians	• Universal Jobmatch (or other Jobcentre Plus online service) for jobs based in England, Scotland or Wales, or JobCentre Online for jobs based in Northern Ireland, and • At least one other medium listed in Table 11C	At least 28 days within the **2 years** immediately before the Sponsor assigned the Certificate of Sponsorship to the applicant
Positions in the NHS where the Resident Labour Market Test includes advertising on NHS Jobs between 19 November 2012 and 6 April 2014	• NHS Jobs	At least 28 days within the **6 months** immediately before the Sponsor assigned the Certificate of Sponsorship to the applicant
All other jobs	• Universal Jobmatch (or other Jobcentre Plus online service) for jobs based in England, Scotland or Wales, or JobCentre Online for jobs based in Northern Ireland, and • At least one other medium listed in Table 11C	At least 28 days within the **6 months** immediately before the Sponsor assigned the Certificate of Sponsorship to the applicant

Table 11C: Advertising media which satisfy the Resident Labour Market Test

Type of medium	Criteria for suitable media
Newspaper	Must be: • marketed throughout the UK or throughout the whole of the devolved nation in which the job is located, and • published at least once a week
Professional journal	Must be: • available nationally through retail outlets or through subscription, • published at least once a month, and • related to the nature of the job i.e. a relevant trade journal, official journal of a professional occupational body, or subject-specific publication
Website	Must be one of the following: • Universal Jobmatch (or other Jobcentre Plus online service), for jobs based in England, Scotland or Wales, • JobCentre Online, for jobs based in Northern Ireland, • an online version of a newspaper or professional journal which would satisfy the criteria above, • the website of a prominent professional or recruitment organisation, which does not charge a fee to jobseekers to view job advertisements or to apply for jobs via those advertisements, or • if the Sponsor is a multinational organisation or has over 250 permanent employees in the UK, the Sponsor's own website

Resident Labour Market Test exemption applies

Shortage occupation

78A.   In order for a Resident Labour Market Test exemption to apply for a job offer in a shortage occupation:

(a)   the job must, at the time the Certificate of Sponsorship was assigned to the applicant, have appeared on the shortage occupation list in Appendix K,

(b)   in all cases, contracted working hours must be for at least 30 hours a week, and

(c)   in all cases, if the UK Border Agency list of shortage occupations indicates that the job appears on the 'Scotland only' shortage occupation list, the job offer must be for employment in which the applicant will be working at a location in Scotland.

Post-Study Work

78B.   In order for a Resident Labour Market Test exemption to apply for post-study work:

(a)   the applicant must be applying for leave to remain,

(b)   the applicant must have, or have last been granted, entry clearance, leave to enter or leave to remain as:

(1)   a Tier 1 (Graduate Entrepreneur) Migrant,

(2)   a Tier 1 (Post-Study Work) Migrant,

(3)   a Participant in the International Graduates Scheme (or its predecessor, the Science and Engineering Graduates Scheme),

(4)   a Participant in the Fresh Talent: Working in Scotland Scheme,

(5)   a Tier 4 Migrant,

(6)   a Student,

(7)   a Student Nurse,

(8)   a Student Re-Sitting an Examination,

(9)   a Person Writing Up a Thesis,

(10)   an Overseas Qualified Nurse or Midwife,

(11)   a Postgraduate Doctor or Dentist, or

(12)   a Student Union Sabbatical Officer,

and

(c)   Where (b)(5) to (12) apply, the applicant must meet the requirements of paragraph 245HD(d) of these Rules.

Other exemptions

78C.   In order for another Resident Labour Market Test exemption to apply, either:

(a)   the Certificate of Sponsorship Checking Service entry must show that the applicant's gross annual salary (including such allowances as are specified as acceptable for this purpose in paragraph 79 of this appendix) to be paid by the Sponsor is £152,100 (or £150,000, if the recruitment took place before 6 April 2013) or higher; or

(b)   the job offer must be in a supernumerary research position where the applicant has been issued a non-transferable scientific research Award or Fellowship by an external organisation which is not the Sponsor, meaning that the role is over and above the Sponsor's normal requirements and if the applicant was not there, the role would not be filled by anyone else; or

(c)   the job offer must be to continue working as a Doctor or Dentist in training, under the same NHS Training Number which was assigned to the applicant for previous lawful employment as a Doctor or Dentist in Training in the UK; or

(d)   the job offer must be as a Doctor in Speciality Training where the applicant's salary and the costs of his training are being met by the government of another country under an agreement with that country and the United Kingdom Government;

and the Certificate of Sponsorship Checking Service entry must provide full details of why an exemption applies.

Continuing to work in the same occupation for the same Sponsor

78D.   In order for the applicant to be awarded points for continuing to work in the same occupation for the same Sponsor:

(a)   the applicant must be applying for leave to remain,

(b)   the applicant must have entry clearance or leave to remain as:

(i)   a Tier 2 (General) Migrant,

(ii)   a Qualifying Work Permit Holder,

(iii)   a Representative of an Overseas Newspaper, News Agency or Broadcasting Organisation,

(iv)   a Member of the Operational Ground Staff of an Overseas-owned Airline or

(v)   a Jewish Agency Employee,

(b)   the Sponsor must be the same employer:

 (i)   as the Sponsor on the previous application that was granted, in the case of an applicant whose last grant of leave was as a Tier 2 (General) Migrant,

 (ii)   that the work permit was issued to, in the case of an applicant whose last grant of leave was as a Qualifying Work Permit Holder,

 (iii)   for whom the applicant was working or stated he was intending to work when last granted leave, in the case of an applicant whose last grant of leave was a Representative of an Overseas Newspaper, News Agency or Broadcasting Organisation, a Member of the Operational Ground Staff of an Overseas-owned Airline, or a Jewish Agency Employee.

(c)   the job that the Certificate of Sponsorship Checking Service entry records the applicant as having been engaged to do must be the same occupation:

 (i)   in respect of which the Certificate of Sponsorship that led to the previous grant was issued, in the case of an applicant whose last grant of leave was as a Tier 2 (General) Migrant,

 (ii)   in respect of which the previous work permit was issued, in the case of an applicant whose last grant of leave was as a Qualifying Permit Holder, or

 (iii)   that the applicant was doing, or intended to do, when he received his last grant of leave, in the case of an applicant whose last grant of leave was a Representative of an Overseas Newspaper, News Agency or Broadcasting Organisation, a Member of the Operational Ground Staff of an Overseas-owned Airline, or a Jewish Agency Employee,

 (iv)   If the applicant has exchanged some of his UK employment rights for shares as an employee-owner, the value of those shares will not be included.

Appropriate salary

79.   The points awarded for appropriate salary will be based on the applicant's gross annual salary to be paid by the Sponsor, subject to the following conditions:

(i)   Points will be awarded based on basic pay (excluding overtime);

(ii)   Allowances, such as London weighting, will be included in the salary for the awarding of points where they are part of the guaranteed salary package and would be paid to a local settled worker in similar circumstances;

(iii)   Other allowances and benefits, such as bonus or incentive pay, employer pension contributions, travel and subsistence (including travel to and from the applicant's home country), will not be included.

79A.   No points will be awarded if the salary referred to in paragraph 79 above is less than £20,300 per year, unless:

(a)   the applicant is applying for leave to remain and has, or last had entry clearance, leave to enter or leave to remain as:

 (i)   a Qualifying Work Permit Holder,

 (ii)   a Representative of an Overseas Newspaper, News Agency or Broadcasting Organisation,

 (iii)   a Member of the operational Ground Staff of an Overseas-owned Airline

 (iv)   a Jewish Agency Employee, or

 (v)   a Tier 2 (General) Migrant under the Rules in place before 6 April 2011

 or

(b)   the Certificate of Sponsorship checking service entry records the applicant is being sponsored as a nurse or midwife, will continue to be sponsored as a nurse or midwife by the Sponsor after achieving Nursing and Midwifery Council registration, and the salary will not be less than £20,300 per year once that registration is achieved.

79B.   No points will be awarded for appropriate salary if the salary referred to in paragraph 79 above is less than the appropriate rate for the job as stated in the codes of practice in Appendix J, unless the applicant is an established entertainer as defined in paragraph 6 of these Rules.

79C.   Where the applicant is paid hourly, the appropriate salary consideration will be based on earnings up to a maximum of 48 hours a week, even if the applicant works for longer than this. for example, an applicant who works 60 hours a week for £8 per hour be considered to have a salary of £19,968 (8x48x52) and not £25,960 (8x60x52), and will therefore not be awarded points for appropriate salary.

79D.   No points will be awarded for appropriate salary if the applicant does not provide a valid Certificate of Sponsorship reference number with his application.

Tier 2 (General) limit

Overview

80.   The Secretary of State shall be entitled to limit the number of Certificates of Sponsorship available to be allocated to Sponsors in any specific period under the Tier 2 (General) limit referred to in paragraph 77B(a) above;

80A.   The Tier 2 (General) limit is 20,700 Certificates of Sponsorship in each year (beginning on 6 April and ending on 5 April).

80B.   The process by which Certificates of Sponsorship shall be allocated to Sponsors under the Tier 2 (General) limit is set out in paragraphs 80C to 84a and Tables 11D below.

80C.   A Sponsor must apply to the Secretary of State for a Certificate of Sponsorship.

80D.   Available points for an application for a Certificate of Sponsorship are shown in Table 11D. No application will be

granted unless it scores a minimum of 30 points under the heading 'Type of Job' and a minimum of 2 points under the heading 'Salary on Offer'.

80E.   Notes to accompany Table 11D appear below the table.

Table 11D Applications for Certificates of Sponsorship under the Tier 2 (General) limit

Type of job	Points	Salary on offer	Points
Shortage Occupation	75	£20,300–£20,999.99	2
PhD-level occupation code and job passes Resident Labour Market Test	50	£21,000–£21,999.99	3
Job passes Resident Labour Market Test or an exemption applies as set out in paragraphs 78B or 78C	30	£22,000–£22,999.99	4
		£23,000–£23,999.99	5
		£24,000–£24,999.99	6
		£25,000–£25,999.99	7
		£26,000–£26,999.99	8
		£27,000–£27,999.99	9
		£28,000–£31,999.99	10
		£32,000–£45,999.99	15
		£46,000–£74,999.99	20
		£75,000–£99,999.99	25
		£100,000–£152,099.99	30

Notes

81.   Points may only be scored for one entry in each column.

81A.   No points will be awarded under the heading 'Type of Job' unless the job described in the Sponsor's application for a Certificate of Sponsorship:

(a)   appears on:

   (i)   the list of occupations skilled to National Qualifications Framework level 6 or above, as stated in the codes of practice in Appendix J, or

   (ii)   one of the following creative sector occupations skilled to National Qualifications Framework level 4 or above:

      (1)   3411 Artists,

      (2)   3412 Authors, writers and translators,

      (3)   3413 Actors, entertainers and presenters,

      (4)   3414 Dancers and choreographers, or

      (5)   3422 Product, clothing and related designers,

or

    (b)   is skilled to National Qualifications Framework level 4 or above, and appears on the shortage occupation list in Appendix K.

81B.   In order for the Sponsor's application to be awarded points for a job in a shortage occupation, the job must, at the time the application for a Certificate of Sponsorship is decided, appear on the the shortage occupation list in Appendix K, and contracted working hours must be for at least 30 hours a week. Furthermore, if the shortage occupation list in Appendix K,indicates that the job appears on the 'Scotland only' shortage occupation list, the job must be for employment in Scotland.

81C.   In order for the Sponsor's application to be awarded points for a job in a PhD-level occupation code, the job must be in an occupation code which appears on the list of PhD-level occupation codes as stated in the codes of practice in Appendix J. The Sponsor's application must also meet the requirements of paragraph 81D.

81D.   In order for the Sponsor's application to be awarded points for a job that passes the resident labour market test or an exemption applies, the Sponsor must certify that it has met the requirements of that test, as defined in guidance published by the UK Border Agency, in respect of the job, or that one of the exemptions set out in paragraphs 78B or 78C of this Appendix applies.

81E.   The points awarded under the heading 'Salary on Offer' will be based on the gross annual salary on offer to be paid by the Sponsor, as stated in the Sponsor's application, subject to the following conditions:

    (i)   Points will be awarded based on basic pay (excluding overtime);

    (ii)   Allowances, such as London weighting, will be included in the salary for the awarding of points where they are part of the guaranteed salary package and would be paid to a local settled worker in similar circumstances;

    (iii)   Other allowances and benefits, such as bonus or incentive pay, travel and subsistence (including travel to and from the applicant's home country), will not be included.

81F.   No points will be awarded for the salary on offer if the salary referred to in paragraph 81e above is less than the appropriate rate for the job as stated in the codes of practice for Tier 2 Sponsors published by the UK Border Agency.

81G.   Where the salary on offer will be paid hourly, the salary on offer will be calculated on the basis of earnings up to a maximum of 48 hours a week, even if the jobholder works for longer than this.

82.–84A.   OMITTED

Attributes for Tier 2 (Ministers of Religion) Migrants

85.   An applicant applying for entry clearance or leave to remain as a Tier 2(Ministers of Religion) Migrant must score 50 points for attributes.

86.   Available points are shown in Table 12 below.

87.   Notes to accompany Table 12 appear below that table.

Table 12

Criterion	Points
Certificate of Sponsorship	50

88.–92A.   OMITTED

Attributes for Tier 2 (Sportsperson) Migrants

93.   An applicant applying for entry clearance or leave to remain as a Tier 2 (Sportsperson) Migrant must score 50 points for attributes.

94.   Available points are shown in Table 13 below

95.   Notes to accompany Table 13 appear below that table.

Criterion	Points
Certificate of Sponsorship	50

96.–100   OMITTED

Attributes for Tier 5 (Youth Mobility Scheme) Temporary Migrants

101.   An applicant applying for entry clearance as a Tier 5 (Youth Mobility Scheme) Temporary Migrant must score 40 points for attributes

102. Available points are shown in Table 14 below.

103. Notes to accompany Table 14 below.

Table 14

Criterion	Points
Citizen of a country or rightful holder of a passport issued by a territory listed in Appendix G or Is a British Overseas Citizen, British Territories Overseas Citizen or British National (Overseas.)	30
Will be 18 or over when his entry clearance becomes valid for use and was under the age of 31 on the date his application was made.	10

Notes

104. The applicant must provide a valid passport as evidence of all of the above.

Attributes for Tier 5 (Temporary Worker) Migrants

105. An applicant applying for entry clearance or leave enter or remain as a Tier 5 (Temporary Worker) Migrant must score 30 points for attributes.

106. Available points are shown in Table 15 below.

107. Notes to accompany Table 15 appear below in that table.

Table 15

Criterion	Points awarded
Holds a Tier 5 (Temporary Worker) Certificate of Sponsorship	30

108.–112. OMITTED

Attributes for Tier 4 (General) Students

113. An applicant applying for entry clearance or leave to remain as a Tier 4 (General) Student must score 30 points for attributes.

114. Available points are shown in Table 16 below.

115. Notes to accompany Table 16 appear below that table.

Table 16

Criterion	Points awarded
Confirmation of Acceptance for Studies	30

Notes

115A. In order to obtain points for a Confirmation of Acceptance for Studies, the applicant must provide a valid Confirmation of Acceptance for Studies reference number.

Tier 4 Interim Limit

115B. The Secretary of State shall be entitled to limit the number of Confirmations of Acceptance for Studies allocated to any specific Sponsor in any one period.

115C. The limit on the number of Confirmations of Acceptance for Studies allocated to specific Sponsors shall be known as the Tier 4 Interim Limit.

115CA. The interim limit implemented by HC1888 and effective in relation to Tier 4 between 6 April 2012 and 31 December 2012 shall be known as the Former Interim Limit.

115D. The Tier 4 Interim Limit will apply from 1 January 2013 to 30 June 2013 (inclusive) (the 'Tier 4 Interim Limit Period').

115E. The Tier 4 Interim Limit will be applied to any Tier 4 Sponsor who

　　(i)　is still subject to the former interim limit on 31 December 2012 and has applied for but not yet achieved HTS status and a valid and satisfactory full institutional inspection, review or audit from one of the following bodies:

　　　　(a)　the Bridge Schools Inspectorate; or

　　　　(b)　the Education and Training Inspectorate; or

    (c)   Estyn; or

    (d)   Education Scotland; or

    (e)   the Independent Schools Inspectorate; or

    (f)   Ofsted; or

    (g)   the Quality Assurance Agency for Higher Education; or

    (h)   The Schools Inspection Service; or is not:

         (ii)   the Foundation Programme Office;(iii) the Yorkshire and Humber Strategic Health Authority;

         (iv)   an overseas higher education institution which has Highly Trusted Sponsor Status.

115F. A Tier 4 Sponsor who does not satisfy the requirements of paragraph 115E and is therefore subject to the Tier 4 Interim Limit is known as a Limited Sponsor.

115FA. No Confirmations of Acceptance for Studies will be allocated to a Limited Sponsor where:

    (i)   The Limited Sponsor did not apply for inspection, review or audit by the appropriate specified body by the relevant deadline, as listed below:

Specified body	Deadline
Quality Assurance Agency	9 September 2011
Independent Schools Inspectorate	9 September 2011
Bridge Schools Inspectorate	7 October 2011
School Inspection Service	7 October 2011
Education Scotland	11 November 2011
Education and Training Inspectorate N.I.	30 April 2012

or

    (ii)   The Limited Sponsor applied by the deadline specified in (i) above, and failed to meet the required standard to obtain a full institutional audit, inspection or review, except for where The Limited Sponsor requires a second institutional audit, inspection or review within 6 months of the initial audit, inspection or review as determined by the relevant body listed above; or

    (iii)   The Limited Sponsor applied for Highly Trusted Sponsor status on two occasions and has not been granted Highly Trusted Sponsor status.

115FB. A Limited Sponsor that is allocated no Confirmations of Acceptance for Studies further to paragraph 115FA is known as a Legacy Sponsor

115G. All Confirmations of Acceptance for Studies allocated by the Secretary of State to Limited Sponsors prior to 1 January 2013 and which have not been assigned to an applicant for entry clearance, leave to enter or leave to remain under Tier 4 prior to 1 January 2013 are withdrawn and the only Confirmations of Acceptance for Studies allocated to a Limited Sponsor are the Confirmations of Acceptance for Studies allocated in accordance with paragraph 115H below.

115H. The Tier 4 Interim Limit will be calculated as follows:

    (i)   A Limited Sponsor who has that status as at 1 January 2013 will be allocated:

         (a)   where the Limited Sponsor was subject to the Former Tier 4 Interim Limit for the entirety of the period 6 April 2012 to 31 December 2012, a number of Confirmations of Acceptance for Studies equal to two thirds of the number of Confirmations of Acceptance for Studies allocated to that Limited Sponsor for the period 6 April 2012 to 31 December 2012;

         (b)   where the Limited Sponsor had a Tier 4 Sponsor Licence for only part of the period 6 April 2012 to 31 December 2012, and was subject to the Former Tier 4 Interim Limit from the date on which it was granted a sponsor licence, a number of Confirmations of Acceptance for Studies equal to:

            (i)   the number of Confirmations of Acceptance for Studies allocated to that Limited Sponsor for the period it was licenced between 6 April 2012 to 31 December 2012;

            (ii)   multiplied by the appropriate factor such that the figure in (i) is equal to the number of Confirmations of Acceptance for Studies that would have been granted to that Limited Sponsor for a period of 6 months;

(c)   where the Limited Sponsor had a Tier 4 Sponsor Licence for the entirety of the period 6 April 2012 to 31 December 2012 and was subject to the Former Tier 4 Interim Limit for only part of that period, a number of Confirmations of Acceptance for Studies equal to:

   (i)   the number of Confirmations of Acceptance for Studies allocated to that Limited Sponsor under the Tier 4 Interim Limit;

   (ii)   multiplied by the appropriate factor such that the figure in (i) is equal to the number of Confirmations of Acceptance for Studies that would have been granted to that Limited Sponsor for a period of 6 months;

(d)   where the calculation in paragraphs (a) to (c) results in 0 or a negative number, the Limited Sponsor will be allocated 0 Confirmations of Acceptance for Studies under the Tier 4 Interim Limit;

(e)   where the calculation in paragraphs (a) to (c) does not result in a whole number, the Limited Sponsor will be allocated a number of Confirmations of Acceptance for Studies equal to the nearest whole number (fractions will be rounded up to the nearest whole number).

115I.   A Limited Sponsor will, on provision to the UK Border Agency of evidence that it meets the criteria set out in paragraph 115E above, be exempt from the Tier 4 Interim Limit from the date the UK Border Agency provides written confirmation that it is so exempt.

116.   A Confirmation of Acceptance for Studies will only be considered to be valid if:

(a)   it was issued no more than 6 months before the application is made,

(b)   the application for entry clearance or leave to remain is made no more than 3 months before the start date of the course of study as stated on the Confirmation of Acceptance for Studies,

(c)   the Sponsor has not withdrawn the offer since the Confirmation of Acceptance for Studies was issued,

(d)   it was issued by an institution with a Tier 4 (General) Student Sponsor Licence,

(da)   where the application for entry clearance or leave to remain is for the applicant to commence a new course of study, not for completion of a course already commenced by way of re-sitting examinations or repeating a module of a course, the Sponsor must hold an A-rated or Highly Trusted Sponsor Licence and must not be a Legacy Sponsor,

(db)   where the Confirmation of Acceptance for Studies is issued by a Legacy Sponsor or a B-rated sponsor, the Confirmation of Acceptance for Studies will only be valid if it is issued for completion of a course already commenced by way of re-sitting examinations or repeating a module of a course and the Confirmation of Acceptance for Studies must be for the same course as the course for which the last period of leave was granted to study with that same sponsor,

(e)   the institution must still hold such a licence at the time the application for entry clearance or leave to remain is determined

(ea)   the migrant must not previously have applied for entry clearance, leave to enter or leave to remain using the same Confirmation of Acceptance for Studies reference number where that application was either approved or refused (not rejected as an invalid application declared void or withdrawn),

(f)   it contains the following mandatory information:

   (i)   the applicant's:

      (1)   name,

      (2)   date of birth,

      (3)   gender,

      (4)   nationality, and

      (5)   passport number;

   (ii)   the course:

      (1)   title,

      (2)   level,

      (3)   start and end dates, and

      (4)   hours per week, including confirmation that the course is full-time;

   (iii)   confirmation if the course is one in which the applicant must hold a valid Academic Technology Approval Scheme clearance certificate from the Counter-Proliferation Department of the Foreign and Commonwealth Office;

(iv)   confirmation if the course is a recognised Foundation Programme for postgraduate doctors or dentists, and requires a certificate from the Postgraduate Dean;

(v)   the main study address;

(vi)   details of how the Tier 4 Sponsor has assessed the applicant's English language ability including, where relevant, the applicant's English language test scores in all four components (reading, writing, speaking and listening);

(vii)   details of any work placements relating to the course;

(viii)   accommodation, fees and boarding costs;

(ix)   details of any partner institution, if the course will be provided by an education provider that is not the Tier 4 Sponsor; and

(x)   the name and address of the overseas higher education institution, if the course is part of a study abroad programme.

(g)   it was not issued for a course of studies, it was issued for a full-time, salaried, elected executive position as a student union sabbatical officer to an applicant who is part-way through their studies or who is being sponsored to fill the position in the academic year immediately after their graduation,

(h)   it was not issued for a course of studies, it was issued within 60 days of the expected end date of a course leading to the award of a PhD and the migrant is sponsored by a Sponsor that is a Recognised Body or a body in receipt of public funding as a higher education institution from the Department of Employment and Learning in Northern Ireland, the Higher Education Funding Council for England, the Higher Education Funding Council for Wales or the Scottish Funding Council, to enable the migrant to remain in the UK as a Tier 4 (General) Student on the doctorate extension scheme.

117.   A Confirmation of Acceptance for Studies reference number will only be considered to be valid if:

(a)   the number supplied links to a Confirmation of Acceptance for Studies Checking Service entry that names the applicant as the migrant and confirms that the Sponsor is sponsoring him in the Tier 4 category indicated by the migrant in his application for leave to remain (that is, as a Tier 4 (General) Student or a Tier 4 (Child) Student), and

(b)   that reference number must not have been withdrawn or cancelled by the Sponsor or the UK Border Agency since it was assigned.

118.   No points will be awarded for a Confirmation of Acceptance for Studies unless:

(a)   the applicant supplies, as evidence of previous qualifications, the specified documents, as set out in paragraph 120-SD(a), that the applicant used to obtain the offer of a place on a course from the Sponsor unless the applicant is sponsored by a Highly Trusted Sponsor, is a national of one of the countries or the rightful holder of a qualifying passport issued by one of the relevant competent authorities, as appropriate, listed in Appendix H, and is applying for entry clearance in his country of nationality or in the territory related to the passport he holds, as appropriate, or leave to remain in the UK. The UK Border Agency reserves the right to request the specified documents from these applicants. The application will be refused if the specified documents are not provided in accordance with the request made; and

(b)   One of the requirements in (i) to (iii) below is met:

(i)   the course is degree level study and the Confirmation of Acceptance for Studies has been assigned by a Sponsor which is a Recognised Body or a body in receipt of funding as a higher education institution from the Department for Employment and Learning in Northern Ireland, the Higher Education Funding Council for England, the Higher Education Funding Council for Wales, or the Scottish Funding Council, and:

(1)   the applicant is a national of one of the following countries: Antigua and Barbuda; Australia; The Bahamas; Barbados; Belize; Canada; Dominica; Grenada; Guyana; Jamaica; New Zealand; St Kitts and Nevis; St Lucia; St Vincent and the Grenadines; Trinidad and Tobago; United States of America, and provides the specified documents set out in paragraph 120-SD(b); or

(2)   has obtained an academic qualification (not a professional or vocational qualification), which is deemed by UK NARIC to meet or exceed the recognised standard of a Bachelor's or Master's degree or a PhD in the UK, from an educational establishment in one of the following countries: Antigua and Barbuda; Australia; The Bahamas; Barbados; Belize; Dominica; Grenada; Guyana; Ireland; Jamaica; New Zealand; St Kitts and Nevis; St

Lucia; St Vincent and The Grenadines; Trinidad and Tobago; the UK; the USA, and provides the specified documents set out in paragraph 120-SD(a); or

(3)   the applicant has successfully completed a course as a Tier 4 (Child) Student (or under the student rules that were in force before 31 March 2009, where the student was granted permission to stay whilst he was under 18 years old) which:

(i)   was at least six months in length, and

(ii)   ended within two years of the date the sponsor assigned the Confirmation of Acceptance for Studies; or

(4)   the Confirmation of Acceptance for Studies Checking Service entry confirms that the applicant has a knowledge of English equivalent to level B2 of the Council of Europe's Common European Framework for Language Learning in all four components (reading, writing, speaking and listening), or above, or that the Sponsor is satisfied that on completion of a pre-sessional course as provided for in paragraph 120(b)(i) of this Appendix, the applicant will have a knowledge of English as set out in this paragraph; or

(ii)   the course is degree level study and the Confirmation of Acceptance for Studies has been assigned by a Sponsor which is not a Recognised Body or is not a body in receipt of funding as a higher education institution from the Department for Employment and Learning in Northern Ireland, the Higher Education Funding Council for England, the Higher Education Funding Council for Wales, or the Scottish Funding Council, and:

(1)   the applicant is a national of one of the following countries: Antigua and Barbuda; Australia; The Bahamas; Barbados; Belize; Canada; Dominica; Grenada; Guyana; Jamaica; New Zealand; St Kitts and Nevis; St Lucia; St Vincent and the Grenadines; Trinidad and Tobago; United States of America, and provides the specified documents set out in paragraph 120-SD(b); or

(2)   has obtained an academic qualification (not a professional or vocational qualification), which is deemed by UK NARIC to meet or exceed the recognised standard of a Bachelor's or Master's degree or a PhD in the UK, from an educational establishment in one of the following countries: Antigua and Barbuda; Australia; The Bahamas; Barbados; Belize; Dominica; Grenada; Guyana; Ireland; Jamaica; New Zealand; St Kitts and Nevis; St Lucia; St Vincent and The Grenadines; Trinidad and Tobago; the UK; the USA, and provides the specified documents set out in paragraph 120-SD(a); or

(3)   the applicant has successfully completed a course as a Tier 4 (Child) Student (or under the student rules that were in force before 31 March 2009, where the student was granted permission to stay whilst he was under 18 years old) which:

(i)   was at least six months in length, and

(ii)   ended within two years of the date the sponsor assigned the Confirmation of Acceptance for Studies; or

(4)   the applicant provides the specified documents from an English language test provider approved by the Secretary of State for these purposes as listed in Appendix O, which clearly show:

(i)   the applicant's name,

(ii)   that the applicant has achieved or exceeded level B2 of the Council of Europe's Common European Framework for Language learning in all four components (reading, writing, speaking and listening), unless exempted from sitting a component on the basis of the applicant's disability,

(iii)   the date of the award, and

(iv)   that the test is within its validity date (where applicable).

Or

(iii)   the course is for below degree level study and:

(1)   the applicant is a national of one of the following countries: Antigua and Barbuda; Australia; The Bahamas; Barbados; Belize; Canada; Dominica; Grenada; Guyana; Jamaica; New Zealand; St Kitts and Nevis; St Lucia; St Vincent and the Grenadines; Trinidad and Tobago; United States of America, and provides the specified documents set out in paragraph 120-SD(b); or

(2)   has obtained an academic qualification (not a professional or vocational qualification), which is deemed by UK NARIC to meet or exceed the recognised standard of a Bachelor's or Master's degree or a PhD in the UK, from an educational establishment in one of the following countries: Antigua and Barbuda; Australia; The Bahamas; Barbados; Belize; Dominica; Grenada; Guyana; Ireland; Jamaica; New Zealand; St Kitts and Nevis; St Lucia; St Vincent and The Grenadines; Trinidad and Tobago; the UK; the USA, and provides the specified documents set out in paragraph 120-SD(a); or

(3)   the applicant has successfully completed a course as a Tier 4 (Child) student (or under the student rules that were in force before 31 March 2009, where the student was granted permission to stay whilst he was under 18 years old) which:

   (i)   was at least six months in length, and

   (ii)   ended within two years of the date the sponsor assigned the Confirmation of Acceptance for Studies; or

(4)   the applicant provides the specified documents from an English language test provider approved by the Secretary of State for these purposes as listed in Appendix O, which clearly show:

   (i)   the applicant's name,

   (ii)   that the applicant has achieved or exceeded level B1 of the Council of Europe's Common European Framework for Language learning in all four components (reading, writing, speaking and listening), unless exempted from sitting a component on the basis of the applicant's disability,

   (iii) the date of the award, and

   (iv)   that the test is within its validity date (where applicable).

119.   If the applicant is re-sitting examinations or repeating a module of a course, the applicant must not previously have re-sat the same examination or repeated the same module more than once, unless the Sponsor is a Highly Trusted Sponsor. If this requirement is not met then no points will be awarded for the Confirmation of Acceptance for Studies, unless the Sponsor is a Highly Trusted Sponsor.

120.   Points will only be awarded for a Confirmation of Acceptance for Studies (even if all the requirements in paragraphs 116 to 119 above are met) if the course in respect of which it is issued meets each of the following requirements:

(a)   The course must meet the following minimum academic requirements:

   (i)   for applicants applying to study in England, Wales or Northern Ireland, the course must be at National Qualifications Framework (NQF) / Qualifications and Credit Framework (QCF) Level 3 or above if the Sponsor is a Highly Trusted Sponsor; or

   (ii)   for applicants applying to study in England, Wales or Northern Ireland, the course must be at National Qualifications Framework (NQF) / Qualifications and Credit Framework (QCF) Level 4 or above if the Sponsor is an A-Rated Sponsor or a B-Rated Sponsor; or

   (iii) for applicants applying to study in Scotland, the course must be accredited at Level 6 or above in the Scottish Credit and Qualifications Framework (SCQF) by the Scottish Qualifications Authority and the Sponsor must be a Highly Trusted Sponsor; or

   (iv)   for applicants applying to study in Scotland, the course must be accredited at Level 7 or above in the Scottish Credit and Qualifications Framework (SCQF) by the Scottish Qualifications Authority if the Sponsor is an A-Rated Sponsor or B-Rated Sponsor; or

   (v)   the course must be a short-term Study Abroad Programme in the United Kingdom as part of the applicant's qualification at an overseas higher education institution, and that qualification must be confirmed as the same as a United Kingdom degree level by the National Recognition Information Centre for the United Kingdom (UK NARIC); or

   (vi)   the course must be an English language course at level B2 or above of the Common European Framework of Reference for Languages; or

   (vii) the course must be a recognised Foundation Programme for postgraduate doctors or dentists.

(b)   The Confirmation of Acceptance for Studies must be for a single course of study except where the Confirmation of Acceptance for Studies is:

   (i)   issued by a Sponsor which is a Recognised Body or a body in receipt of funding as a higher education institution from the Department for Employment and Learning in Northern Ireland, the Higher Education Funding Council for England, the Higher Education Funding Council for Wales, or the Scottish Funding Council to cover both a pre-sessional course of no longer than three months' duration and a course of degree level study at that Sponsor; and

(ii)   the applicant has an unconditional offer of a place on a course of degree level study at that Sponsor or that where the offer is made in respect of an applicant whose knowledge of English is not at B2 level of the Council of Europe's Common European Framework for Language Learning in all four components (reading, writing, speaking and listening) or above, the Sponsor is satisfied that on completion of a pre-sessional course as provided for in (i) above, the applicant will have a knowledge of English at as set out in this paragraph; and

(iii)   the course of degree level study commences no later than one month after the end date of the pre-sessional course.

(c)   The course must, except in the case of a pre-sessional course, lead to an approved qualification as defined in (cb) below.

(ca)   If a student is specifically studying towards an Association of Certified Chartered Accountants (ACCA) qualification or an ACCA Foundations in Accountancy qualification, the sponsor must be an ACCA approved learning partner-student tuition (ALP-st) at either Gold or Platinum level.

(cb)   An approved qualification as one that is:

(1)   validated by Royal Charter,

(2)   awarded by a body that is on the list of recognised bodies produced by the Department for Business, Innovation and Skills,

(3)   recognised by one or more recognised bodies through a formal articulation agreement with the awarding body,

(4)   in England, Wales and Northern Ireland, on the Register of Regulated Qualifications (http://register.ofqual.gov.uk/) at National Qualifications Framework (NQF) / Qualifications and Credit Framework (QCF) level 3 or above,

(5)   in Scotland, accredited at Level 6 or above in the Scottish Credit and Qualifications Framework (SCQF) by the Scottish Qualifications Authority,

(6)   an overseas qualification that UK NARIC assesses as valid and equivalent to National Qualifications Framework (NQF) / Qualifications and Credit Framework (QCF) level 3 or above, or

(7)   covered by a formal legal agreement between a UK-recognised body and another education provider or awarding body. An authorised signatory for institutional agreements within the recognised body must sign this. The agreement must confirm the recognised body's own independent assessment of the level of the Tier 4 Sponsor's or the awarding body's programme compared to the National Qualifications Framework (NQF)/Qualifications and Credit Framework (QCF) or its equivalents. It must also state that the recognised body would admit any student who successfully completes the Tier 4 Sponsor's or the awarding body's named course onto a specific or a range of degree-level courses it offers.

(d)   Other than when the applicant is on a course-related work placement or a pre-sessional course, all study that forms part of the course must take place on the premises of the sponsoring educational institution or an institution which is a partner institution of the migrant's Sponsor.

(e)   The course must meet one of the following requirements:

(i)   be a full time course of degree level study that leads to an approved qualification as defined in (cb) above;

(ii)   be an overseas course of degree level study that is recognised as being equivalent to a UK Higher Education course and is being provided by an overseas Higher Education Institution; or

(iii)   be a full time course of study involving a minimum of 15 hours per week organised daytime study and, except in the case of a pre-sessional course, lead to an approved qualification, below bachelor degree level as defined in (cb) above.

(f)   Where the student is following a course of below degree level study including course –related work placement, the course can only be offered by a Highly Trusted Sponsor. If the course contains a course-related work placement, any period that the applicant will be spending on that placement must not exceed one third of the total length of the course spent in the United Kingdom except :

(i)   where it is a United Kingdom statutory requirement that the placement should exceed one third of the total length of the course; or

(ii) where the placement does not exceed one half of the total length of the course undertaken in the UK and the student is following a course of degree level study and is either:

    (a) sponsored by a Sponsor that is a Recognised Body or a body in receipt of public funding as a higher education institution from the Department of Employment and Learning in Northern Ireland, the Higher Education Funding Council for England, the Higher Education Funding Council for Wales or the Scottish Funding Council; or

    (b) sponsored by an overseas higher education institution to undertake a short-term Study Abroad Programme in the United Kingdom.

Specified documents

120-SD. Where paragraphs 118 to 120 of this Appendix refer to specified documents, those specified documents are as follows:

(a) In the case of evidence relating to previous qualifications, the applicant must provide, for each qualification, either:

    (i) The original certificate(s) of qualification, which clearly shows:

        (1) the applicant's name,

        (2) the title of the award,

        (3) the date of the award, and

        (4) the name of the awarding institution;

    (ii) The transcript of results, which clearly shows:

        (1) the applicant's name,

        (2) the name of the academic institution,

        (3) their course title, and

        (4) confirmation of the award;

    This transcript must be original unless the applicant has applied for their course through UCAS (Universities and Colleges Admissions Service), and:

        (a) the applicant is applying in the UK to study at a Higher Education Institution which has Highly Trusted Sponsor status, and

        (b) the qualification is issued by a UK awarding body for a course that the applicant has studied in the UK;

    or

    (iii) If the applicant's Tier 4 sponsor has assessed the applicant by using one or more references, and the Confirmation of Acceptance for Studies Checking Service entry includes details of the references assessed, the original reference(s) (or a copy, together with an original letter from the Tier 4 sponsor confirming it is a true copy of the reference they assessed), which must contain:

        (1) the applicant's name,

        (2) confirmation of the type and level of course or previous experience; and dates of study or previous experience,

        (3) date of the letter, and

        (4) contact details of the referee.

(b) In the case of evidence of the applicant's nationality, the specified documents are the applicant's current valid original passport or travel document. If the applicant is unable to provide this, the UK Border Agency may exceptionally consider this requirement to have been met where the applicant provides full reasons in the passport section of the application form, and either:

    (1) a current national identity document, or

    (2) an original letter from his home government or embassy, on the letter-headed paper of the government or embassy, which has been issued by an authorised official of that institution and confirms the applicant's full name, date of birth and nationality.

120A. (a) Points will only be awarded for a valid Confirmation of Acceptance for Studies (even if all the requirements in paragraphs 116 to 120A above are met) if the Sponsor has confirmed that the course for which the Confirmation of Acceptance for Studies has been assigned represents academic progress from previous study, as defined in (b) below undertaken during the last period of leave as a Tier 4 (General) Student or as a Student where the applicant has had such leave, except where:

(i) the applicant is re-sitting examinations or repeating modules in accordance with paragraph 119 above, or

(ii) the applicant is making a first application to move to a new institution to complete a course commenced elsewhere.

(b) For a course to represent academic progress from previous study, the course must:

(i) be above the level of the previous course for which the applicant was granted leave as a Tier 4 (General) Student or as a Student, or

(ii) involve further study at the same level, which the Tier 4 Sponsor confirms as complementing the previous course for which the applicant was granted leave as a Tier 4 (General) Student or as a Student.

Attributes for Tier 4 (Child) Students

121. An applicant applying for entry clearance or leave to remain as a Tier 4 (Child) Student must score 30 points for attributes.

122. Available points are show in Table 17 below.

123. Notes to accompany Table 17 appear below that table.

123A. In order to obtain points for a Confirmation of Acceptance for Studies, the applicant must provide a valid Confirmation of Acceptance for Studies reference number.

Table 17

Criterion	Points awarded
Confirmation of Acceptance for Studies	30

Notes

124. A Confirmation of Acceptance for Studies will be considered to be valid only if:

(a) where the applicant is under 16, it was issued by an independent, fee paying school,

(b) it was issued no more than 6 months before the application is made,

(c) the application for entry clearance or leave to remain is made no more than 3 months before the start date of the course of study as stated on the Confirmation of Acceptance for Studies,

(d) the Sponsor has not withdrawn the offer since the Confirmation of Acceptance for Studies was issued,

(e) it was issued by an institution with a Tier 4 (Child) Student Sponsor Licence,

(f) the institution must still hold such a licence at the time the application for entry clearance or leave to remain is determined, and

(fa) the migrant must not previously have applied for entry clearance, leave to enter or leave to remain using the same Confirmation of Acceptance for Studies reference number, if that application was either approved or refused (not rejected as an invalid application declared void or withdrawn), and

(g) it contains such information as is specified as mandatory in these immigration rules.

125. A Confirmation of Acceptance for Studies reference number will only be considered to be valid if:

(a) the number supplied links to a Confirmation of Acceptance for Studies Checking Service entry that names the applicant as the migrant and confirms that the Sponsor is sponsoring him in the Tier 4 category indicated by the migrant in his application for leave to remain (that is, as a Tier 4 (General) Student or a Tier 4 (Child) Student), and

(b) that reference number must not have been withdrawn or cancelled by the Sponsor or the UK Border Agency since it was assigned.

125A. Points will only be awarded for a Confirmation of Acceptance for Studies if the applicant:

(a) supplies, as evidence of previous qualifications, the specified documents set out in paragraph 125-SD that the applicant used to obtain the offer of a place on a course from the Sponsor,

(b) is sponsored by a Highly Trusted Sponsor, is a national of one of the countries or the rightful holder of a qualifying passport issued by one of the relevant competent authorities, as appropriate, listed in Appendix H and is applying for entry clearance in his country of nationality or in the territory related to the passport he holds, as appropriate, or leave to remain in the UK. The UK Border Agency reserves the right to request the specified documents set out in paragraph 125-SD from these applicants. The application will be refused if the specified documents are not provided in accordance with the request made; or

(c)   where the application for entry clearance or leave to remain is for the applicant to commence a new course of study, not for completion of a course already commenced by way of re-sitting examinations or repeating a module of a course, the Sponsor must hold an A-rated or Highly Trusted Sponsor Licence and must not be a Legacy Sponsor, or

(d)   where the Confirmation of Acceptance for Studies is issued by a Legacy Sponsor or a B-rated sponsor, the Confirmation of Acceptance for Studies will only be valid if it is issued for completion of a course already commenced by way of re-sitting examinations or repeating a module of a course and the Confirmation of Acceptance for Studies must be for the same course as the course for which the last period of leave was granted to study with that same sponsor.

Specified documents

125-SD.   Where paragraph 125 of this Appendix refers to specified documents evidence relating to previous qualifications, those specified documents are:

(i)   The original certificate(s) of qualification, which clearly shows:

(1)   the applicant's name,

(2)   the title of the award,

(3)   the date of the award, and

(4)   the name of the awarding institution;

(ii)   The original transcript of results, which clearly shows:

(1)   the applicant's name,

(2)   the name of the academic institution,

(3)   their course title, and

(4)   confirmation of the award;

126.   Points will not be awarded under Table 17 unless the course that the student will be pursuing meets one of the following requirements:

(a)   be taught in accordance with the National Curriculum,

(b)   be taught in accordance with the National Qualification Framework (NQF),

(c)   be accepted as being of equivalent academic status to (a) or (b) above by Ofsted (England), the Education and Training Inspectorate (Northern Ireland), Education Scotland (Scotland) or Estyn (Wales),

(d)   be provided as required by prevailing independent school education inspection standards.

(e)   is a single course of study, except where the Confirmation of Acceptance for Studies is:

(i)   issued by an independent school to cover both a pre-sessional course and a course at an independent school; and

(ii)   the applicant has an unconditional offer of a place at the independent school; and

(iii)   the duration of the pre-sessional course and period of study at the independent school does not exceed the maximum period of entry clearance or leave to remain that can be granted under paragraphs 245ZZB and 245ZZD of the Immigration Rules.

Appendix B – English language

1.   An applicant applying as a Tier 1 Migrant or Tier 2 Migrant must have 10 points for English language, unless applying:

(i)   for entry clearance or leave to remain as a Tier 1 (Exceptional Talent) Migrant, except where applying for leave to remain and the applicant has, or was last granted entry clearance or leave to remain as a Tier 1 (Exceptional Talent) migrant,

(ii)   for entry clearance or leave to remain as a Tier 1 (Investor) Migrant

(iii)   for entry clearance or leave to remain as a Tier 2 (Intra-Company Transfer) Migrant

2.   The levels of English language required are shown in Table 1.

3.   Available points for English language are shown in Table 2.

4.   Notes to accompany the tables are shown below each table.

Table 1 Level of English language required to score points

Tier 1

Row	Category	Applications	Level of English language required
A	Tier 1 (General)	Entry clearance and leave to remain	A knowledge of English equivalent to level C1 or above of the Council of Europe's Common European Framework for Language Learning
B	Tier 1 (Entrepreneur)	Entry clearance and leave to remain	A knowledge of English equivalent to level B1 or above of the Council of Europe's Common European Framework for Language Learning
C	Tier 1 (Graduate Entrepreneur)	Entry clearance and leave to remain	A knowledge of English equivalent to level B1 or above of the Council of Europe's Common European Framework for Language Learning
D	Tier 1 (Exceptional Talent)	Leave to remain, if last granted entry clearance or leave to remain as a Tier 1 (Exceptional Talent) Migrant.	A knowledge of English equivalent to level B1 or above of the Council of Europe's Common European Framework for Language Learning

Tier 2

Row	Category	Applications	Level of English language required
E	Tier 2 (Minister of Religion)	Entry clearance and leave to remain	A knowledge of English equivalent to level B2 or above of the Council of Europe's Common European Framework for Language Learning
F	Tier 2 (General)	Entry clearance and leave to remain, other than the cases in paragraph 5 below	A knowledge of English equivalent to level B1 or above of the Council of Europe's Common European Framework for Language Learning
G	Tier 2 (General)	Leave to remain cases in paragraph 5 below	A knowledge of English equivalent to level A1 or above of the Council of Europe's Common European Framework for Language Learning
H	Tier 2 (Sportsperson)	Entry clearance and leave to remain	A knowledge of English equivalent to level A1 or above of the Council of Europe's Common European Framework for Language Learning

Notes

5. An applicant applying for leave to remain as a Tier 2 (General) Migrant must have competence of English to a level A1 or above as set out in Table 1 above if:

    (i)   he previously had leave as:

        (1)   a Tier 2 (General) Migrant under the rules in place before 6 April 2011,

        (2)   a Qualifying Work Permit Holder,

        (3)   a representative of an overseas newspaper, news agency or Broadcasting organisation,

        (4)   a Member of the Operational Ground Staff of an Overseas-owned Airline, or

        (5)   a Jewish Agency Employee,

        and

    (ii)   he has not been granted leave to remain in any other routes, or entry clearance or leave to enter in any route, since the grant of leave referred to in (i) above.

Table 2 Points available for English language

Factor	Points
National of a majority English speaking country	10
Degree taught in English	10
Passed an English language test	10
Met requirement in a previous grant of leave	10
Transitional arrangements	10

Notes

National of a majority English speaking country

6. 10 points will only be awarded for being a national of a majority English speaking country if the applicant has the relevant level of English language shown in Table 1 and:

    (i)   is a national of one of the following countries:

    Antigua and Barbuda
    Australia
    The Bahamas
    Barbados
    Belize
    Canada
    Dominica
    Grenada
    Guyana
    Jamaica
    New Zealand
    St Kitts and Nevis
    St Lucia
    St Vincent and the Grenadines
    Trinidad and Tobago
    USA
    and

    (ii)   provides his current valid original passport or travel document to show that this requirement is met. If the applicant is unable to do so, the UK Border Agency may exceptionally consider this requirement to have been met where the applicant provides full reasons in the passport section of the application form, and either:

    (1)   a current national identity document, or

    (2)   an original letter from his home government or embassy, on the letter-headed paper of the government or embassy, which has been issued by an authorised official of that institution and confirms the applicant's full name, date of birth and nationality.

Degree taught in English

7. 10 points will be awarded for a degree taught in English if the applicant has the relevant level of English language shown in Table 1 and:

    (i)   has obtained an academic qualification (not a professional or vocational qualification) which either:

    (1)   is deemed by UK NARIC to meet the recognised standard of a Bachelor's degree (not a Master's degree or a PhD) in the UK, and UK NARIC has confirmed that the degree was taught or researched in English to level C1 of the Council of Europe's Common European Framework for Language learning or above

    or:

    (2)   is deemed by UK NARIC to meet or exceed the recognised standard of a Bachelor's or Master's degree or a PhD in the UK, and is from an educational establishment in one of the following countries:

    Antigua and Barbuda
    Australia

The Bahamas
Barbados
Belize
Dominica
Grenada
Guyana
Ireland
Jamaica
New Zealand
St Kitts and Nevis
St Lucia
St Vincent and The Grenadines
Trinidad and Tobago
the UK
the USA,
and

    (ii)   provides the following specified documents to show he has the qualification:

        (1)   the original certificate of the award, or

        (2)   if the applicant is awaiting graduation having successfully completed the qualification, or no longer has the certificate and the awarding institution is unable to provide a replacement, an academic transcript (or original letter in the case of a PhD qualification) from the awarding institution on its official headed paper, which clearly shows:

            (a)   the applicant's name,

            (b)   the name of the awarding institution,

            (c)   the title of the award,

            (d)   confirmation that the qualification has been or will be awarded, and

            (e)   the date that the certificate will be issued (if the applicant has not yet graduated) or confirmation that the institution is unable to reissue the original certificate or award.

8.   If the applicant is required to have competence of English to level A1 as set out in Table 1 above (rows G and H), 10 points will be awarded for a degree taught in English if the applicant has the relevant level of English language shown in Table 1 and:

    (i)   has obtained an academic qualification (not a professional or vocational qualification) which is deemed by UK NARIC to meet or exceed the recognised standard of a Bachelor's or Master's degree or a PhD in the UK,

    (ii)   provides the specified documents in paragraph 7(ii) evidence to show that he has the qualification, and

    (iii)   provides provide an original letter from the awarding institution on its official headed paper, which clearly shows:

        (1)   the applicant's name,

        (2)   the name of the awarding institution,

        (3)   the title of the award,

        (4)   the date of the award, and

        (5)   confirmation that the qualification was taught in English.

9.   An applicant for entry clearance or leave to remain as a Tier 1 (Graduate Entrepreneur) can only score the required 10 points for English language by having a qualification taught in English and scoring 75 points under Table 10, Appendix A, unless he scores points in Appendix A for having a Global Endorsement, in which case he can score points from any of the provisions in paragraphs 1 to 8 above or paragraphs 10 to 15 below.

Passed an English language test

10.   10 points will only be awarded for passing an English language test if the applicant has the relevant level of English language shown in Table 1 and provides the specified documents from an English language test provider approved by the Secretary of State for these purposes, as listed in Appendix O, which clearly show:

    (1)   the applicant's name,

(2)   the qualification obtained, which must meet or exceed the relevant level shown in Table 1 in all four components (reading, writing, speaking and listening), unless the applicant was exempted from sitting a component on the basis of his disability,

(3)   the date of the award, and

(4)   that the test is within its validity date (where applicable).

Met requirement in a previous grant of leave

11.   Subject to paragraph 15 below, 10 points will be awarded for meeting the requirement in a previous grant of leave if the applicant:

(i)   has ever been granted leave as a Tier 1 (General) Migrant or a Tier 1 (Entrepreneur) Migrant or Business person, or

(ii)   has ever been granted leave as a Highly Skilled Migrant under the Rules in place on or after 5 December 2006.

12.   Subject to paragraph 15 below, where the application falls under rows B to H of Table 1 above, 10 points will be awarded for meeting the requirement in a previous grant of leave if the applicant has ever been granted leave:

(a)   as a Minister of Religion (not as a Tier 2 (Minister of Religion) Migrant) under the Rules in place on or after 19 April 2007,

(b)   as a Tier 2 (Minister of Religion) Migrant, provided that when he was granted that leave he obtained points for English language for being a national of a majority English speaking country, a degree taught in English, or passing an English language test, or

(c)   as a Tier 4 (General) student, and the Confirmation of Acceptance for Studies used to support that application was assigned on or after 21 April 2011 for a course of at least degree level study.

13.   Subject to paragraph 15 below, where the application falls under rows B to D or rows F to H of Table 1 above, 10 points will be awarded for meeting the requirement in a previous grant of leave if the applicant has ever been granted leave:

(a)   as a Tier 1 (Exceptional Talent) Migrant,

(b)   as a Tier 2 (General) Migrant under the Rules in place on or after 6 April 2011, or

(c)   as a Tier 4 (General) student, and the Confirmation of Acceptance for Studies used to support that application was assigned on or after 21 April 2011,

provided that when he was granted that leave he obtained points for having a knowledge of English equivalent to level B1 of the Council of Europe's Common European Framework for Language Learning or above.

14.   Subject to paragraph 15 below, where the application falls under rows G and H of table 1 above, 10 points will be awarded for meeting the requirement in a previous grant of leave if the applicant has ever been granted:

(i)   leave as a Minister of Religion (not as a Tier 2 (Minister of Religion) Migrant) under the Rules in place on or after 23 August 2004,

(ii)   leave as a Tier 2 Migrant, provided that when he was granted that leave he obtained points for English language for being a national of a majority English speaking country, a degree taught in English, or passing an English language test.

15.   No points will be awarded for meeting the requirement in a previous grant of leave if false representations were made or false documents or information were submitted (whether or not to the applicant's knowledge) in relation to the requirement in the application for that previous grant of leave.

Transitional arrangements

16.   10 points will be awarded for English language if the applicant:

(a)   is applying for leave to remain as a Tier 2 (General) Migrant, and

(b)   has previously been granted entry clearance, leave to enter or leave to remain as:

(i)   a Jewish Agency Employee,

(ii)   a Member of the Operational Ground Staff of an Overseas-owned Airline,

(iii)   a Minister of Religion, Missionary or Member of a Religious Order,

(iv)   a Qualifying Work Permit Holder,

(v)   a Representative of an Overseas Newspaper, News Agency or Broadcasting Organisation

and

(c) has not been granted leave in any categories other than Tier 2 (General), Tier 2 (Intra-Company Transfer) and those listed in (b) above under the Rules in place since 28 November 2008.

17. 10 points will be awarded for English language if the applicant:

(a) is applying for leave to remain as a Tier 2 (Minister of Religion) Migrant,

(b) has previously been granted entry clearance, leave to enter and/or leave to remain as a Minister of Religion, Missionary or Member of a Religious Order, and

(c) has not been granted leave in any categories other than Tier 2 (Minister of Religion) and those listed in (b) above under the Rules in place since 28 November 2008.

18. 10 points will be awarded for English language if the applicant:

(a) is applying for leave to remain as a Tier 2 (Sportsperson) Migrant,

(b) has previously been granted entry clearance, leave to enter and/or leave to remain as a Qualifying Work Permit Holder, and

(c) has not been granted leave in any categories other than Tier 2 (Sportsperson) and as a Qualifying Work Permit Holder under the Rules in place since 28 November 2008.

Appendix C – Maintenance (funds)

1A. In all cases where an applicant is required to obtain points under Appendix C, the applicant must meet the requirements listed below:

(a) The applicant must have the funds specified in the relevant part of Appendix C at the date of the application;

(b) If the applicant is applying as a Tier 1 Migrant, a Tier 2 Migrant or a Tier 5 (Temporary Worker) Migrant, the applicant must have had the funds referred to in (a) above for a consecutive 90-day period of time, unless applying as a Tier 1 (Exceptional Talent) Migrant or a Tier 1 (Investor) Migrant;

(c) If the applicant is applying as a Tier 4 Migrant, the applicant must have had the funds referred to in (a) above for a consecutive 28-day period of time;

(ca) If the applicant is applying for entry clearance or leave to remain as a Tier 4 Migrant, he must confirm that the funds referred to in (a) above are:

(i) available in the manner specified in paragraph 13 below for his use in studying and living in the UK; and

(ii) that the funds will remain available in the manner specified in paragraph 13 below unless used to pay for course fees and living costs;

(d) If the funds were obtained when the applicant was in the UK, the funds must have been obtained while the applicant had valid leave and was not acting in breach of any conditions attached to that leave;

(e) Where the funds are in one or more foreign currencies, the applicant must have the specified level of funds when converted to pound sterling (£) using the spot exchange rate which appears on www.oanda.com* for the date of the application;

(f) Where the applicant is applying as a Tier 1 Migrant, a Tier 2 Migrant or a Tier 5 Migrant, the funds must have been under his own control on the date of the application and for the period specified in (b) above; and

(g) Where the application is made at the same time as applications by the partner or child of the applicant (such that the applicant is a Relevant Points Based System Migrant for the purposes of paragraph 319AA), each applicant must have the total requisite funds specified in the relevant parts of appendices C and E. If each applicant does not individually meet the requirements of appendices C and / or E, as appropriate, all the applications (the application by the Relevant Points Based System Migrant and applications as the partner or child of that relevant Points Based system Migrant) will be refused.

(h) the end date of the 90-day and 28-day periods referred to in (b) and (c) above will be taken as the date of the closing balance on the most recent of the specified documents (where specified documents from two or more accounts are submitted, this will be the end date for the account that most favours the applicant), and must be no earlier than 31 days before the date of application.

(i) No points will be awarded where the specified documents show that the funds are held in a financial institution listed in Appendix P as being an institution with which the UK Border Agency is unable to make satisfactory verification checks.

(j)   Maintenance must be in the form of cash funds. Other accounts or financial instruments such as shares, bonds, pension funds etc, regardless of notice period are not acceptable.

(k)   If the applicant wishes to rely on a joint account as evidence of available funds, the applicant (or for children under 18 years of age, the applicant's parent or legal guardian who is legally present in the United Kingdom) must be named on the account as one of the account holders.

(l)   Overdraft facilities will not be considered towards funds that are available or under an applicant's own control.

1B.   In all cases where Appendix C or Appendix E states that an applicant is required to provide specified documents, the specified documents are:

(a)   Personal bank or building society statements which satisfy the following requirements:

(i)   The statements must cover:

(1)   a consecutive 90-day period of time, if the applicant is applying as a Tier 1 Migrant, a Tier 2 Migrant a Tier 5 (Temporary Worker) Migrant, or the Partner or Child of a Relevant Points Based System Migrant in any of these categories,

(2)   a single date within 31 days of the date of the application, if the applicant is applying as a Tier 5 (Youth Mobility Scheme) Migrant, or

(3)   a consecutive 28-day period of time, if the applicant is applying as a Tier 4 Migrant or the Partner or Child of a Relevant Points Based System Migrant who is a Tier 4 Migrant

(ii)   The most recent statement must be dated no earlier than 31 days before the date of the application;

(iii)   The statements must clearly show:

(1)   the name of:

(i)   the applicant,

(ii)   the applicant's parent(s) or legal guardian's name, if the applicant is applying as Tier 4 Migrant,

(iii)   the name of the Relevant Points-Based System Migrant, if the applicant is applying as a Partner or Child of a Relevant Points-Based System Migrant, or

(iv)   the name of the applicant's other parent who is legally present in the UK, if the applicant is applying as a Child of a Relevant Points-Based System Migrant,

(2)   the account number,

(3)   the date of each statement,

(4)   the financial institution's name,

(5)   the financial institution's logo,

(6)   any transactions during the specified period, and

(7)   that the funds in the account have been at the required level throughout the specified period;

(iv)   The statements must be be either:

(1)   printed on the bank's or building society's letterhead,

(2)   electronic bank or building society statements, accompanied by a supporting letter from the bank or building society, on company headed paper, confirming the statement provided is authentic, or

(3)   electronic bank or building society statements, bearing the official stamp of the bank or building society on every page,

(v)   The statements must not be mini-statements from automatic teller machines (ATMs);

or

(b)   A building society pass book which satisfies the following requirements:

(i)   The building society pass book must cover:

(1)   a consecutive 90-day period of time, if the applicant is applying as a Tier 1 Migrant, a Tier 2 Migrant a Tier 5 (Temporary Worker) Migrant, or the Partner or Child of a Relevant Points Based System Migrant in any of these categories,

(2)   a single date within 31 days of the date of the application, if the applicant is applying as a Tier 5 (Youth Mobility Scheme) Migrant, or

> (3)   a consecutive 28-day period of time, if the applicant is applying as a Tier 4 Migrant or the Partner or Child of a Relevant Points Based System Migrant who is a Tier 4 Migrant

(ii)   The period covered by the building society pass book must end no earlier than 31 days before the date of the application;

(iii)   The building society pass book must clearly show:

> (1)   the name of:
>
> > (i)   the applicant,
> >
> > (ii)   he applicant's parent(s) or legal guardian's name, if the applicant is applying as Tier 4 Migrant,
> >
> > (iii)   the name of the Relevant Points-Based System Migrant, if the applicant is applying as a Partner or Child of a Relevant Points-Based System Migrant, or
> >
> > (iv)   the name of the applicant's other parent who is legally present in the UK, if the applicant is applying as a Child of a Relevant Points-Based System Migrant,
>
> (2)   the account number,
>
> (3)   the building society's name and logo,
>
> (4)   any transactions during the specified period, and
>
> (5)   that there have been enough funds in the applicant's account throughout the specified period;

or

(c)   A letter from the applicant's bank or building society, or a letter from a financial institution regulated for the purpose of personal savings accounts by the Financial Conduct Authority (FCA) and the Prudential Regulation Authority (PRA) or, for overseas accounts, the official regulatory body for the country in which the institution operates and the funds are located, which satisfies the following requirements:

(i)   The letter must confirm the level of funds and that they have been held for:

> (1)   a consecutive 90-day period of time, if the applicant is applying as a Tier 1 Migrant, a Tier 2 Migrant a Tier 5 (Temporary Worker) Migrant, or the Partner or Child of a Relevant Points Based System Migrant in any of these categories,
>
> (2)   a single date within 31 days of the date of the application, if the applicant is applying as a Tier 5 (Youth Mobility Scheme) Migrant, or
>
> (3)   a consecutive 28-day period of time, if the applicant is applying as a Tier 4 Migrant or the Partner or Child of a Relevant Points Based System Migrant who is a Tier 4 Migrant;

(ii)   The period covered by the letter must end no earlier than 31 days before the date of the application;

(iii)   The letter must be dated no earlier than 31 days before the date of the application;

(iv)   The letter must be on the financial institution's letterhead or official stationery;

(v)   The letter must clearly show:

> (1)   the name of:
>
> > (i)   the applicant,
> >
> > (ii)   the applicant's parent(s) or legal guardian's name, if the applicant is applying as Tier 4 Migrant,
> >
> > (iii)   the name of the Relevant Points-Based System Migrant, if the applicant is applying as a Partner or Child of a Relevant Points-Based System Migrant, or
> >
> > (iv)   the name of the applicant's other parent who is legally present in the UK, if the applicant is applying as a Child of a Relevant Points-Based System Migrant,
>
> (2)   the account number,
>
> (3)   the date of the letter,
>
> (4)   the financial institution's name and logo,
>
> (5)   the funds held in the applicant's account, and
>
> (5)   confirmation that there have been enough funds in the applicant's account throughout the specified period;

or

(d)   If the applicant is applying as a Tier 4 Migrant, an original loan letter from a financial institution regulated for the purpose of student loans by either the Financial Conduct Authority (FCA) and the Prudential Regulation Authority (PRA) or, in the case of overseas accounts, the official regulatory body for the country the institution is in and where the money is held, which is dated no more than 6 months before the date of the application and clearly shows:

(1)   the applicant's name,

(2)   the date of the letter,

(3)   the financial institution's name and logo,

(4)   the money available as a loan,

(5)   for applications for entry clearance, that the loan funds are or will be available to the applicant before he travels to the UK, unless the loan is an academic or student loan from the applicant's country's national government and will be released to the applicant on arrival in the UK,

(6)   there are no conditions placed upon the release of the loan funds to the applicant, other than him making a successful application as a Tier 4 Migrant, and

(7)   the loan is provided by the national government, the state or regional government or a government sponsored student loan company or is part of an academic or educational loans scheme.

Tier 1 Migrants

1.   An applicant applying for entry clearance or leave to remain as a Tier 1 Migrant must score 10 points for funds, unless applying as a Tier 1 (Exceptional Talent) Migrant or a Tier 1 (Investor) Migrant.

2.   10 points will only be awarded if an applicant:

(a)   applying for entry clearance, has the level of funds shown in the table below and provides the specified documents in paragraph 1B above, or

Category	Level of funds	Points
Tier 1 (Entrepreneur)	£3,100	10
Tier 1 (Graduate Entrepreneur)	£1,800	10

(b)   applying for leave to remain, has the level of funds shown in the table below and provides the specified documents in paragraph 1B above, or

Level of funds	Points
£900	10

(c)   applying as a Tier 1 (Graduate Entrepreneur) Migrant scores points from Appendix A for a Global Endorsement, and UK Trade and Investment has confirmed in the endorsement letter that it has awarded funding of at least £1,800 (for entry clearance applications) or £900 (for leave to remain applications) to the applicant.

3.   Where the applicant is applying as a Tier 1 (Entrepreneur) Migrant, he cannot use the same funds to score points for attributes under Appendix A and to score points for maintenance funds for himself or his dependants under this Appendix or Appendix E.

Tier 2 Migrants

4.   An applicant applying for entry clearance or leave to remain as a Tier 2 Migrant must score 10 points for Funds.

5.   10 points will only be awarded if:

(a)   the applicant has the level of funds shown in the table below and provides the specified documents in paragraph 1B above, or

Level of funds	Points awarded
£900	10

(b)   the applicant has entry clearance, leave to enter or leave to remain as:

(i)   a Tier 2 Migrant

(ii)   a Jewish Agency Employee

      (iii)   A member of the Operational Ground Staff of an Overseas-owned Airline,

      (iv)   a Minister of Religion, Missionary or Member of a Religious Order,

      (v)   a Representative of an Overseas Newspaper, News Agency or Broadcasting Organisation, or

      (vi)   a Work Permit Holder, or

(c)   the Sponsor is an a rated Sponsor and has certified on the Certificate of Sponsorship that, should it become necessary, it will maintain and accommodate the migrant up to the end of the first month of his employment. The Sponsor may limit the amount of the undertaking but any limit must be at least £900. Points will only be awarded if the applicant provides a valid Certificate of Sponsorship reference number with his application.

Tier 5 (Youth Mobility) Temporary Migrants

6.   An applicant applying for entry clearance as a Tier 5 (Youth Mobility) Temporary Migrant must score 10 points for funds.

7.   10 points will only be awarded if an applicant has the level of funds shown in the table below and provides the specified documents in paragraph 1B above:

Level of funds	Points awarded
£1800	10

Tier 5 (Temporary Worker) Migrants

8.   A migrant applying for entry clearance or leave to remian as a Tier 5 (Temporary Worker) Migrant must score 10 points for funds.

9.   10 points will only be awarded if an applicant has the level of funds shown in the table below and provides the specified documents in paragraph 1B above:

Criterion	Points awarded
Meets one of the following criteria: Has £900; or The Sponsor is an A rated Sponsor and the Certificate of Sponsorship Checking Service confirms that the Sponsor has certified that the applicant will not claim public funds during his period of leave as a Tier 5 (Temporary Worker) Migrant. Points will only be awarded if the applicant provides a valid Certificate of Sponsorship reference number with his application.	10

Tier 4 (General) Students

10.   A Tier 4 (General) Student must score 10 points for funds.

11.   10 points will only be awarded if the funds shown in the table below are available in the manner specified in paragraph 13 and 13A below to the applicant. The applicant must either:

(a)   provide the specified documents in paragraph 1B above to show that the funds are available to him, or

(b)   where the applicant is sponsored by a Highly Trusted Sponsor, is a national of one of the countries or the rightful holder of a qualifying passport issued by one of the relevant competent authorities, as appropriate, listed in Appendix H, and is applying for entry clearance in his country of nationality or in the territory related to the passport he holds, as appropriate, or leave to remain in the UK, confirm that the funds are available to him in the specified manner. The UK Border Agency reserves the right to request the specified documents in paragraph 1B above from these applicants to support this confirmation. The application will be refused if the specified documents are not provided in accordance with the request made.

Criterion	Points
If studying in inner London: (i) Where the applicant does not have an established presence studying in the United Kingdom, the applicant must have funds amounting to the full course fees for the first academic year of the course, or for the entire course if it is less than a year long, plus £1000 for each month of the course up to a maximum of nine months.	10

Criterion		Points
(ii)	Where the applicant has an established presence studying in the United Kingdom, the applicant must have funds amounting to the course fees required either for the remaining academic year if the applicant is applying part-way through, or for the next academic year if the applicant will continue or commence a new course at the start of the next academic year, or for the entire course if it is less than a year long, plus £1000 for each month of the course up to a maximum of two months.	
If studying in outer London and elsewhere in the United Kingdom:		10
(i)	Where the applicant does not have an established presence studying in the United Kingdom, the applicant must have funds amounting to the full course fees for the first academic year of the course, or for the entire course if it is less than a year long, plus £800 for each month of the course up to a maximum of nine months.	
(ii)	Where the applicant has an established presence studying in the United Kingdom, the applicant must have funds amounting to the course fees required either for the remaining academic year if the applicant is applying part-way through, or for the next academic year if the applicant will continue or commence a new course at the start of the next academic year, or for the entire course if it is less than a year long, plus £800 for each month of the course up to a maximum of two months.	

Notes

12.   An applicant will be considered to be studying in inner London if the institution, or branch of the institution, at which the applicant will be studying is situated in any of the London boroughs of Camden, City of London, Hackney, Hammersmith and Fulham, Haringey, Islington, Kensington and Chelsea, Lambeth, Lewisham, Newham Southwark, Tower Hamlets, Wandsworth, or Westminster. If the applicant will be studying at more than one site, one or more of which is in inner London and one or more outside, then the applicant will be considered to be studying in inner London if the applicant's Confirmation of Acceptance for Studies states that the applicant will be spending the majority of time studying at a site or sites situated in inner London.

12A.   If the length of the applicant's course includes a part of a month, the time will be rounded up to the next full month.

13.   Funds will be available to the applicant only where the specified documents show or, where permitted by these Rules, the applicant confirms that the funds are held or provided by:

(i)   the applicant (whether as a sole or joint account holder); and/or

(ii)   the applicant's parent(s) or legal guardian(s), and the parent(s) or legal guardian(s) have provided written consent that their funds may be used by the applicant in order to study in the UK; and/or

(iii)   an official financial sponsor which must be Her Majesty's Government, the applicant's home government, the British Council or any international organisation, international company, University or Independent school.

13A.   In assessing whether the requirements of Appendix C, paragraph 11 are met, where an applicant pays a deposit on account to the sponsor for accommodation costs this amount, up to a maximum of £1000, can be offset against the total maintenance requirement if he will be staying in accommodation arranged by the Tier 4 sponsor and he has paid this money to that Tier 4 sponsor.

13B.   If the applicant is relying on the provisions in paragraph 13(ii) above, he must provide:

(a)   one of the following original (or notarised copy) documents:

(i)   his birth certificate showing names of his parent(s),

(ii)   his certificate of adoption showing the names of both parent(s) or legal guardian, or

(iii)   a Court document naming his legal guardian;

and

(b)   a letter from his parent(s) or legal guardian, confirming:

(1)   the relationship between the applicant and his parent(s) or legal guardian, and

(2)   that the parent(s) or legal guardian give their consent to the applicant using their funds to study in the UK.

13C.   If the applicant has already paid all or part of the course fees to his Tier 4 Sponsor:

(a)   the Confirmation of Acceptance for Studies Checking Service entry must confirm details of the fees already paid; or

(b)   the applicant must provide an original paper receipt issued by the Tier 4 Sponsor, confirming details of the fees already paid.

13D.   If the applicant has an official financial sponsor as set out in paragraph 13(iii) above:

(a)   the Confirmation of Acceptance for Studies Checking Service entry must confirm details of the official financial sponsorship, if it is the Tier 4 Sponsor who is the official financial sponsor; or

(b)   the applicant must provide a letter of confirmation from his official financial sponsor, on official letter-headed paper or stationery of that organisation and bearing the official stamp of that organisation, which clearly shows:

(1)   the applicant's name,

(2)   the name and contact details of the official financial sponsor,

(3)   the date of the letter,

(4)   the length of the official financial sponsorship, and

(5)   the amount of money the official financial sponsor is giving to the applicant, or a statement that the official financial sponsor will cover all of the applicant's fees and living costs.

14.   An applicant will have an established presence studying in the UK if the applicant has current entry clearance, leave to enter or leave to remain as a Tier 4 migrant, Student or as a Postgraduate Doctor or Dentist and at the date of application:

(i)   has finished a single course that was at least six months long within the applicant's last period of entry clearance, leave to enter or leave to remain, or

(ii)   is applying for continued study on a single course where the applicant has completed at least six months of that course, or

(iii)   is applying for leave to remain as a Tier 4 (General) Student on the doctorate extension scheme.

Tier 4 (Child) Students

15.   A Tier 4 (Child) Student must score 10 points for funds.

16.   10 points will only be awarded if the funds shown in the table below are available in the manner specified in paragraph 21 *and* 21A below to the applicant. The applicant must either:

(a)   provide the specified documents in paragraph 1B above to show that the funds are available to him, or

(b)   where the applicant is sponsored by a Highly Trusted Sponsor, is a national of one of the countries or the rightful holder of a qualifying passport issued by one of the relevant competent authorities, as appropriate, listed in Appendix H, and is applying for entry clearance in his country of nationality or in the territory related to the passport he holds, as appropriate, or leave to remain in the UK, confirm that the funds are available to him in the specified manner. The UK Border Agency reserves the right to request the specified documents in paragraph 1B above from these applicants to support this confirmation. The application will be refused if the specified documents are not provided in accordance with the request made.(

Criterion	Points
Where the child is (or will be) studying at a residential independent school: sufficient funds are available to the applicant to pay boarding fees (being course fees plus board/lodging fees) for an academic year.	10
Where the child is (or will be) studying at a non-residential independent school and is in a private foster care arrangement (see notes below) or staying with and cared for by a close relative (see notes below): sufficient funds are available to the applicant to pay school fees for an academic year, the foster carer or relative (who must meet the requirements specified in paragraph 19 of this Appendix) has undertaken to maintain and accommodate the child for the duration of the course, and that foster carer or relative has funds equivalent to at least £550 per month, for up to a maximum of nine months, to support the child while he is in the United Kingdom.	10

Criterion	Points
Where the child is (or will be) studying at a non-residential independent school, is under the age of 12 and is (or will be) accompanied by a parent, sufficient funds are available to the applicant to pay school fees for an academic year, plus: if no other children are accompanying the applicant and the parent, £1500 per month of stay up to a maximum of nine months; or if other children are accompanying the applicant and the parent, £1500 per month, plus £600 per month for each additional child, up to a maximum of nine months.	10
Where the child is aged 16 or 17 years old and is living independently and studying in inner London: (i) Where the applicant does not have an established presence studying in the United Kingdom, the applicant must have funds amounting to the full course fees for the first academic year of the course, or for the entire course if it is less than a year long, plus £900 for each month of the course up to a maximum of nine months. (ii) Where the applicant has an established presence studying in the United Kingdom, the applicant must have funds amounting to the course fees required either for the remaining academic year if the applicant is applying part-way through, or for the next academic year if the applicant will continue or commence a new course at the start of the next academic year, or for the entire course if it is less than a year long, plus £900 for each month of the course up to a maximum of two months.	10
Where the child is aged 16 or 17 years old, is living independently and studying in outer London or elsewhere in the United Kingdom: (iii) Where the applicant does not have an established presence studying in the United Kingdom, the applicant must have funds amounting to the full course fees for the first academic year of the course, or for the entire course if it is less than a year long, plus £700 for each month of the course up to a maximum of nine months. (iv) Where the applicant has an established presence studying in the United Kingdom, the applicant must have funds amounting to the course fees required either for the remaining academic year if the applicant is applying part-way through, or for the next academic year if the applicant will continue or commence a new course at the start of the next academic year, or for the entire course if it is less than a year long, plus £700 for each month of the course up to a maximum of two months.	10

17.–22.   OMITTED

Appendix D – OMITTED

Appendix E – Maintenance (funds) for the family of Relevant Points Based Systems Migrants

A sufficient level of funds must be available to an applicant applying as the Partner or Child of a Relevant Points Based System Migrant. A sufficient level of funds will only be available if the requirements below are met.

(aa)   Paragraphs 1A and 1B of Appendix C also apply to this Appendix.

(ab)   Where the application is connected to a Tier 1 (Entrepreneur) Migrant, the applicant cannot use the same funds to score points for maintenance funds from this Appendix as the Tier 1 (Entrepreneur) Migrant used to score points for attributes under Appendix A.

(a)   Where the application is connected to a Tier 1 Migrant (other than a Tier 1 (Investor) Migrant or a Tier 1 (Exceptional Talent) Migrant) who is outside the UK or who has been in the UK for a period of less than 12 months, there must be:

  (i)   £1,200 in funds, where the application is connected to a Tier 1 (Graduate Entrepreneur) Migrant;

  (ii)   £1,800 in funds in other cases.

(b)   Where:

(i)   paragraph (a) does not apply, and

(ii)   the application is connected to a Relevant Points Based System Migrant who is not a Tier 1 (Investor) Migrant a Tier 1 (Exceptional Talent) Migrant or a Tier 4 (General) Student there must be £600 in funds.

(ba)   (i)   Where the application is connected to a Tier 4 (General) Student:

        (1)   if the Tier 4 (General) Student is studying in inner London (as defined in paragraph 12 of Appendix C), there must be £600 in funds for each month for which the applicant would, if successful, be granted leave under paragraph 319D(a), up to a maximum of £5,400, or

        (2)   if the Tier 4 (General) Student is not studying in inner London, there must be £450 in funds for each month for which the applicant would, if successful, be granted leave under paragraph 319D(a), up to a maximum of £4,050,

    and in each case

        (3)   the applicant must confirm that the funds referred to in (1) or (2) above are:

            (i)   available in the manner specified in paragraph (f) below for use in living costs in the UK; and

            (ii)   that the funds will remain available in the manner specified in paragraph (f) below unless used to pay for living costs.

(c)   Where the applicant is applying as the Partner of a Relevant Points Based System Migrant the relevant amount of funds must be available to either the applicant or the Relevant Points Based System Migrant.

(d)   Where the applicant is applying as the Child of a Relevant Points Based System Migrant, the relevant amount of funds must be available to the applicant, the Relevant Points Based System Migrant, or the applicant's other parent who is Lawfully present in the UK or being granted entry clearance, or leave to enter or remain, at the same time.

(e)   Where the Relevant Points Based System Migrant is applying for entry clearance or leave to remain at the same time as the applicant, the amount of funds available to the applicant must be in addition to the level of funds required separately of the Relevant Points Based System Migrant.

(f)   In all cases, the funds in question must be available to:

(i)   the applicant, or

(ii)   where he is applying as the partner of a Relevant Points Based System Migrant, either to him or to that Relevant Points Based System Migrant, or

(iii)   where he is applying as the child of a Relevant Points Based System Migrant, either to him, to the Relevant Points Based System Migrant or to the child's other parent who is lawfully present in the UK or being granted entry clearance, or leave to enter or remain, at the same time;

(g)   The funds in question must have been available to the person referred to in (f) above on the date of the application and for:

(i)   a consecutive 90-day period of time, if the applicant is applying as the Partner or Child of a Tier 1 Migrant (other than a Tier 1 (Investor) Migrant) or a Tier 1 (Exceptional Talent) Migrant, a Tier 2 Migrant or a Tier 5 (Temporary Worker) Migrant;

(ii)   a consecutive 28-day period of time, if the applicant is applying as the Partner or Child of a Tier 4 (General) Student;

(h)   If the funds in question were obtained when the person referred to in (f) above was in the UK, the funds must have been obtained while that person had valid leave and was not acting in breach of any conditions attached to that leave; and

(i)   In the following cases, sufficient funds will be deemed to be available where all of the following conditions are met:

(1)   the Relevant Points Based System Migrant to whom the application is connected has, or is being granted, leave as a Tier 2 Migrant,

(2)   the Sponsor of that Relevant Points Based System Migrant is A-rated, and

(3)   that Sponsor has certified on the Certificate of Sponsorship that, should it become necessary, it will maintain and accommodate the dependants of the relevant Points Based System Migrant up to the end of the first month of the dependant's leave, if granted. The undertaking may be limited provided the limit is at least £600 per dependant. If the relevant Points Based System Migrant is applying at the same time as the applicant, points will only be awarded if the Relevant

Points Based System Migrant provides a valid Certificate of Sponsorship reference number with his application.

(ia)   Sufficient funds will not be deemed to be available to the Partner or Child if the specified documents, as set out in paragraph 1B of Appendix C, show that the funds are held in a financial institution listed in Appendix P as being an institution with which the UK Border Agency is unable to make satisfactory verification checks.

(ib)   Sufficient funds will be deemed to be available where the application is connected to a Tier 1 (Graduate Entrepreneur) Migrant who scores, or scored, points from Appendix A for a Global Endorsement, and UK Trade and Investment has confirmed in the endorsement letter that it has awarded funding that is at least sufficient to cover the required maintenance funds for the Tier 1 (Graduate Entrepreneur) Migrant, the applicant and any other dependants.

(j)   In all cases the applicant must provide the specified documents as set out in paragraph 1B of Appendix C, unless the applicant is applying at the same time as the Relevant Points Based System Migrant who is a Tier 4 (General) Student sponsored by a Highly Trusted Sponsor, is a national of one of the countries or the rightful holder of a qualifying passport issued by one of the relevant competent authorities, as appropriate, listed in Appendix H, and is applying for entry clearance in his country of nationality or in the territory related to the passport he holds, as appropriate, or leave to remain in the UK and the applicant is also a national of the same country, and confirms these requirements are met, in which case the specified documents shall not be required. The UK Border Agency reserves the right to request the specified documents from these applicants. The application will be refused if the specified documents are not provided in accordance with the request made.

(k)   Where the funds are in one or more foreign currencies, the applicant must have the specified level of funds when converted to pound sterling (£) using the spot exchange rate which appears on www.oanda.com* for the date of the application.

(l)   Where the application is one of a number of applications made at the same time as a partner or child of a Relevant Points Based System Migrant (as set out in paragraphs 319A and 319F) each applicant, including the Relevant Points Based System Migrant if applying at the same time, must have the total requisite funds specified in the relevant parts of appendices C and E. if each applicant does not individually meet the requirements of appendices C and / or E, as appropriate, all the applications (the application by the Relevant Points Based System Migrant and applications as the partner or child of that Relevant Points Based System Migrant) will be refused.

(m)   The end date of the 90-day and 28-day periods referred to in (g) above will be taken as the date of the closing balance on the most recent of the specified documents (where specified documents from two or more accounts are submitted, this will be the end date for the account that most favours the applicant), as set out in paragraph 1B of Appendix C, and must be no earlier than 31 days before the date of application.

(n)   If:

(i)   the Relevant Points-Based System Migrant is a Tier 4 (General) Student who has official financial sponsorship as set out in paragraph 13(iii) of Appendix C, and

(ii)   this sponsorship is intended to cover costs of the Relevant Points-Based System Migrant's family member(s),

the applicant must provide a letter of confirmation from the Tier 4 (General) Student's official financial sponsor which satisfies the requirements in paragraph 13D of Appendix C, and confirms that the sponsorship will cover costs of the applicant in addition to costs of the Relevant Points-Based System Migrant.

(o)   Where the Relevant Points Based System Migrant is applying for entry clearance or leave to remain at the same time as the applicant, and is not required to provide evidence of maintenance funds because of the provisions in paragraph 5(b) of Appendix C, the applicant is also not required to provide evidence of maintenance funds.

(p)   Overdraft facilities will not be considered towards funds that are available or under an applicant's own control.

Appendix F – OMITTED

Appendix FM family members

Section GEN: General

Purpose

GEN.1.1. This route is for those seeking to enter or remain in the UK on the basis of their family life with a person who is a British Citizen, is settled in the UK, or is in the UK with limited leave as a refugee or person granted humanitarian protection (and the applicant cannot seek leave to enter or remain in the UK as their family member under Part 11 of these rules). It sets out the requirements to be met and, in considering applications under this route, it reflects how, under Article 8 of the Human Rights Convention, the balance will be struck between the right to respect for private and family life and the legitimate aims of protecting national security, public safety and the economic well-being of the UK; the prevention of disorder and crime; the protection of health or morals; and the protection of the rights and freedoms of others. It also takes into account the need to safeguard and promote the welfare of children in the UK.

Definitions

GEN.1.2. For the purposes of this Appendix 'partner' means–

(i)   the applicant's spouse;

(ii)   the applicant's civil partner;

(iii)   the applicant's fiancé(e) or proposed civil partner; or

(iv)   a person who has been living together with the applicant in a relationship akin to a marriage or civil partnership for at least two years prior to the date of application,

unless the context otherwise requires.

GEN.1.3. For the purposes of this Appendix

(a)   'application for leave to remain' also includes an application for variation of leave to enter or remain by a person in the UK;

(b)   references to a person being present and settled in the UK also include a person who is being admitted for settlement on the same occasion as the applicant; and

(c)   references to a British Citizen in the UK also include a British Citizen who is coming to the UK with the applicant as their partner or parent.

GEN.1.4. In this Appendix 'specified' means specified in Appendix FM-SE, unless otherwise stated.

GEN.1.5. If the Entry Clearance Officer, or Secretary of State, has reasonable cause to doubt the genuineness of any document submitted in support of an application, and having taken reasonable steps to verify the document, is unable to verify that it is genuine, the document will be discounted for the purposes of the application.

GEN.1.6. For the purposes of paragraph E-ECP.4.1.(a); E-LTRP.4.1.(a); EECPT. 4.1(a) and E-LTRPT.5.1.(a) the applicant must be a national of Antigua and Barbuda; Australia; the Bahamas; Barbados; Belize; Canada; Dominica; Grenada; Guyana; Jamaica; New Zealand; St Kitts and Nevis; St Lucia; St Vincent and the Grenadines; Trinidad and Tobago; or the United States of America.

GEN.1.7. In this Appendix references to paragraphs are to paragraphs of this Appendix unless the context otherwise requires.

GEN.1.8. Paragraphs 277–280, 289AA, 295AA and 296 of Part 8 of these Rules shall apply to this Appendix.

GEN.1.9. In this Appendix (a) the requirement to make a valid application will not apply when the Article 8 claim is raised:

(i)   as part of an asylum claim, or as part of a further submission in person after an asylum claim has been refused;

(ii)   where a migrant is in immigration detention;

(iii)   where removal directions have been set pending an imminent removal;

(iv)   in an appeal; or

(v)   in response to a (one stop) notice issued under section 120 of the Nationality, Immigration and Asylum Act 2002 and (b) where the Article 8 claim is raised in any of the circumstances specified in paragraph GEN.1.9.(a), or is considered by the Secretary of State under paragraph A277C of these rules, the requirements of paragraphs R-LTRP.1.1.(c) and R-LTRPT.1.1.(c) are not met.

Leave to enter

GEN.2.1.   The requirements to be met by a person seeking leave to enter the UK under this route are that the person–

(a)   must have a valid entry clearance for entry under this route; and

(b)   must produce to the Immigration Officer on arrival a valid national passport or other document satisfactorily establishing their identity and nationality.

GEN.2.2.   If a person does not meet the requirements of paragraph GEN.2.1. entry will be refused.

Family life with a Partner

Section EC-P: Entry clearance as a partner

EC-P.1.1.   The requirements to be met for entry clearance as a partner are that–

(a)   the applicant must be outside the UK;

(b)   the applicant must have made a valid application for entry clearance as a partner;

(c)   the applicant must not fall for refusal under any of the grounds in Section S-EC: Suitability–entry clearance; and

(d)   the applicant must meet all of the requirements of Section E-ECP:

Eligibility for entry clearance as a partner.

Section S-EC: Suitability-entry clearance

S-EC.1.1.   The applicant will be refused entry clearance on grounds of suitability if any of paragraphs S-EC.1.2. to 1.8. apply.

S-EC.1.2.   The Secretary of State has personally directed that the exclusion of the applicant from the UK is conducive to the public good.

S-EC.1.3.   The applicant is at the date of application the subject of a deportation order.

S-EC.1.4.   The exclusion of the applicant from the UK is conducive to the public good because they have:

(a)   been convicted of an offence for which they have been sentenced to a period of imprisonment of at least 4 years; or

(b)   been convicted of an offence for which they have been sentenced to a period of imprisonment of at least 12 months but less than 4 years, unless a period of 10 years has passed since the end of the sentence; or

(c)   been convicted of an offence for which they have been sentenced to a period of imprisonment of less than 12 months, unless a period of 5 years has passed since the end of the sentence.

Where this paragraph applies, unless refusal would be contrary to the Human Rights Convention or the Convention and Protocol Relating to the Status of Refugees, it will only be in exceptional circumstances that the public interest in maintaining refusal will be outweighed by compelling factors.

S-EC.1.5.   The exclusion of the applicant from the UK is conducive to the public good because, for example, the applicant's conduct (including convictions which do not fall within paragraph S-EC.1.4.), character, associations, or other reasons, make it undesirable to grant them entry clearance.

S-EC.1.6.   The applicant has failed without reasonable excuse to comply with a requirement to–

(a)   attend an interview;

(b)   provide information;

(c)   provide physical data; or

(d)   undergo a medical examination or provide a medical report.

S-EC.1.7.   It is undesirable to grant entry clearance to the applicant for medical reasons.

S-EC.1.8.   The applicant left or was removed from the UK as a condition of a caution issued in accordance with section 134 of the Legal Aid, Sentencing and Punishment of Offenders Act 2012 less than 5 years prior to the date on which the application is decided.

S-EC.2.1.   The applicant will normally be refused on grounds of suitability if any of paragraphs S-EC.2.2. to 2.5. apply.

S-EC.2.2.   Whether or not to the applicant's knowledge–

(a)   false information, representations or documents have been submitted in relation to the application (including false information submitted to any person to obtain a document used in support of the application); or

(b)   there has been a failure to disclose material facts in relation to the application.

S-EC.2.3.   One or more relevant NHS body has notified the Secretary of State that the applicant has failed to pay charges in accordance with the relevant NHS regulations on charges to overseas visitors and the outstanding charges have a total value of at least £1000.

S-EC.2.4.   A maintenance and accommodation undertaking has been requested or required under paragraph 35 of these Rules or otherwise and has not been provided.

S-EC.2.5.   The exclusion of the applicant from the UK is conducive to the public good because:

(a)   within the 12 months preceding the date of the application, the person has been convicted of or admitted an offence for which they received a non-custodial sentence or other out of court disposal that is recorded on their criminal record; or

(b)   in the view of the Secretary of State:

(i)   the person's offending has caused serious harm; or

(ii)   the person is a persistent offender who shows a particular disregard for the law.

Section E-ECP: Eligibility for entry clearance as a partner

E-ECP.1.1.   To meet the eligibility requirements for entry clearance as a partner all of the requirements in paragraphs E-ECP.2.1. to 4.2. must be met.

Relationship requirements

E-ECP.2.1.   The applicant's partner must be–

(a)   a British Citizen in the UK, subject to paragraph GEN.1.3.(c); or

(b)   present and settled in the UK, subject to paragraph GEN.1.3.(b); or

(c)   in the UK with refugee leave or with humanitarian protection.

E-ECP.2.2.   The applicant must be aged 18 or over at the date of application.

E-ECP.2.3.   The partner must be aged 18 or over at the date of application.

E-ECP.2.4.   The applicant and their partner must not be within the prohibited degree of relationship.

E-ECP.2.5.   The applicant and their partner must have met in person.

E-ECP.2.6.   The relationship between the applicant and their partner must be genuine and subsisting.

E-ECP.2.7.   If the applicant and partner are married or in a civil partnership it must be a valid marriage or civil partnership, as specified.

E-ECP.2.8.   If the applicant is a fiancé(e) or proposed civil partner they must be seeking entry to the UK to enable their marriage or civil partnership to take place.

E-ECP.2.9.   Any previous relationship of the applicant or their partner must have broken down permanently, unless it is a relationship which falls within paragraph 278(i) of these Rules.

E-ECP.2.10.   The applicant and partner must intend to live together permanently in the UK.

Financial requirements

E-ECP.3.1.   The applicant must provide specified evidence, from the sources listed in paragraph E-ECP.3.2., of–

(a)   a specified gross annual income of at least–

(i)   £18,600;

(ii)   an additional £3,800 for the first child; and

(iii)   an additional £2,400 for each additional child; alone or in combination with

(b)   specified savings of–

(i)   £16,000; and

(ii)   additional savings of an amount equivalent to 2.5 times the amount which is the difference between the gross annual income from the sources listed in paragraph E-ECP.3.2.(a)–(d) and the total amount required under paragraph E-ECP.3.1.(a); or

(c)   the requirements in paragraph E-ECP.3.3.being met.

In this paragraph 'child' means a dependent child of the applicant who is–

(a)   under the age of 18 years, or who was under the age of 18 years when they were first granted entry under this route;

(b)   applying for entry clearance as a dependant of the applicant, or has limited leave to enter or remain in the UK;

(c)   not a British Citizen or settled in the UK; and

(d)   not an EEA national with a right to be admitted under the Immigration (EEA) Regulations 2006.

E-ECP.3.2.   When determining whether the financial requirement in paragraph EECP.3.1. is met only the following sources will be taken into account–

(a)   income of the partner from specified employment or self-employment, which, in respect of a partner returning to the UK with the applicant, can include specified employment or self-employment overseas and in the UK;

(b)   specified pension income of the applicant and partner;

(c)   any specified maternity allowance or bereavement benefit received by the partner in the UK;

(d)   other specified income of the applicant and partner; and

(e)   specified savings of the applicant and partner.

E-ECP.3.3.   The requirements to be met under this paragraph are–

(a)   the applicant's partner must be receiving one or more of the following –

(i)   disability living allowance;

(ii)   severe disablement allowance;

(iii)   industrial injury disablement benefit;

(iv)   attendance allowance;

(v)   carer's allowance; or

(vi)   personal independence payment; and

(b)   the applicant must provide evidence that their partner is able to maintain and accommodate themselves, the applicant and any dependants adequately in the UK without recourse to public funds.

E-ECP.3.4.   The applicant must provide evidence that there will be adequate accommodation, without recourse to public funds, for the family, including other family members who are not included in the application but who live in the same household, which the family own or occupy exclusively: accommodation will not be regarded as adequate if–

(a)   it is, or will be, overcrowded; or

(b)   it contravenes public health regulations.

English language requirement

E-ECP.4.1.   The applicant must provide specified evidence that they–

(a)   are a national of a majority English speaking country listed in paragraph GEN.1.6.;

(b)   have passed an English language test in speaking and listening at a minimum of level A1 of the Common European Framework of Reference for Languages with a provider approved by the Secretary of State;

(c)   have an academic qualification recognised by UK NARIC to be equivalent to the standard of a Bachelor's or Master's degree or PhD in the UK, which was taught in English; or

(d)   are exempt from the English language requirement under paragraph EECP. 4.2.

E-ECP.4.2.   The applicant is exempt from the English language requirement if at the date of application–

(a)   the applicant is aged 65 or over;

(b)   the applicant has a disability (physical or mental condition) which prevents the applicant from meeting the requirement; or

(c)   there are exceptional circumstances which prevent the applicant from being able to meet the requirement prior to entry to the UK.

Section D-ECP: Decision on application for entry clearance as a partner

D-ECP.1.1.   If the applicant meets the requirements for entry clearance as a partner the applicant will be granted entry clearance for an initial period not exceeding 33 months, and subject to a condition of no recourse to public funds; or, where the applicant is a fiancé(e) or proposed civil partner, the applicant will be granted entry clearance for a period not exceeding 6 months, and subject to a condition of no recourse to public funds and a prohibition on employment.

D-ECP.1.2. Where the applicant does not meet the requirements for entry clearance as a partner the application will be refused.

Section R-LTRP: Requirements for limited leave to remain as a partner

R-LTRP.1.1. The requirements to be met for limited leave to remain as a partner are—

  (a) the applicant and their partner must be in the UK;

  (b) the applicant must have made a valid application for limited or indefinite leave to remain as a partner; and either

  (c) (i) the applicant must not fall for refusal under Section S-LTR: Suitability leave to remain; and

    (ii) the applicant meets all of the requirements of Section E-LTRP: Eligibility for leave to remain as a partner; or

  (d) (i) the applicant must not fall for refusal under Section S-LTR: Suitability leave to remain; and

    (ii) the applicant meets the requirements of paragraphs E-LTRP.1.2-1.12. and E-LTRP.2.1.; and

    (iii) paragraph EX.1. applies.

Section S-LTR: Suitability-leave to remain

S-LTR.1.1. The applicant will be refused limited leave to remain on grounds of suitability if any of paragraphs S-LTR.1.2. to 1.7. apply.

S-LTR.1.2. The applicant is at the date of application the subject of a deportation order.

S-LTR.1.3. The presence of the applicant in the UK is not conducive to the public good because they have been convicted of an offence for which they have been sentenced to imprisonment for at least 4 years.

S-LTR.1.4. The presence of the applicant in the UK is not conducive to the public good because they have been convicted of an offence for which they have been sentenced to imprisonment for less than 4 years but at least 12 months.

S-LTR.1.5. The presence of the applicant in the UK is not conducive to the public good because, in the view of the Secretary of State, their offending has caused serious harm or they are a persistent offender who shows a particular disregard for the law.

S-LTR.1.6. The presence of the applicant in the UK is not conducive to the public good because their conduct (including convictions which do not fall within paragraphs S-LTR.1.3. to 1.5.), character, associations, or other reasons, make it undesirable to allow them to remain in the UK.

S-LTR.1.7. The applicant has failed without reasonable excuse to comply with a requirement to—

  (a) attend an interview;

  (b) provide information;

  (c) provide physical data; or

  (d) undergo a medical examination or provide a medical report.

S-LTR.2.1. The applicant will normally be refused on grounds of suitability if any of paragraphs S-LTR.2.2. to 2.4. apply.

S-LTR.2.2. Whether or not to the applicant's knowledge –

  (a) false information, representations or documents have been submitted in relation to the application (including false information submitted to any person to obtain a document used in support of the application); or

  (b) there has been a failure to disclose material facts in relation to the application.

S-LTR.2.3. One or more relevant NHS body has notified the Secretary of State that the applicant has failed to pay charges in accordance with the relevant NHS regulations on charges to overseas visitors and the outstanding charges have a total value of at least £1000.

S-LTR.2.4. A maintenance and accommodation undertaking has been requested under paragraph 35 of these Rules and has not been provided.

S-LTR.3.1. When considering whether the presence of the applicant in the UK is not conducive to the public good any legal or practical reasons why the applicant cannot presently be removed from the UK must be ignored.

Section E-LTRP: Eligibility for limited leave to remain as a partner

E-LTRP.1.1. To qualify for limited leave to remain as a partner all of the requirements of paragraphs E-LTRP.1.2. to 4.2. must be met.

Relationship requirements

E-LTRP.1.2.   The applicant's partner must be–

(a)   a British Citizen in the UK;

(b)   present and settled in the UK; or

(c)   in the UK with refugee leave or as a person with humanitarian protection.

E-LTRP.1.3.   The applicant must be aged 18 or over at the date of application.

E-LTRP.1.4.   The partner must be aged 18 or over at the date of application.

E-LTRP.1.5.   The applicant and their partner must not be within the prohibited degree of relationship.

E-LTRP.1.6.   The applicant and their partner must have met in person.

E-LTRP.1.7.   The relationship between the applicant and their partner must be genuine and subsisting.

E-LTRP.1.8.   If the applicant and partner are married or in a civil partnership it must be a valid marriage or civil partnership, as specified.

E-LTRP.1.9.   Any previous relationship of the applicant or their partner must have broken down permanently, unless it is a relationship which falls within paragraph 278(i) of these Rules.

E-LTRP.1.10.   The applicant and their partner must intend to live together permanently in the UK and, in any application for further leave to remain as a partner (except where the applicant is in the UK as a fiancé(e) or proposed civil partner) and in any application for indefinite leave to remain as a partner, the applicant must provide evidence that, since entry clearance as a partner was granted under paragraph D-ECP1.1. or since the last grant of limited leave to remain as a partner, the applicant and their partner have lived together in the UK or there is good reason, consistent with a continuing intention to live together permanently in the UK, for any period in which they have not done so.

E-LTRP.1.11.   If the applicant is in the UK with leave as a fiancé(e) or proposed civil partner and the marriage or civil partnership did not take place during that period of leave, there must be good reason why and evidence that it will take place within the next 6 months.

E-LTRP.1.12.   The applicant's partner cannot be the applicant's fiancé(e) or proposed civil partner, unless the applicant was granted entry clearance as that person's fiancé(e) or proposed civil partner.

Immigration status requirements

E-LTRP.2.1.   The applicant must not be in the UK–

(a)   as a visitor;

(b)   with valid leave granted for a period of 6 months or less, unless that leave is as a fiancé(e) or proposed civil partner, or was granted pending the outcome of family court or divorce proceedings; or

(c)   on temporary admission or temporary release (unless paragraph EX.1. applies).

E-LTRP.2.2.   The applicant must not be in the UK in breach of immigration laws (disregarding any period of overstaying for a period of 28 days or less), unless paragraph EX.1. applies.

Financial requirements

E-LTRP.3.1.   The applicant must provide specified evidence, from the sources listed in paragraph E-LTRP.3.2., of–

(a)   a specified gross annual income of at least–

(i)   £18,600;

(ii)   an additional £3,800 for the first child; and

(iii)   an additional £2,400 for each additional child; alone or in combination with

(b)   specified savings of–

(i)   £16,000; and

(ii)   additional savings of an amount equivalent to 2.5 times the amount which is the difference between the gross annual income from the sources listed in paragraph E-LTRP.3.2.(a)–(f) and the total amount required under paragraph E-LTRP.3.1.(a); or

(c)   the requirements in paragraph E-LTRP.3.3.being met, unless paragraph EX.1. applies.

In this paragraph 'child' means a dependent child of the applicant who is–

(a)   under the age of 18 years, or who was under the age of 18 years when they were first granted entry under this route;

(b)   applying for entry clearance or is in the UK as a dependant of the applicant;

(c)   not a British Citizen or settled in the UK; and

(d)   not an EEA national with a right to remain in the UK under the Immigration (EEA) Regulations 2006.

E-LTRP.3.2.   When determining whether the financial requirement in paragraph ELTRP.3.1. is met only the following sources may be taken into account–

    (a)   income of the partner from specified employment or self-employment;

    (b)   income of the applicant from specified employment or self-employment unless they are working illegally;

    (c)   specified pension income of the applicant and partner;

    (d)   any specified maternity allowance or bereavement benefit received by the applicant and partner in the UK;

    (e)   other specified income of the applicant and partner;

    (f)   income from the sources at (b), (d) or (e) of a dependent child of the applicant under paragraph E-LTRP.3.1. who is aged 18 years or over; and

    (g)   specified savings of the applicant, partner and a dependent child of the applicant under paragraph E-LTRP.3.1. who is aged 18 years or over.

E-LTRP.3.3.   The requirements to meet this paragraph are–

    (a)   the applicant's partner must be receiving one or more of the following –

        (i)   disability living allowance;

        (ii)   severe disablement allowance;

        (iii)   industrial injury disablement benefit;

        (iv)   attendance allowance;

        (v)   carer's allowance; or

        (vi)   personal independence payment; and

    (b)   the applicant must provide evidence that their partner is able to maintain and accommodate themselves, the applicant and any dependants adequately in the UK without recourse to public funds.

E-LTRP.3.4.   The applicant must provide evidence that there will be adequate accommodation, without recourse to public funds, for the family, including other family members who are not included in the application but who live in the same household, which the family own or occupy exclusively, unless paragraph EX.1. applies: accommodation will not be regarded as adequate if–

    (a)   it is, or will be, overcrowded; or

    (b)   it contravenes public health regulations.

English language requirement

E-LTRP.4.1.   If the applicant has not met the requirement in a previous application for leave as a partner, the applicant must provide specified evidence that they–

    (a)   are a national of a majority English speaking country listed in paragraph GEN.1.6.;

    (b)   have passed an English language test in speaking and listening at a minimum of level A1 of the Common European Framework of Reference for Languages with a provider approved by the Secretary of State;

    (c)   have an academic qualification recognised by UK NARIC to be equivalent to the standard of a Bachelor's or Master's degree or PhD in the UK, which was taught in English; or

    (d)   are exempt from the English language requirement under paragraph ELTRP. 4.2;

    unless paragraph EX.1. applies.

E-LTRP.4.2.   The applicant is exempt from the English language requirement if at the date of application–

    (a)   the applicant is aged 65 or over;

    (b)   the applicant has a disability (physical or mental condition) which prevents the applicant from meeting the requirement; or

    (c)   there are exceptional circumstances which prevent the applicant from being able to meet the requirement.

Section D-LTRP: Decision on application for limited leave to remain as a partner

D-LTRP.1.1.   If the applicant meets the requirements in paragraph R-LTRP.1.1.(a) to (c) for limited leave to remain as a partner the applicant will be granted limited leave to remain for a period not exceeding 30 months, and subject to a condition of no recourse to public funds, and they will be eligible to apply for settlement after a continuous period of at least 60 months with such leave or in the UK with entry clearance as a partner under paragraph D-ECP1.1. (excluding in all cases any period of entry clearance or limited leave as a fiance(e) or proposed civil partner); or, if paragraph E-LTRP.1.11. applies, the applicant will be granted limited leave for a period not exceeding 6 months and subject to a condition of no recourse to public funds and a prohibition on employment.

D-LTRP.1.2.   If the applicant meets the requirements in paragraph R-LTRP.1.1.(a), (b) and (d) for limited leave to remain as a partner they will be granted leave to remain for a period not exceeding 30 months and subject to a condition of no recourse to public funds unless the Secretary of State deems such recourse to be appropriate, and they will be eligible to apply for settlement after a continuous period of at least 120 months with such leave, with limited leave as a partner under paragraph D-LTRP.1.1., or in the UK with entry clearance as a partner under paragraph D-ECP1.1. (excluding in all cases any period of entry clearance or limited leave as a fiancé(e) or proposed civil partner), or, if paragraph E-LTRP.1.11. applies, the applicant will be granted limited leave for a period not exceeding 6 months and subject to a condition of no recourse to public funds and a prohibition on employment.

D-LTRP.1.3.   If the applicant does not meet the requirements for limited leave to remain as a partner the application will be refused.

Section R-ILRP: Requirements for indefinite leave to remain (settlement) as a partner

R-ILRP.1.1.   The requirements to be met for indefinite leave to remain as a partner are that–

(a)   the applicant and their partner must be in the UK;

(b)   the applicant must have made a valid application for indefinite leave to remain as a partner;

(c)   the applicant must not fall for refusal under any of the grounds in Section S-ILR: Suitability-indefinite leave to remain;

(d)   the applicant must meet all of the requirements of Section E-LTRP: Eligibility for leave to remain as a partner (but in applying paragraph E-LTRP.3.1.(b)(ii) delete the words '2.5 times'); and

(e)   the applicant must meet all of the requirements of Section E-ILRP: Eligibility for indefinite leave to remain as a partner.

Section S-ILR: Suitability for indefinite leave to remain

S-ILR.1.1.   The applicant will be refused indefinite leave to remain on grounds of suitability if any of paragraphs S-ILR.1.2. to 1.9. apply.

S-ILR.1.2.   The applicant is at the date of application the subject of a deportation order.

S-ILR.1.3.   The presence of the applicant in the UK is not conducive to the public good because they have been convicted of an offence for which they have been sentenced to imprisonment for at least 4 years.

S-ILR.1.4.   The presence of the applicant in the UK is not conducive to the public good because they have been convicted of an offence for which they have been sentenced to imprisonment for less than 4 years but at least 12 months, unless a period of 15 years has passed since the end of the sentence.

S-ILR.1.5.   The presence of the applicant in the UK is not conducive to the public good because they have been convicted of an offence for which they have been sentenced to imprisonment for less than 12 months, unless a period of 7 years has passed since the end of the sentence.

S-ILR.1.6.   The applicant has, within the 24 months preceding the date of the application, been convicted of or admitted an offence for which they received a non-custodial sentence or other out of court disposal that is recorded on their criminal record.

S-ILR.1.7.   The presence of the applicant in the UK is not conducive to the public good because, in the view of the Secretary of State, their offending has caused serious harm or they are a persistent offender who shows a particular disregard for the law.

S-ILR.1.8.   The presence of the applicant in the UK is not conducive to the public good because their conduct (including convictions which do not fall within paragraphs S-ILR.1.3. to 1.6.), character, associations, or other reasons, make it undesirable to allow them to remain in the UK.

S-ILR.1.9.   The applicant has failed without reasonable excuse to comply with a requirement to–

(a)   attend an interview;

(b)   provide information;

(c)   provide physical data; or

(d)   undergo a medical examination or provide a medical report.

S-ILR.2.1.   The applicant will normally be refused on grounds of suitability if any of paragraphs S-ILR.2.2. to 2.4. apply.

S-ILR.2.2.   Whether or not to the applicant's knowledge–

    (a)   false information, representations or documents have been submitted in relation to the application (including false information submitted to any person to obtain a document used in support of the application); or

    (b)   there has been a failure to disclose material facts in relation to the application.

S-ILR.2.3.   One or more relevant NHS body has notified the Secretary of State that the applicant has failed to pay charges in accordance with the relevant NHS regulations on charges to overseas visitors and the outstanding charges have a total value of at least £1000.

S-ILR.2.4.   A maintenance and accommodation undertaking has been requested under paragraph 35 of these Rules and has not been provided.

S-ILR.3.1.   When considering whether the presence of the applicant in the UK is not conducive to the public good, any legal or practical reasons why the applicant cannot presently be removed from the UK must be ignored.

Section E-ILRP: Eligibility for indefinite leave to remain as a partner

E-ILRP.1.1.   To meet the eligibility requirements for indefinite leave to remain as a partner all of the requirements of paragraphs E-ILRP.1.2. to 1.6. must be met.

E-ILRP.1.2.   The applicant must be in the UK with valid leave to remain as a partner (disregarding any period of overstaying for a period of 28 days or less).

E-ILRP.1.3.   The applicant must have completed a continuous period of at least 60 months with limited leave as a partner under paragraph R-LTRP.1.1.(a) to (c) or in the UK with entry clearance as a partner under paragraph D-ECP.1.1.; or a continuous period of at least 120 months with limited leave as a partner under paragraph R-LTR.P.1.1(a), (b) and (d) or in the UK with entry clearance as a partner under paragraph D-ECP.1.1.; or a continuous period of at least 120 months with limited leave as a partner under a combination of these paragraphs, excluding in all cases any period of entry clearance or limited leave as a fiancé(e) or proposed civil partner.

E-ILRP.1.4.   In calculating the periods under paragraph E-ILRP.1.3. only the periods when the applicant's partner is the same person as the applicant's partner for the previous period of limited leave shall be taken into account.

E-ILRP.1.5.   DELETED.

E-ILRP.1.6.   The applicant must have demonstrated sufficient knowledge of the English language and sufficient knowledge about life in the United Kingdom in accordance with the requirements of Appendix KoLL of these Rules.

Section D-ILRP: Decision on application for indefinite leave to remain as a partner

D-ILRP.1.1.   If the applicant meets all of the requirements for indefinite leave to remain as a partner the applicant will be granted indefinite leave to remain.

D-ILRP.1.2.   If the applicant does not meet the requirements for indefinite leave to remain as a partner only for one or both of the following reasons–

    (a)   paragraph S-ILR.1.5. or S-ILR.1.6. applies;

    (b)   The applicant has not demonstrated sufficient knowledge of the English language or about life in the United Kingdom in accordance with Appendix KoLL,

the applicant will be granted further limited leave to remain as a partner for a period not exceeding 30 months, and subject to a condition of no recourse to public funds.

D-ILRP.1.3.   If the applicant does not meet all the eligibility requirements for indefinite leave to remain as a partner, and does not qualify for further limited leave to remain as a partner under paragraph DILRP. 1.2., the application will be refused, unless the applicant meets the requirements in paragraph R-LTRP.1.1.(a), (b) and (d) for limited leave to remain as a partner. Where they do, the applicant will be granted further limited leave to remain as a partner for a period not exceeding 30 months under paragraph D-LTRP.1.2. and subject to a condition of no recourse to public funds unless the Secretary of State deems such recourse to be appropriate.

Family members

Section EX: Exception

EX.1.   This paragraph applies if

    (a)   (i)   the applicant has a genuine and subsisting parental relationship with a child who–

(aa)   is under the age of 18 years, or was under the age of 18 years when the applicant was first granted leave on the basis that this paragraph applied;

(bb)   is in the UK;

(cc)   is a British Citizen or has lived in the UK continuously for at least the 7 years immediately preceding the date of application ;and

(ii)   it would not be reasonable to expect the child to leave the UK; or

(b)   the applicant has a genuine and subsisting relationship with a partner who is in the UK and is a British Citizen, settled in the UK or in the UK with refugee leave or humanitarian protection, and there are insurmountable obstacles to family life with that partner continuing outside the UK.

Bereaved partner

Section BPILR: Indefinite leave to remain (settlement) as a bereaved partner

BPILR.1.1.   The requirements to be met for indefinite leave to remain in the UK as a bereaved partner are that–

(a)   the applicant must be in the UK;

(b)   the applicant must have made a valid application for indefinite leave to remain as a bereaved partner;

(c)   the applicant must not fall for refusal under any of the grounds in Section S-ILR: Suitability-indefinite leave to remain; and

(d)   the applicant must meet all of the requirements of Section E-BPILR: Eligibility for indefinite leave to remain as a bereaved partner.

Section E-BPILR: Eligibility for indefinite leave to remain as a bereaved partner

E-BPILR.1.1.   To meet the eligibility requirements for indefinite leave to remain as a bereaved partner all of the requirements of paragraphs E-BPILR1.2. to 1.4. must be met.

E-BPILR.1.2.   The applicant's last grant of limited leave must have been as–

(a)   a partner (other than a fiancé(e) or proposed civil partner) of a British Citizen or a person settled in the UK; or

(b)   a bereaved partner.

E-BPILR.1.3.   The person who was the applicant's partner at the time of the last grant of limited leave as a partner must have died.

E-BPILR.1.4.   At the time of the partner's death the relationship between the applicant and the partner must have been genuine and subsisting and each of the parties must have intended to live permanently with the other in the UK.

Section D-BPILR: Decision on application for indefinite leave to remain as a bereaved partner

D-BPILR.1.1.   If the applicant meets all of the requirements for indefinite leave to remain as a bereaved partner the applicant will be granted indefinite leave to remain.

D-BPILR.1.2.   If the applicant does not meet the requirements for indefinite leave to remain as a bereaved partner only because paragraph S-ILR.1.5. or S-ILR.1.6. applies, the applicant will be granted further limited leave to remain for a period not exceeding 30 months, and subject to a condition of no recourse to public funds.

D-BPILR.1.3.   If the applicant does not meet the requirements for indefinite leave to remain as a bereaved partner, or limited leave to remain as a bereaved partner under paragraph D-BPILR.1.2., the application will be refused.

Victim of domestic violence

Section DVILR: Indefinite leave to remain (settlement) as a victim of domestic violence

DVILR.1.1.   The requirements to be met for indefinite leave to remain in the UK as a victim of domestic violence are that–

(a)   the applicant must be in the UK;

(b)   the applicant must have made a valid application for indefinite leave to remain as a victim of domestic violence;

(c)   the applicant must not fall for refusal under any of the grounds in Section S-ILR: Suitability-indefinite leave to remain; and

(d)   the applicant must meet all of the requirements of Section E-DVILR:

Eligibility for indefinite leave to remain as a victim of domestic violence.

Section E-DVILR: Eligibility for indefinite leave to remain as a victim of domestic violence

E-DVILR.1.1. To meet the eligibility requirements for indefinite leave to remain as a victim of domestic violence all of the requirements of paragraphs E-DVILR.1.2. and 1.3. must be met.

E-DVILR.1.2. The applicant's last grant of limited leave must have been–

(a) as a partner (other than a fiancé(e) or proposed civil partner) of a British Citizen or a person settled in the UK;

(b) granted to enable access to public funds pending an application under DVILR.; or

(c) granted under paragraph D-DVILR.1.2.

E-DVILR.1.3. The applicant must provide evidence that during the last period of limited leave as a partner the applicant's relationship with their partner broke down permanently as a result of domestic violence.

Section D-DVILR: Decision on application for indefinite leave to remain as a victim of domestic violence

D-DVILR.1.1. If the applicant meets all of the requirements for indefinite leave to remain as a victim of domestic violence the applicant will be granted indefinite leave to remain.

D-DVILR.1.2. If the applicant does not meet the requirements for indefinite leave to remain as a victim of domestic violence only because paragraph S-ILR.1.5. or S-ILR.1.6. applies, the applicant will be granted further limited leave to remain for a period not exceeding 30 months.

D-DVILR.1.3. If the applicant does not meet the requirements for indefinite leave to remain as a victim of domestic violence, or further limited leave to remain under paragraph D-DVILR.1.2. the application will be refused.

Family life as a child of a person with limited leave as a partner or parent

This route is for a child whose parent is applying for entry clearance or leave, or who has limited leave, as a partner or parent. For further provision on a child seeking to enter or remain in the UK for the purpose of their family life see Part 8 of these Rules.

Section EC-C: Entry clearance as a child

EC-C.1.1. The requirements to be met for entry clearance as a child are that–

(a) the applicant must be outside the UK;

(b) the applicant must have made a valid application for entry clearance as a child;

(c) the applicant must not fall for refusal under any of the grounds in Section S-EC: Suitability for entry clearance; and

(d) the applicant must meet all of the requirements of Section E-ECC: Eligibility for entry clearance as a child.

Section E-ECC: Eligibility for entry clearance as a child

E-ECC.1.1. To meet the eligibility requirements for entry clearance as a child all of the requirements of paragraphs E-ECC.1.2. to 2.4. must be met.

Relationship requirements

E-ECC.1.2. The applicant must be under the age of 18 at the date of application.

E-ECC.1.3. The applicant must not be married or in a civil partnership.

E-ECC.1.4. The applicant must not have formed an independent family unit.

E-ECC.1.5. The applicant must not be leading an independent life.

E-ECC.1.6. One of the applicant's parents must be in the UK with limited leave to enter or remain, or be applying, or have applied, for entry clearance, as a partner or a parent under this Appendix (referred to in this section as the 'applicant's parent'), and

(a) the applicant's parent's partner under Appendix FM is also a parent of the applicant; or

(b) the applicant's parent has had and continues to have sole responsibility for the child's upbringing; or

(c) there are serious and compelling family or other considerations which make exclusion of the child undesirable and suitable arrangements have been made for the child's care.

Financial requirement

E-ECC.2.1. The applicant must provide specified evidence, from the sources listed in paragraph E-ECC.2.2., of–

    (a)   a specified gross annual income of at least–

        (i)   £18,600;

        (ii)   an additional £3,800 for the first child; and

        (iii)   an additional £2,400 for each additional child; alone or in combination with

    (b)   specified savings of

        (i)   £16,000; and

        (ii)   additional savings of an amount equivalent to 2.5 times the amount which is the difference between the gross annual income from the sources listed in paragraph E-ECC.2.2.(a)–(f) and the total amount required under paragraph E-ECC.2.1.(a); or

    (c)   the requirements in paragraph E-ECC.2.3. being met.

In this paragraph 'child' means the applicant and any other dependent child of the applicant's parent who is–

    (a)   under the age of 18 years, or who was under the age of 18 years when they were first granted entry under this route;

    (b)   in the UK;

    (c)   not a British Citizen or settled in the UK; and

    (d)   not an EEA national with a right to remain in the UK under the Immigration (EEA) Regulations 2006.

E-ECC.2.2.   When determining whether the financial requirement in paragraph EECC. 2.1. is met only the following sources may be taken into account–

    (a)   income of the applicant's parent's partner from specified employment or self-employment, which, in respect of an applicant's parent's partner returning to the UK with the applicant, can include specified employment or self-employment overseas and in the UK;

    (b)   income of the applicant's parent from specified employment or self employment if they are in the UK unless they are working illegally;

    (c)   specified pension income of the applicant's parent and that parent's partner;

    (d)   any specified maternity allowance or bereavement benefit received by the applicant's parent and that parent's partner in the UK;

    (e)   other specified income of the applicant's parent and that parent's partner;

    (f)   income from the sources at (b), (d) or (e) of a dependent child of the applicant's parent under paragraph E-ECC.2.1. who is aged 18 years or over; and

    (g)   specified savings of the applicant's parent, that parent's partner and a dependent child of the applicant's parent under paragraph E-ECC.2.1. who is aged 18 years or over.

E-ECC.2.3.   The requirements to be met under this paragraph are–

    (a)   the applicant's parent's partner must be receiving one or more of the following–

        (i)   disability living allowance;

        (ii)   severe disablement allowance;

        (iii)   industrial injury disablement benefit;

        (iv)   attendance allowance;

        (v)   carer's allowance; or

        (vi)   personal independence payment; and

    (b)   the applicant must provide evidence that their parent's partner is able to maintain and accommodate themselves, the applicant's parent, the applicant and any dependants adequately in the UK without recourse to public funds.

E-EEC.2.4.   The applicant must provide evidence that there will be adequate accommodation, without recourse to public funds, for the family, including other family members who are not included in the application but who live in the same household, which the family own or occupy exclusively: accommodation will not be regarded as adequate if–

    (a)   it is, or will be, overcrowded; or

    (b)   it contravenes public health regulations.

Section D-ECC: Decision on application for entry clearance as a child

D-ECC.1.1. If the applicant meets the requirements for entry clearance as a child they will be granted entry clearance of a duration which will expire at the same time as the leave granted to the applicant's parent, and subject to a condition of no recourse to public funds.

D-ECC.1.2. If the applicant does not meet the requirements for entry clearance as a child the application will be refused.

Section R-LTRC: Requirements for leave to remain as a child

R-LTRC.1.1. The requirements to be met for leave to remain as a child are that–

(a) the applicant must be in the UK;

(b) the applicant must have made a valid application for leave to remain as a child;

and either

(c) (i) the applicant must not fall for refusal under any of the grounds in Section S-LTR: Suitability-leave to remain; and

(ii) the applicant meets all of the requirements of Section E-LTRC: Eligibility for leave to remain as a child; or

(d) (i) the applicant must not fall for refusal under any of the grounds in Section S-LTR: Suitability-leave to remain; and

(ii) the applicant meets the requirements of paragraphs E-LTRC.1.2.–1.6.; and

(iii) a parent of the applicant has been or is at the same time being granted leave to remain under paragraph D-LTRP.1.2. or D-LTRPT.1.2. or indefinite leave to remain under this Appendix (except as an adult dependent relative).

Section E-LTRC: Eligibility for leave to remain as a child

E-LTRC.1.1. To qualify for limited leave to remain as a child all of the requirements of paragraphs E-LTRC.1.2. to 2.4. must be met (except where paragraph R-LTRC.1.1.(d)(ii) applies).

Relationship requirements

E-LTRC.1.2. The applicant must be under the age of 18 at the date of application or when first granted leave as a child under this route.

E-LTRC.1.3. The applicant must not be married or in a civil partnership.

E-LTRC.1.4. The applicant must not have formed an independent family unit.

E-LTRC.1.5. The applicant must not be leading an independent life.

E-LTRC.1.6. One of the applicant's parents (referred to in this section as the 'applicant's parent') must be in the UK and have leave to enter or remain or indefinite leave to remain, or is at the same time being granted leave to remain or indefinite leave to remain, under this Appendix (except as an adult dependent relative), and

(a) the applicant's p and compelling family or other considerations which make exclusion of the child undesirable and suitable arrangements have been made for the child's care.

Financial requirements

E-LTRC.2.1. The applicant must provide specified evidence, from the sources listed in paragraph E-LTRC.2.2., of –

(a) a specified gross annual income of at least–

(i) £18,600;

(ii) an additional £3,800 for the first child; and

(iii) an additional £2,400 for each additional child; alone or in combination with

(b) specified savings of–

(i) £16,000; and

(ii) additional savings of an amount equivalent to 2.5 times (or if the parent is applying for indefinite leave to remain 1 times) the amount which is the difference between the gross annual income from the sources listed in paragraph E-LTRC.2.2.(a)–(f) and the total amount required under paragraph E-LTRC.2.1.(a); or

(c) the requirements in paragraph E-LTRC.2.3. being met.

In this paragraph 'child' means the applicant and any other dependent child of the applicant's parent who is–

(i) under the age of 18 years, or who was under the age of 18 years when they were first granted entry under this route;

    (ii) in the UK;

    (iii) not a British Citizen or settled in the UK; and

    (iv) not an EEA national with a right to remain in the UK under the Immigration (EEA) Regulations 2006.

E-LTRC.2.2. When determining whether the financial requirement in paragraph ELTRC. 2.1. is met only the following sources may be taken into account–

   (a) income of the applicant's parent's partner from specified employment or self-employment;

   (b) income of the applicant's parent from specified employment or selfemployment;

   (c) specified pension income of the applicant's parent and that parent's partner;

   (d) any specified maternity allowance or bereavement benefit received by the applicant's parent and that parent's partner in the UK;

   (e) other specified income of the applicant's parent and that parent's partner;

   (f) income from the sources at (b), (d) or (e) of a dependent child of the applicant's parent under paragraph E-LTRC.2.1. who is aged 18 years or over; and

   (g) specified savings of the applicant's parent, that parent's partner and a dependent child of the applicant's parent under paragraph E-ECC.2.1. who is aged 18 years or over.

E-LTRC.2.3. The requirements to be met under this paragraph are–

   (a) the applicant's parent's partner must be receiving one or more of the following–

    (i) disability living allowance;

    (ii) severe disablement allowance;

    (iii) industrial injury disablement benefit;

    (iv) attendance allowance;

    (v) carer's allowance; or

    (vi) personal independence payment; and

   (b) the applicant must provide evidence that their parent's partner is able to maintain and accommodate themselves, the applicant's parent, the applicant and any dependants adequately in the UK without recourse to public funds.

E-LTRC.2.4. The applicant must provide evidence that there will be adequate accommodation in the UK, without recourse to public funds, for the family, including other family members who are not included in the application but who live in the same household, which the family own or occupy exclusively: accommodation will not be regarded as adequate if–

   (a) it is, or will be, overcrowded; or

   (b) it contravenes public health regulations.

Section D-LTRC: Decision on application for leave to remain as a child

D-LTRC.1.1. If the applicant meets the requirements for leave to remain as a child the applicant will be granted leave to remain of a duration which will expire at the same time as the leave granted to the applicant's parent, and subject to a condition of no recourse to public funds. To qualify for indefinite leave to remain as a child of a person with indefinite leave to remain as a partner or parent, the applicant must meet the requirements of paragraph 298 of these rules.

D-LTRC.1.2. If the applicant does not meet the requirements for leave to remain as a child the application will be refused.

Family life as a parent

Family life as a parent of a child in the UK

Section EC-PT: Entry clearance as a parent of a child in the UK

EC-PT.1.1. The requirements to be met for entry clearance as a parent are that–

   (a) the applicant must be outside the UK;

   (b) the applicant must have made a valid application for entry clearance as a parent;

   (c) the applicant must not fall for refusal under any of the grounds in Section S-EC: Suitability– entry clearance; and

   (d) the applicant must meet all of the requirements of Section E-ECPT: Eligibility for entry clearance as a parent.

Section E-ECPT: Eligibility for entry clearance as a parent

E-ECPT.1.1.   To meet the eligibility requirements for entry clearance as a parent all of the requirements in paragraphs E-ECPT.2.1. to 4.2. must be met.

Relationship requirements

E-ECPT.2.1.   The applicant must be aged 18 years or over.

E-ECPT.2.2.   The child of the applicant must be–

(a)   under the age of 18 years at the date of application;

(b)   living in the UK; and

(c)   a British Citizen or settled in the UK.

E-ECPT.2.3.   Either–

(a)   the applicant must have sole parental responsibility for the child; or

(b)   the parent or carer with whom the child normally lives must be–

(i)   a British Citizen in the UK or settled in the UK;

(ii)   not the partner of the applicant; and

(iii)   the applicant must not be eligible to apply for entry clearance as a partner under this Appendix.

E-ECPT.2.4.   (a)   The applicant must provide evidence that they have either–

(i)   sole parental responsibility for the child; or

(ii)   access rights to the child; and

(b)   The applicant must provide evidence that they are taking, and intend to continue to take, an active role in the child's upbringing.

Financial requirements

E-ECPT.3.1.   The applicant must provide evidence that they will be able to adequately maintain and accommodate themselves and any dependants in the UK without recourse to public funds

E-ECPT.3.2.   The applicant must provide evidence that there will be adequate accommodation in the UK, without recourse to public funds, for the family, including other family members who are not included in the application but who live in the same household, which the family own or occupy exclusively: accommodation will not be regarded as adequate if–

(a)   it is, or will be, overcrowded; or

(b)   it contravenes public health regulations.

English language requirement

E-ECPT.4.1.   The applicant must provide specified evidence that they–

(a)   are a national of a majority English speaking country listed in paragraph GEN.1.6.;

(b)   have passed an English language test in speaking and listening at a minimum of level A1 of the Common European Framework of Reference for Languages with a provider approved by the Secretary of State;

(c)   have an academic qualification recognised by UK NARIC to be equivalent to the standard of a Bachelor's or Master's degree or PhD in the UK, which was taught in English; or

(d)   are exempt from the English language requirement under paragraph EECPT. 4.2.

E-ECPT.4.2.   The applicant is exempt from the English language requirement if at the date of application–

(a)   the applicant is aged 65 or over;

(b)   the applicant has a disability (physical or mental condition) which prevents the applicant from meeting the requirement; or

(c)   there are exceptional circumstances which prevent the applicant from being able to meet the requirement prior to entry to the UK.

Section D-ECPT: Decision on application for entry clearance as a parent

D-ECPT.1.1.   If the applicant meets the requirements for entry clearance as a parent they will be granted entry clearance for an initial period not exceeding 33 months, and subject to a condition of no recourse to public funds.

D-ECPT.1.2.   If the applicant does not meet the requirements for entry clearance as a parent the application will be refused.

Section R-LTRPT: Requirements for limited leave to remain as a parent

R-LTRPT.1.1.   The requirements to be met for limited or indefinite leave to remain as a parent or partner are–

    (a)   the applicant and the child must be in the UK;

    (b)   the applicant must have made a valid application for limited or indefinite leave to remain as a parent or partner; and either

    (c)   (i)   the applicant must not fall for refusal under Section S-LTR: Suitability leave to remain; and

        (ii)   the applicant meets all of the requirements of Section ELTRPT: Eligibility for leave to remain as a parent, or

    (d)   (i)   the applicant must not fall for refusal under S-LTR:

        Suitability leave to remain; and

        (ii)   the applicant meets the requirements of paragraphs E-LTRPT.2.2-2.4. and E-LTRPT.3.1.; and

        (iii)   paragraph EX.1. applies.

Section E-LTRPT: Eligibility for limited leave to remain as a parent

E-LTRPT.1.1.   To qualify for limited leave to remain as a parent all of the requirements of paragraphs E-LTRPT.2.2. to 5.2. must be met.

Relationship requirements

E-LTRPT.2.2.   The child of the applicant must be–

    (a)   under the age of 18 years at the date of application, or where the child has turned 18 years of age since the applicant was first granted entry clearance or leave to remain as a parent under this Appendix, must not have formed an independent family unit or be leading an independent life;

    (b)   living in the UK; and

    (c)   a British Citizen or settled in the UK; or

    (d)   has lived in the UK continuously for at least the 7 years immediately preceding the date of application and paragraph EX.1. applies.

E-LTRPT.2.3.   Either–

    (a)   the applicant must have sole parental responsibility for the child or the child normally lives with the applicant and not their other parent (who is a British Citizen or settled in the UK); or

    (b)   the parent or carer with whom the child normally lives must be–

        (i)   a British Citizen in the UK or settled in the UK;

        (ii)   not the partner of the applicant (which here includes a person who has been in a relationship with the applicant for less than two years prior to the date of application); and

        (iii)   the applicant must not be eligible to apply for leave to remain as a partner under this Appendix.

E-LTRPT.2.4.   (a)   The applicant must provide evidence that they have either–

        (i)   sole parental responsibility for the child, or that the child normally lives with them; or

        (ii)   access rights to the child; and

    (b)   The applicant must provide evidence that they are taking, and intend to continue to take, an active role in the child's upbringing.

Immigration status requirement

E-LTRPT.3.1.   The applicant must not be in the UK–

    (a)   as a visitor;

    (b)   with valid leave granted for a period of 6 months or less, unless that leave was granted pending the outcome of family court or divorce proceedings;

    (c)   on temporary admission or temporary release (unless paragraph EX.1. applies).

E-LTRPT.3.2.   The applicant must not be in the UK in breach of immigration laws, (disregarding any period of overstaying for a period of 28 days or less), unless paragraph EX.1. applies.

Financial requirements

E-LTRPT.4.1.   The applicant must provide evidence that they will be able to adequately maintain and accommodate themselves and any dependants in the UK without recourse to public funds, unless paragraph EX.1. applies.

E-LTRPT.4.2.   The applicant must provide evidence that there will be adequate accommodation in the UK, without recourse to public funds, for the family, including other family members who are not included in the application but who live in the same household, which the family own or occupy exclusively, unless paragraph EX.1. applies: accommodation will not be regarded as adequate if–

    (a)   it is, or will be, overcrowded; or

    (b)   it contravenes public health regulations.

English language requirement

E-LTRPT.5.1.   The applicant must provide specified evidence that they–

    (a)   are a national of a majority English speaking country listed in paragraph GEN.1.6.;

    (b)   have passed an English language test in speaking and listening at a minimum of level A1 of the Common European Framework of Reference for Languages with a provider approved by the Secretary of State;

    (c)   have an academic qualification recognised by UK NARIC to be equivalent to the standard of a Bachelor's or Master's degree or PhD in the UK, which was taught in English; or

    (d)   are exempt from the English language requirement under paragraph ELTRPT. 5.2, unless paragraph EX.1. applies.

E-LTRPT.5.2.   The applicant is exempt from the English language requirement if at the date of application–

    (a)   the applicant is aged 65 or over;

    (b)   the applicant has a disability (physical or mental condition) which prevents the applicant from meeting the requirement; or

    (c)   there are exceptional circumstances which prevent the applicant from being able to meet the requirement.

Section D-LTRPT: Decision on application for limited leave to remain as a parent

D-LTRPT.1.1.   If the applicant meets the requirements in paragraph LTRPT.1.1. (a) to (c) for limited leave to remain as a parent the applicant will be granted limited leave to remain for a period not exceeding 30 months, and subject to a condition of no recourse to public funds, and they will be eligible to apply for settlement after a continuous period of at least 60 months with such leave or in the UK with entry clearance as a parent under paragraph D-ECPT.1.1.

D-LTRPT.1.2.   If the applicant meets the requirements in paragraph LTRPT.1.1. (a), (b) and (d) for limited leave to remain as a parent they will be granted leave to remain for a period not exceeding 30 months and subject to a condition of no recourse to public funds unless the Secretary of State deems such recourse to be appropriate, and they will be eligible to apply for settlement after a continuous period of at least 120 months with such leave, with limited leave as a parent under paragraph D-LTRPT.1.1., or in the UK with entry clearance as a parent under paragraph D-ECPT.1.1.

D-LTRPT.1.3.   If the applicant does not meet the requirements for limited leave to remain as a parent the application will be refused.

Section R-ILRPT: Requirements for indefinite leave to remain (settlement) as a parent

R-ILRPT.1.1.   The requirements to be met for indefinite leave to remain as a parent are that–

    (a)   the applicant must be in the UK;

    (b)   the applicant must have made a valid application for indefinite leave to remain as a parent;

    (c)   the applicant must not fall for refusal under any of the grounds in Section S-ILR: Suitability-indefinite leave to remain;

    (d)   the applicant must meet all of the requirements of Section E-LTRPT: Eligibility for leave to remain as a parent; and

    (e)   the applicant must meet all of the requirements of Section E-ILRPT: Eligibility for indefinite leave to remain as a parent.

Section E-ILRPT: Eligibility for indefinite leave to remain as a parent

E-ILRPT.1.1.   To meet the eligibility requirements for indefinite leave to remain as a parent all of the requirements of paragraphs E-ILRPT.1.2. to 1.5. must be met.

E-ILRPT.1.2.   The applicant must be in the UK with valid leave to remain as a parent (disregarding any period of overstaying for 28 days or less).

E-ILRPT.1.3.   The applicant must have completed a continuous period of at least 60 months with limited leave as a parent under paragraph R-LTRPT.1.1.(a) to (c) or in the UK with entry clearance as a parent under paragraph D-ECPT.1.1.; or a continuous period of at least 120 months with limited leave as a parent, under paragraphs R-LTRPT.1.1(a), (b) and (d) or in the UK with entry clearance as a parent under paragraph D-ECPT.1.1.; or a continuous period of at least 120 months with limited leave as a parent under a combination of these paragraphs.

E-ILRPT.1.4.   DELETED.

E-ILRPT.1.5.   The applicant must have demonstrated sufficient knowledge of the English language and sufficient knowledge about life in the United Kingdom in accordance with the requirements of Appendix KoLL of these Rules.

Section D-ILRPT: Decision on application for indefinite leave to remain as a parent

D-ILRPT.1.1.   If the applicant meets all of the requirements for indefinite leave to remain as a parent the applicant will be granted indefinite leave to remain.

D-ILRPT.1.2.   If the applicant does not meet the requirements for indefinite leave to remain as a parent only for one or both of the following reasons–

(a)   paragraph S-ILR.1.5. or S-ILR.1.6. applies; or

(b)   The applicant has not demonstrated sufficient knowledge of the English language or about life in the United Kingdom in accordance with Appendix KoLL,

the applicant will be granted further limited leave to remain as a parent for a period not exceeding 30 months, and subject to a condition of no recourse to public funds.

D-ILRPT.1.3.   If the applicant does not meet all the eligibility requirements for indefinite leave to remain as a parent, and does not qualify for further limited leave to remain under paragraph D-ILRPT.1.2., the application will be refused, unless the applicant meets the requirements in paragraph R-LTRPT.1.1.(a), (b) and (d) for limited leave to remain as a parent. Where they do, the applicant will be granted further limited leave to remain as a parent for a period not exceeding 30 months under paragraph D-LTRPT.1.2. and subject to a condition of no recourse to public funds unless the Secretary of State deems such recourse to be appropriate.

Adult dependent relatives

Section EC-DR: Entry clearance as an adult dependent relative

EC-DR.1.1.   The requirements to be met for entry clearance as an adult dependent relative are that–

(a)   the applicant must be outside the UK;

(b)   the applicant must have made a valid application for entry clearance as an adult dependent relative;

(c)   the applicant must not fall for refusal under any of the grounds in Section S-EC: Suitability for entry clearance; and

(d)   the applicant must meet all of the requirements of Section E-ECDR: Eligibility for entry clearance as an adult dependent relative.

Section E-ECDR: Eligibility for entry clearance as an adult dependent relative

E-ECDR.1.1.   To meet the eligibility requirements for entry clearance as an adult dependent relative all of the requirements in paragraphs E-ECDR.2.1. to 3.2. must be met.

Relationship requirements

E-ECDR.2.1.   The applicant must be the–

(a)   parent aged 18 years or over;

(b)   grandparent;

(c)   brother or sister aged 18 years or over; or

(d)   son or daughter aged 18 years or over

of a person ('the sponsor') who is in the UK.

E-ECDR.2.2.   If the applicant is the sponsor's parent or grandparent they must not be in a subsisting relationship with a partner unless that partner is also the sponsor's parent or grandparent and is applying for entry clearance at the same time as the applicant.

E-ECDR.2.3.   The sponsor must at the date of application be–

(a)   aged 18 years or over; and

(b)   (i)   a British Citizen in the UK; or

(ii)   present and settled in the UK; or

(iii)   in the UK with refugee leave or humanitarian protection.

E-ECDR.2.4.   The applicant or, if the applicant and their partner are the sponsor's parents or grandparents, the applicant's partner, must as a result of age, illness or disability require long-term personal care to perform everyday tasks.

E-ECDR.2.5.   The applicant or, if the applicant and their partner are the sponsor's parents or grandparents, the applicant's partner, must be unable, even with the practical and financial help of the sponsor, to obtain the required level of care in the country where they are living, because–

(a)   it is not available and there is no person in that country who can reasonably provide it; or

(b)   it is not affordable.

Financial requirements

E-ECDR.3.1.   The applicant must provide evidence that they can be adequately maintained, accommodated and cared for in the UK by the sponsor without recourse to public funds.

E-ECDR.3.2.   If the applicant's sponsor is a British Citizen or settled in the UK, the applicant must provide an undertaking signed by the sponsor confirming that the applicant will have no recourse to public funds, and that the sponsor will be responsible for their maintenance, accommodation and care, for a period of 5 years from the date the applicant enters the UK if they are granted indefinite leave to enter.

Section D-ECDR: Decision on application for entry clearance as an adult dependent relative

D-ECDR.1.1.   If the applicant meets the requirements for entry clearance as an adult dependent relative of a British Citizen or person settled in the UK they will be granted indefinite leave to enter.

D-ECDR.1.2.   If the applicant meets the requirements for entry clearance as an adult dependent relative and the sponsor has limited leave the applicant will be granted limited leave of a duration which will expire at the same time as the sponsor's limited leave, and subject to a condition of no recourse to public funds. If the sponsor applies for further limited leave, the applicant may apply for further limited leave of the same duration, if the requirements in EC-DR.1.1. (c) and (d) continue to be met, and subject to no recourse to public funds.

D-ECDR.1.3.   If the applicant does not meet the requirements for entry clearance as an adult dependent relative the application will be refused.

Section R-ILRDR: Requirements for indefinite leave to remain as an adult dependent relative

R-ILRDR.1.1.   The requirements to be met for indefinite leave to remain as an adult dependent relative are that–

(a)   the applicant is in the UK;

(b)   the applicant must have made a valid application for indefinite leave to remain as an adult dependent relative;

(c)   the applicant must not fall for refusal under any of the grounds in Section S-ILR: Suitability-indefinite leave to remain; and

(d)   the applicant must meet all of the requirements of Section E-ILRDR: Eligibility for indefinite leave to remain as an adult dependent relative.

Section E-ILRDR: Eligibility for indefinite leave to remain as an adult dependent relative

E-ILRDR.1.1.   To qualify for indefinite leave to remain as an adult dependent relative all of the requirements of paragraphs E-ILRDR.1.2. to 1.5. must be met.

E-ILRDR.1.2.   The applicant must be in the UK with valid leave to remain as an adult dependent relative (disregarding any period of overstaying for a period of 28 days or less).

E-ILRDR.1.3.   The applicant's sponsor must at the date of application be

(a)   present and settled in the UK; or

(b)   in the UK with refugee leave or as a person with humanitarian protection and have made an application for indefinite leave to remain.

E-ILRDR.1.4.   The applicant must provide evidence that they can be adequately maintained, accommodated and cared for in the UK by the sponsor without recourse to public funds.

E-ILRDR.1.5.   The applicant must provide an undertaking signed by the sponsor confirming that the applicant will have no recourse to public funds, and that the sponsor will be responsible for their maintenance, accommodation and care, for a period ending 5 years from the date the applicant entered the UK with limited leave as an adult dependent relative.

Section D-ILRDR: Decision on application for indefinite leave to remain as an adult dependent relative

D-ILRDR.1.1.   If the applicant meets the requirements for indefinite leave to remain as an adult dependent relative and the applicant's sponsor is settled in the UK, the applicant will be granted indefinite leave to remain as an adult dependent relative.

D-ILRDR.1.2.   If the applicant does not meet the requirements for indefinite leave to remain as an adult dependent relative because paragraph S-ILR.1.5. or S-ILR.1.6. applies, the applicant will be granted further limited leave to remain as an adult dependent relative for a period not exceeding 30 months, and subject to a condition of no recourse to public funds.

D-ILRDR.1.3.   If the applicant's sponsor has made an application for indefinite leave to remain and that application is refused, the applicant's application for indefinite leave to remain will be refused. If the sponsor is granted limited leave, the applicant will be granted further limited leave as an adult dependent relative of a duration which will expire at the same time as the sponsor's further limited leave, and subject to a condition of no recourse to public funds.

D-ILRDR.1.4.   Where an applicant does not meet the requirements for indefinite leave to remain, or further limited leave to remain under paragraphs D-ILRDR.1.2. or 1.3., the application will be refused.

Deportation and removal

Where the Secretary of State or an immigration officer is considering deportation or removal of a person who claims that their deportation or removal from the UK would be a breach of the right to respect for private and family life under Article 8 of the Human Rights Convention that person may be required to make an application under this Appendix or paragraph 276ADE, but if they are not required to make an application Part 13 of these Rules will apply.

Appendix FM-SE

Family Members – Specified Evidence

A.   This Appendix sets out the specified evidence applicants need to provide to meet the requirements of rules contained in Appendix FM and, where those requirements are also contained in other rules and unless otherwise stated, the specified evidence applicants need to provide to meet the requirements of those rules.

B.   Where evidence is not specified by Appendix FM, but is of a type covered by this Appendix, the requirements of this Appendix shall apply.

C.   In this Appendix references to paragraphs are to paragraphs of this Appendix unless the context otherwise requires.

D.   (a)   In deciding an application in relation to which this Appendix states that specified documents must be provided, the Entry Clearance Officer or Secretary of State ('the decision-maker') will consider documents that have been submitted with the application, and will only consider documents submitted after the application where sub-paragraph (b) or (e) applies.

    (b)   If the applicant:

       (i)   Has submitted:

         (aa)   A sequence of documents and some of the documents in the sequence have been omitted (e.g. if one bank statement from a series is missing);

         (bb)   A document in the wrong format (for example, if a letter is not on letterhead paper as specified); or

         (cc)   A document that is a copy and not an original document; or

         (dd)   A document which does not contain all of the specified information; or

       (ii)   Has not submitted a specified document,

    the decision-maker may contact the applicant or his representative in writing or otherwise, and request the document(s) or the correct version(s). The material requested must be received at the address specified in the request within a reasonable timescale specified in the request.

(c)   The decision-maker will not request documents where he or she does not anticipate that addressing the error or omission referred to in sub-paragraph (b) will lead to a grant because the application will be refused for other reasons.

(d)   If the applicant has submitted:

    (i)   A document in the wrong format; or

    (ii)   A document that is a copy and not an original document, or

    (iii)   A document that does not contain all of the specified information, but the missing information is verifiable from:

        (1)   other documents submitted with the application,

        (2)   the website of the organisation which issued the document, or

        (3)   the website of the appropriate regulatory body,

the application may be granted exceptionally, providing the decision-maker is satisfied that the document(s) is genuine and that the applicant meets the requirement to which the document relates. The decision-maker reserves the right to request the specified original document(s) in the correct format in all cases where sub-paragraph (b) applies, and to refuse applications if this material is not provided as set out in sub-paragraph (b).

(e)   Where the decision-maker is satisfied that there is a valid reason why a specified document(s) cannot be supplied, e.g. because it is not issued in a particular country or has been permanently lost, he or she may exercise discretion not to apply the requirement for the document(s) or to request alternative or additional information or document(s) be submitted by the applicant.

(f)   Before making a decision under Appendix FM or this Appendix, the decision-maker may contact the applicant or their representative in writing or otherwise to request further information or documents. The material requested must be received at the address specified in the request within a reasonable timescale specified in the request.

Evidence of Financial Requirements under Appendix FM

A1.   To meet the financial requirement under paragraphs E-ECP.3.1., E-LTRP.3.1., E-ECC.2.1. and E-LTRC.2.1. of Appendix FM, the applicant must meet:

(a)   The level of financial requirement applicable to the application under Appendix FM; and

(b)   The requirements specified in Appendix FM and this Appendix as to:

    (i)   The permitted sources of income and savings;

    (ii)   The time periods and permitted combinations of sources applicable to each permitted source relied upon; and

    (iii)   The evidence required for each permitted source relied upon.

1.   In relation to evidencing the financial requirements in Appendix FM the following general provisions shall apply:

(a)   Bank statements must:

    (i)   be from a financial institution regulated by the appropriate regulatory body for the country in which that institution is operating.

    (ii)   not be from a financial institution on the list of excluded institutions in Appendix P of these rules.

    (iii)   in relation to personal bank statements be only in the name of:

        (1)   the applicant's partner, the applicant or both as appropriate; or

        (2)   if the applicant is a child the applicant parent's partner, the applicant's parent or both as appropriate; or

        (3)   if the applicant is an adult dependent relative, the applicant's sponsor or the applicant,

    unless otherwise stated.

    (iv)   cover the period(s) specified.

    (v)   be:

        (1)   on official bank stationery; or

        (2)   electronic bank statements which are either accompanied by a letter from the bank on its headed stationery confirming that the documents are authentic or which bear the official stamp of the issuing bank on every page.

(aa) Where a bank statement is specified in this Appendix, a building society statement, a building society pass book, a letter from the applicant's bank or building society, or a letter from a financial institution regulated by the Financial Conduct Authority and the Prudential Regulation Authority or, for overseas accounts, the appropriate regulatory body for the country in which the institution operates and the funds are located, may be submitted as an alternative to a bank statement(s) provided that:

(1) the requirements in paragraph 1(a)(i)–(iv) are met as if the document were a bank statement; and

(2) a building society pass book must clearly show:

(i) the account number;

(ii) the building society's name and logo; and

(iii) the information required on transactions, funds held and time period(s) or as otherwise specified in this Appendix in relation to bank statements; and/or

(3) a letter must be on the headed stationery of the bank, building society or other financial institution and must clearly show:

(i) the account number,

(ii) the date of the letter;

(iii) the financial institution's name and logo; and

(iv) the information required on transactions, funds held and time period(s) or as otherwise specified in this Appendix in relation to bank statements.

(b) Promises of third party support will not be accepted. Third party support will only be accepted in the form of:

(i) maintenance payments from a former partner of an applicant in relation to the applicant and former partner's child or children or in relation to the applicant;

(ii) income from a dependent child who has turned 18, remains in the same UK household as the applicant and continues to be counted towards the financial requirement under Appendix FM;

(iii) gift of cash savings (whose souce must be declared) evidenced at paragraph 1(a)(iii), provided that the cash savings have been held by the person or persons at paragraph 1(a)(iii) for at least 6 months prior to the date of application and are under their control; and

(iv) a maintenance grant or stipend associated with undergraduate study or postgraduate study or research.

(bb) Payslips must be:

(i) original formal payslips issued by the employer and showing the employer's name; or

(ii) accompanied by a letter from the employer, on the employer's headed paper and signed by a senior official, confirming the payslips are authentic;

(c) The employment income of an applicant will only be taken into account if they are in the UK, aged 18 years or over and working legally, and prospective employment income will not be taken into account (except that of an applicant's partner or parent's partner who is returning to employment or self-employment in the UK at paragraphs E-ECP.3.2.(a) and E-ECC.2.2.(a) of Appendix FM).

(d) All income and savings must be lawfully derived.

(e) Savings must be held in cash.

(f) Income or cash savings in a foreign currency will be converted to pounds sterling using the closing spot exchange rate which appears on www.oanda.com* on the date of application.

(g) Where there is income or cash savings in different foreign currencies, each will be converted into pounds sterling before being added together, and then added to any UK income or savings to give a total amount.

(h) All documentary evidence must be original, unless otherwise stated.

(i) Evidence of profit from the sale of a business, property, investment, bond, stocks, shares or other asset will:

(i) not be accepted as evidence of income, but

(ii) the associated funds will be accepted as cash savings subject to the requirements of this Appendix and Appendix FM.

(j) Where any specified documents provided are not in English or Welsh, the applicant must provide the original and a full translation that can be independently verified by the Entry Clearance Officer, Immigration Officer or the Secretary of State. The translation must be dated and include:

    (i) confirmation that it is an accurate translation of the original document;

    (ii) the full name and original signature of the translator or an authorised official of the translation company;

    (iii) the translator or translation company's contact details; and

    (iv) if the applicant is applying for leave to remain or indefinite leave to remain, certification by a qualified translator and details of the translator or translation company's credentials.

(k) Where the gross (pre-tax) amount of any income cannot be properly evidenced, the net (post-tax) amount will be counted, including towards a gross income requirement.

(l) Where this Appendix requires the applicant to provide specified evidence relating to a period which ends with the date of application, that evidence, or the most recently dated part of it, must be dated no earlier than 28 days before the date of application.

(m) Cash income on which the correct tax has been paid may be counted as income under this Appendix, subject to the relevant evidential requirements of this Appendix.

(n) In this Appendix, a reference to the 'average' is a reference to the mean average.

2. In respect of salaried employment in the UK (except where paragraph 9 applies), all of the following evidence must be provided:

(a) Payslips covering:

    (i) a period of 6 months prior to the date of application if the person has been employed by their current employer for at least 6 months (and where paragraph 13(b) of this Appendix does not apply); or

    (ii) any period of salaried employment in the period of 12 months prior to the date of application if the person has been employed by their current employer for less than 6 months (or at least 6 months but the person does not rely on paragraph 13(a) of this Appendix), or in the financial year(s) relied upon by a self-employed person.

(b) A letter from the employer(s) who issued the payslips at paragraph 2(a) confirming:

    (i) the person's employment and gross annual salary;

    (ii) the length of their employment;

    (iii) the period over which they have been or were paid the level of salary relied upon in the application; and

    (iv) the type of employment (permanent, fixed-term contract or agency).

(c) Personal bank statements corresponding to the same period(s) as the payslips at paragraph 2(a), showing that the salary has been paid into an account in the name of the person or in the name of the person and their partner jointly.

(d) Where the person is a director of a limited company based in the UK, evidence that the company is not of a type specified in paragraph 9(a). This can include the latest Annual Return filed at Companies House.

2A. (i) In respect of salaried employment in the UK (paragraph 2 of this Appendix), statutory or contractual maternity, paternity, adoption or sick pay in the UK (paragraph 5 or 6 of this Appendix), or a director's salary paid to a self-employed person (paragraph 9 of this Appendix), the applicant may, in addition to the payslips and personal bank statements required under that paragraph, submit the P60 for the relevant period(s) of employment relied upon (if issued). If they do not, the Entry Clearance Officer or Secretary of State may grant the application if otherwise satisfied that the requirements of this Appendix relating to that employment are met. The Entry Clearance Officer or Secretary of State may request that the applicant submit the document(s) in accordance with paragraph D of this Appendix.

    (ii) In respect of salaried employment in the UK (paragraph 2 of this Appendix), or statutory or contractual maternity, paternity, adoption or sick pay in the UK (paragraph 5 or 6 of this Appendix), the applicant may, in addition to the letter from the employer(s) required under that paragraph, submit a signed contract of employment. If they do not, the Entry Clearance Officer or Secretary of State may grant the application if otherwise satisfied that the requirements of this Appendix relating to that employment are met. The Entry Clearance Officer or Secretary of State may request that the applicant submit the document(s) in accordance with paragraph D of this Appendix.

3.   In respect of salaried employment outside of the UK, evidence should be a reasonable equivalent to that set out in paragraph 2 and (where relevant) paragraph 2A.

4.   In respect of a job offer in the UK (for an applicant's partner or parent's partner returning to salaried employment in the UK at paragraphs E-ECP.3.2.(a) and E-ECC.2.2.(a) of Appendix FM) a letter from the employer must be provided:

   (a)   confirming the job offer, the gross annual salary and the starting date of the employment which must be within 3 months of the applicant's partner's return to the UK; or

   (b)   enclosing a signed contract of employment, which must have a starting date within 3 months of the applicant's partner's return to the UK.

5.   In respect of statutory or contractual maternity, paternity or adoption pay in the UK all of the following, and in respect of parental leave in the UK only the evidence at paragraph 5(c), must be provided:

   (a)   Personal bank statements corresponding to the same period(s) as the payslips at paragraph 5(b), showing that the salary has been paid into an account in the name of the person or in the name of the person and their partner jointly.

   (b)   Payslips covering:

      (i)   a period of 6 months prior to the date of application or to the commencement of the maternity, paternity or adoption leave, if the applicant has been employed by their current employer for at least 6 months (and where paragraph 13(b) does not apply); or

      (ii)   any period of salaried employment in the period of 12 months prior to the date of application or to the commencement of the maternity, paternity or adoption leave, if the applicant has been employed by their current employer for less than 6 months (or at least 6 months but the person does not rely on paragraph 13(a)).

   (c)   A letter from the employer confirming:

      (i)   the length of the person's employment;

      (ii)   the gross annual salary and the period over which it has been paid at this level;

      (iii) the entitlement to maternity, paternity, parental or adoption leave; and

      (iv)   the date of commencement and the end-date of the maternity, paternity, parental or adoption leave.

6.   In respect of statutory or contractual sick pay in the UK all of the following must be provided:

   (a)   Personal bank statements corresponding to the same period(s) as the payslips at paragraph 6(b), showing that the salary has been paid into an account in the name of the person or in the name of the person and their partner jointly.

   (b)   Payslips covering:

      (i)   a period of 6 months prior to the date of application or to the commencement of the sick leave, if the applicant has been employed by their current employer for at least 6 months (and where paragraph 13(b) does not apply); or,

      (ii)   any period of salaried employment in the period of 12 months prior to the date of application or to the commencement of the sick leave, if the applicant has been employed by their current employer for less than 6 months (or at least 6 months but the person does not rely on paragraph 13(a)).

   (c)   A letter from employer confirming:

      (i)   the length of the person's employment;

      (ii)   the gross annual salary and the period over which it has been paid at this level;

      (iii) that the person is in receipt of statutory or contractual sick pay; and

      (iv)   the date of commencement of the sick leave.

7.   In respect of self-employment in the UK as a partner, as a sole trader or in a franchise all of the following must be provided:

   (a)   Evidence of the amount of tax payable, paid and unpaid for the last financial year.

   (b)   The latest:

      (i)   annual self-assessment tax return to HMRC (a copy or print-out);

      (ii)   Statement of Account (SA300 or SA302); and,

      (iii) the same for the previous financial year if the latest return does not show the necessary level of gross income, but the average of the last 2 financial years does.

(c)   Proof of registration with HMRC as self-employed if available.

(d)   Each partner's Unique Tax Reference Number (UTR) and/or the UTR of the partnership or business.

(e)   Where the person holds or held a separate business bank account(s), bank statements for the same 12-month period as the tax return(s).

(f)   personal bank statements for the same 12-month period as the tax return(s) showing that the income from self-employment has been paid into an account in the name of the person or in the name of the person and their partner jointly.

(g)   Evidence of ongoing self-employment through evidence of payment of Class 2 National Insurance contributions.

(h)   One of the following documents must also be submitted:

        (i)   (aa)   If the business is required to produce annual audited accounts, the latest such accounts; or

               (bb)   If the business is not required to produce annual audited accounts, the latest unaudited accounts and an accountant's certificate of confirmation, from an accountant who is a member of a UK Recognised Supervisory Body (as defined in the Companies Act 2006);

        (ii)   A certificate of VAT registration and the latest VAT return (a copy or print-out) confirming the VAT registration number, if turnover is in excess of £73,000;

        (iii)   Evidence to show appropriate planning permission or local planning authority consent is held to operate the type/class of business at the trading address (where this is a local authority requirement); or

        (iv)   A franchise agreement signed by both parties.

(i)   The document referred to in paragraph 7(h)(iv) must be provided if the organisation is a franchise.

8.   In respect of self-employment outside of the UK, evidence should be a reasonable equivalent to that set out in paragraph 7.

9.   In respect of income from employment and/or shares in a limited company based in the UK of a type specified in paragraph 9(a), the requirements of paragraph 9(b)–(d) shall apply in place of the requirements of paragraphs 2 and 10(b).

    (a)   The specified type of limited company is one in which:

        (i)   the person is a director of the company (or another company within the same group); and

        (ii)   shares are held (directly or indirectly) by the person, their partner or the following family members of the person or their partner: parent, grandparent, child, stepchild, grandchild, brother, sister, uncle, aunt, nephew, niece or first cousin; and

        (iii)   any remaining shares are held (directly or indirectly) by fewer than five other persons.

    (b)   All of the following must be provided:

        (i)   Company Tax Return CT600 (a copy or print-out) for the last full financial year and evidence this has been filed with HMRC, such as electronic or written acknowledgment from HMRC.

        (ii)   Evidence of registration with the Registrar of Companies at Companies House.

        (iii)   If the company is required to produce annual audited accounts, the latest such accounts.

        (iv)   If the company is not required to produce annual audited accounts, the latest unaudited accounts and an accountant's certificate of confirmation, from an accountant who is a member of a UK Recognized Supervisory Body (as defined in the Companies Act 2006).

        (v)   Corporate/business bank statements covering the same 12-month period as the Company Tax Return CT600.

        (vi)   A current Appointment Report from Companies House.

        (vii)   One of the following documents must also be provided:

               (1)   A certificate of VAT registration and the latest VAT return (a copy or print-out) confirming the VAT registration number, if turnover is in excess of £73,000.

               (2)   Proof of ownership or lease of business premises.

               (3)   Original proof of registration with HMRC as an employer for the purposes of PAYE and National Insurance, proof of PAYE reference number and Accounts Office reference number. This evidence may be in the form of a certified copy of the documentation issued by HMRC.

(c)   Where the person is listed as a director of the company and receives a salary from the company, all of the following documents must also be provided:

    (i)   Payslips and P60 (if issued) covering the same period as the Company Tax Return CT600.

    (ii)   Personal bank statements covering the same 12-month period as the Company Tax Return CT600 showing that the salary as a director was paid into an account in the name of the person or in the name of the person and their partner jointly.

(d)   Where the person receives dividends from the company, all of the following documents must also be provided:

    (i)   Dividend vouchers for all dividends declared in favour of the person during or in respect of the period covered by the Company Tax Return CT600 showing the company's and the person's details with the person's net dividend amount and tax credit.

    (ii)   Personal bank statement(s) showing that those dividends were paid into an account in the name of the person or in the name of the person and their partner jointly.

10.   In respect of non-employment income all the following evidence, in relation to the form of income relied upon, must be provided:

(a)   To evidence property rental income:

    (i)   Confirmation that the person or the person and their partner jointly own the property for which the rental income is received, through:

        (1)   A copy of the title deeds of the property or of the title register from the Land Registry (or overseas equivalent); or

        (2)   A mortgage statement.

    (ii)   personal bank statements for the 12-month period prior to the date of application showing the rental income was paid into an account in the name of the person or of the person and their partner jointly.

    (iii)   A rental agreement or contract.

(b)   To evidence dividends (except where paragraph 9 applies) or other income from investments, stocks, shares, bonds or trust funds:

    (i)   A certificate showing proof of ownership and the amount(s) of any investment(s).

    (ii)   A portfolio report (for a financial institution regulated by the Financial Conduct Authority (and the Prudential Regulation Authority where applicable) in the UK) or a dividend voucher showing the company and person's details with the person's net dividend amount and tax credit.

    (iii)   personal bank statements for the 12-month period prior to the date of application showing that the income relied upon was paid into an account in the name of the person or of the person and their partner jointly.

    (iv)   Where the person is a director of a limited company based in the UK, evidence that the company is not of a type specified in paragraph 9(a). This can include the latest Annual Return filed at Companies House.

(c)   To evidence interest from savings:

    (i)   personal bank statements for the 12-month period prior to the date of application showing the amount of the savings held and that the interest was paid into an account in the name of the person or of the person and their partner jointly.

(d)   To evidence maintenance payments (from a former partner to maintain their and the applicant's child or children or the applicant):

    (i)   Evidence of a maintenance agreement through any of the following:

        (1)   A court order;

        (2)   Written voluntary agreement; or

        (3)   Child Support Agency documentation.

    (ii)   personal bank statements for the 12-month period prior to the date of application showing the income relied upon was paid into an account in the name of the applicant.

(e)   To evidence a pension:

    (i)   Official documentation from:

(1) The Department for Work and Pensions (in respect of the Basic State Pension and the Additional or Second State Pension) or other government department or agency;

(2) An overseas pension authority; or

(3) A pension company,

confirming pension entitlement and amount.

(ii) At least one personal bank statement in the 12-month period prior to the date of application showing payment of the pension into the person's account.

(f) To evidence UK Maternity Allowance, Bereavement Allowance, Bereavement Payment and Widowed Parent's Allowance:

(i) Department for Work and Pensions documentation confirming the person or their partner is or was in receipt of the benefit in the 12-month period prior to the date of application.

(ii) personal bank statements for the 12-month period prior to the date of application showing the income was paid into the person's account.

(g) To evidence a maintenance grant or stipend (not a loan) associated with undergraduate study or postgraduate study or research:

(i) Documentation from the body or company awarding the grant or stipend confirming that the person is currently in receipt of the grant or stipend or will be within 3 months of the date of application, confirming that the grant or stipend will be paid for a period of at least 12 months from the date of application or from the date on which payment of the grant or stipend will commence, and confirming the annual amount of the grant or stipend. Where the grant or stipend is or will be paid on a tax-free basis, the amount of the gross equivalent may be counted as income under this Appendix.

(ii) personal bank statements for any part of the 12-month period prior to the date of the application during which the person has been in receipt of the grant or stipend showing the income was paid into the person's account.

11. In respect of cash savings the following must be provided:

(a) personal bank statements showing that at least the level of cash savings relied upon in the application has been held in an account(s) in the name of the person or of the person and their partner jointly throughout the period of 6 months prior to the date of application.

(b) A declaration by the account holder(s) of the source(s) of the cash savings.

11A. In respect of cash savings:

(a) The savings may be held in any form of bank/savings account (whether a deposit or investment account), provided that the account allows the savings to be accessed immediately (with or without a penalty for withdrawing funds without notice). This can include savings held in a pension savings account which can be immediately withdrawn.

(b) Paid out competition winnings or a legacy which has been paid can contribute to cash savings.

(c) Funds held as cash savings by the applicant, their partner or both jointly at the date of application can have been transferred from investments, stocks, shares, bonds or trust funds within the period of 6 months prior to the date of application, provided that:

(i) The funds have been in the ownership and under the control of the applicant, their partner or both jointly for at least the period of 6 months prior to the date of application.

(ii) The ownership of the funds in the form of investments, stocks, shares, bonds or trust funds; the cash value of the funds in that form at or before the beginning of the period of 6 months prior to the date of application; and the transfer of the funds into cash, are evidenced by a portfolio report or other relevant documentation from a financial institution regulated by the appropriate regulatory body for the country in which that institution is operating.

(iii) The requirements of this Appendix in respect of the cash savings held at the date of application are met, except that the period of 6 months prior to the date of application in paragraph 11(a) will be reduced by the amount of that period in which the relevant funds were held in the form of investments, stocks, shares, bonds or trust funds.

(d) Funds held as cash savings by the applicant, their partner or both jointly at the date of application can be from the proceeds of the sale of property, in the form only of a dwelling, other building or land, which took place within the period of 6 months prior to the date of application, provided that:

    (i)   The property (or relevant share of the property) was owned at the beginning of the period of 6 months prior to the date of application and at the date of sale by the applicant, their partner or both jointly.

    (ii)   Where ownership of the property was shared with a third party, only the proceeds of the sale of the share of the property owned by the applicant, their partner or both jointly may be counted.

    (iii)   The funds deposited as cash savings are the net proceeds of the sale, once any mortgage or loan secured on the property (or relevant share of the property) has been repaid and once any taxes and professional fees associated with the sale have been paid.

    (iv)   The decision-maker is satisfied that the requirements in sub-paragraphs (i)–(iii) are met on the basis of information and documents submitted in support of the application. These may include for example:

        (1)   Registration information or documentation (or a copy of this) from the Land Registry (or overseas equivalent).

        (2)   A letter from a solicitor (or other relevant professional, if the sale takes place overseas) instructed in the sale of the property confirming the sale price and other relevant information.

        (3)   A letter from a lender (a bank or building society) on its headed stationery regarding the repayment of a mortgage or loan secured on the property.

        (4)   Confirmation of payment of taxes or professional fees associated with the sale.

        (5)   Any other relevant evidence that the requirements in subparagraphs (i)–(iii) are met.

    (v)   The requirements of this Appendix in respect of the cash savings held at the date of application are met, except that the period of 6 months mentioned in paragraph 11(a) will be reduced by the amount of time which passed between the start of that 6-month period and the deposit of the proceeds of the sale in an account mentioned in paragraph 11(a).

12.   Where the applicant's partner is in receipt of Carer's Allowance, Disability Living Allowance, Severe Disablement Allowance, Industrial Injuries Disablement Benefit, Attendance Allowance or Personal Independence Payment, all the following must be provided:

    (a)   Official documentation from the Department for Work and Pensions confirming the entitlement and the amount received.

    (b)   At least one personal bank statement in the 12-month period prior to the date of application.showing payment of the benefit or allowance into the person's account.

12A.   Where the financial requirement the applicant must meet under Appendix FM relates to adequate maintenance, paragraphs 2 to 12 apply only to the extent and in the manner specified by this paragraph. Where such a financial requirement applies, the applicant must provide the following evidence:

    (a)   Where the current salaried employment in the UK of the applicant or their partner, parent, parent's partner or sponsor is relied upon:

        (i)   A letter from the employer confirming the employment, the gross annual salary and the annual salary after income tax and National Insurance contributions have been paid, how long the employment has been held, and the type of employment (permanent, fixed-term contract or agency).

        (ii)   Payslips covering the period of 6 months prior to the date of application or such shorter period as the current employment has been held.

        (iii)   personal bank statement covering the same period as the payslips, showing that the salary has been paid into an account in the name of the person or in the name of the person and their partner jointly.

    (b)   Where statutory or contractual maternity, paternity, adoption or sick pay in the UK of the applicant or their partner, parent, parent's partner or sponsor are relied upon, paragraph 5(b)(i) and (c) or paragraph 6(b)(i) and (c) apply as appropriate.

    (c)   Where self-employment in the UK of the applicant or their partner, parent, parent's partner or sponsor, or income from employment and/or shares in a limited company based in the UK of a type to which paragraph 9 applies, is relied upon, paragraph 7 or 9 applies as appropriate.

    (d)   Where the non-employment income of the applicant or their partner, parent, parent's partner or sponsor is relied upon, paragraph 10 applies and paragraph 10(f) shall apply as if it referred to any UK welfare benefit or tax credit relied upon and to HMRC as well as Department for Work and Pensions documentation.

(e) Where the cash savings of the applicant or their partner, parent, parent's partner or sponsor are relied upon, paragraphs 11 and 11A apply.

(f) The monthly housing and Council Tax costs for the accommodation in the UK in which the applicant (and any other family members who are or will be part of the same household) lives or will live if the application is granted.

(g) Where the applicant is an adult dependent relative applying for entry clearance, the applicant must in addition provide details of the care arrangements in the UK planned for them by their sponsor (which can involve other family members in the UK), of the cost of these arrangements and of how that cost will be met by the sponsor.

Calculating Gross Annual Income under Appendix FM

13. Based on evidence that meets the requirements of this Appendix, and can be taken into account with reference to the applicable provisions of Appendix FM, gross annual income under paragraphs E-ECP.3.1., E-LTRP.3.1., E-ECC.2.1. and E-LTRC.2.1. will be calculated in the following ways:

(a) Where the person is in salaried employment in the UK at the date of application, has been employed by their current employer for at least 6 months and has been paid throughout the period of 6 months prior to the date of application at a level of gross annual salary which equals or exceeds the level relied upon in paragraph 13(a)(i), their gross annual income will be (where paragraph 13(b) does not apply) the total of:

(i) The level of gross annual salary relied upon in the application;

(ii) The gross amount of any specified non-employment income (other than pension income) received by them or their partner in the 12 months prior to the date of application; and

(iii) The gross annual income from a UK or foreign State pension or a private pension received by them or their partner.

(b) Where the person is in salaried employment in the UK at the date of application and has been employed by their current employer for less than 6 months (or at least 6 months but the person does not rely on paragraph 13(a)), their gross annual income will be the total of:

(i) The gross annual salary from employment as it was at the date of application;

(ii) The gross amount of any specified non-employment income (other than pension income) received by them or their partner in the 12 months prior to the date of application; and

(iii) The gross annual income from a UK or foreign State pension or a private pension received by them or their partner.

In addition, the requirements of paragraph 15 must be met.

(c) Where the person is the applicant's partner, is in salaried employment outside of the UK at the date of application, has been employed by their current employer for at least 6 months, and is returning to the UK to take up salaried employment in the UK starting within 3 months of their return, the person's gross annual income will be calculated:

(i) On the basis set out in paragraph 13(a); and also

(ii) On that basis but substituting for the gross annual salary at paragraph 13(a)(i) the gross annual salary in the salaried employment in the UK to which they are returning.

(d) Where the person is the applicant's partner, has been in salaried employment outside of the UK within 12 months of the date of application, and is returning to the UK to take up salaried employment in the UK starting within 3 months of their return, the person's gross annual income will be calculated:

(i) On the basis set out in paragraph 13(a) but substituting for the gross annual salary at paragraph 13(a)(i) the gross annual salary in the salaried employment in the UK to which they are returning; and also

(ii) On the basis set out in paragraph 15(b).

(e) Where the person is self-employed, their gross annual income will be the total of their gross income from their self-employment, from any salaried employment they have had, from specified non-employment income received by them or their partner, and from income from a UK or foreign State pension or a private pension received by them or their partner, in the last full financial year or as an average of the last two full financial years. The requirements of this Appendix for specified evidence relating to these forms of income shall apply as if references to the date of application were references to the end of the relevant financial year(s). The relevant financial year(s) cannot be combined with any financial year(s) to which paragraph 9 applies and vice versa.

(f)   Where the person is self-employed, they cannot combine their gross annual income at paragraph 13(e) with specified savings in order to meet the level of income required under Appendix FM.

(g)   Where the person is not relying on income from salaried employment or self-employment, their gross annual income will be the total of:

(i)   The gross amount of any specified non-employment income (other than pension income) received by them or their partner in the 12 months prior to the date of application; and

(ii)   The gross annual income from a UK or foreign State pension or a private pension received by them or their partner.

(h)   Where the person is the applicant's partner and is in self-employment outside the UK at the date of application and is returning to the UK to take up salaried employment in the UK starting within 3 months of their return, the person's gross annual income will be calculated:

(i)   On the basis set out in paragraph 13(a) but substituting for the gross annual salary at paragraph 13(a)(i) the gross annual salary in the salaried employment in the UK to which they are returning; and also

(ii)   On the basis set out in paragraph 13(e).

(i)   Any period of unpaid maternity, paternity, adoption, parental or sick leave in the 12 months prior to the date of application will not be counted towards any period relating to employment, or any period relating to income from employment, for which this Appendix provides.

(j)   The provisions of paragraph 13 which apply to self-employment and to a person who is self-employed also apply to income from employment and/or shares in a limited company based in the UK of a type to which paragraph 9 applies and to a person in receipt of such income.

14.   Where the requirements of this Appendix and Appendix FM are met by the combined income or cash savings of more than one person, the income or the cash savings must only be counted once unless stated otherwise.

15.   In respect of paragraph 13(b) and paragraph 13(d), the provisions in this paragraph also apply:

(a)   In order to evidence the level of gross annual income required by Appendix FM, the person must meet the requirements in paragraph 13(b) or paragraph 13(d)(i); and

(b)   The person must also meet the level of gross annual income required by Appendix FM on the basis that their income is the total of:

(i)   The gross income from salaried employment in the UK or overseas earned by the person in the 12 months prior to the date of application;

(ii)   The gross amount of any specified non-employment income (other than pension income) received by the person or their partner in the 12 months prior to the date of application;

(iii)   The gross amount received from a UK or foreign State pension or a private pension by the person or their partner in the 12 months prior to the date of application; and

(iv)   The person cannot combine the gross annual income at paragraph 15(b)(i)–(iii) with specified savings in order to meet the level of income required.

16.   Where a person is in receipt of maternity, paternity, adoption or sick pay or has been so in the 6 months prior to the date of application, this paragraph applies:

(a)   the relevant date for considering the length of employment with their current employer will be the date that the maternity, paternity, adoption or sick leave commenced or the date of application; and

(b)   the relevant period for calculating income from their salaried employment will be the period prior to the commencement of the maternity, paternity, adoption or sick pay or to the date of application.

17.   If a person is an equity partner, for example in a law firm, the income they draw from the partnership will be treated as salaried employment for the purposes of this Appendix and Appendix FM.

17A.   Where a person is a subcontractor under the Construction Industry Scheme administered by HMRC and does not rely on paragraph 13(e), the income they receive as a subcontractor under the Construction Industry Scheme may be treated as income from salaried employment for the purposes of this Appendix and Appendix FM. In that case, the requirements for specified evidence in paragraph 2 must be met, subject to applying those requirements so as to reflect the person's status as a subcontractor under the Construction Industry Scheme.

18.   When calculating income from salaried employment under paragraphs 12A and 13 to 16, this paragraph applies:

(a) Basic pay, skills-based allowances, and UK location-based allowances will be counted as income provided that:

    (i) They are contractual; and

    (ii) Where these allowances make up more than 30% of the total salary, only the amount up to 30% is counted.

(b) Overtime, commission-based pay and bonuses will be counted as income, where they have been received in the relevant period(s) of employment or self-employment relied upon in the application.

(bb) In respect of a person in salaried employment at the date of application, the amount of income in sub-paragraph (b) which may be added to their gross annual salary, and counted as part of that figure for the purposes of paragraph 13(a)(i) or 13(b)(i), is the annual equivalent of the person's average gross monthly income from that income in their current employment in the 6 months prior to the date of application.

(c) UK and overseas travel, subsistence and accommodation allowances, and allowances relating to the cost of living overseas will not be counted as income.

(d) Gross income from non-salaried employment will be calculated on the same basis as income from salaried employment, except as provided in paragraph 18(e) and 18(f), and the requirements of this Appendix for specified evidence relating to salaried employment shall apply as if references to salary were references to income from non-salaried employment. Non-salaried employment includes that paid at an hourly or other rate (and the number and/or pattern of hours required to be worked may vary), or paid an amount which varies according to the work undertaken, whereas salaried employment includes that paid at a minimum fixed rate (usually annual) and is subject usually to a contractual minimum number of hours to be worked.

(e) For the purpose of paragraph 13(a)(i), in respect of a person in non-salaried employment at the date of application 'the level of gross annual salary relied upon in the application' shall be no greater than the annual equivalent of the person's average gross monthly income from non-salaried employment in the 6 months prior to the date of application, where that employment was held throughout that period.

(f) For the purpose of paragraph 13(b)(i), 'the gross annual salary from employment as it was at the date of application' of a person in non-salaried employment at the date of application shall be considered to be the annual equivalent of the person's average gross monthly income from non-salaried employment in the 6 months prior to the date of application, regardless of whether that employment was held throughout that period.

(g) For the purpose of paragraphs 13(c)(ii) and 13(d)(i), 'the gross annual salary in the salaried employment in the UK to which they are returning' of a person who is returning to the UK to take up non-salaried employment in the UK starting within 3 months of their return is the gross annual income from that employment, based on the rate or amount of pay, and the standard or core hours of work, set out in the document(s) from the employer provided under paragraph 4. Notwithstanding paragraph 18(b), this may include the gross 'on-target' earnings which may be expected from satisfactory performance in the standard or core hours of work.

19. When calculating income from self-employment under paragraphs 12A and 13(e), and in relation to income from employment and/or shares in a limited company based in the UK of a type to which paragraph 9 applies, this paragraph applies:

(a) There must be evidence of ongoing self-employment, and (where income from salaried employment is also relied upon or where paragraph 9(c) applies) ongoing employment, at the date of application.

(b) Where the self-employed person is a sole trader or is in a partnership or franchise agreement, the income will be:

    (i) the gross taxable profits from their share of the business; and

    (ii) allowances or deductable expenses which are not taxed will not be counted towards income.

(c) Where income to which paragraph 19 applies is being used to meet the financial requirement for an initial application for leave to remain as a partner under Appendix FM by an applicant who used such income to meet that requirement in an application for entry clearance as a fiancé(e) or proposed civil partner under that Appendix in the last 12 months, the Secretary of State may continue to accept the same level and evidence of income to which paragraph 19 applies that was accepted in granting the application for entry clearance, provided that there is evidence of ongoing self-employment, and (where income from salaried employment is also relied upon or where paragraph 9(c) applies) ongoing employment, at the date of the application for leave to remain.

(d)   The financial year(s) to which paragraph 7 refers is the period of the last full financial year(s) to which the required Statement(s) of Account (SA300 or SA302) relates.

(e)   The financial year(s) to which paragraph 9 refers is the period of the last full financial year(s) to which the required Company Tax Return(s) CT600 relates.

20.   When calculating income from specified non-employment sources under paragraphs 12A and 13 to 15, this paragraph applies:

(a)   Assets or savings must be in the name of the person, or jointly with their partner.

(b)   Any asset or savings on which income is based must be held or owned by the person at the date of application.

(c)   Any rental income from property, in the UK or overseas, must be from a property that is:

(i)   owned by the person;

(ii)   not their main residence and will not be so if the application is granted, except in the circumstances specified in paragraph 20(e); and

(iii)   if ownership of the property is shared with a third party, only income received from their share of the property can be counted.

(cc)   The amount of rental income from property received before any management fee was deducted may be counted.

(d)   Equity in a property cannot be used to meet the financial requirement.

(e)   Where the applicant and their partner are resident outside the UK at the date of application, rental income from a property in the UK that will become their main residence if the application is granted may only be counted under paragraph 13(c)(i) and paragraph 13(d)(ii).

(f)   Any future entitlement to a maintenance grant or stipend of the type specified in paragraph 10(g) may be counted as though the person had received the annual amount of that grant or stipend in the 12 months prior to the date of application.

20A.   When calculating the gross annual income from pension under paragraph 13, the gross annual amount of any pension received may be counted where the pension has become a source of income at least 28 days prior to the date of application.

21.   When calculating income under paragraphs 13 to 16, the following sources will not be counted:

(a)   Loans and credit facilities.

(b)   Income-related benefits: Income Support, income-related Employment and Support Allowance, Pension Credit, Housing Benefit, Council Tax Benefit and income-based Jobseeker's Allowance.

(c)   The following contributory benefits: contribution-based Jobseeker's Allowance, contribution-based Employment and Support Allowance and Incapacity Benefit.

(d)   Child Benefit.

(e)   Working Tax Credit.

(f)   Child Tax Credit.

(g)   Any other source of income not specified in this appendix.

Evidence of Marriage or Civil Partnerships

22.   A claim to have been married in the United Kingdom must be evidenced by a marriage certificate.

23.   A claim to be divorced in the United Kingdom must be evidenced by a decree absolute from a civil court.

24.   A civil partnership in the United Kingdom must be evidenced by a civil partnership certificate.

25.   The dissolution of a civil partnership in the UK must be evidenced by a final order of civil partnership dissolution from a civil court.

26.   Marriages, civil partnerships or evidence of divorce or dissolution from outside the UK must be evidenced by a reasonable equivalent to the evidence detailed in paragraphs 22 to 25, valid under the law in force in the relevant country.

Evidence of English Language Requirements

27.   Evidence of passing an English language test in speaking and listening must take the form of either:

(a)   a certificate and/or other document(s) for the relevant test as specified in Appendix O that:

(i)   is from an English language test provider approved by the Secretary of State for these purposes as specified in Appendix O of these rules

        (ii)   is a test approved by the Secretary of State for these purposes as specified in Appendix O of these rules

        (iii)   shows the applicant's name;

        (iv)   shows the qualification obtained (which must meet or exceed level A1 of the Common European Framework of Reference); and,

        (v)   shows the date of award.

      Or,

(b)   a print out of the online score from a PTE (Pearson) test which:

        (i)   is a test approved by the Secretary of State for these purposes as specified in Appendix O of these rules;

        (ii)   can be used to show that the qualification obtained (which must meet or exceed level A1 of the Common European Framework of Reference); and,

        (iii)   is from an English language test provider approved by the Secretary of State for these purposes as specified in Appendix O of these rules

28.   The evidence required to show that a person is a citizen or national of a majority English speaking country is a valid passport or travel document, unless paragraphs 29 and 30 apply. A dual national may invoke either of their nationalities.

29.   If the applicant has not provided their passport or travel document other evidence of nationality can be supplied in the following circumstances only (as indicated by the applicant on their application form):

    (a)   where the passport has been lost or stolen;

    (b)   where the passport has expired and been returned to the relevant authorities; or

    (c)   where the passport is with another part of the Home Office.

30.   Alternative evidence as proof of nationality, if acceptable, must be either:

    (a)   A current national identity document; or

    (b)   An original letter from the applicant's Home Government or Embassy confirming the applicant's full name, date of birth and nationality.

31.   Evidence of an academic qualification (recognised by UK NARIC to be equivalent to the standard of a Bachelor's or Master's degree or PhD in the UK) and was taught in English must be either:

    (a)   A certificate issued by the relevant institution confirming the award of the academic qualification showing:

        (i)   the applicant's name;

        (ii)   the title of award;

        (iii)   the date of award;

        (iv)   the name of the awarding institution; and,

        (v)   that the qualification was taught in English

      Or,

    (b)   If the applicant is awaiting graduation or no longer has the certificate and cannot get a new one, the evidence must be:

        (i)   an original academic reference from the institution awarding the academic qualification that;

            (1)   is on official letter headed paper;

            (2)   shows the applicant's name;

            (3)   shows the title of award;

            (4)   confirms that the qualification was taught in English;

            (5)   explains when the academic qualification has been, or will be awarded; and

            (6)   states either the date that the certificate will be issued (if the applicant has not yet graduated) or confirms that the institution is unable to re-issue the original certificate of award.

        or

        (ii)   an original academic transcript that

            (1)   is on official letter headed paper

            (2)   shows the applicant's name;

            (3)   the name of the academic institution;

      (4)   the course title;

      (5)   confirms that the qualification was taught in English; and,

      (6)   provides confirmation of the award.

32.   If the qualification was taken in one of the following countries, it will be assumed for the purpose of paragraph 31 that it was taught in English: Antigua and Barbuda, Australia, the Bahamas, Barbados, Belize, Dominica, Grenada, Guyana, Ireland, Jamaica, New Zealand, St Kitts and Nevis, St Lucia, St Vincent and the Grenadines, Trinidad and Tobago, the UK, the USA.

Adult dependent relatives

33.   Evidence of the family relationship between the applicant(s) and the sponsor should take the form of birth or adoption certificates, or other documentary evidence.

34.   Evidence that, as a result of age, illness or disability, the applicant requires long-term personal care should take the form of:

      (a)   Medical evidence that the applicant's physical or mental condition means that they cannot perform everyday tasks; and

      (b)   This must be from a doctor or other health professional.

35.   Evidence that the applicant is unable, even with the practical and financial help of the sponsor in the UK, to obtain the required level of care in the country where they are living should be from:

      (a)   a central or local health authority;

      (b)   a local authority; or

      (c)   a doctor or other health professional.

36.   If the applicant's required care has previously been provided through a private arrangement, the applicant must provide details of that arrangement and why it is no longer available.

37.   If the applicant's required level of care is not, or is no longer, affordable because payment previously made for arranging this care is no longer being made, the applicant must provide records of that payment and an explanation of why that payment cannot continue. If financial support has been provided by the sponsor or other close family in the UK, the applicant must provide an explanation of why this cannot continue or is no longer sufficient to enable the required level of care to be provided.

Appendix G – Countries and Territories participating in the Tier 5 Youth Mobility Scheme and annual allocations of places for 2014

Places available for use by Countries and Territories with Deemed Sponsorship Status:

Australia – 38,500 places
Canada – 5,500 places
Japan – 1,000 places
New Zealand – 9,500 places
Monaco – 1,000 places

Places available for use by Countries and Territories without Deemed Sponsorship Status:

Taiwan – 1,000 places
South Korea – 1,000 places
Hong Kong – 1,000 places

Appendix H – Applicants who are subject to different documentary requirements under Tier 4 of the Points Based System

An applicant will be subject to different documentary requirements under Tier 4 of the Points Based System where he is a national of one of the following countries and he is applying for entry clearance in his country of nationality or leave to remain in the UK:

Argentina
Australia
Barbados
Botswana

Brunei
Canada
Chile
Japan
Malaysia
New Zealand
Singapore
South Korea
Trinidad and Tobago
United States of America

Where an applicant is a dual national, and only one of their nationalities is listed above, he will be able to apply using the different documentary requirements that apply to these nationals, provided he is applying either for entry clearance in his country of nationality listed above or for leave to remain in the UK.

An applicant will be subject to different documentary requirements under Tier 4 of the Points Based System where he is the rightful holder of one of the following passports, which has been issued by the relevant competent authority, and where he is applying for leave to remain in the UK or for entry clearance in the territory related to the passport he holds:

British National (Overseas)

Hong Kong

Taiwan (those who hold a passport issued by Taiwan that includes the number of the identification card issued by the competent authority in Taiwan)

Where an applicant is the rightful holder of a passport issued by a relevant competent authority listed above and also holds another passport or is the national of a country not listed above, he will be able to apply using the different documentary requirements that apply to rightful holders of those passports listed in this Appendix provided he is applying either for entry clearance in the territory related to the passport he holds or for leave to remain in the UK.

Appendix I, J – OMITTED

Appendix K: Shortage Occupation List

1. Where these Rules refer to jobs which appear on the Shortage Occupation List, this means only those specific jobs within each Standard Occupational Classification code stated in Tables 1 and 2 below and, where stated, where the further specified criteria are met.
2. Jobs which appear on the United Kingdom Shortage Occupation List are set out in Table 1.
3. Jobs which appear on the Scotland Only Shortage Occupation List are set out in Table 2.

Table 1: United Kingdom Shortage Occupation List

Standard Occupational Classification (SOC) code and description	Job titles included on the United Kingdom Shortage Occupation List and further criteria

Production managers and directors in mining and energy (1123)	**Only** the following jobs in this occupation code:
	The following jobs in the decommissioning and waste management areas of the nuclear industry:
	  – managing director
	  – programme director
	  – site director
	The following jobs in the electricity transmission and distribution industry:
	  – project manager
	  – site manager

2112 Biological scientists and biochemists	**Only** the following job in this occupation code: clinical neurophysiologist

Standard Occupational Classification (SOC) code and description	Job titles included on the United Kingdom Shortage Occupation List and further criteria
2113 Physical Scientists	**Only** the following jobs in this occupation code: the following jobs in the construction-related ground engineering industry: – engineering geologist – hydrogeologist – geophysicist the following jobs in the oil and gas industry: – geophysicist – geoscientist – geologist – geochemist technical services manager in the decommissioning and waste areas of the nuclear industry nuclear medicine scientist radiotherapy physicist senior resource geologist and staff geologist in the mining sector
2119 Natural and social science professionals not elsewhere classified	**Only** the following jobs in this occupation code: informatician bio-informatician
2121 Civil engineers	**Only** the following jobs in this occupation code: the following jobs in the construction-related ground engineering industry: – geotechnical engineer – tunnelling engineer the following jobs in the oil and gas industry: – petroleum engineer – drilling engineer – completions engineer – fluids engineer – reservoir engineer – offshore and subsea engineer – control and instrument engineer – process safety engineer – wells engineer senior mining engineer in the mining sector
2122 Mechanical engineers	**Only** the following job in this occupation code: mechanical engineer in the oil and gas industry

Standard Occupational Classification (SOC) code and description	Job titles included on the United Kingdom Shortage Occupation List and further criteria
2123 Electrical engineers	**Only** the following jobs in this occupation code: electrical engineer in the oil and gas industry the following jobs in the electricity transmission and distribution industry: — power system engineer — control engineer — protection engineer the following jobs in the aerospace industry: — electrical machine design engineer — power electronics engineer
2124 Electronics Engineers	**Only** the following jobs in this occupation code: the following jobs in the railway industry: — signalling design manager — signalling design engineer — signalling principles designer — senior signalling design checker — signalling design checker — signalling systems engineer specialist electronics engineer in the automotive manufacturing and design industry
2126 Design and development engineers	**Only** the following jobs in this occupation code: design engineer in the electricity transmission and distribution industry the following jobs in the automotive design and manufacturing industry: — product development engineer — product design engineer the following jobs in the electronics system industry: — integrated circuit design engineer — integrated circuit test engineer
2127 Production and process engineers	**Only** the following jobs in this occupation code: chemical engineer manufacturing engineer (process planning) in the aerospace industry technical services representative in the decommissioning and waste areas of the nuclear industry

Standard Occupational Classification (SOC) code and description	Job titles included on the United Kingdom Shortage Occupation List and further criteria
2129 Engineering professionals not elsewhere classified	**Only** the following jobs in this occupation code: the following jobs in the electricity transmission and distribution industry: – project engineer – proposals engineer the following jobs in the aerospace industry: – aerothermal engineer – stress engineer – chief of engineering – advance tool and fixturing engineer the following jobs in the decommissioning and waste management areas of the civil nuclear industry: – operations manager – decommissioning specialist manager – project/planning engineer – radioactive waste manager – radiological protection advisor The following jobs in the civil nuclear industry: – nuclear safety case engineer – mechanical design engineer (pressure vehicles) – piping design engineer – mechanical design engineer (stress) – thermofluids/process engineer
2135 IT Business analysts, architects and systems designers	**Only** the following jobs in this occupation code: systems engineer in visual effects and 2D/3D computer animation for the film, television or video games sectors
2136 Programmers and software development professionals	**Only** the following jobs in this occupation code: the following jobs in visual effects and 2D/3D computer animation for the film, television or video games sectors: – software developer – shader writer – games designer the following jobs in the electronics system industry: – driver developer – embedded communications engineer
2142 Environmental Professionals	**Only** the following jobs in this occupation code: the following jobs in the construction-related ground engineering industry: – contaminated land specialist – geoenvironmental specialist – landfill engineer

Standard Occupational Classification (SOC) code and description	Job titles included on the United Kingdom Shortage Occupation List and further criteria
2211 Medical practitioners	**Only** the following jobs in this occupation code: consultant in the following specialities: – emergency medicine – haematology – old age psychiatry non-consultant, non-training, medical staff post in the following specialities: – anaesthetics – general medicine specialities delivering acute care services (intensive care medicine, general internal medicine (acute), emergency medicine (including specialist doctors working in accident and emergency)) – rehabilitation medicine – psychiatry
2217 Medical Radiographers	**Only** the following jobs in this occupation code: HPC registered diagnostic radiographer HPC registered therapeutic radiographer sonographer Sponsors must retain evidence of the individual's HPC registration and provide this to the UK Border Agency on request. (Registration may need to be done after the individual has entered the United Kingdom but must be done before starting work).
2231 Nurses	**Only** the following job in this occupation code: specialist nurse working in neonatal intensive care units Sponsors must retain evidence of the individual's provisional / full NMC registration and provide this to the UK Border Agency on request.
2314 Secondary education teaching professionals	**Only** the following jobs in this occupation code: secondary education teachers in the subjects of maths and science (chemistry and physics only)
2442 Social workers	**Only** the following jobs in this occupation code: social worker working in children's and family services
2461 Quality control and planning engineers	**Only** the following jobs in this occupation code: the following jobs in the electricity transmission and distribution industry: – planning / development engineer – quality, health, safety and environment (QHSE) engineer
3113 Engineering technicians	**Only** the following jobs in this occupation code: the following jobs in the electricity transmission and distribution industry: – commissioning engineer – substation electrical engineer
3218 Medical and dental technicians	**Only** the following jobs in this occupation code: nuclear medicine technologist radiotherapy technologist

Standard Occupational Classification (SOC) code and description	Job titles included on the United Kingdom Shortage Occupation List and further criteria
3411 Artist	**Only** the following jobs in this occupation code: Animator in visual effects and 2D/3D computer animation for the film, television or video games sectors
3414 Dancers and choreographers	**Only** the following jobs in this occupation code: skilled classical ballet dancers who meet the standard required by internationally recognised United Kingdom ballet companies (e.g. Birmingham Royal Ballet, English National Ballet, Northern Ballet Theatre, The Royal Ballet and Scottish Ballet). The company must either: – have performed at or been invited to perform at venues of the calibre of the Royal Opera House, Sadler's Wells or Barbican, either in the United Kingdom or overseas; or – attract dancers and/or choreographers and other artists from other countries; or – be endorsed as being internationally recognised by a United Kingdom industry body such as the Arts Councils (of England, Scotland and/or Wales) skilled contemporary dancers who meet the standard required by internationally recognised United Kingdom contemporary dance companies (e.g. Shobana Jeyasingh Dance Company, Scottish Dance Theatre and Rambert Dance Company). The company must either: – have performed at or been invited to perform at venues of the calibre of Sadler's Wells, the Southbank Centre or The Place, either in the United Kingdom or overseas; or – attract dancers and/or choreographers and other artists from all over the world; or – be endorsed as being internationally recognised by a United Kingdom industry body such as the Arts Councils (of England, Scotland and/or Wales)
3415 Musicians	**Only** the following jobs in this occupation code: skilled orchestral musicians who are leaders, principals, sub-principals or numbered string positions, and who meet the standard required by internationally recognised UK orchestras (including London Symphony Orchestra, London Philharmonic Orchestra, Philharmonia Orchestra and Royal Philharmonic Orchestra)
3416 Arts officers, producers and directors	**Only** the following jobs in this occupation code: the following jobs in visual effects and 2D/3D computer animation for the film, television or video games sectors: – 2D supervisor – 3D supervisor – computer graphics supervisor – producer – production manager – technical director – visual effects supervisor

Standard Occupational Classification (SOC) code and description	Job titles included on the United Kingdom Shortage Occupation List and further criteria

3421 Graphic designers	Only the following jobs in this occupation code:
	the following jobs in visual effects and 2D/3D computer animation for the film, television or video games sectors:
	  – compositing artist
	  – matte painter
	  – modeller
	  – rigger
	  – stereo artist
	  – texture artist

3541 Buyers and purchasing officers	Only the following job in this occupation code: manufacturing engineer (purchasing) in the aerospace industry
5215 Welding trades	Only the following job in this occupation code: high integrity pipe welder where the job requires three or more years' related on-the-job experience Sponsors must retain references from the individual's past employer(s) detailing three or more years' related on-the-job experience and provide these to the UK Border Agency on request. Sponsors must also retain relevant evidence to enable them to justify the following: 1) – Why does the job require someone with three or more years' related on-the-job experience? What elements of the job require this experience and why? 2) – Why could the job not be carried out to the required standard by someone with less experience? 3) – How would you expect a settled worker to gain this experience before being appointed to the post?
5235 Aircraft maintenance and related trades	Only the following jobs in this occupation code: licensed and military certifying engineer/inspector technician
5249 Line repairers and cable jointers	Only the following job in this occupation code: overhead linesworker, working on high voltage lines that carry at least 275,000 volts

Standard Occupational Classification (SOC) code and description	Job titles included on the United Kingdom Shortage Occupation List and further criteria

5434 Chefs	**Only** the following job in this occupation code:
	skilled chef where:
	   – the pay is at least £29,570 per year after deductions for accommodation, meals etc; **and**
	   – the job requires five or more years relevant experience in a role of at least equivalent status to the one they are entering; **and**
	   – the job is not in either a fast food outlet, a standard fare outlet, or an establishment which provides a take-away service; **and**
	   – the job is in one of the following roles:
	   – executive chef – limited to one per establishment
	   – head chef – limited to one per establishment
	   – sous chef – limited to one for every four kitchen staff per establishment
	   – specialist chef – limited to one per speciality per establishment
	
	A fast food outlet is one where food is prepared in bulk for speed of service, rather than to individual order.
	
	A standard fare outlet is one where the menu is designed centrally for outlets in a chain / franchise, rather than by a chef or chefs in the individual restaurant. Standard fare outlets also include those where dishes and / or cooking sauces are bought in ready-made, rather than prepared from fresh / raw ingredients.
	
	Sponsors must retain references from the individual's past employer(s) detailing five or more years' relevant experience in a role of at least equivalent status and provide these to the UK Border Agency on request.
	
	Sponsors must also retain relevant evidence to enable them to justify the following:
	
	1) – Why does the job require someone with at least five years' previous experience in a role of at least equivalent status? What elements of the job require this experience and why?
	
	2) – Why could the job not be carried out to the required standard by someone with less experience?
	
	3) – How would you expect a settled worker to gain this experience before being appointed to the post?

Table 2: Scotland Only Shortage Occupation List

Standard Occupational Classification (SOC) code and description	Job titles included on the Scotland Only Shortage Occupation List and further specified criteria
All	**All** job titles and occupations on the United Kingdom Shortage Occupation List
2113 Physical scientists	**Only** the following jobs in this occupation code: jobs on the United Kingdom Shortage Occupation List staff working in diagnostics radiology (including magnetic resonance imaging)

Standard Occupational Classification (SOC) code and description	Job titles included on the Scotland Only Shortage Occupation List and further specified criteria
2211 Medical practitioners	**Only** the following jobs in this occupation code: jobs on the United Kingdom Shortage Occupation List ST3, ST4, ST5 and ST6 trainees in paediatrics or anaesthetics SAS staff doctors in paediatrics or anaesthetics consultants in paediatrics or anaesthetics non-consultant, non-training doctors in the specialty obstetrics and gynaecology

APPENDIX KOLL

PART 1. GENERAL

Purpose

1.1   This Appendix sets out the way in which an applicant for leave to enter or remain must demonstrate sufficient knowledge of the English language and about life in the United Kingdom where it is a requirement of the Rules to demonstrate this for the purposes of an application for indefinite leave to enter or remain. It also sets out general exemptions to the requirement on grounds of age and enables the decision maker to waive the requirement in light of special circumstances in any particular case.

'Specified' in this Appendix means 'specified in Part 4 of this appendix'

PART 2 – KNOWLEDGE OF LANGUAGE AND LIFE

2.1   An applicant for leave to enter or remain has sufficient knowledge of the English language and about life in the United Kingdom for the purpose of an application for indefinite leave to enter or remain made under these Rules if the requirements set out in paragraphs 2.2 and 2.3 are met unless the exceptions set out in Part 3 apply.

2.2   For the purposes of paragraph 2. 1, an applicant has sufficient knowledge of the English language if:

(a)   the applicant has provided specified documentary evidence that:

(i)   the applicant is a national or citizen of one of the following countries:

Antigua and Barbuda
Australia
The Bahamas Barbados
Belize
Canada
Dominica
Grenada
Guyana
Jamaica
New Zealand
St Kitts and Nevis
St Lucia
St Vincent and the Grenadines
Trinidad and Tobago
USA.

or

(ii)   the applicant has passed an English language test in speaking and listening at a minimum level B 1 of the Common European Framework of Reference for Languages with a provider approved by the Secretary of State as specified in Appendix O to these Rules; or

(iii)   the applicant has obtained an academic qualification(not a professional or vocational qualification), which is deemed by UK NARIC to meet the recognised standard of a Bachelor's or Master's degree or PhD in the UK, from an educational establishment in one of the following countries: Antigua and Barbuda; Australia; The Bahamas; Barbados; Belize; Dominica; Grenada; Guyana; Ireland; Jamaica; New Zealand; St Kitts and Nevis; St Lucia; St Vincent and

The Grenadines; Trinidad and Tobago; the UK; the USA; and provides the specified documents; or

(iv)   the applicant has obtained an academic qualification (not a professional or vocational qualification) which is deemed by UK NARIC to meet the recognised standard of a Bachelor's or Master's degree or PhD in the UK, and

    (1)   provides the specified documentary evidence to show he has the qualification, and

    (2)   UK NARIC has confirmed that the qualification was taught or researched in English; or

(v)   the applicant has obtained an academic qualification (not a professional or vocational qualification) which is deemed by UK NARIC to meet the recognised standard of a Bachelor's or Master's degree or PhD in the UK, and provides the specified evidence to show:

    (1)   he has the qualification, and

    (2)   that the qualification was taught or researched in English; or.

(vi)   the applicant has taken and passed in England, Wales or Northern Ireland a qualification in English for Speakers of Other Languages (ESOL) which:

    (aa)   includes speaking and listening;

    (bb)   is at ESOL Entry level 3, level 1, level 2 or level 3,

    (cc)   is regulated by the Office of Qualifications and Examinations Regulation (OFQUAL), the Welsh Government or the Council for Curriculum, Examinations and Assessment (CCEA), and

    (dd)   is listed as an ESOL qualification on the Register of Regulated Qualifications,

    or

(vii)   the applicant has passed in Scotland a National Qualification in English for Speakers of Other Languages at Scottish Credit and Qualifications Framework (SCQF) level 4, 5 or 6 awarded by the Scottish Qualifications Authority;

    or

(b)   the applicant–

    (i)   has limited leave to enter or remain in the UK, and

    (ii)   that leave (or a grant of leave which preceded it provided any periods of leave since have been unbroken) was given on the basis that the applicant had an English language qualification at a minimum level of B 1 on the Common European Framework of Reference for Languages.

2.3   For the purposes of sub-paragraph (1), an applicant has sufficient knowledge about life in the United Kingdom if:

(a)   the applicant has passed the test known as the 'Life in the UK test administered by learndirect limited; or

(b)   in respect of an applicant who was resident in the Isle of Man, the applicant took and passed the test in the Isle of Man known as the 'Life in the UK test' and which was administered by an educational institution or other person approved for that purpose by the Lieutenant Governor; or

(c)   in respect of an applicant who was resident in the Bailiwick of Guernsey or in the Bailiwick of Jersey, the applicant took and passed the test known as the 'Citizenship Test' and which was administered by an educational institution or other person approved for that purpose by the Lieutenant Governor of Guernsey or Jersey (as the case may be).

PART 3 EXCEPTIONS

3.1   Notwithstanding any requirement to the contrary in these Rules, for the purposes of this appendix, an applicant will not be required to demonstrate sufficient knowledge of the English language and about life in the UK where:

(a)   the applicant is under 18 years of age at the date of his or her application, or

(b)   the applicant is at least 65 years of age at the date of his or her application, or

(c)   in all the circumstances of the case, the decision maker considers that, because of the applicant's mental or physical condition, it would be unreasonable to expect the applicant to fulfil that requirement.

3.2   In the following circumstances an applicant will be deemed to have demonstrated sufficient knowledge of the English language and about life in the UK:

(a) Where the application for indefinite leave to remain in the United Kingdom is made under:

    (i) paragraph 196D and the applicant has had, as at the day on which the application is made, continuous leave to enter or remain in the United Kingdom for at least 15 years as the spouse or civil partner of a person who has or has had leave to enter or remain under paragraphs 128–193 (but not paragraphs 135I –135K), or

    (ii) paragraph 198 and the applicant has had, as at the day on which the application was made, continuous leave to enter or remain in the United Kingdom for at least 15 years as the child of a person who has or has had leave to enter or remain in the United Kingdom under paragraphs 128–193 (but not paragraphs 135l–135K), or

    (iii) paragraph 248D and the applicant has had, as at the day on which the application was made, continuous leave to enter or remain in the United Kingdom for at least 15 years as a person exercising rights of access to a child resident in the United Kingdom and that child is under the age of 18 at the day on which the applicant's application for indefinite leave is made under paragraph 248D, or

    (iv) paragraph 273D and the applicant has had, as at the day on which the application is made, continuous leave to enter or remain in the United Kingdom for at least 15 years as a spouse or civil partner of a person who has or has had leave to enter or remain in the United Kingdom as a retired person of independent means, or

    (v) paragraph 275A and the applicant has had, as at the day on which the application was made, continuous leave to enter or remain in the United Kingdom for at least 15 years as the child of a person who has or has had leave to enter or remain in the United Kingdom as a retired person of independent means, or

    (vi) paragraph 287 and the applicant has had, as at the day on which the application is made, continuous leave to enter or remain in the United Kingdom for at least 15 years under paragraph 281 or paragraph 284, or

    (vii) paragraph 295G and the applicant has had, as at the day on which the application is made, continuous leave to enter or remain in the United Kingdom for at least 15 years under paragraph 295B or paragraph 295D, or

    (viii) paragraph 298 and the applicant has had, as at the day on which the application is made, continuous leave to enter or remain in the United Kingdom for at least 15 years under paragraph 302 or Appendix FM or paragraph 319R or paragraph 319X, or

    (ix) paragraph 319E and the applicant has had, as at the day on which the application is made, continuous leave to enter or remain in the United Kingdom for at least 15 years as the partner of a relevant points based system migrant

    (x) paragraph 319J and the applicant has had, as at the day on which the application is made, continuous leave to enter or remain in the United Kingdom for at least 15 years as the child of a relevant points based system migrant

    (xi) section E-ILRP of Appendix FM and the applicant has had, as at the day on which the application is made, continuous leave to enter or remain in the United Kingdom for at least 15 years on the day on which the application is made as a partner (except where leave is as a fiancé or proposed civil partner) under section D-LTRP of Appendix FM; or

    (xii) section E-ILRPT of Appendix FM and the applicant has had, as at the day on which the application is made, continuous leave to enter or remain in the United Kingdom for at least 15 years on the day on which the application is made as a parent under section D-ILRPT of Appendix FM,

    and

(b) the applicant has provided specified documentary evidence of an English language speaking and listening qualification at A2 CEFR or ESOL entry level 2 or Scottish Credit and Qualification Framework level 3:

    and

(c) the applicant has provided specified documentary evidence from a qualified English language teacher that the applicant has made efforts to learn English but does not yet have sufficient knowledge of the English language to pass a qualification at B1 CEFR, or ESOL entry level 3 or Scottish Credit and Qualification Framework level 4.

    and

(d)   the applicant is not a national or a citizen of one of the following countries:

Antigua and Barbuda
Australia
The Bahamas
Barbados Belize
Canada
Dominica
Grenada
Guyana
Jamaica
New Zealand
St Kitts and Nevis
St Lucia
St Vincent and the Grenadines
Trinidad and Tobago
USA.

PART 4 SPECIFIED DOCUMENTS

4.1   Where these Rules require an applicant to demonstrate sufficient knowledge of the English language and of life in the United Kingdom, the applicant must supply the documents specified in paragraphs 4.6 to 4.14 below.

4.2   The decision maker will only consider evidence submitted after the date on which an application is made where the circumstances in paragraphs 4.3 or 4.6 apply.

4.3   Where an applicant has submitted:

(i)   a document in the wrong format (for example, if a letter is not on letterhead paper as specified); or

(ii)   a document that is a copy and not an original document, or

(iii) a document which does not contain all of the specified information,

or

(iv)   fails to submit a specified document,

the decision-maker may contact the applicant or his or her representative (in writing or otherwise), and request the document or the correct version of the document. The document must be received by the Home Office at the address specified in the request within such timescale (which will not be unreasonable) as is specified.

4.4   A decision-maker may decide not to request a document under paragraph 4.3 where he or she does not anticipate that the supply of that document will lead to a grant of leave to enter or remain in the United Kingdom because the application may be refused for other reasons.

4.5   Without prejudice to the decision maker's discretion under paragraph 4.2 and also his or her right in all cases to request the original or specified document and refuse an application in circumstances in which they are not provided, where an applicant submits a specified document:

(i)   in the wrong format, or

(ii)   which is a copy and not an original document, or

(iii) which does not contain all of the specified information but the missing information is verifiable from,

    (aa)   other documents submitted with the application,

    (bb)   the website of the organisation which issued the document,

        or

    (cc)   the website of the appropriate regulatory body;

the application for leave to enter or remain in the United Kingdom may be granted exceptionally providing the decision-maker is satisfied that the specified documents are genuine and that the applicant meets all the other requirements.

4.6   Where the decision-maker is satisfied that there is a valid reason why a document has not been and cannot be supplied, (for example, because the document has been permanently lost or destroyed), he or she may waive the requirement for the document to be provided or may instead request alternative or additional evidence (which may include confirmation of evidence from the organisation which issued the original document).

4.7   The evidence specified for the purposes of paragraph 2.2 of this Appendix is:

(a)   a cerificate that:

    (i)   is from an English language test provider approved by the Secretary of State for the purposes of limited leave to enter or remain as specified in Appendix O of these Rules, and is in respect of a test approved by the Secretary of State as specified in that Appendix, and

    (ii)   shows the applicant's name; and

    (iii)   shows the qualification obtained, and

    (iv)   shows that the level of speaking and listening skills attained by the applicant met or exceeded level B 1 of the Common European Framework of Reference, and

    (v)   shows the date of award of the qualification;

    or,

(b)   a print out of the online score from a PTE Academic (Pearson) test which:

    (i)   is from an English language test provider approved by the Secretary of State for the purposes of limited (ii)leave to enter or remain as specified in Appendix O of these rules, and

    (ii)   is in respect of a test approved by the Secretary of State as specified in that Appendix , and

    (iii)   can be used to show the qualification obtained; and,

    (iv)   shows that the level of speaking and listening skills attained by the applicant met or exceeded level B 1 of the Common European Framework of Reference;

    or

(c)   a certificate or other document issued by an awarding organisation that is recognised either by Ofqual, the Welsh Government, or CCEA that

    (i)   is issued in England, Wales or Northern Ireland in respect of a qualification listed as an ESOL qualification in the OFQUAL Register of Regulated Qualifications, and

    (ii)   shows that the level of speaking and listening skills attained by the applicant met or exceeded ESOL entry level 3;

    or

(d)   a certificate that

    (i)   is issued in Scotland in respect of a National Qualification in English for Speakers of Other Languages awarded by the Scottish Qualifications Authority, and

    (ii)   shows that the level of speaking and listening skills attained by the applicant met or exceeded Scottish Credit and Qualifications Framework level 4

4.8   Subject to paragraphs 4.9 and 4.10 the documentary evidence specified for the purposes of paragraph 2.2 of this Appendix as showing that a person is a national or a citizen of one of the countries listed in paragraph 2.2 is a valid passport or travel document which satisfactorily establishes the applicant's nationality.

4.9   If the applicant cannot provide their passport or travel document other evidence of nationality of the type described in paragraph 4.10 may exceptionally be supplied in the following circumstances (the reason for which must be indicated by the applicant on their application form), where:

(a)   the applicant's passport has been lost or stolen, or

(b)   the applicant's passport has expired and has been returned to the relevant authorities, or

(c)   the applicant's passport is with another part of the Home Office.

4.10   Where paragraph 4.9 applies, the alternative evidence specified for the purposes of establishing the applicant's nationality is:

(a)   a valid national identity document; or

(b)   an original letter from the applicant's Home Government or Embassy confirming the applicant's full name, date of birth and nationality.

4.11   The evidence specified for the purposes of paragraph 2.2(iii) and 2.2(iv) (academic qualification recognised by UK NARIC) is:

(a)   a certificate issued by the relevant institution confirming the award of the academic qualification and showing:

    (i)   the applicant's name,

    (ii)   the title of the award,

    (iii)   the date of the award,

    (iv)   the name of the awarding institution, and,

(v) for paragraph 2.2 (iii) that the qualification was taught in English or,

(b) where an applicant has not, at the date of application, formally graduated or no longer has his or her certificate and is unable to obtain a duplicate certificate:

(i) an original academic reference from the institution awarding the academic qualification that:

(aa) is on official letter headed paper,

(bb) shows the applicant's name,

(cc) shows the title of the award,

(dd) confirms that the qualification was taught in English,

(ee) states when the academic qualification was (or as the case may be, will be) awarded, and

(ff) confirms that the institution is unable to issue a duplicate certificate of award or (as the case may be in respect of an applicant who has not yet graduated) the date on which the certificate will be issued.

or

(ii) an original academic transcript that;

(aa) is on official letter headed paper,

(bb) shows the applicant's name,

(cc) shows the name of the academic institution,

(dd) shows the course title,

(ee) confirms that the qualification was taught in English, and, (ff) confirms the award given.

4.12 In the absence of any evidence to the contrary, a qualification obtained in one of the following countries will be assumed for the purposes of this Appendix to have been taught in English: Antigua and Barbuda, Australia, the Bahamas, Barbados, Belize, Dominica, Grenada, Guyana, Ireland, Jamaica, New Zealand, St Kitts and Nevis, St Lucia, St Vincent and the Grenadines, Trinidad and Tobago, the UK or the USA.

4.13 The evidence specified for the purposes of paragraph 3.2(b) (evidence of English language speaking and listening) is the same as that specified for the purposes of paragraph 2.3 (vi) and 2.3 (vii) except that:

(a) references to B 1 are to be read as references to A2,

(b) references to ESOL levels Entry 3, level 1, level 2 and level 3 are to be read as references to ESOL Entry level 2, and

(c) references to Scottish Credit and Qualification Framework Level 4, 5 and 6 are to be read as references to Scottish Qualification Framework Level 3.

4.14 (a) The evidence specified for the purposes of paragraph 3.2(d) (evidence from qualified English teacher) is a letter from the teacher which is signed by him or her and dated no more than 3 months before the date on which the application for indefinite leave to remain is made and which includes the following information:

(i) the applicant's name,

(ii) confirmation that the applicant has attended an English language class taught by that teacher for at least 75 guided learning hours and which was taught during the period of 12 months immediately preceding the date on which the application for indefinite leave to remain was made,

(iii) confirmation that the teacher has assessed that the speaking and listening level attained by the applicant is not at B 1 level or above,

(iv) confirmation that the applicant is considered unlikely to attain B 1 level through further study

(v) confirmation of the teacher's qualifications as an English language teacher within the meaning of this Appendix.

(b) For the purposes of paragraph (a)(ii) 'guided learning hours' means the time during which a person is taught or given instruction and does not include any time spent on unsupervised preparation or study.

4.15 The documentary evidence specified for the purposes of paragraph 2.3 of this Appendix is:

(a) a pass notification letter issued by learndirect limited in respect of the test known as the 'Life in the UK test', or

(b) where the 'Life in the UK test' was taken and passed in the Isle of Man, a pass certificate in respect of the test issued by the relevant educational institution or other person approved for that purpose by the Lieutenant Governor, or

(c)   where the 'Citizenship test' was taken in the Bailiwick of Guernsey or, as the case may be, in the Bailiwick of Jersey, a pass certificate issued by the relevant educational institution or other person approved for that purpose by the Lieutenant Governor of Guernsey or Jersey (as the case may be).

PART 5 INTERPRETATION

5.1   For the purposes of this Appendix 'decision maker' means an Entry Clearance Officer or the Secretary of State.

5.2   For the purposes of this Appendix, 'qualified English language teacher' means a person who holds a qualification in teaching English as a foreign language or in teaching English to speakers of other languages which was awarded by an awarding organisation regulated by OFQUAL or the Welsh Government or the CCEA or the Scottish Qualification Authority.

Appendix L–T – OMITTED

The European Union and Associated States

Member States of the European Union (see Chapter 4)

Austria

Belgium

Bulgaria

Croatia (but see the Accession of Croatia (Immigration and Worker Authorisation) Regulations 2013
  (SI 2013/1460)

Cyprus

Czech Republic

Denmark

Estonia

Finland

France

Germany

Greece

Hungary

Republic of Ireland

Italy

Latvia

Lithuania

Luxembourg

Malta

The Netherlands

Poland

Portugal

Romania

Slovakia

Slovenia

Spain

Sweden

United Kingdom

Other Members of the European Economic Area (see Chapter 4)

Iceland

Norway

Liechtenstein

(As to Switzerland, see **4.1**)

Directive 2004/38/EC

CHAPTER I – GENERAL PROVISIONS

Article 1 – Subject

This Directive lays down:

(a) the conditions governing the exercise of the right of free movement and residence within the territory of the Member States by Union citizens and their family members;

(b) the right of permanent residence in the territory of the Member States for Union citizens and their family members;

(c) the limits placed on the rights set out in (a) and (b) on grounds of public policy, public security or public health.

Article 2 – Definitions

For the purposes of this Directive:

1. 'Union citizen' means any person having the nationality of a Member State;

2. 'family member' means:

   (a) the spouse;

   (b) the partner with whom the Union citizen has contracted a registered partnership, on the basis of the legislation of a Member State, if the legislation of the host Member State treats registered partnerships as equivalent to marriage and in accordance with the conditions laid down in the relevant legislation of the host Member State;

   (c) the direct descendants who are under the age of 21 or are dependants and those of the spouse or partner as defined in point (b);

   (d) the dependent direct relatives in the ascending line and those of the spouse or partner as defined in point (b);

3. 'host Member State' means the Member State to which a Union citizen moves in order to exercise his/her right of free movement and residence.

Article 3 – Beneficiaries

1. This Directive shall apply to all Union citizens who move to or reside in a Member State other than that of which they are a national, and to their family members as defined in point 2 of Article 2 who accompany or join them.

2. Without prejudice to any right to free movement and residence the persons concerned may have in their own right, the host Member State shall, in accordance with its national legislation, facilitate entry and residence for the following persons:

   (a) any other family members, irrespective of their nationality, not falling under the definition in point 2 of Article 2 who, in the country from which they have come, are dependants or members of the household of the Union citizen having the primary right of residence, or where serious health grounds strictly require the personal care of the family member by the Union citizen;

   (b) the partner with whom the Union citizen has a durable relationship, duly attested.

   The host Member State shall undertake an extensive examination of the personal circumstances and shall justify any denial of entry or residence to these people.

CHAPTER II – RIGHT OF EXIT AND ENTRY

Article 4 – Right of exit

1. Without prejudice to the provisions on travel documents applicable to national border controls, all Union citizens with a valid identity card or passport and their family members who are not nationals of a Member State and who hold a valid passport shall have the right to leave the territory of a Member State to travel to another Member State.

2. No exit visa or equivalent formality may be imposed on the persons to whom paragraph 1 applies.

3. Member States shall, acting in accordance with their laws, issue to their own nationals, and renew, an identity card or passport stating their nationality.

4. The passport shall be valid at least for all Member States and for countries through which the holder must pass when travelling between Member States. Where the law of a Member State does not provide for identity cards to be issued, the period of validity of any passport on being issued or renewed shall be not less than five years.

Article 5 – Right of entry

1. Without prejudice to the provisions on travel documents applicable to national border controls, Member States shall grant Union citizens leave to enter their territory with a valid identity card or passport and shall grant family members who are not nationals of a Member State leave to enter their territory with a valid passport.

    No entry visa or equivalent formality may be imposed on Union citizens.

2. Family members who are not nationals of a Member State shall only be required to have an entry visa in accordance with Regulation (EC) No 539/2001 or, where appropriate, with national law. For the purposes of this Directive, possession of the valid residence card referred to in Article 10 shall exempt such family members from the visa requirement.

    Member States shall grant such persons every facility to obtain the necessary visas. Such visas shall be issued free of charge as soon as possible and on the basis of an accelerated procedure.

3. The host Member State shall not place an entry or exit stamp in the passport of family members who are not nationals of a Member State provided that they present the residence card provided for in Article 10.

4. Where a Union citizen, or a family member who is not a national of a Member State, does not have the necessary travel documents or, if required, the necessary visas, the Member State concerned shall, before turning them back, give such persons every reasonable opportunity to obtain the necessary documents or have them brought to them within a reasonable period of time or to corroborate or prove by other means that they are covered by the right of free movement and residence.

5. The Member State may require the person concerned to report his/her presence within its territory within a reasonable and non-discriminatory period of time. Failure to comply with this requirement may make the person concerned liable to proportionate and non-discriminatory sanctions.

CHAPTER III – RIGHT OF RESIDENCE

Article 6 – Right of residence for up to three months

1. Union citizens shall have the right of residence on the territory of another Member State for a period of up to three months without any conditions or any formalities other than the requirement to hold a valid identity card or passport.

2. The provisions of paragraph 1 shall also apply to family members in possession of a valid passport who are not nationals of a Member State, accompanying or joining the Union citizen.

Article 7 – Right of residence for more than three months

1. All Union citizens shall have the right of residence on the territory of another Member State for a period of longer than three months if they:

(a)   are workers or self-employed persons in the host Member State; or

(b)   have sufficient resources for themselves and their family members not to become a burden on the social assistance system of the host Member State during their period of residence and have comprehensive sickness insurance cover in the host Member State; or

(c)   —   are enrolled at a private or public establishment, accredited or financed by the host Member State on the basis of its legislation or administrative practice, for the principal purpose of following a course of study, including vocational training; and

          —   have comprehensive sickness insurance cover in the host Member State and assure the relevant national authority, by means of a declaration or by such equivalent means as they may choose, that they have sufficient resources for themselves and their family members not to become a burden on the social assistance system of the host Member State during their period of residence; or

(d)   are family members accompanying or joining a Union citizen who satisfies the conditions referred to in points (a), (b) or (c).

2.   The right of residence provided for in paragraph 1 shall extend to family members who are not nationals of a Member State, accompanying or joining the Union citizen in the host Member State, provided that such Union citizen satisfies the conditions referred to in paragraph 1(a), (b) or (c).

3.   For the purposes of paragraph 1(a), a Union citizen who is no longer a worker or self-employed person shall retain the status of worker or self-employed person in the following circumstances:

(a)   he/she is temporarily unable to work as the result of an illness or accident;

(b)   he/she is in duly recorded involuntary unemployment after having been employed for more than one year and has registered as a job-seeker with the relevant employment office;

(c)   he/she is in duly recorded involuntary unemployment after completing a fixed-term employment contract of less than a year or after having become involuntarily unemployed during the first twelve months and has registered as a job-seeker with the relevant employment office. In this case, the status of worker shall be retained for no less than six months;

(d)   he/she embarks on vocational training. Unless he/she is involuntarily unemployed, the retention of the status of worker shall require the training to be related to the previous employment.

4.   By way of derogation from paragraphs 1(d) and 2 above, only the spouse, the registered partner provided for in Article 2(2)(b) and dependent children shall have the right of residence as family members of a Union citizen meeting the conditions under 1(c) above. Article 3(2) shall apply to his/her dependent direct relatives in the ascending lines and those of his/her spouse or registered partner.

Article 8 – Administrative formalities for Union citizens

1.   Without prejudice to Article 5(5), for periods of residence longer than three months, the host Member State may require Union citizens to register with the relevant authorities.

2.   The deadline for registration may not be less than three months from the date of arrival. A registration certificate shall be issued immediately, stating the name and address of the person registering and the date of the registration. Failure to comply with the registration requirement may render the person concerned liable to proportionate and non-discriminatory sanctions.

3.   For the registration certificate to be issued, Member States may only require that

    —   Union citizens to whom point (a) of Article 7(1) applies present a valid identity card or passport, a confirmation of engagement from the employer or a certificate of employment, or proof that they are self-employed persons,

    —   Union citizens to whom point (b) of Article 7(1) applies present a valid identity card or passport and provide proof that they satisfy the conditions laid down therein,

    —   Union citizens to whom point (c) of Article 7(1) applies present a valid identity card or passport, provide proof of enrolment at an accredited establishment and of comprehensive sickness insurance cover and the declaration or equivalent means referred to in point (c) of Article 7(1). Member States may not require this declaration to refer to any specific amount of resources.

4.   Member States may not lay down a fixed amount which they regard as 'sufficient resources', but they must take into account the personal situation of the person concerned. In all cases this amount shall not be higher than the threshold below which nationals of the host Member State become eligible for

social assistance, or, where this criterion is not applicable, higher than the minimum social security pension paid by the host Member State.

5.   For the registration certificate to be issued to family members of Union citizens, who are themselves Union citizens, Member States may require the following documents to be presented:

(a)   a valid identity card or passport;

(b)   a document attesting to the existence of a family relationship or of a registered partnership;

(c)   where appropriate, the registration certificate of the Union citizen whom they are accompanying or joining;

(d)   in cases falling under points (c) and (d) of Article 2(2), documentary evidence that the conditions laid down therein are met;

(e)   in cases falling under Article 3(2)(a), a document issued by the relevant authority in the country of origin or country from which they are arriving certifying that they are dependants or members of the household of the Union citizen, or proof of the existence of serious health grounds which strictly require the personal care of the family member by the Union citizen;

(f)   in cases falling under Article 3(2)(b), proof of the existence of a durable relationship with the Union citizen.

Article 9 – Administrative formalities for family members who are not nationals of a Member State

1.   Member States shall issue a residence card to family members of a Union citizen who are not nationals of a Member State, where the planned period of residence is for more than three months.

2.   The deadline for submitting the residence card application may not be less than three months from the date of arrival.

3.   Failure to comply with the requirement to apply for a residence card may make the person concerned liable to proportionate and non-discriminatory sanctions.

Article 10 – Issue of residence cards

1.   The right of residence of family members of a Union citizen who are not nationals of a Member State shall be evidenced by the issuing of a document called 'Residence card of a family member of a Union citizen' no later than six months from the date on which they submit the application. A certificate of application for the residence card shall be issued immediately.

2.   For the residence card to be issued, Member States shall require presentation of the following documents:

(a)   a valid passport;

(b)   a document attesting to the existence of a family relationship or of a registered partnership;

(c)   the registration certificate or, in the absence of a registration system, any other proof of residence in the host MemberState of the Union citizen whom they are accompanying or joining;

(d)   in cases falling under points (c) and (d) of Article 2(2), documentary evidence that the conditions laid down therein are met;

(e)   in cases falling under Article 3(2)(a), a document issued by the relevant authority in the country of origin or country from which they are arriving certifying that they are dependants or members of the household of the Union citizen, or proof of the existence of serious health grounds which strictly require the personal care of the family member by the Union citizen;

(f)   in cases falling under Article 3(2)(b), proof of the existence of a durable relationship with the Union citizen.

Article 11 – Validity of the residence card

1.   The residence card provided for by Article 10(1) shall be valid for five years from the date of issue or for the envisaged period of residence of the Union citizen, if this period is less than five years.

2.   The validity of the residence card shall not be affected by temporary absences not exceeding six months a year, or by absences of a longer duration for compulsory military service or by one absence of

a maximum of 12 consecutive months for important reasons such as pregnancy and childbirth, serious illness, study or vocational training, or a posting in another Member State or a third country.

Article 12 – Retention of the right of residence by family members in the event of death or departure of the Union citizen

1.   Without prejudice to the second subparagraph, the Union citizen's death or departure from the host Member State shall not affect the right of residence of his/her family members who are nationals of a Member State.

Before acquiring the right of permanent residence, the persons concerned must meet the conditions laid down in points (a), (b), (c) or (d) of Article 7(1).

2.   Without prejudice to the second subparagraph, the Union citizen's death shall not entail loss of the right of residence of his/her family members who are not nationals of a Member State and who have been residing in the host Member State as family members for at least one year before the Union citizen's death.

Before acquiring the right of permanent residence, the right of residence of the persons concerned shall remain subject to the requirement that they are able to show that they are workers or self-employed persons or that they have sufficient resources for themselves and their family members not to become a burden on the social assistance system of the host Member State during their period of residence and have comprehensive sickness insurance cover in the host Member State, or that they are members of the family, already constituted in the host Member State, of a person satisfying these requirements. 'Sufficient resources' shall be as defined in Article 8(4).

Such family members shall retain their right of residence exclusively on a personal basis.

3.   The Union citizen's departure from the host Member State or his/her death shall not entail loss of the right of residence of his/her children or of the parent who has actual custody of the children, irrespective of nationality, if the children reside in the host Member State and are enrolled at an educational establishment, for the purpose of studying there, until the completion of their studies.

Article 13 – Retention of the right of residence by family members in the event of divorce, annulment of marriage or termination of registered partnership

1.   Without prejudice to the second subparagraph, divorce, annulment of the Union citizen's marriage or termination of his/her registered partnership, as referred to in point 2(b) of Article 2 shall not affect the right of residence of his/her family members who are nationals of a Member State.

Before acquiring the right of permanent residence, the persons concerned must meet the conditions laid down in points (a), (b), (c) or (d) of Article 7(1).

2.   Without prejudice to the second subparagraph, divorce, annulment of marriage or termination of the registered partnership referred to in point 2(b) of Article 2 shall not entail loss of the right of residence of a Union citizen's family members who are not nationals of a Member State where:

(a)   prior to initiation of the divorce or annulment proceedings or termination of the registered partnership referred to in point 2(b) of Article 2, the marriage or registered partnership has lasted at least three years, including one year in the host Member State; or

(b)   by agreement between the spouses or the partners referred to in point 2(b) of Article 2 or by court order, the spouse or partner who is not a national of a Member State has custody of the Union citizen's children; or

(c)   this is warranted by particularly difficult circumstances, such as having been a victim of domestic violence while the marriage or registered partnership was subsisting; or

(d)   by agreement between the spouses or partners referred to in point 2(b) of Article 2 or by court order, the spouse or partner who is not a national of a Member State has the right of access to a minor child, provided that the court has ruled that such access must be in the host Member State, and for as long as is required.

Before acquiring the right of permanent residence, the right of residence of the persons concerned shall remain subject to the requirement that they are able to show that they are workers or self-employed persons or that they have sufficient resources for themselves and their family members not to become a burden on the social assistance system of the host Member State during their period of residence and have comprehensive sickness insurance cover in the host Member State, or that they are members of the family, already constituted in the host Member State, of a person satisfying these requirements. 'Sufficient resources' shall be as defined in Article 8(4).

Such family members shall retain their right of residence exclusively on personal basis.

Article 14 – Retention of the right of residence

1. Union citizens and their family members shall have the right of residence provided for in Article 6, as long as they do not become an unreasonable burden on the social assistance system of the host Member State.

2. Union citizens and their family members shall have the right of residence provided for in Articles 7, 12 and 13 as long as they meet the conditions set out therein.

   In specific cases where there is a reasonable doubt as to whether a Union citizen or his/her family members satisfies the conditions set out in Articles 7, 12 and 13, Member States may verify if these conditions are fulfilled. This verification shall not be carried out systematically.

3. An expulsion measure shall not be the automatic consequence of a Union citizen's or his or her family member's recourse to the social assistance system of the host Member State.

4. By way of derogation from paragraphs 1 and 2 and without prejudice to the provisions of Chapter VI, an expulsion measure may in no case be adopted against Union citizens or their family members if:

   (a)   the Union citizens are workers or self-employed persons, or

   (b)   the Union citizens entered the territory of the host Member State in order to seek employment. In this case, the Union citizens and their family members may not be expelled for as long as the Union citizens can provide evidence that they are continuing to seek employment and that they have a genuine chance of being engaged.

Article 15 – Procedural safeguards

1. The procedures provided for by Articles 30 and 31 shall apply by analogy to all decisions restricting free movement of Union citizens and their family members on grounds other than public policy, public security or public health.

2. Expiry of the identity card or passport on the basis of which the person concerned entered the host Member State and was issued with a registration certificate or residence card shall not constitute a ground for expulsion from the host Member State.

3. The host Member State may not impose a ban on entry in the context of an expulsion decision to which paragraph 1 applies.

CHAPTER IV – RIGHT OF PERMANENT RESIDENCE

Section I – Eligibility

Article 16 – General rule for Union citizens and their family members

1. Union citizens who have resided legally for a continuous period of five years in the host Member State shall have the right of permanent residence there. This right shall not be subject to the conditions provided for in Chapter III.

2. Paragraph 1 shall apply also to family members who are not nationals of a Member State and have legally resided with the Union citizen in the host Member State for a continuous period of five years.

3. Continuity of residence shall not be affected by temporary absences not exceeding a total of six months a year, or by absences of a longer duration for compulsory military service, or by one absence of a maximum of 12 consecutive months for important reasons such as pregnancy and childbirth, serious illness, study or vocational training, or a posting in another Member State or a third country.

4. Once acquired, the right of permanent residence shall be lost only through absence from the host Member State for a period exceeding two consecutive years.

Article 17 – Exemptions for persons no longer working in the host Member State and their family members

1. By way of derogation from Article 16, the right of permanent residence in the host Member State shall be enjoyed before completion of a continuous period of five years of residence by:

    (a) workers or self-employed persons who, at the time they stop working, have reached the age laid down by the law of that Member State for entitlement to an old age pension or workers who cease paid employment to take early retirement, provided that they have been working in that Member State for at least the preceding twelve months and have resided there continuously for more than three years.

    If the law of the host Member State does not grant the right to an old age pension to certain categories of self-employed persons, the age condition shall be deemed to have been met once the person concerned has reached the age of 60;

    (b) workers or self-employed persons who have resided continuously in the host Member State for more than two years and stop working there as a result of permanent incapacity to work.

    If such incapacity is the result of an accident at work or an occupational disease entitling the person concerned to a benefit payable in full or in part by an institution in the host Member State, no condition shall be imposed as to length of residence;

    (c) workers or self-employed persons who, after three years of continuous employment and residence in the host Member State, work in an employed or self-employed capacity in another Member State, while retaining their place of residence in the host Member State, to which they return, as a rule, each day or at least once a week.

    For the purposes of entitlement to the rights referred to in points (a) and (b), periods of employment spent in the Member State in which the person concerned is working shall be regarded as having been spent in the host Member State.

    Periods of involuntary unemployment duly recorded by the relevant employment office, periods not worked for reasons not of the person's own making and absences from work or cessation of work due to illness or accident shall be regarded as periods of employment.

2. The conditions as to length of residence and employment laid down in point (a) of paragraph 1 and the condition as to length of residence laid down in point (b) of paragraph 1 shall not apply if the worker's or the self-employed person's spouse or partner as referred to in point 2(b) of Article 2 is a national of the host Member State or has lost the nationality of that Member State by marriage to that worker or self-employed person.

3. Irrespective of nationality, the family members of a worker or a self-employed person who are residing with him in the territory of the host Member State shall have the right of permanent residence in that Member State, if the worker or self-employed person has acquired himself the right of permanent residence in that Member State on the basis of paragraph 1.

4. If, however, the worker or self-employed person dies while still working but before acquiring permanent residence status in the host Member State on the basis of paragraph 1, his family members who are residing with him in the host Member State shall acquire the right of permanent residence there, on condition that:

    (a) the worker or self-employed person had, at the time of death, resided continuously on the territory of that Member State for two years; or

    (b) the death resulted from an accident at work or an occupational disease; or

    (c) the surviving spouse lost the nationality of that Member State following marriage to the worker or self-employed person.

Article 18 – Acquisition of the right of permanent residence by certain family members who are not nationals of a Member State

Without prejudice to Article 17, the family members of a Union citizen to whom Articles 12(2) and 13(2) apply, who satisfy the conditions laid down therein, shall acquire the right of permanent residence after residing legally for a period of five consecutive years in the host Member State.

Section II – Administrative formalities

Article 19 – Document certifying permanent residence for Union citizens

1.   Upon application Member States shall issue Union citizens entitled to permanent residence, after having verified duration of residence, with a document certifying permanent residence.

2.   The document certifying permanent residence shall be issued as soon as possible.

Article 20 – Permanent residence card for family members who are not nationals of a Member State

1.   Member States shall issue family members who are not nationals of a Member State entitled to permanent residence with a permanent residence card within six months of the submission of the application. The permanent residence card shall be renewable automatically every 10 years.

2.   The application for a permanent residence card shall be submitted before the residence card expires. Failure to comply with the requirement to apply for a permanent residence card may render the person concerned liable to proportionate and non-discriminatory sanctions.

3.   Interruption in residence not exceeding two consecutive years shall not affect the validity of the permanent residence card.

Article 21 – Continuity of residence

For the purposes of this Directive, continuity of residence may be attested by any means of proof in use in the host Member State. Continuity of residence is broken by any expulsion decision duly enforced against the person concerned.

CHAPTER V – PROVISIONS COMMON TO THE RIGHT OF RESIDENCE AND THE RIGHT OF PERMANENT RESIDENCE

Article 22 – Territorial scope

The right of residence and the right of permanent residence shall cover the whole territory of the host Member State. Member States may impose territorial restrictions on the right of residence and the right of permanent residence only where the same restrictions apply to their own nationals.

Article 23 – Related rights

Irrespective of nationality, the family members of a Union citizen who have the right of residence or the right of permanent residence in a Member State shall be entitled to take up employment or self-employment there.

Article 24 – Equal treatment

1.   Subject to such specific provisions as are expressly provided for in the Treaty and secondary law, all Union citizens residing on the basis of this Directive in the territory of the host Member State shall enjoy equal treatment with the nationals of that Member State within the scope of the Treaty. The benefit of this right shall be extended to family members who are not nationals of a Member State and who have the right of residence or permanent residence.

2.   By way of derogation from paragraph 1, the host Member State shall not be obliged to confer entitlement to social assistance during the first three months of residence or, where appropriate, the longer period provided for in Article 14(4)(b), nor shall it be obliged, prior to acquisition of the right of permanent residence, to grant maintenance aid for studies, including vocational training, consisting in student grants or student loans to persons other than workers, self-employed persons, persons who retain such status and members of their families.

Article 25 – General provisions concerning residence documents

1. Possession of a registration certificate as referred to in Article 8, of a document certifying permanent residence, of a certificate attesting submission of an application for a family member residence card, of a residence card or of a permanent residence card, may under no circumstances be made a precondition for the exercise of a right or the completion of an administrative formality, as entitlement to rights may be attested by any other means of proof.

2. All documents mentioned in paragraph 1 shall be issued free of charge or for a charge not exceeding that imposed on nationals for the issuing of similar documents.

Article 26 – Checks

Member States may carry out checks on compliance with any requirement deriving from their national legislation for non-nationals always to carry their registration certificate or residence card, provided that the same requirement applies to their own nationals as regards their identity card. In the event of failure to comply with this requirement, Member States may impose the same sanctions as those imposed on their own nationals for failure to carry their identity card.

CHAPTER VI – RESTRICTIONS ON THE RIGHT OF ENTRY AND THE RIGHT OF RESIDENCE ON GROUNDS OF PUBLIC POLICY, PUBLIC SECURITY OR PUBLIC HEALTH

Article 27 – General principles

1. Subject to the provisions of this Chapter, Member States may restrict the freedom of movement and residence of Union citizens and their family members, irrespective of nationality, on grounds of public policy, public security or public health. These grounds shall not be invoked to serve economic ends.

2. Measures taken on grounds of public policy or public security shall comply with the principle of proportionality and shall be based exclusively on the personal conduct of the individual concerned. Previous criminal convictions shall not in themselves constitute grounds for taking such measures.

    The personal conduct of the individual concerned must represent a genuine, present and sufficiently serious threat affecting one of the fundamental interests of society. Justifications that are isolated from the particulars of the case or that rely on considerations of general prevention shall not be accepted.

3. In order to ascertain whether the person concerned represents a danger for public policy or public security, when issuing the registration certificate or, in the absence of a registration system, not later than three months from the date of arrival of the person concerned on its territory or from the date of reporting his/her presence within the territory, as provided for in Article 5(5), or when issuing the residence card, the host Member State may, should it consider this essential, request the Member State of origin and, if need be, other Member States to provide information concerning any previous police record the person concerned may have. Such enquiries shall not be made as a matter of routine. The Member State consulted shall give its reply within two months.

4. The Member State which issued the passport or identity card shall allow the holder of the document who has been expelled on grounds of public policy, public security, or public health from another Member State to re-enter its territory without any formality even if the document is no longer valid or the nationality of the holder is in dispute.

Article 28 – Protection against expulsion

1. Before taking an expulsion decision on grounds of public policy or public security, the host Member State shall take account of considerations such as how long the individual concerned has resided on its territory, his/her age, state of health, family and economic situation, social and cultural integration into the host Member State and the extent of his/her links with the country of origin.

2. The host Member State may not take an expulsion decision against Union citizens or their family members, irrespective of nationality, who have the right of permanent residence on its territory, except on serious grounds of public policy or public security.

3. An expulsion decision may not be taken against Union citizens, except if the decision is based on imperative grounds of public security, as defined by Member States, if they:

    (a) have resided in the host Member State for the previous 10 years; or

    (b) are a minor, except if the expulsion is necessary for the best interests of the child, as provided for in the United Nations Convention on the Rights of the Child of 20 November 1989.

Article 29 – Public health

1. The only diseases justifying measures restricting freedom of movement shall be the diseases with epidemic potential as defined by the relevant instruments of the World Health Organisation and other infectious diseases or contagious parasitic diseases if they are the subject of protection provisions applying to nationals of the host Member State.

2. Diseases occurring after a three-month period from the date of arrival shall not constitute grounds for expulsion from the territory.

3. Where there are serious indications that it is necessary, Member States may, within three months of the date of arrival, require persons entitled to the right of residence to undergo, free of charge, a medical examination to certify that they are not suffering from any of the conditions referred to in paragraph 1. Such medical examinations may not be required as a matter of routine.

Article 30 – Notification of decisions

1. The persons concerned shall be notified in writing of any decision taken under Article 27(1), in such a way that they are able to comprehend its content and the implications for them.

2. The persons concerned shall be informed, precisely and in full, of the public policy, public security or public health grounds on which the decision taken in their case is based, unless this is contrary to the interests of State security.

3. The notification shall specify the court or administrative authority with which the person concerned may lodge an appeal, the time limit for the appeal and, where applicable, the time allowed for the person to leave the territory of the Member State. Save in duly substantiated cases of urgency, the time allowed to leave the territory shall be not less than one month from the date of notification.

Article 31 – Procedural safeguards

1. The persons concerned shall have access to judicial and, where appropriate, administrative redress procedures in the host Member State to appeal against or seek review of any decision taken against them on the grounds of public policy, public security or public health.

2. Where the application for appeal against or judicial review of the expulsion decision is accompanied by an application for an interim order to suspend enforcement of that decision, actual removal from the territory may not take place until such time as the decision on the interim order has been taken, except:

    — where the expulsion decision is based on a previous judicial decision; or

    — where the persons concerned have had previous access to judicial review; or

    — where the expulsion decision is based on imperative grounds of public security under Article 28(3).

3. The redress procedures shall allow for an examination of the legality of the decision, as well as of the facts and circumstances on which the proposed measure is based. They shall ensure that the decision is not disproportionate, particularly in view of the requirements laid down in Article 28.

4. Member States may exclude the individual concerned from their territory pending the redress procedure, but they may not prevent the individual from submitting his/her defence in person, except when his/her appearance may cause serious troubles to public policy or public security or when the appeal or judicial review concerns a denial of entry to the territory.

Article 32 – Duration of exclusion orders

1. Persons excluded on grounds of public policy or public security may submit an application for lifting of the exclusion order after a reasonable period, depending on the circumstances, and in any event after

three years from enforcement of the final exclusion order which has been validly adopted in accordance with Community law, by putting forward arguments to establish that there has been a material change in the circumstances which justified the decision ordering their exclusion.

The Member State concerned shall reach a decision on this application within six months of its submission.

2.   The persons referred to in paragraph 1 shall have no right of entry to the territory of the Member State concerned while their application is being considered.

Article 33 – Expulsion as a penalty or legal consequence

1.   Expulsion orders may not be issued by the host Member State as a penalty or legal consequence of a custodial penalty, unless they conform to the requirements of Articles 27, 28 and 29.

2.   If an expulsion order, as provided for in paragraph 1, is enforced more than two years after it was issued, the Member State shall check that the individual concerned is currently and genuinely a threat to public policy or public security and shall assess whether there has been any material change in the circumstances since the expulsion order was issued.

CHAPTER VII – FINAL PROVISIONS

Article 34 – Publicity

Member States shall disseminate information concerning the rights and obligations of Union citizens and their family members on the subjects covered by this Directive, particularly by means of awareness-raising campaigns conducted through national and local media and other means of communication.

Article 35 – Abuse of rights

Member States may adopt the necessary measures to refuse, terminate or withdraw any right conferred by this Directive in the case of abuse of rights or fraud, such as marriages of convenience. Any such measure shall be proportionate and subject to the procedural safeguards provided for in Articles 30 and 31.

Article 36 – Sanctions

Member States shall lay down provisions on the sanctions applicable to breaches of national rules adopted for the implementation of this Directive and shall take the measures required for their application. The sanctions laid down shall be effective and proportionate. Member States shall notify the Commission of these provisions not later than 30 April 2006 and as promptly as possible in the case of any subsequent changes.

Article 37 – More favourable national provisions

The provisions of this Directive shall not affect any laws, regulations or administrative provisions laid down by a Member State which would be more favourable to the persons covered by this Directive.

Article 38 – Repeals

1.   Articles 10 and 11 of Regulation (EEC) No 1612/68 shall be repealed with effect from 30 April 2006.

2.   Directives 64/221/EEC, 68/360/EEC, 72/194/EEC, 73/148/EEC, 75/34/EEC, 75/35/EEC, 90/364/EEC, 90/365/EEC and 93/96/EEC shall be repealed with effect from 30 April 2006.

3.   References made to the repealed provisions and Directives shall be construed as being made to this Directive.

Article 39 – Report

No later than 30 April 2006 the Commission shall submit a report on the application of this Directive to the European Parliament and the Council, together with any necessary proposals, notably on the opportunity to extend the period of time during which Union citizens and their family members may reside in the territory of the host Member State without any conditions. The Member States shall provide the Commission with the information needed to produce the report.

Article 40 – Transposition

1.   Member States shall bring into force the laws, regulations and administrative provisions necessary to comply with this Directive by 30 April 2006.

    When Member States adopt those measures, they shall contain a reference to this Directive or shall be accompanied by such a reference on the occasion of their official publication. The methods of making such reference shall be laid down by the Member States.

2.   Member States shall communicate to the Commission the text of the provisions of national law which they adopt in the field covered by this Directive together with a table showing how the provisions of this Directive correspond to the national provisions adopted.

Article 41 – Entry into force

This Directive shall enter into force on the day of its publication in the *Official Journal of the European Union*.

Article 42 – Addressees

This Directive is addressed to the Member States.

Done at Strasbourg, 29 April 2004.

Immigration (European Economic Area) Regulations 2006 (SI 2006/1003, as amended)

PART I

INTERPRETATION ETC

1. **Citation and commencement**

   These Regulations may be cited as the Immigration (European Economic Area) Regulations 2006 and shall come into force on 30th April 2006.

2. **General interpretation**

   (1) In these Regulations—

   'the 1971 Act' means the Immigration Act 1971;

   'the 1999 Act' means the Immigration and Asylum Act 1999;

   'the 2002 Act' means the Nationality, Immigration and Asylum Act 2002;

   'the Accession Regulations' means the Accession (Immigration and Worker Registration) Regulations 2004;

   'civil partner' does not include—

   (a) a party to a civil partnership of convenience; or

   (b) the civil partner ('C') of a person ('P') where a spouse, civil partner or durable partner of C or P is already present in the United Kingdom;

   'decision maker' means the Secretary of State, an immigration officer or an entry clearance officer (as the case may be);

   'deportation order' means an order made pursuant to regulation 24(3);

   'derivative residence card' means a card issued to a person, in accordance with regulation 18A, as proof of the holder's derivative right to reside in the United Kingdom as at the date of issue;

   'document certifying permanent residence' means a document issued to an EEA national, in accordance with regulation 18, as proof of the holder's permanent right of residence under regulation 15 as at the date of issue;

   'durable partner' does not include the durable partner ('D') of a person ('P') where a spouse, civil partner or durable partner of D or P is already present in the United Kingdom and where that marriage, civil partnership or durable partnership is subsisting;

   'EEA decision' means a decision under these Regulations that concerns—

   (a) a person's entitlement to be admitted to the United Kingdom;

   (b) a person's entitlement to be issued with or have renewed, or not to have revoked, a registration certificate, residence card, derivative residence card, document certifying permanent residence or permanent residence card;

   (c) a person's removal from the United Kingdom; or

   (d) the cancellation, pursuant to regulation 20A, of a person's right to reside in the United Kingdom;

   'EEA family permit' means a document issued to a person, in accordance with regulation 12, in connection with his admission to the United Kingdom;

   'EEA national' means a national of an EEA State who is not also a British citizen;

   'EEA State' means—

   (a) a member State, other than the United Kingdom;

   (b) Norway, Iceland or Liechtenstein; or

   (c) Switzerland;

   'entry clearance' has the meaning given in section 33(1) of the 1971 Act;

   'entry clearance officer' means a person responsible for the grant or refusal of entry clearance;

   'exclusion order' means an order made under regulation 19(1B);

'immigration rules' has the meaning given in section 33(1) of the 1971 Act;

'military service' means service in the armed forces of an EEA State;

'permanent residence card' means a card issued to a person who is not an EEA national, in accordance with regulation 18, as proof of the holder's permanent right of residence under regulation 15 as at the date of issue;

'registration certificate' means a certificate issued to an EEA national, in accordance with regulation 16, as proof of the holder's right of residence in the United Kingdom as at the date of issue;

'relevant EEA national' in relation to an extended family member has the meaning given in regulation 8(6);

'residence card' means a card issued to a person who is not an EEA national, in accordance with regulation 17, as proof of the holder's right of residence in the United Kingdom as at the date of issue;

'spouse' does not include—

(a)   a party to a marriage of convenience; or

(b)   the spouse ('S') of a person ('P') where a spouse, civil partner or durable partner of S or P is already present in the United Kingdom;

(2)   Paragraph (1) is subject to paragraph 1(a) of Schedule 4 (transitional provisions).

(3)   Section 11 of the 1971 Act (construction of references to entry) shall apply for the purpose of determining whether a person has entered the United Kingdom for the purpose of these Regulations as it applies for the purpose of determining whether a person has entered the United Kingdom for the purpose of that Act.

3.   Continuity of residence

(1)   This regulation applies for the purpose of calculating periods of continuous residence in the United Kingdom under regulation 5(1) and regulation 15.

(2)   Continuity of residence is not affected by—

(a)   periods of absence from the United Kingdom which do not exceed six months in total in any year;

(b)   periods of absence from the United Kingdom on military service; or

(c)   any one absence from the United Kingdom not exceeding twelve months for an important reason such as pregnancy and childbirth, serious illness, study or vocational training or an overseas posting.

(3)   But continuity of residence is broken if a person is removed from the United Kingdom under these Regulations.

4.   'Worker', 'self-employed person', 'self-sufficient person' and 'student'

(1)   In these Regulations —

(a)   'worker' means a worker within the meaning of Article 39 of the Treaty establishing the European Community;

(b)   'self-employed person' means a person who establishes himself in order to pursue activity as a self-employed person in accordance with Article 43 of the Treaty establishing the European Community;

(c)   'self-sufficient person' means a person who has—

(i)   sufficient resources not to become a burden on the social assistance system of the United Kingdom during his period of residence; and

(ii)   comprehensive sickness insurance cover in the United Kingdom;

(d)   'student' means a person who—

(i)   is enrolled, for the principal purpose of following a course of study (including vocational training), at a public or private establishment which is—

(aa)   financed from public funds; or

(bb)   otherwise recognised by the Secretary of State as an establishment which has been accredited for the purpose of providing such courses or training within the law or administrative practice of the part of the United Kingdom in which the establishment is located;

(ii)   has comprehensive sickness insurance cover in the United Kingdom; and

(iii)   assures the Secretary of State, by means of a declaration, or by such equivalent means as the person may choose, that he has sufficient resources not to become a burden on the social assistance system of the United Kingdom during his period of residence.

(2)   For the purposes of paragraph (1)(c), where family members of the person concerned reside in the United Kingdom and their right to reside is dependent upon their being family members of that person—

(a)   the requirement for that person to have sufficient resources not to become a burden on the social assistance system of the United Kingdom during his period of residence shall only be satisfied if his resources and those of the family members are sufficient to avoid him and the family members becoming such a burden;

(b)   the requirement for that person to have comprehensive sickness insurance cover in the United Kingdom shall only be satisfied if he and his family members have such cover.

(3)   For the purposes of paragraph (1)(d), where family members of the person concerned reside in the United Kingdom and their right to reside is dependent upon their being family members of that person, the requirement for that person to assure the Secretary of State that he has sufficient resources not to become a burden on the social assistance system of the United Kingdom during his period of residence shall only be satisfied if he assures the Secretary of State that his resources and those of the family members are sufficient to avoid him and the family members becoming such a burden.

(4)   For the purposes of paragraphs (1)(c) and (d) and paragraphs (2) and (3), the resources of the person concerned and, where applicable, any family members, are to be regarded as sufficient if—

(a)   they exceed the maximum level of resources which a British citizen and his family members may possess if he is to become eligible for social assistance under the United Kingdom benefit system; or

(b)   paragraph (a) does not apply but, taking into account the personal situation of the person concerned and, where applicable, any family members, it appears to the decision maker that the resources of the person or persons concerned should be regarded as sufficient.

(5)   For the purpose of regulation 15A(2) references in this regulation to 'family members' includes a 'primary carer' as defined in regulation 15A(7).

5.   'Worker or self-employed person who has ceased activity'

(1)   In these Regulations, 'worker or self-employed person who has ceased activity' means an EEA national who satisfies the conditions in paragraph (2), (3), (4) or (5).

(2)   A person satisfies the conditions in this paragraph if he—

(a)   terminates his activity as a worker or self-employed person and—

(i)   has reached the age at which he is entitled to a state pension on the date on which he terminates his activity; or

(ii)   in the case of a worker, ceases working to take early retirement;

(b)   pursued his activity as a worker or self-employed person in the United Kingdom for at least twelve months prior to the termination; and

(c)   resided in the United Kingdom continuously for more than three years prior to the termination.

(3)   A person satisfies the conditions in this paragraph if—

(a)   he terminates his activity in the United Kingdom as a worker or self-employed person as a result of a permanent incapacity to work; and

(b)   either—

(i)   he resided in the United Kingdom continuously for more than two years prior to the termination; or

(ii)   the incapacity is the result of an accident at work or an occupational disease that entitles him to a pension payable in full or in part by an institution in the United Kingdom.

(4)   A person satisfies the conditions in this paragraph if—

(a)   he is active as a worker or self-employed person in an EEA State but retains his place of residence in the United Kingdom, to which he returns as a rule at least once a week; and

(b)   prior to becoming so active in that EEA State, he had been continuously resident and continuously active as a worker or self-employed person in the United Kingdom for at least three years.

(5)   A person who satisfies the condition in paragraph (4)(a) but not the condition in paragraph (4)(b) shall, for the purposes of paragraphs (2) and (3), be treated as being active and resident in the United Kingdom during any period in which he is working or self-employed in the EEA State.

(6)   The conditions in paragraphs (2) and (3) as to length of residence and activity as a worker or self-employed person shall not apply in relation to a person whose spouse or civil partner is a British citizen.

(7)   Subject to regulation 7A(3), for the purposes of this regulation—

    (a)   periods of inactivity for reasons not of the person's own making;

    (b)   periods of inactivity due to illness or accident; and

    (c)   in the case of a worker, periods of involuntary unemployment duly recorded by the relevant employment office,

shall be treated as periods of activity as a worker or self-employed person, as the case may be.

6.   **'Qualified person'**

(1)   In these Regulations, 'qualified person' means a person who is an EEA national and in the United Kingdom as—

    (a)   a jobseeker;

    (b)   a worker;

    (c)   a self-employed person;

    (d)   a self-sufficient person; or

    (e)   a student.

(2)   Subject to regulation 7A(4), a person who is no longer working shall not cease to be treated as a worker for the purpose of paragraph (1)(b) if—

    (a)   he is temporarily unable to work as the result of an illness or accident;

    (b)   he is in duly recorded involuntary unemployment after having been employed in the United Kingdom, provided that he has registered as a jobseeker with the relevant employment office and—

        (i)   he was employed for one year or more before becoming unemployed;

        (ii)   he has been unemployed for no more than six months; or

        (iii)   he can provide evidence that he is seeking employment in the United Kingdom and has a genuine chance of being engaged;

    (c)   he is involuntarily unemployed and has embarked on vocational training; or

    (d)   he has voluntarily ceased working and embarked on vocational training that is related to his previous employment.

(3)   A person who is no longer in self-employment shall not cease to be treated as a self-employed person for the purpose of paragraph (1)(c) if he is temporarily unable to pursue his activity as a self-employed person as the result of an illness or accident.

(4)   For the purpose of paragraph (1)(a), 'jobseeker' means a person who enters the United Kingdom in order to seek employment and can provide evidence that he is seeking employment and has a genuine chance of being engaged.

7.   **Family member**

(1)   Subject to paragraph (2), for the purposes of these Regulations the following persons shall be treated as the family members of another person—

    (a)   his spouse or his civil partner;

    (b)   direct descendants of his, his spouse or his civil partner who are—

        (i)   under 21; or

        (ii)   dependants of his, his spouse or his civil partner;

    (c)   dependent direct relatives in his ascending line or that of his spouse or his civil partner;

    (d)   a person who is to be treated as the family member of that other person under paragraph (3).

(2)   A person shall not be treated under paragraph (1)(b) or (c) as the family member of a student residing in the United Kingdom after the period of three months beginning on the date on which the student is admitted to the United Kingdom unless—

(a)   in the case of paragraph (b), the person is the dependent child of the student or of his spouse or civil partner; or

(b)   the student also falls within one of the other categories of qualified persons mentioned in regulation 6(1).

(3)   Subject to paragraph (4), a person who is an extended family member and has been issued with an EEA family permit, a registration certificate or a residence card shall be treated as the family member of the relevant EEA national for as long as he continues to satisfy the conditions in regulation 8(2), (3), (4) or (5) in relation to that EEA national and the permit, certificate or card has not ceased to be valid or been revoked.

(4)   Where the relevant EEA national is a student, the extended family member shall only be treated as the family member of that national under paragraph (3) if either the EEA family permit was issued under regulation 12(2), the registration certificate was issued under regulation 16(5) or the residence card was issued under regulation 17(4).

7A.   Application of the Accession Regulations

(1)   This regulation applies to an EEA national who was an accession State worker requiring registration on 30th April 2011 ('an accession worker').

(2)   In this regulation—

'accession State worker requiring registration' has the same meaning as in regulation 1(2)(d) of the Accession Regulations;

'legally working' has the same meaning as in regulation 2(7) of the Accession Regulations.

(3)   In regulation 5(7)(c), where the worker is an accession worker, periods of involuntary unemployment duly recorded by the relevant employment office shall be treated only as periods of activity as a worker—

(a)   during any period in which regulation 5(4) of the Accession Regulations applied to that person; or

(b)   when the unemployment began on or after 1st May 2011.

(4)   Regulation 6(2) applies to an accession worker where he—

(a)   was a person to whom regulation 5(4) of the Accession Regulations applied on 30th April 2011; or

(b)   became unable to work, became unemployed or ceased to work, as the case maybe, on or after 1st May 2011.

(5)   For the purposes of regulation 15, an accession worker shall be treated as having resided in accordance with these Regulations during any period before 1st May 2011 in which the accession worker—

(a)   was legally working in the United Kingdom; or

(b)   was a person to whom regulation 5(4) of the Accession Regulations applied.

(6)   Subject to paragraph (7), a registration certificate issued to an accession worker under regulation 8 of the Accession Regulations shall, from 1st May 2011, be treated as if it was a registration certificate issued under these Regulations where the accession worker was legally working in the United Kingdom for the employer specified in that certificate on—

(a)   30th April 2011; or

(b)   the date on which the certificate is issued where it is issued after 30th April 2011.

(7)   Paragraph (6) does not apply—

(a)   if the Secretary of State issues a registration certificate in accordance with regulation 16 to an accession worker on or after 1st May 2011; and

(b)   from the date of registration stated on that certificate.

8.   'Extended family member'

(1)   In these Regulations 'extended family member' means a person who is not a family member of an EEA national under regulation 7(1)(a), (b) or (c) and who satisfies the conditions in paragraph (2), (3), (4) or (5).

(2)   A person satisfies the condition in this paragraph if the person is a relative of an EEA national, his spouse or his civil partner and—

(a)   the person is residing in a country other than the United Kingdom and is dependent upon the EEA national or is a member of his household;

(b)   the person satisfied the condition in paragraph (a) and is accompanying the EEA national to the United Kingdom or wishes to join him there; or

(c)   the person satisfied the condition in paragraph (a), has joined the EEA national in the United Kingdom and continues to be dependent upon him or to be a member of his household.

(3)   A person satisfies the condition in this paragraph if the person is a relative of an EEA national or his spouse or his civil partner and, on serious health grounds, strictly requires the personal care of the EEA national his spouse or his civil partner.

(4)   A person satisfies the condition in this paragraph if the person is a relative of an EEA national and would meet the requirements in the immigration rules (other than those relating to entry clearance) for indefinite leave to enter or remain in the United Kingdom as a dependent relative of the EEA national were the EEA national a person present and settled in the United Kingdom.

(5)   A person satisfies the condition in this paragraph if the person is the partner of an EEA national (other than a civil partner) and can prove to the decision maker that he is in a durable relationship with the EEA national.

(6)   In these Regulations 'relevant EEA national' means, in relation to an extended family member, the EEA national who is or whose spouse or civil partner is the relative of the extended family member for the purpose of paragraph (2), (3) or (4) or the EEA national who is the partner of the extended family member for the purpose of paragraph (5).

9.   **Family members of British citizens**

(1)   If the conditions in paragraph (2) are satisfied, these Regulations apply to a person who is the family member of a British citizen as if the British citizen were an EEA national.

(2)   The conditions are that—

(a)   the British citizen is residing in an EEA State as a worker or self-employed person or was so residing before returning to the United Kingdom; and

(b)   if the family member of the British citizen is his spouse or civil partner, the parties are living together in the EEA State or had entered into the marriage or civil partnership and were living together in that State before the British citizen returned to the United Kingdom.

(3)   Where these Regulations apply to the family member of a British citizen the British citizen shall be treated as holding a valid passport issued by an EEA State for the purpose of the application of regulation 13 to that family member.

10.   **'Family member who has retained the right of residence'**

(1)   In these Regulations, 'family member who has retained the right of residence' means, subject to paragraph (8), a person who satisfies the conditions in paragraph (2), (3), (4) or (5).

(2)   A person satisfies the conditions in this paragraph if—

(a)   he was a family member of a qualified person or of an EEA national with a permanent right residence when that person died;

(b)   he resided in the United Kingdom in accordance with these Regulations for at least the year immediately before the death of the qualified person or the EEA national with a permanent right of residence; and

(c)   he satisfies the condition in paragraph (6).

(3)   A person satisfies the conditions in this paragraph if—

(a)   he is the direct descendant of—

(i)   qualified person or an EEA national with a permanent right of residence who has died;

(ii)   a person who ceased to be a qualified person on ceasing to reside in the United Kingdom; or

(iii)   the person who was the spouse or civil partner of the qualified person or an EEA national with a permanent right of residence mentioned in sub-paragraph (i) when he died or is the spouse or civil partner of the person mentioned in sub-paragraph (ii); and

(b)   he was attending an educational course in the United Kingdom immediately before the qualified person or an EEA national with a permanent right of residence died or ceased to be a qualified person and continues to attend such a course.

(4)   A person satisfies the conditions in this paragraph if the person is the parent with actual custody of a child who satisfies the condition in paragraph (3).

(5)   A person satisfies the conditions in this paragraph if—

    (a)   he ceased to be a family member of a qualified person or of an EEA national with a permanent right of residence on the termination of the marriage or civil partnership of that person;

    (b)   he was residing in the United Kingdom in accordance with these Regulations at the date of the termination;

    (c)   he satisfies the condition in paragraph (6); and

    (d)   either—

        (i)   prior to the initiation of the proceedings for the termination of the marriage or the civil partnership the marriage or civil partnership had lasted for at least three years and the parties to the marriage or civil partnership had resided in the United Kingdom for at least one year during its duration;

        (ii)   the former spouse or civil partner of the qualified person or the EEA national with a permanent right of residence has custody of a child of the qualified person;

        (iii)   the former spouse or civil partner of the qualified person or the EEA national with a permanent right of residence has the right of access to a child of the qualified person or the EEA national with a permanent right of residence, where the child is under the age of 18 and where a court has ordered that such access must take place in the United Kingdom; or

        (iv)   the continued right of residence in the United Kingdom of the person is warranted by particularly difficult circumstances, such as he or another family member having been a victim of domestic violence while the marriage or civil partnership was subsisting.

(6)   The condition in this paragraph is that the person—

    (a)   is not an EEA national but would, if he were an EEA national, be a worker, a self-employed person or a self-sufficient person under regulation 6; or

    (b)   is the family member of a person who falls within paragraph (a).

(7)   In this regulation, 'educational course' means a course within the scope of Article 12 of Council Regulation (EEC) No. 1612/68 on freedom of movement for workers.

(8)   A person with a permanent right of residence under regulation 15 shall not become a family member who has retained the right of residence on the death or departure from the United Kingdom of the qualified person or the EEA national with a permanent right of residence or the termination of the marriage or civil partnership, as the case may be, and a family member who has retained the right of residence shall cease to have that status on acquiring a permanent right of residence under regulation 15.

PART 2

EEA RIGHTS

11.   Right of admission to the United Kingdom

(1)   An EEA national must be admitted to the United Kingdom if he produces on arrival a valid national identity card or passport issued by an EEA State.

(2)   A person who is not an EEA national must be admitted to the United Kingdom if he is a family member of an EEA national, a family member who has retained the right of residence, a person who meets the criteria in paragraph (5) or a person with a permanent right of residence under regulation 15 and produces on arrival—

    (a)   a valid passport; and

    (b)   an EEA family permit, a residence card, a derivative residence card or a permanent residence card.

(3)   An immigration officer may not place a stamp in the passport of a person admitted to the United Kingdom under this regulation who is not an EEA national if the person produces a residence card, a derivative residence card or permanent residence card.

(4)   Before an immigration officer refuses admission to the United Kingdom to a person under this regulation because the person does not produce on arrival a document mentioned in paragraph (1) or (2), the immigration officer must give the person every reasonable opportunity to obtain the document or have it brought to him within a reasonable period of time or to prove by other means that he is—

    (a)   an EEA national;

(b)   a family member of an EEA national with a right to accompany that national or join him in the United Kingdom;

(ba)   a person who meets the criteria in paragraph (5); or

(c)   a family member who has retained the right of residence or a person with a permanent right of residence under regulation 15.

(5)   A person ('P') meets the criteria in this paragraph where—

(a)   P previously resided in the United Kingdom pursuant to regulation 15A(3) and would be entitled to reside in the United Kingdom pursuant to that regulation were P in the country;

(b)   P is accompanying an EEA national to, or joining an EEA national in, the United Kingdom and P would be entitled to reside in the United Kingdom pursuant to regulation 15A(2) were P and the EEA national both in the United Kingdom;

(c)   P is accompanying a person ('the relevant person') to, or joining the relevant person in, the United Kingdom and—

(i)   the relevant person is residing, or has resided, in the United Kingdom pursuant to regulation 15A(3); and

(ii)   P would be entitled to reside in the United Kingdom pursuant to regulation 15A(4) were P and the relevant person both in the United Kingdom;

(d)   P is accompanying a person who meets the criteria in (b) or (c) ('the relevant person') to the United Kingdom and—

(i)   P and the relevant person are both—

(aa)   seeking admission to the United Kingdom in reliance on this paragraph for the first time; or

(bb)   returning to the United Kingdom having previously resided there pursuant to the same provisions of regulation 15A in reliance on which they now base their claim to admission; and

(ii)   P would be entitled to reside in the United Kingdom pursuant to regulation 15A(5) were P and the relevant person there; or

(e)   P is accompanying a British citizen to, or joining a British citizen in, the United Kingdom and P would be entitled to reside in the United Kingdom pursuant to regulation 15A(4A) were P and the British citizen both in the United Kingdom.

(6)   Paragraph (7) applies where—

(a)   a person ('P') seeks admission to the United Kingdom in reliance on paragraph (5)(b), (c) or (e); and

(b)   if P were in the United Kingdom, P would have a derived right of residence by virtue of regulation 15A(7)(b)(ii).

(7)   Where this paragraph applies a person ('P') will only be regarded as meeting the criteria in paragraph (5)(b), (c) or (e) where P—

(a)   is accompanying the person with whom P would on admission to the United Kingdom jointly share care responsibility for the purpose of regulation 15A(7)(b)(ii); or

(b)   has previously resided in the United Kingdom pursuant to regulation 15A(2), (4) or (4A) as a joint primary carer and seeks admission to the United Kingdom in order to reside there again on the same basis.

(8)   But this regulation is subject to regulations 19(1) and (2).

12.   Issue of EEA family permit

(1)   An entry clearance officer must issue an EEA family permit to a person who applies for one if the person is a family member of an EEA national and—

(a)   the EEA national—

(i)   is residing in the UK in accordance with these Regulations; or

(ii)   will be travelling to the United Kingdom within six months of the date of the application and will be an EEA national residing in the United Kingdom in accordance with these Regulations on arrival in the United Kingdom; and

(b)   the family member will be accompanying the EEA national to the United Kingdom or joining the EEA national there.

(1A)   An entry clearance officer must issue an EEA family permit to a person who applies and provides proof that, at the time at which he first intends to use the EEA family permit, he—

    (a)   would be entitled to be admitted to the United Kingdom by virtue of regulation 11(5); and

    (b)   will (save in the case of a person who would be entitled to be admitted to the United Kingdom by virtue of regulation 11(5)(a)) be accompanying to, or joining in, the United Kingdom any person from whom his right to be admitted to the United Kingdom under regulation 11(5) will be derived.

(1B)   An entry clearance officer must issue an EEA family permit to a family member who has retained the right of residence.

(2)   An entry clearance officer may issue an EEA family permit to an extended family member of an EEA national who applies for one if—

    (a)   the relevant EEA national satisfies the condition in paragraph (1)(a);

    (b)   the extended family member wishes to accompany the relevant EEA national to the United Kingdom or to join him there; and

    (c)   in all the circumstances, it appears to the entry clearance officer appropriate to issue the EEA family permit.

(3)   Where an entry clearance officer receives an application under paragraph (2) he shall undertake an extensive examination of the personal circumstances of the applicant and if he refuses the application shall give reasons justifying the refusal unless this is contrary to the interests of national security.

(4)   An EEA family permit issued under this regulation shall be issued free of charge and as soon as possible.

(5)   But an EEA family permit shall not be issued under this regulation if the applicant or the EEA national concerned is is not entitled to be admitted to the United Kingdom as a result of regulation 19(1A) or falls to be excluded in accordance with regulation 19(1B).

(6)   An EEA family permit will not be issued under this regulation to a person ('A') who is the spouse, civil partner or durable partner of a person ('B') where a spouse, civil partner or durable partner of A or B holds a valid EEA family permit.

13.   Initial right of residence

(1)   An EEA national is entitled to reside in the United Kingdom for a period not exceeding three months beginning on the date on which he is admitted to the United Kingdom provided that he holds a valid national identity card or passport issued by an EEA State.

(2)   A family member of an EEA national or a family member who has retained the right of residence who is residing in the United Kingdom under paragraph (1) who is not himself an EEA national is entitled to reside in the United Kingdom provided that he holds a valid passport.

(3)   An EEA national or his family member who becomes an unreasonable burden on the social assistance system of the United Kingdom will cease to have a right to reside under this regulation.

(4)   A person who otherwise satisfies the criteria in this regulation will not be entitled to reside in the United Kingdom under this regulation where the Secretary of State has made a decision under regulation 19(3)(b), 20(1) or 20A(1).

(5)   But—

    (a)   this regulation is subject to regulation 19(3)(b); and

    (b)   an EEA national or his family member who becomes an unreasonable burden on the social assistance system of the United Kingdom shall cease to have the right to reside under this regulation.

14.   Extended right of residence

(1)   A qualified person is entitled to reside in the United Kingdom for so long as he remains a qualified person.

(2)   A family member of a qualified person residing in the United Kingdom under paragraph (1) or of an EEA national with a permanent right of residence under regulation 15 is entitled to reside in the United Kingdom for so long as he remains the family member of the qualified person or EEA national.

(3)   A family member who has retained the right of residence is entitled to reside in the United Kingdom for so long as he remains a family member who has retained the right of residence.

(4)   A right to reside under this regulation is in addition to any right a person may have to reside in the United Kingdom under regulation 13 or 15.

(5)   A person who otherwise satisfies the criteria in this regulation will not be entitled to a right to reside in the United Kingdom under this regulation where the Secretary of State has made a decision under regulation 19(3)(b), 20(1) or 20A(1).

15.   Permanent right of residence

(1)   The following persons shall acquire the right to reside in the United Kingdom permanently—

   (a)   an EEA national who has resided in the United Kingdom in accordance with these Regulations for a continuous period of five years;

   (b)   a family member of an EEA national who is not himself an EEA national but who has resided in the United Kingdom with the EEA national in accordance with these Regulations for a continuous period of five years;

   (c)   a worker or self-employed person who has ceased activity;

   (d)   the family member of a worker or self-employed person who has ceased activity;

   (e)   a person who was the family member of a worker or self-employed person where—

      (i)   the worker or self-employed person has died;

      (ii)   the family member resided with him immediately before his death; and

      (iii)   the worker or self-employed person had resided continuously in the United Kingdom for at least the two years immediately before his death or the death was the result of an accident at work or an occupational disease;

   (f)   a person who—

      (i)   has resided in the United Kingdom in accordance with these Regulations for a continuous period of five years; and

      (ii)   was, at the end of that period, a family member who has retained the right of residence.

(1A)   Residence in the United Kingdom as a result of a derivative right of residence does not constitute residence for the purpose of this regulation.

(2)   The right of permanent residence under this regulation shall be lost only through absence from the United Kingdom for a period exceeding two consecutive years.

(3)   A person who satisfies the criteria in this regulation will not be entitled to a permanent right to reside in the United Kingdom where the Secretary of State has made a decision under regulation 19(3)(b), 20(1) or 20A(1).

15A.   Derivative right of residence

(1)   A person ('P') who is not an exempt person and who satisfies the criteria in paragraph (2), (3), (4), (4A) or (5) of this regulation is entitled to a derivative right to reside in the United Kingdom for as long as P satisfies the relevant criteria.

(2)   P satisfies the criteria in this paragraph if—

   (a)   P is the primary carer of an EEA national ('the relevant EEA national'); and

   (b)   the relevant EEA national—

      (i)   is under the age of 18;

      (ii)   is residing in the United Kingdom as a self-sufficient person; and

      (iii)   would be unable to remain in the United Kingdom if P were required to leave.

(3)   P satisfies the criteria in this paragraph if—

   (a)   P is the child of an EEA national ('the EEA national parent');

   (b)   P resided in the United Kingdom at a time when the EEA national parent was residing in the United Kingdom as a worker; and

   (c)   P is in education in the United Kingdom and was in education there at a time when the EEA national parent was in the United Kingdom.

(4)   P satisfies the criteria in this paragraph if—

   (a)   P is the primary carer of a person meeting the criteria in paragraph (3) ('the relevant person'); and

   (b)   the relevant person would be unable to continue to be educated in the United Kingdom if P were required to leave.

(4A)   P satisfies the criteria in this paragraph if—

   (a)   P is the primary carer of a British citizen ('the relevant British citizen');

    (b)   the relevant British citizen is residing in the United Kingdom; and

    (c)   the relevant British citizen would be unable to reside in the UK or in another EEA State if P were required to leave.

(5)   P satisfies the criteria in this paragraph if—

    (a)   P is under the age of 18;

    (b)   P's primary carer is entitled to a derivative right to reside in the United Kingdom by virtue of paragraph (2) or (4);

    (c)   P does not have leave to enter, or remain in, the United Kingdom; and

    (d)   requiring P to leave the United Kingdom would prevent P's primary carer from residing in the United Kingdom.

(6)   For the purpose of this regulation—

    (a)   'education' excludes nursery education;

    (b)   'worker' does not include a jobseeker or a person who falls to be regarded as a worker by virtue of regulation 6(2); and

    (c)   'an exempt person' is a person—

        (i)   who has a right to reside in the United Kingdom as a result of any other provision of these Regulations;

        (ii)   who has a right of abode in the United Kingdom by virtue of section 2 of the 1971 Act;

        (iii)   to whom section 8 of the 1971 Act, or any order made under subsection (2) of that provision, applies; or

        (iv)   who has indefinite leave to enter or remain in the United Kingdom.

(7)   P is to be regarded as a 'primary carer' of another person if

    (a)   P is a direct relative or a legal guardian of that person; and

    (b)   P—

        (i)   is the person who has primary responsibility for that person's care; or

        (ii)   shares equally the responsibility for that person's care with one other person who is not an exempt person.

(7A)   Where P is to be regarded as a primary carer of another person by virtue of paragraph (7)(b)(ii) the criteria in paragraphs (2)(b)(iii), (4)(b) and (4A)(c) shall be considered on the basis that both P and the person with whom care responsibility is shared would be required to leave the United Kingdom.

(7B)   Paragraph (7A) does not apply if the person with whom care responsibility is shared acquired a derivative right to reside in the United Kingdom as a result of this regulation prior to P assuming equal care responsibility.

(8)   P will not be regarded as having responsibility for a person's care for the purpose of paragraph (7) on the sole basis of a financial contribution towards that person's care.

(9)   A person who otherwise satisfies the criteria in paragraph (2), (3), (4), (4A) or (5) will not be entitled to a derivative right to reside in the United Kingdom where the Secretary of State has made a decision under regulation 19(3)(b), 20(1) or 20A(1).

15B.   **Continuation of a right of residence**

(1)   This regulation applies during any period in which, but for the effect of regulation 13(4), 14(5), 15(3) or 15A(9), a person ('P') who is in the United Kingdom would be entitled to reside here pursuant to these Regulations.

(2)   Where this regulation applies, any right of residence will (notwithstanding the effect of regulation 13(4), 14(5), 15(3) or 15A(9)) be deemed to continue during any period in which—

    (a)   an appeal under regulation 26 could be brought, while P is in the United Kingdom, against a relevant decision (ignoring any possibility of an appeal out of time with permission); or

    (b)   an appeal under regulation 26 against a relevant decision, brought while P is in the United Kingdom, is pending (within the meaning of section 104 of the 2002 Act).

(3)   Periods during which residence pursuant to regulation 14 is deemed to continue as a result of paragraph (2) will not constitute residence for the purpose of regulation 15 unless and until—

    (a)   a relevant decision is withdrawn by the Secretary of State; or

    (b)   an appeal against a relevant decision is allowed and that appeal is finally determined (within the meaning of section 104 of the 2002 Act).

(4)   Periods during which residence is deemed to continue as a result of paragraph (2) will not constitute residence for the purpose of regulation 21(4)(a) unless and until—

(a)   a relevant decision is withdrawn by the Secretary of State; or

(b)   an appeal against a relevant decision is allowed and that appeal is finally determined (within the meaning of section 104 of the 2002 Act).

(5)   A 'relevant decision' for the purpose of this regulation means a decision pursuant to regulation 19(3)(b), 20(1) or 20A(1) which would, but for the effect of paragraph (2), prevent P from residing in the United Kingdom pursuant to these Regulations.

PART 3
RESIDENCE DOCUMENTATION

16.   Issue of registration certificate

(1)   The Secretary of State must issue a registration certificate to a qualified person immediately on application and production of—

(a)   a valid identity card or passport issued by an EEA State;

(b)   proof that he is a qualified person.

(2)   In the case of a worker, confirmation of the worker's engagement from his employer or a certificate of employment is sufficient proof for the purposes of paragraph (1)(b).

(3)   The Secretary of State must issue a registration certificate to an EEA national who is the family member of a qualified person or of an EEA national with a permanent right of residence under regulation 15 immediately on application and production of—

(a)   a valid identity card or passport issued by an EEA State; and

(b)   proof that the applicant is such a family member.

(4)   The Secretary of State must issue a registration certificate to an EEA national who is a family member who has retained the right of residence on application and production of—

(a)   a valid identity card or passport; and

(b)   proof that the applicant is a family member who has retained the right of residence.

(5)   The Secretary of State may issue a registration certificate to an extended family member not falling within regulation 7(3) who is an EEA national on application if—

(a)   the relevant EEA national in relation to the extended family member is a qualified person or an EEA national with a permanent right of residence under regulation 15; and

(b)   in all the circumstances it appears to the Secretary of State appropriate to issue the registration certificate.

(6)   Where the Secretary of State receives an application under paragraph (5) he shall undertake an extensive examination of the personal circumstances of the applicant and if he refuses the application shall give reasons justifying the refusal unless this is contrary to the interests of national security.

(7)   A registration certificate issued under this regulation shall state the name and address of the person registering and the date of registration.

(8)   But this regulation is subject to regulation 7A(6) and 20(1).

17.   Issue of residence card

(1)   The Secretary of State must issue a residence card to a person who is not an EEA national and is the family member of a qualified person or of an EEA national with a permanent right of residence under regulation 15 on application and production of—

(a)   a valid passport; and

(b)   proof that the applicant is such a family member.

(2)   The Secretary of State must issue a residence card to a person who is not an EEA national but who is a family member who has retained the right of residence on application and production of—

(a)   a valid passport; and

(b)   proof that the applicant is a family member who has retained the right of residence.

(3)   On receipt of an application under paragraph (1) or (2) and the documents that are required to accompany the application the Secretary of State shall immediately issue the applicant with a certificate of application for the residence card and the residence card shall be issued no later than six months after the date on which the application and documents are received.

(4)   The Secretary of State may issue a residence card to an extended family member not falling within regulation 7(3) who is not an EEA national on application if—

    (a)   the relevant EEA national in relation to the extended family member is a qualified person or an EEA national with a permanent right of residence under regulation 15; and

    (b)   in all the circumstances it appears to the Secretary of State appropriate to issue the residence card.

(5)   Where the Secretary of State receives an application under paragraph (4) he shall undertake an extensive examination of the personal circumstances of the applicant and if he refuses the application shall give reasons justifying the refusal unless this is contrary to the interests of national security.

(6)   A residence card issued under this regulation may take the form of a stamp in the applicant's passport and shall be valid for—

    (a)   five years from the date of issue; or

    (b)   in the case of a residence card issued to the family member or extended family member of a qualified person, the envisaged period of residence in the United Kingdom of the qualified person,

whichever is the shorter.

(6A)   A residence card issued under this regulation shall be entitled 'Residence card of a family member of an EEA national' or 'Residence card of a family member who has retained the right of residence', as the case may be.

(7)   ...

(8)   But this regulation is subject to regulations 20(1) and (1A).

18.   Issue of a document certifying permanent residence and a permanent residence card

(1)   The Secretary of State must issue an EEA national with a permanent right of residence under regulation 15 with a document certifying permanent residence as soon as possible after an application for such a document and proof that the EEA national has such a right is submitted to the Secretary of State.

(2)   The Secretary of State must issue a person who is not an EEA national who has a permanent right of residence under regulation 15 with a permanent residence card no later than six months after the date on which an application for a permanent residence card and proof that the person has such a right is submitted to the Secretary of State.

(3)   Subject to paragraph (5), a permanent residence card shall be valid for ten years from the date of issue and must be renewed on application.

(4)   ...

(5)   A document certifying permanent residence and a permanent residence card shall cease to be valid if the holder ceases to have a right of permanent residence under regulation 15.

(6)   But this regulation is subject to regulation 20.

18A.   Issue of a derivative residence card

(1)   The Secretary of State must issue a person with a derivative residence card on application and on production of—

    (a)   a valid identity card issued by an EEA State or a valid passport; and

    (b)   proof that the applicant has a derivative right of residence under regulation 15A.

(2)   On receipt of an application under paragraph (1) the Secretary of State must issue the applicant with a certificate of application as soon as possible.

(3)   A derivative residence card issued under paragraph (1) may take the form of a stamp in the applicant's passport and will be valid until—

    (a)   a date five years from the date of issue; or

    (b)   any other date specified by the Secretary of State when issuing the derivative residence card.

(4)   A derivative residence card issued under paragraph (1) must be issued as soon as practicable.

(5)   But this regulation is subject to regulations 20(1) and 20(1A).

PART 4

REFUSAL OF ADMISSION AND REMOVAL ETC

19.   Exclusion and removal from the United Kingdom

(1)   A person is not entitled to be admitted to the United Kingdom by virtue of regulation 11 if his exclusion is justified on grounds of public policy, public security or public health in accordance with regulation 21.

(1A)   A person is not entitled to be admitted to the United Kingdom by virtue of regulation 11 if that person is subject to a deportation or exclusion order.

(1B)   If the Secretary of State considers that the exclusion of an EEA national or the family member of an EEA national is justified on the grounds of public policy, public security or public health in accordance with regulation 21 the Secretary of State may make an order for the purpose of these Regulations prohibiting that person from entering the United Kingdom.

(2)   A person is not entitled to be admitted to the United Kingdom as the family member of an EEA national under regulation 11(2) unless, at the time of his arrival—

(a)   he is accompanying the EEA national or joining him in the United Kingdom; and

(b)   the EEA national has a right to reside in the United Kingdom under these Regulations.

(3)   Subject to paragraphs (4) and (5), an EEA national who has entered the United Kingdom or the family member of such a national who has entered the United Kingdom may be removed if—

(a)   that person does not have or ceases to have a right to reside under these Regulations; or

(b)   the Secretary of State has decided that the person's removal is justified on grounds of public policy, public security or public health in accordance with regulation 21.

(4)   A person must not be removed under paragraph (3) as the automatic consequence of having recourse to the social assistance system of the United Kingdom.

(5)   A person must not be removed under paragraph (3) if he has a right to remain in the United Kingdom by virtue of leave granted under the 1971 Act unless his removal is justified on the grounds of public policy, public security or public health in accordance with regulation 21.

20.   Refusal to issue or renew and revocation of residence documentation

(1)   The Secretary of State may refuse to issue, revoke or refuse to renew a registration certificate, a residence card, a document certifying permanent residence or a permanent residence card if the refusal or revocation is justified on grounds of public policy, public security or public health.

(1A)   A decision under regulation 19(3) to remove a person from the United Kingdom will (save during any period in which a right of residence is deemed to continue as a result of regulation 15B(2)) invalidate a registration certificate, residence card, document certifying permanent residence or permanent residence card held by that person or an application made by that person for such a certificate, card or document.

(2)   The Secretary of State may revoke a registration certificate or a residence card or refuse to renew a residence card if the holder of the certificate or card has ceased to have a right to reside under these Regulations.

(3)   The Secretary of State may revoke a document certifying permanent residence or a permanent residence card or refuse to renew a permanent residence card if the holder of the certificate or card has ceased to have a right of permanent residence under regulation 15.

(4)   An immigration officer may, at the time of a person's arrival in the United Kingdom—

(a)   revoke that person's residence card if he is not at that time the family member of a qualified person or of an EEA national who has a right of permanent residence under regulation 15, a family member who has retained the right of residence or a person with a right of permanent residence under regulation 15;

(b)   revoke that person's permanent residence card if he is not at that time a person with a right of permanent residence under regulation 15.

(5)   An entry clearance officer or immigration officer may at any time revoke a person's s EEA family permit if—

(a)   the revocation is justified on grounds of public policy, public security or public health; or

(b)   the person is not at that time the family member of an EEA national with the right to reside in the United Kingdom under these Regulations or is not accompanying that national or joining him in the United Kingdom.

(6)   Any action taken under this regulation on grounds of public policy, public security or public health shall be in accordance with regulation 21.

20A. Cancellation of a right of residence

(1)   Where the conditions in paragraph (2) are met the Secretary of State may cancel a person's right to reside in the United Kingdom pursuant to these Regulations.

(2)   The conditions in this paragraph are met where—

(a)   a person has a right to reside in the United Kingdom as a result of these Regulations;

(b)   the Secretary of State has decided that the cancellation of that person's right to reside in the United Kingdom is justified on grounds of public policy, public security or public health in accordance with regulation 21;

(c)   the circumstances are such that the Secretary of State cannot make a decision under regulation 20(1); and

(d)   it is not possible for the Secretary of State to remove the person from the United Kingdom pursuant to regulation 19(3)(b).

21. Decisions taken on public policy, public security and public health grounds

(1)   In this regulation a 'relevant decision' means an EEA decision taken on the grounds of public policy, public security or public health.

(2)   A relevant decision may not be taken to serve economic ends.

(3)   A relevant decision may not be taken in respect of a person with a permanent right of residence under regulation 15 except on serious grounds of public policy or public security.

(4)   A relevant decision may not be taken except on imperative grounds of public security in respect of an EEA national who—

(a)   has resided in the United Kingdom for a continuous period of at least ten years prior to the relevant decision; or

(b)   is under the age of 18, unless the relevant decision is necessary in his best interests, as provided for in the Convention on the Rights of the Child adopted by the General Assembly of the United Nations on 20th November 1989.

(5)   Where a relevant decision is taken on grounds of public policy or public security it shall, in addition to complying with the preceding paragraphs of this regulation, be taken in accordance with the following principles—

(a)   the decision must comply with the principle of proportionality;

(b)   the decision must be based exclusively on the personal conduct of the person concerned;

(c)   the personal conduct of the person concerned must represent a genuine, present and sufficiently serious threat affecting one of the fundamental interests of society;

(d)   matters isolated from the particulars of the case or which relate to considerations of general prevention do not justify the decision;

(e)   a person's previous criminal convictions do not in themselves justify the decision.

(6)   Before taking a relevant decision on the grounds of public policy or public security in relation to a person who is resident in the United Kingdom the decision maker must take account of considerations such as the age, state of health, family and economic situation of the person, the person's length of residence in the United Kingdom, the person's social and cultural integration into the United Kingdom and the extent of the person's links with his country of origin.

(7)   In the case of a relevant decision taken on grounds of public health—

(a)   a disease that does not have epidemic potential as defined by the relevant instruments of the World Health Organisation or is not a disease listed in Schedule 1 to the Health Protection (Notification) Regulations 2010 shall not constitute grounds for the decision; and

(b)   if the person concerned is in the United Kingdom, diseases occurring after the three month period beginning on the date on which he arrived in the United Kingdom shall not constitute grounds for the decision.

21A. Application of Part 4 to persons with a derivative right of residence

(1)   Where this regulation applies Part 4 of these Regulations applies subject to the modifications listed in paragraph (3).

(2)   This regulation applies where a person—

    (a)   would, notwithstanding Part 4 of these Regulations, have a right to be admitted to, or reside in, the United Kingdom by virtue of a derivative right of residence arising under regulation 15A(2), (4), (4A) or (5);

    (b)   holds a derivative residence card; or

    (c)   has applied for a derivative residence card.

(3)   Where this regulation applies Part 4 applies in relation to the matters listed in paragraph (2) as if—

    (a)   references to a matter being 'justified on grounds of public policy, public security or public health in accordance with regulation 21' referred instead to a matter being 'conducive to the public good';

    (b)   the reference in regulation 20(5)(a) to a matter being 'justified on grounds of public policy, public security or public health' referred instead to a matter being 'conducive to the public good';

    (c)   references to 'the family member of an EEA national' referred instead to 'a person with a derivative right of residence';

    (d)   references to 'a registration certificate, a residence card, a document certifying permanent residence or a permanent residence card' referred instead to 'a derivative residence card';

    (e)   the reference in regulation 19(1A) to a deportation or exclusion order referred also to a deportation or exclusion order made under any provision of the immigration Acts.

    (f)   regulation 20(4) instead conferred on an immigration officer the power to revoke a derivative residence card where the holder is not at that time a person with a derivative right of residence; and

    (g)   regulations 20(3), 20(6) and 21 were omitted.

PART 5

PROCEDURE IN RELATION TO EEA DECISIONS

22.   **Person claiming right of admission**

(1)   This regulation applies to a person who claims a right of admission to the United Kingdom under regulation 11 as—

    (a)   a person, not being an EEA national, who is a family member of an EEA national, a family member who has retained the right of residence or a person with a permanent right of residence under regulation 15; or

    (b)   an EEA national, where there is reason to believe that he may fall to be excluded under regulation 19(1) or (1A).

(2)   A person to whom this regulation applies is to be treated as if he were a person seeking leave to enter the United Kingdom under the 1971 Act for the purposes of paragraphs 2, 3, 4, 7, 16 to 18 and 21 to 24 of Schedule 2 to the 1971 Act (administrative provisions as to control on entry etc), except that—

    (a)   the reference in paragraph 2(1) to the purpose for which the immigration officer may examine any persons who have arrived in the United Kingdom is to be read as a reference to the purpose of determining whether he is a person who is to be granted admission under these Regulations;

    (b)   the references in paragraphs 4(2A), 7 and 16(1) to a person who is, or may be, given leave to enter are to be read as references to a person who is, or may be, granted admission under these Regulations; and

    (c)   a medical examination is not be carried out under paragraph 2 or paragraph 7 as a matter of routine and may only be carried out within three months of a person's arrival in the United Kingdom.

(3)   For so long as a person to whom this regulation applies is detained, or temporarily admitted or released while liable to detention, under the powers conferred by Schedule 2 to the 1971 Act, he is deemed not to have been admitted to the United Kingdom.

23.   **Person refused admission**

(1)   This regulation applies to a person who is in the United Kingdom and has been refused admission to the United Kingdom—

    (a)   because he does not meet the requirement of regulation 11 (including where he does not meet those requirements because his EEA family permit, residence card, derivative residence card or permanent residence card has been revoked by an immigration officer in accordance with regulation 20); or

(b)   in accordance with regulation 19(1), (1A) or (2).

(2)   A person to whom this regulation applies, is to be treated as if he were a person refused leave to enter under the 1971 Act for the purpose of paragraphs 8, 10, 10A, 11, 16 to 19 and 21 to 24 of Schedule 2 to the 1971 Act, except that the reference in paragraph 19 to a certificate of entitlement, entry clearance or work permit is to be read as a reference to an EEA family permit, residence card, derivative residence card or a permanent residence card.

24. Person subject to removal

(1)   If there are reasonable grounds for suspecting that a person is someone who may be removed from the United Kingdom under regulation 19(3)(b), that person may be detained under the authority of the Secretary of State pending a decision whether or not to remove the person under that regulation, and paragraphs 17 and 18 of Schedule 2 to the 1971 Act shall apply in relation to the detention of such a person as those paragraphs apply in relation to a person who may be detained under paragraph 16 of that Schedule.

(2)   Where a decision is taken to remove a person under regulation 19(3)(a), the person is to be treated as if he were a person to whom section 10(1)(a) of the 1999 Act applied, and section 10 of that Act (removal of certain persons unlawfully in the United Kingdom) is to apply accordingly.

(3)   Where a decision is taken to remove a person under regulation l9(3)(b), the person is to be treated as if he were a person to whom section 3(5)(a) of the 1971 Act (liability to deportation) applied, and section 5 of that Act (procedure for deportation) and Schedule 3 to that Act (supplementary provision as to deportation) are to apply accordingly.

(4)   A person who enters the United Kingdom in breach of a deportation or exclusion order shall be removable as an illegal entrant under Schedule 2 to the 1971 Act and the provisions of that Schedule shall apply accordingly.

(5)   Where such a deportation order is made against a person but he is not removed under the order during the two year period beginning on the date on which the order is made, the Secretary of State shall only take action to remove the person under the order after the end of that period if, having assessed whether there has been any material change in circumstances since the deportation order was made, he considers that the removal continues to be justified on the grounds of public policy, public security or public health.

(6)   A person to whom this regulation applies shall be allowed one month to leave the United Kingdom, beginning on the date on which he is notified of the decision to remove him, before being removed pursuant to that decision except—

(a)   in duly substantiated cases of urgency;

(b)   where the person is detained pursuant to the sentence or order of any court;

(c)   where a person is a person to whom regulation 24(4) applies.

(7)   Paragraph (6) of this regulation does not apply where a decision has been taken under regulation 19(3) on the basis that the relevant person—

(a)   has ceased to have a derivative right of residence; or

(b)   is a person who would have had a derivative right of residence but for the effect of a decision to remove under regulation 19(3)(b).

24A. Revocation of deportation and exclusion orders

(1)   A deportation or exclusion order shall remain in force unless it is revoked by the Secretary of State under this regulation.

(2)   A person who is subject to a deportation or exclusion order may apply to the Secretary of State to have it revoked if the person considers that there has been a material change in the circumstances that justified the making of the order.

(3)   An application under paragraph (2) shall set out the material change in circumstances relied upon by the applicant and may only be made whilst the applicant is outside the United Kingdom.

(4)   On receipt of an application under paragraph (2), the Secretary of State shall revoke the order if the Secretary of State considers that the criteria for making such an order are no longer satisfied.

(5)   The Secretary of State shall take a decision on an application under paragraph (2) no later than six months after the date on which the application is received.

PART 6
APPEALS UNDER THESE REGULATIONS

25.   Interpretation of Part 6

(1)   In this Part—

'Asylum claim' has the meaning given in section 113(1) of the 2002 Act;

'Commission' has the same meaning as in the Special Immigration Appeals Commission Act 1997;

'Human rights claim' has the meaning given in section 113(1) of the 2002 Act.

(2)   For the purposes of this Part, and subject to paragraphs (3) and (4), an appeal is to be treated as pending during the period when notice of appeal is given and ending when the appeal is finally determined, withdrawn or abandoned.

(3)   An appeal is not to be treated as finally determined while a further appeal may be brought; and, if such a further appeal is brought, the original appeal is not to be treated as finally determined until the further appeal is determined, withdrawn or abandoned.

(4)   A pending appeal is not to be treated as abandoned solely because the appellant leaves the United Kingdom.

26.   Appeal rights

(1)   Subject to the following paragraphs of this regulation, a person may appeal under these Regulations against an EEA decision.

(2)   If a person claims to be an EEA national, he may not appeal under these Regulations unless he produces a valid national identity card or passport issued by an EEA State.

(2A)   If a person claims to be in a durable relationship with an EEA national he may not appeal under these Regulations unless he produces—

(a)   a passport; and

(b)   either—

(i)   an EEA family permit; or

(ii)   sufficient evidence to satisfy the Secretary of State that he is in a relationship with that EEA national.

(3)   If a person to whom paragraph (2) does not apply claims to be a family member who has retained the right of residence or the family member or relative of an EEA national he may not appeal under these Regulations unless he produces—

(a)   a passport; and

(b)   either—

(i)   an EEA family permit;

(ii)   proof that he is the family member or relative of an EEA national; or

(iii)   in the case of a person claiming to be a family member who has retained the right of residence, proof that he was a family member of the relevant person.

(3A)   If a person claims to be a person with a derivative right of entry or residence he may not appeal under these Regulations unless he produces a valid national identity card issued by an EEA State or a passport, and either—

(a)   an EEA family permit; or

(b)   proof that—

(i)   where the person claims to have a derivative right of entry or residence as a result of regulation 15A(2), he is a direct relative or guardian of an EEA national who is under the age of 18;

(ii)   where the person claims to have a derivative right of entry or residence as a result of regulation 15A(3), he is the child of an EEA national;

(iii)   where the person claims to have a derivative right of entry or residence as a result of regulation 15A(4), he is a direct relative or guardian of the child of an EEA national;

(iv)   where the person claims to have a derivative right of entry or residence as a result of regulation 15A(5), he is under the age of 18 and is a dependant of a person satisfying the criteria in (i) or (iii);

(v)   where the person claims to have a derivative right of entry or residence as a result of regulation 15A(4A), he is a direct relative or guardian of a British citizen.

(4)   A person may not bring an appeal under these Regulations on a ground certified under paragraph (5) or rely on such a ground in an appeal brought under these Regulations.

(5)   The Secretary of State or an immigration officer may certify a ground for the purposes of paragraph (4) if it has been considered in a previous appeal brought under these Regulations or under section 82(1) of the 2002 Act.

(6)   Except where an appeal lies to the Commission, an appeal under these Regulations lies to the First-tier Tribunal or Upper Tribunal.

(7)   The provisions of or made under the 2002 Act referred to in Schedule 1 shall have effect for the purposes of an appeal under these Regulations to the First-tier Tribunal or Upper Tribunal in accordance with that Schedule.

27. Out of country appeals

(1)   Subject to paragraphs (2) and (3), a person may not appeal under regulation 26 whilst he is in the United Kingdom against an EEA decision—

    (a)   to refuse to admit him to the United Kingdom;

    (aa)   to make an exclusion order against him;

    (b)   to refuse to revoke a deportation or exclusion order made against him;

    (c)   to refuse to issue him with an EEA family permit;

    (ca)   to revoke, or to refuse to issue or renew any document under these Regulations where that decision is taken at a time when the relevant person is outside the United Kingdom; or

    (d)   to remove him from the United Kingdom after he has entered the United Kingdom in breach of a deportation or exclusion order.

(2)   Paragraphs (1)(a) and (aa) do not apply where the person is in the United Kingdom and—

    (a)   the person held a valid EEA family permit, registration certificate, residence card, derivative residence card, document certifying permanent residence or permanent residence card on his arrival in the United Kingdom or can otherwise prove that he is resident in the United Kingdom;

    (b)   the person is deemed not to have been admitted to the United Kingdom under regulation 22(3) but at the date on which notice of the decision to refuse to admit him is given he has been in the United Kingdom for at least 3 months; or

    (c)   has made an asylum or human rights claim (or both), unless the Secretary of State has certified that the claim or claims is or are clearly unfounded.

(3)   Paragraph (1)(d) does not apply where the person has made an asylum or human rights claim (or both), unless the Secretary of State has certified that the claim or claims is or are clearly unfounded.

28. Appeals to the Commission

(1)   An appeal against an EEA decision lies to the Commission where paragraph (2) or (4) applies.

(2)   This paragraph applies if the Secretary of State certifies that the EEA decision was taken—

    (a)   by the Secretary of State wholly or partly on a ground listed in paragraph (3); or

    (b)   in accordance with a direction of the Secretary of State which identifies the person to whom the decision relates and which is given wholly or partly on a ground listed in paragraph (3).

(3)   The grounds mentioned in paragraph (2) are that the person's exclusion or removal from the United Kingdom is—

    (a)   in the interests of national security; or

    (b)   in the interests of the relationship between the United Kingdom and another country.

(4)   This paragraph applies if the Secretary of State certifies that the EEA decision was taken wholly or partly in reliance on information which in his opinion should not be made public—

    (a)   in the interests of national security;

    (b)   in the interests of the relationship between the United Kingdom and another country; or

    (c)   otherwise in the public interest.

(5)   In paragraphs (2) and (4) a reference to the Secretary of State is to the Secretary of State acting in person.

(6)   Where a certificate is issued under paragraph (2) or (4) in respect of a pending appeal to the First-tier Tribunal or Upper Tribunal the appeal shall lapse.

(7)   An appeal against an EEA decision lies to the Commission where an appeal lapses by virtue of paragraph (6).

(8)   The Special Immigration Appeals Commission Act 1997 shall apply to an appeal to the Commission under these Regulations as it applies to an appeal under section 2 of that Act to which subsection (2) of that section applies (appeals against an immigration decision) but paragraph (i) of that subsection shall not apply in relation to such an appeal.

29.   Effect of appeals to the Asylum and Immigration Tribunal

(1)   This Regulation applies to appeals under these Regulations made to the First-tier Tribunal or Upper Tribunal.

(2)   If a person in the United Kingdom appeals against an EEA decision to refuse to admit him to the United Kingdom, any directions for his removal from the United Kingdom previously given by virtue of the refusal cease to have effect, except in so far as they have already been carried out, and no directions may be so given while the appeal is pending.

(3)   If a person in the United Kingdom appeals against an EEA decision to remove him from the United Kingdom, any directions given under section 10 of the 1999 Act or Schedule 3 to the 1971 Act for his removal from the United Kingdom are to have no effect, except in so far as they have already been carried out, while the appeal is pending.

(4)   But the provisions of Part I of Schedule 2, or as the case may be, Schedule 3 to the 1971 Act with respect to detention and persons liable to detention apply to a person appealing against a refusal to admit him or a decision to remove him as if there were in force directions for his removal from the United Kingdom, except that he may not be detained on board a ship or aircraft so as to compel him to leave the United Kingdom while the appeal is pending.

(5)   In calculating the period of two months limited by paragraph 8(2) of Schedule 2 to the 1971 Act for—

(a)   the giving of directions under that paragraph for the removal of a person from the United Kingdom; and

(b)   the giving of a notice of intention to give such directions,

any period during which there is pending an appeal by him under is to be disregarded.

(6)   If a person in the United Kingdom appeals against an EEA decision to remove him from the United Kingdom, a deportation order is not to be made against him under section 5 of the 1971 Act while the appeal is pending.

(7)   Paragraph 29 of Schedule 2 to the 1971 Act (grant of bail pending appeal) applies to a person who has an appeal pending under these Regulations as it applies to a person who has an appeal pending under section 82(1) of the 2002 Act.

29A.   Alternative evidence of identity and nationality

(1)   Subject to paragraph (2), where a provision of these Regulations requires a person to hold or produce a valid identity card issued by an EEA State or a valid passport the Secretary of State may accept alternative evidence of identity and nationality where the person is unable to obtain or produce the required document due to circumstances beyond his or her control.

(2)   This regulation does not apply to regulation 11.

SCHEDULE 1   Regulation 26(7)
APPEALS TO THE FIRST-TIER TRIBUNAL

1.   The following provisions of, or made under, the 2002 Act have effect in relation to an appeal under these Regulations to the First-tier Tribunal as if it were an appeal against an immigration decision under section 82(1) of that Act:

section 84(1), except paragraphs (a) and (f);

sections 85 to 87;

section 105 and any regulations made under that section; and

section 106 and any rules made under that section.

2.   Tribunal Procedure Rules have effect in relation to appeals under these Regulations.

SCHEDULE 2   Regulation 30
EFFECT ON OTHER LEGISLATION

1.   Leave under the 1971 Act

(1)   In accordance with section 7 of the Immigration Act 1988, a person who is admitted to or acquires a right to reside in the United Kingdom under these Regulations shall not require leave to remain in the United Kingdom under the 1971 Act during any period in which he has a right to reside under these

Regulations but such a person shall require leave to remain under the 1971 Act during any period in which he does not have such a right.

(2) Subject to sub-paragraph (3), where a person has leave to enter or remain under the 1971 Act which is subject to conditions and that person also has a right to reside under these Regulations, those conditions shall not have effect for as long as the person has that right to reside.

(3) Where the person mentioned in sub-paragraph (2) is an accession State national subject to worker authorisation working in the United Kingdom during the accession period and the document endorsed to show that the person has leave is an accession worker authorisation document, any conditions to which that leave is subject restricting his employment shall continue to apply.

(4) In sub-paragraph (3)—

    (a) 'accession period' has the meaning given in regulation 1(2)(c) of the Accession (Immigration and Worker Authorisation) Regulations 2006;

    (b) 'accession State national subject to worker authorisation' has the meaning given in regulation 2 of those Regulations; and

    (c) 'accession worker authorisation document' has the meaning given in regulation 9(2) of those Regulations.

2. Persons not subject to restriction on the period for which they may remain

(1) For the purposes of the 1971 Act and the British Nationality Act 1981, a person who has a permanent right of residence under regulation 15 shall be regarded as a person who is in the United Kingdom without being subject under the immigration laws to any restriction on the period for which he may remain.

(2) But a qualified person, the family member of a qualified person, a person with a derivative right of residence and a family member who has retained the right of residence shall not, by virtue of that status, be so regarded for those purposes.

3. Carriers' liability under the 1999 Act

For the purposes of satisfying a requirement to produce a visa under section 40(1)(b) of the 1999 Act (charges in respect of passenger without proper documents), 'a visa of the required kind' includes an EEA family permit, a residence card, a derivative residence card, or a permanent residence card required for admission under regulation 11(2).

4. Appeals under the 2002 Act and previous immigration Acts

(1) The following EEA decisions shall not be treated as immigration decisions for the purpose of section 82(2) of the 2002 Act (right of appeal against an immigration decision)—

    (a) a decision that a person is to be removed under regulation 19(3)(a) by way of a direction under section 10(1)(a) of the 1999 Act (as provided for by regulation 24(2));

    (b) a decision to remove a person under regulation 19(3)(b) by making a deportation order under section 5(1) of the 1971 Act (as provided for by regulation 24(3));

    (c) a decision to remove a person mentioned in regulation 24(4) by way of directions under paragraphs 8 to 10 of Schedule 2 to the 1971 Act.

(2) A person who has been issued with a registration certificate, residence card, derivative residence card, a document certifying permanent residence or a permanent residence card under these Regulations or a registration certificate under the Accession (Immigration and Worker Registration) Regulations 2004, or an accession worker card under the Accession (Immigration and Worker Authorisation) Regulations 2006, or a person whose passport has been stamped with a family member residence stamp, shall have no right of appeal under section 2 of the Special Immigration Appeals Commission Act 1997 or section 82(1) of the 2002 Act. Any existing appeal under those sections of those Acts or under the Asylum and Immigration Appeals Act 1993, the Asylum and Immigration Act 1996 or the 1999 Act shall be treated as abandoned.

(3) Subject to paragraph (4), a person may appeal to the First-tier Tribunal under section 83(2) of the 2002 Act against the rejection of his asylum claim where—

    (a) that claim has been rejected, but

    (b) he has a right to reside in the United Kingdom under these Regulations.

(4) Paragraph (3) shall not apply if the person is an EEA national and the Secretary of State certifies that the asylum claim is clearly unfounded.

(5)   The Secretary of State shall certify the claim under paragraph (4) unless satisfied that it is not clearly unfounded.

(6)   In addition to the national of a State which is a contracting party to the Agreement referred to in section 84(2) of the 2002 Act, a Swiss national shall also be treated as an EEA national for the purposes of section 84(1)(d) of that Act.

(7)   An appeal under these Regulations against an EEA decision (including an appeal made on or after 1st April 2003 which is treated as an appeal under these Regulations under Schedule 4 but not an appeal made before that date) shall be treated as an appeal under section 82(1) of the 2002 Act against an immigration decision for the purposes of section 96(1)(a) of the 2002 Act.

(8)   Section 120 of the 2002 Act shall apply to a person if an EEA decision has been taken or may be taken in respect of him and, accordingly, the Secretary of State or an immigration officer may by notice require a statement from that person under subsection (2) of that section and that notice shall have effect for the purpose of section 96(2) of the 2002 Act.

(9)   In sub-paragraph (2), 'family member residence stamp' means a stamp in the passport of a family member of an EEA national confirming that he is the family member of an accession State worker requiring registration or an accession State national subject to worker authorisation working in the United Kingdom and with a right of residence under these Regulations as the family member of that worker; and in this sub-paragraph 'accession State worker requiring registration' has the same meaning as in regulation 2 of the Accession (Immigration and Worker Registration) Regulations 2004 and 'accession State national subject to worker authorisation' has the meaning given in regulation 2 of the Accession (Immigration and Worker Authorisation) Regulations 2006.

Extracts from the European Convention on Human Rights

Article 2 – right to life

1. Everyone's right to life shall be protected by law. No one shall be deprived of his life intentionally save in the execution of a sentence of a court following his conviction of a crime for which this penalty is provided by law.

2. Deprivation of life shall not be regarded as inflicted in contravention of this Article when it results from the use of force which is no more than absolutely necessary:

Article 3 – prohibition of torture

No one shall be subjected to torture or to inhuman or degrading treatment or punishment.

Article 5 – right to liberty and security

1. Everyone has the right to liberty and security of person. No one shall be deprived of his liberty save in the following cases and in accordance with a procedure prescribed by law:

    (a) the lawful detention of a person after conviction by a competent court;

    (b) the lawful arrest or detention of a person for non-compliance with the lawful order of a court or in order to secure the fulfilment of any obligation prescribed by law;

    (c) the lawful arrest or detention of a person effected for the purpose of bringing him before the competent legal authority on reasonable suspicion of having committed an offence or when it is reasonably considered necessary to prevent his committing an offence or fleeing after having done so;

    (d) the detention of a minor by lawful order for the purpose of educational supervision or his lawful detention for the purpose of bringing him before the competent legal authority;

    (e) the lawful detention of persons for the prevention of the spreading of infectious diseases, of persons of unsound mind, alcoholics or drug addicts or vagrants;

    (f) the lawful arrest or detention of a person to prevent his effecting an unauthorised entry into the country or of a person against whom action is being taken with a view to deportation or extradition.

2. Everyone who is arrested shall be informed promptly, in a language which he understands, of the reasons for his arrest and of any charge against him.

3. Everyone arrested or detained in accordance with the provisions of paragraph 1(c) of this Article shall be brought promptly before a judge or other officer authorised by law to exercise judicial power and shall be entitled to trial within a reasonable time or to release pending trial. Release may be conditioned by guarantees to appear for trial.

4. Everyone who is deprived of his liberty by arrest or detention shall be entitled to take proceedings by which the lawfulness of his detention shall be decided speedily by a court and his release ordered if the detention is not lawful.

5. Everyone who has been the victim of arrest or detention in contravention of the provisions of this Article shall have an enforceable right to compensation.

Article 6 – right to a fair trial

1. In the determination of his civil rights and obligations or of any criminal charge against him, everyone is entitled to a fair and public hearing within a reasonable time by an independent and impartial tribunal established by law. Judgment shall be pronounced publicly but the press and public may be excluded from all or part of the trial in the interest of morals, public order or national security in a democratic society, where the interests of juveniles or the protection of the private life of the parties so

require, or to the extent strictly necessary in the opinion of the court in special circumstances where publicity would prejudice the interests of justice.

2.   Everyone charged with a criminal offence shall be presumed innocent until proved guilty according to law.

3.   Everyone charged with a criminal offence has the following minimum rights:

   (a)   to be informed promptly, in a language which he understands and in detail, of the nature and cause of the accusation against him;

   (b)   to have adequate time and facilities for the preparation of his defence;

   (c)   to defend himself in person or through legal assistance of his own choosing or, if he has not sufficient means to pay for legal assistance, to be given it free when the interests of justice so require;

   (d)   to examine or have examined witnesses against him and to obtain the attendance and examination of witnesses on his behalf under the same conditions as witnesses against him;

   (e)   to have the free assistance of an interpreter if he cannot understand or speak the language used in court.

Article 8 – right to respect for private and family life

1.   Everyone has the right to respect for his private and family life, his home and his correspondence.

2.   There shall be no interference by a public authority with the exercise of this right except such as is in accordance with the law and is necessary in a democratic society in the interests of national security, public safety or the economic well-being of the country, for the prevention of disorder or crime, for the protection of health or morals, or for the protection of the rights and freedoms of others.

Article 9 – freedom of thought, conscience and religion

1.   Everyone has the right to freedom of thought, conscience and religion; this right includes freedom to change his religion or belief and freedom, either alone or in community with others and in public or private, to manifest his religion or belief, in worship, teaching, practice and observance.

2.   Freedom to manifest one's religion or beliefs shall be subject only to such limitations as are prescribed by law and are necessary in a democratic society in the interests of public safety, for the protection of public order, health or morals, or for the protection of the rights and freedoms of others.

Article 10 – freedom of expression

1.   Everyone has the right to freedom of expression. This right shall include freedom to hold opinions and to receive and impart information and ideas without interference by public authority and regardless of frontiers. This Article shall not prevent States from requiring the licensing of broadcasting, television or cinema enterprises.

2.   The exercise of these freedoms, since it carries with it duties and responsibilities, may be subject to such formalities, conditions, restrictions or penalties as are prescribed by law and are necessary in a democratic society, in the interests of national security, territorial integrity or public safety, for the prevention of disorder or crime, for the protection of health or morals, for the protection of the reputation or rights of others, for preventing the disclosure of information received in confidence, or for maintaining the authority and impartiality of the judiciary.

Article 11 – freedom of assembly and association

1.   Everyone has the right to freedom of peaceful assembly and to freedom of association with others, including the right to form and to join trade unions for the protection of his interests.

2.   No restrictions shall be placed on the exercise of these rights other than such as are prescribed by law and are necessary in a democratic society in the interests of national security or public safety, for the prevention of disorder or crime, for the protection of health or morals or for the protection of the rights and freedoms of others. This Article shall not prevent the imposition of lawful restrictions on the exercise of these rights by members of the armed forces, of the police or of the administration of the State.

Article 12 – right to marry

Men and women of marriageable age have the right to marry and to found a family, according to the national laws governing the exercise of this right.

Article 14 – prohibition of discrimination

The enjoyment of the rights and freedoms set forth in this Convention shall be secured without discrimination on any ground such as sex, race, colour, language, religion, political or other opinion, national or social origin, association with a national minority, property, birth or other status.

The First Protocol, Article 1 – protection of property

Every natural or legal person is entitled to the peaceful enjoyment of his possessions. No one shall be deprived of his possessions except in the public interest and subject to the conditions provided for by law and by the general principles of international law.

The preceding provisions shall not, however, in any way impair the right of a State to enforce such laws as it deems necessary to control the use of property in accordance with the general interest or to secure the payment of taxes or other contributions or penalties.

British Citizenship: A Summary

The BNA 1981 sets out some basic rules for determining who is a British citizen. The following series of questions can be used to work out if a person may be a British citizen. However, remember that nationality law can be complex, and you will not always be able to work out if a person is a British citizen or not without detailed research of the law and facts.

Q1. When was the person born?

    (a)   Before [1st January] 1983: go to Q2.

    (b)   After [31st December] 1982: go to Q9.

Q2. Where was the person born?

    (a)   In the UK: he is a British citizen otherwise than by descent (see **2.2.1**).

    (b)   Outside the UK: go to Q3.

Q3. Was the person's father born [or registered/naturalised before he was born] in the UK?

    (a)   Yes: go to Q4.

    (b)   No: go to Q5.

Q4. Was the person's father married to their mother? [If after the child's birth, did that marriage legitimise the child?]

    (a)   Yes: he is a British citizen by descent (see **2.2.2**).

    (b)   No: go to Q5.

Q5. Was the person's mother born [or registered/naturalised before he was born] in the UK?

    (a)   Yes: go to Q6.

    (b)   No: go to Q7.

Q6. Did the person's mother register him as a British citizen?

    (a)   Yes: he is a British citizen by descent (see **2.2.6.2**).

    (b)   No: go to Q7.

Q7. Has the person registered as a British citizen?

    (a)   Yes: he is a British citizen by descent (see **2.2.6.2**).

    (b)   No: go to Q8.

Q8. Has the person naturalised in the UK as a British citizen?

    (a)   Yes: he is a British citizen otherwise than by descent (see **2.2.7**).

    (b)   No: he is not a British citizen under these rules but a detailed analysis of law and facts is required.

Q9. Was the person born in the UK?

    (a)   Yes: go to Q10.

    (b)   No: go to Q13.

Q10. Was either of the person's parents a British citizen or settled in the UK when he was born?

    (a)   Yes: he is a British citizen otherwise than by descent (see **2.2.3**).

    (b)   No: go to Q11.

Q11. Did either of the person's parents subsequently become a British citizen or settled in the UK?

    (a)   Yes: he can apply to register as a British citizen otherwise than by descent (see **2.2.6.1**).

    (b)   No: go to Q12.

Q12. Has the person remained in the UK for the first 10 years of his life and not been absent for more than 90 days?

(a)   Yes: he is a British citizen otherwise than by descent (see **2.2.6.1**).

(b)   No: he is not a British citizen under these rules but a detailed analysis of law and facts is required.

Q13. Was one of the person's parents a British citizen otherwise than by birth, registration or naturalisation in the UK before he was born?

(a)   Yes: he is a British citizen by descent (see **2.2.4**).

(b)   No: he is not a British citizen under these rules but a detailed analysis of the law and facts is required.

Note 1: a parent in this context includes the father of an illegitimate child born on or after 1 July 2006 if certain conditions are met (see **2.2.3** and **2.2.4**).

Note 2: as to second generation children born outside UK, see **2.2.5**.

Naturalisation: A Summary

The following series of questions can be used to work out if a person may be eligible to apply for naturalisation as a British citizen.

Q1. Is the person settled in the UK (this includes an EEA national who has permanent residence in the UK)?

    (a)   Yes: go to Q2.

    (b)   No: ineligible.

Q2. Is the person married to a British citizen or in a civil partnership with a British citizen?

    (a)   Yes: go to Q3.

    (b)   No: go to Q7.

Q3. Has the person been living in the UK legally for three years continuously before making the application?

    (a)   Yes: go to Q4.

    (b)   No: ineligible.

Q4. Has the person been absent for less than 270 days in total and not more than 90 days in the year immediately before the application?

    (a)   Yes: go to Q5.

    (b)   No: ineligible but check Home Office policy.

Q5. Can the person produce written evidence to show sufficient knowledge of English (Welsh or Scottish Gaelic) and Life in the UK?

    (a)   Yes: go to Q6.

    (b)   No: ineligible but check to see if Home Office might waive this requirement.

Q6. Can the person show good character?

    (a)   Yes: may be granted naturalisation as a British citizen at discretion of Home Secretary.

    (b)   No: application will be refused.

Q7. Has the person been settled in the UK (this includes an EEA national who has permanent residence in the UK) for at least one year before making the application?

    (a)   Yes: go to Q8.

    (b)   No: ineligible.

Q8. Has the person been living in the UK legally for five years continuously before making the application?

    (a)   Yes: go to Q9.

    (b)   No: ineligible.

Q9. Has the person been absent for less than 450 days in total and not more than 90 days in the year immediately before the application?

    (a)   Yes: go to Q10.

    (b)   No: ineligible but check Home Office policy.

Q10. Can the person produce written evidence to show sufficient knowledge of English (Welsh or Scottish Gaelic) and Life in the UK?

    (a)   Yes: go to Q11.

    (b)   No: ineligible but check to see if Home Office might waive this requirement.

Q11. Can the person show good character?

    (a)   Yes: go to Q12.

    (b)   No: application will be refused.

Q12. Can the person show an intention to live in the UK?

    (a)   Yes: may be granted naturalisation as a British citizen at discretion of Home Secretary.

    (b)   No: application will be refused.

APPENDIX 8

Criminality under the Immigration Rules

Criminality grounds on which entry clearance or leave to enter the UK will be refused under the Immigration Rules

A. By paragraph 320(2) a person seeking entry to the UK will be refused if he:

   (a) is currently the subject of a deportation order; or

   (b) has been convicted of an offence for which he has been sentenced to a period of imprisonment of at least 4 years; or

   (c) has been convicted of an offence for which he has been sentenced to a period of imprisonment of at least 12 months but less than 4 years, unless a period of 10 years has passed since the end of the sentence; or

   (d) has been convicted of an offence for which he has been sentenced to a period of imprisonment of less than 12 months, unless a period of 5 years has passed since the end of the sentence.

   Where this paragraph applies, unless refusal would be contrary to the Human Rights Convention or the Convention and Protocol Relating to the Status of Refugees, it will only be in exceptional circumstances that the public interest in maintaining refusal will be outweighed by compelling factors.

B. By paragraph 320(7B)(vii) a person who left or was removed from the UK as a condition of a caution issued in accordance with s134 Legal Aid, Sentencing and Punishment of Offenders Act 2012 will be refused entry clearance or leave to enter unless a period of 5 years has passed since he left or was removed.

Criminality grounds on which entry clearance or leave to enter the UK is normally refused

A. By paragraph 320(18A) a person seeking entry to the UK will normally be refused if within the 12 months preceding the date of the application he has been convicted of or admitted an offence for which he received a non-custodial sentence or other out of court disposal that is recorded on his criminal record.

B. By paragraph 320(18B) a person seeking entry to the UK will normally be refused if in the view of the Secretary of State: (a) his offending has caused serious harm; or (b) he is a persistent offender who shows a particular disregard for the law.

C. By paragraph 320(19) a person seeking entry to the UK will normally be refused if the immigration officer deems their exclusion from the UK to be conducive to the public good. For example, because the person's conduct (including convictions which do not fall within paragraph 320(2)), character, associations, or other reasons, make it undesirable to grant them leave to enter.

Criminality grounds on which leave to remain and variation of leave to enter or remain in the UK will be refused

A. By paragraph 322(1B) an applicant will be refused if, at the date of application, he is the subject of a deportation order or a decision to make a deportation order;

B. By paragraph 322(1C) where the person is seeking indefinite leave to enter or remain the application will be refused if:

   (i) he has been convicted of an offence for which he has been sentenced to imprisonment for at least 4 years; or

   (ii) he has been convicted of an offence for which he has been sentenced to imprisonment for at least 12 months but less than 4 years, unless a period of 15 years has passed since the end of the sentence; or

   (iii) he has been convicted of an offence for which he has been sentenced to imprisonment for less than 12 months, unless a period of 7 years has passed since the end of the sentence; or

   (iv) he has, within the 24 months preceding the date of the application, been convicted of or admitted an offence for which he has received a non-custodial sentence or other out of court disposal that is recorded on their criminal record.

Criminality grounds on which leave to remain and variation of leave to enter or remain in the UK is normally refused

By paragraph 322(5A) that it is undesirable to permit the person concerned to enter or remain in the UK because, in the view of the Secretary of State (a) his offending has caused serious harm; or (b) he is a persistent offender who shows a particular disregard for the law.

Commonwealth Citizens

Citizens of the following countries are currently Commonwealth citizens according to Sch 3 to the British Nationality Act 1981 (as amended).

Antigua and Barbuda	Mozambique
Australia	Namibia
The Bahamas	Nauru
Bangladesh	New Zealand
Barbados	Nigeria
Belize	Pakistan
Botswana	Papua New Guinea
Brunei	Saint Christopher and Nevis
Cameroon	Saint Lucia
Canada	Saint Vincent and the Grenadines
Republic of Cyprus	Seychelles
Dominica	Sierra Leone
Fiji	Singapore
The Gambia	Solomon Islands
Ghana	South Africa
Grenada	Sri Lanka
Guyana	Swaziland
India	Tanzania
Jamaica	Tonga
Kenya	Trinidad and Tobago
Kiribati	Tuvalu
Lesotho	Uganda
Malawi	Vanuatu
Malaysia	Western Samoa
Maldives	Zambia
Malta	Zimbabwe
Mauritius	

Note that British citizens, and some other categories of British Nationals (including British dependent territories citizens and British overseas citizens) are Commonwealth citizens by virtue of s 37 of the 1981 Act.

It is important to note that as Cameroon, Mozambique, Namibia, Pakistan and South Africa were not members of the Commonwealth on 31 December 1982, then nationals of those countries cannot take advantage of the provisions dealt with at **2.3.**

APPENDIX 10

Commonwealth Citizen with Right of Abode: A Summary

APPENDIX 11

British Overseas Territories

The following are currently British Overseas Territories according to Sch 6 to the British Nationality Act 1981 (as amended).

Anguilla

Bermuda

British Antarctic Territory

British Indian Ocean Territory

Cayman Islands

Gibraltar

Montserrat

Pitcairn, Henderson, Ducie and Oeno Islands

St Helena and Dependencies

South Georgia

South Sandwich Islands

The Sovereign Base Areas of Akrotiri and Dhekelia

Turks and Caicos Islands

Virgin Islands

Note that people from the Falkland Islands were made into full British citizens under the British Nationality (Falkland Islands) Act 1983.

Tier 1 Entrepreneur: Overview

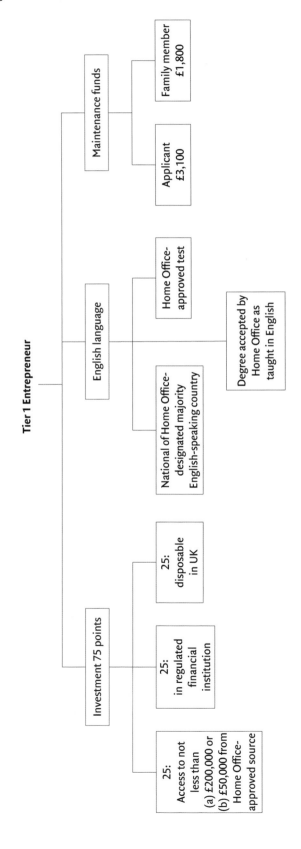

Home Office Definition of Common Ownership or Control

The Home Office states that common ownership or control may be defined as follows:

- one entity controls the composition of the other entity's board; or

- one entity is in a position to cast, or control the casting of, more than half the maximum number of votes that might be cast at a general meeting of the other entity; or

- one entity holds more than half the issued share capital of the other entity (excluding any part of that issued share capital that carries no right to participate beyond a specified amount in a distribution of either profits or capital); or

- both entities have a common parent entity that itself or through other entities meets one of the requirements of the first three bullet points above in relation to both entities that are the subject of the intra-company transfer; or

- one entity is related to the other entity as both entities are party to a joint venture agreement; or

- one entity is related to the other entity in that one entity is party to a joint venture agreement and the other entity is the entity formed by that joint venture agreement; or

- one entity is related to the other entity by agreement that would constitute a joint venture agreement other than for the fact that joint venture agreements are not permitted in the country of operation or one of the entities is not permitted to enter into joint ventures in the country of operation; or

- one entity is related to the other entity in that one entity is party to an agreement that would constitute a joint venture agreement other than for the fact that joint venture agreements are not permitted in the country of operation or that entity is not permitted to enter into joint ventures in the country of operation and the other entity is the entity formed by that agreement; or

- where both entities are either accountancy or law firms, one entity is related to the other entity by agreement which allows both entities to use a trademark which is registered or established under the laws of the United Kingdom and the jurisdiction of the other entity's country of operation; or

- where both entities are either accountancy or law firms, one entity is related to the other entity by agreement which allows both entities to operate under the same name in the United Kingdom and in the jurisdiction of the other entity's country of operation; or

- in the case of unincorporated associations, the receiving entity is a linked company if it is a registered company and its Articles of Association with the sending entity indicate a relationship of control (for example, one Member has the power to appoint the other's trustees).

Refugee or Person in Need of International Protection (Qualification) Regulations 2006

SI 2006/2525

1. Citation and commencement

    (1) These Regulations may be cited as The Refugee or Person in Need of International Protection (Qualification) Regulations 2006 and shall come into force on 9th October 2006.

    (2) These Regulations apply to any application for asylum which has not been decided and any immigration appeal brought under the Immigration Acts (as defined in section 64(2) of the Immigration, Asylum and Nationality Act 2006) which has not been finally determined.

2. Interpretation

    In these Regulations—

    'application for asylum' means the request of a person to be recognised as a refugee under the Geneva Convention;

    'Geneva Convention' means the Convention Relating to the Status of Refugees done at Geneva on 28 July 1951 and the New York Protocol of 31 January 1967;

    'immigration rules' means rules made under section 3(2) of the Immigration Act 1971;

    'persecution' means an act of persecution within the meaning of Article 1(A) of the Geneva Convention;

    'person eligible for humanitarian protection' means a person who is eligible for a grant of humanitarian protection under the immigration rules;

    'refugee' means a person who falls within Article 1(A) of the Geneva Convention and to whom regulation 7 does not apply;

    'residence permit' means a document confirming that a person has leave to enter or remain in the United Kingdom whether limited or indefinite;

    'serious harm' means serious harm as defined in the immigration rules;

    'person' means any person who is not a British citizen.

3. Actors of persecution or serious harm

    In deciding whether a person is a refugee or a person eligible for humanitarian protection, persecution or serious harm can be committed by:

    (a) the State;

    (b) any party or organisation controlling the State or a substantial part of the territory of the State;

    (c) any non-State actor if it can be demonstrated that the actors mentioned in paragraphs (a) and (b), including any international organisation, are unable or unwilling to provide protection against persecution or serious harm.

4. Actors of protection

    (1) In deciding whether a person is a refugee or a person eligible for humanitarian protection, protection from persecution or serious harm can be provided by:

        (a) the State; or

        (b) any party or organisation, including any international organisation, controlling the State or a substantial part of the territory of the State.

    (2) Protection shall be regarded as generally provided when the actors mentioned in paragraph (1)(a) and (b) take reasonable steps to prevent the persecution or suffering of serious harm by operating an effective legal system for the detection, prosecution and punishment of acts constituting persecution or serious harm, and the person mentioned in paragraph (1) has access to such protection.

(3)   In deciding whether a person is a refugee or a person eligible for humanitarian protection the Secretary of State may assess whether an international organisation controls a State or a substantial part of its territory and provides protection as described in paragraph (2).

5.   Act of persecution

(1)   In deciding whether a person is a refugee an act of persecution must be:

(a)   sufficiently serious by its nature or repetition as to constitute a severe violation of a basic human right, in particular a right from which derogation cannot be made under Article 15 of the Convention for the Protection of Human Rights and Fundamental Freedoms; or

(b)   an accumulation of various measures, including a violation of a human right which is sufficiently severe as to affect an individual in a similar manner as specified in (a).

(2)   An act of persecution may, for example, take the form of:

(a)   an act of physical or mental violence, including an act of sexual violence;

(b)   a legal, administrative, police, or judicial measure which in itself is discriminatory or which is implemented in a discriminatory manner;

(c)   prosecution or punishment, which is disproportionate or discriminatory;

(d)   denial of judicial redress resulting in a disproportionate or discriminatory punishment;

(e)   prosecution or punishment for refusal to perform military service in a conflict, where performing military service would include crimes or acts falling under regulation 7.

(3)   An act of persecution must be committed for at least one of the reasons in Article 1(A) of the Geneva Convention.

6.   Reasons for persecution

(1)   In deciding whether a person is a refugee:

(a)   the concept of race shall include consideration of, for example, colour, descent, or membership of a particular ethnic group;

(b)   the concept of religion shall include, for example, the holding of theistic, non-theistic and atheistic beliefs, the participation in, or abstention from, formal worship in private or in public, either alone or in community with others, other religious acts or expressions of view, or forms of personal or communal conduct based on or mandated by any religious belief;

(c)   the concept of nationality shall not be confined to citizenship or lack thereof but shall include, for example, membership of a group determined by its cultural, ethnic, or linguistic identity, common geographical or political origins or its relationship with the population of another State;

(d)   a group shall be considered to form a particular social group where, for example:

(i)   members of that group share an innate characteristic, or a common background that cannot be changed, or share a characteristic or belief that is so fundamental to identity or conscience that a person should not be forced to renounce it, and

(ii)   that group has a distinct identity in the relevant country, because it is perceived as being different by the surrounding society;

(e)   a particular social group might include a group based on a common characteristic of sexual orientation but sexual orientation cannot be understood to include acts considered to be criminal in accordance with national law of the United Kingdom;

(f)   the concept of political opinion shall include the holding of an opinion, thought or belief on a matter related to the potential actors of persecution mentioned in regulation 3 and to their policies or methods, whether or not that opinion, thought or belief has been acted upon by the person.

(2)   In deciding whether a person has a well-founded fear of being persecuted, it is immaterial whether he actually possesses the racial, religious, national, social or political characteristic which attracts the persecution, provided that such a characteristic is attributed to him by the actor of persecution.

7.   Exclusion

(1)   A person is not a refugee, if he falls within the scope of Article 1D, 1E or 1F of the Geneva Convention.

(2)   In the construction and application of Article 1F(b) of the Geneva Convention:

(a)   the reference to serious non-political crime includes a particularly cruel action, even if it is committed with an allegedly political objective;

(b)   the reference to the crime being committed outside the country of refuge prior to his admission as a refugee shall be taken to mean the time up to and including the day on which a residence permit is issued.

(3)   Article 1F(a) and (b) of the Geneva Convention shall apply to a person who instigates or otherwise participates in the commission of the crimes or acts specified in those provisions.

Pre-Action Protocol for Judicial Review

INTRODUCTION

This protocol applies to proceedings *within England and Wales only*. It does not affect the time limit specified by Rule 54.5(1) of the Civil Procedure Rules which requires that any claim form in an application for judicial review must be filed promptly and in any event not later than 3 months after the grounds to make the claim first arose.[1]

1   Judicial review allows people with a sufficient interest in a decision or action by a public body to ask a judge to review the lawfulness of:

- an enactment; or

- a decision, action or failure to act in relation to the exercise of a public function.[2]

2   Judicial review may be used where there is no right of appeal or where all avenues of appeal have been exhausted.

Alternative Dispute Resolution

3.1   The parties should consider whether some form of alternative dispute resolution procedure would be more suitable than litigation, and if so, endeavour to agree which form to adopt. Both the Claimant and Defendant may be required by the Court to provide evidence that alternative means of resolving their dispute were considered. The Courts take the view that litigation should be a last resort, and that claims should not be issued prematurely when a settlement is still actively being explored. Parties are warned that if the protocol is not followed (including this paragraph) then the Court must have regard to such conduct when determining costs. However, parties should also note that a claim for judicial review 'must be filed promptly and in any event not later than 3 months after the grounds to make the claim first arose'.

3.2   It is not practicable in this protocol to address in detail how the parties might decide which method to adopt to resolve their particular dispute. However, summarised below are some of the options for resolving disputes without litigation:

- Discussion and negotiation.

- Ombudsmen – the Parliamentary and Health Service and the Local Government Ombudsmen have discretion to deal with complaints relating to maladministration. The British and Irish Ombudsman Association provide information about Ombudsman schemes and other complaint handling bodies and this is available from their website at www.bioa.org.uk . Parties may wish to note that the Ombudsmen are not able to look into a complaint once court action has been commenced.

- Early neutral evaluation by an independent third party (for example, a lawyer experienced in the field of administrative law or an individual experienced in the subject matter of the claim).

- Mediation – a form of facilitated negotiation assisted by an independent neutral party.

3.3   The Legal Services Commission has published a booklet on 'Alternatives to Court', CLS Direct Information Leaflet 23 (www.clsdirect.org.uk), which lists a number of organisations that provide alternative dispute resolution services.

3.4   *It is expressly recognised that no party can or should be forced to mediate or enter into any form of ADR.*

4   **Judicial review may not be appropriate in every instance.**

Claimants are strongly advised to seek appropriate legal advice when considering such proceedings and, in particular, before adopting this protocol or making a claim. Although the Legal Services Commission will not normally grant full representation before a letter before claim has been sent and the proposed defendant given a reasonable time to respond, initial funding may be available, for eligible claimants, to cover the work necessary to write this. (See Annex C for more information.)

5   This protocol sets out a code of good practice and contains the steps which parties should generally follow before making a claim for judicial review.

6   This protocol does not impose a greater obligation on a public body to disclose documents or give reasons for its decision than that already provided for in statute or common law. However, where the court considers that

a public body should have provided relevant documents and/or information, particularly where this failure is a breach of a statutory or common law requirement, it may impose sanctions.

This protocol *will not be appropriate* where the defendant does not have the legal power to change the decision being challenged, for example decisions issued by tribunals such as the Asylum and Immigration Tribunal.

This protocol *will not be appropriate* in urgent cases, for example, when directions have been set, or are in force, for the claimant's removal from the UK, or where there is an urgent need for an interim order to compel a public body to act where it has unlawfully refused to do so (for example, the failure of a local housing authority to secure interim accomodation for a homeless claimant) a claim should be made immediately. A letter before claim will not stop the implementation of a disputed decision in all instances.

7   All claimants will need to satisfy themselves whether they should follow the protocol, depending upon the circumstances of his or her case. Where the use of the protocol is appropriate, the court will normally expect all parties to have complied with it and will take into account compliance or non-compliance when giving directions for case management of proceedings or when making orders for costs.[3] However, even in emergency cases, it is good practice to fax to the defendant the draft Claim Form which the claimant intends to issue. A claimant is also normally required to notify a defendant when an interim mandatory order is being sought.

The letter before claim

8   Before making a claim, the claimant should send a letter to the defendant. The purpose of this letter is to identify the issues in dispute and establish whether litigation can be avoided.

9   Claimants should normally use the suggested **standard format** for the letter outlined at Annex A.

10   The letter should contain **the date and details of the decision, act or omission being challenged and a clear summary of the facts** on which the claim is based. It should also contain the **details of any relevant information** that the claimant is seeking and an explanation of why this is considered relevant.

11   The letter should normally contain the **details of any interested parties**[4] known to the claimant. They should be sent a *copy* of the letter before claim *for information*. **Claimants are *strongly advised to seek appropriate legal advice* when considering such proceedings and, in particular, before sending the letter before claim to other interested parties or making a claim.**

12   A claim should not normally be made until the proposed reply date given in the letter before claim has passed, unless the circumstances of the case require more immediate action to be taken.

The letter of response

13   Defendants should normally respond within 14 days using the standard format at Annex B. Failure to do so will be taken into account by the court and sanctions may be imposed unless there are good reasons.[5]

14   Where it is not possible to reply within the proposed time limit the defendant should send an interim reply and propose a reasonable extension. Where an extension is sought, reasons should be given and, where required, additional information requested. *This will not affect the time limit for making a claim for judicial review*[6] nor will it bind the claimant where he or she considers this to be unreasonable. However, where the court considers that a subsequent claim is made prematurely it may impose sanctions.

15   If the **claim is being conceded in full**, the reply should say so in clear and unambiguous terms.

16   If the **claim is being conceded in part or not being conceded at all**, the reply should say so in clear and unambiguous terms, and:

   (a)   where appropriate, contain a new decision, clearly identifying what aspects of the claim are being conceded and what are not, or, give a clear timescale within which the new decision will be issued;

   (b)   provide a fuller explanation for the decision, if considered appropriate to do so;

   (c)   address any points of dispute, or explain why they cannot be addressed;

   (d)   enclose any **relevant** documentation requested by the claimant, or explain why the documents are not being enclosed; and

   (e)   where appropriate, confirm whether or not they will oppose any application for an interim remedy.

17   The response should be sent to **all interested parties**[7] identified by the claimant and contain details of any other parties who the defendant considers also have an interest.

A LETTER BEFORE CLAIM

SECTION 1. INFORMATION REQUIRED IN A LETTER BEFORE CLAIM

Proposed claim for judicial review

1 **To**

(*Insert the name and address of the proposed defendant – see details in section 2*)

2 **The claimant**

(*Insert the title, first and last name and the address of the claimant*)

3 **Reference details**

(*When dealing with large organisations it is important to understand that the information relating to any particular individual's previous dealings with it may not be immediately available, therefore it is important to set out the relevant reference numbers for the matter in dispute and/or the identity of those within the public body who have been handling the particular matter in dispute – see details in section 3*)

4 **The details of the matter being challenged**

(*Set out clearly the matter being challenged, particularly if there has been more than one decision*)

5 **The issue**

(*Set out the date and details of the decision, or act or omission being challenged, a brief summary of the facts and why it is contented to be wrong*)

6 **The details of the action that the defendant is expected to take**

(*Set out the details of the remedy sought, including whether a review or any interim remedy are being requested*)

7 **The details of the legal advisers, if any, dealing with this claim**

(*Set out the name, address and reference details of any legal advisers dealing with the claim*)

8 **The details of any interested parties**

(*Set out the details of any interested parties and confirm that they have been sent a copy of this letter*)

9 **The details of any information sought**

(*Set out the details of any information that is sought. This may include a request for a fuller explanation of the reasons for the decision that is being challenged*)

10 **The details of any documents that are considered relevant and necessary**

(*Set out the details of any documentation or policy in respect of which the disclosure is sought and explain why these are relevant. If you rely on a statutory duty to disclose, this should be specified*)

11 **The address for reply and service of court documents**

(*Insert the address for the reply*)

12 **Proposed reply date**

(*The precise time will depend upon the circumstances of the individual case. However, although a shorter or longer time may be appropriate in a particular case, 14 days is a reasonable time to allow in most circumstances*)

SECTION 2. ADDRESS FOR SENDING THE LETTER BEFORE CLAIM

Public bodies have requested that, for certain types of cases, in order to ensure a prompt response, letters before claim should be sent to specific addresses.

- **Where the claim concerns a decision in an Immigration, Asylum or Nationality case:**

  Judicial Review Unit,
  UK Border Agency
  St Anne's House
  20-26 Wellesley Road
  Croydon CR9 2RL

- Where the claim concerns a decision by the Legal Services Commission:

  — The address on the decision letter/notification; and

  Legal Director
  Corporate Legal Team
  Legal Services Commission
  4 Abbey Orchard Street
  London SW1P 2BS

- **Where the claim concerns a decision by a local authority:**
  — The address on the decision letter/notification; and
  — Their legal department[8]
- **Where the claim concerns a decision by a department or body for whom Treasury Solicitor acts and Treasury Solicitor has already been involved in the case a copy should also be sent, quoting the Treasury Solicitor's reference, to:**

  The Treasury Solicitor,
  One Kemble Street,
  London WC2B 4TS

In all other circumstances, the letter should be sent to the address on the letter notifying the decision.

SECTION 3. SPECIFIC REFERENCE DETAILS REQUIRED

Public bodies have requested that the following information should be provided in order to ensure prompt response.

- **Where the claim concerns an Immigration, Asylum or Nationality case, dependent upon the nature of the case:**
  — The Home Office reference number
  — The Port reference number
  — The Asylum and Immigration Tribunal reference number
  — The National Asylum Support Service reference number
  Or, if these are unavailable:
  — The full name, nationality and date of birth of the claimant.
- **Where the claim concerns a decision by the Legal Services Commission:**
  — The certificate reference number.

B RESPONSE TO A LETTER BEFORE CLAIM

INFORMATION REQUIRED IN A RESPONSE TO A LETTER BEFORE CLAIM

Proposed claim for judicial review

1 **The claimant**
(Insert the title, first and last names and the address to which any reply should be sent)

2 **From**
(Insert the name and address of the defendant)

3 **Reference details**
(Set out the relevant reference numbers for the matter in dispute and the identity of those within the public body who have been handling the issue)

4 **The details of the matter being challenged**
(Set out details of the matter being challenged, providing a fuller explanation of the decision, where this is considered appropriate)

5 **Response to the proposed claim**
(Set out whether the issue in question is conceded in part, or in full, or will be contested. Where it is not proposed to disclose any information that has been requested, explain the reason for this. Where an interim reply is being sent and there is a realistic prospect of settlement, details should be included)

6 **Details of any other interested parties**
(Identify any other parties who you consider have an interest who have not already been sent a letter by the claimant)

7 **Address for further correspondence and service of court documents**
(Set out the address for any future correspondence on this matter)

C NOTES ON PUBLIC FUNDING FOR LEGAL COSTS IN JUDICIAL REVIEW

Public funding for legal costs in judicial review is available from legal professionals and advice agencies which have contracts with the Legal Services Commission as part of the Community Legal Service. Funding may be provided for:

- **Legal Help** to provide initial advice and assistance with any legal problem; or
- **Legal Representation** to allow you to be represented in court if you are taking or defending court proceedings. This is available in two forms:

— **Investigative Help** is limited to funding to investigate the strength of the proposed claim. It includes the issue and conduct of proceedings only so far as is necessary to obtain disclosure of relevant information or to protect the client's position in relation to any urgent hearing or time limit for the issue of proceedings. This includes the work necessary to write a **letter before claim** to the body potentially under challenge, setting out the grounds of challenge, and giving that body a reasonable opportunity, typically 14 days, in which to respond.

— **Full Representation** is provided to represent you in legal proceedings and includes litigation services, advocacy services, and all such help as is usually given by a person providing representation in proceedings, including steps preliminary or incidental to proceedings, and/or arriving at or giving effect to a compromise to avoid or bring to an end any proceedings. Except in emergency cases, a proper **letter before claim** must be sent and the other side must be given an opportunity to respond before *Full Representation* is granted.

Further information on the type(s) of help available and the criteria for receiving that help may be found in the Legal Service Manual Volume 3: *"The Funding Code"*. This may be found on the Legal Services Commission website at:

www.legalservices.gov.uk

A list of contracted firms and Advice Agencies may be found on the Community Legal Services website at:

www.justask.org.uk

Footnotes

1. While the court does have the discretion under Rule 3.1(2)(a) of the Civil Procedure Rules to allow a late claim, this is only used in exceptional circumstances. **Compliance with the protocol alone is unlikely to be sufficient to persuade the court to allow a late claim.**

2. Civil Procedure Rule 54.1(2).

3. Civil Procedure Rules Costs Practice Direction.

4. See Civil Procedure Rule 54.1(2)(f).

5. See Civil Procedure Rules Pre-action Protocol Practice Direction paragraphs 2–3.

6. See Civil Procedure Rule 54.5(1).

7. See Civil Procedure Rule 54.1(2)(f).

8. The relevant address should be available from a range of sources such as the Phone Book; Business and Services Directory, Thomson's Local Directory, CAB, etc.

Index